THE WESTERN HERITAGE

Tenth Edition

VOLUME ONE: TO 1740

Donald Kagan
YALE UNIVERSITY

Steven Ozment
HARVARD UNIVERSITY

Frank M. Turner
YALE UNIVERSITY

Prentice Hall
Upper Saddle River   London Singapore
Toronto   Tokyo   Sydney   Hong Kong   Mexico City

VP, Editorial Director: Leah Jewell
Executive Editor: Charles Cavaliere
Editorial Project Manager: Rob DeGeorge
Production Project Manager: Lynn Savino Wendel
Editorial Assistant: Lauren Aylward
Senior Managing Editor: Ann Marie McCarthy
Director of Marketing: Brandy Dawson
Senior Marketing Manager: Sue Westmoreland
Marketing Assistant: Ashley Fallon
Senior Operations Supervisor: Mary Ann Gloriande
Senior Art Director: Maria Lange
Text and Cover Designer: Liz Harasymczuk

AV Project Manager: Mirella Signoretto
Manager, Visual Research: Beth Brenzel
Manager, Rights and Permissions: Zina Arabia
Image Permission Coordinator: Michelina Viscusi
Manager, Cover Visual Research & Permissions: Karen Sanatar
Media Director: Brian Hyland
Lead Media Project Manager: Sarah Kinney
Supplements Editor: Emsal Hasan
Composition/Full-Service Project Management: Rebecca Dunn, Prepare, Inc.
Printer/Binder: Courier Kendallville
Cover Printer: Lehigh-Phoenix Color

This book was set in 10/12 Trump Mediaeval

Credits and acknowledgments borrowed from other sources and reproduced, with permission, in this textbook appear on appropriate page within text.

Cover photo credits: Jacques Louis David (1748–1825), "The Death of Socrates". Oil on canvas. H. 51 in. W. 77-1/4 in. (129.5 x 196.2 cm.). The Metropolitan Museum of Art, Catharine Lorillard Wolfe Collection, Wolfe Fund, 1931. (31.45). Photograph © 1995 The Metropolitan Museum of Art / Art Resource, NY (top illustration); Private Collection/The Bridgeman Art Library (bottom illustration).

Library of Congress Cataloging-in-Publication Data

Kagan, Donald
    The Western Heritage / Donald Kagan, Steven Ozment, Frank M. Turner.—10th ed.
      p. cm.
    "Combined volume."
    Includes bibliographical references and index.
    ISBN 978-0-205-66072-8 (combined)—ISBN 978-0-205-69967-4 (exam)—ISBN 978-0-205-70515-3 (v. 1)—ISBN 978-0-205-70516-0 (v. 2) ISBN 978-0-205-69978-0 (v. A)—ISBN 978-0-205-69979-7 (v. B)—ISBN 978-0-205-70514-6 (v. C)—ISBN 978-0-205-70517-7 (since 1300)
    1. Civilization, Western—History—Textbooks. I. Ozment, Steven E. II. Turner, Frank M. (Frank Miller), 1994 III. Title.
CB245.K28 2010
909'.09821—dc22

2009012769

1 0 9 8 7 6 5 4 3 2

Prentice Hall
is an imprint of

PEARSON

www.pearsonhighered.com

Student edition ISBN 10:0-205-70515-4
                  ISBN 13:978-0-205-70515-3
A La Carte   ISBN 10:0-205-72358-6
                  ISBN 13:978-0-205-72358-4

BRIEF CONTENTS

CONTENTS

DOCUMENTS

MAPS

PREFACE

Students undertaking the study of the Western heritage on the threshold of the second decade of the twenty-first century do so at a remarkable historical moment. In 2008, the United States elected its first African-American president, a Democrat backed by larger Democratic congressional majorities pledged to undertaking major new policy directions at home and abroad. Both the Western and non-Western worlds confront a changing global economy that gave birth to a financial crisis with the most serious implications for economic stability since the 1930s. The August 2008 invasion of Georgia by Russian Federation troops signaled the possibility of a move from a period of relative quietude to one of military resurgence that may bring into question numerous strategic military assumptions that prevailed for almost two decades after the collapse of the Soviet Union. The United States and Western Europe, after several years of controversial military engagement in Iraq and Afghanistan, continue efforts to reshape foreign policy with an emphasis on diplomacy instead of preemptive warfare. Christians in the northern and southern hemispheres continue to be sharply divided as they debate the character of their faith and its relationship to other faiths and the social questions of the day. A growing consensus of opinion recognizes the dangers posed by environmental change.

The authors of this volume continue to believe that the heritage of Western civilization remains a major point of departure for understanding and defining the challenges of this no longer new century. The unprecedented globalization of daily life that is a hallmark of our era has occurred largely through the spread of Western influences. From the sixteenth century onward, the West has exerted vast influences throughout the globe for both good and ill, and today's global citizens continue to live in the wake of that impact. It is the goal of this book to introduce its readers to the Western heritage, so that they may be better informed and more culturally sensitive citizens of the increasingly troubled and challenging global age. The events of recent years and the hostility that has arisen in many parts of the world to the power and influence of the West require new efforts to understand how the West sees itself and how other parts of the world see the West.

Since *The Western Heritage* first appeared, we have sought to provide our readers with a work that does justice to the richness and variety of Western civilization and its many complexities. We hope that such an understanding of the West will foster lively debate about its character, values, institutions, and global influence. Indeed, we believe such a critical outlook on their own culture has characterized the peoples of the West since the dawn of history. Through such debates we define ourselves and the values of our culture. Consequently, we welcome the debate and hope that *The Western Heritage*, Tenth Edition, can help foster an informed discussion through its history of the West's strengths and weaknesses and the controversies surrounding Western history. To further that debate, we have included a new introductory essay entitled "What Is the Western Heritage?" to introduce students to the concept of the West and to allow instructors and students to have a point of departure for debating this concept in their course of study.

We also believe that any book addressing the experience of the West must also look beyond its historical European borders. Students reading this book come from a wide variety of cultures and experiences. They live in a world of highly interconnected economies and instant communication between cultures. In this emerging multicultural society it seems both appropriate and necessary to recognize how Western civilization has throughout its history interacted with other cultures, both influencing and being influenced by them. For this reason, we have introduced in this edition a new chapter on the nineteenth-century European age of imperialism. Further examples of Western interaction with other parts of the world, such as with Islam, appear throughout the text. To further highlight the theme of cultural interaction, *The Western Heritage* includes a series of comparative essays, "The West & the World." (A more complete description follows.)

In this edition as in past editions, our goal has been to present Western civilization fairly, accurately, and in a way that does justice to this great, diverse legacy of human enterprise. History has many facets, no single one of which can alone account for the others. Any attempt to tell the story of the West from a single overarching perspective, no matter how timely, is bound to neglect or suppress some important parts of this story. Like all other authors of introductory texts, we have had to make choices, but we have attempted to provide the broadest possible introduction to Western civilization.

GOALS OF THE TEXT

Our primary goal has been to present a strong, clear, narrative account of the central developments in Western history. We have also sought to call attention to certain critical themes:

- The capacity of Western civilization, from the time of the Greeks to the present, to transform itself through self-criticism.
- The development in the West of political freedom, constitutional government, and concern for the rule of law and individual rights.
- The shifting relations among religion, society, and the state.
- The development of science and technology and their expanding impact on Western thought, social institutions, and everyday life.
- The major religious and intellectual currents that have shaped Western culture.

We believe that these themes have been fundamental in Western civilization, shaping the past and exerting a continuing influence on the present.

Flexible Presentation *The Western Heritage*, Tenth Edition, is designed to accommodate a variety of approaches to a course in Western civilization, allowing teachers to stress what is most important to them. Some teachers will ask students to read all the chapters. Others will select among them to reinforce assigned readings and lectures. We believe the documents as well as the "Encountering the Past" and "A Closer Look" features may also be adopted selectively by instructors for purposes of classroom presentation and debate and as the basis for short written assignments.

Integrated Social, Cultural, and Political History *The Western Heritage* provides one of the richest accounts of the social history of the West available today, with strong coverage of family life, the changing roles of women, and the place of the family in relation to broader economic, political, and social developments. This coverage reflects the explosive growth in social historical research in the past half-century, which has enriched virtually all areas of historical study.

We have also been told repeatedly by teachers that no matter what their own historical specialization, they believe that a political narrative gives students an effective tool to begin to understand the past. Consequently, we have sought to integrate such a strong political narrative with our treatment of the social, cultural, and intellectual factors in Western history.

We also believe that religious faith and religious institutions have been fundamental to the development of the West. No other survey text presents so full an account of the religious and intellectual development of the West. People may be political and social beings, but they are also reasoning and spiritual beings. What they think and believe are among the most important things we can know about them. Their ideas about God, society, law, gender, human nature, and the physical world have changed over the centuries and continue to change. We cannot fully grasp our own approach to the world without understanding the religious and intellectual currents of the past and how they have influenced our thoughts and conceptual categories. We seek to recognize the impact of religion in the expansion of the West, including the settlement the Americas in the sixteenth century and the role of missionaries in nineteenth-century Western imperialism.

Clarity and Accessibility Good narrative history requires clear, vigorous prose. As with earlier editions, we have paid careful attention to our writing, subjecting every paragraph to critical scrutiny. Our goal has been to make the history of the West accessible to students without compromising vocabulary or conceptual level. We hope this effort will benefit both teachers and students.

THE TENTH EDITION

New to This Edition

- We include a new introductory essay entitled "What Is the Western Heritage?" designed to introduce students to the concept of Western civilization as it has changed over the centuries and at the same to provide instructors the opportunity to debate this concept and its implications with their students.
- Each chapter includes a new feature entitled "**Compare and Connect**" that juxtaposes two or more documents in which an important question is debated or a comparison between a document and an illustration is presented. Each "Compare and Connect" feature contains three to five questions on each of the documents, one of which asks students to make connections between and among the viewpoints presented in the feature. These features are intended to encourage students to debate different points of view in class and to learn to read and evaluate differing viewpoints or to analyze documentary and visual evidence. An interactive version of this feature is available on www.myhistorylab.com

- An entirely new chapter, "The Age of Western Imperialism" (Chapter 25), provides an in-depth global overview of nineteenth-century Western imperial expansion. Topics covered in this chapter include the nineteenth-century shift in Western imperial ventures from the Americas to Africa and Asia, the significance of the British Empire, British imperial rule in India, the New Imperialism, the partition of Africa, the role of missionaries in European colonialism, the relationship of technology and science to imperialism, and international colonial rivalries.
- The new chapter on imperialism has led to a streamlining of the chapter on World War I and its aftermath as well as more extensive comments on the colonial ramifications of the peace settlement (Chapter 26).
- A single, more sharply focused chapter on the twentieth-century interwar years (Chapter 27) has replaced two longer chapters on this period.
- The two closing chapters of the book (Chapters 29 and 30) carry the narrative through important recent events such as the Russian invasion of Georgia and the collapse of financial institutions in Europe and the United States in the fall of 2008.

Features That Enliven Student Interest and Understanding

"A Closer Look" Reflecting the increased use of visual sources to interpret the Western heritage, one illustration per chapter is examined and analyzed using leader lines to point out important and historically significant details.

Examples include a Greek trireme, the cover of the Lindau Gospels, a statue of St. Maurice, and a French imperialist poster from the early twentieth century. This feature further enhances the already rich visual presentation of *The Western Heritage*. An interactive version of this feature is available on www.myhistorylab.com

"Encountering the Past" Each chapter includes an essay on a significant issue of everyday life or popular culture. These essays explore a variety of subjects, including gladiatorial bouts and medieval games, smoking in early modern Europe, and the politics of rock music in the late twentieth century. These thirty essays, each of which includes an illustration and study questions, expand *The Western Heritage*'s rich coverage of social and cultural history.

"The West & The World" In this feature, we focus on six subjects that compare Western institutions with those in other parts of the world or discuss how developments in the West have influenced other cultures. In the Tenth Edition, the essays are

Part 1:	Ancient Warfare (page 164)
Part 2:	The Invention of Printing in China and Europe (page 252)
Part 3:	The Columbian Exchange, Disease, Animals, and Agriculture (page 489)
Part 4:	The Abolition of Slavery in the Transatlantic Economy (page 655)
Part 5:	Imperialism: Ancient and Modern (page 793)
Part 6:	Energy and the Modern World (page 979)

Recent Scholarship As in previous editions, changes in this edition reflect our determination to incorporate the most recent developments in historical scholarship and the concerns of professional historians.

Maps and Illustrations To help students understand the relationship between geography and history, approximately half of the maps include relief features. One or two maps in each chapter feature interactive exercises that can be found in MyHistoryLab. All maps have been carefully edited for accuracy. The text also contains close to 500 color and black and white illustrations, many of which are new to the Tenth Edition.

Pedagogical Features This edition retains the pedagogical features of previous editions, including a list of key topics at the beginning of each chapter, glossary terms, chapter review questions, and questions accompanying the more than 200 source documents in the text. Each of these features is designed to make the text more accessible to students and to reinforce key concepts.

- **Primary-source documents,** many of which are new to this edition, acquaint students with the raw material of history and provide intimate contact with the people of the past and their concerns. Questions accompanying the source documents direct students toward important, thought-provoking issues and help them relate the documents to the material in the text. They can be used to stimulate class discussion or as topics for essays and study groups.
- **An outline, a list of key topics, and an introduction** are included in each chapter. Together these features provide a succinct overview of each chapter.
- **Chronologies** follow each major section in a chapter, listing significant events and their dates.

- **In Perspective** sections summarize the major themes of each chapter and provide a bridge to the next chapter.
- **Chapter Review Questions** help students review the material in a chapter and relate it to broader themes. These too can be used for class discussion and essay topics.
- **Suggested Readings** lists following each chapter have been updated with new titles reflecting recent scholarship.
- **Map Explorations** prompt students to engage with maps in an interactive fashion. Each Map Exploration can be found in MyHistoryLab.

A Note on Dates and Transliterations This edition of *The Western Heritage* continues the practice of using B.C.E. (before the common era) and C.E. (common era) instead of B.C. (before Christ) and A.D. (anno Domini, the year of the Lord) to designate dates. We also follow the most accurate currently accepted English transliterations of Arabic words. For example, today *Koran* has been replaced by the more accurate *Qur'an*; similarly *Muhammad* is preferable to *Mohammed* and *Muslim* to *Moslem*.

ANCILLARY INSTRUCTIONAL MATERIALS

The ancillary instructional materials that accompany *The Western Heritage*, Tenth Edition, are designed to reinforce and enliven the richness of the past and inspire students with the excitement of studying the history of Western civilization.

For Instructors

Instructor's Manual The Instructor's Manual contains chapter summaries, key points and vital concepts, and information on audiovisual resources that can be used in developing and preparing lecture presentations. (ISBN 0-205-66073-8)

Test Item File The Test Item File includes over 1,500 multiple-choice, identification, map, and essay test questions. (ISBN 0-205-66076-2)

MyTest MyTest is a browser-based test management program. The program allows instructors to select items from the Test Item File in order to create tests. It also allows for online testing. (ISBN 0-205-66075-4)

The Instructor's Resource Center (www.pearsonhighered.com) Text-specific materials, such as the Instructor's Manual and the Test Item File, are available for downloading by adopters.

For Instructors and Students

 MyHistoryLab (www.myhistorylab.com) MyHistoryLab provides students with an online package complete with the electronic textbook and numerous study aids. With several hundred primary sources, many of which are assignable and link to a gradebook, pre- and post-tests that link to a gradebook and result in individualized study plans, "Closer Look" investigations, videos and images, as well as map activities with gradable quizzes, the site offers students a unique, interactive experience that brings history to life. The comprehensive site also includes a History Bookshelf with fifty of the most commonly assigned books in history classes and a History Toolkit with tutorials and helpful links. Other features include gradable assignments and chapter review materials as well as a Test Item File.

For Students

Primary Source: Documents in Western Civilization DVD This DVD-ROM offers a rich collection of textual and visual—many never before available to a wide audience—and serves as an indispensable tool for working with sources. Extensively developed with the guidance of historians and teachers, *Primary Source: Documents in Western Civilization* includes over 800 sources in Western civilization history—from cave art, to text documents, to satellite images of Earth from space. All sources are accompanied by headnotes and focus questions and are searchable by topic, region, or theme. In addition, a built-in tutorial guides students through the process of working with documents. The DVD can be bundled with *The Western Heritage*, Tenth Edition, at no charge. Please contact your Pearson Arts and Sciences representative for ordering information (ISBN 0-13-134407-2).

A two-volume print version of *Primary Source: Documents in Western Civilization* is also available:

Primary Sources in Western Civilization, Volume 1: To 1700, Second Edition (ISBN 0-13-175583-8)
Primary Sources in Western Civilization, Volume 2: Since 1400, Second Edition (ISBN 0-13-175584-6)

Please contact your Pearson Arts and Sciences representative for ordering information.

***Lives and Legacies: Biographies in Western Civilization*, Second Edition** Extensively revised, *Lives and*

Legacies includes brief, focused biographies of sixty individuals whose lives provide insight into the key developments of Western civilization. Each biography includes an introduction, prereading questions, and suggestions for additional reading. Available in two volumes:

Lives and Legacies, Volume 1, Second Edition (ISBN 0-205-64915-7)
Lives and Legacies, Volume 2, Second Edition (ISBN 0-205-64914-9)

 CourseSmart Textbooks Online This is an exciting new choice for students looking to save money. As an alternative to purchasing the print textbook, students can subscribe to the same content online and save up to 50 percent off the suggested list price of the print text. With a CourseSmart eTextbook, students can search the text, make notes online, print out reading assignments that incorporate lecture notes, and bookmark important passages for later review. For more information, or to subscribe to the Course-Smart eTextbook, visit www.coursesmart.com.

Western Civilization Study Site (www.ablongman.com/ longmanwesterncivilization/) This course-based, open-access online companion provides both students and professors with links for further research as well as test questions in multiple choice, true/false, and fill-in-the-blank formats.

Penguin Classics Selected titles from the renowned Penguin Classics series can be bundled with *The Western Heritage*, Tenth Edition, for a nominal charge. Please contact your Pearson Arts and Sciences sales representative for details.

Longman Atlas of Western Civilization This 52-page atlas features carefully selected historical maps that provide comprehensive coverage for the major historical periods. Contact your Pearson Arts and Sciences representative for details. (ISBN 0-321-21626-1)

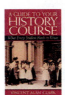 *The Prentice Hall Atlas of Western Civilization*, **Second Edition** Produced in collaboration with Dorling Kindersley, the leader in cartographic publishing, the updated second edition of *The Prentice Hall Atlas of Western Civilization* applies the most innovative cartographic techniques to present Western civilization in all of its complexity and diversity. Contact your Pearson Arts and Sciences sales representative for details. (ISBN 0-13-604246-5)

A Guide to Your History Course: What Every Student Needs to Know Written by Vincent A. Clark, this concise, spiral-bound guidebook orients students to the issues and problems they will face in the history classroom. Available at a discount when bundled with *The Western Heritage*, Tenth Edition. (ISBN 0-13-185087-3)

A Short Guide to Writing about History, **Seventh Edition** Written by Richard Marius, late of Harvard University, and Melvin E. Page, Eastern Tennessee State University, this engaging and practical text helps students get beyond merely compiling dates and facts. Covering both brief essays and the documented resource paper, the text explores the writing and researching processes, identifies different modes of historical writing, including argument, and concludes with guidelines for improving style. (ISBN 0-205-67370-8)

Interpretations of the Western World (www.pearsoncustom.com/custom-library/interpretations-of-the-western-world) The selections in this customizable database of secondary source readings are grouped together topically so instructors can assign readings that illustrate different points of view on a given historical debate.

ACKNOWLEDGMENTS

We are grateful to the scholars and teachers whose thoughtful and often detailed comments helped shape this revision:

Mark Baker, California State University at Bakersfield
Fred Baumgartner, Virginia Tech
Jane Bishop, The Citadel, The Military College of South Carolina
Eugene Boia, Cleveland State University
Kristen Burkholder, Oklahoma State University
Joseph Byrnes, Oklahoma State University
Anthony Cardoza, Loyola University, Chicago
Marcus Cox, The Citadel, The Military College of South Carolina
Delores Davison, Foothill College
Paul Deslandes, University of Vermont
Petra DeWitt, University of Missouri, Rolla
Richard Eller, Catawaba Valley Community College
Axel Fair-Schulz, State University of New York at Potsdam
Sean Field, University of Vermont
Shannon Fogg, Missouri S&T
Stephen Gibson, Ranken Technical College
Stephanie Hallock, Harford Community College
Michael Hickey, Bloomsburg University
Anthony Heideman, Range Community College
William Hudon, Bloomsburg University
Terry Jones, Oklahoma State University
Kevin Keating, Broward Community College
Michael Khodarkovsky, Loyola University, Chicago
Martha Kinney, Suffolk County Community College
Helena Krohn, Tidewater Community College
Eugene Larson, Los Angeles Pierce College
Karl Loewenstein, University of Wisconsin at Oshkosh
Arthur Lysiak, Bloomsburg University

William Martin, University of Utah
Lisa McClain, Boise State University
Daniel Miller, University of West Florida
Eva Mo, Meridian Junior College
Michelle Mouton, University of Wisconsin at Oshkosh
Tonia Sharlach Nash, Oklahoma State University
Charles Odahl, Boise State University
Mark Orsag, Doane College
Michael Pascale, SUNY at Suffolk, Farmingdale College
Neal Pease, University of Wisconsin at Milwaukee
Norman Raiford, Greenville Technical College
Pete Rottier, Cleveland State University
Thomas Rowland, University of Wisconsin at Oshkosh
Michael Rutz, University of Wisconsin at Oshkosh
Stephen Ruzicka, University of North Carolina at Greensboro
Mark Schumann, Eastern Michigan University
Patrick Speelman, The Citadel, The Military College of South Carolina
Frank W. Thackeray, Indiana University Southeast
Daniel Trifan, Missouri Western State University
Miriam Vivian, California State University at Bakersfield
Andrew Zimmerman, George Washington University

We would like to thank the dedicated people who helped produce this new edition. Our acquisitions editor, Charles Cavaliere; our development editor, Gerald Lombardi; our project manager, Rob DeGeorge; our production liaison, Lynn Savino Wendel; Maria Lange who created the beautiful new design of this edition; Mary Ann Gloriande, our operations specialist; and Rebecca Dunn, production editor.

D.K.
S.O.
F.M.T.

ABOUT THE AUTHORS

DONALD KAGAN is Sterling Professor of History and Classics at Yale University, where he has taught since 1969. He received the A.B. degree in history from Brooklyn College, the M.A. in classics from Brown University, and the Ph.D. in history from Ohio State University. During 1958 to 1959 he studied at the American School of Classical Studies as a Fulbright Scholar. He has received three awards for undergraduate teaching at Cornell and Yale. He is the author of a history of Greek political thought, *The Great Dialogue* (1965); a four-volume history of the Peloponnesian war, *The Origins of the Peloponnesian War* (1969); *The Archidamian War* (1974); *The Peace of Nicias and the Sicilian Expedition* (1981); *The Fall of the Athenian Empire* (1987); and a biography of Pericles, *Pericles of Athens and the Birth of Democracy* (1991); *On the Origins of War* (1995) and *The Peloponnesian War* (2003). He is coauthor, with Frederick W. Kagan, of *While America Sleeps* (2000). With Brian Tierney and L. Pearce Williams, he is the editor of *Great Issues in Western Civilization*, a collection of readings. He was awarded the National Humanities Medal for 2002 and was chosen by the National Endowment for the Humanities to deliver the Jefferson Lecture in 2004.

▼

STEVEN OZMENT is McLean Professor of Ancient and Modern History at Harvard University. He has taught Western Civilization at Yale, Stanford, and Harvard. He is the author of eleven books. *The Age of Reform, 1250–1550* (1980) won the Schaff Prize and was nominated for the 1981 National Book Award. Five of his books have been selections of the History Book Club: *Magdalena and Balthasar: An Intimate Portrait of Life in Sixteenth Century Europe* (1986), *Three Behaim Boys: Growing Up in Early Modern Germany* (1990), *Protestants: The Birth of a Revolution* (1992), *The Burgermeister's Daughter: Scandal in a Sixteenth Century German Town* (1996), and *Flesh and Spirit: Private Life in Early Modern Germany* (1999). His most recent publications are *Ancestors: The Loving Family of Old Europe* (2001), *A Mighty Fortress: A New History of the German People* (2004), and "Why We Study Western Civ," *The Public Interest*, 158 (2005).

▼

FRANK M. TURNER is John Hay Whitney Professor of History at Yale University and Director of the Beinecke Rare Book and Manuscript Library at Yale University, where he served as University Provost from 1988 to 1992. He received his B.A. degree at the College of William and Mary and his Ph.D. from Yale. He has received the Yale College Award for Distinguished Undergraduate Teaching. He has directed a National Endowment for the Humanities Summer Institute. His scholarly research has received the support of fellowships from the National Endowment for the Humanities and the Guggenheim Foundation and the Woodrow Wilson Center. He is the author of *Between Science and Religion: The Reaction to Scientific Naturalism in Late Victorian England* (1974), *The Greek Heritage in Victorian Britain* (1981), which received the British Council Prize of the Conference on British Studies and the Yale Press Governors Award, *Contesting Cultural Authority: Essays in Victorian Intellectual Life* (1993), and *John Henry Newman: The Challenge to Evangelical Religion* (2002). He has also contributed numerous articles to journals and has served on the editorial advisory boards of *The Journal of Modern History, Isis*, and *Victorian Studies*. He edited *The Idea of a University* by John Henry Newman (1996), *Reflections on the Revolution in France* by Edmund Burke (2003), and *Apologia Pro Vita Sua and Six Sermons* by John Henry Newman (2008). Between 1996 and 2006 he served as a Trustee of Connecticut College and between 2004 and 2008 as a member of the Connecticut Humanities Council. In 2003, Professor Turner was appointed Director of the Beinecke Rare Book and Manuscript Library at Yale University.

WHAT IS THE WESTERN HERITAGE?

This book invites students and instructors to explore the Western Heritage. What is that heritage? The Western Heritage emerges from an evolved and evolving story of human actions and interactions, peaceful and violent, that arose in the eastern Mediterranean, then spread across the western Mediterranean into northern Europe, and eventually to the American continents, and in their broadest impact, to the peoples of Africa and Asia as well.

The Western Heritage as a distinct portion of world history descends from the ancient Greeks. They saw their own political life based on open discussion of law and policy as different from that of Mesopotamia, Persia, and Egypt, where kings ruled without regard to public opinion. The Greeks invented the concept of citizenship, defining it as engagement in some form of self-government. Furthermore, through their literature and philosophy, the Greeks established the conviction, which became characteristic of the West, that reason can shape and analyze physical nature, politics, and morality.

The city of Rome, spreading its authority through military conquest across the Mediterranean world, embraced Greek literature and philosophy. Through their conquests and imposition of their law, the Romans created the Western world as a vast empire stretching from Egypt and Syria in the east to Britain in the west. Although the Roman Republic, governed by a Senate and popular political institutions, gave way after civil wars to the autocratic rule of the Roman Empire, the idea of a free republic of engaged citizens governed by public law and constitutional arrangements limiting political authority survived centuries of arbitrary rule by emperors. As in the rest of the world, the Greeks, the Romans, and virtually all other ancient peoples excluded women and slaves from political life and tolerated considerable social inequality.

In the early fourth century C.E., the Emperor Constantine reorganized the Roman Empire in two fundamental ways that reshaped the West. First, he moved the imperial capital from Rome to Constantinople (Istanbul), establishing separate emperors in the East and West. Thereafter, large portions of the Western empire became subject to the rulers of Germanic tribes. In the confusion of these times, most of the texts embodying ancient philosophy, literature, and history became lost in the West, and for centuries Western Europeans were intellectually severed from that ancient heritage, which would later be recovered in a series of renaissances, or cultural rebirths, beginning in the eighth century.

Constantine's second fateful major reshaping of the West was his recognition of Christianity as the official religion of the empire. Christianity had grown out of the ancient monotheistic religion of the Hebrew people living in ancient Palestine. With the ministry of Jesus of Nazareth and the spread of his teachings by the Apostle Paul, Christianity had established itself as one of many religions in the empire. Because Christianity was monotheistic, Constantine's official embrace of it led to the eradication of pagan polytheism. Thereafter, the West became more or less coterminous with Latin Christianity, or that portion of the Christian Church acknowledging the Bishop of Rome as its head.

As the emperors' rule broke down, bishops became the effective political rulers in many parts of Western Europe. But the Christian Church in the West never governed without negotiation or conflict with secular rulers, and religious law never replaced secular law. Nor could secular rulers govern if they ignored the influence of the church. Hence from the fourth century C.E. to the present day, rival claims to political and moral authority between ecclesiastical and political officials have characterized the West.

In the seventh century the Christian West faced a new challenge from the rise of Islam. This new monotheistic religion originating in the teachings of the prophet Muhammad arose on the Arabian Peninsula and spread through rapid conquests across North Africa and eventually into Spain, turning the Mediterranean into what one historian has termed "a Muslim lake." Between the eleventh and the thirteenth centuries, Christians attempted to reclaim the Holy Land from Muslim control in church-inspired military crusades that still resonate negatively in the Islamic world.

It was, however, in the Muslim world that most of the texts of ancient Greek and Latin learning survived and were studied, while intellectual life languished in the West. Commencing in the twelfth century, knowledge of those texts began to work its way back into Western Europe. By the fourteenth century, European thinkers redefined themselves and their intellectual ambitions by recovering the literature and science from the ancient world, reuniting Europe with its Graeco-Roman past.

From the twelfth through the eighteenth centuries, a new European political system slowly arose based on centralized monarchies characterized by large armies, navies, and bureaucracies loyal to the monarch, and by

In his painting *The School of Athens*, the great Italian Renaissance painter Raphael portrayed the ancient Greek philosopher Plato and his student, Aristotle, engaged in debate. Plato, who points to the heavens, believed in a set of ideal truths that exist in their own realm distinct from the earth. Aristotle urged that all philosophy must be in touch with lived reality and confirms this position by pointing to the earth. Such debate has characterized the intellectual, political, and social experience of the West. Indeed, the very concept of "Western Civilization" has itself been subject to debate, criticism, and change over the centuries.
© Scala/Art Resource, NY

the capacity to raise revenues. Whatever the personal ambitions of individual rulers, for the most part these monarchies recognized both the political role of local or national assemblies drawn from the propertied elites and the binding power of constitutional law on themselves. Also, in each of these monarchies, church officials and church law played important roles in public life. The monarchies, their military, and their expanding commercial economies became the basis for the extension of European and Western influence around the globe.

In the late fifteenth and early sixteenth centuries, two transforming events occurred. The first was the European discovery and conquest of the American continents, thus opening the Americas to Western institutions, religion, and economic exploitation. Over time the labor shortages of the Americas led to the forced migration of millions of Africans as slaves to the "New World." By the mid-seventeenth century, the West consequently embraced the entire transatlantic world and its multiracial societies.

Second, shortly after the American encounter, a religious schism erupted within Latin Christianity. Reformers rejecting both many medieval Christian doctrines as unbiblical and the primacy of the Pope in Rome established Protestant churches across much of northern Europe. As a consequence, for almost two centuries religious warfare between Protestants and Roman Catholics overwhelmed the continent as monarchies chose to defend one side or the other. This religious turmoil meant that the Europeans who conquered and settled the Americas carried with them particularly energized religious convictions, with Roman Catholics dominating Latin America and English Protestants most of North America.

By the late eighteenth century, the idea of the West denoted a culture increasingly dominated by two new forces. First, science arising from a new understanding of nature achieved during the sixteenth and seventeenth centuries persuaded growing numbers of the educated elite that human beings can rationally master nature for ever-expanding productive purposes improving the health and well-being of humankind. From this era to the present, the West has been associated with advances in technology, medicine, and scientific research. Second, during the eighteenth century, a drive for economic improvement that vastly increased agricultural production and then industrial manufacturing transformed economic life, especially in Western Europe and later the United States. Both of these economic developments went hand in hand with urbanization and the movement of the industrial economy into cities where the new urban populations experienced major social dislocation.

During these decades certain West European elites came to regard advances in agricultural and manufacturing economies that were based on science and tied to commercial expansion as "civilized" in contrast to cultures that lacked those characteristics. From these ideas emerged the concept of Western Civilization defined to suggest that peoples dwelling outside Europe or inside Europe east of the Elbe River were less than civilized. Whereas Europeans had once defined themselves against the rest of the world as free citizens and then later as Christians, they now defined themselves as "civilized." Europeans would carry this self-assured superiority into their nineteenth- and early twentieth-century encounters with the peoples of Asia, Africa, and the Pacific.

During the last quarter of the eighteenth century, political revolution erupted across the transatlantic world. The British colonies of North America revolted. Then revolution occurred in France and spread across much of Europe. From 1791 through 1830, the Wars of Independence liberated Latin America from its European conquerors. These revolutions created bold new modes of political life, rooting the legitimacy of the state in some form of popular government and generally written constitutions. Thereafter, despite the presence of authoritarian governments on the European continent, the idea of the West, now including the new republics of the United States and Latin America, became associated with liberal democratic governments.

Furthermore, during the nineteenth century, most major European states came to identify themselves in terms of nationality—language, history, and ethnicity—

rather than loyalty to a monarch. Nationalism eventually inflamed popular opinion and unloosed unprecedented political ambition by European governments.

These ambitions led to imperialism and the creation of new overseas European empires in the late nineteenth century. For the peoples living in European-administered Asian and African colonies, the idea and reality of the West embodied foreign domination and often disadvantageous involvement in a world economy. When in 1945 the close of World War II led to a sharp decline in European imperial authority, colonial peoples around the globe challenged that authority and gained independence. These former colonial peoples, however, often still suspected the West of seeking to control them. Hence, anticolonialism like colonialism before it redefined definitions of the West far from its borders.

Late nineteenth-century nationalism and imperialism also unleashed with World War I in 1914 unprecedented military hostilities among European nations that spread around the globe, followed a quarter century later by an even greater world war. As one result of World War I, revolution occurred in Russia with the establishment of the communist Soviet Union. During the interwar years a Fascist Party seized power in Italy and a Nazi Party took control of Germany. In response to these new authoritarian regimes, West European powers and the United States identified themselves with liberal democratic constitutionalism, individual freedom, commercial capitalism, science and learning freely pursued, and religious liberty, all of which they defined as the Western Heritage. During the Cold War, conceived of as an East-West, democratic versus communist struggle that concluded with the collapse of the Soviet Union in 1991, the Western Powers led by the United States continued to embrace those values in conscious opposition to the Soviet government, which since 1945 had also dominated much of Eastern Europe.

Since 1991 the West has again become redefined in the minds of many people as a world political and economic order dominated by the United States. Europe clearly remains the West, but political leadership has moved to North America. That American domination and recent American foreign policy have led throughout the West and elsewhere to much criticism of the United States.

Such self-criticism itself embodies one of the most important and persistent parts of the Western Heritage. From the Hebrew prophets and Socrates to the critics of European imperialism, American foreign policy, social inequality, and environmental devastation, voices in the West have again and again been raised to criticize often in the most strident manner the policies of

Western governments and the thought, values, social conditions, and inequalities of Western societies.

Consequently, we study the Western Heritage not because the subject always or even primarily presents an admirable picture, but because the study of the Western Heritage like the study of all history calls us to an integrity of research, observation, and analysis that clarifies our minds and challenges our moral sensibilities. The challenge of history is the challenge of thinking, and it is to that challenge that this book invites its readers.

QUESTIONS

1. How have people in the West defined themselves in contrast with civilizations of the ancient East, and later in contrast with Islamic civilization, and still later in contrast with less economically developed regions of the world? Have people in the West historically viewed their own civilization to be superior to civilizations in other parts of the world? Why or why not?

2. How did the Emperor Constantine's adoption of Christianity as the official religion of the Roman Empire change the concept of the West? Is the presence of Christianity still a determining characteristic of the West?

3. How has the geographical location of what has been understood as the West changed over the centuries?

4. In the past two centuries Western nations established empires around the globe. How did these imperial ventures and the local resistance to them give rise to critical definitions of the West that contrasted with the definitions that had developed in Europe and the United States? How have those non-Western definitions of the West contributed to self-criticism within Western nations?

5. How useful is the concept of Western civilization in understanding today's global economy and global communications made possible by the Internet? Is the idea of Western civilization synonymous with the concept of modern civilization? Do you think the concept of the West will once again be redefined ten years from now?

To view a video of the authors discussing the Western heritage, go to www.myhistorylab.com

This depiction of the Pharaoh Tutankahmun (r. 1336–1327 B.C.E.) and his queen comes from his tomb, which was discovered in the 1920s. "King Tut" died at the age of eighteen. Robert Frerck/Odyssey Production/Woodfin Camp & Associates

1

The Birth of Civilization

KEY TOPICS

• The earliest history of humanity, including the beginnings of human culture in the Paleolithic Age, the agricultural revolution and the shift from food gathering to food production

• The ancient civilizations of Mesopotamia and Egypt

• The great Near Eastern empires, 1500–486 B.C.E.

• The emergence of Judaism

• The difference in outlook between ancient Near Eastern and Greek civilizations

HISTORY, IN ITS two senses—as the events of the past that make up the human experience on earth and as the written record of those events—is a subject of both interest and importance. We naturally want to know how we came to be who we are, and how the world we live in came to be what it is. But beyond its intrinsic interest, history provides crucial insight into present human behavior. To understand who we are now, we need to know the record of the past and to try to understand the people and forces that shaped it.

For hundreds of thousands of years after the human species emerged, people lived by hunting, fishing, and collecting wild plants. Only some 10,000 years ago did they learn to cultivate plants, herd animals, and make airtight pottery for storage. These discoveries transformed them from gatherers to producers and allowed them to grow in number and to lead a settled life. About 5,000 years ago humans learned how to control the waters of great river valleys, making possible much richer harvests and supporting a further increase in population. The peoples of these river valley societies created the earliest civilizations. They invented writing, which, among other things, enabled them to keep inventories of food and other resources. They discovered the secret of smelting metal to make tools and weapons of bronze far superior to the stone implements of earlier times. They came together in towns and cities, where industry and commerce flourished. Complex religions took form, and social divisions increased. Kings—considered to be representatives of the gods or to be themselves divine—emerged as rulers, assisted by priests and defended by well-organized armies.

The first of these civilizations appeared among the Sumerians before 3500 B.C.E. in the Tigris-Euphrates Valley we call Mesopotamia. From the Sumerians to the Assyrians and Babylonians, a series of peoples ruled Mesopotamia, each shaping and passing along its distinctive culture, before the region fell under the control of great foreign empires. A second early civilization emerged in the Nile Valley around 3100 B.C.E. Egyptian civilization developed a remarkably continuous pattern, in part because Egypt was largely protected from invasion by the formidable deserts surrounding the valley. The essential character of Egyptian civilization changed little for nearly 3,000 years. Influences from other areas, however, especially Nubia to the south, Syria-Palestine to the northeast, and the Aegean to the north, may be seen during many periods of Egyptian history.

By the fourteenth century B.C.E., several powerful empires had arisen and were vying for dominance in regions that included Egypt, Mesopotamia, and **Asia Minor**. Northern warrior peoples, such as the Hittites who dominated Asia Minor, conquered and ruled peoples in various areas. For two centuries, the Hittite and Egyptian Empires struggled with each other for control of Syria-Palestine. By about 1200 B.C.E., however, both these empires had collapsed. Beginning about 850 B.C.E., the Assyrians arose in northern Mesopotamia and ultimately established a mighty new empire, even invading Egypt in the early seventh century B.C.E. The Assyrians were dominant until the late seventh century B.C.E., when they fell to a combination of enemies. Their vast empire was overtaken by the Babylonians, but these people, too, would soon become only a small, though important, part of the enormous empire of Persia.

Among all these great empires nestled a people called the Israelites, who maintained a small, independent kingdom in the region between Egypt and Syria for several centuries. This kingdom ultimately fell to the Assyrians and later remained subject to other conquerors. The Israelites possessed little worldly power or wealth, but they created a powerful religion, Judaism, the first certain and lasting worship of a single god in a world of polytheism. Judaism was the seedbed of two other religions that have played a mighty role in the history of the world: Christianity and Islam. The great empires have collapsed, their power forgotten for millennia until the tools of archaeologists uncovered their remains, but the religion of the Israelites, in itself and through its offshoots, has endured as a powerful force.

▼ Early Humans and Their Culture

Scientists estimate the earth may be as many as 6 billion years old and that creatures very much like humans appeared perhaps 3 to 5 million years ago, probably in Africa. Some 1 to 2 million years ago, erect and tool-using early humans spread over much of Africa, Europe, and Asia. Our own species, *Homo sapiens*, probably emerged some 200,000 years ago, and the earliest remains of fully modern humans date to about 90,000 years ago.

Humans, unlike other animals, are cultural beings. **Culture** may be defined as the ways of living built up by a group and passed on from one generation to another. It includes behavior such as courtship or child-rearing practices; material things such as tools, clothing, and shelter; and ideas, institutions, and beliefs. Language, apparently a uniquely human trait, lies behind our ability to create ideas and institutions and to transmit culture from one generation to another. Our flexible and dexterous hands enable us to hold and make tools and so to create the material artifacts of culture. Because culture is learned and not inherited, it permits rapid adaptation to changing conditions, making possible the spread of humanity to almost all the lands of the globe.

The Paleolithic Age

Anthropologists designate early human cultures by their tools. The earliest period—the **Paleolithic** (from Greek, "old stone")—dates from the earliest use of stone tools some 1 million years ago to about 10,000 B.C.E. During this immensely long period, people were hunters, fishers, and gatherers, but not producers, of food. They learned to make and use increasingly sophisticated tools of stone and perishable materials like wood; they learned to make and control fire; and they acquired language and the ability to use it to pass on what they had learned.

These early humans, dependent on nature for food and vulnerable to wild beasts and natural disasters, may have developed responses to the world rooted in fear of the unknown—of the uncertainties of human life or the overpowering forces of nature. Religious and magical beliefs and practices may have emerged in an effort to propitiate or coerce the superhuman forces thought to animate or direct the natural world. Evidence of religious faith and practice, as well as of magic, goes as far back as archaeology can take us. Fear or awe, exaltation, gratitude, and empathy with the natural world must all have figured in the cave art and in the ritual practices, such as burial, that we find evidenced at Paleolithic sites around the globe. The sense that there is more to the world than meets the eye—in other words, the religious response to the world—seems to be as old as humankind.

The style of life and the level of technology of the Paleolithic period could support only a sparsely settled society. If hunters were too numerous, game would not suffice. In Paleolithic times, people were subject to the same natural and ecological constraints that today maintain a balance between wolves and deer in Alaska.

Evidence from Paleolithic art and from modern hunter-gatherer societies suggests that human life in the Paleolithic Age was probably characterized by a division of labor by sex. Men engaged in hunting, fishing, making tools and weapons, and fighting against other families, clans, and tribes. Women, less mobile because of childbearing, gathered nuts, berries, and wild grains, wove baskets, and made clothing. Women gathering food probably discovered how to plant and care for seeds. This knowledge eventually made possible the development of agriculture and animal husbandry.

The Neolithic Age

Only a few Paleolithic societies made the initial shift from hunting and gathering to agriculture. Anthropologists and archaeologists disagree as to why, but however it happened, some 10,000 years ago parts of what we now call the Near East began to change from a nomadic hunter-gatherer culture to a more settled agricultural one. Because the shift to agriculture coincided with advances in stone tool technology—the development of greater precision, for example, in chipping and grinding—this period is called the **Neolithic Age** (from Greek, "new stone," the later period in the Stone Age). Productive animals, such as sheep and goats, and food crops, such as wheat and barley, were first domesticated in the mountain foothills where they already lived or grew in the wild. Once domestication had taken place, people could move to areas where these plants and animals did not occur naturally, such as the river valleys of the Near East. The invention of pottery during the Neolithic Age enabled people to store surplus foods and liquids and to transport them, as well as to cook agricultural products that were difficult to eat or digest raw. Cloth was made from flax and wool. Crops required constant care from planting to harvest, so Neolithic farmers built permanent dwellings. The earliest of these tended to be circular huts, large enough to house only one or two people and clustered in groups around a central storage place. Later people built square and rectangular family-sized houses with individual storage places and enclosures to house livestock. Houses in a Neolithic village were normally all the

same size and were built on the same plan, suggesting that most Neolithic villagers had about the same level of wealth and social status. A few items, such as stones and shells, were traded long distance, but Neolithic villages tended to be self-sufficient.

Two larger Neolithic settlements do not fit this village pattern. One was found at Çatal Höyük, in a fertile agricultural region about 150 miles south of Ankara, the capital of present-day Turkey. This was a large town covering over fifteen acres, with a population probably well over 6,000 people. The houses were clustered so closely that they had no doors but were entered by ladders from the roofs. Many were decorated inside with sculptures of animal heads and horns, as well as paintings that were apparently redone regularly. Some appear to depict ritual or festive occasions involving men and women. One is the world's oldest landscape picture, showing a nearby volcano exploding. The agriculture, arts, and crafts of this town were astonishingly diversified and at a much higher level of attainment than other, smaller settlements of the period. The site of Jericho, an oasis around a spring near the Dead Sea, was occupied as early as 12,000 B.C.E. Around 8000 B.C.E., a town of eight to ten acres grew up, surrounded by a massive stone wall with at least one tower against the inner face. Although this wall may have been for defense, its use is disputed because no other Neolithic settlement has been found with fortifications. The inhabitants of Neolithic Jericho had a mixed agricultural, herding, and hunting economy and may have traded salt. They had no pottery but plastered the skulls of their dead to make realistic memorial portraits of them. These two sites show that the economy and the settlement patterns of the Neolithic period may be more complicated than many scholars have thought.

Throughout the Paleolithic Age, the human population had been small and relatively stable. The shift from food gathering to food production may not have been associated with an immediate change in population, but over time in the regions where agriculture and animal husbandry appeared, the number of human beings grew at an unprecedented rate. One reason for this is that farmers usually had larger families than hunters. Their children began to work and matured at a younger age than the children of hunters. When animals and plants were domesticated and brought to the river valleys, the relationship between human beings and nature was changed forever. People had learned to control nature, a vital prerequisite for the emergence of civilization. But farmers had to work harder and longer than hunters did, and they had to stay in one place. Herders, in contrast, often moved from place to place in search of pasture and water, returning to their villages in the spring. Some scholars refer to the dramatic changes in subsistence, settlement, technology, and population of this time as the **Neolithic Revolution**. The earliest Neolithic societies appeared in the Mideast about 8000 B.C.E., in China about 4000 B.C.E., and in India about 3600 B.C.E. Neolithic agriculture was based on wheat and barley in the Mideast, on millet and rice in China, and on corn in Mesoamerica, several millennia later.

In 1991 a discovery in the Ötztal Tyrolean Alps on the border between Italy and Austria shed new light on the Neolithic period. A tourist came upon a frozen body, which turned out to be the oldest mummified human being yet discovered. Dated to about 3300 B.C.E., it was the remains of a man between 25 and 35 years old, 5 feet 2 inches tall, weighing 110 pounds. He has been called Ötzi, the Ice Man from the place of his discovery. He had not led a peaceful life, for his nose was broken, and several of his ribs were fractured. An arrowhead in his shoulder suggests he bled to death in the ice and snow. He wore a fur robe made of the skins of mountain animals, and under it he wore a woven grass cape. His shoes were made of leather stuffed with grass. He was heavily armed for his time, carrying a dagger of flint and a bow with arrows also tipped in flint. He also carried an axe whose blade was made of copper, indicating that metallurgy was already under way. His discovery provides a vivid evidence of the beginning of the transition from the Stone Age to the Bronze Age.

Ötzi is the nickname scientists have given to the remains of the oldest mummified human body yet discovered. This reconstruction shows his probable appearance and the clothing and weapons found on and with him.
Wieslaw Smetek/Stern/Black Star

hundreds and even thousands of people over many years. Elaborate representational artwork appeared, sometimes made of rare and imported materials. New technologies, such as smelting and the manufacture of metal tools and weapons, were characteristic of urban life. Commodities, like pottery and textiles that had been made in individual houses in villages, were mass produced in cities, which also were characterized by social stratification—that is, the grouping of people into classes based on factors such as control of resources, family, religious or political authority, and personal wealth. The earliest writing is also associated with the growth of cities. Writing, like representational art, was a powerful means of communicating over space and time and was probably invented to deal with urban problems of management and record keeping.

These attributes—urbanism; technological, industrial, and social change; long-distance trade; and new methods of symbolic communication—are defining characteristics of the form of human culture called **civilization**. At about the time the earliest civilizations were emerging, someone discovered how to combine tin and copper to make a stronger and more useful material—bronze. Archaeologists coined the term *Bronze Age* to refer to the period 3100 to 1200 B.C.E. in the Near East and eastern Mediterranean.

The Bronze Age and the Birth of Civilization

Neolithic agricultural villages and herding cultures gradually replaced Paleolithic culture in much of the world. Then another major shift occurred, first in the plains along the Tigris and Euphrates Rivers in the region the Greeks and Romans called **Mesopotamia** (modern Iraq), later in the valley of the Nile River in Egypt, and somewhat later in India and the Yellow River basin in China. This shift was associated initially with the growth of towns alongside villages, creating a hierarchy of larger and smaller settlements in the same region. Some towns then grew into much larger urban centers and often drew population into them, so that nearby villages and towns declined. The urban centers, or cities, usually had monumental buildings, such as temples and fortifications. These were vastly larger than individual houses and could be built only by the sustained effort of

▼ Early Civilizations to about 1000 B.C.E.

By 4000 B.C.E., people had settled in large numbers in the river-watered lowlands of Mesopotamia and Egypt. By about 3000 B.C.E., when the invention of writing gave birth to history, urban life and the organization of society into centralized states were well established in the valleys of the Tigris and Euphrates Rivers in Mesopotamia and of the Nile River in Egypt.

Much of the population of cities consists of people who do not grow their own food, so urban life is possible only where farmers and stockbreeders can be made to produce a substantial surplus beyond their own needs. Also, some process has to be in place so this surplus can be collected and redeployed to sustain city dwellers. Efficient farming of plains alongside rivers, moreover, requires intelligent management of water resources for irrigation. In Mesopotamia, irrigation was essential, because in the south (later Babylonia), there was not enough rainfall to sustain crops. Furthermore, the rivers, fed by melting snows in Armenia, rose to flood the fields in the spring, about the time for harvest, when water was not needed. When water was needed for the autumn planting, less was available. This meant that people had to build dikes to keep the rivers from flooding the fields in the spring and had to devise means to store water for use in the autumn. The Mesopotamians became skilled at that activity early on. In Egypt, however, the Nile River flooded at the right moment for cultivation, so irrigation was simply a matter of directing the water to the fields. In Mesopotamia, villages, towns, and cities tended to be strung along natural watercourses and, eventually, manmade canal systems. Thus, control of water could be important in warfare, because an enemy could cut off water upstream of a city to force it to submit. Since the Mesopotamian plain was flat, branches of the rivers often changed their courses, and people would have to abandon their cities and move to new locations. Archeologists once believed that urban life and centralized government arose in response to the need to regulate irrigation. This theory supposed that only a strong, central authority could construct and maintain the necessary waterworks. However, archeologists have now shown that large-scale irrigation appeared only long after urban civilization had already developed, so major waterworks were a *consequence* of urbanism, not a cause of it.

Mesopotamian Civilization

The first civilization appears to have arisen in Mesopotamia. The region is divided into two ecological zones, roughly north and south of modern Baghdad. In the south (Babylonia), as noted, irrigation is vital; in the north (later Assyria), agriculture is possible with rainfall and wells. The south has high yields from irrigated lands, whereas the north has lower yields, but much more land under cultivation, so it can produce more than the south. The oldest Mesopotamian cities seem to have been founded by a people called the Sumerians during the fourth millennium B.C.E. in the land of Sumer, which is the southern half of Babylonia. By 3000 B.C.E., the Sumerian city of Uruk was the largest city in the world. (See Map 1–1.) Colonies of people from Uruk built cities and

Map 1–1 **THE ANCIENT NEAR EAST** There were two ancient river valley civilizations. Egypt was united into a single state, and Mesopotamia was long divided into a number of city-states.

outposts in northern Syria and southern Anatolia. One of these, at Habubah Kabirah on the Euphrates River in Syria, was built on a regular plain on virgin ground, with strong defensive walls, but was abandoned after a few generations and never inhabited again. No one knows how the Sumerians were able to establish colonies so far from their homeland or even what their purpose was. They may have been trading centers.

From about 2800 to 2370 B.C.E., in what is called the Early Dynastic period, several Sumerian city-states, independent political units consisting of a major city and its surrounding territory, existed in southern Mesopotamia, arranged in north-south lines along the major watercourses. Among these cities were Uruk, Ur, Nippur, Shuruppak, and Lagash. Some of the city-states formed leagues among themselves that apparently had both political and religious significance. Quarrels over water and agricultural land led to incessant warfare, and in time, stronger towns and leagues conquered weaker ones and expanded to form kingdoms ruling several city-states.

Peoples who, unlike the Sumerians, mostly spoke Semitic languages (that is, languages in the same family as Arabic and Hebrew) occupied northern Mesopotamia and Syria. The Sumerian language is not related to any language known today. Many of these Semitic peoples absorbed aspects of Sumerian culture, especially writing. At the western end of this broad territory, at Ebla in northern Syria, scribes kept records using Sumerian writing and studied Sumerian word lists. In northern Babylonia, the Mesopotamians believed the large city of Kish had the first kings in history. In the far east of this territory, not far from modern Baghdad, a people known as the Akkadians established their own kingdom at a capital city called Akkade, under their first king, Sargon, who had been a servant of the king of Kish.

The Akkadians conquered all the Sumerian city-states and invaded southwestern Iran and northern Syria. This was the first empire in history, having a heartland, provinces, and an absolute ruler. It included numerous peoples, cities, languages, and cultures, as well as different ecological zones, under one rule. Sargon's name became legendary as the first great conqueror of history. His grandson, Naram-Sin, ruled from the Persian Gulf to the Mediterranean Sea, with a standardized administration, unheard-of wealth and power, and a grand style that to later Mesopotamians was a high point of their history. Naram-Sin even declared himself a god and had temples built to himself, something no Sumerian ruler had ever done. External attack and internal weakness destroyed the Akkadian Empire, but several smaller states flourished independently, notably Lagash in Sumer, under its ruler Gudea.

About 2125 B.C.E., the Sumerian city of Ur rose to dominance, and the rulers of the Third Dynasty of Ur established an empire built on the foundation of the

The Victory Stele of Naram-Sin, the Akkadian ruler, commemorates the king's campaign (c. 2230 B.C.E.) against the Lullubi, a people living in the northern Zagros Mountains, along the eastern frontier of Mesopotamia. Kings set up monuments like this one in the courtyards of temples to record their deeds. They were also left in remote corners of the empire to warn distant peoples of the death and enslavement awaiting the king's enemies (pink sandstone).   Victory stele of Naram-Sin, King of Akkad, over the mountain-dwelling Lullubi, Mesopotamian, Akkadian Period, c. 2230 B.C. (pink sandstone). Louvre, Paris, France/The Bridgeman Art Library International Ltd.

Akkadian Empire, but far smaller. In this period, Sumerian culture and literature flourished. Epic poems were composed, glorifying the deeds of the ancestors of the kings of Ur. A highly centralized administration kept detailed records of agriculture, animal husbandry, commerce, and other matters. Over 100,000 of these documents have been found in the ruins of Sumerian cities. After little more than a century of prominence,

KEY EVENTS AND PEOPLE IN MESOPOTAMIAN HISTORY

ca. 3500 B.C.E.	Development of Sumerian cities, especially Uruk
ca. 2800–2370 B.C.E.	Early Dynastic period of Sumerian city-states
ca. 2370 B.C.E.	Sargon establishes Akkadian dynasty and Akkadian Empire
ca. 2125–2027 B.C.E.	Third Dynasty of Ur
ca. 2000–1800 B.C.E.	Establishment of Amorites in Mesopotamia
ca. 1792–1750 B.C.E.	Reign of Hammurabi

the kingdom of Ur disintegrated in the face of famine and invasion. From the east, the Elamites attacked the city of Ur and captured the king. From the north and west, a Semitic-speaking people, the Amorites, invaded Mesopotamia in large numbers, settling around the Sumerian cities and eventually founding their own dynasties in some of them, such as at Uruk, Babylon, Isin, and Larsa.

The fall of the Third Dynasty of Ur put an end to Sumerian rule, and the Sumerians gradually disappeared as an identifiable group. The Sumerian language survived only in writing as the learned language of Babylonia taught in schools and used by priests and scholars. So great was the respect for Sumerian that seventeen centuries after the fall of Ur, when Alexander the Great arrived in Babylon in 331 B.C.E., Sumerian was still used as a scholarly and religious language there.

For some time after the fall of Ur, there was relative peace in Babylonia under the Amorite kings of Isin, who used Sumerian at their court and considered themselves the successors of the kings of Ur. Eventually, another Amorite dynasty at the city of Larsa contested control of Babylonia, and a period of warfare began, mostly centering around attacks on strategic points on waterways. A powerful new dynasty at Babylon defeated Isin, Larsa, and other rivals and dominated Mesopotamia for nearly 300 years. Its high point was the reign of its most famous king, Hammurabi (r. ca. 1792–1750 B.C.E.), best known today for the collection of laws that bears his name. (See "Hammurabi's Law Code," page 11.) Hammurabi destroyed the great city of Mari on the Euphrates and created a kingdom embracing most of Mesopotamia.

Collections of laws existed as early as the Third Dynasty of Ur, and Hammurabi's owed much to earlier models and different legal traditions. His collection of laws, now referred to as the Code of Hammurabi, reveals a society divided by class. There were nobles, commoners, and slaves, and the law did not treat all of them equally. In general, punishments were harsh, based literally on the principle of "an eye for an eye, a tooth for a tooth," whereas Sumerian law often levied fines instead of bodily mutilation or death. Disputes over property and other complaints were heard in the first instance by local city assemblies of leading citizens and heads of families. Professional judges heard cases for a fee and held court near the city gate. In Mesopotamian trials, witnesses and written evidence had to be produced and a written verdict issued. False testimony was punishable by death. Sometimes the contesting parties would submit to an oath before the gods, on the theory that no one would risk swearing a false oath. In cases where evidence or oath could not establish the truth, the contesting parties might take an ordeal, such as being thrown into the river for the god to decide who was telling the truth. Cases of capital punishment could be appealed to the king. Hammurabi was closely concerned with the details of his kingdom, and his surviving letters often deal with minor local disputes.

About 1600 B.C.E., the Babylonian kingdom fell apart under the impact of invasions from the north by the Hittites, Hurrians, and Kassites, all non-Mesopotamian peoples.

Government From the earliest historical records, it is clear that the Sumerians were ruled by monarchs in some form. The earliest Sumerian rulers are shown in their art leading an army, killing prisoners, and making offerings to the gods. The type of rule varied at different times and places. In later Assyria, for example, the king served as chief priest; in Babylonia, the priesthood was separate from royalty. Royal princesses were sometimes appointed as priestesses of important gods. One of the most famous of these was Enheduanna, daughter of Sargon of Akkad. She is the first author in history whose writings can be identified with a real person. Although she was an Akkadian, she wrote complicated, passionate, and intensely personal poetry in the Sumerian language, in which she tells of important historical events that she experienced. In one passage, she compares the agony of writing a poem to giving birth.

The government and the temples cultivated large areas of land to support their staffs and retinue. Laborers of low social status who were given rations of raw foods and other commodities to sustain them and their families did some of the work on this land. Citizens leased some land for a share of the crop and a cash payment. These lands were carefully surveyed, and sometimes the crop could be estimated in advance. The government and temples owned large herds of sheep, goats, cattle, and donkeys. The Sumerian city-states exported wool and textiles to buy metals, such as copper, that were not available in Mesopotamia. Families and private individuals often owned their own farmland or houses in the cities, which they bought and sold as they liked.

A Closer ▶ LOOK

THE ROYAL STANDARD OF UR

THIS MYSTERIOUS OBJECT, dated about 2500 B.C.E., was found in one of the largest graves in the Royal Cemetery at Ur, a major city of the Sumerians, who created the earliest civilization in Mesopotamia, perhaps in the world.

We do not know the original function of the Standard. The archaeologist who discovered it thought that it was carried on a pole. It is made of a wooden frame carrying a mosaic of shell, red limestone, and a blue stone called lapis lazuli. It was found in damaged condition, and the present restoration is only a guess as to how it originally appeared.

The main panels are known as "War" and "Peace." "War" shows one of the earliest representations of a Sumerian army. Chariots, each pulled by four donkeys, trample enemies; infantry with cloaks carry spears; enemy soldiers are killed with axes, others are paraded naked and presented to the king who holds a spear. The "Peace" panel depicts animals, fish, and other goods brought in procession to a banquet.

British Museum, London, UK/Bridgeman Art Library

Seated figures, wearing woolen fleeces or fringed skirts, drink to the accompaniment of a musician playing a lyre.

Picture Desk, Inc./Kobal Collection

To examine this image in an interactive fashion, please go to www.myhistorylab.com

Mathematics Government, business, ... required a good system of writing. The ... ented the writing system now known as ... the Latin *cuneus*, "wedge") because of the wedge-shaped marks they made by writing on clay tablets with a cut reed stylus. At first the writing system was sketchy, giving only a few elements of a sentence to help a reader remember something he probably already knew. Later, people thought to write whole sentences in the order in which they were to be spoken, so writing could communicate new information to a reader. The Sumerian writing system used several thousand characters, some of which stood for words and some for sounds. Some characters stood for many different sounds or words, and some sounds could be written using a choice of many different characters. The result was a writing system that was difficult to learn. Sumerian students were fond of complaining about their unfair teachers, how hard their schoolwork was, and their too-short vacations. Sumerian and Babylonian schools emphasized language and literature, accounting, legal practice, and mathematics, especially geometry, along with memorization of much abstract knowledge that had no relevance to everyday life. The ability to read and write was restricted to an elite who could afford to go to school. Success in school, however, and factors such as good family connections meant a literate Sumerian could find employment as a clerk, surveyor, teacher, diplomat, or administrator.

The Sumerians also began the development of mathematics. The earliest Sumerian records suggest that before 3000 B.C.E. people had not yet thought of the concept of "number" independently of counting specific things. Therefore, the earliest writing used different numerals for counting different things, and the numerals had no independent value. (The same sign could be 10 or 18, for example, depending on what was counted.) Once an independent concept of number was established, mathematics developed rapidly. The Sumerian system was based on the number 60 ("sexagesimal"), rather than the number 10 ("decimal"), the system in general use today. Sumerian counting survives in the modern 60-minute hour and the circle of 360 degrees. By the time of Hammurabi, the Mesopotamians were expert in many types of mathematics, including mathematical astronomy. The calendar the Mesopotamians used had twelve lunar months of thirty days each. To keep it in accordance with the solar year and the seasons, the Mesopotamians occasionally introduced a thirteenth month.

Religion The Sumerians and their successors worshiped many gods and goddesses. They were visualized in human form, with human needs and weaknesses. Most of the gods were identified with some natural phenomenon such as the sky, fresh water, or storms. They differed from humans in their greater power, sublime position in the universe, and immortality. The Mesopotamians believed the human race was created to serve the gods and to relieve the gods of the necessity of providing for themselves. The gods were considered universal, but also residing in specific places, usually one important god or goddess in each city. Mesopotamian temples were run like great households where the gods were fed lavish meals, entertained with music, and honored with devotion and ritual. There were gardens for their pleasure and bedrooms to retire to at night. The images of the gods were dressed and adorned with the finest materials. Theologians organized the gods into families and generations. Human social institutions, such as kingship, or crafts, such as carpentry, were associated with specific gods, so the boundaries between human and divine society were not always clearly drawn. Because the great gods were visualized like human rulers, remote from the common people and their concerns, the Mesopotamians imagined another more personal intercessor god who was supposed to look after a person, rather like a guardian spirit. The public festivals of the gods were important holidays, with parades, ceremonies, and special foods. People wore their best clothes and celebrated their city and its gods. The Mesopotamians were religiously tolerant and readily accepted the possibility that different people might have different gods.

The Mesopotamians had a vague and gloomy picture of the afterworld. The winged spirits of the dead were recognizable as individuals. They were confined to a dusty, dark netherworld, doomed to perpetual hunger and thirst unless someone offered them food and drink. Some spirits escaped to haunt human beings. There was no preferential treatment in the afterlife for those who had led religious or virtuous lives—everyone was in equal misery. Mesopotamian families often had a ceremony to remember and honor their dead. People were usually buried together with goods such as pottery and ornaments. In the Early Dynastic period, certain kings were buried with a large retinue of attendants, including soldiers and musicians, who apparently took poison during the funeral ceremony and were buried where they fell. But this practice soon disappeared. Children were sometimes buried under the floors of houses. Some families used burial vaults; others, large cemeteries. No tombstones or inscriptions identified the deceased. Mesopotamian religion focused on problems of this world and how to lead a good life before dying. (See "Encountering The Past: Divination in Ancient Mesopotamia," page 10.)

Religion played a large part in the literature and art of Mesopotamia. Epic poems told of the deeds of the gods, such as how the world was created and organized, of a great flood the gods sent to wipe out the human race, and of the hero-king Gilgamesh, who tried to

DIVINATION IN ANCIENT MESOPOTAMIA

DIVINATION ATTEMPTS TO foretell the future by the use of magic or occult practices. The ancient Mesopotamians put much thought and effort into discovering signs that they believed would indicate future events, interpreting the meaning of these signs, and taking steps to avert evil. Mesopotamians believed in divination the way many people today put their trust in science.

One of the earliest divination methods the Mesopotamians used involved the sacrifice of sheep and goats. Seers examined the entrails of the sacrificed animals to look for deformations that could foretell the future. Clay tablets recorded particular deformations and the historical events they had foretold. The search for omens in the entrails of sacrificial animals was especially important for Mesopotamian kings, who always performed that ceremony before undertaking important affairs of state.

But animal sacrifice was expensive. Most Mesopotamians, therefore, used other devices. They burned incense and examined the shape of the smoke that arose. They poured oil into water and studied the resulting patterns for signs. They found omens in how people answered questions or in what they overheard strangers say. They collected clay tablets—their books—that described people's appearance and what it might tell them about the future.

The heavens were another source of omens. Astrologers recorded and interpreted the movements of the stars, planets, comets, and other heavenly bodies. Mesopotamia's great progress in astronomy derived in large part from this practice. The study of dreams and of unusual births, both human and animal, was also important. Troubled dreams and monstrous offspring had frightening implications for human affairs.

All these practices derived from the belief that the gods sent omens to warn human beings. Once the omens had been interpreted, the Mesopotamians sought to avert danger with magic and prayers.

How did the Mesopotamians try to learn what would happen in the future, and what did they try to do about what they learned?

How would they explain their great interest in omens?

Astrological calendar. From Uruk, Mesopotamia. Astrological calendar. From Uruk, Mesopotamia. Babylonian, 1st mill. B.C.E. Museum of Oriental Antiquities, Istanbul, Turkey. Photograph © Erich Lessing/Art Resource, NY

HAMMURABI'S LAW CODE

■■

Hammurabi (1792–1750 B.C.E.) ruled the great Babylonian Empire that stretched from the Persian Gulf to the Mediterranean Sea. Building on older Mesopotamian laws, he compiled one of the great ancient codes, the most complete collection of Babylonian laws. His legal decisions were inscribed in the Semitic Akkadian language in cuneiform script placed in Babylon's temple of Marduk. It contains 282 case laws dealing with economics (prices, tariffs, trade, and commerce), family law (marriage and divorce), criminal law (assault, theft), and civil law (slavery, debt). The stone was discovered in the ancient Persian capital of Susa in 1901 and can now be found in the Louvre in Paris.

What principles of justice underlie the cases shown here? By what rights did Hammurabi claim to declare the law?

LAWS

If a son has struck his father, they shall cut off his hand.

If a seignior has destroyed the eye of a member of the aristocracy, they shall destroy his eye.

If he has broken another seignior's bone, they shall break his bone.

If he has destroyed the eye of a commoner or broken the bone of a commoner, he shall pay one mina of silver.

If he has destroyed the eye of a seignior's slave or broken the bone of a seignior's slave, he shall pay one-half his value.

If a seignior has knocked out a tooth of a seignior of his own rank, they shall knock out his tooth.

If he has knocked out a commoner's tooth, he shall pay one-third mina of silver. . . .

EPILOGUE

I, Hammurabi, the perfect king,
was not careless (or) neglectful of the black-headed (people),
whom Enlil had presented to me,
(and) whose shepherding Marduk had committed to me;
I sought out peaceful regions for them;
I overcame grievous difficulties; . . .
With the mighty weapon which Zababa and Inanna entrusted to me,
with the insight that Enki allotted to me,
with the ability that Marduk gave me,
I rooted out the enemy above and below;
I made an end of war;
I promoted the welfare of the land;
I made the peoples rest in friendly habitations; . . .
The great gods called me,
so I became the beneficent shepherd whose scepter is righteous ...

James Pritchard, *The Ancient Near East.* © 1958 Princeton University Press, 1986 renewed PUP. Reprinted by permission of Princeton University Press.

escape death by going on a fantastic journey to find the sole survivor of the great flood. (See "Compare & Connect: The Great Flood," on page 12.) There were also many literary and artistic works that were not religious in character, so we should not imagine religion dominated all aspects of the Mesopotamians' lives. Religious architecture took the form of great temple complexes in the major cities. The most imposing religious structure was the *ziggurat*, a tower in stages, sometimes with a small chamber on top. The terraces may have been planted with trees to resemble a mountain. Poetry about ziggurats often compares them to mountains, with their peaks in the sky and their roots in the netherworld, linking heaven to earth, but their precise purpose is not known. Eroded remains of many of these monumental structures still dot the Iraqi landscape. Through the Bible, they have entered Western tradition as "the tower of Babel."

The Great Flood

STORIES OF A great deluge appeared in many cultures at various times in the ancient world. In the Mesopotamian world the earliest known story of a great flood sent by the gods to destroy mankind appeared in the Sumerian civilization. Later the story was included in the Gilgamesh epic in a Semitic language. The great flood of Noah's time appears in the book of Genesis in the Hebrew Bible.

QUESTIONS

1. In what ways is the story from the *Epic of Gilgamesh* similar to the Story of Noah in the Hebrew Bible?

2. How is the account of a great flood in the Story of Noah different from that in the *Epic of Gilgamesh*?

3. What is the significance of the similarities and differences between the two accounts?

I. The Babylonian Story of the Flood

The passage that follows is part of the Babylonian Epic of Gilgamesh. *An earlier independent Babylonian Story of the Flood suggested that the gods sent a flood because there were too many people on the earth. A version of this story was later combined with the* Epic of Gilgamesh, *a legendary king who became terrified of death when his best friend and companion died. After many adventures, Gilgamesh crossed the distant ocean and the "waters of death" to ask Utanapishtim, who, with his wife, was the only survivor of the great flood, the secret of eternal life. In response, Utanapishtim narrated the story of the great flood, to show that his own immortality derived from a onetime event in the past, so Gilgamesh could not share his destiny.*

Six days and seven nights
The wind continued, the deluge and windstorm
  levelled the land.
When the seventh day arrived,
The windstorm and deluge left off their battle,
Which had struggled, like a woman in labor.
The sea grew calm, the tempest stilled, the deluge
  ceased.
I looked at the weather, stillness reigned,
And the whole human race had turned into clay.
The landscape was flat as a rooftop.
I opened the hatch, sunlight fell upon my face.
Falling to my knees, I sat down weeping,
Tears running down my face.
I looked at the edges of the world, the borders of the sea,

At twelve times sixty double leagues the periphery
  emerged.
The boat had come to rest on Mount Nimush,
Mount Nimush held the boat fast, not letting it move.
One day, a second day Mount Nimush held the boat
  fast, not letting it move.
A third day, a fourth day Mount Nimush held the boat
  fast, not letting it move.
A fifth day, a sixth day Mount Nimush held the boat
  fast, not letting it move.
When the seventh day arrived,
I brought out a dove and set it free.
The dove went off and returned,
No landing place came to its view, so it turned back.
I brought out a swallow and set it free,
The swallow went off and returned,
No landing space came to its view, so it turned back.
I brought out a raven and set it free.
The raven went off and saw the ebbing of the waters.
It ate, preened, left droppings, did not turn back.
I released all to the four directions,
I brought out an offering and offered it to the four
  directions.
I set up an incense burner on the summit of the mountain,
I arranged seven and seven cult vessels,
I heaped reeds, cedar, and myrtle in their bowls.
The gods smelled the savor,
The gods smelled the sweet savor,
The gods crowded round the sacrificer like flies.
As soon as the Belet-ili arrived,
She held up the great fly-ornaments that Anu had made
  in his ardor:

The Flood Tablet (Tablet XI), which relates part of the *Epic of Gilgamesh*. The eleventh tablet describes the meeting of Gilgamesh and Utanapishtim who, along with his wife, survived a great flood that destroyed the rest of humankind.   Art Resource/The British Museum Great Court Ltd. © Copyright The British Museum

'O ye gods, as surely as I shall not forget these lapis
   pendants on my neck,
'I shall be mindful of these days and not forget, not ever!
'The gods should come to the incense burner,
'But Enlil should not come to the incense burner,
'For he, irrationally, brought on the flood,
'And marked my people for destruction!'
As soon as Enlil arrived,
He saw the boat, Enlil flew into a rage,
He was filled with fury at the gods:
'Who came through alive? No man was to survive
   destruction!'
Ninurta made ready to speak,
Said to the valiant Enlil:
'Who but Ea could contrive such a thing?
'For Ea alone knows every artifice.'
Ea made ready to speak,
Said to the valiant Enlil:
'You, O valiant one, are the wisest of the gods,
'How could you, irrationally, have brought on the flood?
'Punish the wrong-doer for his wrong-doing,
'Punish the transgressor for his transgression,
'But be lenient, lest he be cut off,
'Bear with him, lest he [. . .].

'Instead of your bringing on a flood,
'Let the lion rise up to diminish the human race!
'Instead of your bringing on a flood,
'Let the wolf rise up to diminish the human race!
'Instead of your bringing on a flood,
'Let famine rise up to wreak havoc in the land!
  'Instead of your bringing on a flood,
   'Let pestilence rise up to wreak havoc in the land!
    'It was not I who disclosed the secret of the great
    gods,
    'I made Atrahasis have a dream and so he heard
    the secret of the gods.
    'Now then, make some plan for him.'
  Then Enlil came up into the boat,
 Leading me by the hand, he brought me up too.
 He brought my wife up and had her kneel beside me.
 He touched our brows, stood between us to bless us:
'Hitherto Utanapishtim has been a human being,
'Now Utanapishtim and his wife shall become like us
  gods.
'Utanapishtim shall dwell far distant at the source of
  the rivers.'

Source: "The Babylonian Story of the Flood" from *The Babylonian Epic of Gilgamesh*, in *The Epic of Gilgamesh*, trans. by Benjamin R. Foster. Copyright © 2001 by W.W. Norton & Company. Used by permission of W.W. Norton & Company, Inc.

II. Noah's Flood—Genesis 7.11–9.11

In the six hundredth year of Noah's life, in the second month, on the seventeenth day of the month, on that day all the fountains of the great deep burst forth, and the windows of the heavens were opened. The rain fell on the earth forty days and forty nights. . . .

At the end of forty days Noah opened the window of the ark that he had made and sent out the raven; and it went to and fro until the waters were dried up from the earth. Then he sent out the dove from him, to see if the waters had subsided from the face of the ground; but the dove found no place to set its foot, and it returned to him to the ark, for the waters were still on the face of the whole earth. So he put out his hand and took it and brought it into the ark with him. He waited another seven days, and again he sent out the dove from the ark; and the dove came back to him in the evening, and there in its beak was a freshly plucked olive leaf; so Noah knew that the waters had subsided from the earth. Then he waited another seven days, and sent out the dove; and it did not return to him any more. . . .

Then God said to Noah and to his sons with him, "As for me, I am establishing my covenant with you and your descendants after you, and with every living creature that is with you, the birds, the domestic animals, and every animal of the earth with you, as many as came out of the ark." I establish my covenant with you, that never again shall all flesh be cut off by the waters of a flood, and never again shall there be a flood to destroy the earth."

Society Hundreds of thousands of cuneiform texts from the early third millennium B.C.E. until the third century B.C.E. give us a detailed picture of how peoples in ancient Mesopotamia conducted their lives and of the social conditions in which they lived. From the time of Hammurabi, for example, there are many royal letters to and from the various rulers of the age, letters from the king to his subordinates, administrative records from many different cities, and numerous letters and documents belonging to private families.

Categorizing the laws of Hammurabi according to the aspects of life with which they deal reveals much about Babylonian life in his time. The third largest category of laws deals with commerce, relating to such issues as contracts, debts, rates of interest, security, and default. Business documents of Hammurabi's time show how people invested their money in land, moneylending, government contracts, and international trade. Some of these laws regulate professionals, such as builders, judges, and surgeons. The second largest category of laws deals with land tenure, especially land given by the king to soldiers and marines in return for their service. The letters of Hammurabi that deal with land tenure show he was concerned to uphold the individual rights of landholders against powerful officials who tried to take their land from them. The largest category of laws relates to the family and its maintenance and protection, including marriage, inheritance, and adoption.

Parents usually arranged marriages, and betrothal was followed by the signing of a marriage contract. The bride usually left her own family to join her husband's. The husband-to-be could make a bridal payment, and the father of the bride-to-be provided a dowry for his daughter in money, land, or objects. A marriage started out monogamous, but a husband whose wife was childless or sickly could take a second wife. Sometimes husbands also sired children from domestic slave women. Women could possess their own property and do business on their own. Women divorced by their husbands without good cause could get their dowry back. A woman seeking divorce could also recover her dowry if her husband could not convict her of wrongdoing. A married woman's place was thought to be in the home, but hundreds of letters between wives and husbands show them as equal partners in the ventures of life. (See "An Assyrian Woman Writes to Her Husband, ca. 1800 B.C.E.") Single women who were not part of families could set up in business on their own, often as tavern owners or moneylenders, or could be associated with temples, sometimes working as midwives and wet nurses, or taking care of orphaned children.

Slavery: Chattel Slaves and Debt Slaves There were two main types of slavery in Mesopotamia: chattel and debt slavery. Chattel slaves were bought like any other piece of property and had no legal rights. They had to wear their hair in a certain way and were sometimes branded or tattooed on their hands. They were often non-Mesopotamians bought from slave merchants. Prisoners of war could also be enslaved. Chattel slaves were expensive luxuries during most of Mesopotamian history. They were used in domestic service rather than in production, such as fieldwork. A wealthy household might have five or six slaves, male and female.

Debt slavery was more common than chattel slavery. Rates of interest were high, as much as 33.3 percent, so people often defaulted on loans. One reason the interest rates were so high was that the government periodically canceled certain types of debts, debt slavery, and obligations, so lenders ran the risk of losing their money. If debtors had pledged themselves or members of their families as surety for a loan, they became the slave of the creditor; their labor went to pay the interest on the loan. Debt slaves could not be sold but could redeem their freedom by paying off the loan. True chattel slavery did not become common until the Neo-Babylonian period (612–539 B.C.E.).

Although laws against fugitive slaves or slaves who denied their masters were harsh—the Code of Hammurabi permits the death penalty for anyone who sheltered or helped a runaway slave to escape—Mesopotamian slavery appears enlightened compared with other slave systems in history. Slaves were generally of the same people as their masters. They had been enslaved because of misfortune from which their masters were not immune, and they generally labored alongside them. Slaves could engage in business and, with certain restrictions, hold property. They could marry free men or women, and the resulting children would normally be free. A slave who acquired the means could buy his or her freedom. Children of a slave by a master might be allowed to share his property after his death. Nevertheless, slaves were property, subject to an owner's will and had little legal protection.

Egyptian Civilization

As Mesopotamian civilization arose in the valley of the Tigris and Euphrates, another great civilization emerged in Egypt, centered on the Nile River. From its sources in Lake Victoria and the Ethiopian highlands, the Nile flows north some 4,000 miles to the Mediterranean. Ancient Egypt included the 750-mile stretch of smooth, navigable river from Aswan to the sea. South of Aswan the river's course is interrupted by several cataracts—rocky areas of rapids and whirlpools.

The Egyptians recognized two sets of geographical divisions in their country. **Upper** (southern) **Egypt** consisted of the narrow valley of the Nile. **Lower** (northern)

AN ASSYRIAN WOMAN WRITES TO HER HUSBAND, CA. 1800 B.C.E.

■■

The wives of early Assyrian businessmen were often active in their husbands' business affairs. They made extra money for themselves by having slave girls weave textiles that the husbands then sold on business trips. Their letters are one of the largest groups of women's records from the ancient world. The woman writing this letter, Taram-Kubi, complains of her husband's selfishness and points out all the matters she has worked on during his absence on business.

What functions did this woman perform on behalf of the family? How do you judge her real power in regard to her husband? On what evidence do you base that judgment? What does this document reveal about the place of women in Assyrian society?

You wrote to me saying, "You'll need to safeguard the bracelets and rings which are there so they'll be available [to buy] food." In fact, you sent [the man] Ilum-bani a half pound of gold! Which are the bracelets you left me? When you left, you didn't leave me an ounce of silver, you picked the house clean and took away everything! After you left, there was a severe famine in the city. Not so much as a quart of grain did you leave me, I always had to buy grain for our food. Besides that, I paid the assessment for the divine icon (?); in fact, I paid for my part in full. Besides that, I paid over to the Town Hall the grain owed [the man] Atata. What is the extravagance you keep writing to me about? There is nothing for us to eat—we're the ones being extravagant? I picked up whatever I had to hand and sent it to you—today I'm living in an empty house. It's high time you sent me the money realized on my weavings, in silver, from what you have to hand, so I can buy ten quarts of grain!

Trans. by Benjamin R. Foster, 1999.

Egypt referred to the broad triangular area, named by the Greeks after their letter "delta," formed by the Nile as it branches out to empty into the Mediterranean. (See Map 1–2.) They also made a distinction between what they termed the "black land," the dark fertile fields along the Nile, and the "red land," the desert cliffs and plateaus bordering the valley.

The Nile alone made agriculture possible in Egypt's desert environment. Each year the rains of central Africa caused the river to rise over its floodplain, cresting in September and October. In places the plain extends several miles on either side; elsewhere the cliffs slope down to the water's edge. When the floodwaters receded, they left a rich layer of organically fertile silt. The construction and maintenance of canals, dams, and irrigation ditches to control the river's water, together with careful planning and organization of planting and harvesting, produced an agricultural prosperity unmatched in the ancient world.

The Nile served as the major highway connecting Upper and Lower Egypt. There was also a network of desert roads running north and south, as well as routes across the eastern desert to the Sinai and the Red Sea. Other tracks led to oases in the western desert. Thanks to geography and climate, Egypt was more isolated and enjoyed far more security than Mesopotamia. This security, along with the predictable flood calendar, gave Egyptian civilization a more optimistic outlook than the civilizations of the Tigris and Euphrates, which were more prone to storms, flash floods, and invasions.

The 3,000-year span of ancient Egyptian history is traditionally divided into thirty-one royal dynasties, from the first, said to have been founded by Menes, the king who originally united Upper and Lower Egypt, to the last, established by Alexander the Great, who conquered Egypt in 332 B.C.E. (as we see in Chapter 3). Ptolemy, one of Alexander's generals, founded the Ptolemaic Dynasty, whose last ruler was Cleopatra. In 30 B.C.E., the Romans defeated Egypt, effectively ending the independent existence of a civilization that had lasted three millennia.

The unification of Upper and Lower Egypt was vital, for it meant the entire river valley could benefit from an unimpeded distribution of resources. Three times in its history, Egypt experienced a century or more of political and social disintegration, known as Intermediate Periods. During these eras, rival dynasties often set up separate power bases in Upper and Lower Egypt until a strong leader reunified the land.

The Old Kingdom (2700–2200 B.C.E.) The Old Kingdom represents the culmination of the cultural and historical developments of the Early Dynastic

period. For over four hundred years, Egypt enjoyed internal stability and great prosperity. During this period, the **pharaoh** (the term comes from the Egyptian for "great house," much as we use "White House" to refer to the president) was a king who was also a god. From his capital at Memphis, the god-king administered Egypt according to set principles, prime among them being *maat*, an ideal of order, justice, and truth. In return for the king's building and maintaining temples, the gods preserved the equilibrium of the state and en-

MAP EXPLORATION

Interactive map: To explore this map further, go to
www.myhistorylab.com

Map 1–2 **THE NEAR EAST AND GREECE ABOUT 1400 B.C.E.** About 1400 B.C.E., the Near East was divided among four empires. Egypt extended south to Nubia and north through Palestine and Phoenicia. The Kassites ruled in Mesopotamia, the Hittites in Asia Minor, and the Mitannians in Assyrian lands. In the Aegean, the Mycenaean kingdoms were at their height.

MAJOR PERIODS IN ANCIENT EGYPTIAN HISTORY (DYNASTIES IN ROMAN NUMERALS)

3100–2700 B.C.E.	Early Dynastic Period (I–II)
2700–2200 B.C.E.	Old Kingdom (III–VI)
2200–2052 B.C.E.	First Intermediate Period (VII–XI)
2052–1630 B.C.E.	Middle Kingdom (XII–XIII)
1630–1550 B.C.E.	Second Intermediate Period (XIV–XVII)
1550–1075 B.C.E.	New Kingdom (XVIII–XX)

sured the king's continuing power, which was absolute. Since the king was obligated to act infallibly in a benign and beneficent manner, the welfare of the people of Egypt was automatically guaranteed and safeguarded.

Nothing better illustrates the nature of Old Kingdom royal power than the pyramids built as pharaonic tombs. Beginning in the Early Dynastic period, kings constructed increasingly elaborate burial complexes in Upper Egypt. Djoser, a Third Dynasty king, was the first to erect a monumental six-step pyramid of hard stone. Subsequent pharaohs built other stepped pyramids until Snefru, the founder of the Fourth Dynasty, converted a stepped to a true pyramid over the course of putting up three monuments.

His son Khufu (Cheops in the Greek version of his name) chose the desert plateau of Giza, south of Memphis, as the site for the largest pyramid ever constructed. Its dimensions are prodigious: 481 feet high, 756 feet long on each side, and its base covering 13.1 acres. The pyramid is made of 2.3 million stone blocks averaging 2.5 tons each. It is also a geometrical wonder, deviating from absolutely level and square only by the most minute measurements using the latest modern devices. Khufu's successors, Khafre (Chephren) and Menkaure (Mycerinus), built equally perfect pyramids at Giza, and together, the three constitute one of the most extraordinary achievements in human history. Khafre also built the huge composite creature, part lion and part human, that the Greeks named the Sphinx. Recent research has shown that the Sphinx played a crucial role in the solar cult aspects of the pyramid complex.

The pyramids are remarkable not only for the great technical skill they demonstrate, but also for the concentration of resources they represent. They are evidence that the pharaohs controlled vast wealth and had the power to focus and organize enormous human effort over the years it took to build each pyramid. They also provide a visible indication of the nature of the Egyptian state: The pyramids, like the pharaohs, tower above the land; the low tombs at their base, like the officials buried there, seem to huddle in relative unimportance.

Originally, the pyramids and their associated cult buildings contained statuary, offerings, and all the pharaoh needed for the afterlife. Despite great precautions and ingenious concealment methods, tomb robbers took nearly everything, leaving little for modern archeologists to recover. Several full-size wooden boats have been found, however, still in their own graves at the base of the pyramids, ready for the pharaoh's journeys in the next world. Recent excavations have uncovered remains of the large town built to house the thousands of pyramid builders, including the farmers who worked at Giza during the annual flooding of their fields.

Numerous officials, both members of the royal family and nonroyal men of ability, aided the god-kings. The highest office was the *vizier* (a modern term from Arabic). Central offices dealing with granaries, surveys, assessments, taxes, and salaries administered the land. Water management was local rather than on a national level. Upper and Lower Egypt were divided into **nomes**, or districts, each governed by a *nomarch*, or governor, and his local officials. The kings could also appoint royal officials to oversee groups of nomes or to supervise pharaonic landholdings throughout Egypt.

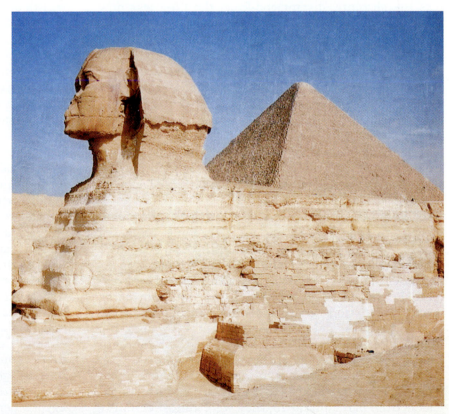

The Great Sphinx has the body of a lion and the head of a man. It was carved at Giza in the reign of the Pharaoh Khafre (c. 2570–2544 B.C.E.).   SEF/Art Resource, NY

The First Intermediate Period and Middle Kingdom (2200–1786 B.C.E.)   Toward the end of the Old Kingdom, for a combination of political and economic reasons, absolute pharaonic power waned as the nomarchs and other officials became more independent and influential. About 2200 B.C.E., the Old Kingdom collapsed and gave way to the decentralization and disorder of the First Intermediate Period, which lasted until about 2052 B.C.E. Eventually, the kings of Dynasty 11, based in Thebes in Upper Egypt, defeated the rival Dynasty 10, based in a city south of Giza.

Amunemhet I, the founder of Dynasty 12 and the Middle Kingdom, probably began his career as a successful vizier under an Eleventh Dynasty king. After reuniting Upper and Lower Egypt, he turned his attention to making three important and long-lasting administrative changes. First, he moved his royal residence from Thebes to a brand-new town, just south of the old capital at Memphis, signaling a fresh start rooted in past glories. Second, he reorganized the nome structure by more clearly defining the nomarchs' duties to the state, granting them some local autonomy within the royal structure. Third, he established a co-regency system to smooth transitions from one reign to another.

Amunemhet I and the other Middle Kingdom pharaohs sought to evoke the past by building pyramid complexes like those of the later Old Kingdom rulers. Yet the events of the First Intermediate Period had irrevocably changed the nature of Egyptian kingship. Gone was the absolute, distant god-king; the king was now more directly concerned with his people. In art, instead of the supremely confident faces of the Old Kingdom pharaohs, the Middle Kingdom rulers seem thoughtful, careworn, and brooding.

Egypt's relations with its neighbors became more aggressive during the Middle Kingdom. To the south, royal fortresses were built to control Nubia and the growing trade in African resources. To the north and east, Syria and Palestine increasingly came under Egyptian influence, even as fortifications sought to prevent settlers from the Levant from moving into the Delta.

The Second Intermediate Period and the New Kingdom (1630–1075 B.C.E.)   For some unknown reason, during Dynasty 13, the kingship changed hands rapidly and the western Delta established itself as an independent Dynasty 14, ushering in the Second Intermediate Period. The eastern Delta, with its expanding Asiatic populations, came under the control of the Hyksos (Dynasty 15) and minor Asiatic kings (Dynasty 16). Meanwhile, the Dynasty 13 kings left their northern capital and regrouped in Thebes (Dynasty 17).

Though much later sources describe the Hyksos ("chief of foreign lands" in Egyptian) as ruthless invaders from parts unknown, they were almost certainly Amorites from the Levant, part of the gradual infiltration of the Delta during the Middle Kingdom. Ongoing excavations at the Hyksos capital of Avaris in the eastern Delta have revealed architecture, pottery, and other goods consistent with that cultural background. After nearly a century of rule, the Hyksos were expelled, a process begun by Kamose, the last king of Dynasty 17, and completed by his brother Ahmose, the first king of the Eighteenth Dynasty and the founder of the New Kingdom.

During Dynasty 18, Egypt pursued foreign expansion with renewed vigor. Military expeditions reached as far north as the Euphrates in Syria, with frequent campaigns in the Levant. To the south, major Egyptian temples were built in the Sudan, almost 1,300 miles from Memphis. Egypt's economic and political power was at its height.

Egypt's position was reflected in the unprecedented luxury and cosmopolitanism of the royal court and in the ambitious palace and temple projects undertaken throughout the country. Perhaps to foil tomb robbers, the Dynasty 18 pharaohs were the first to cut their tombs deep into the rock cliffs of a desolate valley in Thebes, known today as the Valley of the Kings. To date, only one intact royal tomb has been discovered there, that of the young Dynasty 18 king Tutankhamun, and even it had been disturbed shortly after his death. The thousands of goods buried with him, many of them marvels of craftsmanship, give an idea of Egypt's material wealth during this period.

Following the premature death of Tutankhamun in 1323 B.C.E., a military commander named Horemheb assumed the kingship, which passed in turn to his own army commander, Ramses I. The pharaohs Ramessides of Dynasty 19 undertook numerous monumental projects, among them Ramses II's rock-cut temples at Abu Simbel, south of the First Cataract, which had to be moved to a higher location when the Aswan High Dam was built in the 1960s. There and elsewhere, Ramses II left textual and pictorial accounts of his battle in 1285 B.C.E. against the Hittites at Kadesh on the Orontes in Syria. Sixteen years later, the Egyptians and Hittites signed a formal peace treaty, forging an alliance against an increasingly volatile political situation in the Mideast and eastern Mediterranean during the thirteenth century B.C.E.

Merneptah, one of the hundred offspring of Ramses II, held off a hostile Libyan attack, as well as incursions by the Sea Peoples, a loose coalition of Mediterranean raiders who seem to have provoked and taken advantage of unsettled conditions. One of Merneptah's inscriptions commemorating his military triumphs contains the first known mention of Israel.

Despite his efforts, by the end of Dynasty 20, Egypt's period of imperial glory had passed. The next

LOVE POEMS FROM THE NEW KINGDOM

Numerous love poems from ancient Egypt reveal the Egyptians' love of life through their frank sensuality.

How does the girl in the first poem propose to escape the supervision of her parents? What ails the young man in the second poem?

SHE: Love, how I'd love to slip down to the pond,
  bathe with you close by on the bank.
Just for you I'd wear my new Memphis swimsuit,
  made of sheer linen, fit for a queen—
Come see how it looks in the water!
Couldn't I coax you to wade in with me? Let the
  cool creep slowly around us?
Then I'd dive deep down and come up for you
  dripping,
Let you fill your eyes with the little red fish that
  I'd catch.
And I'd say, standing there tall in the shallows:
Look at my fish, love, how it lies in my hand,

How my fingers caress it, slip down its sides . . .
But then I'd say softer, eyes bright with your
  seeing:
A gift, love. No words.
Come closer and look, it's all me.
HE: I think I'll go home and lie very still, feigning
  terminal illness.
Then the neighbors will all troop over to stare, my
  love, perhaps, among them.
How she'll smile while the specialists snarl in
  their teeth!—
she perfectly well knows what ails me.

"Love, how I'd love to slip down to the pond" and "I think I'll go home and lie very still," from *Love Songs of the New Kingdom*, trans. from the Ancient Egyptian by John L. Foster, copyright © 1969, 1970, 1971, 1972, 1973, 1974 by John L. Foster. By permission of the University of Texas Press.

thousand years witnessed a Third Intermediate Period, a Saite Renaissance, Persian domination, conquest by Alexander the Great, the Ptolemaic period, and finally, defeat at the hands of Octavian in 30 B.C.E.

Language and Literature   Writing first appears in Egypt about 3000 B.C.E. Although the impetus for the first Egyptian writing probably came from Mesopotamia, the Egyptians may have invented it on their own. The writing system, dubbed **hieroglyphics** ("sacred carvings") by the Greeks, was highly sophisticated, involving hundreds of picture signs that remained relatively constant in the way they were rendered for over 3,000 years. Many of them formed a syllabary of one, two, or three consonantal sounds; some conveyed a word's meaning or category, either independently or added to the end of the word. Texts were usually written horizontally from right to left, but could be written from left to right, as well as vertically from top to bottom in both horizontal directions. A cursive version of hieroglyphics was used for business documents and literary texts, which were penned rapidly in black and red ink. The Egyptian language, part of the Afro-Asiatic (or

Hamito-Semitic) family, evolved through several stages—Old, Middle, and Late Egyptian, Demotic, and Coptic—thus giving it a history of continuous recorded use well into the medieval period.

Egyptian literature includes narratives, myths, books of instruction in wisdom, letters, religious texts, and poetry, written on papyri, limestone flakes, and postherds. (See "Love Poems from the New Kingdom.") Unfortunately only a small fraction of this enormous literature has survived, and many texts are incomplete. Though they surely existed, we have no epics or dramas from ancient Egypt. Such nonliterary documents as lists of kings, autobiographies in tombs, wine jar labels, judicial records, astronomical observations, and medical and other scientific texts are invaluable for our understanding of Egyptian history and civilization.

Religion: Gods and Temples   Egyptian religion encompasses a multitude of concepts that often seem mutually contradictory to us. Three separate explanations for the origin of the universe were formulated, each based in the philosophical traditions of a venerable

Seated Egyptian scribe, height 21 feet (53 cm) painted limestone, fifth dynasty, c. 2510–2460 B.C.E. One of the hallmarks of the early river valley civilizations was the development of writing. Ancient Egyptian scribes had to undergo rigorous training but were rewarded with a position of respect and privilege. "Seated Scribe" from Saqqara, Egypt. 5th Dynasty, c. 2510–2460 B.C.E. Painted limestone, height 21' (53 cm). Musee du Louvre, Paris. Bridgeman-Giraudon/Art Resource, NY

Egyptian city. The cosmogony of Heliopolis, north of Memphis, held that the creator sun god Atum (also identified as Re) emerged from the darkness of a vast sea to stand upon a primeval mound, containing within himself the life force of the gods he was to create. At Memphis, it was the god Ptah who created the other gods by uttering their names. Further south, at Hermopolis, eight male and female entities within a primordial slime suddenly exploded, and the energy that resulted created the sun and Atum, from which the rest came.

The Egyptian gods, or pantheon, similarly defy neat categorization, in part because of the common tendency to combine the character and function of one or more gods. Amun, one of the eight entities in the Hermopolitan cosmogony, provides a good example. Thebes, Amun's cult center, rose to prominence in the Middle Kingdom. In the New Kingdom, Amun was elevated above his seven cohorts and took on aspects of the sun god Re to become Amun-Re.

Not surprisingly in a nearly rainless land, solar cults and mythologies were highly developed. Much thought was devoted to conceptualizing what happened as the sun god made his perilous way through the underworld in the night hours between sunset and sunrise. Three long texts trace Re's journey as he vanquishes immense snakes and other foes.

The Eighteenth Dynasty was one of several periods during which solar cults were in ascendancy. Early in his reign, Amunhotep IV promoted a single, previously minor aspect of the sun, the Aten ("disk") above Re himself and the rest of the gods. He declared that the Aten was the creator god who brought life to humankind and all living beings, with himself and his queen Nefertiti the sole mediators between the Aten and the people. For religious and political reasons still imperfectly understood, he went further, changing his name to Akhenaten ("the effective spirit of the Aten"), building a new capital called Akhetaten ("the horizon of the Aten") near Amarma north of Thebes, and chiseling out the name of Amun from inscriptions everywhere. Shortly after his death, Amarna was abandoned and partially razed. A large diplomatic archive of tablets written in Akkadian was left at the site, which give us a vivid, if one-sided, picture of the political correspondence of the day. During the reigns of Akhenaten's successors, Tutankhamun (born Tutankhaten) and Horemheb, Amun was restored to his former position, and Akhenaten's monuments were defaced and even demolished.

In representations, Egyptian gods have human bodies, possess human or animal heads, and wear crowns, celestial disks, or thorns. The lone exception is the Aten, made nearly abstract by Akhenaten, who altered its image to a plain disk with solar rays ending in small hands holding the hieroglyphic sign for life to the nostrils of Akhenaten and Nefertiti. The gods were thought to reside in their cult centers, where, from the New Kingdom on, increasingly ostentatious temples were built, staffed by full-time priests. At Thebes, for instance, successive kings enlarged the great Karnak temple complex dedicated to Amun for over 2,000 years. Though the ordinary person could not enter a temple precinct, great festivals took place for all to see. During Amun's major festival of Opet, the statue of the god traveled in a divine boat along the Nile, whose banks were thronged with spectators.

Worship and the Afterlife For most Egyptians, worship took place at small local shrines. They left offerings to the chosen gods, as well as votive inscriptions with simple prayers. Private houses often had niches containing busts for ancestor worship and statues of household deities. The Egyptians strongly believed in the power of magic, dreams, and oracles, and they possessed a wide variety of amulets to ward off evil.

The Egyptians thought the afterlife was full of dangers, which could be overcome by magical means, among them the spells in the *Book of the Dead*. The goals were to join and be identified with the gods, espe-

The Egyptians believed in the possibility of life after death through the god Osiris. Aspects of each person's life had to be tested by forty-two assessor-gods before the person could be presented to Osiris. In the scene from a papyrus manuscript of the *Book of the Dead*, the deceased and his wife (on the left) watch the scales of justice weighing his heart (on the left side of the scales) against the feather of truth. The jackal-headed god Anubis also watches the scales, and the ibis-headed god Thoth keeps the record. British Museum, London, UK/The Bridgeman Art Library International Ltd.

cially Osiris, or to sail in the "boat of millions." Originally only the king could hope to enjoy immortality with the gods, but gradually this became available to all. Since the Egyptians believed the preservation of the body was essential for continued existence in the afterlife, early on they developed mummification, a process that took seventy days by the New Kingdom. How lavishly tombs were prepared and decorated varied over the course of Egyptian history and in accordance with the wealth of a family. A high-ranking Dynasty 18 official, for example, typically had a Theban rock-cut tomb of several rooms embellished with scenes from daily life and funerary texts, as well as provisions and equipment for the afterlife, statuettes of workers, and a place for descendants to leave offerings.

Women in Egyptian Society It is difficult to assess the position of women in Egyptian society, because our pictorial and textual evidence comes almost entirely from male sources. Women's prime roles were connected with the management of the household. They could not hold office, go to scribal schools, or become artisans. Nevertheless, women could own and control property, sue for divorce, and, at least in theory, enjoy equal legal protection.

Royal women often wielded considerable influence, particularly in the Eighteenth Dynasty. The most remarkable was Hatshepsut, daughter of Thutmosis I and widow of Thutmosis II, who ruled as pharaoh for nearly twenty years. Many Egyptian queens held the title "god's wife of Amun," a power base of great importance.

In art, royal and nonroyal women are conventionally shown smaller than their husbands or sons (see illustration). Yet it is probably of greater significance that they are so frequently depicted in such a wide variety of contexts. Much care was lavished on details of their gestures, clothing, and hairstyles. With their husbands, they attend banquets, boat in the papyrus marshes, make and receive offerings, and supervise the myriad affairs of daily life.

Slaves Slaves did not become numerous in Egypt until the growth of Egyptian imperial power in the Middle Kingdom (2052–1786 B.C.E.). During that period, black Africans from Nubia to the south and Asians from the east were captured in war and brought back to Egypt as slaves. The great period of Egyptian imperial expansion, the New Kingdom (1550–1075 B.C.E.), vastly increased the number of slaves and captives in Egypt. Sometimes an entire people was enslaved, as the Bible says the Hebrews were.

Slaves in Egypt performed many tasks. They labored in the fields with the peasants, in the shops of artisans, and as domestic servants. Others worked as policemen and soldiers. Many slaves labored to erect the great temples, obelisks, and other huge monuments of Egypt's imperial age. As in Mesopotamia, slaves were branded for identification and to help prevent their escape. Slaves could be freed in Egypt, but manumission seems to have been rare. Nonetheless, former slaves were not set apart and could expect to be assimilated into the mass of the population.

▼ Ancient Near Eastern Empires

In the time of Dynasty 18 in Egypt, new groups of peoples had established themselves in the Near East: the Kassites in Babylonia, the Hittites in Asia Minor, and the Mitannians in northern Syria and Mesopotamia. (See Map 1–2, page 16.) The Kassites and Mitannians were warrior peoples who ruled as a minority over more civilized folk and absorbed their culture. The Hittites established a kingdom of their own and forged an empire that lasted some two hundred years.

The Hittites

The Hittites were an Indo-European people, speaking a language related to Greek and Sanskrit. By about 1500 B.C.E., they established a strong, centralized government with a capital at Hattusas (near Ankara, the capital of modern Turkey). Between 1400 and 1200 B.C.E., they emerged as a leading military power in the Mideast and contested Egypt's ambitions to control Palestine and Syria. This struggle culminated in a great battle between the Egyptian and Hittite armies at Kadesh in northern Syria (1285 B.C.E.) and ended as a standoff. The Hittites adopted Mesopotamian writing and many aspects of Mesopotamian culture, especially through the Hurrian peoples of northern Syria and southern Anatolia. Their extensive historical records are the first to mention the Greeks, whom the Hittites called Ahhiyawa (the Achaeans of Homer). The Hittite kingdom disappeared by 1200 B.C.E., swept away in the general invasions and collapse of the Mideastern nation-states at that time. Successors to the empire, called the Neo-Hittite states, flourished in southern Asia Minor and northern Syria until the Assyrians destroyed them in the first millennium B.C.E.

The government of the Hittites was different from that of Mesopotamia in that Hittite kings did not claim to be divine or even to be the chosen representatives of the gods. In the early period, a council of nobles limited the king's power, and the assembled army had to ratify his succession to the throne.

The Discovery of Iron An important technological change took place in northern Anatolia, somewhat earlier than the creation of the Hittite kingdom, but perhaps within its region. This was the discovery of how to smelt iron and the decision to use it to manufacture weapons and tools in preference to copper or bronze. Archaeologists refer to the period after 1100 B.C.E. as the Iron Age.

The Assyrians

The Assyrians were originally a people living in Assur, a city in northern Mesopotamia on the Tigris River. They spoke a Semitic language closely related to Babylonian. They had a proud, independent culture heavily influenced by Babylonia. Assur had been an early center for trade but emerged as a political power during the fourteenth century B.C.E. The first Assyrian Empire spread north and west but was brought to an end in the general collapse of Near Eastern states at the end of the second millennium. A people called the Arameans, a Semitic nomadic and agricultural people originally from northern Syria who spoke a language called Aramaic, invaded Assyria. Aramaic is still used in parts of the Near East and is one of the languages of medieval Jewish and Mideastern Christian culture.

The Second Assyrian Empire

After 1000 B.C.E., the Assyrians began a second period of expansion, and by 665 B.C.E., they controlled all of Mesopotamia, much of southern Asia Minor, Syria, Palestine, and Egypt to its southern frontier. They succeeded, thanks to a large, well-disciplined army and a society that valued military skills. Some Assyrian kings boasted of their atrocities, so their names inspired terror throughout the Near East. They constructed magnificent palaces at Nineveh and Nimrud (near modern Mosul, Iraq), surrounded by parks and gardens. The walls of the reception rooms and hallways were decorated with stone reliefs and inscriptions proclaiming the power and conquests of the king.

The Assyrians organized their empire into provinces with governors, military garrisons, and administration for taxation, communications, and intelligence. Important officers were assigned large areas of land throughout the empire, and agricultural colonies were set up in key regions to store up supplies for military actions beyond the frontiers. Vassal kings had to send tribute and delegations to the Assyrian capital every year. Tens of thousands of people were forcibly displaced from their homes and resettled in other areas of the empire, partly to populate sparsely inhabited regions, partly to diminish resistance to Assyrian rule. People of the kingdom of Israel, which the Assyrians invaded and destroyed, were among them.

Relief, Israel, tenth–sixth century: Judean exiles carrying provisions. Detail of the Assyrian conquest of the Jewish fortified town of Lachish (battle 701 B.C.).   Relief, Israel, 10th-6th Century: Judean exiles carrying provisions. Detail of the Assyrian conquest of the Jewish fortified town of Lachish (battle 701 BC). Part of a relief from the palace of Sennacherib at Nineveh, Mesopotamia (Iraq). British Museum, London, Great Britain. Copyright Erich Lessing/Art Resource, NY

and sea routes. For centuries, an astronomical center at Babylon kept detailed records of observations that were the longest-running chronicle of the ancient world. Nebuchadnezzar's dynasty did not last long, and the government passed to various men in rapid succession. The last independent king of Babylon set up a second capital in the Arabian desert and tried to force the Babylonians to honor the Moon-god above all other gods. He allowed dishonest or incompetent speculators to lease huge areas of temple land for their personal profit. These policies proved unpopular—some said that the king was insane—and many Babylonians may have welcomed the Persian conquest that came in 539 B.C.E. After that, Babylonia began another, even more prosperous phase of its history as one of the most important provinces of another great Eastern empire, that of the Persians.

The empire became too large to govern efficiently. The last years of Assyria are obscure, but civil war apparently divided the country. The Medes, a powerful people from western and central Iran, had been expanding across the Iranian plateau. They were feared for their cavalry and archers, against which traditional Mideastern armies were ineffective. The Medes attacked Assyria and were joined by the Babylonians, who had always been restive under Assyrian rule, under the leadership of a general named Nebuchadnezzar. They eventually destroyed the Assyrian cities, including Nineveh in 612 B.C.E., so thoroughly that Assyria never recovered. The ruins of the great Assyrian palaces lay untouched until archaeologists began to explore them in the nineteenth century.

The Neo-Babylonians

The Medes did not follow up on their conquests, so Nebuchadnezzar took over much of the Assyrian Empire. Under him and his successors, Babylon grew into one of the greatest cities of the world. The Greek traveler Herodotus described its wonders, including its great temples, fortification walls, boulevards, parks, and palaces, to a Greek readership that had never seen the like. Babylon prospered as a center of world trade, linking Egypt, India, Iran, and Syria-Palestine by land

▼ The Persian Empire

The great Persian Empire arose in the region now called Iran. The ancestors of the people who would rule it spoke a language from the Aryan branch of the family of Indo-European languages, related to the Greek spoken by the Hellenic peoples and the Latin of the Romans. The most important collections of tribes among them were the Medes and the Persians, peoples so similar in language and customs that the Greeks used both names interchangeably.

The Medes were the first Iranian people to organize their tribes into a union. They were aggressive enough to build a force that challenged the great empires of Mesopotamia. With the help of the ruler of Babylon, they defeated the mighty Assyrian Empire in 612 B.C.E. Until the middle of the sixth century, the Persians were subordinate to the Medes, but when Cyrus II (called the Great) became King of the Persians (r. 559–530 B.C.E.), their positions were reversed. About 550 B.C.E., Cyrus captured the capital at Ecbatana and united the Medes and Persians under his own rule.

Cyrus the Great

Cyrus quickly expanded his power. The territory he inherited from the Medes touched on Lydia, ruled by the rich and powerful king Croesus. Croesus controlled

MAP EXPLORATION

Interactive map: To explore this map further, go to
www.myhistorylab.com

Map 1–3   **THE ACHAEMENID PERSIAN EMPIRE**   The empire created by Cyrus had reached its fullest extent under Darius when Persia attacked Greece in 490 B.C.E. It extended from India to the Aegean, and even into Europe, encompassing the lands formerly ruled by Egyptians, Hittites, Babylonians, and Assyrians.

western Asia Minor, having conquered the Greek cities of the coast about 560 B.C.E. Made confident by his victories, by alliances with Egypt and Babylon, and by what he thought was a favorable signal from the Greek oracle of Apollo at Delphi, he invaded Persian territory in 546 B.C.E. Cyrus achieved a decisive victory, capturing Croesus and his capital city of Sardis. By 539 B.C.E. he had conquered the Greek cities and extended his power as far to the east as the Indus valley and modern Afghanistan.

In that same year he captured Babylon. Because its last king was unpopular, Cyrus was greeted not as a conqueror, but as a liberator. On the cylinder on which was inscribed his version of events, he claimed that the Babylonian god Marduk had "got him into his city Babylon without fighting or battle."[1]

Unlike the harsh Babylonian and Assyrian conquerors who preceded him, Cyrus pursued a policy of

toleration and restoration. He did not impose the Persian religion but claimed to rule by the favor of the Babylonian god. Instead of deporting defeated peoples from their native lands and destroying their cities, he rebuilt their cities and allowed the exiles to return. The conquest of the Babylonian Empire had brought Palestine under Persian rule, so Cyrus permitted the Hebrews, taken into captivity by King Nebuchadnezzar in 586 B.C.E., to return to their native land of **Judah**. This policy, followed by his successors, was effective but not as gentle as it might seem. Wherever they ruled, Cyrus and his successors demanded tribute from their subjects and military service, enforcing these requirements strictly and sometimes brutally.

Darius the Great

Cyrus's son Cambyses succeeded to the throne in 529 B.C.E. His great achievement was the conquest of Egypt, establishing it as a satrapy (province) that ran as far west

[1]"The Cyrus Cylinder," in D. Winton Thomas, *Documents from Old Testament Times* (New York: Harper and Row, 1961), p. 92.

Persian nobles pay homage to King Darius in this relief from the treasury at the Persian capital of Persepolis. Darius is seated on the throne; his son and successor Xerxes stands behind him. Darius and Xerxes are carved in larger scale to indicate their royal status.   Oriental Institute Museum, University of Chicago

as Libya and as far south as Ethiopia. The Persians ruled, as the Bible puts it, "from India to Ethiopia, one hundred and twenty-seven provinces" (Esther 1:1). (See Map 1–3.) On Cambyses's death in 522 B.C.E., a civil war roiled much of the Persian Empire. Darius emerged as the new emperor in 521 B.C.E.

On a great rock hundreds of feet in the air near the mountain Iranian village of Behistun, Darius had carved an inscription in three languages, Babylonian, Old Persian, and Elamite, all in the cuneiform script. They boasted of his victories and the greatness of his rule and, discovered almost two thousand years later, greatly helped scholars decipher all three languages. Darius's long and prosperous reign lasted until 486 B.C.E., during which he brought the empire to its greatest extent. To the east he added new conquests in northern India. In the west he sought to conquer the nomadic people called Scythians who roamed around the Black Sea. For this purpose he crossed into Europe over the Hellespont (Dardanelles) to the Danube River and beyond, taking possession of Thrace and Macedonia on the fringes of the Greek mainland. In 499 B.C.E., the Ionian Greeks of western Asia Minor rebelled, launching the wars between Greeks and Persians that would not end until two decades later. (See Chapter 2.)

Government and Administration

Like the Mesopotamian kingdoms, the Persian Empire was a hereditary monarchy that claimed divine sanction from the god Ahura Mazda. The ruler's title was *Shahanshah*, "king of kings." In theory all the land and the peoples in the empire belonged to him as absolute monarch, and he demanded tribute and service for the use of his property. In practice he depended on the advice and administrative service of aristocratic courtiers, ministers, and provincial governors, the satraps. He was expected, as Ahura Mazda's chosen representative, to rule with justice, in accordance with established custom and the precedents in the Law of the Medes and Persians. Still, the king ruled as a semi-divine autocrat; anyone approaching him prostrated himself as before a god who could demand their wealth, labor, and military service and had the power of life and death. The Greeks would see him as the model of a despot or tyrant who regarded his people as slaves.

The empire was divided into twenty-nine satrapies. The satraps were allowed considerable autonomy. They ruled over civil affairs and commanded the army in war, but the king exercised several means of control. In each satrapy he appointed a secretary and a military commander. He also chose inspectors called "the eyes and ears of the king" who traveled throughout the empire reporting on what they learned in each satrapy. Their travels and those of royal couriers were made swifter and easier by a system of excellent royal roads. The royal postal system was served by a kind of "pony express" that placed men mounted on fast horses at stations along the way. It normally took three months to travel the 1,500 miles from Sardis in Lydia to the Persian capital at Susa. The royal postal service made the trip in less than two weeks. Ruling over a vast empire whose people spoke countless different languages, the Persians did not try to impose their own, but instead adopted Aramaic, the most common language of Middle-Eastern commerce, as the imperial tongue. This practical decision simplified both civil and military administration.

Medes and Persians made up the core of the army. The best of them served in the 10,000 Immortals, while an additional 4,000 composed the Great King's body-guard, divided equally between infantry and cavalry. Royal schools trained aristocratic Median and Persian boys as military officers and imperial administrators. The officers commanded not only the Iranian troops but also drafted large numbers of subject armies when needed. A large Persian army, such as the one that invaded Greece in 480 B.C.E., included hundreds of thousands of non-Iranian soldiers organized by ethnic group, each dressed in its own uniforms, taking orders from Iranian officers.

Religion

Persia's religion was different from that of its neighbors and subjects. Its roots lay in the Indo-European traditions of the Vedic religion that Aryan peoples brought into India about 1500 B.C.E. Their religious practices included animal sacrifices and a reverence for fire. Although the religion was polytheistic, its chief god Ahura Mazda, the "Wise Lord," demanded an unusual emphasis on a stern ethical code. It took a new turn with the appearance of Zarathushtra, a Mede whom the Greeks called Zoroaster, perhaps as early as 1000 B.C.E., as tradition states, although some scholars place him about 600 B.C.E. He was a great religious prophet and teacher who changed the traditional Aryan worship.

Zarathushtra's reform made Ahura Mazda the only god, dismissing the others as demons not to be worshipped but fought. There would be no more polytheism and no sacrifices. The old sacrificial fire was converted into a symbol of goodness and light. Zarathushtra insisted that the people should reject the "Lie" (*druj*) and speak only the "Truth" (*asha*), portraying life as an unending struggle between two great forces, Ahura Mazda, the creator and only god, representing goodness and light, and Ahriman, a demon, representing darkness and evil. He urged human beings to fight for the good, in the expectation that the good would be rewarded with glory and the evil punished with suffering.

Traditions and legends about Zarathustra as well as law, liturgy, and the teachings of the prophet are contained in the *Avesta*, the sacred book of the Persians. By the middle of the sixth century B.C.E., Zoroastrianism had become the chief religion of the Persians. On the great inscribed monument at Behistun, Darius the Great paid public homage to the god of Zarathustra and his teachings: "On this account Ahura Mazda brought me help . . . because I was not wicked, nor was I a liar, nor was I a tyrant, neither I nor any of my line. I have ruled according to righteousness."[2]

KEY EVENTS IN THE HISTORY OF ANCIENT NEAR EASTERN EMPIRES

ca. 1400–1200 B.C.E.	Hittite Empire
ca. 1100 B.C.E.	Rise of Assyrian power
732–722 B.C.E.	Assyrian conquest of Syria-Palestine
671 B.C.E.	Assyrian conquest of Egypt
612 B.C.E.	Destruction of Assyrian capital at Nineveh
612–539 B.C.E.	Neo-Babylonian (Chaldean) Empire
550 B.C.E.	Cyrus the Great unites Persians and Medes
546 B.C.E.	Persia conquers Lydia
521–486 B.C.E.	Reign of Darius the Great

Art and Culture

The Persians learned much from the people they encountered and those they conquered, especially from Mesopotamia and Egypt, but they shaped it to fit comfortably on a Persian base. A good example is to be found in their system of writing. They adapted the Aramaic alphabet of the Semites to create a Persian alphabet and used the cuneiform symbols of Babylon to write the Old Persian language they spoke. They borrowed their calendar from Egypt.

Persian art and architecture contain similar elements of talents and styles borrowed from other societies and blended with Persian traditions to serve Persian purposes. In describing, with justifiable pride, the construction of his palace at Susa, Darius says:

The cedar timber—a mountain by name Lebanon—from there it was brought . . . the yaka-timber was brought from Gandara and from Carmania. The gold was brought from Sardis and from Bactria . . . the precious stone lapis-lazuli and carnelian . . . was brought from Sogdiana. The . . . turquoise from Chorasmia. . . . The silver and ebony . . . from Egypt . . . the ornamentation from Ionia . . . the ivory . . . from Ethiopia and from Sind and from Arachosia. . . . The stone-cutters who wrought the stone, those were Ionians and Sardians. The goldsmiths . . . were Medes and Egyptians. The men who wrought the wood, those were Sardians and Egyptians. The men who wrought the baked brick, those were Babylonians. The men who adorned the wall, those were Medes and Egyptians.[3]

Probably the most magnificent of Persian remains are those of the Royal Palace at Persepolis, built by Darius and his successor Xerxes (r. 485–465 B.C.E.). Its foundation is a high platform supported on three sides by a stone wall 20 or 30 feet high. This was reached by a grand stairway whose sides are covered with carvings.

The complex contained the Hall of a Hundred Columns where the kings did their judicial duties. Better than any other tangible objects, the columns,

---

[2]J. H. Breasted, *Ancient Times: A History of the Early World*, 2nd ed. (Boston: Ginn & Co., 1935), p. 277.

[3]T. Cuyler Young, Jr., "Iran, ancient," *Ecyclopaedia Britannica Online*.

Interactive map: To explore this map further, go to www.myhistorylab.com

MAP EXPLORATION

Map 1–4 **ANCIENT PALESTINE** The Hebrews established a unified kingdom under Kings David and Solomon in the tenth century B.C.E. After Solomon, the kingdom was divided into Israel in the north and Judah, with its capital, Jerusalem, in the south. North of Israel were the great commercial cities of Phoenicia, Tyre, and Sidon.

stairway, and the gateway with winged bulls reveal the grandeur of the ancient Persian Empire.

▼ Palestine

None of the powerful kingdoms of the ancient Near East had as much influence on the future of Western civilization as the small stretch of land between Syria and Egypt, the land called Palestine for much of its history.

The three great religions of the modern world outside the Far East—Judaism, Christianity, and Islam—trace their origins, at least in part, to the people who arrived there a little before 1200 B.C.E. The book that recounts their experiences is the Hebrew Bible.

The Canaanites and the Phoenicians

Before the Israelites arrived in their promised land, it was inhabited by groups of people speaking a Semitic language called Canaanite. The Canaanites lived in walled cities and were farmers and seafarers. They had their own writing system, an alphabet that may have originated among people who were impressed by Egyptian writing, but wanted something much simpler to use. Instead of the hundreds of characters required to read Egyptian or cuneiform, their alphabet used between twenty and thirty characters. The Canaanites, like the other peoples of Syria-Palestine, worshipped many gods, especially gods of weather and fertility, whom they thought resided in the clouds atop the high mountains of northern Syria. The invading Israelites destroyed various Canaanite cities and holy places and may have forced some of the population to move north and west, though Canaanite and Israelite culture also intermingled.

The **Phoenicians** were the descendants of the Canaanites and other peoples of Syria-Palestine, especially those who lived along the coast. They played an important role in Mediterranean trade, sailing to ports in Cyprus, Asia Minor, Greece, Italy, France, Spain, Egypt, and North Africa, as far as Gibraltar and possibly beyond. They founded colonies throughout the Mediterranean as far west as Spain. The most famous of these colonies was Carthage, near modern Tunis in North Africa. Sitting astride the trade routes, the Phoenician cities were important sites for the transmission of culture from east to west. The Greeks, who had long forgotten their older writing system of the Bronze Age, adopted a Phoenician version of the Canaanite alphabet that is the origin of our present alphabet.

The Israelites

The history of the Israelites must be pieced together from various sources. They are mentioned only rarely in the records of their neighbors, so we must rely chiefly on their own account, the Hebrew Bible. This is not a history in our sense, but a complicated collection of historical narrative, pieces of wisdom, poetry, law, and religious witness. Scholars of an earlier time tended to discard it as a historical source, but the most recent trend is to take it seriously while using it with caution.

According to tradition, the patriarch Abraham came from Ur and wandered west to tend his flocks in the land

THE ISRAELITES

ca. 1000–961 B.C.E.	Reign of King David
ca. 961–922 B.C.E.	Reign of King Solomon
722 B.C.E.	Assyrian conquest of Israel (northern kingdom)
586 B.C.E.	Destruction of Jerusalem; fall of Judah (southern kingdom); Babylonian Captivity
539 B.C.E.	Restoration of temple; return of exiles

of the Canaanites. Some of his people settled there, and others wandered into Egypt. By the thirteenth century B.C.E., led by Moses, they had left Egypt and wandered in the desert until they reached and conquered Canaan. They established a united kingdom that reached its peak under David and Solomon in the tenth century B.C.E. The sons of Solomon could not maintain the unity of the kingdom, and it split into two parts: Israel in the north and Judah, with its capital at Jerusalem, in the south. (See Map 1–4, page 27.) The rise of the great empires brought disaster to the Israelites. The northern kingdom fell to the Assyrians in 722 B.C.E., and its people—the **ten lost tribes**—were scattered and lost forever. Only the kingdom of Judah remained. It is from this time that we may call the Israelites Jews.

In 586 B.C.E., Judah was defeated by the Neo-Babylonian king Nebuchadnezzar II. He destroyed the great temple built by Solomon and took thousands of hostages off to Babylon. When the Persians defeated Babylonia, they ended this Babylonian captivity of the Jews and allowed them to return to their homeland. After that, the area of the old kingdom of the Jews in Palestine was dominated by foreign peoples for some 2,500 years, until the establishment of the State of Israel in 1948 C.E.

The Jewish Religion

The fate of the small nation of Israel would be of little interest were it not for its unique religious achievement. The great contribution of the Jews is the development of **monotheism**—the belief in one universal God, the creator and ruler of the universe. Among the Jews, this idea may be as old as Moses, as the Jewish tradition asserts, and it certainly dates as far back as the prophets of the eighth century B.C.E. The Jewish God is neither a natural force nor like human beings or any other creatures; he is so elevated that those who believe in him may not picture him in any form. The faith of the Jews is given special strength by their belief that God made a covenant with Abraham that

his progeny would be a chosen people who would be rewarded for following God's commandments and the law he revealed to Moses.

Like the teachings of Zarathushtra in Iran, Jewish religious thought included a powerful ethical element. God is a severe, but just, judge. Ritual and sacrifice are not enough to achieve his approval. People must be righteous, and God himself appears to be bound to act righteously. The Jewish prophetic tradition was a powerful ethical force. The prophets constantly criticized any falling away from the law and the path of righteousness. They placed God in history, blaming the misfortunes of the Jews on God's righteous and necessary intervention to punish the people for their misdeeds. The prophets also promised the redemption of the Jews if they repented, however. The prophetic tradition expected the redemption to come in the form of a Messiah who would restore the house of David. Christianity, emerging from this tradition, holds that Jesus of Nazareth was that Messiah.

Jewish religious ideas influenced the future development of the West, both directly and indirectly. The Jews' belief in an all-powerful creator (who is righteous himself and demands righteousness and obedience from humankind) and a universal God (who is the father and ruler of all peoples) is a critical part of the Western heritage.

▼ General Outlook of Mideastern Cultures

Our brief account of the history of the ancient Mideast so far reveals that its various peoples and cultures were different in many ways. Yet the distance between all of them and the emerging culture of the Greeks (Chapter 2) is striking. We can see this distance best by comparing the approach of the other cultures to several fundamental human problems with that of the Greeks: What is the relationship of humans to nature? To the gods? To each other? These questions involve attitudes toward religion, philosophy, science, law, politics, and government. Unlike the Greeks, the civilizations of the Mideast seem to have these features in common: Once established, they tended toward cultural uniformity and stability. Reason, though employed for practical and intellectual purposes, lacked independence from religion and the high status to challenge the most basic received ideas. The standard form of government was a monarchy; republics were unknown. Rulers were considered divine or the appointed spokesmen for divinity. Religious and political institutions and beliefs were thoroughly intertwined. Government was not subject to secular, reasoned analysis but rested on religious authority, tradition, and power. Individual freedom had no importance.

Humans and Nature

For the peoples of the Mideast, there was no simple separation between humans and nature or even between animate creatures and inanimate objects. Humanity was part of a natural continuum, and all things partook of life and spirit. These peoples imagined that gods more or less in the shape of humans ruled a world that was irregular and unpredictable, subject to divine whims. The gods were capricious because nature seemed capricious.

A Babylonian story of creation makes it clear that humanity's function is merely to serve the gods. The creator Marduk says,

I shall compact blood, I shall cause bones to be,
I shall make stand a human being, let "Man" be its name.
I shall create humankind,
They shall bear the gods' burden that those may rest.[4]

In a world ruled by powerful deities of this kind, human existence was precarious. Disasters that we would think human in origin, the Mesopotamians saw as the product of divine will. Thus, a Babylonian text depicts the destruction of the city of Ur by invading Elamites as the work of the gods, carried out by the storm god Enlil:

Enlil called the storm.
The people mourn.
Exhilarating winds he took from the land.
The people mourn.
Good winds he took away from Sumer.
The people mourn.
He summoned evil winds.
The people mourn.
Entrusted them to Kingaluda, tender of storms.
He called the storm that will annihilate the land.
The people mourn.
He called disastrous winds.
The people mourn.
Enlil—choosing Gibil as his helper—
Called the (great) hurricane of heaven.
The people mourn.[5]

Both the Egyptian and the Babylonian versions of the destruction of humankind clearly show human vulnerability in the face of divine powers. In one Egyptian tale, Re, the god who had created humans, decided to destroy them because they were plotting evil against him. He sent the goddess Sekhmet to accomplish the deed, and she was resting in the midst of her task, having enjoyed the work and wading in a sea of blood, when Re changed his mind. He ordered 7,000 barrels of blood-colored beer poured in Sekhmet's path. She quickly became too drunk to continue the slaughter and thus humanity was preserved. In the Babylonian story of the flood, the motive for the destruction of humanity is given as follows:

The land had grown numerous, the peoples had increased,
The land was bellowing like a bull.
The god was disturbed by their uproar,
The god Enlil heard their clamor.
He said to the great gods,
"The clamor of mankind has become burdensome to me,
"I am losing sleep to their uproar!"[6]

Utanapishtim and his wife survived because he was friendly with Enki, the god of wisdom, who helped him to pull through by a trick.

In such a universe, humans could not hope to understand nature, much less control it. At best, they could try by magic to use uncanny forces against others. An example of this device is provided by a Mesopotamian incantation to cure sickness. The sufferer tries to use magical powers by acting out the destruction of the powers he thinks caused his illness:

As this garlic is peeled off and thrown into the fire,
[And the Fire God] burns it up with fire,
Which will not be cultivated in a garden patch,
Whose roots will not take hold in the ground,
Whose sprout will not come forth nor see the sun,
Which will not be used for the repast of god or king,
[So] may the curse, something evil, revenge, interrogation,
The sickness of my suffering, wrong-doing, crime, misdeed, sin
The sickness which is in my body, flesh, and sinews
Be peeled off like this garlic,
May [the Fire God] burn it with fire this day,
May the wicked thing go forth, that I may see light.[7]

Humans and the Gods, Law, and Justice

Human relationships to the gods were equally humble. There was no doubt that the gods could destroy human beings and might do so at any time for no good reason. Humans could—and, indeed, had to—try to win the gods over by prayers and sacrifices, but there was no guarantee of success. The gods were bound by no laws and no morality. The best behavior and the greatest devotion to the cult of the gods were no defense against the divine and cosmic caprice.

In the earliest civilizations, human relations were guided by laws, often set down in written codes. The basic question about law concerned its legitimacy: Why, apart from the lawgiver's power to coerce obedience, should anyone obey the law? For Old Kingdom Egyptians, the answer was simple: The king was bound to act

---

[4]Benjamin R. Foster, *From Distant Days, Myths, Tales, and Poetry of Ancient Mesopotamia* (Bethesda, MD: CDL Press, 1999), p. 38.

[5]Thorkild Jacobsen in Henri Frankfort et al., *Before Philosophy* (Baltimore: Penguin, 1949), p. 154.

[6]Foster, pp. 170–171.

[7]Foster, p. 412.

in accordance with maat, and so his laws were righteous. For the Mesopotamians, the answer was almost the same: The king was a representative of the gods, so the laws he set forth were authoritative. The prologue to the most famous legal document in antiquity, the Code of Hammurabi, makes this plain:

I am the king who is preeminent among kings;
my words are choice; my ability has no equal.
By the order of Sharnash, the great judge of heaven and
   earth,
may my justice prevail in the land;
by the word of Marduk, my lord,
may my statutes have no one to rescind them.[8]

The Hebrews introduced some important new ideas. Their unique God was capable of great anger and destruction, but he was open to persuasion and subject to morality. He was therefore more predictable and comforting, for all the terror of his wrath. The biblical version of the flood story, for instance, reveals the great difference between the Hebrew God and the Babylonian deities. The Hebrew God was powerful and wrathful, but he was not arbitrary. He chose to destroy his creatures for their moral failures:

the wickedness of man was great in the earth, and that every imagination of the thought of his heart was evil continually . . . the earth was corrupt in God's sight and the earth was filled with violence.[9]

When he repented and wanted to save someone, he chose Noah because "Noah was a righteous man, blameless in his generation."[10]

The biblical story of Sodom and Gomorrah shows that God was bound by his own definition of righteousness. He had chosen to destroy these wicked cities but felt obliged by his covenant to inform Abraham first.[11] Abraham called on God to abide by his own moral principles, and God saw Abraham's point.

Such a world offers the possibility of order in the universe and on this earth. There is also the possibility of justice among human beings, for the Hebrew God had provided his people with law. Through his prophet Moses, he had provided humans with regulations that would enable them to live in peace and justice. If they would abide by the law and live upright lives, they and their descendants could expect happy and prosperous lives. This idea was different from the uncertainty of the Babylonian view, but like it and its Egyptian partner, it left no doubt of the certainty of the divine. Cosmic order, human survival, and justice all depended on God.

▼ Toward the Greeks and Western Thought

Greek thought offered different approaches and answers to many of the concerns we have been discussing. Calling attention to some of those differences will help convey the distinctive outlook of the Greeks and the later cultures within Western civilization that have drawn heavily on Greek influence.

Greek ideas had much in common with the ideas of earlier peoples. The Greek gods had most of the characteristics of the Mesopotamian deities. Magic and incantations played a part in the lives of most Greeks, and Greek law, like that of earlier peoples, was usually connected with divinity. Many, if not most, Greeks in the ancient world must have lived their lives with notions similar to those other peoples held. The surprising thing is that some Greeks developed ideas that were strikingly different and, in so doing, set part of humankind on an entirely new path.

As early as the sixth century B.C.E., some Greeks living in the Ionian cities of Asia Minor raised questions and suggested answers about the nature of the world that produced an intellectual revolution. In their speculations, they made guesses that were completely naturalistic and made no reference to supernatural powers. One historian of Greek thought, discussing the views of Thales, the first Greek philosopher, put the case particularly well:

In one of the Babylonian legends it says: "All the lands were sea . . . Marduk bound a rush mat upon the face of the waters, he made dirt and piled it beside the rush mat." What Thales did was to leave Marduk out. He, too, said that everything was once water. But he thought that earth and everything else had been formed out of water by a natural process, like the silting up of the Delta of the Nile. . . . It is an admirable beginning, the whole point of which is that it gathers into a coherent picture a number of observed facts without letting Marduk in.[12]

By putting the question of the world's origin in a naturalistic form, Thales, in the sixth century B.C.E., may have begun the unreservedly rational investigation of the universe and, in so doing, initiated both philosophy and science.

The same relentlessly rational approach was used even in regard to the gods themselves. In the same century as Thales, Xenophanes of Colophon expressed the opinion that humans think of the gods as resembling themselves, that, like themselves, they were born, that they wear clothes like theirs, and that they have voices and bodies like theirs. If oxen, horses, and lions had hands and could paint like humans, Xenophanes argued, they would paint gods in their own image; the oxen would draw gods like oxen and the horses like horses. Thus, Africans believed in flat-nosed, black-faced gods,

[8]James B. Pritchard, *Ancient Near Eastern Texts Related to the Old Testament*, 3rd ed. (Princeton: Princeton University Press, 1969), p. 164.
[9]Genesis 6:5, 6:11.
[10]Genesis 6:9.
[11]Genesis 18:20–33.
[12]Benjamin Farrington, *Greek Science* (London: Penguin, 1953), p. 37.

and the Thracians in gods with blue eyes and red hair.[13] In the fifth century B.C.E., Protagoras of Abdera went so far toward agnosticism as to say, "About the gods I can have no knowledge either that they are or that they are not or what is their nature."[14]

This rationalistic, skeptical way of thinking carried over into practical matters. The school of medicine led by Hippocrates of Cos (about 400 B.C.E.) attempted to understand, diagnose, and cure disease without any attention to supernatural forces. One of the Hippocratics wrote, of the mysterious disease epilepsy:

It seems to me that the disease is no more divine than any other. It has a natural cause, just as other diseases have. Men think it divine merely because they do not understand it. But if they called everything divine which they do not understand, why, there would be no end of divine things.[15]

By the fifth century B.C.E., the historian Thucydides could analyze and explain human behavior completely in terms of human nature and chance, leaving no place for the gods or supernatural forces.

The same absence of divine or supernatural forces characterized Greek views of law and justice. Most Greeks, of course, liked to think that, in a vague way, law came ultimately from the gods. In practice, however, and especially in the democratic states, they knew that laws were made by humans and should be obeyed because they represented the expressed consent of the citizens. Law, according to the fourth-century B.C.E. statesman Demosthenes, is "a general covenant of the whole State, in accordance with which all men in that State ought to regulate their lives."[16]

In Perspective

The statement of the following ideas, so different from any that came before the Greeks, opens the discussion of most of the issues that appear in the long history of Western civilization and that remain major concerns in the modern world. What is the nature of the universe, and how can it be controlled? Are there divine powers, and if so, what is humanity's relationship to them? Are law and justice human, divine, or both? What is the place in human society of freedom, obedience, and reverence? These and many other matters were either first considered or first elaborated on by the Greeks.

The Greeks' sharp departure from the thinking of earlier cultures marked the beginning of the unusual ex-

perience that we call Western civilization. Nonetheless, they built on a foundation of lore that people in the Near East had painstakingly accumulated. From ancient Mesopotamia and Egypt, they borrowed important knowledge and skills in mathematics, astronomy, art, and literature. From Phoenicia, they learned the art of writing. The discontinuities, however, are more striking than the continuities.

Hereditary monarchies, often elevated by the aura of divinity, ruled the great civilizations of the river valleys. Powerful priesthoods presented yet another bastion of privilege that stood between the ordinary person and the knowledge and opportunity needed for freedom and autonomy. Religion was an integral part of the world of the ancient Near East, in the kingdoms and city-states of Palestine, Phoenicia, and Syria, just as in the great empires of Egypt, Mesopotamia, and Persia. The secular, reasoned questioning that sought to understand the world in which people lived—that sought explanations in the natural order of things rather than in the supernatural acts of the gods—was not characteristic of the older cultures. Nor would it appear in similar societies at other times in other parts of the world. The new way of looking at things was uniquely the product of the Greeks. We now need to see why they raised fundamental questions in the way that they did.

REVIEW QUESTIONS

1. How would you define "history"? What different academic disciplines do historians rely on, and why is the study of history important?

2. How was life during the Paleolithic Age different from that in the Neolithic Age? What advancements in agriculture and human development had taken place by the end of the Neolithic era? Is it valid to speak of a Neolithic Revolution?

3. What were the political and intellectual outlooks of the civilizations of Egypt and Mesopotamia? How did geography influence the religious outlooks of these two civilizations?

4. To what extent did the Hebrew faith bind the Jews politically? Why was the concept of monotheism so radical for Near Eastern civilizations?

5. How did the Assyrian Empire differ from that of the Hittites or Egyptians? Why did the Assyrian Empire ultimately fail to survive? Why was the Persian Empire so successful? What were the main teachings of Zarathustra? How did his concept of the divine compare to that of the Jews?

6. In what ways did Greek thought develop along different lines from that of Near Eastern civilizations? What new questions about human society did the Greeks ask?

[13]Henri Frankfort et al., *Before Philosophy* (Baltimore: Penguin, 1949), pp. 14–16.
[14]Hermann Diels, *Fragmente der Vorsokratiker*, 5th ed., ed. by Walter Krantz (Berlin: Weidmann, 1934–1938), Frg. 4.
[15]Diels, Frgs. 14–16.
[16]Demosthenes, *Against Aristogeiton* 16.

SUGGESTED READINGS

C. Aldred, *The Egyptians* (1998). Probably the best one-volume history of the subject.

P. Briant, *From Cyrus to Alexander: A History of the Persian Empire* (2002). A scholarly account of ancient Persia with greater knowledge of the Persian evidence than is usual.

T. Bryce, *The Kingdom of the Hittites* (1998). A fine new account.

M. Ehrenberg, *Women in Prehistory* (1989). Discusses the role of women in early times.

B. M. Fagan, *People of the Earth: An Introduction to World Prehistory*, 11th ed. (2003). A narrative account of human prehistory up to the earliest civilizations.

W. W. Hallo and W. K. Simpson, *The Ancient Near East: A History*, rev. ed. (1998). A fine survey of Egyptian and Mesopotamian history.

A. Kamm, *The Israelites: An Introduction* (1999). A brief, excellent, and accessible account.

R. Matthews, *Archaeology of Mesopotamia: Theories and Approaches* (2003). A fascinating investigation of the theories, methods, approaches, and history of Mesopotamian archaeology from its origins in the nineteenth century up to the present day.

J. B. Pritchard, ed., *Ancient Near Eastern Texts Relating to the Old Testament* (1969). A good collection of documents in translation with useful introductory material.

R. Rudgley, *The Lost Civilizations of the Stone Age* (1999). A bold new interpretation that claims that many elements of civilization were already present in the Stone Age.

H. W. F. Saggs, *Babylonians* (1995). A general account of ancient Mesopotamia by an expert scholar.

I. Shaw, ed., *The Oxford History of Ancient Egypt* (2000). An up-to-date survey by leading scholars.

W. K. Simpson et al., *The Literature of Ancient Egypt: An Anthology of Stories, Instructions, Stelae, Autobiographies, and Poetry* (2003). A fine collection of writings from ancient Egypt.

D. C. Snell, *Life in the Ancient Near East, 3100–332 B.C.E.* (1997). A social history with emphasis on culture and daily life.

For additional learning resources related to this chapter, please go to www.myhistorylab.com

PEARSON
myhistorylab

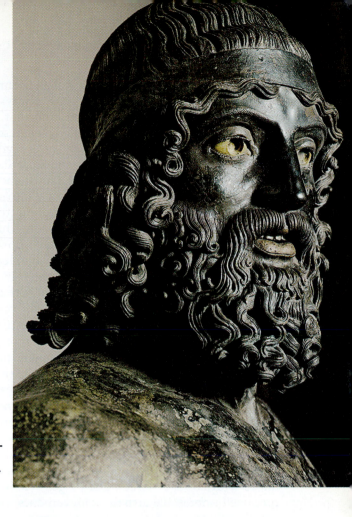

In 1972, this striking bronze statue was found off the coast of Riace, southern Italy. Possibly a votive statue from the sanctuary of Delphi in Greece, it may have been the work of the sculptor Phidias (ca. 490–430 B.C.E.).   Erich Lessing/Art Resource, N.Y.

2

The Rise of Greek Civilization

▼ **The Bronze Age on Crete and on the Mainland to about 1150** B.C.E.
The Minoans • The Mycenaeans

▼ **The Greek "Middle Ages" to about 750** B.C.E.
Greek Migrations • The Age of Homer

▼ **The *Polis***
Development of the *Polis* • The *Hoplite* Phalanx • The Importance of the *Polis*

▼ **Expansion of the Greek World**
Magna Graecia • The Greek Colony • The Tyrants (about 700–500 B.C.E.)

▼ **The Major States**
Sparta • Athens

▼ **Life in Archaic Greece**
Society • Religion • Poetry

▼ **The Persian Wars**
The Ionian Rebellion • The War in Greece

▼ **In Perspective**

KEY TOPICS

• The Bronze Age civilizations that ruled the Aegean area before the development of Hellenic civilization

• The rise, development, and expansion of the *polis*, the characteristic political unit of Hellenic Greece

• The early history of Sparta and Athens

• The wars between the Greeks and the Persians

ABOUT 2000 B.C.E., Greek-speaking peoples settled the lands surrounding the Aegean Sea and established a style of life and formed a set of ideas, values, and institutions that spread far beyond the Aegean corner of the Mediterranean Sea. Preserved and adapted by the Romans, Greek culture powerfully influenced the society of western Europe in the Middle Ages and dominated the Byzantine Empire in the same period. It would ultimately spread across Europe and cross the Atlantic to the Western Hemisphere.

At some time in their history, the Greeks of the ancient world founded cities on every shore of the Mediterranean Sea. Pushing on through the Dardanelles, they placed many settlements on the coasts of the Black Sea in southern Russia and as far east as the approaches to the Caucasus Mountains. The center of Greek life, however, has always been the Aegean Sea and the islands in and around it. This location at the eastern end of the Mediterranean soon put the Greeks in touch with the more advanced civilizations of Mesopotamia, Egypt, Asia Minor, and Syria-Palestine. The Greeks acknowledged the influence of these predecessors. A character in one of Plato's dialogues says, "Whatever the Greeks have acquired from foreigners they have, in the end, turned into something finer."[1] This is a proud statement, but it also shows that the Greeks were aware of how much they had learned from other civilizations.

The Bronze Age Minoan culture of Crete contributed to Greek civilization; and the mainland Mycenaean culture, which conquered Minoan Crete, contributed even more. Both these cultures, however, had more in common with the cultures of the Near East than with the new Hellenic culture established by the Greeks in the centuries after the end of the Bronze Age in the twelfth century B.C.E.

The rugged geography of the Greek peninsula and its nearby islands isolated the Greeks of the early Iron Age from their richer and more culturally advanced neighbors, shaping, in part, their way of life and permitting them to develop that way of life on their own. The aristocratic world of the "Greek Dark Ages" (1150–750 B.C.E.) produced impressive artistic achievements, especially in the development of painted pottery and most magnificently, in the epic poems of Homer. In the eighth century B.C.E., social, economic, and military changes profoundly influenced the organization of Greek political life; the Greek city-state, the *polis*, came into being and thereafter dominated the cultural development of the Greek people.

This change came in the midst of turmoil, for the pressure of a growing population led many Greeks to leave home and establish colonies far away. Those who remained often fell into political conflict, from which tyrannies sometimes emerged. These tyrannies, however, were transitory, and the Greek cities emerged from them as self-governing polities, usually ruled by an oligarchy, broad or narrow. The two most important states, Athens and Sparta, developed in different directions. Sparta formed a mixed constitution in which a small part of the population dominated the vast majority, and Athens developed the world's first democracy.

▼ The Bronze Age on Crete and on the Mainland to about 1150 B.C.E.

The Bronze Age civilizations in the region the Greeks would rule arose on the island of Crete, on the islands of the Aegean, and on the mainland of Greece. Crete was the site of the earliest Bronze Age settlements, and mod-

ern scholars have called the civilization that arose there **Minoan**, after Minos, the legendary king of Crete. A later Bronze Age civilization was centered at the mainland site of Mycenae and is called **Mycenaean**.

The Minoans

With Greece to the north, Egypt to the south, and Asia to the east, Crete was a cultural bridge between the older civilizations and the new one of the Greeks. The Bronze Age came to Crete not long after 3000 B.C.E., and the Minoan civilization, which powerfully influenced the islands of the Aegean and the mainland of Greece, arose in the third and second millennia B.C.E.

Scholars have established links between stratigraphic layers at archaeological sites on Crete and specific styles of pottery and other artifacts found in the layers. On this basis they have divided the Bronze Age on Crete into three major periods—Early, Middle, and Late Minoan—with some subdivisions. Dates for Bronze Age settlements on the Greek mainland, for which the term *Helladic* is used, are derived from the same chronological scheme.

During the Middle and Late Minoan periods in the cities of eastern and central Crete, a civilization developed that was new and unique in its character and beauty. Its most striking creations are the palaces uncovered at such sites as Phaestus, Haghia Triada, and, most important, Cnossus. Each of these palaces was built around a central court surrounded by a labyrinth of rooms. Some sections of the palace at Cnossus were four stories high. The basement contained many storage rooms for oil and grain, apparently paid as taxes to the king. The main and upper floors contained living quarters, and workshops for making pottery and jewelry. There were sitting rooms and even bathrooms, to which water was piped through excellent plumbing. Lovely columns, which tapered downward, supported the ceilings, and many of the walls carried murals showing landscapes and seascapes, festivals, and sports. The palace design and the paintings show the influence of Syria, Asia Minor, and Egypt, but the style and quality are unique to Crete.

In contrast to the Mycenaean cities on the mainland of Greece, Minoan palaces and settlements lacked strong defensive walls. This evidence that the Minoans built without defense in mind has raised questions and encouraged speculation. Some scholars, pointing also to evidence that Minoan religion was more matriarchal than the patriarchal religion of the Mycenaeans and their Greek descendants, have argued that the civilizations of Crete, perhaps reflecting the importance of women, were inherently more tranquil and pacific than others. An earlier and different explanation for the absence of fortifications was that the protection provided by the sea made them unnecessary. The evidence is not strong enough to support either explanation, and the mystery remains.

---

[1]Plato, *Epinomis* 987 d.

Along with palaces, paintings, pottery, jewelry, and other valuable objects, excavations have revealed clay writing tablets like those found in Mesopotamia. The tablets, preserved accidentally when a great fire that destroyed the royal palace at Cnossus hardened them, have three distinct kinds of writing on them: a kind of picture writing called *hieroglyphic*, and two different linear scripts called Linear A and Linear B. The languages of the two other scripts remain unknown, but Linear B proved to be an early form of Greek. The contents of the tablets, primarily inventories, reveal an organization centered on the palace and ruled by a king who was supported by an extensive bureaucracy that kept remarkably detailed records.

This sort of organization is typical of early civilizations in the Near East, but as we shall see, is nothing like that of the Greeks after the Bronze Age. Yet the inventories were written in a form of Greek. If they controlled Crete throughout the Bronze Age, why should Minoans, who were not Greek, have written in a language not their own? This question raises the larger one of what the relationship was between Crete and the Greek mainland in the Bronze Age and leads us to an examination of mainland culture.

The Mycenaeans

In the third millennium B.C.E.—the Early Helladic Period—most of the Greek mainland, including many of the sites of later Greek cities, was settled by people who used metal, built some impressive houses, and traded with Crete and the islands of the Aegean. The names they gave to places, names that were sometimes preserved by later invaders, make it clear they were not Greeks and they spoke a language that was not Indo-European (the language family to which Greek belongs).

Not long after the year 2000 B.C.E., many of these Early Helladic sites were destroyed by fire, some were abandoned, and still others appear to have yielded peacefully to an invading people. These signs of invasion probably signal the arrival of the Greeks.

All over Greece, there was a smooth transition between the Middle and Late Helladic periods. The invaders succeeded in establishing control of the entire mainland. The shaft graves cut into the rock at the royal palace-fortress of Mycenae show that they prospered and sometimes became rich. At Mycenae, the richest finds come from the period after 1600 B.C.E. The city's wealth and power reached their peak during this time, and the culture of the whole mainland during the Late Helladic Period goes by the name *Mycenaean*.

The presence of the Greek Linear B tablets at Cnossus suggests that Greek invaders also established themselves in Crete, and there is good reason to believe that at the height of Mycenaean power (1400–1200 B.C.E.), Crete was part of the Mycenaean world. Although their dating is still controversial, the Linear B tablets at Cnossus seem to belong to Late Minoan III. Thus, what is called the great "palace period" at Cnossus would have followed an invasion by Mycenaeans in 1400 B.C.E. These Greek invaders ruled Crete until the end of the Bronze Age.

Mycenaean Culture The excavation of Mycenae, Pylos, and other Mycenaean sites reveals a culture influenced by, but different from, the Minoan culture. Mycenae and Pylos, like Cnossus, were built some distance from the sea, but defense against attack was foremost in the minds of the founders of the Mycenaean cities. Both Mycenae and Pylos were built on hills in a position commanding the neighboring territory. The Mycenaean people were warriors, as their art, architecture, and weapons reveal. The success of their campaigns and the defense of their territory required strong central authority, and all available evidence shows that the kings provided it. Their palaces, in which the royal family and its retainers lived, were located within the walls; most of the population lived outside the walls. As on Crete, paintings usually covered the palace walls, but instead of peaceful landscapes and games, the Mycenaean murals depicted scenes of war and boar hunting.

About 1500 B.C.E., the already impressive shaft graves were abandoned in favor of *tholos* tombs. These large, beehivelike chambers were built of enormous well-cut and fitted stones and were approached by an unroofed passage (*dromos*) cut horizontally into the side of the hill. The lintel block alone of one of these tombs weighs over one hundred tons. Only a strong king whose wealth was great, whose power was unquestioned, and who commanded the labor of many people could undertake such a project. His wealth probably came from plundering raids, piracy, and trade. Some of this trade went westward to Italy and Sicily, but most of it was with the islands of the Aegean, the coastal towns of Asia Minor, and the cities of Syria, Egypt, and Crete. The Mycenaeans sent pottery, olive oil, and animal hides in exchange for jewels and other luxuries.

This statuette of a female with a snake in each of her hands is thought to represent either the Minoan snake goddess herself or one of her priestesses performing a religious ritual. It was found on Crete and dates from around 1600 B.C.E. Max Alexander/Dorling Kindersley © Archaeological Receipts Fund (TAP)

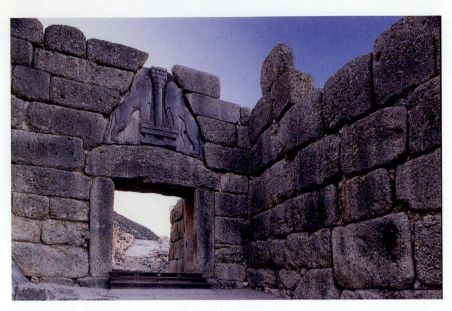

The citadel of Mycenae, a major center of the Greek civilization of the Bronze Age, was built of enormously heavy stones. The lion gate at its entrance was built in the thirteenth century B.C.E.   Joe Cornish/Dorling Kindersley © Archaeological Receipts Fund (TAP)

Tablets containing the Mycenaean Linear B writing have been found all over the mainland; the largest and most useful collection was found at Pylos. These tablets reveal a world similar to the one the records at Cnossus show. The king, whose title was *wanax*, held a royal domain, appointed officials, commanded servants, and kept a close record of what he owned and what was owed to him. This evidence confirms all the rest; the Mycenaean world was made up of several independent, powerful, and well-organized monarchies.

The Rise and Fall of Mycenaean Power At the height of their power (1400–1200 B.C.E.), the Mycenaeans were prosperous and active. They enlarged their cities, expanded their trade, and even established commercial colonies in the East. The archives of the Hittite kings of Asia Minor mention them. Egyptian records name them as marauders of the Nile Delta. Sometime about 1250 B.C.E., they probably sacked Troy, on the coast of northwestern Asia Minor, giving rise to the epic poems of Homer—the *Iliad* and the *Odyssey*. (See Map 2–1.) Around 1200 B.C.E., however, the Mycenaean world showed signs of trouble, and by 1100 B.C.E., it was gone. Its palaces were destroyed, many of its cities were abandoned, and its art, way of life, and system of writing were buried and forgotten.

What happened? Some recent scholars, noting evidence that the Aegean island of Thera (modern Santorini) suffered a massive volcanic explosion in the middle to late second millennium B.C.E., have suggested that this natural disaster was responsible. According to one version of this theory, the explosion occurred around 1400 B.C.E., blackening and poisoning the air for miles around and sending a monstrous tidal wave that destroyed the great palace at Cnossus and, with it, Minoan culture. According to another version, the explosion took place about 1200 B.C.E., destroying Bronze Age culture throughout the Aegean. This second version conveniently accounts for the end of both Minoan and Mycenaean civilizations in a single blow, but the evidence does not support it. The Mycenaean towns were not destroyed all at once; many fell around 1200 B.C.E., but some flourished for another century, and the Athens of the period was never destroyed or abandoned. No theory of natural disaster can account for this pattern, leaving us to seek less dramatic explanations for the end of Mycenaean civilization.

The Dorian Invasion Some scholars have suggested that piratical sea raiders destroyed Pylos and, perhaps, other sites on the mainland. The Greeks themselves believed in a legend that told of the Dorians, a rude people from the north who spoke a Greek dialect different from that of the Mycenaean peoples. According to the legend, the Dorians joined with one of the Greek tribes, the Heraclidae, in an attack on the southern Greek peninsula of Peloponnesus, which was repulsed. One hundred years later, they returned and gained full control. Recent historians have identified this legend of "the return of the Heraclidae" with a Dorian invasion.

Archaeology has not provided material evidence of whether there was a single Dorian invasion or a series of them, and it is impossible as yet to say with any certainty what happened at the end of the Bronze Age in the Aegean. The chances are good, however, that Mycenaean civilization ended gradually over the century between 1200 B.C.E. and 1100 B.C.E. Its end may have been the result of internal conflicts among the Mycenaean kings combined with continuous pressure from outsiders, who raided, infiltrated, and eventually dominated Greece and its neighboring islands. There is reason to believe that Mycenaean society suffered internal weaknesses due to its organization around the centralized control of military force and agricultural production. This rigid organization may have deprived it of flexibility and vitality, leaving it vulnerable to outside challengers. In any case, Cnossus, Mycenae, and Pylos were abandoned, their secrets to be kept for over 3,000 years.

Map 2–1 THE AEGEAN AREA IN THE BRONZE AGE   The Bronze Age in the Aegean area lasted from about 1900 to about 1100 B.C.E. Its culture on Crete is called Minoan and was at its height about 1900–1400 B.C.E. Bronze Age Helladic culture on the mainland flourished from about 1600–1200 B.C.E.

▼ The Greek "Middle Ages" to about 750 B.C.E.

The immediate effects of the Dorian invasion were disastrous for the inhabitants of the Mycenaean world. The palaces and the kings and bureaucrats who managed them were destroyed. The wealth and organization that had supported the artists and merchants were likewise swept away by a barbarous people who did not have the knowledge or social organization to maintain them. Many villages were abandoned and never resettled. Some of their inhabitants probably turned to a nomadic life, and many perished. The chaos resulting from the collapse of the rigidly controlled palace culture produced severe depopulation and widespread poverty that lasted for a long time.

Greek Migrations

Another result of the invasion was the spread of the Greek people eastward from the mainland to the Aegean islands and the coast of Asia Minor. The Dorians themselves, after occupying most of the Peloponnesus, occupied the southern Aegean islands and the southern part of the Anatolian coast.

These migrations made the Aegean a Greek lake. The fall of the advanced Minoan and Mycenaean civilizations, however, virtually ended trade with the old civilizations of the Near East; nor was there much internal trade among the different parts of Greece. The Greeks were forced to turn inward, and each community was left largely to its own devices. The Near East was also in disarray at this time, and no great power arose to impose its ways and its will on the helpless people who lived about the Aegean. The Greeks were allowed time to recover from their disaster and to create their own unique style of life.

Our knowledge of this period in Greek history rests on limited sources. Writing disappeared after the fall of Mycenae, and no new script appeared until about 750 B.C.E., so we have no contemporary author to shed light on the period. Excavation reveals no architecture, sculpture, or painting until after 750 B.C.E.

The Age of Homer

For a picture of society in these "Dark Ages," the best source is Homer. His epic poems, the **Iliad** and the **Odyssey**, emerged from a tradition of oral poetry whose roots extend into the Mycenaean Age. Through the centuries bards had sung tales of the heroes who had fought at Troy, using verse arranged in rhythmic formulas to aid the memory. In this way some old material was preserved into the eighth century B.C.E., when the poems attributed to Homer were finally written down. Although the poems tell of the deeds of Mycenaean Age heroes, the world they describe clearly differs from the Mycenaean world. Homer's heroes are not buried in *tholos* tombs but are cremated; they worship gods in temples, whereas the Mycenaeans had no temples; they have chariots but do not know their proper use in warfare. Certain aspects of the society described in the poems appear instead to resemble the world of the tenth and ninth centuries B.C.E., and other aspects appear to belong to the poet's own time, when population was growing at a swift pace and prosperity was returning, thanks to changes in Greek agriculture, society, and government.

Government In the Homeric poems, the power of the kings is much less than that of the Mycenaean rulers. Homeric kings had to consult a council of nobles before they made important decisions. The nobles felt free to discuss matters in vigorous language and in opposition to the king's wishes. In the *Iliad*, Achilles does not hesitate to address Agamemnon, the "most kingly" commander of the Trojan expedition, in these words: "you with a dog's face and a deer's heart." Such language may have been impolite, but it was not treasonous. The king could ignore the council's advice, but it was risky for him to do so.

Only noblemen had the right to speak in council, but the common people could not be entirely ignored. If a king planned a war or a major change of policy during a campaign, he would not fail to call the common soldiers to an assembly; they could listen and express their feelings by acclamation, though they could not take part in the debate. Homer shows that even in these early times the Greeks, unlike their predecessors and contemporaries, practiced some forms of limited constitutional government.

Society Homeric society, nevertheless, was sharply divided into classes, the most important division being the one between nobles and everyone else. We do not know the origin of this distinction, but we cannot doubt that at this time Greek society was aristocratic. Birth determined noble status, and wealth usually accompanied it. Below the nobles were three other classes: *thetes*, landless laborers, and slaves. We do not know whether the *thetes* owned the land they worked outright (and so were free to sell it) or worked a hereditary plot that belonged to their clan (and was, therefore, not theirs to dispose of as they chose).

The worst condition was that of the free, but landless, hired agricultural laborer. The slave, at least, was attached to a family household and so was protected and fed. In a world where membership in a settled group gave the only security, the free laborers were desperately vulnerable. Slaves were few in number and were mostly women, who served as maids and concubines. Some male slaves worked as shepherds. Few, if any, worked in agriculture, which depended on free labor throughout Greek history.

Homeric Values The Homeric poems reflect an aristocratic code of values that powerfully influenced all future Greek thought. In classical times, Homer was the schoolbook of the Greeks. They memorized his texts, settled diplomatic disputes by citing passages in them, and emulated the behavior and cherished the values they found in them. Those values were physical prowess; courage; fierce protection of one's family, friends, property; and, above all, personal honor and reputation. Speed of foot, strength, and, most of all, excellence at fighting make a man great, and all these attributes promote personal honor. Achilles, the great hero of the *Iliad*, refuses to fight in battle, allowing his fellow Greeks to be slain and almost defeated, because Agamemnon has wounded his honor by taking away his battle prize. He returns not out of a sense of duty to the army, but to avenge the death of his dear friend Patroclus. Odysseus, the hero of the *Odyssey*, returning home after his wanderings, ruthlessly kills the many suitors who had, in his long absence, sought to marry his wife Penelope; they had dishonored him by consuming his wealth, wooing Penelope, and scorning his son.

The highest virtue in Homeric society was **arete**— manliness, courage in the most general sense, and the excellence proper to a hero. This quality was best revealed in a contest, or *agon*. Homeric battles are not primarily group combats, but a series of individual contests between great champions. One of the prime forms of entertainment is the athletic contest, and such a contest celebrates the funeral of Patroclus.

The central ethical idea in Homer can be found in the instructions that Achilles' father gives him when he sends him off to fight at Troy: "Always be the best and distinguished above others." The father of another Homeric hero has given his son exactly the same orders and has added to them the injunction: "Do not bring shame on the family of your fathers who were by far the best in Ephyre and in wide Lycia." Here in a nutshell we have the chief values of the aristocrats of Homer's world: to vie for individual supremacy in *arete* and to defend and increase the honor of the family. These would remain prominent aristocratic values long after Homeric society was only a memory.

Women in Homeric Society In the world described by Homer, the role of women was chiefly to bear and raise children, but the wives of the heroes also had a respected position, presiding over the household, overseeing the servants, and safeguarding the family property. They were prized for their beauty, constancy, and skill at weaving. All these fine qualities are combined in Penelope, the wife of Odysseus, probably the ideal Homeric woman. For the twenty years of her husband's absence, she put off the many suitors who sought to marry her and take his place, remained faithful to him, preserved his property, and protected the future of their son. Far different was the reputation of Agamemnon's wife, Clytemnestra, who betrayed her husband while he was off fighting at Troy and murdered him on his return. Homer contrasts her with the virtuous Penelope in a passage that reveals a streak of hostility to women that can be found throughout the ancient history of the Greeks:

Not so did the daughter of Tyndareus fashion her evil deeds, when she killed her wedded lord, and a song of loathing will be hers among men, to make evil the reputation of womankind, even for those whose acts are virtuous.[2]

Unlike Greek women in later centuries, the women of the higher class depicted in Homer are seen moving freely about their communities in town and country. They have a place alongside their husbands at the banquets in the great halls and take part in the conversation. In the *Odyssey*'s land of Phaeacia, admittedly a kind of fairyland, the wise queen Arete can decide the fate of suppliants and sometimes is asked to settle disputes even between men. A good marriage is seen as essential, admirable, and desirable. The shipwrecked Odysseus tries to win the sympathy of Arete's young daughter by wishing for her "all that you desire in your heart":

A husband and a home and the accompanying unity of mind and feeling
Which is so desirable, for there is nothing nobler or better than this,
When two people, who think alike, keep house
As man and wife; causing pain to their enemies,
And joy to their well-wishers, as they themselves know best.[3]

▼ The *Polis*

The characteristic Greek institution was the **polis** (plural **poleis**). The common translation of that word as "city-state" is misleading, for it says both too much and too little. All Greek *poleis* began as little more than agricultural villages or towns, and many stayed that way, so the word "city" is inappropriate. All of them were states, in the sense of being independent political units, but they were much more than that. The *polis* was thought of as a community of relatives; all its citizens, who were theoretically descended from a common ancestor, belonged to subgroups, such as fighting brotherhoods or *phratries*, clans, and tribes, and worshipped the gods in common ceremonies.

Aristotle argued that the *polis* was a natural growth and the human being was by nature "an animal who lives in a *polis*." Humans alone have the power of speech and from it derive the ability to distinguish good from bad and right from wrong, "and the sharing of these things is what makes a household and a *polis*." Therefore, humans who are incapable of sharing these things or who are so self-sufficient that they have no need of them are not humans at all, but either wild beasts or gods. Without law and justice, human beings are the worst and most dangerous of the animals. With them, humans can be the best, and justice exists only in the *polis*. These high claims were made in the fourth century B.C.E., hundreds of years after the *polis* came into existence, but they accurately reflect an attitude that was present from the first.

Development of the *Polis*

Originally the word *polis* referred only to a citadel—an elevated, defensible rock to which the farmers of the neighboring area could retreat in case of attack. The **Acropolis** in Athens and the hill called Acrocorinth in Corinth are examples. For some time, such high places and the adjacent farms made up the *polis*. The towns grew gradually and without planning, as their narrow, winding, and disorderly streets show. For centuries they had no walls. Unlike the city-states of the Near East, they were not placed for commercial convenience on

[2]Homer, *Odyssey* 24.199–202, trans. by Richmond Lattimore (Chicago: University of Chicago Press, 1965).

[3]Homer, *Odyssey* 6.181–185, in *Ancient Greece*, trans. by M. Dillon and L. Garland (London and New York: Routledge, 2000).

rivers or the sea. Nor did they grow up around a temple to serve the needs of priests and to benefit from the needs of worshippers. The availability of farmland and of a natural fortress determined their location. They were placed either well inland or far enough away from the sea to avoid piratical raids. Only later and gradually did the **agora**—a marketplace and civic center—appear within the *polis*. The *agora* was to become the heart of the Greeks' remarkable social life, distinguished by conversation and argument carried on in the open air.

Some *poleis* probably came into existence early in the eighth century B.C.E. The institution was certainly common by the middle of the century, for all the colonies that were established by the Greeks in the years after 750 B.C.E. took the form of the *polis*. Once the new institution had been fully established, true monarchy disappeared. Vestigial kings survived in some places, but they were almost always only ceremonial figures without power. The original form of the *polis* was an aristocratic republic dominated by the nobility through its council of nobles and its monopoly of the magistracies.

Just as the *polis* emerged from sources within Greek society after the Bronze Age, striking changes also appeared in the creation and decoration of Greek pottery.

About 750 B.C.E., coincident with the development of the *polis*, the Greeks borrowed a writing system from one of the Semitic scripts and added vowels to create the first true alphabet. This new Greek alphabet was easier to learn than any earlier writing system, leading to much wider literacy.

The *Hoplite* Phalanx

A new military technique was crucial to the development of the *polis*. In earlier times, small troops of cavalry and individual "champions" who first threw their spears and then came to close quarters with swords may have borne the brunt of fighting. Toward the end of the eighth century B.C.E., however, the **hoplite phalanx** came into being and remained the basis of Greek warfare thereafter.

The *hoplite* was a heavily armed infantryman who fought with a spear and a large shield. Most scholars believe that these soldiers were formed into a phalanx in close order, usually at least eight ranks deep, although some argue for a looser formation. As long as the *hoplites* fought bravely and held their ground, there would be few casualties and no defeat, but if they gave way, the result was usually a rout. All depended on the discipline, strength, and courage of the individual soldier. At its best, the phalanx could withstand cavalry charges and defeat infantries not as well protected or disciplined. Until defeated by the Roman legion, it was the dominant military force in the eastern Mediterranean.

The usual *hoplite* battle in Greece was between the armies of two *poleis* quarreling over land. One army invaded the territory of the other when the crops were almost ready for harvest. The defending army had to protect its fields. If the army was beaten, its fields were captured or destroyed and its people might starve. In every way, the phalanx was a communal effort that relied not on the extraordinary actions of the individual, but on the courage of a considerable portion of the citizenry. This style of fighting produced a single, decisive battle that reduced the time lost in fighting other kinds of warfare; it spared the houses, livestock, and other capital of the farmer-soldiers who made up the phalanx, and it also reduced the number of casualties. It perfectly suited the farmer-soldier-citizen, who was the backbone of the *polis*, and, by keeping wars short and limiting their destructiveness and expense, it helped the *polis* prosper. (See "Tyrtaeus on the Citizen Soldier.")

The phalanx and the *polis* arose together, and both heralded the decline of the kings. The phalanx, however, was not made up only of aristocrats. Most of the *hoplites* were farmers working small holdings. The immediate beneficiaries of the royal decline were the aristocrats, but because the existence of the *polis* depended on small farmers, their wishes could not long be wholly ignored. The rise of the *hoplite* phalanx created a bond between the aristocrats and the yeomen family farmers who fought in it. This bond helps explain why class conflicts were muted for some time. It also guaranteed, however, that the aristocrats, who dominated at first, would not always be unchallenged.

The Importance of the *Polis*

The Greeks looked to the *polis* for peace, order, prosperity, and honor in their lifetime. They counted on it to preserve their memory and to honor their descendants after death. Some of them came to see it not only as a ruler, but also as the molder of its citizens. Knowing this, we can understand the pride and scorn that underlie the comparison the poet Phocylides made between the Greek state and the capital of the powerful Assyrian Empire: "A little *polis* living orderly in a high place is stronger than a block-headed Nineveh."

▼ Expansion of the Greek World

From the middle of the eighth century B.C.E. until well into the sixth century B.C.E., the Greeks vastly expanded their territory, their wealth, and their contacts with other peoples. A burst of colonizing activity placed *poleis* from Spain to the Black Sea. A century earlier, a few Greeks had established trading posts in Syria. There they had learned new techniques in the arts and crafts and much more from the older civilizations of the Near East.

TYRTAEUS ON THE CITIZEN SOLDIER

■■

The military organization of citizen soldiers for the defense of the polis *and the idea of the* polis *itself that permeated Greek political thought found echoes in Greek poetry. A major example is this part of a poem by Tyrtaeus, who wrote in Sparta about 625* B.C.E.

How do the values expressed in this poem compare with those esteemed in the epic of Homer? Why, according to Tyrtaeus, is the Spartan soldier right and wise to risk his life by showing courage in battle?

I would not say anything for a man nor take
    account of him
for any speed of his feet or wrestling skill he
    might have,
not if he had the size of a Cyclops and strength to
    go with it,
not if he could outrun Bóreas, the North Wind of
    Thrace,
not if he were more handsome and gracefully
    formed than Tithónos,
or had more riches than Midas had, or Kinyras too,
not if he were more of a king than Tantalid Pelops,
or had the power of speech and persuasion
    Adrastos had,
not if he had all splendors except for a fighting spirit.
For no man ever proves himself a good man in war
    unless he can endure to face the blood and the
    slaughter,
go close against the enemy and fight with his hands.
Here is courage, mankind's finest possession, here is
the noblest prize that a young man can endeavor
    to win,
and it is a good thing his city and all the people
    share with him
when a man plants his feet and stands in the
    foremost spears
relentlessly, all thought of foul flight completely
    forgotten,
and has well trained his heart to be steadfast and
    to endure,
and with words encourages the man who is
    stationed beside him.
Here is a man who proves himself to be valiant in
    war.
With a sudden rush he turns to flight the rugged
    battalions
of the enemy, and sustains the beating waves of
    assault.
And he who so falls among the champions and
    loses his sweet life,

so blessing with honor his city, his father, and all
    his people,
with wounds in his chest, where the spear that he
    was facing has transfixed
that massive guard of his shield, and gone through
    his breastplate as well,
why, such a man is lamented alike by the young
    and the elders,
and all his city goes into mourning and grieves for
    his loss.
His tomb is pointed to with pride, and so are his
    children,
and his children's children, and afterward all the
    race that is his.
His shining glory is never forgotten, his name is
    remembered,
and he becomes an immortal, though he lies
    under the ground.
when one who was a brave man has been killed by
    the furious War God
standing his ground and fighting hard for his
    children and land.
But if he escapes the doom of death, the destroyer
    of bodies,
and wins his battle, and bright renown for the
    work of his spear,
all men give place to him alike, the youth and the
    elders,
and much joy comes his way before he goes down
    to the dead.
Aging he has reputation among his citizens. No one
tries to interfere with his honors or all he deserves,
all men withdraw before his presence, and yield
    their seats to him,
and youth, and the men of his age, and even those
    older than he.
Thus a man should endeavor to reach this high
    place of courage
with all his heart, and, so trying, never be
    backward in war.

From *Greek Lyrics*, trans. by Richmond Lattimore, pp. 14–15, 1960. Reprinted by permission of The University of Chicago Press.

Magna Graecia

Syria and its neighboring territory were too strong to penetrate, so the Greeks settled the southern coast of Macedonia. This region was sparsely settled, and the natives were not well enough organized to resist the Greek colonists. Southern Italy and eastern Sicily were even more inviting areas. Before long, there were so many Greek colonies in Italy and Sicily that the Romans called the whole region **Magna Graecia**, "Great Greece." The Greeks also put colonies in Spain and southern France. In the seventh century B.C.E., Greek colonists settled the coasts of the northeastern Mediterranean, the Black Sea, and the straits connecting them. About the same time, they established settlements on the eastern part of the North African coast. The Greeks now had outposts throughout the Mediterranean world. (See Map 2–2.)

The Greek Colony

The Greeks did not lightly leave home to join a colony. The voyage by sea was dangerous and uncomfortable, and at the end of it were uncertainty and danger. Only powerful pressures like overpopulation and hunger for land drove thousands from their homes to establish new *poleis*.

The colony, although sponsored by the mother city, was established for the good of the colonists rather than for the benefit of those they left behind. The colonists tended to divide the land they settled into equal shares, reflecting an egalitarian tendency inherent in the ethical system of the yeoman farmers in the mother cities. They often copied their home constitution, worshipped the same gods as the people of the mother city at the same festivals in the same way, and carried on a busy trade with the mother city. Most colonies, though independent, were friendly with their mother cities. Each might ask the other for aid in time of trouble and expect to receive a friendly hearing, although neither was obligated to help the other.

The Athenians had colonies of this typical kind but introduced innovations during their imperial period (478–404 B.C.E.). At one point they began to treat all the colonies of their empire as though they were Athenian

MAP EXPLORATION

Interactive map: To explore this map further, go to
www.myhistorylab.com

Map 2–2 **GREEK COLONIZATION** The height of Greek colonization was between about 750 and 550 B.C.E. Greek colonies stretched from the Mediterranean coasts of Spain and Gaul (modern France) in the west to the Black Sea and Asia Minor in the east.

settlements, requiring them to bring an offering of a cow and a suit of armor to the Great Panathenaic festival, just like true Athenian colonies. The goal may have been to cloak imperial rule in the more friendly garb of colonial family attachment.

The best known exception to the rule of friendly relations between colony and mother city was the case of Corinth and its colony Corcyra, which quarreled and fought for more than two centuries. Thucydides tells of a fateful conflict between them that played a major role in causing the Peloponnesian War.

Colonization had a powerful influence on Greek life. By relieving the pressure of a growing population, it provided a safety valve that allowed the *poleis* to escape civil wars. By confronting the Greeks with the differences between themselves and the new peoples they met, colonization gave them a sense of cultural identity and fostered a **Panhellenic** ("all-Greek") spirit that led to the establishment of common religious festivals. The most important ones were at Olympia, Delphi, Corinth, and Nemea.

Colonization also encouraged trade and industry. The influx of new wealth from abroad and the increased demand for goods from the homeland stimulated a more intensive use of the land and an emphasis on crops for export, chiefly the olive and the wine grape. The manufacture of pottery, tools, weapons, and fine artistic metalwork, as well as perfumed oil, the soap of the ancient Mediterranean world, was likewise encouraged. New opportunities allowed some men, sometimes outside the nobility, to become wealthy and important. The new rich became a troublesome element in the aristocratic *poleis*, for, although increasingly important in the life of their states, the ruling aristocrats barred them from political power, religious privileges, and social acceptance. These conditions soon created a crisis in many states.

The Tyrants (about 700–500 B.C.E.)

In some cities—perhaps only a small percentage of the more than 1,000 Greek *poleis*—the crisis produced by new economic and social conditions led to or intensified factional divisions within the ruling aristocracy. Between 700 and 500 B.C.E., the result was often the establishment of a tyranny.

The Rise of Tyranny A tyrant was a monarch who had gained power in an unorthodox or unconstitutional, but not necessarily wicked, way and who exercised a strong one-man rule that might well be beneficent and popular.

The founding tyrant was usually a member of the ruling aristocracy who either had a personal grievance or led an unsuccessful faction. He often rose to power because of his military ability and support from the *hoplites*. He generally had the support of the politically powerless group of the newly wealthy and of the poor farmers.

When he took power, he often expelled many of his aristocratic opponents and divided at least some of their land among his supporters. He pleased his commercial and industrial supporters by destroying the privileges of the old aristocracy and by fostering trade and colonization.

The tyrants presided over a period of population growth that saw an increase especially in the number of city dwellers. They responded with a program of public works that included the improvement of drainage systems, care for the water supply, the construction and organization of marketplaces, the building and strengthening of city walls, and the erection of temples. They introduced new local festivals and elaborated the old ones. They patronized the arts, supporting poets and artisans with gratifying results. All this activity contributed to the tyrant's popularity, to the prosperity of his city, and to his self-esteem.

In most cases, the tyrant's rule was secured by a personal bodyguard and by mercenary soldiers. An armed citizenry, necessary for an aggressive foreign policy, would have been dangerous, so the tyrants usually sought peaceful alliances with other tyrants abroad and avoided war.

The End of the Tyrants By the end of the sixth century B.C.E., tyranny had disappeared from the Greek states and did not return in the same form or for the same reasons. The last tyrants were universally hated for their cruelty and repression. They left bitter memories in their own states and became objects of fear and hatred everywhere.

Besides the outrages individual tyrants committed, the very concept of tyranny was inimical to the idea of the *polis*. The notion of the *polis* as a community to which every member must be responsible, the connection of justice with that community, and the natural aristocratic hatred of monarchy all made tyranny seem alien and offensive. The rule of a tyrant, however beneficent,

CHRONOLOGY OF THE RISE OF GREECE

ca. 2900–1150 B.C.E.	Minoan period
ca. 1900 B.C.E.	Probable date of the arrival of the Greeks on the mainland
ca. 1600–1150 B.C.E.	Mycenaean period
ca. 1250 B.C.E.	Sack of Troy (?)
ca. 1200–1150 B.C.E.	Destruction of Mycenaean centers in Greece
ca. 1100–750 B.C.E.	"Greek Dark Ages"
ca. 750–600 B.C.E.	Major period of Greek colonization
ca. 750 B.C.E.	Probable date when Homer flourished
ca. 700 B.C.E.	Probable date when Hesiod flourished
ca. 700–500 B.C.E.	Major period of Greek tyranny

was arbitrary and unpredictable. Tyranny came into being in defiance of tradition and law, and the tyrant governed without either. He was not answerable in any way to his fellow citizens.

From a longer perspective, however, the tyrants made important contributions to the development of Greek civilization. They encouraged economic changes that helped secure the future prosperity of Greece. They increased communication with the rest of the Mediterranean world and cultivated crafts and technology, as well as arts and literature. Most important of all, they broke the grip of the aristocracy and put the productive powers of the most active and talented of its citizens fully at the service of the *polis*.

▼ The Major States

Generalization about the *polis* becomes difficult not long after its appearance, for although the states had much in common, some of them developed in unique ways. Sparta and Athens, which became the two most powerful Greek states, had especially unusual histories.

Sparta

At first Sparta—located on the **Peloponnesus**, the southern peninsula of Greece—seems not to have been strikingly different from other *poleis*. About 725 B.C.E., however, the pressure of population and land hunger led the Spartans to launch a war of conquest against their western neighbor, Messenia. (See Map 2–3.) The First Messenian War gave the Spartans as much land as they would ever need. The reduction of the Messenians to the status of serfs, or **Helots**, meant the Spartans did not even need to work the land that supported them.

The turning point in Spartan history came about 650 B.C.E., when, in the Second Messenian War, the Helots rebelled with the help of Argos and other Peloponnesian cities. The war was long and bitter and at one point threatened the existence of Sparta. After they had suppressed the revolt, the Spartans were forced to reconsider their way of life. They could not expect to keep down the Helots, who outnumbered them perhaps ten to one, and still maintain the old free and easy habits typical of most Greeks. Faced with the choice of making drastic changes and sacrifices or abandoning their con-

Map 2–3 **THE PELOPONNESUS** Sparta's region, Laconia, was in the Peloponnesus. Most nearby states were members of the Peloponnesian League under Sparta's leadership.

trol of Messenia, the Spartans chose to turn their city forever after into a military academy and camp.

Spartan Society

The new system that emerged late in the sixth century B.C.E. exerted control over each Spartan from birth, when officials of the state decided which infants were physically fit to survive. At the age of seven, the Spartan boy was taken from his mother and turned over to young instructors. He was trained in athletics and the military arts and taught to endure privation, to bear physical pain, and to live off the country, by theft if necessary. At twenty, the Spartan youth was enrolled in the army, where he lived in barracks with his companions until the age of thirty. Marriage was permitted, but a strange sort of marriage it was, for the Spartan male could visit his wife only infrequently and by stealth. At thirty, he became a full citizen, an "equal." He took his meals at a public mess in the company of fifteen comrades. His own plot of land, worked by Helots, provided his food, a simple diet without much meat or wine. Military service was required until the age of sixty; only then could the Spartan retire to his home and family.

This educational program extended to women, too, although they were not given military training. Like males, female infants were examined for fitness to survive. Girls were given gymnastic training, were permitted greater freedom of movement than among other Greeks, and were equally indoctrinated with the idea of service to Sparta.

The entire system was designed to change the natural feelings of devotion to family and children into a more powerful commitment to the *polis*. Privacy, luxury, and even comfort were sacrificed to the purpose of producing soldiers whose physical powers, training, and discipline made them the best in the world. Nothing that might turn the mind away from duty was permitted. The very use of coins was forbidden lest it corrupt the desires of Spartans. Neither family nor money was allowed to interfere with the only ambition permitted to a Spartan male: to win glory and the respect of his peers by bravery in war.

Spartan Government

The Spartan constitution was mixed, containing elements of monarchy, oligarchy, and democracy. There were two kings, whose power was limited by law and also by the rivalry that usually existed between the two royal houses. The origins and explanation of this unusual dual kingship are unknown, but both kings ruled together in Sparta and exercised equal powers. Their functions were chiefly religious and military. A Spartan army rarely left home without a king in command.

A council of elders, consisting of twenty-eight men over the age of sixty, elected for life, and the kings, rep-

resented the oligarchic element. These elders had important judicial functions, sitting as a court in cases involving the kings. They also were consulted before any proposal was put before the assembly of Spartan citizens. In a traditional society like Sparta's, they must have had considerable influence.

The Spartan assembly consisted of all males over thirty. This was thought to be the democratic element in the constitution, but its membership included only a small percentage of the entire population. Theoretically, they were the final authority, but in practice, only magistrates, elders, and kings participated in debate, and voting was usually by acclamation. Therefore, the assembly's real function was to ratify decisions already made or to decide between positions favored by the leading figures. Sparta also had a unique institution, the board of *ephors*. This consisted of five men elected annually by the assembly. Originally, boards of *ephors* appear to have been intended to check the power of the kings, but gradually they gained other important functions. They controlled foreign policy, oversaw the generalship of the kings on campaign, presided at the assembly, and guarded against rebellions by the Helots.

The whole system was remarkable both for how it combined participation by the citizenry with significant checks on its power and for its unmatched stability. Most Greeks admired the Spartan state for these qualities and also for its ability to mold citizens so thoroughly to an ideal. Many political philosophers, from Plato to modern times, have based utopian schemes on a version of Sparta's constitution and educational system.

The Peloponnesian League

By about 550 B.C.E., the Spartan system was well established, and its limitations were plain. Suppression of the Helots required all the effort and energy that Sparta had. The Spartans could expand no further, but they could not allow unruly independent neighbors to cause unrest that might inflame the Helots.

When the Spartans defeated Tegea, their northern neighbor, they imposed an unusual peace. Instead of taking away land and subjugating the defeated state, Sparta left the Tegeans their land and their freedom. In exchange, they required the Tegeans to follow the Spartan lead in foreign affairs and to supply a fixed number of soldiers to Sparta on demand. This became the model for Spartan relations with the other states in the Peloponnesus. Soon Sparta was the leader of an alliance that included every Peloponnesian state but Argos; modern scholars have named this alliance the Peloponnesian League. It provided Sparta with security and made it the most powerful *polis* in Hellenic history. By 500 B.C.E., Sparta and the league had given the Greeks a force capable of facing mighty threats from abroad.

Athens

Athens—located in **Attica**—was slow to come into prominence and to join in the new activities that were changing the more advanced states. The reasons were several: Athens was not situated on the most favored trade routes of the eighth and seventh centuries B.C.E.; its large area (about 1,000 square miles) allowed population growth without great pressure; and the many villages and districts within this territory were not fully united into a single *polis* until the seventh century B.C.E. (See Map 2–4.)

Aristocratic Rule   In the seventh century B.C.E., Athens was a typical aristocratic *polis*. Its people were divided into four tribes and into several clans and brotherhoods (*phratries*). The aristocrats held the most land and the best land, and dominated religious and political life. There was no written law, and powerful nobles rendered decisions on the basis of tradition and, most likely, self-interest. The **Areopagus**, a council of nobles deriving its name from the hill where it held its sessions, governed the state. Annually the council elected nine magistrates, called *archons*, who joined the Areopagus after their year in office. Because the *archons* served for only a year, were checked by their colleagues, and looked forward to a lifetime as members of the Areopagus, the aristocratic Areopagus, not the *archons*, was the true master of the state.

Pressure for Change   In the seventh century B.C.E., the peaceful life of Athens was disturbed, in part by quarrels within the nobility and in part by the beginnings of an agrarian crisis. In 632 B.C.E., a nobleman named Cylon attempted a coup to establish himself as tyrant. He was thwarted, but the unrest continued.

In 621 B.C.E., a man named Draco was given special authority to codify and publish laws for the first time. In later years Draco's penalties were thought to be harsh—hence the saying that his laws were written in blood. (We still speak of unusually harsh penalties as Draconian.) Draco's work was probably limited to laws concerning homicide and was aimed at ending blood feuds between clans, but it set an important precedent: The publication of laws strengthened the hand of the state against the local power of the nobles.

Map 2–4   **ATTICA AND VICINITY**   Citizens of all towns in Attica were also citizens of Athens.

The root of Athens's troubles was agricultural. Many Athenians worked family farms, from which they obtained most of their living. It appears that they planted wheat, the staple crop, year after year without rotating fields or using enough fertilizer. Shifting to more intensive agricultural techniques and to the planting of fruit and olive trees and grapevines required capital, leading the less successful farmers to acquire excessive debt. To survive, some farmers had to borrow from wealthy neighbors to get through the year. In return, they promised one sixth of the next year's crop. The deposit of an inscribed stone on the entailed farms marked the arrangement. As their troubles persisted, debtors had to pledge their wives, their children, and themselves as surety for new loans. Inevitably, many Athenians defaulted and were enslaved. Some were even sold abroad. Revolutionary pressures grew among the poor, who began to demand the abolition of debt and a redistribution of the land.

Reforms of Solon In the year 594 B.C.E., as tradition has it, the Athenians elected Solon as the only *archon*, with extraordinary powers to legislate and revise the constitution. Immediately, he attacked the agrarian problem by canceling current debts and forbidding future loans secured by the person of the borrower. He helped bring back many Athenians enslaved abroad and freed those in Athens enslaved for debt. This program was called the "shaking off of burdens." It did not, however, solve the fundamental economic problem, and Solon did not redistribute the land.

In the short run, therefore, Solon did resolve the economic crisis, but his other economic actions had profound success in the long run. He forbade the export of wheat and encouraged that of olive oil. This policy had the initial effect of making wheat more available in Attica and encouraging the cultivation of olive oil (used in the ancient world not only as a food, but as soap and as fuel for lamps) and wine as cash crops. By the fifth century B.C.E., the cultivation of cash crops had become so profitable that much Athenian land was diverted from grain production, and Athens became dependent on imported wheat. Solon also changed the Athenian standards of weights and measures to conform with those of Corinth and Euboea and the cities of the east. This change also encouraged commerce and turned Athens in the direction that would lead it to great prosperity in the fifth century B.C.E. Solon also encouraged industry by offering citizenship to foreign artisans, and the development of the outstanding Attic pottery of the sixth century reflects his success.

Solon also changed the constitution. Citizenship had previously been the privilege of all male adults whose fathers were citizens; to their number he added those immigrants who were tradesmen and merchants. All these Athenian citizens were divided into four classes on the basis of wealth, measured by annual agricultural production. The two highest classes alone could hold the *archonship*, the chief magistracy in Athens, and sit on the Areopagus.

Men of the third class were allowed to serve as *hoplites*. They could be elected to a council of 400 chosen by all the citizens, 100 from each tribe. Solon seems to have meant this council to serve as a check on the Areopagus and to prepare any business that needed to be put before the traditional assembly of all adult male citizens. The *thetes* made up the last class. They voted in the assembly for the *archons* and the council members and on any other business brought before them by the *archons* and the council. They also sat on a new popular court established by Solon. This new court was recognized as a court of appeal, and by the fifth century B.C.E., almost all cases came before it. In Solon's Athens, as everywhere in the world before the twentieth century, women took no part in the political or judicial process.

Pisistratus the Tyrant Solon's efforts to avoid factional strife failed. Within a few years contention reached such a degree that no *archons* could be chosen. Out of this turmoil emerged the first Athenian tyranny. Pisistratus, a nobleman, leader of a faction, and military hero, briefly seized power in 560 B.C.E. and again in 556 B.C.E., but each time his support was inadequate, and he was driven out. At last, in 546 B.C.E., he came back at the head of a mercenary army from abroad and established a successful tyranny. It lasted beyond his death, in 527 B.C.E., until the expulsion of his son Hippias in 510 B.C.E.

In many respects, Pisistratus resembled the other Greek tyrants. His rule rested on the force provided by mercenary soldiers. He engaged in great programs of public works, urban improvement, and religious piety. Temples were built, and religious centers were expanded and improved. Poets and artists were supported to add cultural luster to the court of the tyrant.

Pisistratus sought to increase the power of the central government at the expense of the nobles. The newly introduced festival of the god Dionysus and the improved and expanded Great Panathenaic festival helped fix attention on the capital city, as did the new temples and the reconstruction of the *agora* as the center of public life. Circuit judges were sent out into the country to hear cases, weakening the power of the local barons. All this time Pisistratus made no formal change in the Solonian constitution. The assembly, councils, and courts met; the magistrates and councils were elected. Pisistratus merely saw to it that his supporters dominated these bodies. The intended effect was to blunt the sharp edge of tyranny with the appearance of a constitutional government, and it worked. The rule of Pisistratus was remembered as popular and mild. The unintended effect was to give the Athenians more experience in the procedures of self-government and a growing taste for it.

Aristogeiton and Harmodius were Athenian aristocrats slain in 514 B.C.E. after assassinating Hipparchus, brother of the tyrant Hippias. After the overthrow of the son of Pisistratus in 510 B.C.E., the Athenians erected a statue to honor their memory. This is a Roman copy. Aristogeiton and Harmodius of Athens ("The Tyrant Slayers"). Roman copy of Greek original. Museo Archeologico Nazionale, Naples, Italy. Photograph © Scala/Art Resource, NY

Spartan Intervention Pisistratus was succeeded by his oldest son, Hippias, who followed his father's ways at first. In 514 B.C.E., however, his brother Hipparchus was murdered as a result of a private quarrel. Hippias became nervous, suspicious, and harsh. The Alcmaeonids, one of the noble clans that Hippias and Hipparchus had exiled, won favor with the influential oracle at Delphi and used its support to persuade Sparta to attack the Athenian tyranny. Led by their ambitious king, Cleomenes I, the Spartans marched into Athenian territory in 510 B.C.E. and deposed Hippias, who went into exile to the Persian court. The tyranny was over.

The Spartans must have hoped to leave Athens in friendly hands, and indeed Cleomenes' friend Isagoras, a rival of the Alcmaeonids, held the leading position in Athens after the withdrawal of the Spartan army. Isagoras, however, faced competitors, chief among them Clisthenes of the restored Alcmaeonid clan. Clisthenes lost out in the initial political struggle among the noble factions. Isagoras seems then to have tried to restore a version of the pre-Solonian aristocratic state. As part of his plan, he removed from the citizen lists those whom Solon or Pisistratus had added and any others thought to have a doubtful claim.

Clisthenes then took an unprecedented action—he turned to the people for political support and won it with a program of great popular appeal. In response, Isagoras called in the Spartans again; Cleomenes arrived and allowed Isagoras to expel Clisthenes and many of his supporters. But the fire of Athenian political consciousness, ignited by Solon and kept alive under Pisistratus, had been fanned into flames by the popular appeal of Clisthenes. The people refused to tolerate an aristocratic restoration and drove out the Spartans and Isagoras with them. Clisthenes and his allies returned, ready to put their program into effect.

Clisthenes, the Founder of Democracy A central aim of Clisthenes' reforms was to diminish the influence of traditional localities and regions in Athenian life, for these were an important source of power for the nobility and of factions in the state. He immediately restored to citizenship those Athenians who had supported him whom Isagoras had disenfranchised, and he added new citizens to the rolls. In 508 B.C.E., he made the *deme*, the equivalent of a small town in the country or a ward in the city, the basic unit of civic life. The **deme** was a purely political unit that elected its own officers. The distribution of *demes* in each tribe guaranteed that no region would dominate any of them. Because the tribes had common religious activities and fought as regimental units, the new organization also increased devotion to the *polis* and diminished regional divisions and personal loyalty to local barons.

A new council of 500 replaced the Solonian council of 400. The council's main responsibility was to prepare legislation for the assembly to discuss, but it also had important financial duties and received foreign emissaries. Final authority in all things rested with the assembly of all adult male Athenian citizens. Debate in the assembly was free and open; any Athenian could submit legislation, offer amendments, or argue the merits of any question. In practice, political leaders did most of the talking. We may imagine that in the early days the council had more authority than it did after the Athenians became more confident in their new self-government.

It is fair to call Clisthenes the father of Athenian democracy. He did not alter the property qualifications of Solon, but his enlargement of the citizen rolls, his

Greek houses had no running water. This scene painted ca. 520 B.C.E. shows five women carrying water home from a fountain. "Hydria (water jug)." Greek, Archaic period, ca. 520 B.C. Attributed to the Priam Painter. Greece, Athens. Ceramic, black-figure, H: 0.53 m diam (with handles): 0.37 m. William Francis Warden Fund. © Museum of Fine Arts, Boston. Accession #61.195

diminution of the power of the aristocrats, and his elevation of the role of the assembly, with its effective and manageable council, all give him a firm claim to that title.

As a result of the work of Solon, Pisistratus, and Clisthenes, Athens entered the fifth century B.C.E. well on the way to prosperity and democracy. It was much more centralized and united than it had been, and it was ready to take its place among the major states that would lead the defense of Greece against the dangers that lay ahead.

▼ Life in Archaic Greece

Society

As the "Dark Ages" ended, the features that would distinguish Greek society thereafter took shape. The artisan and the merchant grew more important as contact with the non-Hellenic world became easier. Most people, however, continued to make their living from the land. Wealthy aristocrats with large estates, powerful households, families, and clans led different lives from those of the poorer countryfolk and the independent farmers who had smaller and less fertile fields.

Farmers Ordinary country people rarely leave a written record of their thoughts or activities, and we have no such record from ancient Greece. The poet Hesiod (ca. 700 B.C.E.), however, was certainly no aristocrat. He presented himself as a small farmer, and his *Works and Days* gives some idea of the life of such a farmer. The crops included grain—chiefly barley, but also wheat;

grapes for making wine; olives for food and oil; green vegetables, especially the bean; and some fruit. Sheep and goats provided milk and cheese. The Homeric heroes had great herds of cattle and ate lots of meat, but by Hesiod's time land fertile enough to provide fodder for cattle was needed to grow grain. He and small farmers like him tasted meat chiefly from sacrificial animals at festivals.

These farmers worked hard to make a living. Although Hesiod had the help of oxen and mules and one or two hired helpers for occasional labor, his life was one of continuous toil. The hardest work came in October, at the start of the rainy season, the time for the first plowing. The plow was light and easily broken, and the work of forcing the iron tip into the earth was backbreaking, even with the help of a team of oxen. For the less fortunate farmer, the cry of the crane that announced the time of year to plow "bites the heart of the man without oxen." Autumn and winter were the time for cutting wood, building wagons, and making tools. Late winter was the time to tend to the vines, May was the time to harvest the grain, July to winnow and store it. Only at the height of summer's heat did Hesiod allow for rest, but when September came, it was time to harvest the grapes. As soon as that task was done the cycle started again. The work went on under the burning sun and in the freezing cold.

Hesiod wrote nothing of pleasure or entertainment, but his poetry displays an excitement and pride that reveals the new hopes of a rural population more dynamic and confident than we know of anywhere else in the ancient world. Less austere farmers than Hesiod gathered at the blacksmith's shop for warmth and companionship in winter, and even he must have taken part in religious rites and festivals that were accompanied by some kind of entertainment. Nonetheless, the lives of yeoman farmers were certainly hard and their pleasures few.

Aristocrats Most aristocrats were rich enough to employ many hired laborers, sometimes sharecroppers, and sometimes even slaves, to work their extensive lands. They could therefore enjoy leisure for other activities. The center of aristocratic social life was the drinking party, or **symposium**. This activity was not a mere drinking bout meant to remove inhibitions and produce oblivion. The Greeks, in fact, almost always mixed their wine with water, and one of the goals of the participants was to drink as much as the others without becoming drunk.

The *symposium* was a carefully organized occasion, with a "king" chosen to set the order of events and to determine that night's mixture of wine and water. Only men took part; they ate and drank as they reclined on couches along the walls of the room. The sessions began with prayers and libations to the gods. Usually there were games, such as dice or *kottabos*, in which wine was flicked from the cups at different targets. Sometimes dancing girls or flute girls offered entertainment. Frequently the aristocratic participants provided their own amusements with songs, poetry, or even philosophical disputes. Characteristically, these took the form of contests, with some kind of prize for the winner, for aristocratic values continued to emphasize competition and the need to excel, whatever the arena.

This aspect of aristocratic life appears in the athletic contests that became widespread early in the sixth century. The games included running events; the long jump; the discus and javelin throws; the pentathlon, which included all of these; boxing; wrestling; and the chariot race. Only the rich could afford to raise, train, and race horses, so the chariot race was a special preserve of aristocracy. The nobility also especially favored wrestling, and the *palaestra*, or fields, where they practiced became an important social center for the aristocracy. The contrast between the hard, drab life of the farmers and the leisured and lively one of the aristocrats could hardly have been greater. (See "Encountering the Past: Greek Athletics.")

Religion

Like most ancient peoples, the Greeks were **polytheists**, and religion played an important part in their lives. Much of Greek art and literature was closely connected with religion, as was the life of the *polis* in general.

Olympian Gods The Greek pantheon consisted of the twelve gods who lived on Mount Olympus. These were

- Zeus, the father of the gods
- Hera, his wife

  Zeus's siblings:

- Poseidon, his brother, god of the seas and earthquakes
- Hestia, his sister, goddess of the hearth
- Demeter, his sister, goddess of agriculture and marriage

  and Zeus's children:

- Aphrodite, goddess of love and beauty
- Apollo, god of the sun, music, poetry, and prophecy
- Ares, god of war
- Artemis, goddess of the moon and the hunt
- Athena, goddess of wisdom and the arts
- Hephaestus, god of fire and metallurgy
- Hermes, messenger of the gods, connected with commerce and cunning

These gods were seen as behaving much like mortals, with all the foibles of humans, except they were superhuman in these as well as in their strength and immortality. In contrast, Zeus, at least, was seen as a source of human justice, and even the Olympians were understood to be subordinate to the Fates. Each *polis* had one of the Olympians as its guardian deity and worshipped that god in its own special way, but all the gods were Panhellenic. In the eighth and seventh centuries B.C.E., common shrines were established at Olympia for the worship of Zeus, at Delphi for Apollo, at the Isthmus of Corinth for Poseidon, and at Nemea once again for Zeus. Each held athletic contests in honor of its deity, to which all Greeks were invited and for which a sacred truce was declared.

Immortality and Morality Besides the Olympians, the Greeks also worshipped countless lesser deities connected with local shrines. They even worshipped human heroes, real or legendary, who had accomplished great deeds and had earned immortality and divine status. The worship of these deities was not a very emotional experience. It was a matter of offering prayer, libations, and gifts in return for protection and favors from the god during the lifetime of the worshipper. The average human had no hope of immortality, and these devotions involved little moral teaching.

Most Greeks seem to have held to the common-sense notion that justice lay in paying one's debts. They thought that civic virtue consisted of worshipping the

GREEK ATHLETICS

ATHLETIC CONTESTS WERE central to life in ancient Greece. From the mythical world portrayed in the eighth century B.C.E. in Homer's *Iliad* and *Odyssey* almost until the fall of the Roman Empire in the late fifth century C.E., organized athletic games were the focus of attention not only for the competitors and spectators but throughout the Hellenic world. Victors won praise and everlasting fame in the verses of great poets like Pindar (ca. 522–ca. 440 B.C.E.) and received extraordinary honors from their native cities.

The games were part of religious festivals held all over the Greek lands. The gods—Zeus, Apollo, Poseidon—were thought to enjoy the same pleasures as mortals and so to delight in contests that tested physical excellence. The most famous and prestigious were the Olympic games, held every four years in honor of Zeus at Olympia, which were said to have begun in 776 B.C.E.

Team games were of little interest to the Greeks, who preferred contests among individuals, where each man—and all the contestants were males—could demonstrate his individual excellence. By the fifth century B.C.E., the athletes competed in the nude and anointed their bodies with oil. Running events included the stadium run, a sprint of about 200 meters that carried the most prestige of all; a run of twice that distance; a distance race of about 4,800 meters; and a race in armor. Field events consisted of the long jump, and the discus and javelin throws. Combat sports included wrestling, boxing, and the *pankration*; a kind of no-holds-barred contest that forbade gouging and biting but permitted just about anything else, including kicking and breaking of fingers.

The prizes for victors were wreaths or crowns of olive, laurel, pine leaves, or wild celery. The common conception that ancient Greek athletes were pure amateurs competing merely for laurel wreaths and honors is, however, an oversimplification. The cities of the victors were free to add more tangible rewards. In Athens, Olympic winners were honored with free meals at the town hall for life. Many festivals—but not the Olympics—also awarded cash prizes, some worth far more than the annual salary of a working man. Victors could earn wealth as well as glory.

What kinds of contests made up Greek athletics?

What were the incentives for Greek athletes?

A foot race, probably a sprint, at the Panathenaic Games in Athens, ca. 580 B.C.E. National Archives and Records Administration

A Closer ▶ LOOK

THE TRIREME

THE TRIREME WAS the warship that dominated naval warfare in the Mediterranean in the fifth and fourth centuries B.C.E. The naval battles of the Persian Wars and the Peloponnesian War were fought between fleets of triremes—light, fast, and maneuverable ships powered by oars. This is a picture of the *Olympias*, a modern reconstruction of an ancient trireme, commissioned by the Greek navy.

The trireme was propelled by 170 rowers in three tiers along each side of the vessel: 31 in the top tier, 27 in the middle, and 27 in the bottom. It was about 120 feet long and 18 feet wide, with a hull that was made of a thin shell of planks joined edge-to-edge and then stiffened by a keel and light transverse ribs. The mast supported a sail that could help propel the ship when the wind was favorable. During battle, however, the mast was taken down, and the trireme maneuvered by oars alone.

After the Persian Wars, the Athenians built the largest and best navy in the ancient Mediterranean, developing the trireme to its highest level of skill and efficiency.

The principal armament of the trireme was a bronze-clad ram, which extended from the keel at or below the waterline and was designed to pierce the light hulls of enemy warships. The ship also carried spearmen and bowmen who sometimes attacked enemy crews and could be landed like today's marines to fight on shore.

To examine this image in an interactive fashion, please go to www.myhistorylab.com

PEARSON
myhistorylab

© AAAC/Topham/The Image Works

state deities in the traditional way, performing required public services, and fighting in defense of the state. To them, private morality meant to do good to one's friends and harm to one's enemies.

The Cult of Delphian Apollo In the sixth century B.C.E., the influence of the cult of Apollo at Delphi and of his oracle there became great. The oracle was the most important of several that helped satisfy the human craving for a clue to the future. The priests of Apollo preached moderation; the two famous sayings identified with Apollo: "Know thyself" and "Nothing in excess" exemplified their advice. Humans needed self-control (*sophrosynēe*). Its opposite was arrogance (***hubris***), brought on by excessive wealth or good fortune. *Hubris* led to moral blindness and, finally, to divine vengeance. This theme of moderation and the dire consequences of its absence was central to Greek popular morality and appears frequently in Greek literature.

The Cult of Dionysus and the Orphic Cult The somewhat cold religion of the Olympian gods and of the cult of Apollo did little to assuage human fears or satisfy human hopes and passions. For these needs, the Greeks turned to other deities and rites. Of these deities, the most popular was Dionysus, a god of nature and fertility, of the grapevine, drunkenness, and sexual abandon. In some of his rites, this god was followed by *maenads*, female devotees who cavorted by night, ate raw flesh, and were reputed to tear to pieces any creature they came across.

The Orphic cult, named after its supposed founder, the mythical poet Orpheus, provided its followers with more hope than did the worship of the twelve Olympians. Cult followers are thought to have refused to kill animals or eat their flesh and to have believed in the transmigration of souls, which offered the prospect of some form of life after death.

Poetry

The poetry of the sixth century B.C.E. also reflected the great changes sweeping through the Greek world. The lyric style—poetry meant to be sung, either by a chorus or by one person—predominated. Sappho of Lesbos, Anacreon of Teos, and Simonides of Cos composed personal poetry, often relating the pleasure and agony of love. Alcaeus of Mytilene, an aristocrat driven from his city by a tyrant, wrote bitter invective.

Perhaps the most interesting poet of the century from a political point of view was Theognis of Megara. He was an aristocrat who lived through a tyranny, an unusually chaotic and violent democracy, and an oligarchy that restored order but ended the rule of the old aristocracy. Theognis was the spokesperson for the old, defeated aristocracy of birth. He divided everyone into two classes, the noble and the base; the former were the good, the latter bad. Those nobly born must associate only with others like themselves if they were to preserve their virtue; if they mingled with the base, they became base. Those born base, however, could never become noble. Only nobles could aspire to virtue and possessed the critical moral and intellectual qualities—respect or honor and judgment. These qualities could not be taught; they were innate. Even so, they had to be carefully guarded against corruption by wealth or by mingling with the base. Intermarriage between the noble and the base was especially condemned. These were the ideas of the unreconstructed nobility, whose power had been destroyed or reduced

This Attic cup from the fifth century B.C.E. shows the two great poets from the island of Lesbos, Sappho (right) and Alcaeus. Hirmer Fotoarchiv

in most Greek states by this time. Such ideas remained alive in aristocratic hearts throughout the next century and greatly influenced later thinkers, Plato among them.

▼ The Persian Wars

The Greeks' period of fortunate isolation and freedom ended in the sixth century B.C.E. They had established colonies along most of the coast of Asia Minor from as early as the eleventh century B.C.E. The colonies maintained friendly relations with the mainland but developed a flourishing economic and cultural life independent of their mother cities and of their eastern neighbors. In the middle of the sixth century B.C.E., however, these Greek cities of Asia Minor came under the control of Lydia and its king, Croesus (ca. 560–546 B.C.E.). Lydian rule seems not to have been harsh, but the Persian conquest of Lydia in 546 B.C.E. brought a less pleasant subjugation. (See Chapter 1.)

The Ionian Rebellion

The Ionian Greeks (those living on the central part of the west coast of Asia Minor and nearby islands) had been moving toward democracy and were not pleased to find themselves under the monarchical rule of Persia. That rule, however, was not overly burdensome at first. The Persians required their subjects to pay tribute and to serve in the Persian army. They ruled the Greek cities through local individuals, who governed their cities as "tyrants." Most of the tyrants, however, were not harsh, the Persian tribute was not excessive, and the Greeks enjoyed general prosperity. Neither the death of the Persian king Cyrus the Great fighting on a distant frontier in 530 B.C.E., nor the suicide of his successor Cambyses, nor the civil war that followed it in 522–521 B.C.E. produced any disturbance in the Greek cities. When Darius emerged as Great King in 521 B.C.E., he found **Ionia** perfectly obedient.

The private troubles of the ambitious tyrant of Miletus, Aristagoras, ended this calm. He had urged a Persian expedition against the island of Naxos; when it failed, he feared the consequences and organized the Ionian rebellion of 499 B.C.E. To gain support, he overthrew the tyrannies and proclaimed democratic constitutions. Then he turned to the mainland states for help, petitioning first Sparta, the most powerful Greek state. The Spartans, however, would have none of Aristagoras's promises of easy victory and great wealth. They had no close ties with the Ionians and no national interest in the region. Furthermore, the thought of leaving their homeland undefended against the Helots while their army was far off terrified them.

Aristagoras next sought help from the Athenians, who were related to the Ionians and had close ties of religion and tradition with them. Besides, Hippias, the deposed tyrant of Athens, was an honored guest at the court of Darius, who had already made it plain that he favored the tyrant's restoration. The Persians, moreover, controlled both sides of the Hellespont, the route to the grain fields beyond the Black Sea that were increasingly vital to Athens. Perhaps some Athenians already feared that a Persian attempt to conquer the Greek mainland was only a matter of time. The Athenian assembly agreed to send a fleet of twenty ships to help the rebels. The Athenian expedition was strengthened by five ships from Eretria in Euboea, which participated out of gratitude for past favors.

In 498 B.C.E., the Athenians and their allies made a surprise attack on Sardis, the old capital of Lydia and now the seat of the *satrap*, and burned it. This action caused the revolt to spread throughout the Greek cities of Asia Minor outside Ionia, but the Ionians could not follow it up. The Athenians withdrew and took no further part. Gradually the Persians reimposed their will. In 495 B.C.E., they defeated the Ionian fleet at Lade, and in the next year they wiped out Miletus. The Ionian rebellion was over.

The War in Greece

In 490 B.C.E., the Persians launched an expedition directly across the Aegean to punish Eretria and Athens, to restore Hippias, and to gain control of the Aegean Sea. (See Map 2–5.) They landed their infantry and cavalry forces first at Naxos, destroying it for its successful resistance in 499 B.C.E. Then they destroyed Eretria and deported its people deep into the interior of Persia.

Marathon Rather than submit and accept the restoration of the hated tyranny of Hippias, the Athenians chose to resist the Persian forces bearing down on them and risk the same fate that had just befallen Eretria. Miltiades, an Athenian who had fled from Persian service, led the city's army to confront the Persians at Marathon. There some 10,000 Athenians, and the Plataeans defeated two or three times their number, killing thousands of the enemy while losing only 192 of their own men.

A Persian victory at Marathon would have destroyed Athenian freedom and led to the conquest of all the mainland Greeks. The greatest achievements of Greek culture, most of which lay in the future, would never have occurred. But the Athenians won a decisive victory, instilling them with a sense of confidence and pride in their *polis*, their unique form of government, and themselves.

The Great Invasion Internal troubles prevented the Persians from taking swift revenge for their loss at Marathon. Almost ten years elapsed before Darius's successor, Xerxes, in 481 B.C.E., gathered an army of at least 150,000 men and a navy of more than 600 ships to conquer Greece. In Athens, Themistocles, who favored making Athens into a naval power, had become the leading politician. During his *archonship* in 493 B.C.E., Athens had already built a fortified port at Piraeus. A decade later the Athenians came upon a rich vein of silver in the state mines, and Themistocles persuaded them to use the profits to increase their fleet. By 480 B.C.E., Athens had over two hundred ships, the backbone of a navy that was to defeat the Persians.

Of the hundreds of Greek states, only thirty-one—led by Sparta, Athens, Corinth, and Aegina—were willing to fight as the Persian army gathered south of the Hellespont. In the spring of 480 B.C.E., Xerxes launched his invasion. The Persian strategy was to march into Greece, destroy Athens, defeat the Greek army, and add the Greeks to the number of Persian subjects. The huge Persian army needed to keep in touch with the fleet for supplies. If the Greeks could defeat the Persian navy, the army could not remain in Greece long. Themistocles

Map 2–5 THE PERSIAN INVASION OF GREECE This map traces the route taken by the Persian king Xerxes in his invasion of Greece in 480 B.C.E. The gray arrows show movements of Xerxes' army, the purple arrows show movements of his navy, and the green arrows show movements of the Greek army and navy.

knew that the Aegean was subject to sudden devastating storms. His strategy was to delay the Persian army and then to bring on the kind of naval battle he might hope to win. (See "Compare & Connect: Greek Strategy in the Persian War," on page 56.)

Severe storms wrecked many Persian ships while the Greek fleet waited safely in a protected harbor. Then Xerxes attacked Thermopylae, and for two days the Greeks butchered his best troops without serious loss to themselves. On the third day, however, a traitor

Greek Strategy in the Persian War

IN THE SUMMER of 480 B.C.E., Xerxes, Great King of Persia, took an enormous invading army into Greece. During the previous year those Greeks who meant to resist met to plan a defense. After abandoning an attempt to make a stand at Tempe in Thessaly, they fell back to central Greece, at Thermopylae on land and Artemisium at sea. Herodotus is our main source and his account of the Greek strategy is not clear. How did the Greeks hope to check the Persians? Did they hope to stop them for good at Thermopylae, or was the idea to force a sea battle at Artemisium? Were both the army and the fleet intended only to fight holding actions until the Athenians fled to Salamis and the Peloponnesus? Scholars have long argued these questions, which have been sharpened by the discovery of the "Themistocles Decree," an inscription from the third century B.C.E. which purports to be an Athenian decree passed in 480 B.C.E. before the Battle of Artemisium. The authenticity of the decree is still in question, but if it reflects a reliable tradition, it must influence our view in important ways.

QUESTIONS

1. In Herodotus' account what is the state of the Athenian preparation?

2. What light does it reflect on the original Greek strategy for the war?

3. Was the Themistocles Decree passed before or after the battle at Thermopylae? What light does this decree shed on Greek strategy?

4. How do the two documents compare?

5. Are they incompatible?

I. The Account of Herodotus

In this passage Herodotus describes Athens after the Greek defeat at Thermopylae.

Meanwhile, the Grecian fleet, which had left Artemisium, proceeded to Salamis, at the request of the Athenians, and there cast anchor. The Athenians had begged them to take up this position, in order that they might convey their women and children out of Attica, and further might deliberate upon the course which it now behooved them to follow. Disappointed in the hopes which they had previously entertained, they were about to hold a council concerning the present posture of their affairs. For they had looked to see the Peloponnesians drawn up in full force to resist the enemy in Boeotia, but found nothing of what they had expected; nay, they learnt that the Greeks of those parts, only concerning themselves about their own safety, were building a wall across the Isthmus, and intended to guard the Peloponnese, and let the rest of Greece take its chance. These tidings caused them to make the request whereof I spoke, that the combined fleet should anchor at Salamis.

So while the rest of the fleet lay to off this island, the Athenians cast anchor along their own coast. Immediately upon their arrival, proclamation was made, that every Athenian should save his children and household as he best could; whereupon some sent their families to Aegina, some to Salamis, but the greater number to Troezen. This removal was made with all possible haste, partly from a desire to obey the advice of the oracle, but still more for another reason. The Athenians say they have in their acropolis a huge serpent which lives in the temple, and is the guardian of the whole place. Nor do they only say this, but, as if the serpent really dwelt there, every month they lay out its food, which consists of a honey-cake. Up to this time the honey-cake had always been consumed; but now it lay untouched. So the priestess told the people what had happened; whereupon they left Athens the more readily, since they believed that the goddess had abandoned the citadel.

Source: Herodotus, *Histories* 8.40.41, trans. by George Rawlinson.

II. The Themistocles Decree

THE GODS

Resolved by the Council and the People

Themistocles, son of Neokles, of Phrearroi, made the motion:

To entrust the city to Athena the Mistress of Athens and to all the other Gods to guard and defend from the Barbarian for the sake of the land. The Athenians themselves and the foreigners who live in Athens are to send their children and women to safety in Troizen, their protector being Pittheus, the founding hero of the land. They are to send the old men and their movable possessions to safety on Salamis. The treasurers and priestesses are to remain on the acropolis guarding the property of the gods.

All the other Athenians and foreigners of military age are to embark on the 200 ships that are ready and defend against the Barbarian for the sake of their own freedom and that of the rest of the Greeks along with the Lakedaimonians, the Korinthians, the Aiginetans, and all others who wish to share the danger.

The generals are to appoint, starting tomorrow, 200 trierarchs [captains], one to a ship, from among those who have land and house in Athens and legitimate children and who are not older than fifty; to these men the ships are to be assigned by lot. They are to enlist marines, 10 to each ship, from men between the ages of twenty and thirty, and four archers. They are to distribute the servicemen [the marines and archers] by lot at the same time as they assign the trierarchs to the ships by lot. The generals are to write up the rest ship by ship on white boards, (taking) the Athenians from the lexiarchic registers, the foreigners from those registered with the polemarch. They are to write them up assigning them by divisions, 200 of about one hundred (men) each, and to write above each division the name of the trireme and of the trierarch and the servicemen, so that they may know on which trireme each division is to embark. When all the divisions have been composed and allotted to the triremes, the Council and the generals are to man all the 200 ships, after sacrificing a placatory offering to Zeus the Almighty and Athena and Nike and Poseidon the Securer.

When the ships have been manned, with 100 of them they are to meet the enemy at Artemision in Euboia, and with the other 100 they are to lie off Salamis and the coast of Attica and keep guard over the land. In order that all Athenians may be united in their defense against the Barbarian those who have been sent into exile for ten years are to go to Salamis and to stay there until the People come to some decision about them, while those who have been deprived of citizen rights are to have their rights restored . . .

The Greek League, founded specifically to resist this Persian invasion, met at Corinth as the Persians were ready to cross the Hellespont. They chose Sparta as leader and first confronted the Persians at Thermopylae, the "hot gates," on land and off Artemisium at sea. The opening between the mountains and the sea at Thermopylae was so narrow that a small army could hold it against a much larger one. The Spartans sent their king, Leonidas, with 300 of their own citizens and enough allies to make a total of about 9,000.

A Greek *hoplite* attacks a Persian soldier. The contrast between the Greek's metal body armor, large shield, and long spear and the Persian's cloth and leather garments indicates one reason the Greeks won. This Attic vase was found on Rhodes and dates from ca. 475 B.C.E. Greek. Vase, Red-figured. Attic. ca. 480–470 B.C. Neck amphora, Nolan type. Side 1: "Greek warrior attacking a Persian." Said to be from Rhodes. Terracotta. H. 13-11/16 in. The Metropolitan Museum of Art, Rogers Fund, 1906. (06.1021.117) Photograph © 1986 The Metropolitan Museum of Art

Source: "Waiting for the Barbarian," *Greece and Rome*, second series, 8 trans. by Michael H. Jameson (Oxford, 1961), pp. 5–18. By permission of the Oxford University Press.

THE GREEK WARS AGAINST PERSIA

ca. 560–546 B.C.E.	Greek cities of Asia Minor conquered by Croesus of Lydia
546 B.C.E.	Cyrus of Persia conquers Lydia and gains control of Greek cities
499–494 B.C.E.	Greek cities rebel (Ionian rebellion)
490 B.C.E.	Battle of Marathon
480–479 B.C.E.	Xerxes' invasion of Greece
480 B.C.E.	Battles of Thermopylae, Artemisium, and Salamis
479 B.C.E.	Battles of Plataea and Mycale

showed the Persians a mountain trail that permitted them to come on the Greeks from behind. Many allies escaped, but Leonidas and his 300 Spartans all died fighting. At about the same time, the Greek and Persian fleets fought an indecisive battle at Artemisium. The fall of Thermopylae, however, forced the Greek navy to withdraw.

After Thermopylae, the Persian army moved into Attica and burned Athens. If an inscription discovered in 1959 is authentic, Themistocles had foreseen this possibility before Thermopylae, and the Athenians had begun to evacuate their homeland before they sent their fleet north to fight at Artemisium.

Defeating the Persians A sea battle in the narrow waters to the east of the island of Salamis, to which the Greek fleet withdrew after the battle at Artemisium, decided the fate of Greece. The Peloponnesians were reluctant to confront the Persian fleet at this spot, but Themistocles persuaded them to stay by threatening to resettle all the Athenians in Italy. The Spartans knew that they and the other Greeks could not hope to win without the aid of the Athenians. Because the Greek ships were fewer, slower, and less maneuverable than those of the Persians, the Greeks put soldiers on their ships and relied chiefly on hand-to-hand combat. In the ensuing battle the Persians lost more than half their ships and retreated to Asia with a good part of their army, but the danger was not over yet.

The Persian general Mardonius spent the winter in central Greece, and in the spring he unsuccessfully tried to win the Athenians away from the Greek League. The Spartan regent, Pausanias, then led the largest Greek army up to that time to confront Mardonius in Boeotia. At Plataea, in the summer of 479 B.C.E., the Persians suffered a decisive defeat. Mardonius died in battle, and his army fled.

Meanwhile the Ionian Greeks urged King Leotychidas, the Spartan commander of the fleet, to fight the Persian fleet. At Mycale, on the coast of Samos, Leotychidas destroyed the Persian camp and its fleet. The Persians fled the Aegean and Ionia. For the moment, at least, the Persian threat was gone.

In Perspective

Hellenic civilization, that unique cultural experience at the root of Western civilization, has powerfully influenced the peoples of the modern world. It was itself influenced by the great Bronze Age civilization of Crete called Minoan and emerged from the collapse of the Bronze Age civilization on the Greek mainland called Mycenaean. These earlier Aegean civilizations more closely resembled other early civilizations in Egypt, Mesopotamia, Syria-Palestine, and elsewhere than the Hellenic civilization that sprang from them. They had highly developed cities; a system of writing; a strong, centralized monarchical government with tightly organized, large bureaucracies; hierarchical social systems; professional standing armies; and a regular system of taxation to support it all. To a greater or lesser degree, these early civilizations tended toward cultural stability—changing little over time—and uniformity—all sharing many structural features. The striking thing about the emergence of the Hellenic civilization is its sharp departure from this pattern.

The collapse of the Mycenaean world produced a harsh material and cultural decline for the Greeks. Small farm villages replaced cities. Trade all but ended, and communication among the Greeks themselves and between them and other peoples was sharply curtailed. The art of writing was lost for more than three centuries. During this "Dark Age," the rest of the world ignored the Greeks—poor, few in number, isolated, and illiterate—and left them alone to develop their own society and the matrix of Hellenic civilization.

During the three-and-a-half centuries from about 1100 to 750 B.C.E., the Greeks set the foundations for their great achievements. The crucial unit in the new Greek way of life was the *polis*, the Hellenic city-state. There were hundreds of them, and each evoked a kind of loyalty and attachment by its citizens that made the idea of dissolving one's own *polis* into a larger unit unthinkable. The result was a dynamic, many-faceted, competitive, sometimes chaotic world in which rivalry for excellence and victory had the highest value. This agonistic, or competitive, quality marks Greek life throughout its history. Its negative aspect was constant warfare among the states. Its positive side was an extraordinary achievement in literature and art; competition, sometimes formal and organized, spurred on poets and artists.

Kings had been swept away with the Mycenaean world, and the *poleis* were republics. Since the Greeks were so poor, the differences in wealth among them were relatively small. Therefore, class distinctions were less marked and important than in other civilizations. The introduction of a new mode of fighting, the *hoplite* phalanx, had further leveling effects, for it placed the safety of the state in the hands of the average farmer. Armies were made up of citizen-soldiers, who were not paid and who returned to their farms after a campaign. As a result, a relatively large portion of the people shared political control, and participation in political life was highly valued. There was no bureaucracy, for there were no kings and not much economic surplus to support bureaucrats. Most states imposed no regular taxation. There was no separate caste of priests and little concern with life after death. In this varied, dynamic, secular, and remarkably free context, speculative natural philosophy arose based on observation and reason, the root of modern natural science and philosophy.

Contact with the rest of the world increased trade and wealth and brought in valuable new information and ideas. Egyptian and Near Eastern models that were always adapted and changed, rather than copied, powerfully shaped Greek art. Changes often produced social and economic strain, leading to the overthrow of traditional aristocratic regimes by tyrants. But monarchic rule was anathema to the Greeks, and these regimes were temporary. In Athens, the destruction of the tyranny brought the world's first democracy. Sparta, in contrast, developed a uniquely stable government that avoided tyranny and impressed the other Greeks.

The Greeks' time of independent development, untroubled by external forces, ended in the sixth century, when Persia conquered the Greek cities of Asia Minor. When the Persian kings tried to conquer the Greek mainland, however, the leading states managed to put their quarrels aside and unite against the common enemy. Their determination to preserve their freedom carried them to victory over tremendous odds.

REVIEW QUESTIONS

1. How did the later Bronze Age Mycenaean civilization differ from the Minoan civilization of Crete in political organization, art motifs, and military posture?
2. What are the most important historical sources for the Minoan and Mycenaean civilizations? What is Linear B, and what problems does it raise for the reconstruction of Bronze Age history? How valuable are the Homeric epics as sources of early Greek history?
3. What was a *polis*? What role did geography play in its development, and why did the Greeks consider it a unique and valuable institution?
4. What were the fundamental political, social, and economic institutions of Athens and Sparta in about 500 B.C.E.? Why did Sparta develop its unique form of government?
5. What were the main stages in the transformation of Athens from an aristocratic state to a democracy between 600 and 500 B.C.E.? In what ways did Draco, Solon, Pisistratus, and Clisthenes each contribute to the process?
6. Why did the Greeks and Persians go to war in 490 and 480 B.C.E.? Why did the Persians want to conquer Greece? Why were the Greeks able to defeat the Persians and how did they benefit from the victory?

SUGGESTED READINGS

E. K. Anhalt, *Solon the Singer*. A fine study of the Athenian poet-politician.

W. Burkert, *The Orientalizing Revolution: Near Eastern Influence on Greek Culture in the Early Archaic Age* (1992). A study of the Eastern impact on Greek literature and religion from 750 to 650 B.C.E.

J. Chadwick, *The Mycenaean World* (1976). A readable account by an author who helped decipher Mycenaean writing.

R. Drews, *The Coming of the Greeks* (1988). A fine study of the arrival of the Greeks as part of the movement of Indo-European peoples.

J. V. A. Fine, *The Ancient Greeks* (1983). An excellent survey that discusses historical problems and the evidence that gives rise to them.

M. I. Finley, *World of Odysseus*, rev. ed. (1965). A fascinating attempt to reconstruct Homeric society.

V. D. Hanson, *The Other Greeks* (1995). A revolutionary account of the invention of the family farm by the Greeks and the central role of agrarianism in shaping the Greek city-state.

V. D. Hanson, *The Western Way of War* (1989). A brilliant and lively discussion of the rise and character of the *hoplite* phalanx and its influence on Greek society.

J. M. Hurwit, *The Art and Culture of Early Greece* (1985). A fascinating study of the art of early Greece in its literary and cultural context.

W. K. Lacey, *The Family in Ancient Greece* (1984).

P. B. Manville, *The Origins of Citizenship in Ancient Athens* (1990). An examination of the origins of citizenship in the time of Solon of Athens.

J. F. McGlew, *Tyranny and Political Culture in Ancient Greece* (1993). A study of tyranny and its effect on Greek political tradition.

S. G. Miller, *Ancient Greek Athletics* (2004). The best available account.

R. Osborne, *Greece in the Making, 1200–479 B.C.* (1996). An up-to-date, well-illustrated account of early Greek history.

S. Price, *Religions of the Ancient Greeks* (1999). A valuable survey from early times through the fifth century B.C.E.

R. Sallares, *The Ecology of the Ancient Greek World* (1991). A valuable study of the Greeks and their environment.

D. M. Schaps, *Economic Rights of Women in Ancient Greece* (1981).

B. Strauss, *The Battle of Salamis: The Naval Encounter That Saved Greece—and Western Civilization* (2004). A lively account of the great Persian invasion of Greece.

C. G. Thomas and C. Conant, *Citadel to City-State: The Transformation of Greece, 1200–700 B.C.E.* (1999). A good account of Greece's emergence from the Dark Ages into the world of the *polis*.

H. van Wees, *Greek Warfare: Myths and Realities* (2004). An account of Greek fighting that challenges traditional understandings.

For additional learning resources related to this chapter, please go to www.myhistorylab.com

PEARSON
myhistorylab

The Winged Victory of Samothrace. This is one of the great masterpieces of Hellenistic sculpture. It appears to be the work of the Rhodian sculptor Pythokritos, about 200 B.C.E. The statue stood in the sanctuary of the Great Gods on the Aegean island of Samothrace on a base made in the shape of a ship's prow. The goddess is seen as landing on the ship to crown its victorious commander and crew. The Nike of Samothrace, goddess of victory. Marble figure (190 B.C.E.) from Rhodos, Greece. Height 328 cm, MA 2369, Louvre, Dpt. des Antiquités Grecques/Romaines, Paris, France. Photograph © Erich Lessing/Art Resource, NY

3

Classical and Hellenistic Greece

T HE GREEKS' REMARKABLE victory over the Persians in 480–479 B.C.E. won them another period of freedom and autonomy. They used this time to carry their political and cultural achievement to its height. In Athens, especially, it produced a great sense of confidence and ambition.

Spartan withdrawal from active leadership against the Persians left a vacuum that was filled by the Delian League, which soon turned into the Athenian Empire. At the same time as it tightened its hold over the Greek cities in and around the

Aegean Sea, Athens developed an extraordinarily democratic constitution at home. Fears and jealousies of this new kind of state and empire created a split in the Greek world that led to major wars impoverishing Greece and leaving it vulnerable to conquest. In 338 B.C.E., Philip of Macedon conquered the Greek states, putting an end to the age of the *polis*.

▼ Aftermath of Victory

The unity of the Greeks had shown strain even in the life-and-death struggle against the Persians. Within two years of the Persian retreat, it gave way almost completely and yielded to a division of the Greek world into two spheres of influence, dominated by Sparta and Athens. The need of the Ionian Greeks to obtain and defend their freedom from Persia and the desire of many Greeks to gain revenge and financial reparation for the Persian attack brought on the split. (See Map 3–1.)

The Delian League

Sparta had led the Greeks to victory, and it was natural to look to the Spartans to continue the campaign against Persia. But Sparta was ill-suited to the task, which required both a long-term commitment far from the Peloponnesus and continuous naval action.

Athens had become the leading naval power in Greece, and the same motives that led the Athenians to support the Ionian revolt prompted them to try to drive the Persians from the Aegean and the Hellespont. The Ionians were at least as eager for the Athenians to take the helm as the Athenians were to accept the responsibility and opportunity.

In the winter of 478–477 B.C.E., the islanders and the Greeks from the coast of Asia Minor and other Greek cities on the Aegean met with the Athenians on the sacred island of Delos and swore oaths of alliance. As a symbol that the alliance was meant to be permanent, they dropped lumps of iron into the sea; the alliance was to hold until these lumps of iron rose to the surface. The aims of this new **Delian League** were to free

Map 3–1 **CLASSICAL GREECE** Greece in the Classical period (ca. 480–338 B.C.E.) centered on the Aegean Sea. Although there were important Greek settlements in Italy, Sicily, and all around the Black Sea, the area shown in this general reference map embraced the vast majority of Greek states.

those Greeks who were under Persian rule, to protect all against a Persian return, and to obtain compensation from the Persians by attacking their lands and taking booty. An assembly in which each state, including Athens, had one vote was supposed to determine league policy. Athens, however, was clearly designated the leader.

From the first, the league was remarkably successful. The Persians were driven from Europe and the Hellespont, and the Aegean was cleared of pirates. Some states were forced into the league or were prevented from leaving. The members approved coercion because it was necessary for the common safety. In 467 B.C.E., a great victory at the Eurymedon River in Asia Minor routed the Persians and added several cities to the league.

The Rise of Cimon

Cimon, son of Miltiades, the hero of Marathon, became the leading Athenian soldier and statesman soon after the war with Persia. A coalition of his enemies drove Themistocles from power. Ironically, the author of the Greek victory over Persia of 480 B.C.E. was exiled and ended his days at the court of the Persian king. Cimon, who was to dominate Athenian politics for almost two decades, pursued a policy of aggressive attacks on Persia and friendly relations with Sparta. In domestic affairs Cimon was conservative. He accepted the democratic constitution of Clisthenes, which appears to have become somewhat more limited after the Persian War. Defending this constitution and his interventionist foreign policy, Cimon led the Athenians and the Delian League to victory after victory, and his own popularity grew with his successes.

▼ The First Peloponnesian War: Athens Against Sparta

In 465 B.C.E., the island of Thasos rebelled from the Delian League, and Cimon put it down after a siege of more than two years. The Thasian revolt is the first recorded instance in which Athenian interests alone seemed to determine league policy, a significant step in the league's evolution into the Athenian Empire.

When Cimon returned to Athens from Thasos, he was charged with taking bribes for having refrained from conquering Macedonia, although conquering Macedonia had not been part of his assignment. He was acquitted; the trial was only a device by which his political opponents tried to reduce his influence. Their program at home was to undo the gains made by the Areopagus and bring about further democratic changes. In foreign policy, Cimon's enemies wanted to break with Sparta and contest its claim to leadership over the Greeks. They intended at least to establish the independence of Athens and its alliance. The head of this faction was Ephialtes. His supporter, and the person chosen to be the public prosecutor of Cimon, was Pericles, a member of a distinguished Athenian family. He was still young, and his defeat in court did not do lasting damage to his career.

The Breach with Sparta

When the Thasians began their rebellion, they asked Sparta to invade Athens the next spring, and the *ephors*, the annual magistrates responsible for Sparta's foreign policy, agreed. An earthquake, however, accompanied by a rebellion of the Helots that threatened the survival of Sparta, prevented the invasion. The Spartans asked their allies, the Athenians among them, for help, and Cimon persuaded the Athenians to send it. This policy was disastrous for Cimon and his faction. While Cimon was in the Peloponnesus helping the Spartans, Ephialtes stripped the Areopagus of almost all its power. The Spartans, meanwhile, fearing "the boldness and revolutionary spirit of the Athenians," ultimately sent them home. In 462 B.C.E., Ephialtes was assassinated, and Pericles replaced him as leader of the democratic faction. In the spring of 461 B.C.E., Cimon was ostracized, and Athens made an alliance with Argos, Sparta's traditional enemy. Almost overnight, Cimon's domestic and foreign policies had been overturned.

The Division of Greece

The new regime at Athens, led by Pericles and the democratic faction, was confident and ambitious. When Megara, getting the worst of a border dispute with Corinth, withdrew from the Peloponnesian League, the Athenians accepted the Megarians as allies. This alliance gave Athens a great strategic advantage, for Megara barred the way from the Peloponnesus to Athens. Sparta, however, resented the defection of Megara to Athens, leading to the outbreak of the first of the **Peloponnesian Wars**, the first phase in a protracted struggle between Athens and Sparta. The Athenians conquered Aegina and gained control of Boeotia. At this moment Athens was supreme and apparently invulnerable, controlling the states on its borders and dominating the sea. (See Map 3–2, page 64.)

About 455 B.C.E., however, the tide turned. A disastrous defeat met an Athenian fleet that had gone to aid an Egyptian rebellion against Persia. The great loss of men, ships, and prestige caused rebellions in the empire, forcing Athens to make a truce in Greece to subdue its allies in the Aegean. In 449 B.C.E., the Athenians ended the war against Persia.

In 446 B.C.E., the war on the Greek mainland broke out again. Rebellions in Boeotia and Megara removed

Map 3–2 **THE ATHENIAN EMPIRE ABOUT 450 B.C.E.** The Athenian Empire at its fullest extent shortly before 450 B.C.E. We see Athens and the independent states that provided manned ships for the imperial fleet but paid no tribute; dependent states that paid tribute; and states allied to, but not actually in, the empire.

Athens's land defenses and brought a Spartan invasion. Rather than fight, Pericles, the commander of the Athenian army, agreed to a peace of thirty years by the terms of which he abandoned all Athenian possessions on the Greek mainland outside of Attica. In return, the Spartans gave formal recognition to the Athenian Empire. From then on, Greece was divided into two power blocs: Sparta with its alliance on the mainland, and Athens ruling its empire in the Aegean.

▼ Classical Greece

The Athenian Empire

After the Egyptian disaster, the Athenians moved the Delian League's treasury to Athens and began to keep one sixtieth of the annual revenues for themselves. Because of the peace with Persia, there seemed no further reason for the allies to pay tribute, so the Athenians were compelled to find a new justification for their empire. They called for a Panhellenic congress to meet at Athens to discuss rebuilding the temples the Persians had destroyed and to consider how to maintain freedom

of the seas. When Sparta's reluctance to participate prevented the congress, Athens felt free to continue to collect funds from the allies, both to maintain its navy and to rebuild the Athenian temples. Athenian propaganda suggested that henceforth the allies would be treated as colonies and Athens as their mother city, the whole to be held together by good feeling and common religious observances.

There is little reason, however, to believe the allies were taken in or were truly content with their lot. Nothing could cloak the fact that Athens was becoming the master and its allies mere subjects. By 445 B.C.E., when the Thirty Years' Peace gave formal recognition to an Athenian Empire, only Chios, Lesbos, and Samos were autonomous and provided ships. All the other states paid tribute. The change from alliance to empire came about because of the pressure of war and rebellion and largely because the allies were unwilling to see to their own defense. Although the empire had many friends among the lower classes and the democratic politicians in the subject cities, it was seen more and more as a tyranny. Athenian prosperity and security, however, had come to depend on the empire, and the Athenians were determined to defend it.

An Athenian silver four-drachma coin (*tetradrachm*) from the fifth century B.C.E. (440–430 B.C.E.). On the front (left) is the profile of Athena and on the back (right) is her symbol of wisdom, the owl. The silver from which the coins were struck came chiefly from the state mines at Sunium in southern Attica. Hirmer Fotoarchiv

Athenian Democracy

Even as the Athenians were tightening their control over their empire, they were expanding democracy at home. Under the leadership of Pericles, they evolved the freest government the world had yet seen.

Democratic Legislation   Legislation was passed making the *hoplite* class eligible for the *archonship*, and, in practice, no one was thereafter prevented from serving in this office on the basis of his property class. Pericles himself proposed a law introducing pay for jury members, opening that important duty to the poor. Circuit judges were reintroduced, a policy making swift impartial justice available even to the poorest residents in the countryside.

Finally, Pericles himself introduced a bill limiting citizenship to those who had two citizen parents. From a modern perspective this measure might be seen as a step away from democracy, and, in fact, it would have barred Cimon and one of Pericles's ancestors. In Greek terms, however, it was natural. Democracy was defined as the privilege of those who held citizenship, making citizenship a valuable commodity. Limiting it increased its value. Thus, the bill must have won a large majority. Women, resident aliens, and slaves were also denied participation in government in all the Greek states.

How Did the Democracy Work?   Within the citizen body, the extent of Athenian democracy was remarkable. The popular assembly—a collection of the people, not their representatives—had to approve every decision of the state. Every judicial decision was subject to appeal to a popular court of not fewer than 51 and as many

as 1,501 citizens, chosen from an annual panel of jurors widely representative of the Athenian population. (See Encountering the Past, "Going to Court in Athens," page 66.) Most officials were selected by lot without regard to class. The main elected officials, such as the ten generals (the generalship was an office that had both political and military significance) and the imperial treasurers, were usually nobles and almost always rich men, but the people were free to choose otherwise. All public officials were subject to scrutiny before taking office

KEY EVENTS IN ATHENIAN HISTORY BETWEEN THE PERSIAN WAR AND THE GREAT PELOPONNESIAN WAR

478–477 B.C.E.	Delian League founded
ca. 474–462 B.C.E.	Cimon leading politician
467 B.C.E.	Victory over Persians at Eurymedon River
465–463 B.C.E.	Rebellion of Thasos
462 B.C.E.	Ephialtes murdered; Pericles rises to leadership
461 B.C.E.	Cimon ostracized
461 B.C.E.	Reform of Areopagus
ca. 460 B.C.E.	First Peloponnesian War begins
454 B.C.E.	Athens defeated in Egypt; crisis in the Delian League
449 B.C.E.	Peace with Persia
445 B.C.E.	Thirty Years' Peace ends First Peloponnesian War

GOING TO COURT IN ATHENS

THE ATHENIANS PLACED the administration of justice directly into the hands of their fellow citizens, including the poorest ones. Each year 6,000 Athenian males, between a quarter and a fifth of the citizen body, signed on to a panel. (Because women were not considered citizens, they were not allowed to sit on juries or sue in the courts.) From this panel on any given day, jurors were assigned to specific courts and cases. The usual size of a jury was 501, although there were juries of from 51 to as many as 1,501 members.

Unlike in a modern American court, there was no public prosecutor, no lawyers at all, and no judge. The jury was everything. Private citizens registered complaints and argued their own cases. In deciding fundamental matters of justice and fairness, the Athenian democrat put little faith in experts.

In the courtroom the plaintiff and defendant would each present his case for himself, rebut his opponent, cite the relevant laws and precedents, produce witnesses, and sum up. No trial lasted more than a day. The jury did not deliberate but just voted by secret ballot. A simple majority decided the verdict. If a penalty was called for and not prescribed by law (as few were), the plaintiff proposed one penalty, and the defendant a different one. The jury voted to choose one of these but could not propose any other. Normally, this process led both sides to suggest moderate penalties, for an unreasonable suggestion would alienate the jury. To further deter frivolous lawsuits, the plaintiff had to pay a large fine if he did not win a stated percentage of the jurors' votes.

The Athenian system of justice had obvious flaws. Decisions could be quirky and unpredictable because they were unchecked by precedent. Juries could be prejudiced, and the jurors had no defense except their own intelligence and knowledge against speakers who cited laws incorrectly and distorted history. Speeches—unhampered by rules of evidence and relevance, and without the discipline judges impose—could be fanciful, false, and deceptive.

For all its flaws, however, the Athenian system was simple, speedy, open, and easily understood by the citizens. It counted, as always, on the common sense of the ordinary Athenian and contained provisions aimed at producing moderate penalties and deterring unreasonable lawsuits. No legal technicalities or experts came between the citizens and their laws.

What were the advantages and disadvantages of the Athenian justice system?

Do you think it would lead to fair and just results?

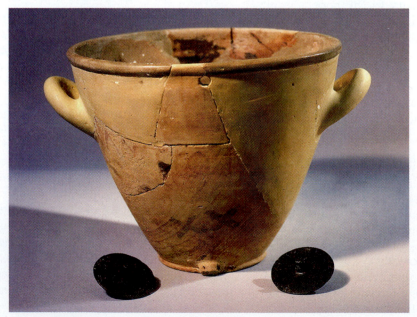

Water-clock and Jury Ballots. Participants in an Athenian trial could speak for only a limited time. A water-clock (Clepsydra) like this kept the time. In front of it are two ballots used by the jurors to vote in favor of the plaintiff or the defendant. Picture Desk/The Art Archive/Agora Museum Athens/Dagli Orti and could be called to account or to be removed from office during their tenure. They were held to compulsory examination and accounting at the end of their term. There was no standing army, no police force, open or secret, and no way to coerce the people.

Pericles was elected to the generalship fifteen years in a row and thirty times in all, not because he was a dictator, but because he was a persuasive speaker, a skillful politician, a respected military leader, an acknowledged patriot, and patently incorruptible. When he lost the people's confidence, they did not hesitate to depose him from office. In 443 B.C.E., however, he stood at the height of his power. The defeat of the Athenian fleet in the Egyptian campaign and the failure of Athens's continental campaigns had persuaded him to favor a conservative policy, seeking to retain the empire in the Aegean and live at peace with the Spartans. It was in this direction that he led Athens's imperial democracy in the years after the First Peloponnesian War. (See "Compare & Connect: Athenian Democracy—Pro and Con," on page 68.)

The Women of Athens: Legal Status and Everyday Life

Men dominated Greek society, as in most other societies all over the world throughout history. This was true of the democratic city of Athens in the great days of Pericles, in the fifth century B.C.E., no less than of any other Greek city. The actual position of women in classical Athens, however, has been the subject of much controversy.

The bulk of the evidence, coming from the law, from philosophical and moral writings, and from information about the conditions of daily life and the organization of society, shows that women were excluded from most aspects of public life. They could not vote, could not take part in the political assemblies, could not hold public office, and could not take any direct part in politics. Since Athens was one of the few places in the ancient world where male citizens of all classes had these public responsibilities and opportunities, the exclusion of women was all the more significant.

The same sources show that in the private aspects of life women were always under the control of a male guardian—a father, a husband, or some other male relative. Women married young, usually between age twelve and eighteen, whereas their husbands were typically over thirty. In many ways, women's relationships with men were similar to father-daughter relationships. Marriages were arranged; women normally had no choice of husband, and male relatives controlled their doweries. To obtain a divorce, women needed the approval of a male relative who was willing to serve as guardian after the dissolution of the marriage. In case of divorce, the dowry returned with the woman, but her father or the appropriate male relative controlled it.

The main function and responsibility of a respectable Athenian woman of a citizen family was to

The Acropolis was both the religious and civic center of Athens. In its final form it is the work of Pericles and his successors in the late fifth century B.C.E. This photograph shows the Parthenon and to its left the Erechtheum.   Meredith Pillon, *Greek National Tourism Organization*

Athenian Democracy—Pro and Con

THE FIRST DEMOCRACY in the world's history appeared in Athens at the end of the sixth century B.C.E. By the middle of the fifth century B.C.E. the Athenian constitution had broadened to give all adult males participation in all aspects of government.

Although most Greek states remained oligarchic, some adopted the Athenian model and became democratic, but democracy was harshly criticized by members of the upper classes, traditionalists, and philosophers. In the following documents Pericles, the most famous Athenian political leader, and an anonymous pamphleteer present contrasting evaluations of the Athenian democracy.

QUESTIONS

1. What virtues does Pericles find in the Athenian constitution?
2. Against what criticisms is he defending it?
3. What are the author's objections to democracy?
4. How would a defender of the Athenian constitution and way of life meet his complaints?
5. To what extent do these descriptions agree?
6. How do they disagree?

I. Pericles' Funeral Oration

In 431 B.C.E., the first year of the Peloponnesian War, Pericles delivered a speech to honor and commemorate the Athenian soldiers who died in the fighting. A key part of it was the praise of the Athenian democratic constitution which, he argued, justified the sacrifice they had made.

Our constitution does not copy the laws of neighbouring states; we are rather a pattern to others than imitators ourselves. Its administration favours the many instead of the few; this is why it is called a democracy. If we look to the laws, they afford equal justice to all in their private differences; if to social standing, advancement in public life falls to reputation for capacity, class considerations not being allowed to interfere with merit; nor again does poverty bar the way, if a man is able to serve the state, he is not hindered by the obscurity of his condition. The freedom which we enjoy in our government extends also to our ordinary life. There, far from exercising a jealous surveillance over each other, we do not feel called upon to be angry with our neighbour for doing what he likes, or even to indulge in those injurious looks which cannot fail to be offensive, although they inflict no positive penalty. But all this ease in our private relations does not make us lawless as

Source: Thucydides, *The Peloponnesian War* 2.37, trans. by Richard Crawley, New York, Random House, 1951.

citizens. Against this fear is our chief safeguard, teaching us to obey the magistrates and the laws, particularly such as regard the protection of the injured, whether they are actually on the statute book, or belong to that code which, although unwritten, yet cannot be broken without acknowledged disgrace.

II. Athenian Democracy: An Unfriendly View

The following selection comes from an anonymous pamphlet thought to have been written in the midst of the Peloponnesian War. Because it has come down to us among the works of Xenophon, but cannot be his work, it is sometimes called "The Constitution of the Athenians" by Pseudo-Xenophon. It is also common to refer to the unknown author as "The Old Oligarch"—although neither his age nor his purpose is known—because of the obviously antidemocratic tone of the work. Such opinions were common among members of the upper classes in Athens late in the fifth century B.C.E. and thereafter.

Now, in discussing the Athenian constitution, I cannot commend their present method of running the state, because in choosing it they preferred that the masses should do better than the respectable citizens; this, then, is my reason for not commending it. Since, however, they have made this choice, I will demonstrate how well they preserve their constitution and handle the other affairs for which the rest of the Greeks criticize them.

Again, some people are surprised at the fact that in all fields they give more power to the masses, the poor, and the common people than they do to the respectable elements of society, but it will become clear that they preserve the democracy by doing precisely this. When the poor, the ordinary people, and the lower classes flourish and increase in numbers, then the power of the democracy will be increased; if, however, the rich and the respectable flourish, the democrats increase the strength of their opponents. Throughout the world the aristocracy are opposed to democracy, for they are naturally least liable to loss of self-control and injustice and most meticulous in their regard for what is respectable, whereas the masses display extreme ignorance, indiscipline, and wickedness, for poverty gives them a tendency towards the ignoble, and in some cases the lack of money leads to their being uneducated and ignorant.

It may be objected that they ought not to grant each and every man the right of speaking in the Ekklesia and serving on the Boule, but only the ablest and best of them; however, in this also they are acting in their own best interests by allowing the mob also a voice. If none but the respectable spoke in the Ekklesia and the Boule, the result would benefit that class and harm the masses; as it is, anyone who wishes rises and speaks, and as a member of the mob he discovers what is to his own advantage and that of those like him.

But someone may say: "How could such a man find out what was advantageous to himself and the common people?" The Athenians realize that this man, despite his ignorance and badness, brings them more advantage because he is well-disposed to them than the ill-disposed, respectable man would, despite his virtue and wisdom. Such practices do not produce the best city, but they are the best way of preserving democracy. For the common people do not wish to be deprived of their rights in an admirably governed city, but to be free and to rule the city; they are not disturbed by inferior laws, for the common people get their strength and freedom from what you define as inferior laws.

Source: *Aristotle and Xenophon on Democracy and Oligarchy*, trans. with introductions and commentary by J. M. Moore (Berkeley and Los Angeles: University of California Press, 1975), pp. 37–38.

ΠΕΡΙΚΛΗΣ
ΞΑΝΘΙΠΠΟΥ
ΑΘΗΝΑΙΟΣ

Pericles (ca. 495–429 B.C.E.) was the leading statesman of Athens for much of the fifth century. This is a Roman copy in marble of the Greek bronze bust that was probably cast in the last decade of Pericles' life. Library of Congress produce male heirs for the **oikos**, or household, of her husband. If, however, her father's *oikos* lacked a male heir, the daughter became an *epikleros*, the "heiress" to the family property. In that case, she was required by law to marry a relative on her father's side to produce the desired male offspring. In the Athenian way of thinking, one household "lent" a woman to another for bearing and raising a male heir to continue the existence of the *oikos*.

Because the pure and legitimate lineage of the offspring was important, women were carefully segregated from men outside the family and were confined to the women's quarters in the house. Men might seek sexual gratification outside the house with prostitutes of high or low style, frequently recruited from abroad. Respectable women stayed home to raise the children, cook, weave cloth, and oversee the management of the household. The only public function of women—an important one—was in the various rituals and festivals of the state religion. Apart from these activities, Athenian women were expected to remain at home out of sight, quiet, and unnoticed. Pericles told the widows and mothers of the Athenian men who died in the first year of the Peloponnesian War only this: "Your great glory is not to fall short of your natural character, and the greatest glory of women is to be least talked about by men, whether for good or bad."

The picture of the legal status of women derived from these sources is largely accurate. It does not fit well, however, with other evidence from mythology, from pictorial art, and from the tragedies and comedies by the great Athenian dramatists. These often show women as central characters and powerful figures in both the public and the private spheres, suggesting that Athenian women may have played a more complex role than their legal status suggests. In Aeschylus's tragedy *Agamemnon*, for example, Clytemnestra arranges the murder of her royal husband and establishes the tyranny of her lover, whom she dominates.

As a famous speech in Euripides' tragedy *Medea* makes clear, we are left with an apparent contradiction. In this speech, Medea paints a bleak picture of the subjugation of women as dictated by their legal status. (See "Medea Bemoans the Condition of Women.") Yet Medea, as Euripides depicted her, is a powerful figure who negotiates with kings. She is the central character in a tragedy bearing her name, produced at state expense before most of the Athenian population and written by one of Athens's greatest poets and dramatists. She is a cause of terror to the audience and, at the same time, an object of their pity and sympathy as a victim of injustice. She is certainly not, what Pericles recommended in his *Funeral Oration*, "least talked about by men, whether for good or for bad." It is also important to remember that she is a foreigner with magical powers, by no means a typical Athenian woman.

An Exceptional Woman: Aspasia   Pericles' life did not conform to his own prescription. After divorcing his first wife, he entered a liaison that was unique in his time, to a woman who was, in her own way, as remarkable as the great Athenian leader. His companion was Aspasia, a young woman who had left her native Miletus and come to live in Athens. The ancient writers refer to her as a *hetaira*, a kind of high-class courtesan who provided men with both erotic and other kinds of entertainment. She clearly had a keen and lively intellect and may well have been trained in the latest ideas and techniques of discussion in her native city, the home of the Greek Enlightenment. Socrates thought it was worth his time to talk with her in the company of his followers and friends. In the dialogue *Menexenus*, Plato jokingly gives her credit for writing Pericles' speeches, including the *Funeral Oration*. There should be no doubt that both Pericles and the men in his circle took her seriously.

Aspasia represented something completely different from Athenian women. She was not a child, not a sheltered and repressed creature confined to the narrow world of slave women, children, and female relatives, but a beautiful, independent, brilliantly witty young woman capable of holding her own in conversation with the best minds in Greece and of discussing and illuminating any question with her husband. There can be no doubt that Pericles loved her passionately. He took her into his house, and whether or not they were formally and legally married, he treated her as his one and only beloved wife. Each morning when he left home and every evening when he returned, he embraced her and kissed her tenderly, by no means the ordinary greeting between an Athenian man and woman.

For an Athenian to consort with courtesans was normal—to take one into his house and treat her as a concubine, perhaps only a little less so. What was shocking and, to many, offensive, was to treat such a woman, a foreigner, as a wife, to lavish such affection on her as few Athenian wives enjoyed, to involve her regularly in conversation with other men, and to discuss important matters with her and treat her opinions with respect. The scandal was immense, and the comic poets made the most of it. Enemies claimed that Pericles was enslaved to a foreign woman who was using her hold over him for political purposes of her own. The Samian War, which arose over a quarrel between Aspasia's native Miletus and Samos, intensified these allegations, for the story spread that Pericles had launched the war at her bidding. After Pericles' death, Aristophanes would pick up these old charges and work them around comically to blame Aspasia for the Peloponnesian War as well.

To some degree, the reality of women's lives in ancient Greece must have depended on their social and

MEDEA BEMOANS THE CONDITION OF WOMEN

In 431 B.C.E., Euripides (ca. 485–406 B.C.E.) presented his play Medea *at the Festival of Dionysus in Athens. The heroine is a foreign woman who has unusual powers. Her description of the condition of women in the speech that follows, however, appears to be an accurate representation of the condition of women in fifth-century B.C.E. Athens.*

Apart from participation in politics, how did the lives of men and women differ in ancient Athens? How well or badly did that aspect of Athenian society suit the needs of the Athenian people and the state in the Classical Age? Since men had a dominant position in the state, and the state managed and financed the presentation of tragedies, how do you explain the sympathetic account of the condition of women Euripides puts into the mouth of Medea?

Of all things which are living and can form a
    judgment
We women are the most unfortunate creatures.
Firstly, with an excess of wealth it is required
For us to buy a husband and take for our bodies
A master; for not to take one is even worse.
And now the question is serious whether we take
A good or bad one; for there is no easy escape
For a woman, nor can she say no to her marriage.
She arrives among new modes of behavior and
    manners,
And needs prophetic power, unless she has
    learned at home,
How best to manage him who shares the bed with
    her.
And if we work out all this well and carefully,

And the husband lives with us and lightly bears
    his yoke,
Then life is enviable. If not, I'd rather die.
A man, when he's tired of the company in his
    home,
Goes out of the house and puts an end to his
    boredom
And turns to a friend or companion of his own age.
But we are forced to keep our eyes on one alone.
What they say of us is that we have a peaceful
    time
Living at home, while they do the fighting in war.
How wrong they are! I would very much rather
    stand
Three times in the front of battle than bear one
    child.

From Euripides, *Medea in Four Tragedies*, trans. by Rex Warner, copyright © 1955, The Bodley Head.

economic status. Poorer women necessarily worked hard at household as well as agricultural tasks and in shops. They also fetched water from the wells and fountains, and both vase paintings and literature show women gathering and chatting at these places. Aristotle asks "How would it be possible to prevent the wives of the poor from going out of doors?"[1] Women of the better classes, however, had no such duties or opportunities. They were more easily and closely supervised. Our knowledge of the experience of women, however, comes from limited sources that do not always agree. Different

scholars arrive at conflicting pictures by emphasizing one kind of a source rather than another. Although the legal subordination of women cannot be doubted, the reality of their place in Greek society remains a lively topic of debate.

Slavery

The Greeks had some form of slavery from the earliest times, but true chattel slavery was initially rare. The most common forms of bondage were different kinds of serfdom in relatively backward areas such as Crete, Thessaly, and Sparta. As noted in Chapter 2, the Spartans

[1] Aristotle, *Politics* 1300a.

conquered the natives of their region and reduced them to the status of Helots, subjects who belonged to the Spartan state and worked the land for their Spartan masters. Another early form of bondage involving a severe, but rarely permanent, loss of freedom resulted from default in debt. In Athens, however, at about 600 B.C.E., such bondsmen, called *hektemoroi*, were sold outside their native land as true slaves until the reforms of Solon put an end to debt bondage entirely.

True chattel slavery began to increase about 500 B.C.E. and remained important to Greek society thereafter. The main sources of slaves were war captives and the captives of pirates. Like the Chinese, Egyptians, and many other peoples, the Greeks regarded foreigners as inferior, and most slaves working for the Greeks were foreigners. Greeks sometimes enslaved Greeks, but not to serve in their home territories.

The chief occupation of the Greeks, as of most of the world before our century, was agriculture. Most Greek farmers worked small holdings too poor to support even one slave, but some had one or two slaves to work alongside them. The upper classes had larger farms that were let out to free tenant farmers or were worked by slaves, generally under an overseer who was himself a slave. Large landowners generally did not have a single great estate but possessed several smaller farms scattered about the *polis.* This arrangement did not encourage the amassing of great numbers of agricultural slaves such as those who would later work the cotton and sugar plantations of the New World. Industry, however, was different.

Larger numbers of slaves labored in industry, especially in mining. Nicias, a wealthy Athenian of the fifth century B.C.E., owned a thousand slaves he rented to a mining contractor for profit, but this is by far the largest number known. Most manufacturing was on a small scale, with shops using one, two, or a handful of slaves. Slaves worked as craftsmen in almost every trade, and, like agricultural slaves on small farms, they worked alongside their masters. Many slaves were domestic servants or shepherds. Publicly held slaves served as policemen, prison attendants, clerks, and secretaries.

The number of slaves in ancient Greece and their importance to Greek society are the subjects of controversy. We have no useful figures of the absolute number of slaves or their percentage of the free population in the classical period (fifth and fourth centuries B.C.E.), and estimates range from 20,000 to 100,000. Accepting the mean between the extremes, 60,000, and estimating the free population at its height at about 40,000 households, would yield a figure of fewer than two slaves per family. Estimates suggest that only a quarter to a third of free Athenians owned any slaves at all.

Some historians have noted that in the American South during the period before the Civil War—where slaves made up less than one third of the total population and three quarters of free Southerners had no slaves—the proportion of slaves to free citizens was similar to that of ancient Athens. Because slavery was so important to the economy of the South, these historians suggest, it may have been equally important and similarly oppressive in ancient Athens. This argument has several problems.[2] First, in the cotton states of the American South before the Civil War, a single cash crop, well suited for exploitation by large groups of slaves, dominated the economy and society. In Athens, in contrast, the economy was mixed, the crops varied, and the land and its distribution were poorly suited to massive slavery.

Different, too, was the likelihood that a slave would become free. Americans rarely freed their slaves, but in Greece liberation was common. The most famous example is that of the Athenian slave Pasion, who began as a bank clerk, earned his freedom, became Athens's richest banker, and was awarded Athenian citizenship. Such cases were certainly rare, but gaining one's freedom was not.

It is important also to distinguish the American South, where skin color separated slaves from their masters, from the different society of classical Athens. Southern masters were increasingly hostile to freeing slaves and afraid of slave rebellions, but in Athens slaves walked the streets with such ease that it offended class-conscious Athenians.

Even more remarkable, the Athenians sometimes considered freeing all their slaves. In 406 B.C.E., when their city was facing defeat in the Peloponnesian War, they freed all slaves of military age and granted citizenship to those who rowed the ships that won the battle of Arginusae. Twice more at crucial moments, similar proposals were made, although without success.

Religion in Public Life

In Athens, as in the other Greek states, religion was more a civic than a private matter. Participation in the rituals of the state religion was not a matter of faith, but of patriotism and good citizenship. In its most basic form, it had little to do with morality. Over time poets and philosophers put forth ethical and moral ideas that among other peoples, like the Hebrews and Persians, were the work of religious prophets and basic to their religious beliefs. Greek religion, however, emphasized not moral conduct to orthodox belief, but the faithful practice of rituals meant to win the favor of the gods. To fail

---

[2] M. I. Finley, "Was Greek Civilization Based on Slave Labor?," *Historia* 8 (1959), p. 151.

to carry out these duties or to attack the gods in any way were seen as blows against the state and were severely punished.

Famous examples of such blasphemies and their punishment occurred late in the fifth and early in the fourth centuries B.C.E. In 415, some men mutilated the statues of Hermes found on every street in Athens. Others were accused of mocking the sacred mysteries of the worship of the goddesses Demeter and Persephone. Suspicions arose at once that the purpose of these sacrilegious acts was to overthrow the Athenian democracy, and the perpetrators were put to death. In 399 B.C.E., the philosopher Socrates was convicted of not honoring the state's gods and of introducing new divinities, and he was also put to death. This was connected with the further charge of corrupting the youths, both acts believed to do harm to the well-being of Athens. In ancient Greece there was no thought of separating religion from civic and political life.

▼ The Great Peloponnesian War

During the first decade after the Thirty Years' Peace of 445 B.C.E., the willingness of each side to respect the new arrangements was tested and not found wanting. About 435 B.C.E., however, a dispute in a remote and unimportant part of the Greek world ignited a long and disastrous war that shook the foundations of Greek civilization.

Causes

The spark that ignited the conflict was a civil war at Epidamnus, a Corcyraean colony on the Adriatic. This civil war caused a quarrel between Corcyra (modern Corfu) and its mother city and traditional enemy, Corinth, an ally of Sparta. The Corcyraean fleet was second in size only to that of Athens, and the Athenians feared that its capture by Corinth would threaten Athenian security. As a result, they made an alliance with the previously neutral Corcyra, angering Corinth and leading to a series of crises in 433–432 B.C.E. that threatened to bring the Athenian Empire into conflict with the Peloponnesian League.

In the summer of 432 B.C.E., the Spartans met to consider the grievances of their allies. Persuaded, chiefly by the Corinthians, that Athens was an insatiably aggressive power seeking to enslave all the Greeks, they voted for war. The treaty of 445 B.C.E. specifically provided that all differences be submitted to arbitration, and Athens repeatedly offered to arbitrate any question. Pericles insisted that the Athenians refuse

THE GREAT PELOPONNESIAN WAR	
435 B.C.E.	Civil war at Epidamnus
432 B.C.E.	Sparta declares war on Athens
431 B.C.E.	Peloponnesian invasion of Athens
421 B.C.E.	Peace of Nicias
415–413 B.C.E.	Athenian invasion of Sicily
405 B.C.E.	Battle of Aegospotami
404 B.C.E.	Athens surrenders

to yield to threats or commands and to uphold the treaty and the arbitration clause. Sparta refused to arbitrate, and in the spring of 431 B.C.E., its army marched into Attica, the Athenian homeland.

Strategic Stalemate

The Spartan strategy was traditional: to invade the enemy's country and threaten the crops, forcing the enemy to defend them in a *hoplite* battle. Such a battle the Spartans were sure to win because they had the better army and they outnumbered the Athenians at least two to one. Any ordinary *polis* would have yielded or fought and lost. Athens, however, had an enormous navy, an annual income from the empire, a vast reserve fund, and long walls that connected the fortified city with the fortified port of Piraeus.

The Athenians' strategy was to allow devastation of their own land to prove that Spartan invasions could not hurt Athens. At the same time, the Athenians launched seaborne raids on the Peloponnesian coast to hurt Sparta's allies. Pericles expected that within a year or two— three at most—the Peloponnesians would become discouraged and make peace, having learned their lesson. If the Peloponnesians held out, Athenian resources were inadequate to continue for more than four or five years without raising the tribute in the empire and running an unacceptable risk of rebellion.

The plan required restraint and the leadership only a Pericles could provide. In 429 B.C.E., however, after a devastating plague and a political crisis that had challenged his authority, Pericles died. After his death, no dominant leader emerged to hold the Athenians to a consistent policy. Two factions vied for influence: One, led by Nicias, wanted to continue the defensive policy, and the other, led by Cleon, preferred a more aggressive strategy. In 425 B.C.E., the aggressive faction was able to win a victory that changed the course of the war. Four hundred Spartans surrendered. Sparta offered peace at once to get them back.

The great victory and the prestige it brought Athens made it safe to raise the imperial tribute, without which Athens could not continue to fight. The Athenians indeed wanted to continue, for the Spartan peace offer gave no adequate guarantee of Athenian security.

In 424 B.C.E., the Athenians undertook a more aggressive policy. They sought to make Athens safe by conquering Megara and Boeotia. Both attempts failed, and defeat helped discredit the aggressive policy, leading to a truce in 423 B.C.E. Meanwhile, Sparta's ablest general, Brasidas, took a small army to Thrace and Macedonia. He captured Amphipolis, the most important Athenian colony in the region. Thucydides was in charge of the Athenian fleet in those waters and was held responsible for the city's loss. He was exiled and was thereby given the time and opportunity to write his famous history of the Great Peloponnesian War. In 422 B.C.E., Cleon led an expedition to undo the work of Brasidas. At Amphipolis, both he and Brasidas died in battle. The removal of these two leaders of the aggressive factions in their respective cities paved the way for the Peace of Nicias, named for its chief negotiator, which was ratified in the spring of 421 B.C.E.

The Fall of Athens

The peace, officially supposed to last fifty years and, with a few exceptions, guarantee the status quo, was in fact fragile. Neither side carried out all its commitments, and several of Sparta's allies refused ratification. In 415 B.C.E., Alcibiades persuaded the Athenians to attack Sicily to bring it under Athenian control. This ambitious and unnecessary undertaking ended in disaster in 413 B.C.E., when the entire expedition was destroyed. The Athenians lost some 200 ships, about 4,500 of their own men, and almost ten times as many allies. It shook Athens's prestige, reduced its power, provoked rebellions, and brought the wealth and power of Persia into the war on Sparta's side.

It is remarkable that the Athenians could continue fighting despite the disaster. They survived a brief oligarchic coup in 411 B.C.E. and won several important victories at sea as the war shifted to the Aegean. Their allies rebelled, however, and Persia paid for fleets to sustain them. Athenian financial resources shrank and finally disappeared. When its fleet was caught napping and was destroyed at Aegospotami in 405 B.C.E., Athens could not build another. The Spartans, under Lysander, a clever and ambitious general who was responsible for obtaining Persian support, cut off the food supply through the Hellespont, and the Athenians were starved into submission. In 404 B.C.E., they surrendered unconditionally; the city walls were dismantled, Athens was permitted no fleet, and the empire was gone. The Great Peloponnesian War was over.

▼ Competition for Leadership in the Fourth Century B.C.E.

Athens's defeat did not bring domination to the Spartans. Instead, the period from 404 B.C.E. until the Macedonian conquest of Greece in 338 B.C.E. was a time of intense rivalry among the Greek cities, each seeking to achieve leadership and control over the others. Sparta, a recovered Athens, and a newly powerful Thebes were the main competitors in a struggle that ultimately weakened all the Greeks and left them vulnerable to outside influence and control.

The Hegemony of Sparta

The collapse of the Athenian Empire created a vacuum of power in the Aegean and opened the way for Spartan leadership or hegemony. Fulfilling the contract that had brought them the funds to win the war, the Spartans handed the Greek cities of Asia Minor back to Persia. Under the leadership of Lysander, the Spartans made a mockery of their promise to free the Greeks by stepping into the imperial role of Athens in the cities along the European coast and the islands of the Aegean. In most of the cities, Lysander installed a board of ten local oligarchs loyal to him and supported them with a Spartan garrison. Tribute brought in an annual revenue almost as great as that the Athenians had collected.

Limited population, the Helot problem, and traditional conservatism all made Sparta a less than ideal state to rule a maritime empire. The increasing arrogance of Sparta's policies alienated some of its allies, especially Thebes and Corinth. In 404 B.C.E., Lysander installed an oligarchic government in Athens, and its leaders' outrageous behavior earned them the title "Thirty Tyrants." Democratic exiles took refuge in Thebes and Corinth and raised an army to challenge the oligarchy. Sparta's conservative king, Pausanias, replaced Lysander, arranging a peaceful settlement and, ultimately, the restoration of democracy. Thereafter, Athenian foreign policy remained under Spartan control, but otherwise Athens was free.

In 405 B.C.E., Darius II of Persia died and was succeeded by Artaxerxes II. His younger brother, Cyrus, received Spartan help in recruiting a Greek mercenary army to help him contest the throne. The Greeks marched inland as far as Mesopotamia, where they defeated the Persians at Cunaxa in 401 B.C.E., but Cyrus was killed in the battle. The Greeks were able to march back to the Black Sea and safety; their success revealed the potential weakness of the Persian Empire.

The Greeks of Asia Minor had supported Cyrus and were now afraid of Artaxerxes' revenge. The Spartans accepted their request for aid and sent an army into Asia, attracted by the prospect of prestige, power, and money. In 396 B.C.E., the command of Sparta's army was given to a new king, Agesilaus, who dominated Sparta until his death in 360 B.C.E. His consistent advocacy of aggressive policies that provided him with opportunities to display his bravery in battle may have been motivated by a psychological need to compensate for his physical lameness and his disputed claim to the throne.

Agesilaus collected much booty and frightened the Persians. They sent a messenger with money and promises of further support to friendly factions in all of the Greek states likely to help them against Sparta. By 395 B.C.E., Thebes was able to organize an alliance that included Argos, Corinth, and a resurgent Athens. The result was the Corinthian War (395–387 B.C.E.), which put an end to Sparta's Asian adventure. In 394 B.C.E., the Persian fleet destroyed Sparta's maritime empire. Meanwhile, the Athenians rebuilt their walls, enlarged their navy, and even recovered some of their lost empire in the Aegean. The war ended when the exhausted Greek states accepted a peace dictated by the Great King of Persia.

The Persians, frightened now by the recovery of Athens, turned the management of Greece over to Sparta. Agesilaus broke up all alliances except the Peloponnesian League. He used or threatened to use the Spartan army to interfere in other *poleis* and put friends of Sparta in power within them. Sparta reached a new level of lawless arrogance in 382 B.C.E., when it seized Thebes during peacetime without warning or pretext. In 379 B.C.E., a Spartan army made a similar attempt on Athens. That action persuaded the Athenians to join with Thebes, which had rebelled from Sparta a few months earlier, to wage war on the Spartans.

In 371 B.C.E., the Thebans, led by their great generals Pelopidas and Epaminondas, defeated the Spartans at Leuctra. The Thebans encouraged the Arcadian cities of the central Peloponnesus to form a league, freed the Helots, and helped them found a city of their own. They deprived Sparta of much of its farmland and of the people who worked it and hemmed Sparta in with hostile neighbors. Sparta's population had shrunk so it could put fewer than 2,000 men into the field at Leuctra. Its aggressive policies had led to ruin. The Theban victory brought the end of Sparta as a power of the first rank.

The Hegemony of Thebes: The Second Athenian Empire

Thebes's power after its victory at Leuctra lay in its democratic constitution, its control over Boeotia, and its two outstanding and popular generals. One of these generals, Pelopidas, died in a successful attempt to gain control of Thessaly. The other, Epaminondas, made Thebes dominant over all of Greece north of Athens and the Corinthian Gulf and challenged the reborn Athenian Empire in the Aegean. All this activity provoked resistance, and by 362 B.C.E., Thebes faced a Peloponnesian coalition as well as Athens. Epaminondas, once again leading a Boeotian army into the Peloponnesus, confronted this coalition at the Battle of Mantinea. His army was victorious, but Epaminondas himself was killed, and Theban dominance died with him.

The Second Athenian Confederation, which Athens had organized in 378 B.C.E., was aimed at resisting Spartan aggression in the Aegean. Its constitution avoided the abuses of the Delian League, but the Athenians soon began to repeat them anyway. This time, however, they did not have the power to put down resistance. When the collapse of Sparta and Thebes and the restraint of Persia removed any reason for voluntary membership, Athens's allies revolted. By 355 B.C.E., Athens had to abandon most of the empire. After two centuries of almost continuous warfare, the Greeks returned to the chaotic disorganization that characterized the time before the founding of the Peloponnesian League.

▼ The Culture of Classical Greece

The repulse of the Persian invasion released a flood of creative activity in Greece that was rarely, if ever, matched anywhere at any time. The century and a half between the Persian retreat and the conquest of Greece by Philip of Macedon (479–338 B.C.E.) produced achievements of such quality as to justify the designation of that era as the Classical Period. Ironically, we often use the term *classical* to suggest calm and serenity, but the word that best describes Greek life, thought, art, and literature in this period is *tension*.

The Fifth Century B.C.E.

Two sources of tension contributed to the artistic outpouring of fifth-century B.C.E. Greece. One arose from the conflict between the Greeks' pride in their accomplishments and their concern that overreaching would bring retribution. Friction among the *poleis* intensified during this period as Athens and Sparta gathered most of them into two competing and menacing blocs. The victory over the Persians brought a sense of exultation in the capacity of humans to accomplish great things and a sense of confidence in the divine justice that had brought low the arrogant pride of Xerxes. But the Greeks recognized that Xerxes' fate awaited all those who reached too far, creating a sense of unease. The

This storage jar (amphora), made about 540 B.C.E., is attributed to the anonymous Athenian master artist called the Amasis painter. It shows Dionysus, the god of wine, revelry, and fertility with two of his ecstatic female worshippers called maenads.
Cliche Bibliotheque Nationale de France—Paris

second source of tension was the conflict between the soaring hopes and achievements of individuals and the claims and limits their fellow citizens in the *polis* put on them. These tensions were felt throughout Greece. They had the most spectacular consequences, however, in Athens in its Golden Age, the time between the Persian and the Peloponnesian wars.

Attic Tragedy

Nothing reflects Athens's concerns better than Attic tragedy, which emerged as a major form of Greek poetry in the fifth century B.C.E. The tragedies were presented in a contest as part of the public religious observations in honor of the god Dionysus. The festivals in which they were shown were civic occasions.

Each poet who wished to compete submitted his work to the *archon*. Each offered three tragedies (which might or might not have a common subject) and a satyr play, or comic choral dialogue with Dionysus, to close. The three best competitors were each awarded three actors and a chorus. The state paid the actors. The state selected a wealthy citizen to provide the chorus as *choregos*, for the Athenians had no direct taxation to support such activities. Most of the tragedies were performed in the theater of Dionysus on the south side of the Acropolis, and as many as 30,000 Athenians could attend. A jury of Athenians chosen by lot voted prizes and honors to the best author, actor, and *choregos*.

Attic tragedy served as a forum in which the poets raised vital issues of the day, enabling the Athenian audience to think about them in a serious, yet exciting, context. On rare occasions, the subject of a play might be a contemporary or historic event, but almost always it was chosen from mythology. Until late in the century, the tragedies always dealt solemnly with difficult questions of religion, politics, ethics, morality, or some combination of these. The plays of the dramatists Aeschylus and Sophocles, for example, follow this pattern. The plays of Euripides, written toward the end of the century, are less solemn and more concerned with individual psychology.

Old Comedy

Comedy was introduced into the Dionysian festival early in the fifth century B.C.E. Cratinus, Eupolis, and the great master of the genre called Old Comedy, Aristophanes (ca. 450–385 B.C.E.), the only one from whom we have complete plays, wrote political comedies. They were filled with scathing invective and satire against such contemporary figures as Pericles, Cleon, Socrates, and Euripides. (See "Lysistrata Ends the War," page 78.)

Architecture and Sculpture

The great architectural achievements of Periclean Athens, as much as Athenian tragedy, illustrate the magnificent results of the union and tension between religious and civic responsibilities, on the one hand, and the transcendent genius of the individual artist, on the other. Beginning in 448 B.C.E. and continuing to the outbreak of the Great Peloponnesian War, Pericles undertook a great building program on the Acropolis. (See Map 3–3.) The income from the empire paid for it. The new buildings included temples to honor the city's gods and a fitting gateway to the temples. Pericles' main purpose seems to have been to represent visually the greatness and power of Athens, by emphasizing intellectual and artistic achievement—civilization rather than military and naval power. It was as though these buildings were tangible proof of Pericles' claim that Athens was "the school of Hellas"—that is, the intellectual center of all Greece.

Philosophy

The tragic dramas, architecture, and sculpture of the fifth century B.C.E. all indicate an extraordinary concern with human beings—their capacities, their limits, their nature, and their place in the universe. The same concern is clear in the development of philosophy.

To be sure, some philosophers continued the speculation about the nature of the cosmos (as opposed to human nature) that began with Thales in the sixth century B.C.E. Parmenides of Elea and his pupil Zeno, in opposition to the earlier philosopher Heraclitus, argued that change was only an illusion of the senses.

of human interpretation and agreement—unlike the atoms themselves, which are natural.

Previous to the atomists, Anaxagoras of Clazomenae, an older contemporary and a friend of Pericles, had spoken of tiny fundamental particles called *seeds*, which were put together on a rational basis by a force called *nous*, or "mind." Anaxagoras was thus suggesting a distinction between matter and mind. The atomists, however, regarded "soul," or mind, as material and believed purely physical laws guided everything. In these conflicting positions, we have the beginning of the enduring philosophical debate between materialism and idealism.

These speculations were of interest to few people, and in fact, most Greeks were suspicious of them. A group of professional teachers who emerged in the mid-fifth century began a far more influential debate. Called *Sophists*, they traveled about and received pay for teaching such practical techniques of persuasion as rhetoric, dialectic, and argumentation. (Persuasive

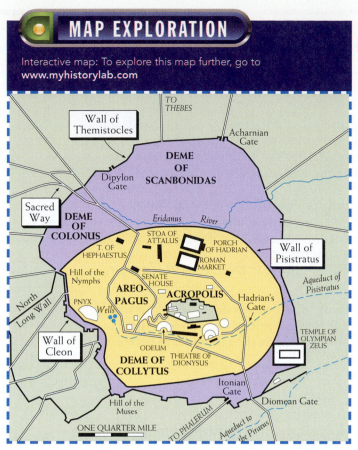

Interactive map: To explore this map further, go to www.myhistorylab.com

MAP EXPLORATION

Map 3–3 ANCIENT ATHENS This sketch locates some of the major features of the ancient city of Athens that have been excavated and are visible today. It includes monuments ranging in age from the earliest times to the period of the Roman Empire. The geographical relation of the Acropolis to the rest of the city is apparent, as is that of the Agora, the Areopagus (where the early council of aristocrats met), and the Pnyx (site of assembly for the larger, more democratic meetings of the entire people).

Reason and reflection showed that reality was fixed and unchanging, because it seemed evident that nothing could be created out of nothingness. Empedocles of Acragas further advanced such fundamental speculations by identifying four basic elements: fire, water, earth, and air. Like Parmenides, he thought that reality was permanent, but he thought it was not immobile; two primary forces, he contended, love and strife—or, as we might say, attraction and repulsion—moved the four elements.

Empedocles' theory is clearly a step on the road to the **atomist** theory of Leucippus of Miletus and Democritus of Abdera. According to this theory, the world consists of innumerable tiny, solid, indivisible, and unchangeable particles—or "atoms"—that move about in the void. The size of the atoms and the arrangements they form when joined produce the secondary qualities that our senses perceive, such as color and shape. These secondary qualities are merely conventional—the result

Diagram of a Doric Column and Entablature:

a *Corner Akroterion*
b *Sima with a lion's head as waterspout*
c *Geison (cornice)*
d *Tympanum*
e *Mutule with Guttae (trops)*
f *Triglyphs*
g *Metopes*
h *Regulae with guttae*
i *Architrave or Epistyle*
k *Abacus*
l *Echinus*
m *Shaft with 20 sharp-edged flutings*
n *Stylobate*
o *Krepis or Krepidoma*
p *Taenia*

Diagram of an Ionic Column and Entablature

a *Sima*
b *Geison (cornice)*
c *Tympanum*
d *Frieze*
e *Architrave or Epistyle (in three parts)*
f *Capital with Volutes*
g *Shaft with 24 flutings separated by fillets*
h *Attic Base with double Torus and a Trochilos*
i *Stylobate*
k *Krepis or Krepidoma*

Corinthian Capital

The three orders of Greek architecture, Doric, Ionic, and Corinthian, have had an enduring impact on Western architecture.

LYSISTRATA ENDS THE WAR

Aristophanes, the greatest of the Athenian comic poets, presented the play Lysistrata *in 411 B.C.E., two decades into the Great Peloponnesian War. The central idea of the plot is that the women of Athens, led by Lysistrata, tired of the privations the war imposed, decide to take matters into their own hands and bring the war to an end. The device they employ is to get the women on both sides to deny their marital favors to their husbands, a kind of sexual strike that quickly achieves its purpose. Before the following passage, Lysistrata has set the terms the Spartans must accept. Next she turns to the Athenians. The play is a masterful example of Athenian Old Comedy, which was almost always full of contemporary and historical political satirical references and sexual puns and jokes. The references to "Peace" in the stage directions are to an actor playing the goddess Peace.*

To what historic event does the passage concerning "the Tyrant's days" refer? To what does the "Promontory of Pylos" refer? What was the real role of women in Athenian political life, and what does the play tell us about it? What is the relationship between humor and reality in this play?

LYSISTRATA
(Turning to the Athenians)
Men of Athens, do you think I'll let you off?
Have you forgotten the Tyrant's days, when you wore
the smock of slavery, when the Spartans turned to the spear,
cut down the pride of Thessaly, despatched the friends
of tyranny, and dispossessed your oppressors?
Recall:
On that great day, your only allies were Spartans;
your liberty came at their hands, which stripped away
your servile garb and clothed you again in Freedom!

SPARTAN
(Indicating Lysistrata)
Hain't never seed no higher type of woman.
    KINESIAS
(Indicating Peace)
Never saw one I wanted so much to top.
    LYSISTRATA
(Oblivious to the byplay, addressing both groups)
With such a history of mutual benefits conferred
and received, why are you fighting? Stop this wickedness!
Come to terms with each other! What prevents you?
    SPARTAN
We'd a heap sight druther make Peace, if we was indemnified with a plumb strategic location.

skills were much valued in democracies like Athens, where so many issues were resolved through open debate.) Some Sophists claimed to teach wisdom and even virtue. Reflecting the human focus characteristic of fifth-century thought, they refrained from speculations about the physical universe, instead applying reasoned analysis to human beliefs and institutions. In doing so, they identified a central problem of human social life and the life of the *polis*: the conflict between nature and custom, or law. The more traditional among them argued that law itself was in accord with nature and was of divine origin, a view that fortified the traditional beliefs of the *polis*.

Others argued, however, that laws were merely the result of convention—an agreement among people—and not in accord with nature. The laws could not pretend to be a positive moral force but merely had the negative function of preventing people from harming each other. The most extreme Sophists argued that law was contrary to nature, a trick whereby the weak control the strong. Critias, an Athenian oligarch and one of the more extreme Sophists, even said that some clever person had invented the gods themselves to deter people from doing what they wished. Such ideas attacked the theoretical foundations of the *polis* and helped provoke the philosophical responses of Plato and Aristotle in the next century.

(Pointing at Peace's rear)
We'll take thet butte.
LYSISTRATA
Butte?
SPARTAN
The Promontory of Pylos—Sparta's Back Door.
We've missed it fer a turrible spell.
(Reaching)
Hev to keep our
hand in.
KINESIAS
(Pushing him away)
The price is too high—you'll never take that!
LYSISTRATA
Oh, let them have it.
KINESIAS
What room will we have left
for maneuvers?
LYSISTRATA
Demand another spot in exchange.
KINESIAS
*(Surveying Peace like a map as he addresses the
Spartan)*
Then you hand over to us—uh, let me see—
let's try Thessaly . . .
(Indicating the relevant portions of Peace)
First of all, Easy Mountain . . .
then the Maniac Gulf behind it . . .
and down to Megara for the legs . . .
SPARTAN
You cain't take all of thet! Yore plumb
out of yore mind!
LYSISTRATA
(To Kinesias)

Don't argue. Let the legs go.
*(Kinesias nods. A pause, general smiles of agree-
ment)*
KINESIAS
(Doffing his cloak)
I feel an urgent desire to plow a few furrows.
SPARTAN
(Doffing his cloak)
Hit's time to work a few loads of fertilizer in.
LYSISTRATA
Conclude the treaty and the simple life is yours.
If such is your decision, convene your councils,
and then deliberate the matter with your allies.
KINESIAS
Deliberate? Allies?
We're over-extended already!
Wouldn't every ally approve of our position—
Union Now?
SPARTAN
I know I kin speak for ourn?
KINESIAS
And I for ours
They're just a bunch of gigolos.
LYSISTRATA
I heartily approve.
Now first attend to your purification,
then we, the women, will welcome you to the
Citadel
and treat you to all the delights of a home-cooked
banquet.
Then you'll exchange your oaths and pledge your
faith,
and every man of you will take his wife
and depart for home.

Aristophanes, *Lysistrata*, trans. by Douglass Parker, in *Four Comedies by Aristophanes*, ed. by W. Arrowsmith (Ann Arbor: University of Michigan Press, 1969), pp. 79–81. Reprinted by permission of the University of Michigan Press.

History The first prose literature in the form of history was Herodotus's account of the Persian War. "The father of history," as he has been deservedly called, was born shortly before the outbreak of the war. His account goes far beyond all previous chronicles, genealogies, and geographical studies and attempts to explain human actions and to draw instruction from them.

Although his work was completed about 425 B.C.E. and shows a few traces of Sophist influence, its spirit is that of an earlier time. Herodotus accepted the evidence of legends and oracles, although not uncritically, and often explained human events in terms of divine intervention. Human arrogance and divine vengeance are key forces that help explain the defeat of Croesus by Cyrus, as well as Xerxes' defeat by the Greeks. Yet the *History* is typical of its time in celebrating the crucial role of human intelligence as exemplified by Miltiades at Marathon and Themistocles at Salamis. Nor was Herodotus unaware of the importance of institutions. His pride in the superiority of the Greek *polis*, in the discipline it inspired in its citizen soldiers, and in the superiority of the Greeks' voluntary obedience to law over the Persians' fear of punishment is unmistakable.

Thucydides, the historian of the Peloponnesian War, was born about 460 B.C.E. and died a few years after the end of the Great Peloponnesian War. He was very much a product of the late fifth century B.C.E. His work, which was influenced by the secular, human-centered, skeptical rationalism of the Sophists, also reflects the scientific attitude of the school of medicine named for his contemporary, Hippocrates of Cos.

The Hippocratic school, known for its pioneering work in medicine and scientific theory, emphasized an approach to the understanding, diagnosis, and treatment of disease that combined careful observation with reason. In the same way, Thucydides took pains to achieve factual accuracy and tried to use his evidence to discover meaningful patterns of human behavior. He believed human nature was essentially unchanging, so a wise person equipped with the understanding history provided might accurately foresee events and thus help to guide them. He believed, however, that only a few had the ability to understand history and to put its lessons to good use. He thought that the intervention of chance, which played a great role in human affairs, could foil even the wisest. Thucydides focused his interest on politics, and in that area his assumptions about human nature do not seem unwarranted. His work has proved to be, as he hoped, "a possession forever." Its description of the terrible civil war between the two basic kinds of *poleis* is a final and fitting example of the tension that was the source of both the greatness and the decline of Classical Greece.

The Fourth Century B.C.E.

Historians often speak of the Peloponnesian War as the crisis of the *polis* and of the fourth century B.C.E. as the period of its decline. The war did bring powerfully important changes: the impoverishment of some Greek cities and, with it, an intensification of class conflict; the development of professionalism in the army; and demographic shifts that sometimes reduced the citizen population and increased the numbers of resident aliens. The Greeks of the fourth century B.C.E. did not know, however, that their traditional way of life was on the verge of destruction. Still, thinkers recognized that they lived in a time of troubles, and they responded in various ways. Some looked to the past and tried to shore up the weakened structure of the *polis*; others tended toward despair and looked for new solutions; and still others averted their gaze from the public arena altogether. All of these responses are apparent in the literature, philosophy, and art of the period.

Drama The tendency of some to turn away from the life of the *polis* and inward to everyday life, the family, and their own individuality is apparent in the poetry of the fourth century B.C.E. A new genre, called Middle Comedy, replaced the political subjects and personal invective of the Old Comedy with a comic-realistic depiction of daily life, plots of intrigue, and a mild satire of domestic situations. Significantly, the role of the cho-

rus, which in some way represented the *polis*, was diminished quite a bit. These trends all continued and were carried even further in the New Comedy. Its leading playwright, Menander (342–291 B.C.E.), completely abandoned mythological subjects in favor of domestic tragicomedy. His gentle satire of the foibles of ordinary people and his tales of lovers temporarily thwarted before a happy and proper ending would not be unfamiliar to viewers of modern situation comedies.

Tragedy faded as a robust and original form. It became common to revive the great plays of the previous century. No tragedies written in the fourth century B.C.E. have been preserved. The plays of Euripides, which rarely won first prize when first produced for Dionysian festival competitions, became increasingly popular in the fourth century and after. Euripides was less interested in cosmic confrontations of conflicting principles than in the psychology and behavior of individual human beings. Some of his late plays, in fact, are less like the tragedies of Aeschylus and Sophocles than forerunners of later forms such as the New Comedy. Plays like *Helena*, *Andromeda*, and *Iphigenia in Tauris* are more like fairy tales, tales of adventure, or love stories than tragedies.

Sculpture The same movement away from the grand, the ideal, and the general, and toward the ordinary, the real, and the individual is apparent in the development of Greek sculpture. To see these developments, one has only to compare the statue of the striding god from Artemisium (ca. 460 B.C.E.), thought to be either Zeus on the point of releasing a thunderbolt or Poseidon about to throw his trident, or the Doryphoros of Polycleitus (ca. 450–440 B.C.E.) with the Hermes of Praxiteles (ca. 340–330 B.C.E.) or the Apoxyomenos attributed to Lysippus (ca. 330 B.C.E.).

Philosophy and the Crisis of the *Polis*

Socrates Probably the most complicated response to the crisis of the *polis* may be found in the life and teachings of Socrates (469–399 B.C.E.). Because he wrote nothing, our knowledge of him comes chiefly from his disciples Plato and Xenophon and from later tradition. Although as a young man he was interested in speculations about the physical world, he later turned to the investigation of ethics and morality; as the Roman writer and statesman Cicero put it, he brought philosophy down from the heavens. Socrates was committed to the search for truth and for the knowledge about human affairs that he believed reason could discover. His method was to question and cross-examine men, particularly those reputed to know something, such as craftsmen, poets, and politicians.

The result was always the same. Those Socrates questioned might have technical information and skills

The theater at Epidaurus was built in the fourth century B.C.E. The city contained the Sanctuary of Asclepius, a god of healing, and drew many visitors who packed the theater at religious festivals. Hirmer Fotoarchiv

but seldom had any knowledge of the fundamental principles of human behavior. It is understandable that Athenians so exposed should be angry with their examiner, and it is not surprising they thought Socrates was undermining the beliefs and values of the *polis.* Socrates' unconcealed contempt for democracy, which seemingly relied on ignorant amateurs to make important political decisions without any certain knowledge, created further hostility. Moreover, his insistence on the primacy of his own individualism and his determination to pursue philosophy even against the wishes of his fellow citizens reinforced this hostility and the prejudice that went with it.

But Socrates, unlike the Sophists, did not accept pay for his teaching; he professed ignorance and denied that he taught at all. His individualism, moreover, was unlike the worldly hedonism of some of the Sophists. It was not wealth or pleasure or power that he urged people to seek, but "the greatest improvement of the soul." Unlike the more radical Sophists, he also denied that the *polis* and its laws were merely conventional. He thought, on the contrary, that they had a legitimate claim on the citizen, and he proved it in the most convincing fashion.

In 399 B.C.E., an Athenian jury condemned him to death on the charges of bringing new gods into the city and of corrupting the youth. His dialectical inquiries had angered many important people. His criticism of democracy must have been viewed with suspicion, especially since Critias and Charmides, who were members of the Thirty Tyrants, and the traitor Alcibiades, who had gone over to the Spartans, had been among his disciples. He was given a chance to escape but, as Plato's *Crito* tells us, he refused to do so because of his veneration of the laws. Socrates' career set the stage for later responses to the travail of the *polis.* He recognized its difficulties and criticized its shortcomings, and he turned away from an active political life, but he did not abandon the idea of the *polis.* He fought as a soldier in its defense, obeyed its laws, and sought to put its values on a sound foundation by reason.

The Cynics One branch of Socratic thought—the concern with personal morality and one's own soul, the disdain of worldly pleasure and wealth, and the withdrawal from political life—was developed and then distorted almost beyond recognition by the **Cynic School**. Antisthenes (ca. 455–360 B.C.E.), a follower of Socrates, is said

A Closer ▶ LOOK

THE ERECHTHEUM: PORCH OF THE MAIDENS

THE ERECHTHEUM, LOCATED on the north side of the Acropolis of Athens, was a temple to the goddess Athena in her oldest form as Athena Polias, the protector of the city. It was built between 421 and 407 B.C.E., probably to replace an older temple the Persians had destroyed in 480.

The new temple included the sites of some of the most ancient and holy relics of the Athenians: a small olive wood statue of Athena Polias; the tombs of Cecrops and Erechtheus, legendary early kings of Athens; the marks of the sea god Poseidon's trident; and the salt water well (the "salt sea") that legend said resulted from Poseidon's strike. In the courtyard, according to the myth, Athena caused an olive tree to grow when she was contesting Poseidon for the honor of being the patron divinity of Athens. Poseidon created a salt-water spring on the Acropolis, but Athena's olive tree won over the judges, and she was victorious. Sculpture in the west pediment of the Parthenon depicted this contest.

Within the foundations the sacred snake of the temple, which represented the spirit of Cecrops and whose well-being was thought essential for the safety of the city, was thought to live. The priestesses of Athena fed the snake honey cakes. The snake's occasional refusal to eat the cakes was considered a disastrous omen.

On the north side, there is another large porch with columns, and on the south, the famous "porch of the maidens," with six draped female figures (Caryatids) used instead of a column as a support. Lord Elgin, an early nineteenth-century British ambassador to the Ottoman Empire, removed one of the Caryatids and sent it to Britain to decorate his Scottish mansion. It was later sold to the British Museum (along with other sculptures plundered from the Parthenon). Today the five original Caryatids are displayed in helium-filled glass cases in the Acropolis Museum and have been replaced on the temple by exact replicas.

Steve Allen/Getty Images, Inc.—Brand × Pictures

Roy Rainford/Robert Harding/Getty Images

To examine this image in an interactive fashion, please go to www.myhistorylab.com

myhistorylab

The need to preserve the many sacred precincts likely explains the complex design. The main structure consists of four compartments, the largest being the east cella, with an Ionic portico on its east end.

to have been its founder, but its most famous exemplar was Diogenes of Sinope (ca. 400–325 B.C.E.). Because Socrates disparaged wealth and worldly comfort, Diogenes wore rags and lived in a tub. He performed shameful acts in public and made his living by begging to show his rejection of convention. He believed happiness lay in satisfying natural needs in the simplest and most direct way; because actions to this end, being natural, could not be indecent, they could and should be done publicly.

Socrates questioned the theoretical basis for popular religious beliefs; the Cynics, in contrast, ridiculed all religious observances. As Plato said, Diogenes was Socrates gone mad. Beyond that, the way of the Cynics contradicted important Socratic beliefs. Socrates, unlike traditional aristocrats such as Theognis, believed virtue was a matter not of birth, but of knowledge and that people do wrong only through ignorance of what is virtuous. The Cynics, in contrast, believed "virtue is an affair of deeds and does not need a store of words and learning."[3] Wisdom and happiness come from pursuing the proper style of life, not from philosophy.

The Cynics moved even further away from Socrates by abandoning the concept of the *polis* entirely. When Diogenes was asked about his citizenship, he answered he was *kosmopolites*, a citizen of the world. The Cynics plainly had turned away from the past, and their views anticipated those of the Hellenistic Age.

Plato Plato (429–347 B.C.E.) was by far the most important of Socrates' associates and is a perfect example of the pupil who becomes greater than his master. He was the first systematic philosopher and therefore the first to place political ideas in their full philosophical context. He was also a writer of genius, leaving us twenty-six philosophical discussions. Almost all are in the form of dialogues, which somehow make the examination of difficult and complicated philosophical problems seem dramatic and entertaining. Plato came from a noble Athenian family, and he looked forward to an active political career until the excesses of the Thirty Tyrants and the execution of Socrates discouraged him from that pursuit. Twice he made trips to Sicily in the hope of producing a model state at Syracuse under the tyrants Dionysius I and II, but without success.

In 386 B.C.E., he founded the Academy, a center of philosophical investigation and a school for training statesmen and citizens. It had a powerful impact on Greek thought and lasted until the emperor Justinian closed it in the sixth century C.E.

Like Socrates, Plato firmly believed in the *polis* and its values. Its virtues were order, harmony, and justice, and one of its main objects was to produce good people. Like his master, and unlike the radical Sophists, Plato thought the *polis* was in accord with nature. He accepted Socrates' doctrine of the identity of virtue and knowl-

The striding god from Artemisium is a bronze statue dating from about 460 B.C.E. It was found in the sea near Artemisium, the northern tip of the large Greek island of Euboea, and is now on display in the Athens Archaeological Museum. Exactly whom he represents is not known. Some have thought him to be Poseidon holding a trident; others believe he is Zeus hurling a thunderbolt. In either case, he is a splendid representative of the early Classical period of Greek sculpture. National Archaeological Museum, Athens

edge. He made it plain what that knowledge was: *episteme*—science—a body of true and unchanging wisdom open to only a few philosophers, whose training, character, and intellect allowed them to see reality. Only such people were qualified to rule; they would prefer the life of pure contemplation, but would accept their responsibility and take their turn as philosopher kings. The training of such an individual required a specialization of function and a subordination of that individual to the community even greater than that at Sparta. This specialization would lead to Plato's definition of justice: Each person should do only that one thing to which his or her nature is best suited. (See "Plato on the Role of Women in His Utopian Republic," page 85.)

Plato understood that the *polis* of his day suffered from terrible internal stress, class struggle, and factional divisions. His solution, however, was not that of some Greeks—that is, conquest and resulting economic prosperity. For Plato, the answer was in moral and political reform. The way to harmony was to destroy the causes

[3] Diogenes Laertius, *Life of Antisthenes* 6.11.

of strife: private property, the family—anything, in short, that stood between the individual citizen and devotion to the *polis*.

Concern for the redemption of the *polis* was at the heart of Plato's system of philosophy. He began by asking the traditional questions: What is a good man, and how is he made? The goodness of a human being belonged to moral philosophy, and when goodness became a function of the state, it became political philosophy. Because goodness depended on knowledge of the good, it required a theory of knowledge and an investigation of what kind of knowledge goodness required. The answer must be metaphysical and so required a full examination of metaphysics. Even when the philosopher knew the good, however, the question remained how the state could bring its citizens to the necessary comprehension of that knowledge. The answer required a theory of education. Even purely logical and metaphysical questions, therefore, were subordinate to the overriding political questions. In this way, Plato's need to find a satisfactory foundation for the beleaguered *polis* contributed to the birth of systematic philosophy.

Aristotle   Aristotle (384–322 B.C.E.) was a pupil of Plato's and owed much to the thought of his master, but his different experience and cast of mind led him in new directions. He was born at Stagirus, the son of the court doctor of neighboring Macedon. As a young man, he went to Athens to study at the Academy, where he stayed until Plato's death. Then he joined a Platonic colony at Assos in Asia Minor, and from there he moved to Mytilene. In both places he did research in marine biology, and biological interests played a large part in all his thoughts. In 342 B.C.E., Philip, the king of Macedon, appointed him tutor to his son, the young Alexander. (See "The Hellenistic World," page 86.)

In 336 B.C.E., Aristotle returned to Athens, where he founded his own school, the Lyceum, or the Peripatos, as it was also called because of the covered walk within it. In later years its members were called *Peripatetics*. On the death of Alexander in 323 B.C.E., the Athenians rebelled against the Macedonian rule, and Aristotle found it wise to leave. He died the following year.

Unlike the Academy, the members of the Lyceum took little interest in mathematics and were concerned with gathering, ordering, and analyzing all human knowledge. Aristotle wrote dialogues on the Platonic model, but none survive. He and his students also prepared many collections of information to serve as the basis for scientific works. Of these, only the *Constitution of the Athenians*, one of 158 constitutional treatises, remains. Almost all of what we possess is in the form of philosophical and scientific studies, whose loose organization and style suggest they were lecture notes. The range of subjects treated is astonishing, including logic, physics, astronomy, biology, ethics, rhetoric, literary criticism, and politics.

In each field, the method is the same. Aristotle began with observation of the empirical evidence, which in some cases was physical and in others was common opinion. To this body of information, he applied reason and discovered inconsistencies or difficulties. To deal with these, he introduced metaphysical principles to explain the problems or to reconcile the inconsistencies.

His view on all subjects, like Plato's, was teleological; that is, both Plato and Aristotle recognized purposes apart from and greater than the will of the individual human being. Plato's purposes, however, were contained in ideas, or forms that were transcendental concepts outside the experience of most people. For Aristotle, the purposes of most things were easily inferred by observation of their behavior in the world. Aristotle's most striking characteristics are his moderation and his common sense. His epistemology finds room for both reason and experience; his metaphysics gives meaning and reality to both mind and body; his ethics aims at the good life, which is the contemplative life, but recognizes the necessity for moderate wealth, comfort, and pleasure.

All these qualities are evident in Aristotle's political thought. Like Plato, he opposed the Sophists' assertion that the *polis* was contrary to nature and the result of mere convention. His response was to apply to politics the teleology he saw in all nature. In his view, matter existed to achieve an end, and it developed until it achieved its form, which was its end. There was constant development from matter to form, from potential to actual. Therefore, human primitive instincts could be seen as the matter out of which the human's potential as a political being could be realized. The *polis* made individuals self-sufficient and allowed the full realization of their potentiality. It was therefore natural.

It was also the highest point in the evolution of the social institutions that serve the human need to continue the species—marriage, household, village, and, finally, *polis*. For Aristotle, the purpose of the *polis* was neither economic nor military, but moral. According to Aristotle, "The end of the state is the good life" (*Politics* 1280b), the life lived "for the sake of noble actions" (1281a), a life of virtue and morality.

Characteristically, Aristotle was less interested in the best state—the utopia that required philosophers to rule it—than in the best state that was practically possible, one that would combine justice with stability. The constitution for that state he called *politeia*, not the best constitution, but the next best, the one most suited to, and most possible, for most states. Its quality was moderation, and it naturally gave power to neither the rich nor the poor, but to the middle class, which must also be the most numerous. The middle class possessed many virtues; because of its moderate wealth, it was free of the arrogance of the rich and the malice of the poor. For this reason, it was the most stable class.

PLATO ON THE ROLE OF WOMEN IN HIS UTOPIAN REPUBLIC

The Greek invention of reasoned intellectual analysis of all things led the philosopher Plato to consider the problem of justice, which is the subject of his most famous dialogue, the Republic. This leads him to sketch out a utopian state in which justice may be found and where the most radical arrangements may be necessary. These include the equality of the sexes and the destruction of the family in favor of the practice of men having wives and children in common. In the following excerpts, he argues for the fundamental equality of men and women and that women are no less appropriate as Guardians—leaders of the state—than men.

Why does Plato treat men and women the same? What objections could be raised to that practice? Would that policy, even if appropriate in Plato's utopia, also be suitable to conditions in the real world of classical Athens? In the world of today?

"If, then, we use the women for the same things as the men, they must also be taught the same things."

"Yes."

"Now music and gymnastics were given to the men."

"Yes."

"Then these two arts, and what has to do with war, must be assigned to the women also, and they must be used in the same ways."

"On the basis of what you say," he said, "it's likely."

"Perhaps," I said, "compared to what is habitual, many of the things now being said would look ridiculous if they were to be done as is said."

"Indeed they would," he said.

"Well," I said, "since we've started to speak, we mustn't be afraid of all the jokes—of whatever kind—the wits might make if such a change took place in gymnastics, in music and, not the least, in the bearing of arms and the riding of horses."

"Then," I said, "if either the class of men or that of women show its superiority in some art or other practice, then we'll say that that art must be assigned to it. But if they look as though they differ in this alone, that the female bears and the male mounts, we'll assert that it has not thereby yet been proved that a woman differs from a man with respect to what we're talking about; rather, we'll still suppose that our guardians and their women must practice the same things."

"And rightly," he said.

"Therefore, my friend, there is no practice of a city's governors which belongs to woman because she's woman, or to man because he's man; but the natures are scattered alike among both animals; and woman participates according to nature in all practices, and man in all, but in all of them woman is weaker than man."

"Certainly."

"So, shall we assign all of them to men and none to women?"

"How could we?"

"For I suppose there is, as we shall assert, one woman apt at medicine and another not, one woman apt at music and another unmusical by nature."

"Of course."

"And isn't there then also one apt at gymnastics and at war, and another unwarlike and no lover of gymnastics?"

"I suppose so."

"And what about this? Is there a lover of wisdom and a hater of wisdom? And one who is spirited and another without spirit?"

"Yes, there are these too."

"There is, therefore, one woman fit for guarding and another not, or wasn't it a nature of this sort we also selected for the men fit for guarding?"

"Certainly, that was it."

The stability of the constitution also came from its being a mixed constitution, blending in some way the laws of democracy and of oligarchy. Aristotle's scheme was unique because of its realism and the breadth of its vision. All the political thinkers of the fourth century B.C.E. recognized the *polis* was in danger, and all hoped to save it. All recognized the economic and social troubles that threatened it. Isocrates, a contemporary of Plato and Aristotle, urged a program of imperial conquest as a cure for poverty and revolution. Plato saw the folly of solving a political and moral problem by purely economic means and resorted to the creation of utopias. Aristotle combined the practical analysis of political and economic realities with the moral and political purposes of the traditional defenders of the *polis.* The result was a passionate confidence in the virtues of moderation and of the middle class, and the proposal of a constitution that would give it power. It is ironic that the ablest defense of the *polis* came soon before its demise.

▼ The Hellenistic World

The term *Hellenistic* was coined in the nineteenth century to describe the period of three centuries during which Greek culture spread far from its homeland to Egypt and deep into Asia. The new civilization formed in this expansion was a mixture of Greek and Near Eastern elements, although the degree of mixture varied from time to time and place to place. The Hellenistic world was larger than the world of Classical Greece, and its major political units were much larger than the city-states, though these persisted in different forms. The new political and cultural order had its roots in the rise to power of a Macedonian dynasty that conquered Greece and the Persian Empire in two generations.

The Macedonian Conquest

The quarrels among the Greeks brought on defeat and conquest by a new power that suddenly rose to eminence in the fourth century B.C.E.: the kingdom of Macedon. The Macedonians inhabited the land to the north of Thessaly (see Map 3–1, page 62), and through the centuries they had unknowingly served the vital purpose of protecting the Greek states from the barbarian tribes further to the north.

By Greek standards, Macedon was a backward, semibarbaric land. It had no *poleis* and was ruled loosely by a king in a rather Homeric fashion. He was chosen partly on the basis of descent, but the acclamation of the army gathered in assembly was required to make him legitimate. Quarrels between pretenders to the throne and even murder to secure it were not uncommon. A council of nobles checked the royal power and could reject a weak or incompetent king. Hampered by

constant wars with the barbarians, internal strife, loose organization, and lack of money, Macedon played no great part in Greek affairs up to the fourth century B.C.E.

The Macedonians were of the same stock as the Greeks and spoke a Greek dialect, and the nobles, at least, thought of themselves as Greeks. The kings claimed descent from Heracles and the royal house of Argos. They tried to bring Greek culture into their court and won acceptance at the Olympic games. If a king could be found to unify this nation, it was bound to play a greater part in Greek affairs.

Philip of Macedon   That king was Philip II (r. 359–336 B.C.E.), who, although still under thirty, took advantage of his appointment as regent to overthrow his infant nephew and make himself king. Like many of his predecessors, he admired Greek culture. Between 367 and 364 B.C.E., he had been a hostage in Thebes, where he learned much about Greek politics and warfare from Epaminondas. His talents for war and diplomacy and his boundless ambition made him the ablest king in Macedonian history. Using both diplomatic and military means, he pacified the tribes on his frontiers and strengthened his own hold on the throne. Then he began to undermine Athenian control of the northern Aegean. He took Amphipolis, which gave him control of gold and silver mines. The income allowed him to found new cities, to bribe

This freestanding statue of the *Charioteer of Delphi* is one of the few full-scale bronze sculptures that survive from the fifth century B.C.E. Polyzalos, the tyrant of the Greek city of Gela in Sicily, dedicated it after winning a victory in the chariot race in the Pythian games, either in 478 or 474. The games were held at the sacred shrine of the god Apollo at Delphi, and the statue was placed within the god's sanctuary, not far from Apollo's temple.   The Charioteer of Delphi. Dedicated by Polyzalos of Gela for a victory either in 478 or 474 B.C.E. Greek (Classical). Bronze, H: 180 cm. Archaeological Museum, Delphi, Greece. Photograph © Nimatallah/Art Resource, NY politicians in foreign towns, and to reorganize his army into the finest fighting force in the world.

The Macedonian Army Philip put to good use what he had learned in Thebes and combined it with the advantages afforded by Macedonian society and tradition. His genius created a versatile and powerful army that was at once national and professional, unlike the amateur armies of citizen-soldiers who fought for the individual *poleis*.

The infantry was drawn from among Macedonian farmers and the frequently rebellious Macedonian hill people. In time, these two elements were integrated to form a loyal and effective national force. Infantrymen were armed with thirteen-foot pikes instead of the more common nine-foot pikes and stood in a more open phalanx formation than the *hoplite* phalanx of the *poleis*. The effectiveness of this formation depended more on the skillful use of the pike than the weight of the charge. In Macedonian tactics, the role of the phalanx was not to be the decisive force, but to hold the enemy until a massed cavalry charge could strike a winning blow on the flank or into a gap. The cavalry was made up of Macedonian nobles and clan leaders, called Companions, who lived closely with the king and developed a special loyalty to him.

Philip also employed mercenaries who knew the latest tactics used by mobile light-armed Greek troops and were familiar with the most sophisticated siege machinery known to the Greeks. With these mercenaries, and with draft forces from among his allies, he could expand on his native Macedonian army of as many as 40,000 men.

The Invasion of Greece So armed, Philip turned south toward central Greece. Since 355 B.C.E., the Phocians had been fighting against Thebes and Thessaly. Philip gladly accepted the request of the Thessalians to be their general, defeated Phocis, and treacherously took control of Thessaly. Swiftly he turned northward again to Thrace and gained domination over the northern Aegean coast and the European side of the straits to the Black Sea. This conquest threatened the vital interests of Athens, which still had a formidable fleet of three hundred ships.

The Athens of 350 B.C.E. was not the Athens of Pericles. It had neither imperial revenue nor allies to share the burden of war, and its own population was smaller than in the fifth century. The Athenians, therefore, were reluctant to go on expeditions themselves or even to send out mercenary armies under Athenian generals, for they had to be paid out of taxes or contributions from Athenian citizens.

The leading spokesman against these tendencies and the cautious foreign policy that went with them was Demosthenes (384–322 B.C.E.), one of the greatest orators in Greek history. He was convinced that Philip was a dangerous enemy to Athens and the other Greeks.

He spent most of his career urging the Athenians to resist Philip's encroachments. He was right, for beginning in 349 B.C.E., Philip attacked several cities in northern and central Greece and firmly planted Macedonian power in those regions. The king of "barbarian" Macedon was elected president of the Pythian Games at Delphi, and the Athenians were forced to concur in the election.

In these difficult times it was Athens's misfortune not to have the kind of consistent political leadership that Cimon or Pericles had offered a century earlier. Many, perhaps most, Athenians accepted Demosthenes' view of Philip, but few were willing to run the risks and make the sacrifices necessary to stop him. Others, like Eubulus, an outstanding financial official and conservative political leader, favored a cautious policy of cooperation with Philip in the hope that his aims were limited and were no real threat to Athens.

Not all Athenians feared Philip. Isocrates (436–338 B.C.E.), the head of an important rhetorical and philosophical school in Athens, looked to him to provide the unity and leadership needed for a Panhellenic campaign against Persia. He and other orators had long urged such a campaign. They saw the conquest of Asia Minor as the solution to the economic, social, and political problems that had brought poverty and civil war to the Greek cities ever since the Peloponnesian War. Finally, there seem to have been some Athenians who were in the pay of Philip, for he used money lavishly to win support.

The years between 346 B.C.E. and 340 B.C.E. were spent in diplomatic maneuvering, each side trying to win useful allies. At last, Philip attacked Perinthus and Byzantium, the lifeline of Athenian commerce; in 340 B.C.E., he besieged both cities and declared war. The Athenian fleet saved both, and so in the following year, Philip marched into Greece. Demosthenes performed wonders in rallying the Athenians and winning Thebes over to the Athenian side. In 338 B.C.E., however, Philip defeated the allied forces at Chaeronea in Boeotia. The decisive blow in this great battle was a cavalry charge led by Alexander, the eighteen-year-old son of Philip.

The Macedonian Government of Greece The Macedonian settlement of Greek affairs was not as harsh as many had feared, although in some cities the friends of Macedon came to power and killed or exiled their enemies. Demosthenes remained free to engage in politics. Athens was spared from attack on the condition that it give up what was left of its empire and follow the lead of Macedon. The rest of Greece was arranged so as to remove all dangers to Philip's rule. To guarantee his security, Philip placed garrisons at Thebes, Chalcis, and Corinth.

In 338 B.C.E., Philip called a meeting of the Greek states to form the federal League of Corinth. The constitution of the league provided for autonomy, freedom from tribute and garrisons, and suppression of piracy and civil war. The league delegates would make foreign policy in theory without consulting their home governments or Philip. All this was a facade; not only was Philip of Macedon president of the league, but he was also its ruler. The defeat at Chaeronea ended Greek freedom and autonomy. Although it maintained its form and way of life for some time, the *polis* had lost control of its own affairs and the special conditions that had made it unique.

Philip did not choose Corinth as the seat of his new confederacy simply from convenience or by accident. It was at Corinth that the Greeks had gathered to resist a Persian invasion almost 150 years earlier. And it was there in 337 B.C.E. that Philip announced his intention to invade Persia in a war of liberation and revenge, as leader of the new league. In the spring of 336 B.C.E., however, as he prepared to begin the campaign, Philip was assassinated.

In 1977, a mound was excavated at the Macedonian village of Vergina. The structures revealed and the extraordinarily rich finds associated with them have led many scholars to conclude this is the royal tomb of Philip II, and the evidence seems persuasive. Philip certainly deserved so distinguished a resting place. He found Macedon a disunited kingdom of semibarbarians, despised and exploited by the Greeks. He left it a united kingdom, master and leader of the Greeks, rich, powerful, and ready to undertake the invasion of Asia.

Alexander the Great

Philip's first son, Alexander III (356–323 B.C.E.), later called Alexander the Great, succeeded his father at the age of twenty. The young king also inherited his father's daring plans to conquer Persia.

The Conquest of the Persian Empire The Persian Empire was vast and its resources enormous. The usurper Cyrus and his Greek mercenaries, however, had shown it to be vulnerable when they penetrated deep into its interior in the fourth century B.C.E. Its size and disparate nature made it hard to control and exploit. Its rulers faced constant troubles on its far-flung frontiers and intrigues within the royal palace. Throughout the fourth century, they had used Greek mercenaries to suppress uprisings. At the time of Philip II's death in 336 B.C.E., a new and inexperienced king, Darius III, was ruling Persia. Yet with a navy that dominated the sea, a huge army, and vast wealth, it remained a formidable opponent.

In 334 B.C.E., Alexander crossed the Hellespont into Asia. His army consisted of about 30,000 infantry and 5,000 cavalry; he had no navy and little money. These facts determined his early strategy—he must seek quick and decisive battles to gain money and supplies from the conquered territory, and he must move along the coast to neutralize the Persian navy by depriving it of ports. Memnon, the commander of the Persian navy, recommended the perfect strategy against this plan: to retreat, to scorch the earth and deprive Alexander of supplies, to avoid battles, to use guerrilla tactics, and to stir up rebellion in Greece. He was ignored. The Persians preferred to stand and fight; their pride and courage were greater than their wisdom.

Alexander met the Persian forces of Asia Minor at the Granicus River, where he won a smashing victory in characteristic style. (See Map 3–4.) He led a cavalry charge across the river into the teeth of the enemy on the opposite bank. He almost lost his life in the process, but he won the devotion of his soldiers. That victory left the coast of Asia Minor open. Alexander captured the coastal cities, thus denying them to the Persian fleet.

In 333 B.C.E., Alexander marched inland to Syria, where he met the main Persian army under King Darius at Issus. Alexander himself led the cavalry charge that broke the Persian line and sent Darius fleeing into central Asia Minor. He continued along the coast and captured previously impregnable Tyre after a long and ingenious siege, putting an end to the threat of the Persian navy. He took Egypt with little trouble and was greeted as liberator, pharaoh, and son of Re (an Egyptian god whose Greek equivalent was Zeus). At Tyre, Darius sent Alexander a peace offer, yielding his entire empire west of the Euphrates River and his daughter in exchange for an alliance and an end to the invasion. But Alexander aimed at conquering the whole empire and probably whatever lay beyond.

In the spring of 331 B.C.E., Alexander marched into Mesopotamia. At Gaugamela, near the ancient Assyrian city of Nineveh, he met Darius, ready for a last stand. Once again, Alexander's tactical genius and personal leadership carried the day. The Persians were broken, and Darius fled once more. Alexander entered Babylon, again hailed as liberator and king.

THE RISE OF MACEDON

359–336 B.C.E.	Reign of Philip II
338 B.C.E.	Battle of Chaeronea; Philip conquers Greece
338 B.C.E.	Founding of League of Corinth
336–323 B.C.E.	Reign of Alexander III (the Great)
334 B.C.E.	Alexander invades Asia
333 B.C.E.	Battle of Issus
331 B.C.E.	Battle of Gaugamela
330 B.C.E.	Fall of Persepolis
327 B.C.E.	Alexander reaches Indus Valley
323 B.C.E.	Death of Alexander

SCYTHIANS

CHORASMIA

Aral Sea

Oxus River

Alexandria Eschate

Western Himalayas

HINDU KUSH

Samarkand

SOGDIANA

BACTRIA

Bactra

Kabul

Bucephala

Nicaea

PUNJAB

INDIA

Indus River

ARACHOSIA

DRANGIANA

ARIA

Herat

Return of Craterus

Kandahar

GEDROSIA

Pattala

IRAN

PARTHIA

Hecatompylos

Caspian Sea

Caucasus Mountains

Trapezus

Ecbatana

MEDIA

CARMANIA

Pasargadae

Persepolis

Alexandria

PERSIS

SUSIANA

Susa

INDIAN OCEAN

Persian Gulf

Gaugamela

Arbela

Opis

Tigris River

Euphrates River

Cunaxa

Babylon

MESOPOTAMIA

ARABIA

Route of Alexander

500 MILES

500 KILOMETERS

Black Sea

Sinope

Byzantium

Ancyra

Cilician Gates

Issus

Tarsus

Gordium

Granicus River

Sardes

Ipsus

Side

Ephesus

Miletus

Xanthus

CRETE

CYPRUS

Byblos

Sidon

Tyre

Damascus

Syrian Desert

Gaza

Pelusium

Memphis

Mediterranean Sea

Alexandria

Heliopolis

Nile River

Thebes

Red Sea

Paraetonium

Oracle of Amon (Siwah)

LIBYA

ILLYRIA

MACEDONIA

THRACE

Pella

N

Map 3–4 **ALEXANDER'S CAMPAIGNS** The route taken by Alexander the Great in his conquest of the Persian Empire, 334 to 323 B.C.E. Starting from the Macedonian capital at Pella, he reached the Indus Valley before being turned back by his own restive troops. He died of fever in Mesopotamia.

In January of 330 B.C.E., he came to Persepolis, the Persian capital, which held splendid palaces and the royal treasury. This bonanza ended his financial troubles and put a vast sum of money into circulation, with economic consequences that lasted for centuries. After a stay of several months, Alexander burned Persepolis to dramatize the destruction of the native Persian dynasty and the completion of Hellenic revenge for the earlier Persian invasion of Greece.

The new regime could not be secure while Darius lived, so Alexander pursued him eastward. Just south of the Caspian Sea, he came on the corpse of Darius, killed by his relative Bessus. The Persian nobles around Darius had lost faith in him and had joined in the plot. The murder removed Darius from Alexander's path, but now he had to catch Bessus, who proclaimed himself successor to Darius. The pursuit of Bessus (who was soon caught), combined with his own great curiosity and longing to go to the most distant places, took Alexander to the frontier of India.

Near Samarkand, in the land of the Scythians, he founded Alexandria Eschate ("Furthest Alexandria"), one of the many cities bearing his name that he founded as he traveled. As part of his grand scheme of amalgamation and conquest, he married the Bactrian princess Roxane and enrolled 30,000 young Bactrians into his army. These were to be trained and sent back to the center of the empire for later use.

In 327 B.C.E., Alexander took his army through the Khyber Pass in an attempt to conquer the lands around the Indus River (modern Pakistan). He reduced the king of these lands, Porus, to vassalage but pushed on in the hope of reaching the river called Ocean that the Greeks believed encircled the world. Finally, his weary men refused to go on. By the spring of 324 B.C.E., the army was back at the Persian Gulf and celebrated in the Macedonian style, with a wild spree of drinking.

The Death of Alexander   Alexander was filled with plans for the future: for the consolidation and organization of his empire; for geographical exploration; for building new cities, roads, and harbors; and perhaps for further conquests in the west. There is even some evidence that he asked to be deified and worshiped as a god, although we cannot be sure if he really did so or why. In June 323 B.C.E., however, he was overcome by a fever and died in Babylon at the age of thirty-three. His memory has never faded, and he soon became the subject of myth, legend, and romance. From the beginning, estimates of him have varied. Some have seen in him a man of grand and noble vision who transcended the narrow limits of Greek and Macedonian ethnocentrism and sought to realize the solidarity of humankind in a great world state. Others have seen him as a calculating despot, given to drunken brawls, brutality, and murder.

The truth is probably somewhere in between. Alexander was one of the greatest generals the world has seen; he never lost a battle or failed in a siege, and with a modest army he conquered a vast empire. He had rare organizational talents, and his plan for creating a multinational empire was the only intelligent way to consolidate his conquests. He established many new cities—seventy, according to tradition—mostly along trade routes. These cities encouraged commerce and prosperity and introduced Hellenic civilization into new areas. It is hard to know if even Alexander could have held together the vast new empire he had created, but his death proved that only he would have had a chance to succeed.

The Successors

Nobody was prepared for Alexander's sudden death, and a weak succession further complicated affairs: Roxane's unborn child and Alexander's weak-minded half brother. His able and loyal Macedonian generals at first hoped to preserve the empire for the Macedonian royal house, and to this end they appointed themselves governors of the various provinces of the empire. The conflicting ambitions of these strong-willed men, however, led to prolonged warfare among them. In these conflicts three of the original number were killed, and all of the direct members of the Macedonian royal house were either executed or murdered. With the murder of Roxane and her son in 310 B.C.E., there was no longer any focus for the enormous empire; and in 306 and 305 B.C.E., the surviving governors proclaimed themselves kings of their various holdings.

Three of these Macedonian generals founded dynasties of significance in the spread of Hellenistic culture:

- Ptolemy I, 367–283 B.C.E.; founder of Dynasty 31 in Egypt, the Ptolemies, of whom Cleopatra, who died in 30 B.C.E., was the last
- Seleucus I, 358–280 B.C.E.; founder of the Seleucid Dynasty in Mesopotamia
- Antigonus I, 382–301 B.C.E.; founder of the Antigonid Dynasty in Asia Minor and Macedon

For the first seventy-five years or so after the death of Alexander, the world ruled by his successors enjoyed considerable prosperity. The vast sums of money that he and they put into circulation greatly increased the level of economic activity. The opportunities for service and profit in the East attracted many Greeks and relieved their native cities of some of the pressure of the poor. The opening of vast new territories to Greek trade, the increased demand for Greek products, and the new availability of desired goods, as well as the conscious policies of the Hellenistic kings, all helped the growth of commerce.

The new prosperity, however, was not evenly distributed. The urban Greeks, the Macedonians, and the

One of the masterpieces of Hellenistic sculpture, the *Laocoön*. This is a Roman copy. According to legend, Laocoön was a priest who warned the Trojans not to take the Greeks' wooden horse within their city. This sculpture depicts his punishment. Great serpents sent by the goddess Athena, who was on the side of the Greeks, devoured Laocoön and his sons before the horrified people of Troy. Direzione Generale Musei Vaticani

Hellenized natives who made up the upper and middle classes lived in comfort and even luxury, but the rural native peasants did not. Unlike the independent men who owned and worked the relatively small and equal lots of the *polis* in earlier times, Hellenistic farmers were reduced to subordinate, dependent peasant status, working on large plantations of decreasing efficiency. During prosperous times these distinctions were bearable, although even then there was tension between the two groups. After a while, however, the costs of continuing wars, inflation, and a gradual lessening of the positive effects of the introduction of Persian wealth all led to economic crisis. The kings bore down heavily on the middle classes, who were skilled at avoiding their responsibilities, however. The pressure on the peasants and the city laborers became great too, and they responded by slowing down their work and even by striking. In Greece, economic pressures brought clashes between rich and poor, demands for the abolition of debt and the redistribution of land, and even, on occasion, civil war.

These internal divisions, along with international wars, weakened the capacity of the Hellenistic kingdoms to resist outside attack. By the middle of the second century B.C.E., they had all, except for Egypt, succumbed to an expanding Italian power, Rome. The two centuries between Alexander and the Roman conquest, however, were of great and lasting importance. They saw the entire eastern Mediterranean coast, Greece, Egypt, Mesopotamia, and the old Persian Empire formed into a single political, economic, and cultural unit.

▼ Hellenistic Culture

The career of Alexander the Great marked a significant turning point in Greek thought as it was represented in literature, philosophy, religion, and art. His conquests and the establishment of the successor kingdoms put an end to the central role of the *polis* in Greek life and thought. Some scholars disagree about the end of the *polis*, denying that Philip's victory at Chaeronea marked its demise. They point to the persistence of *poleis* throughout the Hellenistic period and even see a continuation of them in the Roman *municipia*. These were, however, only a shadow of the vital reality that had been the true *polis*.

Deprived of control of their foreign affairs, and with a foreign monarch determining their important internal arrangements, the post-Classical cities lost the political freedom that was basic to the old outlook. They were cities, perhaps—in a sense, even city-states—but not *poleis*. As time passed, they changed from sovereign states to municipal towns merged into military empires. Never again in antiquity would there be either a serious attack on or defense of the *polis*, for its importance was gone. For the most part, the Greeks after Alexander turned away from political solutions for their problems. Instead, they sought personal responses to their hopes and fears, particularly in religion, philosophy, and magic. The confident, sometimes arrogant, humanism of the fifth century B.C.E. gave way to a kind of resignation to fate, a recognition of helplessness before forces too great for humans to manage.

Philosophy

These developments are noticeable in the changes that overtook the established schools of philosophy as well as in the emergence of two new and influential groups of philosophers: the Epicureans and the Stoics. Athens's position as the center of philosophical studies was reinforced, for the Academy and the Lyceum continued in operation, and the new schools were also located in Athens. The Lyceum turned gradually away from the universal investigations of its founder, Aristotle, even from his scientific interests, to become a center chiefly of literary and especially historical studies.

The Academy turned even further away from its tradition. It adopted the systematic Skepticism of Pyrrho of Elis. Under the leadership of Arcesilaus and Carneades, the Skeptics of the Academy became skilled at pointing out fallacies and weaknesses in the philosophies of the rival schools. They thought that nothing could be known and so consoled themselves and their followers by suggesting that nothing mattered. It was easy for them, therefore, to accept conventional morality and the world as it was. The Cynics, of course, continued to denounce convention and to advocate the crude life in accordance with nature, which some of them practiced publicly to the shock and outrage of respectable citizens. Neither Skepticism nor Cynicism had much appeal to the middle-class city dweller of the third century B.C.E., who sought some basis for choosing a way of life now that the *polis* no longer provided one ready-made.

The Epicureans   Epicurus of Athens (342–271 B.C.E.) formulated a new teaching, embodied in the school he founded in his native city in 306 B.C.E. His philosophy conformed to the mood of the times in that its goal was not knowledge, but human happiness, which he believed a style of life based on reason could achieve. He took sense perception to be the basis of all human knowledge. The reality and reliability of sense perception rested on the acceptance of the physical universe described by the atomists, Democritus and Leucippus. The **Epicureans** proclaimed atoms were continually falling through the void and giving off images that were in direct contact with the senses. These falling atoms could swerve in an arbitrary, unpredictable way to produce the combinations seen in the world.

Epicurus thereby removed an element of determinism that existed in the Democritean system. When a person died, the atoms that composed the body dispersed, so the person had no further existence or perception and therefore nothing to fear after death. Epicurus believed the gods existed, but that they took no interest in human affairs. This belief amounted to a practical atheism, and Epicureans were often thought to be atheists.

The purpose of Epicurean physics was to liberate people from their fear of death, of the gods, and of all nonmaterial or supernatural powers. Epicurean ethics were hedonistic, that is, based on the acceptance of pleasure as true happiness. But pleasure for Epicurus was chiefly negative: the absence of pain and trouble. The goal of the Epicureans was *ataraxia*, the condition of being undisturbed, without trouble, pain, or responsibility. Ideally, a man should have enough means to allow him to withdraw from the world and avoid business and public life. Epicurus even advised against marriage and children. He preached a life of genteel, restrained selfishness that might appeal to intellectual men of means but was not calculated to be widely attractive.

The Stoics   Soon after Epicurus began teaching in his garden in Athens, Zeno of Citium in Cyprus (335–263 B.C.E.) established the **Stoic** school. It derived its name from the *stoa poikile*, or painted portico, in the Athenian *agora*, where Zeno and his disciples walked and talked beginning about 300 B.C.E. From then until about the middle of the second century B.C.E., Zeno and his successors preached a philosophy that owed a good deal to Socrates, by way of the Cynics. It was also fed by a stream of Eastern thought. Zeno, of course, came from Phoenician Cyprus; Chrysippus, one of his successors, came from Cilicia in southern Asia Minor; and other early Stoics came from such places as Carthage, Tarsus, and Babylon.

Like the Epicureans, the Stoics sought the happiness of the individual. Quite unlike them, the Stoics proposed a philosophy almost indistinguishable from religion. They believed humans must live in harmony within themselves and with nature; for the Stoics, God and nature were the same. The guiding principle in nature was divine reason (**Logos**), or fire. Every human had a spark of this divinity, and after death it returned to the eternal divine spirit. From time to time the world was destroyed by fire, from which a new world arose.

The aim of humans, and the definition of human happiness, was the virtuous life: a life lived in accordance with natural law, "when all actions promote the harmony of the spirit dwelling in the individual man with the will of him who orders the universe."[4] To live such a life required the knowledge only the wise possessed. They knew what was good, what was evil, and what was neither, but "indifferent." According to the Stoics, good and evil were dispositions of the mind or soul: prudence, justice, courage, temperance, and so on, were good, whereas folly, injustice, cowardice, and the like, were evil. Life, health, pleasure, beauty, strength, wealth, and so on, were neutral—morally indifferent—for they did not contribute either to happiness or to misery. Human misery came from an irrational mental contraction—from passion, which was a disease of the soul. The wise sought *apatheia*, or freedom from passion, because passion arose from things that were morally indifferent.

Politically, the Stoics fit well into the new world. They thought of it as a single *polis* in which all people were children of the same God. Although they did not forbid political activity, and many Stoics took part in political life, withdrawal was obviously preferable

---

[4] Diogenes Laertius, *Life of Antisthenes* 6.11.

because the usual subjects of political argument were indifferent. Because the Stoics strove for inner harmony of the individual, their aim was a life lived in accordance with the divine will, their attitude fatalistic, and their goal a form of apathy. They fit in well with the reality of post-Alexandrian life. In fact, Stoicism facilitated the task of creating a new political system that relied not on the active participation of the governed, but merely on their docile submission.

Literature

Hellenistic literature reflects the new intellectual currents, the new conditions of literary life, and the new institutions created in that period. The center of literary production in the third and second centuries B.C.E. was the new city of Alexandria in Egypt. There the Ptolemies, the monarchs of Egypt during that time, founded the museum—a great research institute where royal funds supported scientists and scholars—and the library, which contained almost half a million papyrus scrolls.

The library contained much of the great body of past Greek literature, most of which has since been lost. The Alexandrian scholars made copies of what they judged to be the best works. They edited and criticized these works from the point of view of language, form, and content, and wrote biographies of the authors. Their work is responsible for the preservation of most of what remains to us of ancient literature. While some of their work is dry, petty, quarrelsome, and simply foolish, at its best, it is full of learning and perception.

A page from *On Floating Bodies*. Archimedes' work was covered over by a tenth-century manuscript, but ultraviolet radiation reveals the original text and drawings underneath. © 2004 Christie's Images, Inc.

The scholarly atmosphere of Alexandria naturally gave rise to work in history and chronology. Eratosthenes (ca. 275–195 B.C.E.) established a chronology of important events dating from the Trojan War, and others undertook similar tasks. Contemporaries of Alexander, such as Ptolemy I, Aristobulus, and Nearchus, wrote what were apparently sober and essentially factual accounts of his career. We know most of the work of Hellenistic historians only in fragments that later writers cited. It seems, in general, to have emphasized sensational and biographical detail over the kind of rigorous, impersonal analysis that marked the work of Thucydides.

Architecture and Sculpture

The advent of the Hellenistic monarchies greatly increased the opportunities open to architects and sculptors. Money was plentiful, rulers sought outlets for conspicuous display, new cities needed to be built and beautified, and the well-to-do wanted objects of art. The new cities were usually laid out on the grid plan introduced in the fifth century B.C.E. by Hippodamus of Miletus. Temples were built on the classical model, and the covered portico, or *stoa*, became a popular addition to the *agoras* of the Hellenistic towns.

Reflecting the cosmopolitan nature of the Hellenistic world, leading sculptors accepted commissions wherever they were attractive. The result was a certain uniformity of style, although Alexandria, Rhodes, and the kingdom of Pergamum in Asia Minor developed their own distinctive characteristics. For the most part, Hellenistic sculpture moved away from the balanced tension and idealism of the fifth century B.C.E. toward the sentimental, emotional, and realistic mode of the fourth century B.C.E. These qualities are readily apparent in the marble statue called the Laocoon, carved at Rhodes in the second century B.C.E. and afterward taken to Rome.

Mathematics and Science

Among the most spectacular and remarkable intellectual developments of the Hellenistic age were those that came in mathematics and science. The burst of activity in these subjects drew their inspiration from several sources. The stimulation and organization provided by the work of Plato and Aristotle should not be ignored. Alexander's interest in science, evidenced by the scientists he took with him on his expedition and the aid he gave them in collecting data provided further impetus.

The expansion of Greek horizons geographically and the consequent contacts with Egyptian and Babylonian knowledge were also helpful. Finally, the patronage of the Ptolemies and the opportunity for many scientists to work with one another at the museum at Alexandria provided a unique opportunity for scientific work. The work the Alexandrians did formed the greater part of the scientific knowledge available to the Western world until the scientific revolution of the sixteenth and seventeenth centuries C.E.

Euclid's *Elements* (written early in the third century B.C.E.) remained the textbook of plane and solid geometry until recent times. Archimedes of Syracuse (ca. 287–212 B.C.E.) made further progress in geometry, established the theory of the lever in mechanics, and invented hydrostatics.

These advances in mathematics, once they were applied to the Babylonian astronomical tables available to the Hellenistic world, spurred great progress in astronomy. As early as the fourth century B.C.E., Heraclides of Pontus (ca. 390–310 B.C.E.) had argued that Mercury and Venus circulate around the sun and not Earth. He appears to have made other suggestions leading to a **heliocentric theory** of the universe. Most scholars, however, give credit for that theory to Aristarchus of Samos (ca. 310–230 B.C.E.), who asserted that the sun, along with the other fixed stars, did not move and that Earth revolved around the sun in a circular orbit and rotated on its axis while doing so. The heliocentric theory ran contrary not only to the traditional view codified by Aristotle, but also to what seemed to be common sense.

Hellenistic technology was not up to proving the theory, and, of course, the planetary orbits are not circular. The heliocentric theory did not, therefore, take hold. Hipparchus of Nicea (b. ca. 190 B.C.E.) constructed a model of the universe on the geocentric theory; his ingenious and complicated model did a good job of accounting for the movements of the sun, the moon, and the planets. Ptolemy of Alexandria (second century C.E.) improved Hipparchus's system, which remained dominant until the work of Copernicus, in the sixteenth century C.E.

Hellenistic scientists mapped the earth as well as the sky. Eratosthenes of Cyrene (ca. 275–195 B.C.E.) calculated the circumference of Earth to within about two hundred miles. He wrote a treatise on geography based on mathematical and physical reasoning and the reports of travelers. Despite the new data that were available to later geographers, Eratosthenes' map was in many ways more accurate than the one Ptolemy of Alexandria constructed, which became standard in the Middle Ages. (See Map 3–5.)

The Hellenistic Age contributed little to the life sciences, such as biology, zoology, and medicine. Even the

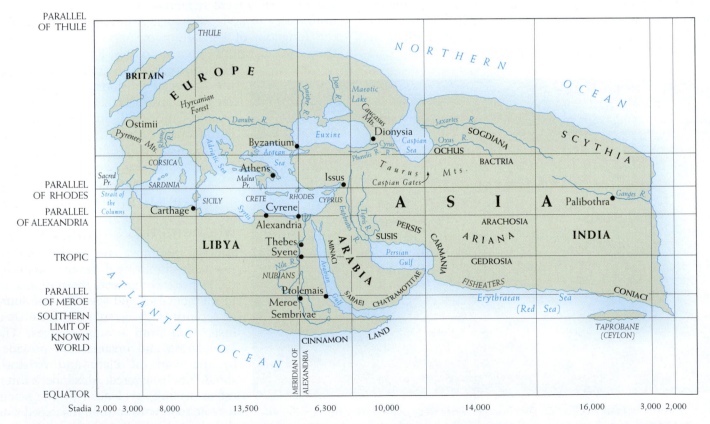

Map 3–5 **THE WORLD ACCORDING TO ERATOSTHENES** Eratosthenes of Alexandria (ca. 275–195 B.C.E.) was a Hellenistic geographer. His map, reconstructed here, was remarkably accurate for its time. The world was divided by lines of "latitude" and "longitude," thus anticipating our global divisions.

sciences that had such impressive achievements to show in the third century B.C.E. made little progress thereafter. In fact, to some extent, there was a retreat from science. Astrology and magic became subjects of great interest as scientific advance lagged.

In Perspective

The Classical Age of Greece was a period of unparalleled achievement. Whereas monarchical, hierarchical, command societies continued to characterize the rest of the world, in Athens democracy was carried as far as it would go before modern times. Although Athenian citizenship was limited to adult males of native parentage, citizens were granted full and active participation in every decision of the state without regard to wealth or class. Democracy disappeared late in the fourth century B.C.E. with the end of Greek autonomy. When it returned in the modern world more than two millennia later, it was broader, but shallower. Democratic citizenship did not again imply the active, direct participation of every citizen in the government of the state.

It was in this democratic, imperial Athens that the greatest artistic, literary, and philosophical achievements of Classical Greece took place. Analytical, secular history, tragedy and comedy, the philosophical dialogue, an organized system of logic, and the logical philosophical treatise were among the achievements of the Classical Age. The tradition of rational, secular speculation in natural philosophy and science was carried forward, but more attention was devoted to human questions in medicine and ethical and political philosophy. A naturalistic style of art evolved that showed human beings first as they ideally might look and then as they really looked, an approach that dominated Greek and Roman art until the late stages of the Roman Empire. This naturalistic style had a powerful effect on the Italian Renaissance and, through it, the modern world.

These Hellenic developments, it should be clear, diverge sharply from the experience of previous cultures and of contemporary ones in the rest of the world. To a great degree, they sprang from the unique political experience of the Greeks, based on the independent city-states. That unique experience and the Classical period ended with the Macedonian conquest, which introduced the Hellenistic Age and ultimately made the Greeks subject to, or part of, a great national state or empire.

The Hellenistic Age speaks to us less fully and vividly than that of Classical Greece, chiefly because it had no historian to compare with Herodotus and Thucydides. We lack the clear picture that a continuous, rich, lively, and meaningful narrative provides. This deficiency should not obscure the great achievements of the age. Its literature, art, scholarship, and science deserve attention in their own right.

The Hellenistic Age did perform a vital civilizing function. It spread Greek culture over a remarkably wide area and made a significant and lasting impression on much of it. Greek culture also adjusted to its new surroundings, unifying and simplifying its cultural cargo to make it more accessible to outsiders. The various Greek dialects gave way to a version of the Attic tongue, the koine, or common language.

In the same way, the scholarship of Alexandria established canons of literary excellence and the scholarly tools with which to make the great treasures of Greek culture understandable to later generations. The syncretism of thought and belief introduced in this period also made understanding and accord more likely among different peoples. When the Romans came into contact with Hellenism, it powerfully impressed them. When they conquered the Hellenistic world, they became, as their poet Horace said, captives of its culture.

REVIEW QUESTIONS

1. How was the Delian League transformed into the Athenian Empire during the fifth century B.C.E.? Did the empire offer any advantages to its subjects? Why was there such resistance to Athenian efforts to unify the Greek world in the fifth and fourth centuries B.C.E.?

2. Why did Athens and Sparta come to blows in the Great Peloponnesian War? What was each side's strategy for victory? Why did Sparta win the war?

3. Give examples from art, literature, and philosophy of the tension that characterized Greek life and thought in the Classical Age. How does Hellenistic art differ from that of the Classical Age?

4. Between 431 and 362 B.C.E., why did Athens, Sparta, and Thebes each fail to impose hegemony over the city-states of Greece? What does your analysis tell you about the components of successful rule?

5. How and why did Philip II conquer Greece between 359 and 338 B.C.E.? How was he able to turn Macedon into a formidable military and political power? Why was Athens unable to defend itself against Macedon? Where does more of the credit for Philip's success lie—in Macedon's strength or in the weakness of the Greek city-states?

6. What were the major consequences of Alexander's death? What did he achieve? Was he a conscious promoter of Greek civilization or just an egomaniac drunk with the lust of conquest?

SUGGESTED READINGS

J. Buckler, *Aegean Greece in the Fourth Century* BC (2003). A political, diplomatic, and military history of the Aegean Greeks of the fourth century B.C.E.

W. Burkert, *Greek Religion* (1985). A fine general study.

P. Cartledge, *Alexander the Great: The Hunt for a New Past* (2004). A learned and lively biography.

P. Cartledge, *Spartan Reflections* (2001). A collection of valuable essays by a leading scholar of ancient Sparta.

G. Cawkwell, *Philip of Macedon* (1978). A brief but learned account of Philip's career.

Y. Garlan, *Slavery in Ancient Greece* (1988). An up-to-date survey.

R. Garland, *Daily Life of the Ancient Greeks* (1998). A good account of the way the Greeks lived.

P. Green, *From Alexander to Actium* (1990). A brilliant synthesis of the Hellenistic period.

P. Green, *The Greco-Persian War* (1996). A lively account by a fine scholar with a keen feeling for the terrain.

E. S. Gruen, *Heritage and Hellenism: The Reinvention of Jewish Tradition* (1998). A fine account of the interaction between Jews and Greeks in Hellenistic times.

C. D. Hamilton, *Agesilaus and the Failure of Spartan Hegemony* (1991). An excellent biography of the king who was the central figure in Sparta during its domination in the fourth century B.C.E.

R. Just, *Women in Athenian Law and Life* (1988). A good study of the place of women in Athenian life.

D. Kagan, *The Peloponnesian War* (2003). An analytic narrative of the great war between Athens and Sparta.

D. Kagan, *Pericles of Athens and the Birth of Athenian Democracy* (1991). An account of the life and times of the great Athenian statesman.

B. M. W. Knox, *The Heroic Temper: Studies in Sophoclean Tragedy* (1964). A brilliant analysis of tragic heroism.

D. M. Lewis, *Sparta and Persia* (1977). A valuable discussion of relations between Sparta and Persia in the fifth and fourth centuries B.C.E.

C. B. Patterson, *The Family in Greek History* (1998). An interesting interpretation of the relationship between family and state in ancient Greece.

J. J. Pollitt, *Art and Experience in Classical Greece* (1972). A scholarly and entertaining study of the relationship between art and history in Classical Greece, with excellent illustrations.

J. J. Pollitt, *Art in the Hellenistic Age* (1986). An extraordinary analysis that places the art in its historical and intellectual context.

R. W. Sharples, *Stoics, Epicureans, and Sceptics. An Introduction to Hellenistic Philosophy* (1996). A brief and useful introduction.

B. S. Strauss, *Athens after the Peloponnesian War* (1987). An excellent discussion of Athens's recovery and of the nature of Athenian society and politics in the fourth century B.C.E.

I. Worthington, *Demosthenes, Statesman and Orator* (2000). A useful collection of essays on the career and importance of the Athenian political leader.

For additional learning resources related to this chapter, please go to www.myhistorylab.com

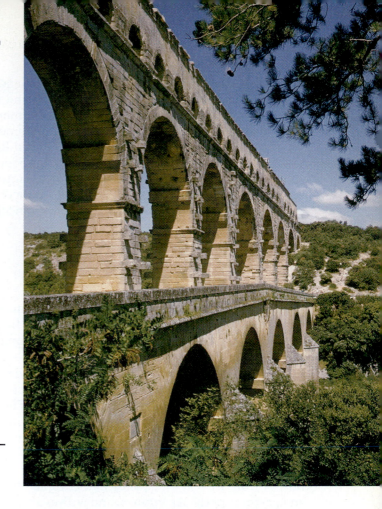

The Pont du Gard, an aqueduct and bridge, was built in the first century B.C.E. in southern France in Rome's first province beyond the Alps.   Walter S. Clark/Photo Researchers, Inc.

4

Rome: From Republic to Empire

THE ACHIEVEMENT OF the Romans was one of the most remarkable in human history. The descendants of the inhabitants of a small village in central Italy, they came eventually to rule the entire Italian peninsula, then the entire Mediterranean coastline. They conquered most of the Near East and, finally, much of continental Europe. They ruled this vast empire under a single government that provided considerable peace and prosperity for centuries. Never before the Romans nor since has that area been united, and rarely, if ever, has it enjoyed a stable peace. But

Rome's legacy was not merely military excellence and political organization. The Romans adopted and transformed the intellectual and cultural achievements of the Greeks and combined them with their own outlook and historical experience. The resulting Graeco-Roman tradition in literature, philosophy, and art provided the core of learning for the Middle Ages and pointed the way to the new paths taken in the Renaissance. It remains at the heart of Western civilization to this day.

▼ Prehistoric Italy

The culture of Italy developed late. Paleolithic settlements gave way to the Neolithic mode of life only around 2500 B.C.E. The Bronze Age came around 1500 B.C.E. About 1000 B.C.E., bands of new arrivals—warlike peoples speaking a set of closely related languages we call *Italic*—began to infiltrate Italy from across the Adriatic Sea and around its northern end. These invaders cremated their dead and put the ashes in tombs stocked with weapons and armor. Their bronzework was of a higher quality than that of the people they displaced, and they were soon making weapons, armor, and tools of iron. By 800 B.C.E., they had occupied the highland pastures of the Apennines, and within a short time, they began to challenge the earlier settlers for control of the tempting western plains. It would be the descendants of these tough mountain people—Umbrians, Sabines, Samnites, and Latins—together with others soon to arrive—Etruscans, Greeks, and Celts—who would shape the future of Italy.

▼ The Etruscans

The **Etruscans** exerted the most powerful external influence on the Romans. Their civilization arose in Etruria (now Tuscany), west of the Apennines between the Arno and Tiber Rivers, about 800 B.C.E. (See Map 4–1.) Since antiquity their origin has been debated, some arguing that they were indigenous and others that they came from the east. The evidence does not permit any certainty, and scholarship today focuses on the formation of a people rather than its origins.

Government

The Etruscans brought civilization with them. Their settlements were self-governing, fortified city-states, of which twelve formed a loose religious confederation. At first, kings ruled these cities, but they were replaced by an agrarian aristocracy, which ruled through a council and elected annual magistrates. The Etruscans were a military ruling class that exploited the native Italians

(the predecessors of the later Italic speakers), who worked the Etruscans' land and mines and served as infantry in Etruscan armies. This aristocracy accumulated wealth through agriculture, industry, piracy, and commerce with the Carthaginians and the Greeks.

Religion

The Etruscans' influence on the Romans was greatest in religion. They imagined a world filled with gods and spirits, many of them evil. To deal with such demons, the Etruscans developed complicated rituals and powerful priesthoods. Divination by sacrifice and omens in

Map 4–1 **ANCIENT ITALY** This map of ancient Italy and its neighbors before the expansion of Rome shows major cities and towns as well as several geographical regions and the locations of some of the Italic and non-Italic peoples.

nature helped discover the divine will, and careful attention to precise rituals directed by priests helped please the gods. After a while the Etruscans, influenced by the Greeks, worshipped gods in the shape of humans and built temples for them.

Women

Etruscan women had a more significant role in family and society than did Greek women in the world of the *polis*. Etruscan wives appeared in public, in religious festivals, and at public banquets together with their husbands. Many of them were literate, and women both took part in athletic contests and watched them as spectators alongside men. Inscriptions on tombs and paintings on coffins mention both father and mother of the deceased and often show husbands and wives together in respectful and loving attitudes.

Dominion

The Etruscan aristocracy remained aggressive and skillful in the use of horses and war chariots. In the seventh and sixth centuries B.C.E., they expanded their power in Italy and across the sea to Corsica and Elba. They conquered **Latium** (a region that included the small town of Rome) and Campania, where they became neighbors of the Greeks of Naples. In the north, they got as far as the Po Valley. Small bands led by Etruscan chieftains who did not work in concert and would not necessarily aid one another in distress carried out these conquests. As a result, the conquests outside Etruria were not firmly based and did not last long.

Etruscan power reached its height some time before 500 B.C.E. and then rapidly declined. About 400 B.C.E., Celtic peoples from the area the Romans called **Gaul** (modern France) broke into the Po Valley and drove out the Etruscans. They settled this land so firmly that the Romans thereafter called it *Cisalpine Gaul* (Gaul on this side of the Alps). Eventually, even the Etruscan heartland in Etruria lost its independence and was incorporated into Roman Italy. The Etruscan language was forgotten, and Etruscan culture gradually became only a memory, but its influence on the Romans remained.

▼ Royal Rome

Rome was an unimportant town in Latium until the Etruscans conquered it, but its location—fifteen miles from the mouth of the Tiber River at the point at which hills made further navigation impossible—gave it advantages over its Latin neighbors. The island in the Tiber southwest of the Capitoline Hill made the river fordable, so Rome was naturally a center for communication and trade, both east-west and north-south.

This elaborate Etruscan coffin was discovered in a tomb at Cerveteri in the Italian region of Tuscany, the heart of ancient Etruria. It has been dated to about 520 B.C.E. Made of terra cotta, it shows wife and husband reclining affectionately together.
Sarcophagus of a Couple. Etruscan, 6th B.C.E. Terracotta. H: 114 cm. Louvre, Paris, France. Copyright Erich Lessing/Art Resource, NY

Government

In the sixth century B.C.E., Rome came under Etruscan control. Led by Etruscan kings, the Roman army, equipped and organized like the Greek phalanx, gained control of most of Latium. An effective political and social order that gave extraordinary power to the ruling figures in both public and private life made this success possible. To their kings the Romans gave the awesome power of **imperium**—the right to issue commands and to enforce them by fines, arrests, and corporal, or even capital, punishment. Although it tended apparently to remain in the same family, kingship was elective. The Roman Senate had to approve the candidate for the office, and a vote of the people gathered in an assembly formally granted the *imperium*. A basic characteristic of later Roman government—the granting of great power to executive officers contingent on the approval of the Senate and, ultimately, the people—was already apparent in this structure. The same word is at the root of *imperator*, a military title, the source of our word *emperor*, that would eventually become the title of Rome's rulers. The union of military and political power would be a major theme in the transformation of the Roman Republic into a monarchical empire.

In theory and law, the king was the commander of the army, the chief priest, and the supreme judge. He could make decisions in foreign affairs, call out the army, lead it in battle, and impose discipline on his troops, all by virtue of his *imperium*. In practice, the royal power was much more limited.

The Senate was the second branch of the early Roman government. According to tradition, it originated when Romulus, Rome's legendary first king, chose one hundred of Rome's leading men to advise him. The number of senators ultimately rose to three hundred, where it stayed through most of the history of the republic. Ostensibly, the Senate had neither executive nor legislative power; it met only when the king summoned it to advise him. In reality its authority was great, for the senators, like the king, served for life. The Senate, therefore, had continuity and experience, and its members were the most powerful men in the state. It could not be lightly ignored.

The third branch of government, the curiate assembly, was made up of all citizens, as divided into thirty groups. (In early Rome, citizenship required descent from Roman parents on both sides.) The assembly met only when the king summoned it; he determined the agenda, made proposals, and recognized other speakers, if any. Usually, the assembly was called to listen and approve. Voting was not by head, but by group; a majority within each group determined its vote, and the majority vote of the groups determined decisions. Group voting would be typical of all future forms of Roman assembly.

The Family

The center of Roman life was the family. At its head stood the father, whose power and authority within the family resembled those of the king within the state. Over his children, the father held broad powers analogous to *imperium* in the state; he had the right to sell

his children into slavery, and he even had the power of life and death over them. Over his wife, he had less power; he could not sell or kill her. In practice, consultation within the family, public opinion, and, most of all, tradition limited his power to dispose of his children. The father was the chief priest of the family. He led it in daily prayers to the dead, which reflected the ancestor worship central to the Roman family and state.

Women in Early Rome

Early Roman society was hierarchical and dominated by males. Throughout her life, a woman was under the control of some adult male. Before her marriage it was her father, afterward her husband or, when neither was available, a guardian chosen from one of their male relatives. One of them had to approve her right to buy or sell property or make contracts. Roman law gave control of a woman from father to husband by the right of *manus* (hand). This was conferred by one of two formal marriage ceremonies that were typical in early Rome. Over time, however, a third form of marriage became popular that left the power of *manus* in the hands of the woman's father, even after her marriage. This kind of union was similar to what we would call common-law marriage, in which a woman could stay out of her husband's control of her and her dowry by absenting herself from her husband's home for at least three consecutive nights each year. This gave her greater rights of inheritance in her father's family and greater independence in her marriage.

In early Rome, marriage with *manus* was most common, but women of the upper classes had a position of influence and respect greater than the classical Greeks had and more like what appears to have been true of the Etruscans. Just as the husband was *paterfamilias*, the wife was *materfamilias*. She was mistress within the home, controlling access to the storerooms, keeping the accounts, and supervising the slaves and the raising of the children. She also was part of the family council and a respected adviser on all questions concerning the family. Divorce was difficult and rare, limited to a few specific transgressions by the wife, one of which was drunkenness. Even when divorced for cause, the wife retained her dowry.

Busts of a Roman couple from the period of the Republic. Although some have identified the individuals as Cato the Younger and his daughter Porcia, no solid evidence confirms this claim. Bust of Cato and Porcia. Roman sculpture. Vatican Museums, Vatican State. Photograph © Scala/Art Resource, NY

Clientage

Clientage was one of Rome's most important institutions. The client was "an inferior entrusted, by custom or by himself, to the protection of a stranger more powerful than he, and rendering certain services and observances in return for this protection."[1] The Romans spoke of a client as being in the *fides*, or trust, of his patron, and so the relationship always had moral implications. The patron provided his client with protection, both physical and legal. He gave him economic assistance in the form of a land grant, the opportunity to work as a tenant farmer or a laborer on the patron's land, or simply handouts. In return, the client would fight for his patron, work his land, and support him politically. Public opinion and tradition reinforced these mutual obligations. When early custom was codified in the mid-fifth century B.C.E., one of the twelve tablets of laws announced, "Let the patron who has defrauded his client be accursed."

In the early history of Rome, patrons were rich and powerful, whereas clients were poor and weak, but as time passed, rich and powerful members of the upper classes became clients of even more powerful men, chiefly for political purposes. Because the client-patron relationship was hereditary and sanctioned by religion and custom, it played an important part in the life of the Roman Republic.

Patricians and Plebeians

In the royal period, a class distinction based on birth divided Roman society in two. The wealthy **patrician** upper class held a monopoly of power and influence. Its members alone could conduct state religious ceremonies, sit in the Senate, or hold office. They formed a closed caste by forbidding marriage outside their own group.

The **plebeian** lower class must have consisted originally of poor, dependent small farmers, laborers, and artisans, the clients of the nobility. As Rome and its population grew, families that were rich, but outside the charmed circle of patricians, grew wealthy. From early times, therefore, there were rich plebeians, and incompetence and bad luck must have produced some poor patricians. The line between the classes and the monopoly of privileges remained firm, nevertheless, and the struggle of the plebeians to gain equality occupied more than two centuries of republican history.

▼ The Republic

Roman tradition tells us that the outrageous behavior of the last kings led the noble families to revolt in 509 B.C.E., bringing the monarchy to a sudden close and leading to the creation of the Roman Republic.

[1] E. Badian, *Foreign Clientelae* (264–70 B.C.E.), Clarendon Press (Oxford, 1958), p. 1.

Constitution

The Consuls   The Roman constitution was an unwritten accumulation of laws and customs. The Romans were a conservative people and were never willing to deprive their chief magistrates of the great powers the monarchs had exercised. They elected two patricians to the office of consul and endowed them with *imperium*. Two financial officials called *quaestors*, whose number ultimately reached eight, assisted them. Like the kings, the **consuls** led the army, had religious duties, and served as judges. They retained the visible symbols of royalty—the purple robe, the ivory chair, and the *lictors* (minor officials), who accompanied them bearing rods and axe. The power of the consuls, however, was limited legally and institutionally as well as by custom.

The power of the consulship was granted not for life, but only for a year. Each consul could prevent any action by his colleague simply by saying no to his proposal, and the consuls shared their religious powers with others. Even the *imperium* was limited. Although the consuls had full powers of life and death while leading an army, within the sacred boundary of the city of Rome, the citizens had the right to appeal all cases involving capital punishment to the popular assembly. Besides, after their one year in office, the consuls would spend the rest of their lives as members of the Senate. It was a reckless consul who failed to ask the advice of the Senate or to follow it when there was general agreement.

The many checks on consular action tended to prevent initiative, swift action, and change, but this was just what a conservative, traditional, aristocratic republic wanted. Only in the military sphere did divided counsel and a short term of office create important problems. The Romans tried to get around the difficulties by sending only one consul into the field or, when this was impossible, allowing each consul sole command on alternate days. In serious crises, the consuls, with the advice of the Senate, could appoint a *dictator* to the command and could retire in his favor. The *dictator*'s term of office was limited to six months, but his own *imperium* was valid both inside and outside the city without appeal.

These devices worked well enough in the early years of the republic, when Rome's battles were near home. Longer wars and more sophisticated opponents, however, revealed the system's weaknesses and required significant changes. Long campaigns prompted the invention of the **proconsulship** in 325 B.C.E., whereby the term of a consul serving in the field was extended. This innovation contained the seeds of many troubles for the constitution.

The creation of the office of *praetor* also helped provide commanders for Rome's many campaigns. The basic function of the *praetors* was judicial, but they also had *imperium* and served as generals. *Praetors'* terms were also for one year. By the end of the republic, there were eight *praetors*, whose annual terms, like the consuls', could be extended for military commands when necessary.

At first, the consuls identified citizens and classified them according to age and property. After the middle of the fifth century B.C.E., this job was delegated to a new office, that of **censor**. The Senate elected two *censors* every five years. They conducted a census and drew up the citizen rolls. Their task was not just clerical; the classification of the citizens fixed taxation and status, so the *censors* had to be men of fine reputation, former consuls. They soon acquired additional powers. By the fourth century B.C.E., they compiled the roll of senators and could strike senators from that roll not only for financial but also for moral reasons. As the prestige of the office grew, it became the ultimate prize of a Roman political career.

The Senate and the Assembly With the end of the monarchy, the Senate became the single continuous, deliberative body in the Roman state, greatly increasing its influence and power. Its members were prominent patricians, often leaders of clans and patrons of many clients. The Senate soon gained control of the state's finances and of foreign policy. Neither magistrates nor popular assemblies could lightly ignore its formal advice.

The most important assembly in the early republic was the *centuriate assembly*, which was, in a sense, the Roman army acting in a political capacity. Its basic unit was the *century*, theoretically one hundred fighting men classified according to their weapons, armor, and equipment. Because each man equipped himself, this meant the organization was by classes according to wealth.

Voting was by *century* and proceeded in order of classification from the cavalry down. The assembly elected the consuls and several other magistrates, voted on bills put before it, made decisions of war and peace, and also served as the court of appeal against decisions of the magistrates affecting the life or property of a citizen. In theory, the assembly had final authority, but the Senate exercised great, if informal, influence.

The Struggle of the Orders The laws and constitution of the early republic gave to the patricians almost a monopoly of power and privilege. Plebeians were barred from public office, from priesthoods, and from other public religious offices. They could not serve as judges and could not even know the law, for there was no published legal code. The only law was traditional practice, and that existed only in the minds and actions of patrician magistrates. Plebeians were subject to the *imperium* but could not exercise its power. They were not allowed to marry patricians. When Rome gained new land by conquest, patrician magistrates distributed it in a way that favored patricians. The patricians dominated the assemblies and the Senate. The plebeians undertook a cam-

paign to achieve political, legal, and social equality, and this attempt, which succeeded after two centuries of intermittent effort, is called the *Struggle of the Orders*.

The most important source of plebeian success was the need for their military service. According to tradition, the plebeians, angered by patrician resistance to their demands, withdrew from the city and camped on the Sacred Mount. There they formed a plebeian tribal assembly and elected plebeian **tribunes** to protect them from the arbitrary power of the magistrates. They declared the tribune inviolate and sacrosanct; anyone laying violent hands on him was accursed and liable to death without trial. By extension of his right to protect the plebeians, the tribune gained the power to veto any action of a magistrate or any bill in a Roman assembly or the Senate. The plebeian assembly voted by tribe, and a vote of the assembly was binding on plebeians. They tried to make their decisions binding on all Romans, but could not do so until 287 B.C.E.

Next, the plebeians obtained access to the laws, when early Roman custom in all its harshness and simplicity was codified in the Twelve Tables around 450 B.C.E. In 445 B.C.E., plebeians gained the right to marry patricians. The main prize, the consulship, the patricians did not yield easily. Not until 367 B.C.E. did legislation—the Licinian-Sextian Laws—provide that at least one consul could be a plebeian. Before long, plebeians held other offices—even the dictatorship and the censorship. In 300 B.C.E., they were admitted to the most important priesthoods, the last religious barrier to equality. In 287 B.C.E., the plebeians completed their triumph. They once again withdrew from the city and secured the passage of a law whereby decisions of the plebeian assembly bound all Romans and did not require the approval of the Senate.

It might seem that the Roman aristocracy had given way under the pressure of the lower class. Yet the victory of the plebeians did not bring democracy. An aristocracy based strictly on birth had given way to an aristocracy more subtle, but no less restricted, based on

THE RISE OF THE PLEBEIANS TO EQUALITY IN ROME

509 B.C.E.	Kings expelled; republic founded
450–449 B.C.E.	Laws of the Twelve Tables published
445 B.C.E.	Plebeians gain right of marriage with patricians
367 B.C.E.	Licinian-Sextian Laws open consulship to plebeians
300 B.C.E.	Plebeians attain chief priesthoods
287 B.C.E.	Laws passed by Plebeian Assembly made binding on all Romans

A Closer LOOK

LICTORS

THE LICTORS WERE attendants of the Roman magistrates who held the power of *imperium*, the right to command. In republican times these magistrates were the consuls, praetors, and proconsuls. The lictors were men from the lower classes—some were even former slaves. They constantly attended the magistrates when the latter appeared in public. The lictors cleared a magistrate's way in crowds, and summoned, arrested, and punished offenders for him. They also served as their magistrate's house guard.

The axe carried by the man on the left is a symbol of the magistrate's power, when he was acting as a military commander outside the city, to put a Roman citizen to death.

The bundle of sticks, called *fasces*, the other two lictors carry indicates the magistrates' right to employ corporal punishment, but their bindings symbolize the right of citizens not on military duty not to be punished without a trial.

The traditional dress of a lictor was a toga when in Rome, and a red coat called a *sagum* when outside the city or when taking part in a triumph.

Alinari/Art Resource, NY

To examine this image in an interactive fashion, please go to www.myhistorylab.com

myhistorylab

---

a combination of wealth and birth. A relatively small group of rich and powerful families, both patrician and plebeian, known as *nobiles*, attained the highest offices in the state. The significant distinction was no longer between patrician and plebeian but between the *nobiles* and everyone else.

The absence of the secret ballot in the assemblies enabled the *nobiles* to control most decisions and elections through intimidation and bribery. The leading families constantly competed with one another for office, power, and prestige, but they often combined in marriage and less formal alliances to keep the political plums within their own group. In the century from 233 to 133 B.C.E., for instance, twenty-six families provided 80 percent of the consuls, and only ten families accounted for almost 50 percent. These same families dominated the Senate, whose power became ever greater. Rome's success brought the Senate prestige, increased control of policy, and increased confidence in its capacity to rule. The end of the Struggle of the Orders brought domestic peace under a republican constitution dominated by a capable, if narrow, senatorial aristocracy. This outcome satisfied most Romans outside the ruling group, because Rome conquered Italy and brought many benefits to its citizens.

The Conquest of Italy

Not long after the fall of the monarchy in 509 B.C.E., a coalition of Romans, Latins, and Italian Greeks drove the Etruscans out of Latium for good. Throughout the fifth century B.C.E., the powerful Etruscan city of Veii, only twelve miles north of the Tiber River, raided Roman territory. After a hard struggle and a long siege, the Romans took Veii in 392 B.C.E., more than doubling the size of Rome.

Roman policy toward defeated enemies used both the carrot and the stick. When the Romans made friendly alliances with some, they gained new soldiers for their army. When they treated others more harshly by annexing their land, they achieved a similar end. Service in the Roman army was based on property, and the distribution to poor Romans of conquered land made soldiers of previously useless men. It also gave the poor a stake in Rome and reduced the pressure against its aristocratic regime. The long siege of Veii kept soldiers from their farms during the campaign. From that time on, the Romans paid their soldiers, thus giving their army greater flexibility and a more professional quality.

Gallic Invasion and Roman Reaction

At the beginning of the fourth century B.C.E., a disaster struck. In 387 B.C.E., the Gauls, barbaric Celtic tribes from across the Alps, defeated the Roman army and burned Rome. The Gauls sought plunder, not conquest, so they extorted a ransom from the Romans and returned to the north. Rome's power appeared to be wiped out.

By about 350 B.C.E., however, the Romans were more dominant than ever. Their success in turning back new Gallic raids added to their power and prestige. As the Romans tightened their grip on Latium, the Latins became resentful. In 340 B.C.E., they demanded independence from Rome or full equality and launched a war of independence that lasted until 338 B.C.E. The victorious Romans dissolved the Latin League, and their treatment of the defeated opponents provided a model for the settlement of Italy.

Roman Policy Toward the Conquered

The Romans did not destroy any of the Latin cities or their people, nor did they treat them all alike. Some near Rome received full Roman citizenship. Others farther away gained municipal status, which gave them the private rights of intermarriage and commerce with Romans, but not the public rights of voting and holding office in Rome. They retained the rights of local self-government and could obtain full Roman citizenship if they moved to Rome. They followed Rome in foreign policy and provided soldiers to serve in the Roman legions. (See "Rome's Treatment of Conquered Italian Cities.")

Still other states became allies of Rome on the basis of treaties, which differed from city to city. Some were given the private rights of intermarriage and commerce with Romans, and some were not; the allied states were always forbidden to exercise these rights with one another. Some, but not all, were allowed local autonomy. Land was taken from some, but not from others, nor was the percentage taken always the same. All the allies supplied troops to the army, in which they fought in auxiliary battalions under Roman officers, but they did not pay taxes to Rome.

On some of the conquered land, the Romans placed colonies, permanent settlements of veteran soldiers in the territory of recently defeated enemies. The colonists retained their Roman citizenship and enjoyed home rule; in return for the land they had been given, they were a kind of permanent garrison to deter or suppress rebellion. These colonies were usually connected to Rome by a network of military roads built as straight as possible and so durable that some are used even today. The roads guaranteed that a Roman army could swiftly reinforce an embattled colony or put down an uprising in any weather.

The Roman settlement of Latium reveals even more clearly than before the principles by which Rome was able to conquer and dominate Italy. The excellent army and the diplomatic skill that allowed Rome to separate its enemies help explain its conquests. The reputation for harsh punishment of rebels, and the sure promise that such punishment would be delivered, was made unmistakably clear: Both the colonies and military roads help explain the reluctance to revolt. But the positive side, represented by Rome's organization of the defeated states, is at least as important. The Romans did not regard the status given each newly conquered city as permanent. They held out to loyal allies the prospect of improving their status—even of achieving the ultimate prize, full Roman citizenship. In so doing, the Romans gave their allies a stake in Rome's future success and a sense of being colleagues, though subordinate ones, rather than subjects. The result, in general, was that most of Rome's allies remained loyal even when put to the severest test.

Defeated Samnites

The next great challenge to Roman arms came in a series of wars with a tough mountain people of the southern Apennines, the Samnites. Some of Rome's allies rebelled, and soon the Etruscans and Gauls joined in the war against Rome. But most of

---

ROMAN EXPANSION IN ITALY

392 B.C.E.	Fall of Veii; Etruscans defeated
387 B.C.E.	Gauls burn Rome
338 B.C.E.	Latin League defeated
295 B.C.E.	Battle of Sentinum; Samnites and allies defeated
275 B.C.E.	Pyrrhus driven from Italy
265 B.C.E.	Rome rules Italy south of the Po River

ROME'S TREATMENT OF CONQUERED ITALIAN CITIES

Titus Livius (59 B.C.E.–17 C.E.), called Livy in English-speaking countries, wrote a history of Rome from its origins until his own time. In the following excerpt from it he describes the kind of settlement they imposed on various Italian cities after crushing their revolt in the years 340–338 B.C.E.

What principles and purposes underlay Rome's treatment of the different cities? What purposes were intended in settling Roman colonists among them?

The principal members of the senate applauded the consul's statement on the business on the whole; but said that, as the states were differently circumstanced, their plan might be readily adjusted and determined according to the desert of each, if they should put the question regarding each state specifically. The question was therefore so put regarding each separately and a decree passed. To the people of Lanuvium the right of citizenship was granted, and the exercise of their religious rights was restored to them with this provision, that the temple and grove of Juno Sospita should be common between the Lanuvian burghers and the Roman people. The peoples of Aricia, Nomentum, and Pedum were admitted into the number of citizens on the same terms as the Lanuvians. To the Tusculans the rights of citizenship which they already possessed were continued; no public penalty was imposed and the crime of rebellion was visited on its few instigators. On the people of Velitrae, Roman citizens of long standing, measures of great severity were inflicted because they had so often rebelled; their walls were razed, and their senate deported and ordered to dwell on the other side of the Tiber; any individual who should be caught on the hither side of the river should be fined one thousand asses, and the person who had apprehended him should not discharge his prisoner from confinement until the money was paid down. Into the lands of the senators colonists were sent; by their addition Velitrae recovered its former populous appearance.

From *History of Rome by Livy*, trans. by D. Spillan et al. (New York: American Book Company, n.d.). Vol. 1, p. 561, 1896.

the allies remained loyal. In 295 B.C.E., at Sentinum, the Romans defeated an Italian coalition, and by 280 B.C.E., they were masters of central Italy. Their power extended from the Po Valley south to Apulia and Lucania.

Now the Romans were in direct contact with the Greek cities of southern Italy. Roman intervention in a quarrel between Greek cities brought them face to face with Pyrrhus, king of Epirus. Pyrrhus, probably the best general of his time, commanded a well-disciplined and experienced mercenary army, which he hired out for profit, and a new weapon: twenty war elephants. He defeated the Romans twice but suffered many casualties. When one of his officers rejoiced at the victory, Pyrrhus told him, "If we win one more battle against the Romans, we shall be completely ruined." This "Pyrrhic victory" led him to withdraw to Sicily in 275 B.C.E. The Greek cities that had hired him were forced to join the Roman confederation. By 265 B.C.E., Rome ruled all Italy as far north as the Po River, an area of 47,200 square miles. The year after the defeat of Pyrrhus, Ptolemy Philadelphus, king of Egypt, sent a message of congratulations to establish friendly relations with Rome. This act recognized Rome's new status as a power in the Hellenistic world.

Rome and Carthage

The conquest of southern Italy brought the Romans face to face with the great naval power of the western Mediterranean, Carthage. (See Map 4–2, page 106.) Late in the ninth century B.C.E., the Phoenician city of Tyre had planted a colony on the coast of northern Africa near modern Tunis, calling it the New City, or Carthage. In the sixth century B.C.E., the conquest of Phoenicia by the Assyrians and the Persians left Carthage independent and free to exploit its advantageous

Map 4–2 **THE WESTERN MEDITERRANEAN AREA DURING THE RISE OF ROME** This map covers the theater of conflict between the growing Roman dominions and those of Carthage in the third century B.C.E. The Carthaginian Empire stretched westward from the city (in modern Tunisia) along the North African coast and into southern Spain.

situation. The city was located on a defensible site and commanded an excellent harbor that encouraged commerce. The coastal plain grew abundant grains, fruits, and vegetables. An inland plain allowed sheepherding. The Phoenician settlers conquered the native inhabitants and used them to work the land.

Beginning in the sixth century B.C.E., the Carthaginians expanded their domain to include the coast of northern Africa west beyond the Straits of Gibraltar and eastward into Libya. Overseas, they came to control the southern part of Spain, Sardinia, Corsica, Malta, the Balearic Islands, and western Sicily. The people of these territories, though originally allies, were all reduced to subjection like the natives of the Carthaginian home territory. They all served in the Carthaginian army or navy and paid tribute. Carthage also profited greatly from the mines of Spain and from an absolute monopoly of trade imposed on the western Mediterranean.

An attack by Hiero, tyrant of Syracuse, on the Sicilian city of Messana just across from Italy, first caused trouble between Rome and Carthage. Messana had been seized by a group of Italian mercenary soldiers who called themselves *Mamertines*, the sons of the war god Mars. When Hiero defeated the Mamertines, some of them called on the Carthaginians to help save their city. Carthage agreed and sent a garrison, for the Carthagi-

nians wanted to prevent Syracuse from dominating the straits. One Mamertine faction, however, fearing that Carthage might take undue advantage of the opportunity, asked Rome for help.

In 264 B.C.E., the request came to the Senate. Because a Punic garrison (the Romans called the Carthaginians *Phoenicians*; in Latin the word is *Poeni* or *Puni*—hence the adjective *Punic*) was in place at Messana, any intervention would be not against Syracuse, but against the mighty empire of Carthage. Unless Rome intervened, however, Carthage would gain control of all Sicily and the straits. The assembly voted to send an army to Messana and expelled the Punic garrison. The First **Punic War** was on.

The First Punic War (264–241 B.C.E.) The war in Sicily soon settled into a stalemate until the Romans built a fleet to cut off supplies to the besieged Carthaginian cities at the western end of Sicily. When Carthage sent its own fleet to raise the siege, the Romans destroyed it. In 241 B.C.E., Carthage signed a treaty giving up Sicily and the islands between Italy and Sicily; it also agreed to pay a war indemnity in ten annual installments. Neither side was to attack the allies of the other. The peace was realistic and not unduly harsh; Rome had earned Sicily, and Carthage could well afford

Rome became a naval power late in its history to defeat Carthage in the First Punic War (264–241 B.C.E.). This sculpture in low relief shows a Roman ship, propelled by oars, with both ram and soldiers, ready either to ram or board an enemy ship. A *Roman Warship. Direzione Generale Musei Vaticani*

the indemnity. If it had been carried out in good faith, it might have brought lasting peace.

A rebellion, however, broke out in Carthage among the mercenaries, newly recruited from Sicily, who now demanded their pay. In 238 B.C.E., while Carthage was still preoccupied with the rebellion, Rome seized Sardinia and Corsica and demanded that Carthage pay an additional indemnity. This was a harsh and cynical action by the Romans; even the historian Polybius, a great champion of Rome, could find no justification for it. It undid the calming effects of the peace of 241 B.C.E. without preventing the Carthaginians from recovering their strength to seek vengeance in the future.

The conquest of overseas territory presented the Romans with new administrative problems. Instead of following the policy they had pursued in Italy, they made Sicily a province and Sardinia and Corsica another. It became common to extend the term of the governors of these provinces beyond a year. The governors were unchecked by colleagues and exercised full *imperium*. New magistracies, in effect, were thus created free of the limits put on the power of officials in Rome.

The new populations were neither Roman citizens nor allies; they were subjects who did not serve in the army but paid tribute instead. The old practice of extending citizenship and, with it, loyalty to Rome thus stopped at the borders of Italy. Rome collected taxes on these subjects by "farming" them out at auction to the highest bidder. At first, the tax collectors were natives from the same province. Later they were Roman allies and, finally, Roman citizens below senatorial rank who

could become powerful and wealthy by squeezing the provincials hard. These innovations were the basis for Rome's imperial organization in the future. In time, they strained the constitution and traditions and threatened the existence of the republic.

After the First Punic War, campaigns against the Gauls and across the Adriatic distracted Rome. Meanwhile Hamilcar Barca, the Carthaginian governor of Spain from 237 B.C.E. until his death in 229 B.C.E., was leading Carthage on the road to recovery. Hamilcar sought to build a Punic Empire in Spain. He improved the ports and the commerce conducted in them, exploited the mines, gained control of the hinterland, won over many of the conquered tribes, and built a strong and disciplined army.

Hamilcar's successor, his son-in-law Hasdrubal, pursued the same policies. His success alarmed the Romans. They imposed a treaty in which he promised not to take an army north across the Ebro River in Spain, although Punic expansion in Spain was well south of that river at the time. Though the agreement appeared to put Rome in the position of giving orders to an inferior, it benefited both sides equally. If the Carthaginians accepted the limit of the Ebro on their expansion in Spain, the Romans would not interfere with that expansion.

The Second Punic War (218–202 B.C.E.) On Hasdrubal's assassination in 221 B.C.E., the army chose as his successor Hannibal, son of Hamilcar Barca. Hannibal was at that time twenty-five years old. He quickly consolidated and extended the Punic Empire in Spain. A few years before his accession, Rome had received an offer of alliance from the people of Saguntum, a Spanish town about one hundred miles south of the Ebro. The Romans accepted the friendship and the responsibilities

THE PUNIC WARS	
264–241 B.C.E.	First Punic War
238 B.C.E.	Rome seizes Sardinia and Corsica
221 B.C.E.	Hannibal takes command of Punic army in Spain
218–202 B.C.E.	Second Punic War
216 B.C.E.	Battle of Cannae
209 B.C.E.	Scipio takes New Carthage
202 B.C.E.	Battle of Zama
149–146 B.C.E.	Third Punic War
146 B.C.E.	Destruction of Carthage

it entailed, despite the Ebro treaty. At first, Hannibal avoided any action against Saguntum, but the Saguntines, confident of Rome's protection, began to interfere with some of the Spanish tribes allied with Hannibal. When the Romans sent an embassy to Hannibal warning him to let Saguntum alone and repeating the injunction not to cross the Ebro, he ignored the warning and captured the town. The Romans sent an ultimatum to Carthage demanding the surrender of Hannibal. Carthage refused, and Rome declared war in 218 B.C.E.

Between the close of the First Punic War and the outbreak of the Second, Rome had repeatedly provoked Carthage, taking Sardinia in 238 B.C.E. and interfering in Spain, but had not prevented Carthage from building a powerful and dangerous empire in Spain. Hannibal saw to it that the Romans paid the price for these blunders. By September 218 B.C.E., he was across the Alps, in Italy and among the friendly Gauls.

Hannibal defeated the Romans at the Ticinus River and crushed the joint consular armies at the Trebia River. In 217 B.C.E., he outmaneuvered and trapped another army at Lake Trasimene. The key to success, however, would be defection by Rome's allies. Hannibal released Italian prisoners without harm or ransom and moved his army south of Rome to encourage rebellion. But the allies remained firm.

Sobered by their defeats, the Romans elected Quintus Fabius Maximus dictator. His strategy was to avoid battle while harassing Hannibal's army. He would fight only when his army had recovered and then only on favorable ground.

In 216 B.C.E., Hannibal marched to Cannae in Apulia to tempt the Romans, under different generals, into another open fight. They sent off an army of some 80,000 men to meet him. Almost the entire Roman army was wiped out. It was the worst defeat in Roman history. Rome's prestige was shattered, and most of its allies in southern Italy, as well as Syracuse in Sicily, went over to Hannibal. For more than a decade, no Roman army would dare face Hannibal in the field.

Hannibal, however, had neither the numbers nor the supplies to besiege walled cities, nor did he have the equipment to take them by assault. The Romans appointed Publius Cornelius Scipio (237–183 B.C.E.), later called Africanus, to the command in Spain with proconsular *imperium*. Scipio was not yet twenty-five and had held no high office. But he was a general almost as talented as Hannibal. Within a few years, young Scipio had conquered all of Spain and had deprived Hannibal of any hope of help from that region.

In 204 B.C.E., Scipio landed in Africa and forced the Carthaginians to accept a peace, the main clause of which was the withdrawal of Hannibal and his army from Italy. Hannibal had won every battle but lost the war, for he had not counted on the determination of Rome and the loyalty of its allies. Hannibal's return inspired Carthage to break the peace and to risk all in battle. In 202 B.C.E., Scipio and Hannibal faced each other at the Battle of Zama. The generalship of Scipio and the desertion of Hannibal's mercenaries gave the victory to Rome. The new peace terms reduced Carthage to the status of a dependent ally of Rome. The Second Punic War ended the Carthaginian command of the western Mediterranean and Carthage's term as a great power. Rome ruled the seas and the entire Mediterranean coast from Italy westward.

The Republic's Conquest of the Hellenistic World

The East By the middle of the third century B.C.E., the eastern Mediterranean had reached a condition of stability based on a balance of power among the three great Hellenistic kingdoms that allowed an established place even for lesser states. Two aggressive monarchs: Philip V of Macedon (221–179 B.C.E.) and Antiochus III of the Seleucid kingdom (223–187 B.C.E.) threatened this equilibrium, however. Philip and Antiochus moved swiftly, the latter against Syria and Palestine, the former against cities in the Aegean, in the Hellespontine region, and on the coast of Asia Minor.

The threat that a more powerful Macedon might pose to Rome's friends and, perhaps, even to Italy persuaded the Romans to intervene. Philip had already attempted to meddle in Roman affairs when he formed an alliance with Carthage during the Second Punic War, provoking a conflict known as the First Macedonian War (215–205 B.C.E.). In 200 B.C.E., in an action that began the Second Macedonian War, the Romans sent an ultimatum to Philip ordering him not to attack any Greek city and to pay reparations to Pergamum. These orders were meant to provoke, not avoid, war, and Philip refused to obey. Two years later the Romans sent out a talented young general, Flamininus, who demanded that Philip withdraw from Greece entirely. In 197 B.C.E., with Greek support, Flamininus defeated Philip at Cynoscephalae,

ROMAN ENGAGEMENT OVERSEAS

215–205 B.C.E.	First Macedonian War
200–197 B.C.E.	Second Macedonian War
196 B.C.E.	Proclamation of Greek freedom by Flamininus at Corinth
189 B.C.E.	Battle of Magnesia; Antiochus defeated in Asia Minor
172–168 B.C.E.	Third Macedonian War
168 B.C.E.	Battle of Pydna
154–133 B.C.E.	Roman wars in Spain
134 B.C.E.	Numantia taken

ending the war. The Greek cities freed from Philip were made autonomous, and in 196 B.C.E., Flamininus proclaimed the freedom of the Greeks.

Soon after the Romans withdrew from Greece, they came into conflict with Antiochus, who was expanding his power in Asia and on the European side of the Hellespont. On the pretext of freeing the Greeks from Roman domination, he landed an army on the Greek mainland. The Romans routed Antiochus at Thermopylae and quickly drove him from Greece. In 189 B.C.E., they crushed his army at Magnesia in Asia Minor. The peace of Apamia in the next year deprived Antiochus of his elephants and his navy and imposed a huge indemnity on him. Once again, the Romans took no territory for themselves and left several Greek cities in Asia free. They regarded Greece, and now Asia Minor, as a kind of protectorate in which they could intervene or not as they chose.

This relatively mild policy was destined to end as the stern and businesslike policies of the conservative *censor* Cato gained favor in Rome. A new harshness was to be applied to allies and bystanders, as well as to defeated opponents.

In 179 B.C.E., Perseus succeeded Philip V as king of Macedon. He tried to gain popularity in Greece by favoring the democratic and revolutionary forces in the cities. The Romans, troubled by his threat to stability, launched the Third Macedonian War (172–168 B.C.E.), and in 168 B.C.E. Aemilius Paulus defeated Perseus at Pydna. (See "Plutarch Describes a Roman Triumph," page 110.) The peace that followed this war, reflecting the changed attitude at Rome, was harsh. It divided Macedon into four separate republics, whose citizens were forbidden to intermarry or even to do business across the new national boundaries. Anti-Roman factions in the Greek cities were punished severely.

When Aemilius Paulus returned from his victory, he celebrated for three days by parading the spoils of war, royal prisoners, and great wealth through the streets of Rome. The public treasury benefited to such a degree that the direct property tax on Roman citizens was abolished. Part of the booty went to the general and part to his soldiers. New motives were thereby introduced into Roman foreign policy, or, perhaps, old motives were given new prominence. Foreign campaigns could bring profit to the state, rewards to the army, and wealth, fame, honor, and political power to the general.

The West Harsh as the Romans had become toward the Greeks, they treated the people of the Iberian Peninsula (Spain and Portugal), whom they considered barbarians, even worse. They committed dreadful atrocities, lied, cheated, and broke treaties to exploit and pacify the natives, who fought back fiercely in guerrilla style. From 154 to 133 B.C.E., the fighting waxed, and it became hard to recruit Roman soldiers to participate in the increasingly ugly war. At last, in 134 B.C.E., Scipio Aemilianus took the key city of Numantia by siege and burned it to the ground. This put an end to the war in Spain.

Roman treatment of Carthage was no better. Although Carthage lived up to its treaty with Rome faithfully and posed no threat, some Romans refused to abandon their hatred of the traditional enemy. Cato is said to have ended all his speeches in the Senate with the same sentence: "Ceterum censeo delendam esse Carthaginem" ("Besides, I think that Carthage must be destroyed"). At last the Romans took advantage of a technical breach of the peace to destroy Carthage. In 146 B.C.E., Scipio Aemilianus took the city, plowed up its land, and put salt in the furrows as a symbol of the permanent abandonment of the site. The Romans incorporated it as the province of Africa, one of six Roman provinces, including Sicily, Sardinia-Corsica, Macedonia, Hither Spain, and Further Spain.

▼ Civilization in the Early Roman Republic

Close and continued association with the Greeks of the Hellenistic world wrought important changes in the Roman style of life and thought. The Roman attitude toward the Greeks ranged from admiration for their culture and history to contempt for their constant squabbling, their commercial practices, and their weakness. Conservatives such as Cato might speak contemptuously of the Greeks as "Greeklings" (*Graeculi*), but even he learned Greek and absorbed Greek culture.

Before long, the education of the Roman upper classes was bilingual. Young Roman nobles studied Greek rhetoric, literature, and sometimes philosophy. These studies even affected education and the Latin language. As early as the third century B.C.E., Livius Andronicus, a liberated Greek slave, translated the *Odyssey* into Latin. It became a primer for young Romans and put Latin on the road to becoming a literary language.

Religion

The Greeks influenced Roman religion almost from the beginning. The Romans identified their own gods with Greek equivalents and incorporated Greek mythology into their own. Mostly, however, Roman religious practice remained simple and Italian, until the third century B.C.E. brought important new influences from the East.

Traditional Religion and Character In early Rome the family stood at the center of religious observance, and gods of the household and farm were most important. The *Lares* protected the family property, the *Penates* guarded what was inside the household. The *Genius* protected the life of the family. In the early days, before they were

PLUTARCH DESCRIBES A ROMAN TRIUMPH

In 168 B.C.E., L. Aemilius Paulus defeated King Perseus in the Battle of Pydna, bringing an end to the Third Macedonian War. For his great achievement, the Senate granted Paulus the right to celebrate a triumph, the great honorific procession granted only for extraordinary victories and that all Roman generals sought. The Greek historian. Plutarch (ca. 46–ca. 120 C.E.), who wrote a famous collection of biographies of eminent Greeks and Romans, described Paulus's triumph.

How do you explain the particular elements displayed on each day of the triumph? What purposes do you think a triumph served? What does this account tell us about Roman values? How are they different from the values Americans cherish today? Are there any similarities?

The people erected scaffolds in the forum, in the circuses, as they call their buildings for horse races, and in all other parts of the city where they could best behold the show. The spectators were clad in white garments; all the temples were open, and full of garlands and perfumes; the ways were cleared and kept open by numerous officers, who drove back all who crowded into or ran across the main avenue. This triumph lasted three days. On the first, which was scarcely long enough for the sight, were to be seen the statues, pictures, and colossal images which were taken from the enemy, drawn upon two hundred and fifty chariots. On the second was carried in a great many wagons the finest and richest armour of the Macedonians, both of brass and steel, all newly polished and glittering; the pieces of which were piled up and arranged purposely with the greatest art, so as to seem to be tumbled in heaps carelessly and by chance.

On the third day, early in the morning, first came the trumpeters, who did not sound as they were wont in a procession or solemn entry, but such a charge as the Romans use when they encourage the soldiers to fight. Next followed young men wearing frocks with ornamented borders, who led to the sacrifice a hundred and twenty stalled oxen, with their horns gilded, and their heads adorned with ribbons and garlands; and with these were boys that carried basins for libation, of silver and gold.

After his children and their attendants came Perseus himself, clad all in black, and wearing the boots of his country, and looking like one altogether stunned and deprived of reason, through the greatness of his misfortunes. Next followed a great company of his friends and familiars, whose countenances were disfigured with grief, and who let the spectators see, by their tears and their continual looking upon Perseus, that it was his fortune they so much lamented, and that they were regardless of their own.

After these were carried four hundred crowns, all made of gold, sent from the cities by their respective deputations to Aemilius, in honour of his victory. Then he himself came, seated on a chariot magnificently adorned (a man well worthy to be looked at, even without these ensigns of power), dressed in a robe of purple, interwoven with gold, and holding a laurel branch in his right hand. All the army, in like manner, with boughs of laurel in their hands, divided into their bands and companies, followed the chariot of their commander; some singing verses, according to the usual custom, mingled with raillery; others, songs of triumph and the praise of Aemilius' deeds; who, indeed, was admired and accounted happy by all men, and unenvied by every one that was good; except so far as it seems the province of some god to lessen that happiness which is too great and inordinate, and so to mingle the affairs of human life that no one should be entirely free and exempt from calamities; but, as we read in Homer, that those should think themselves truly blessed whom fortune has given an equal share of good and evil.

From Plutarch, "Aemilius Paulus," in *Lives of the Noble Grecians and Romans*, trans. by John Dryden, rev. by A. H. Clough (New York: Random House, n.d.), pp. 340–341.

influenced by the Etruscans and Greeks, Roman religion knew little of mythology: Their gods were impersonal forces, *numina*, rather than deities in human or superhuman form. To win their favor and protection the Romans developed a detailed and rigid set of rituals that used ceremony as a kind of magical bargain with which they could win and bind the benevolence of divinity. Their image of an afterlife was vague and insubstantial. Rome had no priestly caste, so the father *(paterfamilias)* was the family's priest. In the same way, in the Republic, the head of the state's board of chief priests, *the pontifex maximus*, was elected by the popular assembly. Morality played little role in Roman religion but, since failure to perform the necessary rites correctly could bring harm on the entire state, everyone had to participate in religious observance as a civic duty and evidence of patriotism. (See "Encountering the Past, Two Roman Festivals," page 112.)

In 205 B.C.E., the Senate approved the public worship of Cybele, the Great Mother goddess from Phrygia in Asia Minor. Hers was a fertility cult accompanied by ecstatic, frenzied, and sensual rites that so outraged conservative Romans that they soon banned the cult. Similarly, the Senate banned the worship of Dionysus, or Bacchus, in 186 B.C.E. In the second century B.C.E., interest in Babylonian astrology also grew, and the Senate's attempt in 139 B.C.E. to expel the "Chaldaeans," as the astrologers were called, did not prevent the continued influence of their superstition.

Education

Education in the early republic reflected the limited, conservative, and practical nature of that community of plain farmers and soldiers. Education was entirely the responsibility of the family, the father teaching his own son at home. It is not clear whether in these early times girls received any education, though they certainly did later on. The boys learned to read, write, calculate, and how to farm. They memorized the laws of the Twelve Tables, learned how to perform religious rites, heard stories of the great deeds of early Roman history and particularly those of their ancestors, and engaged in the physical training appropriate for potential soldiers. This course of study was practical, vocational, and moral; it aimed to make the boys moral, pious, patriotic, law abiding, and respectful of tradition.

Hellenized Education   In the third century B.C.E., the Romans came into contact with the Greeks of southern Italy, and this contact changed Roman education. Greek teachers introduced the study of language, literature, and philosophy, as well as the idea of a liberal education, or what the Romans called **humanitas**, the root of our concept of the humanities. The aim of education changed from the mastery of practical, vocational skills to an emphasis on broad intellectual training, critical thinking, an interest in ideas, and the development of a well-rounded person.

The new emphasis required students to learn Greek, for Rome did not yet have a literature of its own. Hereafter, educated Romans were expected to be bilingual. Schools were established in which a teacher, called a *grammaticus*, taught students the Greek language and its literature, especially the poets and particularly Homer. After the completion of this elementary education, Roman boys of the upper classes studied rhetoric—the art of speaking and writing well. For the Greeks, rhetoric was less important than philosophy. The more practical Romans took to it avidly, however, for it was of great use in legal disputes and political life.

Some Romans were attracted to Greek literature and philosophy. Scipio Aemilianus, the man who finally defeated and destroyed Carthage, surrounded himself and his friends with such Greek thinkers as the historian Polybius and the philosopher Panaetius.

Equally outstanding Romans, such as Cato the Elder, were more conservative and opposed the new learning on the grounds that it would weaken Roman moral fiber. On more than one occasion they passed laws expelling philosophers and teachers of rhetoric. But these attempts to go back to older ways failed. The new education suited the needs of the Romans of the second century B.C.E. They found themselves changing from a rural to an urban society and were being thrust into the sophisticated world of Hellenistic Greeks.

By the last century of the Roman Republic, the new Hellenized education had become dominant. Latin literature had come into being and, along with Latin translations of Greek poets, formed part of the course of study. But Roman gentlemen still were expected to be bilingual, and Greek language and literature were still central to the curriculum. Many schools were established. The number of educated people grew.

This carved relief from the second century C.E. shows a schoolmaster and his pupils. The pupil at the right is arriving late.   Rheinisches Landesmuseum, Trier, Germany. Alinari/Art Resource, NY

TWO ROMAN FESTIVALS: THE SATURNALIA AND LUPERCALIA

THE ROMANS LOVED festivals, and their calendar contained many of them. The most famous celebrations were the Lupercalia, on February 15, and the Saturnalia, which took place from December 17 to 24. Both festivals were so popular that Christianity later adopted them under different names for its own religious calendar.

The Saturnalia celebrated Saturn, an agricultural god. (Our Saturday is named after him.) During this festival all public and private business gave way to feasting, gambling, wild dancing, and the kind of revelry that still occurs today during Mardi Gras in cities like New Orleans and Rio de Janeiro.

During the Saturnalia, masters permitted slaves to say and do what they liked; moral restrictions were eased; and Romans exchanged presents. Rather than try to abolish the Saturnalia, Christianity established December 25th as the birth date of Jesus, and the irrepressible Roman holiday, including the giving of presents, parties, and elaborate meals, became the celebration of Christmas.

The Lupercalia was dedicated, in part, to Faunus, the ancient Italian god of the countryside. Worshipped as the bringer of fertility to fields and flocks, Faunus was typically represented in art as half man, half goat and was associated with merriment like the Greek god Pan.

On the day of the Lupercalia, young male priests called Luperci sacrificed goats and a dog to Faunus. The Luperci then ran naked around the city, striking any woman who came near them with a thong cut from the skins of the sacrificed goats to render her fertile. Women who had not conceived or who wanted more children made sure that the Luperci struck them. It was at the Lupercalia of 44 B.C.E that the consul Marcus Antonius (Shakespeare's Mark Antony) offered a royal crown to Julius Caesar. In 494 C.E., the Christian church converted the festival into the Feast of the Purification of the Virgin Mary.

Why do you think the Romans loved these festivals?

Why might the Christian Church have chosen to adapt pagan customs instead of trying to abolish them?

This is a bronze statuette of the ancient Italian rural deity Faunus, whom the Romans identified with the Greek god Pan. Christi Graham and Nick Nicholls © The British Museum

In the late republic, Roman education, though still entirely private, became more formal and organized. From the ages of seven to twelve, boys went to elementary school accompanied by a Greek slave called a *paedagogus* (hence our term *pedagogue*), who looked after their physical well-being and their manners and improved their ability in Greek conversation. At school the boys learned to read and write, using a wax tablet and a stylus, and to do simple arithmetic with an abacus and pebbles (*calculi*). Discipline was harsh and corporal punishment frequent. From twelve to sixteen, boys went to a higher school, where the *grammaticus* provided a liberal education, using Greek and Latin literature as his subject matter. He also taught dialectic, arithmetic, geometry, astronomy, and music. Sometimes he included the elements of rhetoric, especially for those boys who would not go on to a higher education.

At sixteen, some boys went on to advanced study in rhetoric. The instructors were usually Greek. They trained their charges by studying models of fine speech of the past and by having them write, memorize, and declaim speeches suitable for different occasions. Sometimes the serious student attached himself to some famous public speaker to learn what he could. Sometimes a rich Roman would support a Greek philosopher in his own home. His son could converse with the philosopher and acquire the learning and polished thought necessary for the fully cultured gentleman. Some, like the great orator Cicero, undertook what we might call postgraduate study by traveling abroad to study with great teachers of rhetoric and philosophy in the Greek world.

This style of education broadened the Romans' understanding through the careful study of a foreign language and culture. It made them a part of the older and wider culture of the Hellenistic world, a world they had come to dominate and needed to understand.

Education for Women Though the evidence is limited, we can be sure that girls of the upper classes received an education equivalent at least to the early stages of a boy's education. They were probably taught by tutors at home rather than going to school, as was increasingly the fashion among boys in the late republic. Young women did not study with philosophers and rhetoricians, for they were usually married by the age at which the men were pursuing their higher education. Still, some women continued their education and became prose writers or poets. By the first century C.E., there were apparently enough learned women to provoke the complaints of a crotchety and conservative satirist:

Still more exasperating is the woman who begs as soon as she sits down to dinner, to discourse on poets and poetry, comparing Virgil with Homer; professors, critics, lawyers, auctioneers—even another woman—can't get a word in. She rattles on at such a rate that you'd think that all the pots and pans in the kitchen were crashing to the floor or that every bell in town was clanging. All by herself she makes as much noise as some primitive tribe chasing away an eclipse. She should learn the philosopher's lesson: "moderation is necessary even for intellectuals." And, if she still wants to appear educated and eloquent, let her dress as a man, sacrifice to men's gods and bathe in the men's baths. Wives shouldn't try to be public speakers; they shouldn't use rhetorical devices; they shouldn't read all the classics—there should be some things women don't understand. I myself cannot understand a woman who can quote the rules of grammar and never make a mistake and cites obscure, long-forgotten poets—as if men cared about such things. If she has to correct somebody let her correct her girl friends and leave her husband alone.[2] (See also "Women's Uprising in Republican Rome," page 114.)

Slavery

Like most ancient peoples, the Romans had slaves from early in their history, but among the shepherds and family farmers of early Rome, they were relatively few. Slavery became a basic element in the Roman economy and society only during the second century B.C.E., after the Romans had conquered most of the lands bordering the Mediterranean. In the time between the beginning of Rome's first war against Carthage (264 B.C.E.) and the conquest of Spain (133 B.C.E.), the Romans enslaved some 250,000 prisoners of war, greatly increasing the availability of slave labor and reducing its price. Many slaves worked as domestic servants, feeding the growing appetite for luxury of the Roman upper class; at the other end of the spectrum, many worked in the mines of Spain and Sardinia. Some worked as artisans in small factories and shops or as public clerks. Slaves were permitted to marry, and they produced sizable families. As in Greece, domestic slaves and those used in crafts and commerce could earn money, keep it, and, in some cases, use it to purchase their own freedom. *Manumission* (the freeing of slaves) was common among the Romans. After a time, a considerable proportion of the Roman people included freedmen who had been slaves themselves or whose ancestors had been bondsmen. It was not uncommon to see the son or grandson of a slave become wealthy as a freedman and the slave himself or his son become a Roman citizen.

The unique development in the Roman world was the emergence of an agricultural system that employed and depended on a vast number of slaves. By the time of Jesus, there were between 2 and 3 million slaves in Italy, about 35 to 40 percent of the total population, most of them part of great slave gangs that worked the vast plantations the Romans called *latifundia*. The life of Rome's agricultural slaves appears to have been much harder than that of other Roman slaves and of slaves in other ancient societies, with the possible exception of slaves working in

[2]Juvenal, *Satires* 6.434–456, trans. by Roger Killian, Richard Lynch, Robert J. Rowland, and John Sims, cited by Sarah B. Pomeroy in *Goddesses, Whores, Wives, and Slaves* (New York: Schocken Books, 1975), p. 172.

WOMEN'S UPRISING IN REPUBLICAN ROME

■■

In 195 B.C.E., Roman women staged a rare public political protest when they demanded the repeal of a law passed two decades earlier during the Second Punic War, which they believed limited their rights unfairly. Livy (59 B.C.E.–17 C.E.) describes the affair and the response of the traditionalist Marcus Porcius Cato (234–149 B.C.E.).

Why did the women complain? How did they try to achieve their goals? Which of Cato's objections to their behavior do you think were most important? Since women did not vote or sit in assemblies, why did the affair end as it did?

Amid the anxieties of great wars, either scarce finished or soon to come, an incident occurred, trivial to relate, but which, by reason of the passions it aroused, developed into a violent contention. [Two] tribunes of the people, proposed to the assembly the abrogation of the Oppian law. The tribune Gaius Oppius had carried this law in the heat of the Punic War, . . . that no woman should possess more than half an ounce of gold or wear a parti-coloured garment or ride in a carriage in the City or in a town within a mile thereof, except on the occasion of a religious festival . . . . [T]he Capitoline was filled with crowds of supporters and opponents of the ill. The matrons could not be kept at home by . . . their husbands' orders, but blocked all the streets and approaches to the Forum, begging the men as they came down to the Forum that, in the prosperous condition of the state, when the private fortunes of all men were daily increasing, they should allow the woman too to have their former distinctions restored. The crowd of women grew larger day by day; for they were now coming in from the towns and rural districts. Soon they dared even to approach and appeal to the consuls, the praetors, and the other officials, but one consul, at least, they found adamant, Marcus Porcius Cato, who spoke thus in favour of the law whose repeal was being urged:

"If each of us, citizens, had determined to assert his rights and dignity as a husband with 'respect to his own spouse,' we should have less trouble with the sex as a whole; as it is, our liberty, destroyed at home by female violence, even here in the Forum is crushed and trodden underfoot, and because we have not kept them individually under control, we dread them collectively . . . . But from no class is there not the greatest danger if you permit them meetings . . . and secret consultations.

"I should have said, 'What sort of practice is this, of running out into the streets and blocking the roads and speaking to other women's husbands? Could you not have made the same requests, each of your own husband, at home? And yet, not even at home, if modesty would keep matrons within the limits of their proper rights, did it become you to concern yourselves with the question of what laws should be adopted in this place or repealed.' Our ancestors permitted no woman to conduct even personal business without a guardian to intervene in her behalf; they wished them to be under the control of fathers, brothers, husbands; we (Heaven help us!) allow them now even to interfere in public affairs, yes, and to visit the Forum and our informal and formal sessions. Give loose rein to their uncontrollable nature and to this untamed creature and expect that they will themselves set bounds to their licence; unless you act, this is the least of the things enjoined upon women by custom or law and to which they submit with a feeling of injustice. It is complete liberty or, rather, if we wish to speak the truth, complete licence that they desire.

"If they win in this, what will they not attempt? Review all the laws with which your forefathers restrained their licence and made them subject to their husbands; even with all these bonds you can scarcely control them. What of this? If you suffer them to seize these bonds one by one and wrench themselves free and finally to be placed on a parity with their husbands, do you think that you will be able to endure them? The moment they begin to be your equals, they will be your superiors."

The next day an even greater crowd of women appeared in public, and all of them in a body beset the doors of those tribunes, who were vetoing their colleagues' proposal, and they did not desist until the threat of veto was withdrawn by the tribunes. After that there was no question that all the tribes would vote to repeal the law. The law was repealed twenty years after it was passed.

From *Livy*, trans. by Evan T. Stage (Cambridge, MA: Harvard University Press, 1935), XXXIV, i–iii; viii, pp. 413–419, 439.

mines. *Latifundia* owners sought maximum profits and treated their slaves simply as means to that end. The slaves often worked in chains, were oppressed by brutal foremen, and lived in underground prisons.

Such harsh treatment led to serious slave rebellions of a kind we do not hear of in other ancient societies. A rebellion in Sicily in 134 B.C.E. kept the island in turmoil for more than two years, and the rebellion of the gladiators led by Spartacus in 73 B.C.E. produced an army of 70,000 slaves that repeatedly defeated the Roman legions and overran southern Italy before it was brutally crushed.

Slavery retained its economic and social importance in the first century of the imperial period, but its centrality began to decline in the second. The institution was never abolished, nor did it disappear while the Roman Empire lasted, but over time it became less important. The reasons for this decline are rather obscure. A rise in the cost of slaves and a consequent reduction in their economic value

seem to have been factors. More important, it appears, was a general economic decline that permitted increasing pressure on the free lower classes. More and more they were employed as *coloni*—tenant farmers—tied by imperial law to the land they worked, ostensibly free, but bonded and obligated. Over centuries, these increasingly serf-like *coloni* replaced most agricultural slave labor. Pockets of slave labor remained as late as the eighth century C.E., but the system of ancient slavery had essentially been replaced by the time the Roman Empire fell in the West.

▼ Roman Imperialism: The Late Republic

Rome's expansion in Italy and overseas was accomplished without a grand general plan. (See Map 4–3.) The Romans gained the new territories as a result of wars

MAP EXPLORATION

Interactive map: To explore this map further, go to
www.myhistorylab.com

Territorial Extent of the Republic, 44 B.C.E.

1,000 MILES

1,000 KILOMETERS

Map 4–3 **ROMAN DOMINIONS OF THE LATE REPUBLIC** The Roman Republic's conquest of Mediterranean lands—and beyond—until the death of Julius Caesar is shown here. Areas conquered before Tiberius Gracchus (ca. 133 B.C.E.) are distinguished from later ones and from client areas owing allegiance to Rome.

that they believed were either defensive or preventive. Their foreign policy was aimed at providing security for Rome on Rome's terms, but these terms were often unacceptable to other nations and led to continued conflict. Whether intended or not, Rome's expansion brought the Romans an empire and, with it, power, wealth, and responsibilities. The need to govern an empire beyond the seas would severely test the republican constitution that had served Rome well during its years as a city-state and that had been well adapted to the mastery of Italy. Roman society and the Roman character had maintained their integrity through the period of expansion in Italy, but the temptations and strains the wealth and the complicated problems of an overseas empire presented would test them.

The Aftermath of Conquest

War and expansion changed the economic, social, and political life of Italy. Before the Punic Wars, most Italians owned their own farms, which provided the greater part of the family's needs. Some families owned larger holdings, but their lands chiefly grew grain, and they used the labor of clients, tenants, and hired workers rather than slaves. Fourteen years of fighting in the Second Punic War did terrible damage to Italian farmland. Many veterans returning from the wars found it impossible or unprofitable to go back to their farms. Some moved to Rome, where they could find work as laborers, but most stayed in the country as tenant farmers or hired hands. Often, the wealthy converted the abandoned land into *latifundia* for growing cash crops—grain, olives, and grapes for wine—or into cattle ranches.

The upper classes had plenty of capital to operate these estates because of profits from the war and from exploiting the provinces. Land was cheap, and so was slave labor. By fair means and foul, large landholders obtained great quantities of public land and forced small farmers from it. These changes separated the people of Rome and Italy more sharply into rich and poor, landed and landless, privileged and deprived. The result was political, social, and, ultimately, constitutional conflict that threatened the existence of the republic.

The Gracchi

By the middle of the second century B.C.E., the problems caused by Rome's rapid expansion troubled perceptive Roman nobles. The fall in status of peasant farmers made it harder to recruit soldiers and came to present a political threat as well. The patron's traditional control over his clients was weakened when they fled from their land. Even those former landowners who worked on the land of their patrons as tenants or hired hands were less reliable. The introduction of the secret ballot in the 130s B.C.E. made them even more independent.

Tiberius Gracchus In 133 B.C.E., Tiberius Gracchus tried to solve these problems. He became tribune for 133 B.C.E. on a program of land reform; some of the most powerful members of the Roman aristocracy helped him draft the bill. They meant it to be a moderate attempt at solving Rome's problems. The bill's target was public land that had been acquired and held illegally, some of it for many years. The bill allowed holders of this land to retain as many as five hundred iugera (approximately 320 acres), but the state would reclaim

This wall painting from the first century B.C.E. comes from the villa of Publius Fannius Synistor at Pompeii and shows a woman playing a cithera.   Roman. Paintings. Pompeian, Boscoreale. 1st Century B.C. "Lady Playing the Cithara." Wall painting from the east wall of large room in the villa of Publius Fannius Synistor. Fresco on lime plaster. H. 6 ft. 1 1/2 in. W. 6 ft. 1 1/2 in. (187 × 187 cm.) The Metropolitan Museum of Art, Rogers Fund, 1903. (03.14.5) Photograph © 1986 The Metropolitan Museum of Art

THE RUIN OF THE ROMAN FAMILY FARM AND THE GRACCHAN REFORMS

The independent family farm was the backbone both of the Greek polis *and of the early Roman Republic. Rome's conquests, the long wars that kept the citizen-soldier away from his farm, and the availability of great numbers of slaves at a low price, however, badly undercut the traditional way of farming and with it the foundations of republican society. In the following passage, Plutarch describes the process of agricultural change and the response to it of the reformer Tiberius Gracchus, tribune in 133* B.C.E.

Why did Roman farmers face troubles? What were the social and political consequences of the changes in agricultural life? What solution did Tiberius Gracchus propose? Why, besides selfishness and greed, did people oppose his plan?

Of the territory which the Romans won in war from their neighbours, a part they sold, and a part they made common land, and assigned it for occupation to the poor and indigent among the citizens, on payment of a small rent into the public treasury. And when the rich began to offer larger rents and drove out the poor, a law was enacted forbidding the holding by one person of more than five hundred [iugera] of land. For a short time this enactment gave a check to the rapacity of the rich, and was of assistance to the poor, who remained in their places on the land which they had rented and occupied the allotment which each had held from the outset. But later on the neighbouring rich men, by means of fictitious personages, transferred these rentals to themselves, and finally held most of the land openly in their own names. Then the poor, who had been ejected from their land, no longer showed themselves eager for military service, and neglected the bringing up of children, so that soon all Italy was conscious of a dearth of freemen, and was filled with gangs of foreign slaves, by whose aid the rich cultivated their estates, from which they had driven away the free citizens.

And it is thought that a law dealing with injustice and rapacity so great was never drawn up in milder and gentler terms. For men who ought to have been punished for their disobedience and to have surrendered with payment of a fine the land which they were illegally enjoying, these men it merely ordered to abandon their injust acquisitions upon being paid their value, and to admit into ownership of them such citizens as needed assistance. But although the rectification of the wrong was so considerate, the people were satisfied to let bygones be bygones if they could be secure from such wrong in the future; the men of wealth and substance, however, were led by their greed to hate the law, and by their wrath and contentiousness to hate the lawgiver, and tried to dissuade the people by alleging that Tiberius was introducing a re-distribution of land for the confusion of the body politic, and was stirring up a general revolution.

From Plutarch, "Tiberius Gracchus," in *Lives* 8–9, Vol. 10, trans. by Bernadotte Perrin and William Heinemann (London and New York: G. P. Putnam's Sons, 1921), pp. 159–167.

anything over that and redistribute it in small lots to the poor, who would pay a small rent to the state and could not sell what they had received.

The bill aroused great hostility. Its passage would hurt many senators who held vast estates. Others thought it would be a bad precedent to allow any interference with property rights, even if they involved illegally held public land. Still others feared the political gains that Tiberius and his associates would make if the beneficiaries of their law were properly grateful to its drafters. (See "The Ruin of the Roman Family Farm and the Gracchan Reforms.")

When Tiberius put the bill before the tribal assembly, one of the tribunes, M. Octavius, interposed his veto. Tiberius went to the Senate to discuss his proposal, but the senators continued their opposition. Tiberius now had to choose between dropping the matter and undertaking a revolutionary course. Unwilling to give up, he put his bill before the tribal assembly again. Again Octavius vetoed. So Tiberius, strongly supported by the people, had Octavius removed from office, violating the constitution. The assembly's removal of a magistrate implied a fundamental shift of power from the Senate to the people. If the assembly could pass laws the Senate opposed and a tribune vetoed, and if they could remove magistrates, then Rome would become a democracy like Athens instead of a traditional oligarchy. At this point, many of Tiberius's senatorial allies deserted him.

Tiberius proposed a second bill, harsher than the first and more appealing to the people, for he had given up hope of conciliating the Senate. This bill, which passed the assembly, provided for a commission to carry it out. When King Attalus of Pergamum died and left his kingdom to Rome, Tiberius proposed using the Pergamene revenue to finance the commission. This proposal challenged the Senate's control both of finances and of foreign affairs. Hereafter there could be no compromise: Either Tiberius or the Roman constitution must go under.

Tiberius understood the danger he would face if he stepped down from the tribunate, so he announced his candidacy for a second successive term, striking another blow at tradition. His opponents feared he might go on to hold office indefinitely, to dominate Rome in what appeared to them a demagogic tyranny. They concentrated their fire on the constitutional issue, the deposition of the tribune. They appear to have had some success, for many of Tiberius's supporters did not come out to vote. At the elections a riot broke out, and a mob of senators and their clients killed Tiberius and some three hundred of his followers and threw their bodies into the Tiber River. The Senate had put down the threat to its rule, but at the price of the first internal bloodshed in Roman political history.

The tribunate of Tiberius Gracchus changed Roman politics. Heretofore Roman political struggles had generally been struggles for honor and reputation between great families or coalitions of such families. Fundamental issues were rarely at stake. The revolutionary proposals of Tiberius, however, and the senatorial resort to bloodshed created a new situation. Tiberius's use of the tribunate to challenge senatorial rule encouraged imitation despite his failure. From then on, Romans could pursue a political career that was not based solely on influence within the aristocracy; pressure from the people might be an effective substitute. In the last century of the republic, politicians who sought such backing were called **populares**, whereas those who supported the traditional role of the Senate were called **optimates**, or "the best men."

These groups were not political parties with formal programs and party discipline, but they were more than merely vehicles for the political ambitions of unorthodox politicians. Fundamental questions—such as those about land reform, the treatment of the Italian allies, the power of the assemblies versus the power of the Senate, and other problems—divided the Roman people, from the time of Tiberius Gracchus to the fall of the republic. Some popular leaders, of course, were cynical self-seekers who used the issues only for their own ambitions. Some few may have been sincere advocates of a principled position. Most, no doubt, were a mixture of the two, like most politicians in most times.

Gaius Gracchus   The tribunate of Gaius Gracchus (brother of Tiberius) was much more dangerous than that of Tiberius. All the tribunes of 123 B.C.E. were his supporters, so there could be no veto, and a recent law permitted the reelection of tribunes. Gaius's program appealed to a variety of groups. First, he revived the agrarian commission, which had been allowed to lapse. Because there was not enough good public land left to meet the demand, he proposed to establish new colonies: two in Italy and one on the old site of Carthage. Among other popular acts, he put through a law stabilizing the price of grain in Rome, which involved building granaries to guarantee an adequate supply.

Gaius broke new ground in appealing to the equestrian order in his struggle against the Senate. The **equestrians** (so called because they served in the Roman cavalry) were neither peasants nor senators. Some were businesspeople who supplied goods and services to the Roman state and collected its taxes. Almost continuous warfare and the need for tax collection in the provinces had made many of them rich. Most of the time, these wealthy men had the same outlook as the Senate; generally, they used their profits to purchase land and to try to reach senatorial rank themselves. Still, they had a special interest in Roman expansion and in the exploitation of the provinces. In the late second century B.C.E., they developed a clear sense of group interest and exerted political influence.

In 129 B.C.E., Pergamum became the new province of Asia. Gaius put through a law turning over to the equestrian order the privilege of collecting its revenue. He also barred senators from serving as jurors on the courts that tried provincial governors charged with extortion. The combination was a wonderful gift for wealthy equestrian businessmen, who were now free to squeeze profits out of the rich province of Asia without much fear of interference from the governors. The results for Roman provincial administration were bad, but the immediate political consequences for Gaius were excellent. The equestrians were now given reality as a class; as a political unit they might be set against the Senate or be formed into a coalition to serve Gaius's purposes.

Gaius easily won reelection as tribune for 122 B.C.E. He aimed at giving citizenship to the Italians, both to resolve their dissatisfaction and to add them to his political coalition. But the common people did not want to share the advantages of Roman citizenship. The Senate seized on this proposal to drive a wedge between Gaius and his supporters.

The Romans did not reelect Gaius for 121 B.C.E., leaving him vulnerable to his enemies. A hostile consul provoked an incident that led to violence. The Senate invented an extreme decree ordering the consuls to see to it that no harm came to the republic; in effect, this decree established martial law. Gaius was hunted down and killed, and a senatorial court condemned and put to death some 3,000 of his followers without any trial.

Marius and Sulla

For the moment, the senatorial oligarchy had fought off the challenge to its traditional position. Before long, it faced more serious dangers arising from troubles abroad. The first grew out of a dispute over the succession to the throne of Numidia, a client kingdom of Rome's near Carthage.

Marius and the Jugurthine War   The victory of Jugurtha, who became king of Numidia, and his massacre of Roman and Italian businessmen in the province, gained Roman attention. Although the Senate was reluctant to become involved, pressure from the equestrians and the people forced the declaration of what became known as the Jugurthine War in 111 B.C.E.

As the war dragged on, the people, sometimes with good reason, suspected the Senate of taking bribes from Jugurtha. They elected C. Marius (157–86 B.C.E.) to the consulship for 107 B.C.E. The assembly, usurping the role of the Senate, assigned him to Numidia. This action was significant in several ways. Marius was a *novus homo*, a "new man"—that is, the first in the history of his family to reach the consulship. Although a wealthy equestrian, he had been born in the town of Arpinum and was outside the closed circle of the old Roman aristocracy. His earlier career had won him a reputation as an outstanding soldier and a political maverick.

Marius quickly defeated Jugurtha, but Jugurtha escaped, and guerrilla warfare continued. Finally, Marius's subordinate, L. Cornelius Sulla (138–78 B.C.E.), trapped Jugurtha and brought the war to an end. Marius celebrated the victory, but Sulla, an ambitious though impoverished descendant of an old Roman family, resented being cheated of the credit he thought he deserved. Rumors credited Sulla with the victory and diminished Marius's role. Thus were the seeds planted for a mutual hostility that would last until Marius's death.

While the Romans were fighting Jugurtha, a far greater danger threatened Rome from the north. In 105 B.C.E., two barbaric tribes, the Cimbri and the Teutones, had come down the Rhone Valley and crushed a Roman army at Arausio (Orange) in southern France. When these tribes threatened again, the Romans elected Marius to his second consulship to meet the danger. He served five consecutive terms until 100 B.C.E., when the crisis was over.

While the barbarians were occupied elsewhere, Marius used the time to make important changes in the army. He began using volunteers for the army, mostly the dispossessed farmers and rural proletarians whose problems the Gracchi had not solved. They enlisted for a long term of service and looked on the army not as an unwelcome duty, but as an opportunity and a career. They became semiprofessional clients of their general and sought guaranteed food, clothing, shelter, and booty from victories. They came to expect a piece of land as a form of mustering-out pay, or veteran's bonus, when they retired.

Volunteers were most likely to enlist with a man who was a capable soldier and influential enough to obtain what he needed for them. They looked to him rather than to the state for their rewards. He, however, had to obtain these favors from the Senate if he was to maintain his power and reputation. Marius's innovation created both the opportunity and the necessity for military leaders to gain enough power to challenge civilian authority. The promise of rewards won these leaders the personal loyalty of their troops, and that loyalty allowed them to frighten the Senate into granting their demands.

The Wars against the Italians (90–88 B.C.E.)   For a decade Rome avoided serious troubles, but in that time the Senate took no action to deal with Italian discontent. The Italians were excluded from the land bill for Marius's veterans. Their discontent caused the Senate to expel all Italians from Rome in 95 B.C.E. Four years later, the tribune M. Livius Drusus put forward a bill to enfranchise the Italians. Drusus seems to have been a sincere aristocratic reformer, but he was assassinated in 90 B.C.E. Frustrated, the Italians revolted and established a separate confederation with its own capital and coinage.

Employing the traditional device of divide and conquer, the Romans immediately offered citizenship to those cities that remained loyal and soon made the same offer to the rebels if they laid down their arms. Even then, hard fighting was needed to put down the uprising, but by 88 B.C.E., the war against the allies was over. All the Italians became Roman citizens with the protections that citizenship offered. However, they retained local self-government and a dedication to their own municipalities that made Italy flourish. The passage of time blurred the distinction between Romans and Italians and forged them into a single nation.

Sulla's Dictatorship   During the war against the allies, Sulla had performed well. He was elected consul for 88 B.C.E. and was given command of the war against Mithridates, who was leading a major rebellion in Asia. At this point, the seventy-year-old Marius emerged from obscurity and sought the command for himself. With popular and equestrian support, he got the assembly to transfer the command to him. Sulla, defending the rights of the Senate and his own interests, marched his army against Rome. This was the first time a Roman general had used his army against fellow citizens. Marius and his friends fled, and Sulla regained the command. No sooner had he left again for Asia, than Marius joined with the consul Cinna and seized Rome. He outlawed Sulla and massacred the senatorial opposition. Marius died soon after his election to a seventh consulship, for 86 B.C.E.

Cinna now was the chief man at Rome. Supported by Marius's men, he held the consulship from 87 to 84 B.C.E. His future depended on Sulla's fortunes in the East.

By 85 B.C.E., Sulla had driven Mithridates from Greece and had crossed over to Asia Minor. Eager to regain control of Rome, he negotiated a compromise peace. In 83 B.C.E., he returned to Italy and fought a civil war that lasted for more than a year. Sulla won and drove the followers of Marius from Italy. He had himself appointed dictator, not in the traditional sense, but to remake the state.

Sulla's first step was to wipe out the opposition. The names of those proscribed were posted in public. As outlaws, anyone could kill them and receive a reward. Sulla proscribed not only political opponents, but also his personal enemies and men whose only crime was their wealth. With the proceeds from the confiscations, Sulla rewarded his veterans, perhaps as many as 100,000 men, and thereby built a solid base of support.

Sulla had enough power to make himself the permanent ruler of Rome. He was traditional enough to want to restore senatorial government, but reformed so as to prevent the misfortunes of the past. To deal with the decimation of the Senate caused by the proscriptions and the civil war, he enrolled three hundred new members, many of them from the equestrian order and the upper classes of the Italian cities. The office of tribune, which the Gracchi had used to attack senatorial rule, was made into a political dead end.

Sulla's most valuable reforms improved the quality of the courts and the entire legal system. He created new courts to deal with specified crimes, bringing the number of courts to eight. Because both judge and jurors were senators, the courts, too, enhanced senatorial power. These actions were the most permanent of Sulla's reforms, laying the foundation for Roman criminal law.

Sulla retired to a life of ease and luxury in 79 B.C.E. He could not, however, undo the effect of his own example—that of a general using the loyalty of his own troops to take power and to massacre his opponents, as well as innocent men. These actions proved to be more significant than his constitutional arrangements.

▼ The Fall of the Republic

Within a year of Sulla's death, his constitution came under assault. To deal with an armed threat to its powers, the Senate violated the very procedures meant to defend them.

Pompey, Crassus, Caesar, and Cicero

The Senate gave the command of the army to Pompey (106–48 B.C.E.), who was only twenty-eight and had never been elected to a magistracy. Then, when Sertorius, a Marian general, resisted senatorial control, the Senate appointed Pompey proconsul in Spain in 77 B.C.E. These actions ignored Sulla's rigid rules for office holding, which had been meant to guarantee experienced, loyal, and safe commanders. In 71 B.C.E., Pompey returned to Rome with new glory, having put down the rebellion of Sertorius. In 73 B.C.E., the Senate made another extraordinary appointment to put down a great slave rebellion led by the gladiator Spartacus. Marcus Licinius Crassus, a rich and ambitious senator, received powers that gave him command of almost all of Italy. Together with the newly returned Pompey, he crushed the rebellion in 71 B.C.E. Extraordinary commands of this sort proved to be the ruin of the republic.

Crassus and Pompey were ambitious men whom the Senate feared. Both demanded special honors and election to the consulship for the year 70 B.C.E. Pompey was legally ineligible because he had never gone through the strict course of offices Sulla's constitution prescribed, and Crassus needed Pompey's help. They joined forces, though they disliked and were jealous of each other. They gained popular support by promising to restore the full powers of the tribunes, which Sulla had curtailed, and they gained equestrian backing by promising to restore equestrians to the extortion court juries. They both won election and repealed most of Sulla's constitution. This opened the way for further attacks on senatorial control and for collaboration between ambitious generals and demagogic tribunes.

In 67 B.C.E., a special law gave Pompey *imperium* for three years over the entire Mediterranean and fifty miles in from the coast. It also gave him the power to raise troops and money to rid the area of pirates. The assembly passed the law over senatorial opposition, and in three months Pompey cleared the seas of piracy. Meanwhile, a new war had broken out with Mithridates. In 66 B.C.E., the assembly transferred the command to Pompey, giving him unprecedented powers. He held *imperium* over all Asia, with the right to make war and peace at will. His *imperium* was superior to that of any proconsul in the field.

Once again, Pompey justified his appointment. He defeated Mithridates and drove him to suicide. By 62 B.C.E., he had extended Rome's frontier to the Euphrates River and had organized the territories of Asia so well that his arrangements remained the basis of Roman rule well into the imperial period. When Pompey returned to Rome in 62 B.C.E., he had more power, prestige, and popular support than any Roman in history. The Senate and his personal enemies had reason to fear he might emulate Sulla and establish his own rule.

Rome had not been quiet in Pompey's absence. Crassus was the foremost among those who had reason to fear Pompey's return. Although rich and influential, Crassus did not have the confidence of the Senate, a firm political base of his own, or the kind of military glory needed to rival Pompey. During the 60s B.C.E., therefore, he allied himself with various popular leaders.

The ablest of these men was Gaius Julius Caesar (100–44 B.C.E.). He was a descendant of an old, but politically obscure, patrician family that claimed descent from the kings and even from the goddess Venus. Despite this noble lineage, Caesar was connected to the popular party through his aunt, the wife of Marius, and through his own wife, Cornelia, the daughter of Cinna. Caesar was an ambitious young politician whose daring and rhetorical skill made him a valuable ally in winning the discontented of every class to the cause of the *populares*. Though Crassus was the senior partner, each needed the other to achieve what both wanted: significant military commands with which to build a reputation, a political following, and a military force to compete with Pompey's.

The chief opposition to Crassus's candidates for the consulship for 63 B.C.E. came from Cicero (106–43 B.C.E.), a *novus homo*, from Marius's hometown of Arpinum. He had made a spectacular name as the leading lawyer in Rome. Cicero, though he came from outside the senatorial aristocracy, was no *populPopularis*. His program was to preserve the republic against demagogues and ambitious generals by making the government more liberal. He wanted to unite the stable elements of the state—the Senate and the equestrians—in a harmony of the orders. This program did not appeal to the senatorial oligarchy, but the Senate preferred Cicero to Catiline, a dangerous and popular politician thought to be linked with Crassus. Cicero and Antonius were elected consuls for 63 B.C.E., with Catiline running third.

Cicero soon learned of a plot hatched by Catiline. Catiline had run in the previous election on a platform of cancellation of debts; this appealed to discontented elements in general, but especially to the heavily indebted nobles and their many clients. Made desperate by defeat, Catiline planned to stir up rebellions around Italy, to cause confusion in the city, and to take it by force. Quick action by Cicero defeated Catiline.

The First Triumvirate

Toward the end of 62 B.C.E., Pompey landed at Brundisium. Surprisingly, he disbanded his army, celebrated a great triumph, and returned to private life. He had delayed his return in the hope of finding Italy in such a state as to justify his keeping the army and dominating the scene. Cicero's quick suppression of Catiline prevented his plan. Pompey, therefore, had either to act illegally or to lay down his arms. Because he had not thought of monarchy or revolution, but merely wanted to be recognized and treated as the greatest Roman, he chose the latter course.

Pompey had achieved amazing things for Rome and simply wanted the Senate to approve his excellent arrangements in the East and to make land allotments to his veterans. His demands were far from unreasonable, and a prudent Senate would have granted them and tried to employ his power in defense of the constitution. But the Senate was jealous and fearful of overmighty individuals and refused his requests. Pompey was driven to an alliance with his natural enemies, Crassus and Caesar, because the Senate blocked what all three wanted.

In 60 B.C.E., Caesar returned to Rome from his governorship of Spain. He wanted to celebrate a triumph, the great victory procession that the Senate granted certain generals to honor especially great achievements, and to run for consul. The law did not allow him to do both, however, requiring him to stay outside the city with his army but demanding that he canvass for votes personally within the city. He asked for a special dispensation, but the Senate refused. Caesar then performed a political miracle. He reconciled Crassus with Pompey and gained the support of both for his own ambitions. So was born the First Triumvirate, an informal agreement among three Roman politicians, each seeking his private goals, which further undermined the republic.

Julius Caesar and His Government of Rome

Though he was forced to forgo his triumph, Caesar was elected to the consulship for 59 B.C.E. His fellow consul was M. Calpernius Bibulus, the son-in-law of Cato and a conservative hostile to Caesar and the other *populares*. Caesar did not hesitate to override his colleague. The triumvirs' program was quickly enacted. Caesar got the extraordinary command that would give him a chance to earn the glory and power with which to rival Pompey: the governorship of Illyricum and Gaul for five years. A land bill settled Pompey's veterans comfortably, and his eastern settlement was ratified. Crassus, much of whose influence came from his position as champion of the equestrians, won for them a great windfall by having the government renegotiate a tax contract in their favor. To guarantee themselves against any reversal of these actions, the triumvirs continued their informal but effective collaboration, arranging for the election of friendly consuls and the departure of potential opponents.

A bust of Julius Caesar.   Bust of Julius Caesar (100–44 B.C.E.).
Roman statesman. Museo Archeologico Nazionale, Naples, Italy.
Photograph © Scala/Art Resource, NY

Caesar was now free to seek the military success he craved. His province included Cisalpine Gaul in the Po Valley (by now occupied by many Italian settlers as well as Gauls) and Narbonese Gaul beyond the Alps (modern Provence).

Relying first on the excellent quality of his army and the experience of his officers and then on his own growing military ability, Caesar made great progress. By 56 B.C.E., he had conquered most of Gaul, but he had not yet consolidated his victories firmly. He therefore sought an extension of his command, but quarrels between Crassus and Pompey so weakened the Triumvirate that the Senate was prepared to order Caesar's recall.

To prevent the dissolution of his base of power, Caesar persuaded Crassus and Pompey to meet with him at Luca in northern Italy to renew the coalition. They agreed that Caesar would get another five-year command in Gaul, and Crassus and Pompey would be consuls again in 55 B.C.E. After that, they would each receive an army and a five-year command. Caesar was free to return to Gaul and finish the job. The capture of

Alesia in 51 B.C.E. marked the end of the serious Gallic resistance and of Gallic liberty. For Caesar, it brought the wealth, fame, and military power he wanted. He commanded thirteen loyal legions, a match for his enemies as well as for his allies.

By the time Caesar was ready to return to Rome, the Triumvirate had dissolved and a crisis was at hand. At Carrhae, in 53 B.C.E., Crassus died trying to conquer the Parthians, successors to the Persian Empire. His death broke one link between Pompey and Caesar. The death of Caesar's daughter Julia, who had been Pompey's wife, dissolved another.

As Caesar's star rose, Pompey became jealous and fearful. He did not leave Rome but governed his province through a subordinate. In the late 50s B.C.E., political rioting at Rome caused the Senate to appoint Pompey sole consul. This grant of unprecedented power and responsibility brought Pompey closer to the senatorial aristocracy in mutual fear of, and hostility to, Caesar. The Senate wanted to bring Caesar back to Rome as a private citizen after his proconsular command expired. He would then be open to attack for past illegalities. Caesar tried to avoid the trap by asking permission to stand for the consulship in absentia.

Early in January of 49 B.C.E., the more extreme faction in the Senate had its way. It ordered Pompey to defend the state and Caesar to lay down his command by a specified day. For Caesar, this meant exile or death, so he ordered his legions to cross the Rubicon River, the boundary of his province. (See Map 4–4.) This action started a civil war. In 45 B.C.E., Caesar defeated the last forces of his enemies under Pompey's sons at Munda in Spain. The war was over, and Caesar, in Shakespeare's words, bestrode "the narrow world like a Colossus."

From the beginning of the civil war until his death in 44 B.C.E., Caesar spent less than a year and a half in Rome, and many of his actions were attempts to deal with immediate problems between campaigns. His innovations generally sought to make rational and orderly what was traditional and chaotic. An excellent example is Caesar's reform of the calendar. By 46 B.C.E., it was 80 days ahead of the proper season, because the official year was lunar, containing only 355 days. Using the best scientific advice, Caesar instituted a new calendar, now known as the **Julian Calendar**: With minor changes by Pope Gregory XIII in the sixteenth century, it is the calendar in use today.

Another general tendency of his reforms in the political area was the elevation of the role of Italians and even provincials at the expense of the old Roman families, most of whom were his political enemies. He raised the number of senators to nine hundred and filled the Senate's depleted ranks with Italians and even Gauls. He was free with grants of Roman citizenship, giving the franchise to Cisalpine Gaul as a whole and to many individuals of various regions.

Map 4–4 **THE CIVIL WARS OF THE LATE ROMAN REPUBLIC** This map shows the extent of the territory controlled by Rome at the time of Caesar's death and the sites of the major battles of the civil wars of the late republic.

Caesar made few changes in the government of Rome. The Senate continued to play its role, in theory. But its increased size, its packing with supporters of Caesar, and his own monopoly of military power made the whole thing a sham. He treated the Senate as his creature, sometimes with disdain. His legal position rested on several powers. In 46 B.C.E., he was appointed dictator for ten years, and in the next year he was appointed for life. He also held the consulship, the immunity of a tribune (although, being a patrician, he had never been a tribune), the chief priesthood of the state, and a new position, prefect of morals, which gave him the censorial power. Usurping the elective power of the assemblies, he even named the magistrates for the next few years, because he expected to be away in the East.

The enemies of Caesar were quick to accuse him of aiming at monarchy. (See "Compare & Connect: Did Caesar Want to Be King?," page 124.) A conspiracy under the leadership of Gaius Cassius Longinus and Marcus Junius Brutus included some sixty senators.

Did Caesar Want to Be King?

AFTER THE RETIREMENT and death of Sulla, his constitution was quickly destroyed, his attempt to restore the rule of the Senate proven a failure. The remaining years of the Roman Republic were occupied with a struggle among dynasts and senatorial factions to achieve dominance. From 49 to 46 B.C.E. Caesar and Pompey fought a great civil war that ended in total defeat for Pompey and the senatorial forces. Caesar was unchallenged master of the Roman world. His problem was to invent a system of government that would avoid the pitfalls of divided rule and yet rest upon widespread popular support. From antiquity to the present time, men have argued that his solution was nothing less than monarchy pure and simple. Others have denied that this was his goal. The question cannot be settled, for Caesar was assassinated before he could put his plans into practice, yet it is important to consider the problem both because of its intrinsic interest and because it represents a significant stage in the transition from republic to empire.

QUESTIONS

1. What does Cassius Dio think Caesar wanted?
2. What is the opinion of Nicolaus of Damascus?
3. What is the significance of the debate?

I. Cassius Dio

Cassius Dio was a Greek of the third century C.E. who became a senator under the Roman Empire. He wrote an eighty-book history of Rome from the beginning to 229 C.E. Here he tells the story of the growing suspicion among his enemies and the plots arising among them.
When he had reached this point, the conduct of the men plotting against him became no longer doubtful, and in order to embitter even his best friends against him they did their best to traduce the man and finally called him "king,"—a name which was often heard in their consultations. When he refused the title and rebuked in a way those that so saluted him, yet did nothing by which he could be thought to be really displeased at it, they secretly adorned his statue, which stood on the rostra, with a diadem. And when Gaius Epidius Marullus and Lucius Cassetius Flavus, tribunes, took it down, he became thoroughly angry, although they uttered no insulting word and furthermore spoke well of him before the people as not desiring anything of the sort. At this time, though vexed, he remained quiet; subsequently, however, when he was riding in from Albanum, some men again called him king, and he said that his name was not king but Caesar: then when those tribunes brought suit against the first man that termed him king, he no longer restrained his wrath but showed evident irritation, as if these officials were actually aiming at the stability of his government. . . .

Something else that happened not long after these events proved still more clearly that while pretendedly he shunned the title, in reality he desired to assume it. When he had entered the Forum at the festival of the Lupercalia . . . Antony with his fellow priests saluted him as king and surrounding his brows with a diadem said: "The people gives this to you through my hands." He answered that Jupiter alone was king of the Romans and sent the diadem to him to the Capitol, yet he was not angry and caused it to be inscribed in the records that the royalty presented to him by the people through the consul he had refused to receive. It was accordingly suspected that this had been done by some prearranged plan and that he was anxious for the name but wished to be somehow compelled to take it, and the consequent hatred against him was intense.

II. Nicolaus of Damascus

Nicolaus was born to a distinguished Greek family in the first century B.C. He served as adviser and court historian to Herod the Great of Judea. In addition to the biography of the young Augustus, from which the following selection is taken, he wrote dramas, philosophical works, and a multivolume history of the world.
Such was the people's talk at that time. Later, in the course of the winter, a festival was held in Rome,

Source: CassiusDio, 44.8–11, trans. by H. B. Foster, pp. 414–417, Cambridge, MA, Harvard University Press, 1961.

called Lupercalia, in which old and young men together take part in a procession, naked except for a girdle, and anointed, railing at those whom they meet and striking them with pieces of goat's hide. When this festival came on Marcus Antonius was chosen director. He proceeded through the Forum, as was the custom, and the rest of the throng followed him. Caesar was sitting in a golden chair on the Rostra, wearing a purple toga. At first Licinius advanced toward him carrying a laurel wreath, though inside it a diadem was plainly visible. He mounted up, pushed up by his colleagues (for the place from which Caesar was accustomed to address the assembly was high), and set the diadem down before Caesar's feet. Amid the cheers of the crowd he placed it on Caesar's head. Thereupon Caesar called Lepidus, the master of horse, to ward him off, but Lepidus hesitated. In the meanwhile Cassius Longinus, one of the conspirators, pretending to be really well disposed toward Caesar so that he might the more readily escape suspicion, hurriedly removed the diadem and placed it in Caesar's lap. Publius Casca was also with him. While Caesar kept rejecting it, and among the shouts of the people, Antonius suddenly rushed up, naked and anointed, just as he was in the procession, and placed it on his head. But Caesar snatched it off, and threw it into the crowd. Those who were standing at some distance applauded this action, but those who were near at hand clamored that he should accept it

A profile of Brutus, one of Caesar's assassins, appeared on this silver coin. The reverse shows a cap of liberty between two daggers and reads "Ides of March." Getty Images, Inc–Liaison

and not repel the people's favor. Various individuals held different views of the matter. Some were angry, thinking it an indication of power out of place in a democracy; others, thinking to court favor, approved; still others spread the report that Antonius had acted as he did not without Caesar's connivance. There were many who were quite willing that Caesar be made king openly. All sorts of talk began to go through the crowd. When Antonius crowned Caesar a second time, the people shouted in chorus, 'Hail, King,' but Caesar still refusing the crown, ordered it to be taken to the temple of Capitolme Jupiter, saying that it was more appropriate there. Again the same people applauded as before. There is told another story, that Antonius acted thus wishing to ingratiate himself with Caesar, and at the same time was cherishing the hope of being adopted as his son. Finally, he embraced Caesar and gave the crown to some of the men standing near to place it on the head of the statue of Caesar which was near by. This they did. Of all the occurrences of that time this was not the least influential in hastening the action of the conspirators, for it proved to their very eyes the truth of the suspicions they entertained.

Source: Nicolaus of Damascus, *Life of Augustus*, 19–22, trans. by Clayton M. Hall (Menascha, WI: George Banta, 1923), p. 41. Reprinted by permission of Clayton M. Hall.

On 15 March 44 B.C.E., Caesar entered the Senate, characteristically without a bodyguard, and was stabbed to death. The assassins regarded themselves as heroic tyrannicides but did not have a clear plan of action to follow the tyrant's death. No doubt they simply expected the republic to be restored in the old way, but things had gone too far for that. There followed instead thirteen more years of civil war, at the end of which the republic received its final burial.

The Second Triumvirate and the Triumph of Octavian

Caesar had had legions of followers, and he had a capable successor in Mark Antony. But the dictator had named his eighteen-year-old grandnephew, Gaius Octavius (63 B.C.E.–14 C.E.), as his heir and had left him three quarters of his vast wealth. To everyone's surprise, the sickly and inexperienced young man came to Rome to claim his legacy. He gathered an army, won the support of many of Caesar's veterans, and became a figure of importance—the future **Augustus**.

THE FALL OF THE ROMAN REPUBLIC

133 B.C.E.	Tribunate of Tiberius Gracchus
123–122 B.C.E.	Tribunate of Gaius Gracchus
111–105 B.C.E.	Jugurthine War
104–100 B.C.E.	Consecutive consulships of Marius
90–88 B.C.E.	War against the Italian allies
88 B.C.E.	Sulla's march on Rome
82 B.C.E.	Sulla assumes dictatorship
71 B.C.E.	Crassus crushes rebellion of Spartacus
71 B.C.E.	Pompey defeats Sertorius in Spain
70 B.C.E.	Consulship of Crassus and Pompey
60 B.C.E.	Formation of First Triumvirate
58–50 B.C.E.	Caesar in Gaul
53 B.C.E.	Crassus killed in Battle of Carrhae
49 B.C.E.	Caesar crosses Rubicon; civil war begins
48 B.C.E.	Pompey defeated at Pharsalus; killed in Egypt
46–44 B.C.E.	Caesar's dictatorship
45 B.C.E.	End of civil war
43 B.C.E.	Formation of Second Triumvirate
42 B.C.E.	Triumvirs defeat Brutus and Cassius at Philippi
31 B.C.E.	Octavian and Agrippa defeat Antony at Actium

At first, the Senate tried to use Octavius against Antony, but when the conservatives rejected his request for the consulship, Octavius broke with them. Following Sulla's grim precedent, he took his army and marched on Rome. There he finally assumed his adopted name, C. Julius Caesar Octavianus. Modern historians refer to him at this stage in his career as Octavian, although he insisted on being called Caesar. In August 43 B.C.E., he became consul and declared the assassins of Caesar outlaws. Brutus and Cassius had an army of their own, so Octavian made a pact with Mark Antony and M. Aemilius Lepidus, a Caesarean governor of the western provinces. They took control of Rome and had themselves appointed "triumvirs to put the republic in order," with great powers. This was the Second Triumvirate, and unlike the first, it was legally empowered to rule almost dictatorially.

The need to pay their troops, their own greed, and the passion that always emerges in civil wars led the triumvirs to start a wave of proscriptions that outdid even those of Sulla. In 42 B.C.E., the triumviral army defeated Brutus and Cassius at Philippi in Macedonia, and the last hope of republican restoration died with the tyrannicides. Each of the triumvirs received a command. The junior partner, Lepidus, was given Africa, Antony took the rich and inviting East, and Octavian got the West and the many troubles that went with it.

Octavian had to fight a war against Sextus, the son of Pompey, who held Sicily. He also had to settle 100,000 veterans in Italy, confiscating much property and making many enemies. Helped by his friend Agrippa, he defeated Sextus Pompey in 36 B.C.E. Among his close associates was Maecenas, who served him as adviser and diplomatic agent. Maecenas helped manage the delicate relations with Antony and Lepidus, but perhaps equally important was his role as a patron of the arts. Among his clients were the poets Vergil and Horace, both of whom did important work for Octavian. They painted him as a restorer of Roman values, as a man of ancient Roman lineage and of traditional Roman virtues, and as the culmination of Roman destiny. More and more he was identified with Italy and the West, as well as with order, justice, and virtue.

Meanwhile Antony was in the East, chiefly at Alexandria with Cleopatra, the queen of Egypt. In 36 B.C.E., he attacked Parthia, with disastrous results. Octavian had promised to send troops to support Antony's Parthian campaign but never sent them. Antony was forced to depend on the East for support, and this meant reliance on Cleopatra. Octavian understood the advantage of representing himself as the champion of the West, Italy, and Rome. Meanwhile he represented Antony as the man of the East and the dupe of Cleopatra, her tool in establishing Alexandria as the center of an empire and herself as its ruler. Such propaganda made it easier for Caesareans to abandon Antony in favor of the young heir of Caesar. It did not help Antony's cause that he agreed to a public festival at Alexandria in 34 B.C.E., where he and Cleopatra sat on golden thrones. She was proclaimed "Queen of Kings," her son by Julius Caesar was named "King of Kings," and her other children received parts of the Roman Empire.

By 32 B.C.E., all pretense of cooperation ended. Octavian and Antony each tried to put the best face on what was essentially a struggle for power. Lepidus had been put aside some years earlier. Antony sought senatorial support and promised to restore the republican constitution. Octavian seized and published what was alleged to be the will of Antony, revealing his gifts of provinces to the children of Cleopatra. This caused the conflict to take the form of East against West, Rome against Alexandria.

In 31 B.C.E., the matter was settled at Actium in western Greece. Agrippa, Octavian's best general, cut off the enemy by land and sea, forcing and winning a naval battle. Octavian pursued Antony and Cleopatra to Alexandria, where both committed suicide. The civil wars were over, and at the age of thirty-two, Octavian was absolute master of the Mediterranean world. His power was enormous, but he had to restore peace, prosperity, and confidence. All of these required establishing a constitution that would reflect the new realities without offending unduly the traditional republican prejudices that still had so firm a grip on Rome and Italy.

In Perspective

The history of the Roman Republic was almost as sharp a departure from the common experiences of ancient civilizations as that of the Greek city-states. A monarchy in its earliest known form, Rome not long thereafter expelled its king and established an aristocratic republic somewhat like the *poleis* of the Greek "Dark Ages." But unlike the Greeks, the Romans continued to be in touch with foreign neighbors, including the far more civilized urban monarchies of the Etruscans. Nonetheless, the Romans clung to their republican institutions. For a long time the Romans remained a nation of farmers and herdsmen, to whom trade was relatively unimportant, especially outside of Italy.

Over time, the caste distinctions between patricians and plebeians were replaced by distinctions based on wealth and, even more important, aristocracy, wherein the significant distinction was between noble families, who held the highest elected offices in the state, and those outside the nobility. The Roman Republic from the first found itself engaged in almost continuous warfare with its neighbors—either in defense of its own territory, in fights over disputed territory, or in defense of other cities or states who were friends and allies of Rome.

Both internally and in their foreign relations, the Romans were a legalistic people, placing great importance on traditional behavior encoded into laws. Although backed by the powerful authority of the magistrates at home and the potent Roman army abroad, the laws were based on experience, common sense, and equity. Roman law aimed at stability and fairness, and it succeeded well enough that few people who lived under it wanted to do away with it. It lived on and grew during the imperial period and beyond. During the European Middle Ages, it played an important part in the revival of the West and continued to exert an influence into modern times.

The force of Roman arms, the high quality of Roman roads and bridges, and the pragmatic character of Roman law helped create something unique: an empire ruled by a republic, first a large one on land that included all of Italy and later one that commanded the shores of the entire Mediterranean and extended far inland in many places. Rome controlled an area that bears comparison with some of the empires of the East. It acquired that territory, wealth, and power in a state managed by annual magistrates elected by the male Roman citizens and by an aristocratic Senate, which had to take notice of popular assemblies and a published, impersonal code of law. It achieved its greatness with an army of citizens and allies, without a monarchy or a regular bureaucracy.

The temptations and responsibilities of governing a vast and rich empire, however, finally proved too much for the republican constitution. Trade grew, and with it a class of merchants and financiers—equestrians—that was neither aristocratic nor agricultural, but increasingly powerful. The influx of masses of slaves captured in war undermined the small farmers who had been the backbone of the Roman state and its army. As many of them were forced to leave their farms, they moved to the cities, chiefly to Rome, where they had no productive role. Conscripted armies of farmers serving relatively short terms gave way to volunteer armies of landless men serving as professionals and expecting to be rewarded for their services with gifts of land or money. The generals of these armies were not annual magistrates whom the Senate and the constitution controlled, but ambitious military leaders seeking glory and political advantage.

The result was civil war and the destruction of the republic. The conquest of a vast empire moved the Romans away from their unusual historical traditions toward the more familiar path of an empire that older rulers in Egypt and Mesopotamia had trodden.

REVIEW QUESTIONS

1. How did the institutions of family and clientage and the establishment of patrician and plebeian classes contribute to the stability of the early Roman Republic? How important were education and slavery to the success of the republic?

2. What was the Struggle of the Orders? How did plebeians get what they wanted? How was Roman society different after the struggle ended?

3. How was Rome able to conquer and control Italy? In their relations with Greece and Asia Minor in the second century B.C.E., were the Romans looking for security? Wealth? Power? Fame?

4. Why did the Romans and the Carthaginians clash in the First and Second Punic Wars? Could the wars have been avoided? How did Rome benefit from its victory over Carthage? What problems did this victory create?

5. What social, economic, and political problems did Italy have in the second century B.C.E.? What were the main proposals of Tiberius and Gaius Gracchus? What questions about Roman society did they raise? Why did the proposals fail?

6. What problems plagued the Roman Republic in its last century? What caused these problems and how did the Romans try to solve them? To what extent was the republic destroyed by ambitious generals who loved power more than Rome itself?

SUGGESTED READINGS

G. Barker and T. Rasmussen, *The Etruscans* (2000). A valuable new study of a mysterious people.

R. Baumann, *Women and Politics in Ancient Rome* (1995). A study of the role of women in Roman public life.

A. H. Bernstein, *Tiberius Sempronius Gracchus: Tradition and Apostasy* (1978). An interpretation of Tiberius's place in Roman politics.

T. J. Cornell, *The Beginnings of Rome: Italy and Rome from the Bronze Age to the Punic Wars* (1995). A fine new study of early Rome.

T. Cornell and J. Matthews, *Atlas of the Roman World* (1982). Presents a comprehensive view of the Roman world in its physical and cultural setting.

J-M. David, *The Roman Conquest of Italy* (1997). A good analysis of how Rome united Italy.

E. S. Gruen, *The Hellenistic World and the Coming of Rome* (1984). A new interpretation of Rome's conquest of the eastern Mediterranean.

W. V. Harris, *War and Imperialism in Republican Rome, 327–70 B.C.E.* (1975). An analysis of Roman attitudes and intentions concerning imperial expansion and war.

T. Holland, *Rubicon: The Last Years of the Roman Republic* (2004). A lively account of the fall of the republic.

S. Lancel, *Carthage, A History* (1995). A good account of Rome's great competitor.

H. Mouritsen, *Plebs and Politics in the Late Roman Republic* (2001). A new study of Roman republican politics and the place of the common people in them.

J. Powell and J. Patterson, *Cicero the Advocate* (2004). A careful study of the Roman statesman's legal career.

H. H. Scullard, *A History of the Roman World 753–146 B.C.E.*, 4th ed. (1980). An unusually fine narrative history with useful critical notes.

For additional learning resources related to this chapter, please go to www.myhistorylab.com

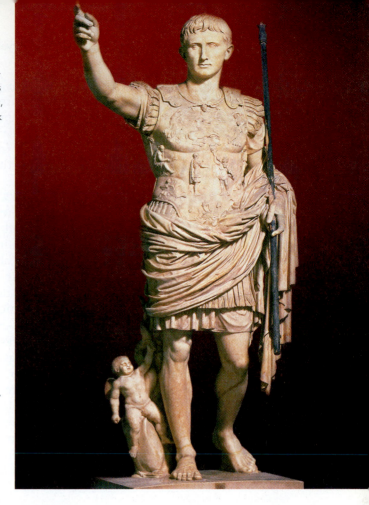

This statue of Emperor Augustus (r. 27 B.C.E.–14 C.E.), now in the Vatican, stood in the villa of Augustus's wife Livia. The figures on the elaborate breastplate are all of symbolic significance. At the top, for example, Dawn in her chariot brings in a new day under the protective mantle of the sky god; in the center, Tiberius, Augustus's future successor, accepts the return of captured Roman army standards from a barbarian prince; and at the bottom, Mother Earth offers a horn of plenty.   Vatican Museums & Galleries, Vatican City/Superstock

The Roman Empire

KEY TOPICS

• The Augustan constitution

• The organization and government of the Roman Empire

• Culture and civilization from the late republic through the imperial period

• The early history of Christianity

• The decline and fall of Rome in the West

THE VICTORY OF Augustus put an end to the deadly period of civil strife that had begun with the murder of Tiberius Gracchus. The establishment of a monarchy, at first concealed in republican forms but gradually more obvious, brought a long period of peace. Rome's unquestioned control of the entire Mediterranean permitted the growth of trade and a prosperity in the first two centuries of the Roman Empire not to be equaled for more than a millennium.

Management of the empire outside Italy became more benign and efficient. With shared citizenship, the provinces usually accepted Roman rule readily and even enthusiastically. Latin became the official language of the western part of the empire and Greek the official language in the east. This permitted the growth and spread of a common culture, today called *classical civilization*, throughout the empire. The same conditions fostered a great outburst of activity and excellence in the arts. The loss of political freedom, however, brought a decline in the vitality of the great Roman genre of rhetoric.

Christianity emerged in the first century C.E. as one of many competing Eastern cults. It continued to spread and attract converts, winning toleration and finally dominance in the fourth century. The world of imperial Rome powerfully shaped Christianity, which absorbed and used classical culture even while fighting it.

The third century C.E. brought serious attacks on Rome's frontiers, causing political and economic chaos. For a time, such emperors as Diocletian (r. 284–305) and Constantine (r. 306–337) instituted heroic measures to restore order. Their solutions involved increased centralization, militarization, and attempts to control every aspect of life. The emperors became more exalted and remote, the people increasingly burdened with heavy taxes even as the loss of economic freedom reduced their ability to pay. At last a new wave of barbarian attacks proved irresistible, and the Roman Empire in the West ended in the second half of the fifth century.

▼ The Augustan Principate

If the problems facing Octavian after the Battle of Actium in 31 B.C.E. were great, so were his resources for addressing them. He was the master of a vast military force, the only one in the Roman world, and he had loyal and capable assistants. Of enormous importance was the rich treasury of Egypt, which Octavian treated as his personal property. The people of Italy were eager for an end to civil war and a return to peace, order, and prosperity. In exchange for these, most people were prepared to accept a considerable abandonment of republican practices and to give power to an able ruler. The memory of Julius Caesar's fate, however, was still fresh in Octavian's mind. Its lesson was that it was dangerous to flaunt unprecedented powers and to disregard all republican traditions.

Octavian did not create his constitutional solution at a single stroke. It developed gradually as he tried new devices to fit his perception of changing conditions. Behind all the republican trappings and the apparent sharing of authority with the Senate, the government of Octavian, like that of his successors, was a monarchy. All real power, both civil and military, lay with the ruler—whether he was called by the unofficial title of *princeps*, or "first citizen," like Octavian, the founder of the regime, or *imperator*, "emperor," like those who followed. During the civil war Octavian's powers came from his triumviral status, whose dubious legality and

unrepublican character were an embarrassment. From 31 B.C.E. on, he held the consulship each year, but this circumstance was neither strictly legal nor satisfactory.

On 13 January 27 B.C.E., Octavian put forward a new plan in dramatic style, coming before the Senate to give up all his powers and provinces. In what was surely a rehearsed response, the Senate begged him to reconsider. At last he agreed to accept the provinces of Spain, Gaul, and Syria with proconsular power for military command and to retain the consulship in Rome. The other provinces would be governed by the Senate as before. Because the provinces he retained were border provinces that contained twenty of Rome's twenty-six legions, his true power was undiminished. The Senate, however, responded with almost hysterical gratitude, voting him many honors. Among them was the semireligious title Augustus, which implied veneration, majesty, and holiness. From this time on, historians speak of Rome's first emperor as Augustus and of his regime as the *Principate*. This would have pleased him, for it helps conceal the novel, unrepublican nature of the regime and the naked power on which it rested.

In 23 B.C.E., Augustus resigned his consulship and held that office only rarely thereafter. Instead, he was voted two powers that were to be the base of his rule thenceforth: the proconsular *imperium maius* and the *tribunician power*. The former made his proconsular power greater than that of any other proconsul and permitted him to exercise it even within the city of Rome. The latter gave him the right to conduct public business in the assemblies and the Senate, gave him the power of the veto, the *tribunician sacrosanctity* (immunity from arrest and punishment), and a connection with the Roman popular tradition. Thereafter, with only minor changes, Augustus's powers remained those conferred by the settlement of 23 B.C.E.

Administration

Augustus made important changes in the government of Rome, Italy, and the provinces. Most of his reforms reduced inefficiency and corruption, ended the danger to peace and order from ambitious individuals, and lessened the distinction between Romans and Italians, senators and equestrians. The assemblies lost their significance as a working part of the constitution, and the Senate took on most of the functions of the assemblies. Augustus purged the old Senate of undesirable members and fixed its number at six hundred. He recruited its members from wealthy men of good character, who entered after serving as lesser magistrates. Augustus controlled the elections and ensured that promising young men, whatever their origin, served the state as administrators and provincial governors. In this way, many equestrians and Italians who had no connection with the Roman aristocracy entered the Senate. For

This scene from Augustus's Ara Pacis, the Altar of Peace, in Rome shows the general Marcus Agrippa (63–12 B.C.E.) in procession with the imperial family. Agrippa was a powerful deputy, close friend, and son-in-law of Augustus. He was chiefly responsible for the victory over Mark Antony at the Battle of Actium in 31 B.C.E.   *Museum of the Ara Pacis, Rome, Italy*

all his power, Augustus was always careful to treat the Senate with respect and honor.

Augustus divided Rome into regions and wards with elected local officials. He gave the city, with its rickety wooden tenements, its first public fire department and police force. He carefully controlled grain distribution to the poor and created organizations to provide an adequate water supply. The Augustan period was one of great prosperity, based on the wealth brought in by the conquest of Egypt, on the great increase in commerce and industry made possible by general peace, on a vast program of public works, and on the revival of small farming by Augustus's resettled veterans.

The union of political and military power in the hands of the *princeps* enabled him to install rational, efficient, and stable government in the provinces for the first time. The emperor, in effect, chose the governors, removed the incompetent or rapacious, and allowed the effective ones to keep their provinces for longer periods. Also, he allowed much greater local autonomy, giving considerable responsibility to the upper classes in the provincial cities and towns and to the tribal leaders in less civilized areas.

The Army and Defense

The main external problem facing Augustus—and one that haunted all his successors—was the northern frontier. (See Map 5–1 on page 132.) Rome needed to pacify the regions to the north and the northeast of Italy and to find defensible frontiers against the recurring waves of barbarians. Augustus's plan was to push forward into central Europe to create the shortest possible defensive line. The eastern part of the plan succeeded, and the campaign in the West started well. In 9 C.E., however, the German tribal leader Herrmann, or Arminius, as the Romans called him, ambushed and destroyed three Roman legions, and the aged Augustus abandoned the campaign, leaving a problem of border defense that bedeviled his successors.

Under Augustus, the armed forces achieved professional status. Enlistment, chiefly by Italians, was for twenty years, but the pay was good, with occasional bonuses and the promise of a pension on retirement in the form of money or a plot of land. Together with the auxiliaries from the provinces, these forces formed a

Map 5–1 **THE ROMAN EMPIRE, 14 C.E.** This map shows the growth of the empire under Augustus and its extent at his death.

frontier army of about 300,000 men. In normal times, this was barely enough to hold the line.

The army permanently based in the provinces brought Roman culture to the natives. The soldiers spread their language and customs, often marrying local women and settling down in the area of their service. They attracted merchants, as new towns and cities that grew into centers of Roman civilization grew up around the military camps. As time passed, the provincials on the frontiers became Roman citizens who helped strengthen Rome's defenses against the barbarians outside.

Religion and Morality

A century of political strife and civil war had undermined many of the foundations of traditional Roman society. To repair the damage, Augustus sought to preserve and restore the traditional values of the family and religion in Rome and Italy. He introduced laws curbing adultery and divorce and encouraging early marriage and the procreation of legitimate children. He set an example of austere behavior in his own household and even banished his daughter, Julia, whose immoral behavior had become public knowledge.

Augustus worked at restoring the dignity of formal Roman religion, building many temples, reviving old cults, and invigorating the priestly colleges. He banned the worship of newly introduced foreign gods. Writers he patronized, such as Vergil, pointed out his family's legendary connection with Venus. During his lifetime he did not accept divine honors, though he was deified after his death. As with Julius Caesar, a state cult was dedicated to his worship.

▼ Civilization of the Ciceronian and Augustan Ages

The high point of Roman culture came in the last century of the republic and during the Principate of Augustus. Both periods reflected the dominant influence of Greek culture, especially its Hellenistic mode. Upper-class Romans were educated in Greek rhetoric, philosophy, and literature, which also served as the models for Roman writers and artists. Yet in spirit and sometimes in form, the art and writing of both periods show uniquely Roman qualities, though each in different ways.

The Late Republic

Cicero   The towering literary figure of the late republic was Cicero (106–43 B.C.E.). He is most famous for the orations he delivered in the law courts and in the Senate. Together with a considerable body of his private letters, these orations provide us with a clearer and fuller insight into his mind than into that of any other figure in antiquity. We see the political life of his period largely through his eyes. He also wrote treatises on rhetoric, ethics, and politics that put Greek philosophical ideas into Latin terminology and at the same time changed them to suit Roman conditions and values.

Cicero's own views provide support for his moderate and conservative practicality. He believed in a world governed by divine and natural law that human reason could perceive and human institutions reflect. He looked to law, custom, and tradition to produce both stability and liberty. His literary style, as well as his values and ideas, were an important legacy for the Middle Ages and, reinterpreted, for the Renaissance. He was killed at the order of Mark Antony, whose political opponent he had been during the civil wars after the death of Julius Caesar.

History   The last century of the republic produced some historical writing, much of which is lost to us. Sallust (86–35 B.C.E.) wrote a history of the years 78 to 67 B.C.E., but only a few fragments remain to remind us of his reputation as the greatest of republican historians. His surviving work consists of two pamphlets on the Jugurthine War and on the conspiracy of Catiline of 63 B.C.E. They reveal his Caesarean and antisenatorial prejudices and the stylistic influence of Thucydides.

Julius Caesar wrote important treatises on the Gallic and civil wars. They are not fully rounded historical accounts, but chiefly military narratives written from Caesar's point of view and to enhance his reputation. Their objective manner (Caesar always referred to himself in the third person) and their direct, simple, and vigorous style make them persuasive even today. They must have been most effective with the citizens of Rome who were their immediate audience.

Law   The period from the Gracchi to the fall of the republic was important in the development of Roman law. Before that time, Roman law was essentially national and had developed chiefly by juridical decisions, case by case. Contact with foreign peoples and the influence of Greek ideas, however, forced a change. From the last century of the republic on, the edicts of the *praetors* had increasing importance in developing the Roman legal code. They interpreted and even changed and added to existing law. Quite early, the edicts of the magistrates who dealt with foreigners developed the idea of the ***jus gentium***, or "law of peoples," as opposed to that arising strictly from the experience of the Romans. In the first century B.C.E., the influence of Greek thought made the idea of *jus gentium* identical with that of the ***jus naturae***, or "natural law," taught by the Stoics. It was this view of a world ruled by divine reason that Cicero enshrined in his treatise on the law, *De Legibus*.

Poetry   The time of Cicero was also the period of two of Rome's greatest poets, Lucretius and Catullus, each representing a different aspect of Rome's poetic tradition. The Hellenistic poets and literary theorists saw two functions for the poet: entertainer and teacher. They thought the best poet combined both roles, and the Romans adopted the same view. When Naevius and Ennius wrote epics on Roman history, they combined historical and moral instruction with pleasure. Lucretius (ca. 99–55 B.C.E.) pursued a similar path in his epic poem *De Rerum Natura* (*On the Nature of the World*). In it, he set forth the scientific and philosophical ideas of Epicurus and Democritus with the zeal of a missionary trying to save society from fear and superstition. He knew his doctrine might be bitter medicine to the reader: "That is why I have tried to administer it to you in the dulcet strain of poesy, coated with the sweet honey of the Muses."[1]

Catullus (ca. 84–54 B.C.E.) was a thoroughly different kind of poet. He wrote poems that were personal—even autobiographical. Imitating the Alexandrians, he wrote short poems filled with learned allusions to mythology, but he far surpassed his models in intensity of feeling. He wrote of the joys and pains of love, he hurled invective at important contemporaries like Julius Caesar, and he amused himself in witty poetic exchanges with others. He offered no moral lessons and was not interested in Rome's glorious history and in contemporary politics. In a sense, he is an example of the proud, independent, pleasure-seeking nobleman who characterized part of the aristocracy at the end of the republic.

The Age of Augustus

The spirit of the Augustan Age, the Golden Age of Roman literature, was different, reflecting the new conditions of society. The old aristocratic order, with its independent nobles following their own particular interests, was gone. So was the world of poets of the lower orders, receiving patronage from individual aristocrats. Under Augustus, all patronage flowed from the *princeps*, usually through his chief cultural adviser, Maecenas.

The major poets of this time, Vergil and Horace, had lost their property during the civil wars. The patronage of the *princeps* allowed them the leisure and the security to write poetry, but it also made them dependent on him and limited their freedom of expression. They wrote on subjects that were useful for his policies and

---

[1]Lucretius, *De Rerum Natura*, lines 931 ff.

glorified him and his family. These poets were not mere propagandists, however. It seems clear that mostly they believed in the virtues of Augustus and his reign and sang its praises with some degree of sincerity. Because they were poets of genius, they were also able to maintain a measure of independence in their work.

Vergil   Vergil (70–19 B.C.E.) was the most important of the Augustan poets. His first important works, the *Eclogues*, or *Bucolics*, are pastoral idylls in a somewhat artificial mode. The subject of the *Georgics*, however, was suggested to Vergil by Maecenas. The model here was the early Greek poet Hesiod's *Works and Days* (see Chapter 2), but Vergil's poem pays homage to the heroic human effort to forge order and social complexity out of a hostile and sometimes brutal natural environment. It was also a hymn to the cults, traditions, and greatness of Italy.

   All this served the purpose of glorifying Augustus's resettlement of the veterans of the civil wars on Italian farms and his elevation of Italy to special status in the empire. Vergil's greatest work is the *Aeneid*, a long national epic that placed the history of Rome in the great tradition of the Greeks and the Trojan War. Its hero, the Trojan warrior Aeneas, personifies the ideal Roman qualities of duty, responsibility, serious purpose, and patriotism. As the Romans' equivalent of Homer, Vergil glorified not the personal honor and excellence of the Greek epic heroes, but the civic greatness, peace, and prosperity that Augustus and the Julian family had given to imperial Rome.

This mosaic found in Tunisia shows the poet Vergil reading from his Aeneid to the Muses of Epic and Tragedy.   Roger Wood/CORBIS/Bettmann

Horace   Horace (65–8 B.C.E.) was the son of a freedman and fought on the republican side until its defeat at Philippi. The patronage of Maecenas and the attractions of the Augustan reforms won him over to the Augustan side. His *Satires* are genial and humorous. His *Odes*, which are ingenious in their adaptation of Greek meters to the requirements of Latin verse, best reveal his great skills as a lyric poet. Two of the *Odes* are directly in praise of Augustus, and many of them glorify the new Augustan order, the imperial family, and the empire.

Propertius   Sextus Propertius lived in Rome in the second half of the first century B.C.E., a contemporary of Vergil and Horace. Like them, he was part of the poetic circle around Augustus's friend Maecenas. He wrote witty and graceful elegies.

Ovid   The career of Ovid (43 B.C.E.–18 C.E.) reveals the darker side of Augustan influence on the arts. He wrote light and entertaining love elegies that reveal the sophistication and the loose sexual code of a notorious sector of the Roman aristocracy whose values and amusements were contrary to the seriousness and family-centered life Augustus was trying to foster. Ovid's *Ars Amatoria*, a poetic textbook on the art of seduction, angered Augustus and was partly responsible for the poet's exile in 8 C.E. Ovid tried to recover favor, especially with his *Fasti*, a poetic treatment of Roman religious festivals, but to no avail. His most popular work is the *Metamorphoses*, a kind of mythological epic that turns Greek myths into charming stories in a graceful and lively style. Ovid's fame did not fade with his exile and death, but his fate was an effective warning to later poets.

History   The achievements of Augustus, his emphasis on tradition, and the continuity of his regime with the glorious history of Rome encouraged both historical and antiquarian prose works. Some Augustan writers wrote scholarly treatises on history and geography in Greek. By far the most important and influential prose writer of the time, however, was Livy (59 B.C.E.–17 C.E.), an Italian from Padua. His *History of Rome* was written in Latin and treated the period from the legendary origins of Rome until 9 B.C.E. Only a fourth of his work is extant; of the rest we have only pitifully brief summaries. He based his history on earlier accounts and made no effort at original research. His great achievement was to tell the story of Rome in a continuous and impressive narrative. Its purpose was moral, and he set up historical models as examples of good and bad behavior and, above all, patriotism. He glorified Rome's greatness and connected it with Rome's past, as Augustus tried to do.

Architecture and Sculpture   Augustus was as great a patron of the visual arts as he was of literature. His building program beautified Rome, glorified his reign, and contributed to the general prosperity and his own popularity. He filled the Campus Martius with beautiful new buildings, theaters, baths, and basilicas; the Roman Forum was rebuilt, and Augustus built a forum of his own. At its heart was the temple of Mars the Avenger, which commemorated Augustus's victory and the greatness of his ancestors. On Rome's Palatine Hill, he built a splendid temple to his patron god, Apollo, to further his religious policy.

The Greek classical style, which aimed at serenity and the ideal type, influenced most of the building. The same features were visible in the portrait sculpture of Augustus and his family. The greatest monument of the age is the *Ara Pacis*, or "Altar of Peace," dedicated in 9 B.C.E. Part of it shows a procession in which Augustus and his family appear to move forward, followed in order by the magistrates, the Senate, and the people of Rome. There is no better symbol of the new order.

▼ Imperial Rome, 14 to 180 C.E.

The central problem for Augustus's successors was the position of the ruler and his relationship to the ruled. Augustus tried to cloak the monarchical nature of his government, but his successors soon abandoned all pretense. The ruler came to be called *imperator*—from which comes our word "emperor"—as well as Caesar. The latter title signified connection with the imperial house, and the former indicated the military power on which everything was based.

The Emperors

Because Augustus was ostensibly only the "first citizen" of a restored republic and the Senate and the people theoretically voted him his powers, he could not legally name his successor. In fact, however, he plainly designated his heirs by lavishing favors on them and by giving them a share in the imperial power and responsibility. Tiberius (r. 14–37 C.E.),[2] his immediate successor, was at first embarrassed by the ambiguity of his new role, but soon the monarchical and hereditary nature of the regime became clear. Gaius (Caligula, r. 37–41 C.E.), Claudius (r. 41–54 C.E.), and Nero (r. 54–68 C.E.) were all descended from either Augustus or his wife, Livia, and all were elevated because of that fact.

Gaius Caesar Germanicus succeeded Tiberius in 37 at the age of twenty-five. When he was a boy, the soldiers of his father's legions gave him the nickname Caligula (little boot), which stayed with him for the rest of his life. Recovered from a severe illness that struck him soon after becoming emperor, he launched a series of wild, tyrannical actions. He restored the use of trials

for treason that had darkened the reign of Tiberius and was vicious and cruel. He claimed to be divine even while alive and was thought to aim at a despotic monarchy like that of the Ptolemies in Egypt. Caligula spent the large amount of money in the state treasury and tried to get more by seizing the property of wealthy Romans. He was widely thought to be insane.

In 41 C.E., the naked military basis of imperial rule was revealed when the Praetorian Guard, having assassinated Caligula, dragged the lame, stammering, and frightened Claudius from behind a curtain and made him emperor. In 68 C.E., the frontier legions learned what the historian Tacitus (ca. 55–120) called "the secret of Empire . . . that an emperor could be made elsewhere than at Rome." Nero's incompetence and unpopularity, and especially his inability to control his armies, led to a serious rebellion in Gaul in 68 C.E. The year 69 saw four different emperors assume power in quick succession as different Roman armies took turns placing their commanders on the throne.

Vespasian (r. 69–79 C.E.) emerged victorious from the chaos, and his sons, Titus (r. 79–81 C.E.) and Domitian (r. 81–96 C.E.), carried forward his line, the Flavian dynasty. Vespasian, a tough soldier from the Italian middle class, was the first emperor who did not come from the old Roman nobility. A good administrator and a hardheaded realist of rough wit, he resisted all attempts by flatterers to find noble ancestors for him. On his deathbed he is said to have ridiculed the practice of deifying emperors by saying, "Alas, I think I am becoming a god."

RULERS OF THE EARLY EMPIRE	
27 B.C.E.–14 C.E.	Augustus
The Julio-Claudian Dynasty	
14–37 C.E.	Tiberius
37–41 C.E.	Gaius (Caligula)
41–54 C.E.	Claudius
54–68 C.E.	Nero
69 C.E.	Year of the Four Emperors
The Flavian Dynasty	
69–79 C.E.	Vespasian
79–81 C.E.	Titus
81–96 C.E.	Domitian
The "Good Emperors"	
96–98 C.E.	Nerva
98–117 C.E.	Trajan
117–138 C.E.	Hadrian
138–161 C.E.	Antoninus Pius
161–180 C.E.	Marcus Aurelius

---

[2]Dates for emperors give the years of their reigns, indicated by "r."

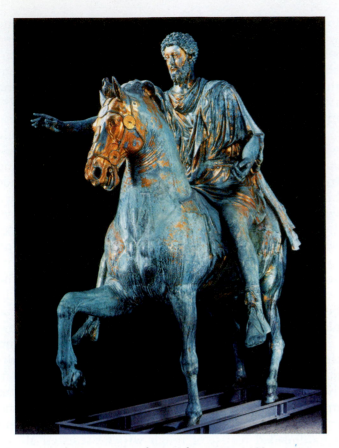

Marcus Aurelius, emperor of Rome from 161 to 180 C.E., was one of the five "good emperors" who brought a period of relative peace and prosperity to the empire. This is the only Roman bronze equestrian statue that has survived. Capitoline Museums, Rome, Italy/Canali PhotoBank, Milan/Superstock

The assassination of Domitian put an end to the Flavian dynasty. Because Domitian had no close relative who had been designated as successor, the Senate put Nerva (r. 96–98 C.E.) on the throne to avoid chaos. He was the first of the five "good emperors," who included Trajan (r. 98–117 C.E.), Hadrian (r. 117–138 C.E.), Antoninus Pius (r. 138–161 C.E.), and Marcus Aurelius (r. 161–180 C.E.). Until Marcus Aurelius, none of these emperors had sons, so they each followed the example set by Nerva of adopting an able senator and establishing him as successor. This rare solution to the problem of monarchical succession was, therefore, only a historical accident. The result, nonetheless, was almost a century of peaceful succession and competent rule, which ended when Marcus Aurelius allowed his incompetent son, Commodus (r. 180–192 C.E.), to succeed him, with unfortunate results.

The genius of the Augustan settlement lay in its capacity to enlist the active cooperation of the upper classes and their effective organ, the Senate. The election of magistrates was taken from the assemblies and given to the Senate, which became the major center for legislation and exercised important judicial functions.

This semblance of power persuaded some contemporaries and even some modern scholars that Augustus had established a *dyarchy*—a system of joint rule by *princeps* and Senate. That was never true.

The hollowness of the senatorial role became more apparent as time passed. Some emperors, like Vespasian, took pains to maintain, increase, and display the prestige and dignity of the Senate. Others, like Caligula, Nero, and Domitian, degraded the Senate and paraded their own despotic power. But from the first, the Senate's powers were illusory. The emperors controlled magisterial elections, and the Senate's legislative function quickly degenerated into mere assent to what the emperor or his representatives put before it. The true function of the Senate was to be a legislative and administrative extension of the emperor's rule.

Real opposition to the imperial rule sometimes took the form of plots against the life of the emperor. Plots and the suspicion of plots led to repression, the use of spies and paid informers, book burning, and executions. The opposition consisted chiefly of senators who looked back to republican liberty for their class and who found justification in the Greek and Roman traditions of tyrannicide as well as in the precepts of Stoicism. Plots and repression were most common under Nero and Domitian. From Nerva to Marcus Aurelius, however, the emperors, without yielding any power, again learned to enlist the cooperation of the upper class by courteous and modest deportment.

The Administration of the Empire

The provinces flourished economically and generally accepted Roman rule easily. (See Map 5–2.) In the eastern provinces, the emperor was worshiped as a god; even in Italy, most emperors were deified after their death as long as the imperial cult established by Augustus continued. Imperial policy usually combined an attempt to unify the empire and its various peoples with a respect for local customs and differences. Roman citizenship was spread ever more widely, and by 212 C.E., almost every free inhabitant of the empire was a citizen. Latin became the language of the western provinces. Although the East remained essentially Greek in language and culture, even it adopted many aspects of Roman life. The spread of **Romanitas**, or "Roman-ness," was more than nominal, for senators and even emperors began to be drawn from provincial families.

Local Municipalities From an administrative and cultural standpoint, the empire was a collection of cities and towns and had little to do with the countryside. Roman policy during the Principate was to raise urban centers to the status of Roman municipalities, with the rights and privileges attached to them. A typical municipal charter left much responsibility in the hands of local councils and

MAJOR ROADS OF THE ROMAN EMPIRE

Rome

Mediterranean Sea

500 MILES
500 KILOMETERS

Caspian Sea

PARTHIAN EMPIRE

Persian Gulf

Tigris R.
Euphrates R.

ARMENIA
ASSYRIA
MESOPOTAMIA
CAPPADOCIA
ASIA
ARABIA
ARABIA PETRAEA

PONTUS
BITHYNIA
GALATIA
CILICIA
PISIDIA
LYCIA
CYPRUS
PALESTINE
Jerusalem

Red Sea

EGYPT

Black Sea

LOWER MOESIA
THRACE
Byzantium

DACIA

SARMATIA

UPPER MOESIA
MACEDONIA
ILLYRIA
GREECE
ACHAEA
CRETE

LIBYA

CYRENAICA

DALMATIA
PANNONIA (INF.)
PANNONIA (SUP.)
NORICUM
RHAETIA
Alps Mts.
CISALPINE GAUL

Mediterranean Sea

N

Danube R.

GERMANIA

GERMANIA (SUP.)
GERMANIA (INF.)
Cologne

ITALY
Rome

SARDINIA
CORSICA

SICILY

AFRICA
Carthage
NUMIDIA

AFRICA

LUGDUNENSIS
GAUL
NARBONENSIS
AQUITANIA

BALEARIC ISLANDS

MAURETANIA

North Sea

BRITAIN

Wall of Antoninus
Wall of Hadrian

ATLANTIC OCEAN

HIBERNIA

TARRACONENSIS
LUSITANIA
BAETICA

500 MILES
500 KILOMETERS

14 C.E. – Death of Augustus
14–98 C.E. – Acquisitions, Augustus to Trajan
98–117 C.E. – Acquisitions during the Reign of Trajan

Map 5–2 **PROVINCES OF THE ROMAN EMPIRE TO 117 C.E.** The growth of the empire to its greatest extent is here shown in three stages—at the death of Augustus in 14 C.E., at the death of Nerva in 98, and at the death of Trajan in 117. The division into provinces is also shown. The insert shows the main roads that tied the far-flung empire together.

A Closer LOOK

SPOILS FROM JERUSALEM ON THE ARCH OF TITUS IN ROME

THE ARCH OF the Emperor Titus (r. 79–81 C.E.) stands at the highest point of the ancient Sacred Way that leads to the Roman Forum. It commemorates Titus's conquest of Judea, which ended the Jewish Wars (66–70 C.E.).

Carved on one of the internal faces of the passageway is a scene showing the triumphal procession with the booty from the Temple at Jerusalem—the sacred Menorah, the Table of the Shewbread shown at an angle, and the silver trumpets that called the Jews to celebrate the holy days of Rosh Hashanah.

Scala/Art Resource, NY

To examine this image in an interactive fashion, please go to www.myhistorylab.com

myhistorylab

The bearers of the booty wear laurel crowns and those carrying the candlestick have pillows on their shoulders. Placards in the background explain the spoils and the victories Titus won. These few figures, standing for hundreds in the actual procession, move toward the carved arch at the right.

Flavius Josephus, a first-century C.E. historian and eyewitness to the event, described Titus's triumph: "The spoils in general were borne in promiscuous heaps; but conspicuous above all stood out those captured in the Temple at Jerusalem. These consisted of a golden table, many talents in weight, and a lampstand, likewise made of gold, but constructed on a different pattern from those we use in ordinary life. Affixed to a pedestal was a central shaft, from which there extended slender branches, arranged trident-fashion, a wrought lamp being attached to the extremity of each branch; of these there were seven, indicating the honor paid to the number among the Jews. After these, and last of all the spoils, was carried a copy of the Jewish Law."
(The Jewish War 7.148–50).

The largest city of the ancient region of Tripolitania, Leptis Magna was located 62 miles southeast of Tripoli on the Mediterranean coast of Libya in North Africa. In its heyday, it was one of the richest cities in the Roman Empire, and it contains some of the finest remains of Roman architecture. The city was lavishly rebuilt by the Emperor Septimius Severus (r. 193–211 C.E.), who was born at Leptis in 146 C.E.
Peter Wilson/Rough Guides DK

magistrates elected from the local aristocracy. Moreover, the holding of a magistracy, and later a seat on the council, carried Roman citizenship with it. Therefore, the Romans enlisted the upper classes of the provinces in their own government, spread Roman law and culture, and won the loyalty of the influential people. (For a glimpse into the lives of ordinary people, see "Daily Life in a Roman Provincial Town: Graffiti from Pompeii," page 140.)

There were exceptions to this picture of success. The Jews found their religion incompatible with Roman demands and were savagely repressed when they rebelled in 66–70, 115–117, and 132–135 C.E. In Egypt, the Romans exploited the peasants with exceptional ruthlessness and did not pursue a policy of urbanization.

As the efficiency of the bureaucracy grew, so did the number and scope of its functions and therefore its size. The emperors came to take a broader view of their responsibilities for the welfare of their subjects than before. Nerva conceived and Trajan introduced the *alimenta*, a program of public assistance for the children of the poor. More and more the emperors intervened when municipalities got into difficulties, usually financial, sending imperial troubleshooters to deal with problems. The importance and autonomy of the municipalities shrank as the central administration took a greater part in local affairs. The provincial aristocracy came to regard public service in its own cities as a burden rather than an opportunity. The price paid for the increased efficiency that centralized control offered was the loss of the vitality of the cities throughout the empire.

The success of Roman civilization also came at great cost to the farmers who lived outside of Italy. Taxes, rents, mandatory gifts, and military service drew capital away from the countryside to the cities on a scale not previously seen in the Graeco-Roman world. More and more the rich life of the urban elite came at the expense of millions of previously stable farmers.

Foreign Policy Augustus's successors, for the most part, accepted his conservative and defensive foreign policy. Trajan was the first emperor to take the offensive in a sustained way. Between 101 and 106 C.E., he crossed the Danube and, after hard fighting, established the new province of Dacia between the Danube and the Carpathian Mountains. He was tempted, no doubt, by its gold mines, but he probably was also pursuing a new general strategy: to defend the empire more aggressively by driving wedges into the territory of threatening barbarians. The same strategy dictated the invasion of the Parthian Empire in the East (113–117 C.E.). Trajan's early success was astonishing, and he established three new provinces in Armenia, Assyria, and Mesopotamia. But his lines were overextended. Rebellions sprang up, and the campaign crumbled. Trajan was forced to retreat, and he died before getting back to Rome.

Hadrian's reign marked an important shift in Rome's frontier policy. Heretofore, Rome had been on the offensive against the barbarians. Although the Romans rarely gained new territory, they launched frequent attacks to chastise and pacify troublesome tribes. Hadrian hardened the Roman defenses, building a stone wall in the south of Scotland and a wooden one across the Rhine-Danube triangle.

The Roman defense became rigid, and initiative passed to the barbarians. Marcus Aurelius was compelled to spend most of his reign resisting dangerous attacks in the East and on the Danube frontier.

Agriculture: The Decline of Slavery and the Rise of the *Coloni* The defense of its frontiers put enormous pressure on the human and financial resources of the empire, but the effect of these pressures was not immediately felt. The empire generally experienced considerable economic growth well into the reigns of the "good emperors." Internal peace and efficient administration benefited agriculture as well as trade and industry. Farming and trade developed together as political conditions made it easier to sell farm products at a distance.

Small farms continued to exist, but the large estate, managed by an absentee owner and growing cash

DAILY LIFE IN A ROMAN PROVINCIAL TOWN: GRAFFITI FROM POMPEII

On the walls of the houses of Pompeii, buried and preserved by the eruption of Mount Vesuvius in 79 C.E., many scribblings give us an idea of what the life of ordinary people was like.

How do these graffiti differ from those one sees in a modern American city? What do they reveal about the similarities and differences between the ordinary people of ancient Rome and the people of today? How would you account for the differences?

I

Twenty pairs of gladiators of Decimus Lucretius Satrius Valens, lifetime flamen of Nero son of Caesar Augustus, and ten pairs of gladiators of Decimus Lucretius Valens, his son, will fight at Pompeii on April 8, 9, 10, 11, 12. There will be a full card of wild beast combats, and awnings [for the spectators]. Aemilius Celer [painted this sign], all alone in the moonlight.

II

Market days: Saturday in Pompeii, Sunday in Nuceria, Monday in Atella, Tuesday in Nola, Wednesday in Cumae, Thursday in Puteoli, Friday in Rome.

III

Pleasure says: "You can get a drink here for an as [a few cents], a better drink for two, Falernian for four."

IV

A copper pot is missing from this shop. 65 sesterces reward if anybody brings it back, 20 sesterces if he reveals the thief so we can get our property back.

V

The weaver Successus loves the innkeeper's slave girl, Iris by name. She doesn't care for him, but he begs her to take pity on him. Written by his rival. So long.

[Answer by the rival:] Just because you're bursting with envy, don't pick on a handsomer man, a lady-killer and a gallant.

[Answer by the first writer:] There's nothing more to say or write. You love Iris, who doesn't care for you.

VI

Take your lewd looks and flirting eyes off another man's wife, and show some decency on your face!

VII

Anybody in love, come here. I want to break Venus' ribs with a club and cripple the goddess' loins. If she can pierce my tender breast, why can't I break her head with a club?

VIII

I write at Love's dictation and Cupid's instruction;
But damn it! I don't want to be a god without you.

IX

[A prostitute's sign:] I am yours for 2 asses cash.

Excerpt from N. Lewis and M. Reinhold, *Roman Civilization*, Vol. 2 (New York: Columbia University Press, 1955). Reprinted by permission of Columbia University Press.

ROME'S INDEPENDENT WOMEN: TWO VIEWS

In the last years of the republic and into the transition to the empire, Roman writers begin to describe what might be called the "new woman." These women are pictured as wearing makeup, dressing and behaving shamelessly, and engaging in adulterous affairs. Perhaps the most shocking of their practices was to engage in sexual activity, but to refuse to have children. The following passages reveal two different approaches to the newly popular means of birth control. The first comes from Soranus, a doctor who practiced in Rome late in the first century C.E. The second comes from Ovid's poems about love.

According to the doctors, when might abortion and contraception be appropriate? What reasons do they have for their opinions? What arguments does Ovid make against the use of abortion? How do these ancient arguments compare with modern ones?

SORANUS

For one party [of doctors] banishes abortives, citing the testimony of Hippocrates who says: "I will give to no one an abortive"; moreover, because it is the specific task of medicine to guard and preserve what has been engendered by nature. The other party prescribes abortives, but with discrimination, that is, they do not prescribe them when a person wishes to destroy the embryo because of adultery or out of consideration for youthful beauty; but only to prevent subsequent danger in parturition if the uterus is small and not capable of accommodating the complete development, or if the uterus at its orifice has knobbly swellings and fissures, or if some similar difficulty is involved.

And they say the same about contraceptives as well, and we too agree with them.

OVID

She who first began the practice of tearing out her tender progeny deserved to die in her own warfare. Can it be that, to be free of the flaw of stretchmarks, you have to scatter the tragic sands of carnage? Why will you subject your womb to the weapons of abortion and give dread poisons to the unborn? The tigress lurking in Armenia does no such thing, nor does the lioness dare destroy her young. Yet tender girls do so—though not with impunity; often she who kills what is in her womb dies herself.

Soranus, *Gynecology* 1.19.60 in O. Temkin, *Soranus: Gynecology* (Baltimore: Johns Hopkins Press, 1956).

Ovid, *Amores* 2.14.5–9, 27–28, 35–38, trans. by Natalie Kampen in E. Fantham, E. P. Foley, N. B. Kampen, S. B. Pomeroy and H. A. Shapiro, *Women in the Classical World* (New York: Oxford University Press 1994), pp. 301–302.

---

crops, dominated agriculture. At first, as in the republican period, slaves mostly worked these estates, but in the first century, this began to change. Economic pressures forced many of the free lower classes to become tenant farmers, or *coloni*, and eventually the *coloni* replaced slaves as the mainstay of agricultural labor. Typically, these sharecroppers paid rent in labor or in kind, though sometimes they made cash payments. Eventually, they were tied to the land they worked, much as were the manorial serfs of the Middle Ages. Whatever its social costs, the system was economically efficient, however, and contributed to the general prosperity.

Women of the Upper Classes

By the late years of the Roman republic, women of the upper classes had achieved a considerable independence and influence. Some of them had become wealthy through inheritance and they were well educated. Women conducted literary salons and took part in literary groups. Marriage without the husband's right of *manus* became common, and some women conducted their sexual lives as freely as men. (See "Rome's Independent Women: Two Views.") The notorious Clodia, from one of Rome's noblest and most powerful families, is described as conducting many affairs, the most famous with the poet Catullus, who reviles her even as he describes the pangs of his love. Such women were reluctant to have children and increasingly employed contraception and abortion to avoid childbirth.

During the Principate, Augustus's daughter and granddaughter, both named Julia, were the subject of scandal and they were punished for adultery. Augustus tried to restore Rome to an earlier ideal of decency and family integrity that reduced the power and sexual freedom of women. He also introduced legislation to encourage the procreation of children, but the new laws seem to have had little effect. In the first imperial century, several powerful women played an important, if unofficial, political role. Augustus's wife Livia had great influence during his reign, and he honored her with the title Augusta in his will. Even in the reign of her son (and Augustus's stepson) Tiberius, she exercised great influence. It was said that he fled Rome to live in Capri in order to escape her domination. The Emperor Claudius's wife Messalina took part in a plot to overthrow him. The Elder Agrippina, wife of the general Germanicus, was active in opposition to Tiberius, and her daughter, also called Agrippina, helped bring her son Nero to the throne. In later centuries, women were permitted to make wills and inherit from children. At the turn of the first century, the Emperor Domitian freed women from the need for guardianship.

Life in Imperial Rome: The Apartment House

The civilization of the Roman Empire depended on the vitality of its cities. The typical city had about 20,000 inhabitants, and perhaps only three or four had a population of more than 75,000. The population of Rome, however, was certainly greater than 500,000, perhaps more than a million. People coming to Rome for the first time found it overwhelming and its size, bustle, and noise either thrilled or horrified them. The rich lived in elegant homes called *domūs*. These were single-storied houses with plenty of space, an open central courtyard, and rooms designed for specific and different purposes, such as dining, sitting, or sleeping, in privacy and relative quiet. Though only a small portion of Rome's population lived in them, *domūs* took up as much as a third of the city's space. Public space for temples, markets, baths, gymnasiums, theaters, forums, and governmental buildings took up another quarter of Rome's territory.

This left less than half of Rome's area to house the mass of its inhabitants, who were squeezed into multiple dwellings that grew increasingly tall. Most Romans during the imperial period lived in apartment buildings called **insulae**, or "islands," that rose to a height of five or six stories and sometimes even more. The most famous of them, the Insula of Febiala, seems to have

"towered above the Rome of the Antonines like a skyscraper."[3]

These buildings were divided into separate apartments (*cenicula*) of undifferentiated rooms, the same plan on each floor. The apartments were cramped and uncomfortable. They had neither central heating nor open fireplaces; heat and fire for cooking came from small portable stoves. The apartments were hot in summer, cold in winter, and stuffy and smoky when the stoves were lit. There was no plumbing, so tenants needed to go into the streets to wells or fountains for water and to public baths and latrines, or to less regulated places. The higher up one lived, the more difficult were these trips, so chamber pots and commodes were kept in the rooms. These receptacles were emptied into vats on the staircase landings or in the alleys outside; on occasion, the contents, and even the containers, were tossed out the window. Roman satirists complained of the discomforts and dangers of walking the streets beneath such windows. Roman law tried to find ways to assign responsibilities for the injuries done to dignity and person.

Despite these difficulties, the attractions of the city and the shortage of space caused rents to rise, making life in the *insulae* buildings expensive, uncomfortable, and dangerous. The houses were lightly built of concrete and brick and were far too high for the limited area of their foundations, and so they often collapsed. Laws limiting the height of buildings were not always obeyed and did not, in any case, always prevent disaster. The satirist Juvenal did not exaggerate much when he wrote, "We inhabit a city held up chiefly by slats, for that is how the landlord patches up the cracks in the old wall, telling the tenants to sleep peacefully under the ruin that hangs over their heads." (See "Juvenal on Life in Rome," page 144.)

Even more serious was the threat of fire. Wooden beams supported the floors, and torches, candles, and oil lamps lit the rooms and braziers heated them. Fires broke out easily and, without running water, they usually led to disaster.

When we compare these apartments with the attractive public places in the city, we can understand why the Romans spent most of their time out of doors.

The Culture of the Early Empire

The years from 14 to 180 C.E. were a time of general prosperity and a flourishing material and artistic culture, but one not so brilliant and original as in the Age of Augustus.

Literature   In Latin literature, the period between the death of Augustus and the time of Marcus Aurelius is known as the Silver Age. As the name implies,

[3]J. Carcopino, *Daily Life in Ancient Rome* (New Haven, CT: Yale University Press, 1940), p. 26.

Map 5–3 **ANCIENT ROME** This map of Rome during the late empire shows the seven hills on and around which the city was built, as well as the major walls, bridges, and other public sites and buildings.

this age produced work of high quality although probably less high than in the Augustan era. In contrast to the hopeful, positive optimists of the Augustans, the writers of the Silver Age were gloomy, negative, and pessimistic. In the works of the former period, praise of the emperor, his achievements, and the world abounds; in the latter, criticism and satire lurk everywhere. Some of the most important writers of the Silver Age came from the Stoic opposition and reflected its hostility to the growing power and personal excesses of the emperors.

The writers of the second century C.E. appear to have turned away from contemporary affairs and even recent history. Historical writing was about remote periods so there would be less danger of irritating imperial sensibilities. Scholarship was encouraged, but we hear little of poetry, especially that dealing with dangerous subjects. In the third century C.E., romances written in Greek became popular and offer further evidence of the tendency of writers of the time to seek and offer escape from contemporary realities.

Architecture The main contribution of the Romans lay in two new kinds of buildings—the great public bath and a new freestanding kind of amphitheater—and in the advances in engineering that made these large struc-

tures possible. While keeping the basic post-and-lintel construction used by the Greeks, the Romans added to it the principle of the semicircular arch, borrowed from the Etruscans. They also made good use of concrete, a building material the Hellenistic Greeks first used and the Romans fully developed. The arch, combined with the post and lintel, produced the great Colosseum built by the Flavian emperors. When used internally in the form of vaults and domes, the arch permitted great buildings like the baths, of which the most famous and best preserved are those of the later emperors Caracalla (r. 211–217) and Diocletian (r. 284–305). (See Map 5–3.)

One of Rome's most famous buildings, the Pantheon, begun by Augustus's friend Agrippa and rebuilt by Hadrian, combined all these elements. Its portico of Corinthian columns is of Greek origin, but its rotunda of brick-faced concrete with its domed ceiling and relieving arches is thoroughly Roman. The new engineering also made possible the construction of more mundane, but useful, structures like bridges and aqueducts.

Society Seen from the harsh perspective of human history, the first two centuries of the Roman Empire deserve their reputation of a "golden age." One of the dark sides of Roman society, at least since the third century B.C.E., had been its increasing addiction to the brutal

JUVENAL ON LIFE IN ROME

The satirical poet Juvenal lived and worked in Rome in the late first and early second centuries C.E. His poems present a vivid picture of the material and cultural world of the Romans of his time. In the following passages, he tells of the discomforts and dangers of life in the city, both indoors and out.

What dangers awaited pedestrians in Juvenal's Rome? Who had responsibility for the condition of Rome? If the situation was as bad as he says, why was nothing done about it? Why did people choose to live in Rome at all under the conditions he describes?

Who, in Praeneste's cool, or the wooded Volsinian
   uplands,
Who, on Tivoli's heights, or a small town like
   Gabii, say,
Fears the collapse of his house? But Rome is
   supported on pipestems,
Matchsticks; it's cheaper, so, for the landlord to
   shore up his ruins,
Patch up the old cracked walls, and notify all the
   tenants
They can sleep secure, though the beams are in
   ruins above them.
No, the place to live is out there, where no cry of
   Fire!
Sounds the alarm of the night, with a neighbor
   yelling for water,
Moving his chattels and goods, and the whole
   third story is smoking.

Look at other things, the various dangers of
   nighttime.
How high it is to the cornice that breaks, and a
   chunk beats my brains out,
Or some slob heaves a jar, broken or cracked, from
   a window.
Bang! It comes down with a crash and proves its
   weight on the sidewalk.
You are a thoughtless fool, unmindful of sudden
   disaster,
If you don't make your will before you go out to
   have dinner.
There are as many deaths in the night as there are
   open windows
Where you pass by; if you're wise, you will pray, in
   your wretched devotions,
People may be content with no more than
   emptying slop jars.

From Juvenal, *The Satires of Juvenal*, trans. by Rolfe Humphries. Copyright © 1958 Indiana University Press, pp. 40, 43. Reprinted by permission of Indiana University Press.

contests involving gladiators. By the end of the first century C.E., emperors regularly appealed to this barbaric entertainment as a way of winning the acclaim of their people. On broader fronts in Roman society, by the second century C.E., troubles were brewing that foreshadowed the difficult times ahead. The literary efforts of the time reveal a flight from the present, from reality, and from the public realm to the past, to romance, and to private pursuits. Some of the same aspects may be seen in everyday life, especially in the decline of vitality in the local government.

In the first century C.E., members of the upper classes vied with one another for election to municipal office and for the honor of doing service to their communities. By the second century C.E., the emperors had to intervene to correct abuses in local affairs and even to force unwilling members of the ruling classes to accept public

office. Magistrates and council members were held personally and collectively responsible for the revenues due. Some magistrates even fled to avoid their office, a practice that became widespread in later centuries.

These difficulties reflected more basic problems. The prosperity that the end of civil war and the influx of wealth from the East brought could not sustain itself beyond the first half of the second century C.E. Population also appears to have declined for reasons that remain mysterious. The cost of government kept rising. The emperors were required to maintain a standing army, minimal in size, but costly, to keep the people in Rome happy with "bread and circuses," to pay for an increasingly numerous bureaucracy, and to wage expensive wars to defend the frontiers against dangerous and determined barbarian enemies. The ever-increasing need for money compelled the emperors to raise taxes, to press hard on their subjects, and to bring on inflation by debasing the coinage. These elements brought about the desperate crises that ultimately destroyed the empire.

▼ The Rise of Christianity

Christianity emerged, spread, survived, and ultimately conquered the Roman Empire despite its origin among poor people from an unimportant and remote province of the empire. Christianity faced the hostility of the established religious institutions of its native Judea. It also had to compete against the official cults of Rome and the highly sophisticated philosophies of the educated classes and against such other "**mystery**" **religions** as the cults of Mithra, Isis, and Osiris. The Christians also faced the opposition of the imperial government and formal persecution. Yet Christianity achieved toleration and finally exclusive command as the official religion of the empire.

Jesus of Nazareth

An attempt to understand this amazing outcome must begin with the story of Jesus of Nazareth. The most important evidence about his life is in the Gospel accounts, all of them written well after his death. The earliest, by Mark, is dated about 70 C.E. and the latest, by John, about 100 C.E. They are not, moreover, attempts at simply describing the life of Jesus with historical accuracy. Rather, they are statements of faith by true believers. The authors of the Gospels believed Jesus was the son of God and that he had come into the world to redeem humanity and to bring immortality to those who believed in him and followed his way. To the Gospel writers, Jesus' resurrection was striking proof of his teachings. At the same time, the Gospels regard Jesus as a figure in history, and they recount events in his life as well as his sayings.

There is no reason to doubt that Jesus was born in the province of Judea in the time of Augustus and that he was a most effective teacher in the tradition of the prophets. This tradition promised the coming of a **Messiah** (in Greek, *christos*—so Jesus Christ means "Jesus the Messiah"), the redeemer who would make Israel triumph over its enemies and establish the kingdom of God on earth. In fact, Jesus seems to have insisted the Messiah would not establish an earthly kingdom but would bring an end to the world as human beings knew it at the Day of Judgment. On that day, God would reward the righteous with immortality and happiness in heaven and condemn the wicked to eternal suffering in hell. Until then (a day his followers believed would come soon), Jesus taught the faithful to abandon sin and worldly concerns; to follow him and his way; to follow the moral code described in the Sermon on the Mount, which preached love, charity, and humility; and to believe in him and his divine mission.

Jesus won a considerable following, especially among the poor, which caused great suspicion among the upper classes. His novel message and his criticism of the religious practices connected with the temple at Jerusalem and its priests provoked the hostility of the religious establishment. A misunderstanding of the movement made it easy to convince the Roman governor, Pontius Pilate, that Jesus and his followers might be dangerous revolutionaries. He was put to death in Jerusalem by the cruel and degrading device of crucifixion, probably in 30 C.E. His followers believed he was resurrected on the third day after his death, and that belief became a critical element in the religion they propagated throughout the Roman Empire and beyond.

The new belief spread quickly to the Jewish communities of Syria and Asia Minor. It might, however, have had only a short life as a despised Jewish heresy were it not for the conversion and career of Paul.

Paul of Tarsus

Paul was born Saul, a citizen of the Cilician city of Tarsus in Asia Minor. He had been trained in Hellenistic culture and was a Roman citizen. But he was also a zealous member of the Jewish sect known as the **Pharisees**, the group that was most strict in its adherence to Jewish law. He took part in the persecution of the early Christians until his own conversion outside Damascus about 35 C.E., after which he changed his name from Saul to Paul.

The great problem facing the early Christians was to resolve their relationship to Judaism. If the new faith was a version of Judaism, then it must adhere to the Jewish law and seek converts only among Jews. James, called the brother of Jesus, was a conservative who held to that view, whereas the Hellenist Jews tended to see Christianity as a new and universal religion. To force all converts to follow Jewish law would have been fatal to the growth of the new sect. Jewish law's many technicalities and dietary prohibitions were strange to Gentiles, and the necessity of circumcision—a frightening, painful, and dangerous operation for adults—would have been a tremendous deterrent to conversion. Paul supported the position of the Hellenists and soon won many converts among the Gentiles. After some conflict within the sect, Paul won out. Consequently, the "apostle to the Gentiles" deserves recognition as a crucial contributor to the success of Christianity.

Paul believed that the followers of Jesus should be *evangelists* (messengers), to spread the gospel, or "good news," of God's gracious gift. He taught that Jesus would soon return for the Day of Judgment, and that all who would, should believe in him and accept his way.

CHARIOT RACING

FROM THEIR EARLIEST history the Romans enjoyed watching chariot races. As early as the period of the kings (seventh and sixth centuries B.C.E.), they built chariot racecourses, which they called "circuses" because of their curved or circular shape. Of these, the most famous, and one of the earliest, was the Circus Maximus ("largest"). Over the centuries politicians of the republic and, later, emperors of Rome, used the structures to provide such other free entertainments for the Roman public as trick riding displays and exhibitions and hunts of wild animals, but the chariot races were the most popular.

Spectators watched the races in tiers of seats along the two parallel sides of the course, which came together as a semicircle at one end. At the other end were stations called *carceres*, or barriers, for the chariots. Down the center of the course ran a fence that separated the two lanes for about two-thirds of the way, and at each end was a post around which the chariots had to make their turns. The races consisted of seven laps, the last one ending in a dash down the final straightaway. The full distance of a race in the Circus Maximus has been estimated at about 2.7 miles.

The earliest races may have been run for fun by rich aristocrats competing for glory, but the first written evidence shows the sport in the hands of racing companies called *factiones* who supplied the horses, chariots, and professional drivers. These companies were distinguished by their colors: At first there was only one red and one white company; later blue, green, purple, and gold *factiones* joined the competition. Each stable gained great numbers of fanatical supporters who bet large sums of money on the races. All kinds of devices were used to win. Horses were drugged; drivers were bribed or even poisoned when they refused a bribe.

Although various numbers of horses were used to pull the chariots at different times, the *quadriga*, or four-horse team, was the most common. The horse on the far left was the most important, because turns were made to the left and that horse's quick response was critical to the team's safety and success. As many as twelve chariots could compete in a race. Because of the short stretches, sharp turns, and crowded track, sheer speed was less important than strength, courage, and endurance. The races were dangerous to horse and rider, and the risk of collisions, falls, injury, and death appears to have provided the chief thrills to the Roman audience.

Why did Romans go to see the chariot races? Why did politicians and emperors sponsor them?

Romans bet heavily on the kind of chariot races shown on this low relief and were fanatically attached to their favorite riders and stables. © Araldo de Luca/CORBIS

Faith in Jesus as the Christ was necessary, but not sufficient, for salvation, nor could good deeds alone achieve it. That final blessing of salvation was a gift of God's grace that would be granted to all who asked for it.

Organization

Paul and the other apostles did their work well. The new religion spread throughout the Roman Empire and even beyond its borders. It had its greatest success in the cities and among the poor and uneducated. The rites of the early communities appear to have been simple and few. Baptism by water removed original sin and permitted participation in the community and its activities. The central ritual was a common meal called the *agape*, or "love feast," followed by the ceremony of the *Eucharist*, or "thanksgiving," a celebration of the Lord's Supper in which unleavened bread was eaten and unfermented wine was drunk. There were also prayers, hymns, or readings from the Gospels.

Not all the early Christians were poor, and the rich provided for the poor at the common meals. The sense of common love fostered in these ways focused the community's attention on the needs of the weak, the sick, the unfortunate, and the unprotected. This concern gave the early Christian communities a warmth and a human appeal that stood in marked contrast to the coldness and impersonality of the pagan cults. No less attractive were the promise of salvation, the importance to God of each human soul, and the spiritual equality of all in the new faith. As Paul put it, "There is neither Jew nor Greek, there is neither slave nor free, there is neither male nor female; for you are all one in Christ Jesus."[4]

The future of Christianity depended on its communities finding an organization that would preserve unity within the group and help protect it against enemies outside. At first, the churches had little formal organization. Soon, it appears, affairs were placed in the hands of boards of prebyters or "elders," and **deacons**, or "those who serve." By the second century C.E., as their numbers grew, the Christians of each city tended to accept the authority and leadership of **bishops** (*episkopoi*, or "overseers"). The congregations elected bishops to lead them in worship and to supervise funds. As time passed, the bishops extended their authority over the Christian communities in outlying towns and the countryside. The power and almost monarchical authority of the bishops were soon enhanced by the doctrine of **Apostolic Succession**, which asserted that ordination passed on the powers Jesus had given his original disciples from bishop to bishop.

The bishops kept in touch with one another, maintained communications between different Christian communities, and prevented doctrinal and sectarian splintering, which would have destroyed Christian

[4]Galatians 3:28, Revised Standard Version of the Bible.

This second-century statue in the Lateran Museum in Rome shows Jesus as the biblical Good Shepherd. "The Good Shepherd," marble, Height: as restored cm 99, as preserved cm 55, head cm 15.5. Late 3rd century A.D. Vatican Musuems, Pio-Christian Museum, Inv. 28590. Courtesy of the Vatican Museums

unity. They maintained internal discipline and dealt with the civil authorities. After a time they began the practice of coming together in councils to settle difficult questions, to establish orthodox opinion, and even to expel as **heretics** those who would not accept it. It is unlikely that Christianity could have survived the travails of its early years without such strong internal organization and government.

The Persecution of Christians

The new faith soon incurred the distrust of the pagan world and of the imperial government. At first, Christians were thought of as a Jewish sect and were therefore protected by Roman law. It soon became clear, however, that they were different, both mysterious and dangerous. They denied the existence of the pagan gods and so were accused of atheism. Their refusal to worship the emperor was judged treasonous. Because they kept mostly to themselves, took no part in civic affairs, engaged in secret rites, and had an organized network of local associations, they were misunderstood and suspected. The love feasts were erroneously reported to be scenes of sexual scandal. The alarming doctrine of the actual presence of Jesus' body in the Eucharist was distorted into an accusation of cannibalism.

The privacy and secrecy of Christian life and worship ran counter to a traditional Roman dislike of any private association, especially any of a religious nature. Christians thus earned the reputation of being "haters of humanity." Claudius expelled them from Rome, and Nero tried to make them scapegoats for the great fire that struck the city in 64 C.E. By the end of the first century, "the name alone"—that is, simple membership in the Christian community—was a crime.

But, for the most part, the Roman government did not take the initiative in attacking Christians in the first two centuries. When one governor sought instructions for dealing with the Christians, the emperor Trajan urged moderation. Christians were not to be sought out, anonymous accusations were to be disregarded, and anyone denounced could be acquitted merely by renouncing Christ and sacrificing to the emperor. (See "Compare & Connect: Christianity in the Roman Empire—Why Did the Romans Persecute the Christians?" on page 150.) Unfortunately, no true Christian could meet the conditions, and so there were martyrdoms.

Mobs, not the government, started most persecutions in this period, however. Though they lived quiet, inoffensive lives, some Christians must have seemed unbearably smug and self-righteous. Unlike the tolerant, easygoing pagans, who were generally willing to accept the new gods of foreign people and add them to the pantheon, the Christians denied the reality of the pagan gods. They proclaimed the unique rightness of their own way and looked forward to their own salvation and the damnation of nonbelievers. It is not surprising, therefore, that pagans disliked these strange and unsocial people, tended to blame misfortunes on them, and, in extreme cases, turned to violence. But even this adversity had its uses. It weeded out the weaklings among the Christians and brought greater unity to those who remained faithful. It also provided the Church with martyrs around whom legends could grow that would inspire still greater devotion and dedication.

The Emergence of Catholicism

Division within the Christian Church may have been an even greater threat to its existence than persecution from outside. Most Christians never accepted complex, intellectualized opinions but held to what even then were traditional, simple, conservative beliefs. This body of majority opinion, considered to be universal, or catholic, was enshrined by the church that came to be called Catholic. The Catholic Church's doctrines were deemed **orthodox**, that is, "holding the right opinions," whereas those holding contrary opinions were heretics.

The need to combat heretics, however, compelled the orthodox to formulate their own views more clearly and firmly. By the end of the second century C.E., an orthodox canon included the Old Testament, the Gospels, and the Epistles of Paul, among other writings. The process of creating a standard set of holy books was not completed for at least two more centuries, but a vitally important start had been made. The orthodox declared the Catholic Church itself to be the depository of Christian teaching and the bishops to be its receivers. They also drew up a **creed** or brief statements of faith to which true Christians should adhere.

In the first century, all that was required of one to be a Christian was to be baptized, to partake of the Eucharist, and to call Jesus the Lord. By the end of the second century, an orthodox Christian—that is, a member of the Catholic Church—was required to accept its creed, its canon of holy writings, and the authority of the bishops. The loose structure of the apostolic church had given way to an organized body with recognized leaders able to define its faith and to exclude those who did not accept it. Whatever the shortcomings of this development, it provided the clarity, unity, and discipline needed for survival.

Rome as a Center of the Early Church

During this same period, the church in Rome came to have special prominence. As the center of communications and the capital of the empire, Rome had natural advantages. After the Roman destruction of Jerusalem in 135 C.E., no other city had any convincing claim to primacy in the church. Besides having the largest single congregation of Christians, Rome also benefited from the tradition that Jesus' apostles Peter and Paul were martyred there.

Peter, moreover, was thought to be the first bishop of Rome. The Gospel of Matthew (16:18) reported Jesus' statement to Peter: "Thou art Peter [in Greek, *Petros*] and upon this rock [in Greek, *petra*] I will build my church." Eastern Christians might later point out that Peter had been the leader of the Christian community at Antioch before he went to Rome. But in the second century, the church at Antioch, along with the other Christian churches of Asia Minor, was fading in influence, and by 200 C.E., Rome was the most important center of Christianity. Because of the city's early influence and because of the Petrine doctrine derived from the Gospel of Matthew, later bishops of Rome claimed supremacy in the Catholic Church. But as the era of the "good emperors" came to a close, this controversy was far in the future.

▼ The Crisis of the Third Century

Dio Cassius, a historian of the third century C.E., described the Roman Empire after the death of Marcus Aurelius as declining from "a kingdom of gold into one of iron and rust." Although we have seen that the gold contained more than a little impurity, there is no reason to quarrel with Dio's assessment of his own time. Commodus (r. 180–192 C.E.), the son of Marcus Aurelius, proved the wisdom of the "good emperors" in selecting their successors for their talents rather than for family ties. Commodus was incompetent and autocratic. He reduced the respect in which the imperial office was held, and his assassination brought the return of civil war.

Barbarian Invasions

The pressure on Rome's frontiers reached massive proportions in the third century. In the East, a new power threatened the frontiers. In the third century B.C.E., the Parthians had made the Iranians independent of the Hellenistic kings and had established an empire of their own on the old foundations of the Persian Empire. Roman attempts to conquer them had failed, but as late as 198 C.E., the Romans could reach and destroy the Parthian capital and bring at least northern Mesopotamia under their rule.

In 224 C.E., however, a new Iranian dynasty, the Sassanians, seized control from the Parthians and brought new vitality to Persia. They soon recovered Mesopotamia in 260 C.E. and humiliated the Romans by taking the emperor Valerian (r. 253–260) prisoner; he died in captivity.

On the western and northern frontiers, the pressure came not from a well-organized rival empire, but from an ever-increasing number of German tribes. Though the Germans had been in contact with the Romans at least since the second century B.C.E., civilization had not much affected them. The men did no agricultural work, but confined their activities to hunting, drinking, and fighting. They were organized on a family basis by clans, hundreds, and tribes. Their leaders were chiefs, usually from a royal family, elected by the assembly of fighting men. The king was surrounded by a collection of warriors, whom the Romans called his *comitatus*. Always eager for plunder, these tough barbarians were attracted by the civilized delights they knew existed beyond the frontier of the Rhine and Danube Rivers.

The most aggressive of the Germans in the third century C.E. were the Goths. Centuries earlier they had wandered from their ancestral home near the Baltic Sea into southern Russia. In the 220s and 230s C.E., they began to put pressure on the Danube frontier. By about 250 C.E., they were able to penetrate the empire and overrun the Balkans. The need to meet this threat and the one the Persian Sassanids posed in the East made the Romans weaken their western frontiers, and other Germanic peoples—the Franks and the Alemanni—broke through in those regions. There was danger that Rome would be unable to meet this challenge.

The unprecedentedly numerous and simultaneous attacks, no doubt, caused Rome's perils but its internal weakness encouraged these attacks. The Roman army was not what it had been in its best days. By the second century C.E., it was made up mostly of romanized provincials. The pressure on the frontiers and epidemics of plague in the time of Marcus Aurelius forced the emperor to conscript slaves, gladiators, barbarians, and brigands. The training and discipline with which the Romans had conquered the Mediterranean world had declined. The Romans also failed to respond to the new conditions of constant pressure on all the frontiers. A strong, mobile reserve that could meet a threat in one place without causing a weakness elsewhere might have helped, but no such unit was created.

Septimius Severus (r. 193–211 C.E.) and his successors transformed the character of the Roman army. Septimius was a military usurper who owed everything to the support of his soldiers. He meant to establish a family dynasty, in contrast to the policy of the "good emperors" of the second century. He was prepared to make Rome into an undisguised military monarchy. Septimius drew recruits for the army increasingly from peasants of the less civilized provinces.

Economic Difficulties

These changes were a response to the great financial needs the barbarian attacks caused. Inflation had forced Commodus to raise the soldiers' pay. Yet the Severan emperors had to double it to keep up with prices, which increased the imperial budget by as much as 25 percent. To raise money, the emperors invented new taxes, debased the coinage, and even sold the palace furniture. But it was still hard to recruit troops. The new style of military life Septimius introduced—with its laxer discipline, more pleasant duties, and greater opportunity for advancement, not only in the army, but also in Roman society—was needed to attract men into the army. The policy proved effective for a short time but could not prevent the chaos of the late third century.

The same forces that caused problems for the army damaged society at large. The shortage of workers for the large farms, which had all but wiped out the independent family farm, reduced agricultural production. Distracted by external threats, the emperors were less able to preserve domestic peace. Piracy, brigandage, and the neglect of roads and harbors hampered trade. So, too, did the debasement of the coinage and the inflation in general. Imperial taxation and confiscations of the property of the rich removed badly needed capital from productive use.

More and more, the government had to demand services that had been given gladly in the past. Because the empire lived hand to mouth, with no significant reserve fund and no system of credit financing, the emperors had to compel the people to provide food, supplies, money, and labor. The upper classes in the cities were made to serve as administrators without pay and to meet deficits in revenue out of their own pockets. Sometimes these

COMPARE AND CONNECT

Christianity in the Roman Empire—
Why Did the Romans Persecute the Christians?

THE RISE OF Christianity and its spread throughout the Mediterranean presented a serious problem to the magistrates of the Roman Empire. Like most other pagans, the Romans were tolerant of most religious beliefs. Persecution on religious grounds was unusual among the Romans. The Christians, however, were very different from votaries of Isis, Mithra, Magna Mater, even from the Jews. The Romans did, in fact, persecute the Christians with varying degrees of severity. The following passages shed light on the character of and reasons for these persecutions.

QUESTIONS
1. Why did Nero blame the Christians?
2. On what grounds did Pliny punish the Christians?
3. What was the reaction of Trajan?
4. How did the approach of the two emperors compare?

I. The Persecution by Nero

In 64 C.E. a terrible fire broke out in Rome that destroyed a good part of the city. Here the historian Tacitus tells us how the Emperor Nero dealt with its aftermath.

The next thing was to seek means of propitiating the gods, and recourse was had to the Sibylline books, by the direction of which prayers were offered to Vulcanus, Ceres, and Proserpina. Juno, too, was entreated by the matrons, first, in the Capitol, then on the nearest part of the coast, whence water was procured to sprinkle the fane and image of the goddess. And there were sacred banquets and nightly vigils celebrated by married women. But all human efforts, all the lavish gifts of the emperor, and the propitiations of the gods, did not banish the sinister belief that the conflagration was the result of an order. Consequently, to get rid of the report, Nero fastened the guilt and inflicted the most exquisite tortures on a class hated for their abominations, called Christians by the populace. Christus, from whom the name had its origin, suffered the extreme penalty during the reign of Tiberius at the hands of one of our procurators, Pontius Pilatus, and a most mischievous superstition, thus checked for the moment, again broke out not only in Judaea, the first source of the evil, but even in Rome, where all things hideous and shameful from every part of the world find their centre and become popular. Accordingly, an arrest was first made of all who pleaded guilty; then, upon their information, an im-

mense multitude was convicted, not so much of the crime of firing the city, as of hatred against mankind. Mockery of every sort was added to their deaths. Covered with the skins of beasts, they were torn by dogs and perished, or were nailed to crosses, or were doomed to the flames and burnt, to serve as a nightly illumination, when daylight had expired.

Nero offered his gardens for the spectacle, and was exhibiting a show in the circus, while he mingled with the people in the dress of a charioteer or stood aloft on a car. Hence, even for criminals who deserved extreme and exemplary punishment, there arose a feeling of compassion; for it was not, as it seemed, for the public good, but to glut one man's cruelty, that they were being destroyed.

II. The Emperor Trajan and the Christians

Pliny the Younger was governor of the Roman province of Bithynia in Asia Minor about 112 C.E. Confronted by problems caused by Christians, he wrote to the Emperor Trajan to report his policies and to ask for advice. The following exchange between governor and empire provides evidence of the challenge Christianity posed to Rome and the Roman response.

TO THE EMPEROR TRAJAN

Having never been present at any trials of the Christians, I am unacquainted with the method and limits to be observed either in examining or punishing them.

Source: Tacitus, *Annals* 15. 44, trans. by A. J. Church and W. J. Brodribb, Modern Library, N.Y., 1942.

150

In the meanwhile, the method I have observed towards those who have been denounced to me as Christians is this: I interrogated them whether they were Christians; if they confessed it, I repeated the question twice again, adding the threat of capital punishment; if they still persevered, I ordered them to be executed. For whatever the nature of their creed might be, I could at least feel no doubt that contumacy and inflexible obstinacy deserved chastisement. There were others also possessed with the same infatuation, but being citizens of Rome, I directed them to be carried thither. . . .

TRAJAN TO PLINY

The method you have pursued, my dear Pliny, in sifting the cases of those denounced to you as Christians is extremely proper. It is not possible to lay down any general rule which can be applied as the fixed standard in all cases of this nature. No search should be made for these people, when they are denounced and found guilty they must be punished; with the restriction, however, that when the party denies himself to be a Christian, and shall give proof that he is not (that is, by adoring our Gods he shall be pardoned on the ground of repentance even though he may have formerly incurred suspicion). Informations without the accuser's name subscribed must not be admitted in evidence against anyone, as it is introducing a very dangerous precedent, and by no means agreeable to the spirit of the age.

Source: From Pliny the Younger, *Letters*, trans. by W. Melmoth, rev. by W. M. Hutchinson (London: William Heinemann, Ltd; Cambridge, MA: Harvard University Press, 1925).

Thrown to the lions in 275 C.E. by the Romans for refusing to recant his Christian beliefs, St. Mamai is an important martyr in the iconography of Georgia, a Caucasian kingdom that embraced Christianity early in the fourth century. This gilded silver medallion, made in Georgia in the eleventh century, depicts the saint astride a lion while he bears a cross in one hand, symbolizing his triumphant victory over death and ignorance. Kekelidze Institute, Tblisi, Georgia. Courtesy of the Library of Congress demands caused provincial rebellions, as in Egypt and Gaul. More typically, they caused peasants and even town administrators to flee to escape their burdens. All these difficulties weakened Rome's economic strength when it was most needed.

The Social Order

The new conditions caused important changes in the social order. Hostile emperors and economic losses decimated the Senate and the traditional ruling class. Men coming up through the army took their places. The whole state began to take on an increasingly military appearance. Distinctions among the classes by dress had been traditional since the republic; in the third and fourth centuries C.E., the people's everyday clothing became a kind of uniform that precisely revealed status. Titles were assigned to ranks in society as to ranks in the army. The most important distinction was the one Septimius Severus formally established, which drew a sharp line between the **honestiores** (senators, equestrians, the municipal aristocracy, and the soldiers) and the lower classes, or **humiliores**. Septimius gave the *honestiores* a privileged position before the law. They were given lighter punishments, could not be tortured, and alone had the right of appeal to the emperor.

As time passed, it became more difficult to move from the lower order to the higher, another example of the growing rigidity of the late Roman Empire. Peasants were tied to their lands, artisans to their crafts, soldiers to the army, merchants and shipowners to the needs of the state, and citizens of the municipal upper class to the collection and payment of increasingly burdensome taxes. Freedom and private initiative gave way before the needs of the state and its ever-expanding control of its citizens.

Civil Disorder

Commodus was killed on the last day of 192 C.E. The succeeding year was similar to the year 69. Three emperors ruled in swift succession, Septimius Severus emerging, as we have seen, to establish firm rule and a dynasty. The murder of Alexander Severus, the last of the dynasty, in 235 C.E., brought on a half century of internal anarchy and foreign invasion.

The empire seemed on the point of collapse. But the two conspirators who overthrew and succeeded the emperor Gallienus (r. 253–268) proved to be able soldiers. Claudius II Gothicus (268–270 C.E.) and Aurelian (270–275 C.E.) drove back the barbarians and stamped out internal disorder. The soldiers who followed Aurelian on the throne were good fighters who made significant changes in Rome's system of defense. Around Rome, Athens, and other cities, they built heavy walls that could resist barbarian attack. They drew back their best troops from the frontiers, relying chiefly on a newly organized heavy cavalry and a mobile army near the emperor's own residence.

Hereafter, mercenaries, who came from among the least civilized provincials and even from among the Germans, largely made up the army. The officers gave personal loyalty to the emperor rather than to the empire. These officers became a foreign, hereditary caste of aristocrats that increasingly supplied high administrators and even emperors. In effect, the Roman people hired an army of mercenaries, who were only technically Roman, to protect them.

▼ The Late Empire

During the fourth and fifth centuries, the Romans strove to meet the many challenges, internal and external, that threatened the survival of their empire. Growing pressure from barbarian tribes pushing against its frontier intensified the empire's tendency to smother individuality, freedom, and initiative, in favor of an intrusive and autocratic centralized monarchy. Economic and military weakness increased, and it became even harder to keep the vast empire together. Hard and dangerous times may well have helped the rise of Christianity, encouraging people to turn away from the troubles of this world to be concerned about the next.

The Fourth Century and Imperial Reorganization

The period from Diocletian (r. 284–305 C.E.) to Constantine (r. 306–337 C.E.) was one of reconstruction and reorganization after a time of civil war and turmoil. Diocletian was from Illyria (the former Yugoslavia of the twentieth century). A man of undistinguished birth, he rose to the throne through the ranks of the army. He knew that the job of defending and governing the entire empire was too great for one individual.

Diocletian therefore decreed the introduction of the **tetrarchy**, the rule of the empire by four men with power divided territorially. (See Map 5–4.) He allotted the provinces of Thrace, Asia, and Egypt to himself. His co-emperor, Maximian, shared with him the title of Augustus and governed Italy, Africa, and Spain. In addition, two men were given the subordinate title of Caesar: Galerius, who was in charge of the Danube frontier and the Balkans, and Constantius, who governed Britain and Gaul. This arrangement not only afforded a good solution to the military problem but also provided for a peaceful succession.

Diocletian was the senior Augustus, but each tetrarch was supreme in his own sphere. The Caesars were recognized as successors to each half of the empire, and marriages to daughters of the Augusti enhanced their loyalty. It was a return, in a way, to the precedent of the

Map 5–4   **DIVISIONS OF THE ROMAN EMPIRE UNDER DIOCLETIAN**   Diocletian divided the sprawling empire into four prefectures for more effective government and defense. The inset map shows their boundaries, and the larger map gives some details of regions and provinces. The major division between the East and the West was along the line running south between Pannonia and Moesia.

"good emperors" of 96 to 180 C.E., who chose their successors from the ranks of the ablest men. It seemed to promise orderly and peaceful transitions instead of assassinations, chaos, and civil war.

Each man established his residence and capital at a place convenient for frontier defense, and none chose Rome. The effective capital of Italy became the northern city of Milan. Diocletian beautified Rome by constructing his monumental baths, but he visited the city only once and made his own capital at Nicomedia in Asia Minor. This was another step in the long leveling process that had reduced the eminence of Rome and Italy. It was also evidence of the growing importance of the East.

In 305 C.E., Diocletian retired and compelled his co-emperor to do the same. But his plan for a smooth succession failed. In 310, there were five Augusti and no Caesars. Out of this chaos, Constantine, son of Constantius, produced order. In 324, he defeated his last op-

ponent and made himself sole emperor, uniting the empire once again; he reigned until 337. Mostly, Constantine carried forward the policies of Diocletian. He supported Christianity, however, which Diocletian had tried to suppress.

Development of Autocracy   Diocletian and Constantine carried the development of the imperial office toward **autocracy** to the extreme. The emperor ruled by decree, consulting only a few high officials whom he himself appointed. The Senate had no role whatever, and the elimination of all distinctions between senator and equestrian further diminished its dignity.

The emperor was a remote figure surrounded by carefully chosen high officials. He lived in a great palace and was almost unapproachable. Those admitted to his presence had to prostrate themselves before him and kiss the hem of his robe, which was purple and had golden threads woven through it. The emperor was addressed

This porphyry sculpture on the corner of the church of San Marco in Venice shows Emperor Diocletian (r. 284–305 C.E.) and his three imperial colleagues. Dressed for battle, they clasp one another to express their mutual solidarity. John Heseltine © Dorling Kindersley

as *dominus*, or "lord," and his right to rule was not derived from the Roman people, but from heaven. All this remoteness and ceremony had a double purpose: to enhance the dignity of the emperor and to safeguard him against assassination.

Constantine erected the new city of Constantinople on the site of ancient Byzantium on the Bosporus, which leads to both the Aegean and Black Seas. He made it the new capital of the empire. Its strategic location was excellent for protecting the eastern and Danubian frontiers, and, surrounded on three sides by water, it was easily defended. This location also made it easier to carry forward the policies that fostered autocracy and Christianity. Rome was full of tradition, the center of senatorial and even republican memories, and of pagan worship. Constantinople was free from both, and its dedication in 330 C.E. marked the beginning of a new era. Until its fall to the Turks in 1453, it served as a bastion of civilization, the preserver of classical culture, a bulwark against barbarian attack, and the greatest city in Christendom.

A civilian bureaucracy, carefully separated from the military to reduce the chances of rebellion by anyone combining the two kinds of power, carried out the autocratic rule of the emperors. Below the emperor's court, the most important officials were the *praetorian* prefects, each of whom administered one of the four major areas into which the empire was divided: Gaul, Italy, Illyricum,

and the Orient. The four prefectures were subdivided into twelve territorial units called *dioceses*, each under a vicar subordinate to the prefect. The dioceses were further divided into almost a hundred provinces, each under a provincial governor.

A vast system of spies and secret police, without whom the increasingly rigid organization could not be trusted to perform, supervised the entire system. Despite these efforts, the system was corrupt and inefficient.

The cost of maintaining a 400,000-man army, as well as the vast civilian bureaucracy, the expensive imperial court, and the imperial taste for splendid buildings strained an already weak economy. Diocletian's attempts to establish a reliable currency failed, leading instead to increased inflation. To deal with it, he resorted to price control with his Edict of Maximum Prices in 301 C.E. For each product and each kind of labor, a maximum price was set, and violations were punishable by death. The edict still failed.

Peasants unable to pay their taxes and officials unable to collect them tried to escape. Diocletian resorted to stern regimentation to keep all in their places and at the service of the government. The terror of the third century forced many peasants to seek protection in the *villa*, or "country estate," of a large and powerful landowner and to become tenant farmers. As social boundaries hardened, these *coloni* and their descendants became increasingly tied to their estates.

The Arch of Constantine. Built in 315 C.E., it represents a transition between classical and medieval, pagan and Christian. Many of the sculptures incorporated in it were taken from earlier works dating to the first and second centuries. Others, contemporary with the arch, reflect new, less refined style. Scala/Art Resource, NY

REIGNS OF SELECTED LATE EMPIRE RULERS (ALL DATES ARE C.E.)

180–192	Commodus
193–211	Septimius Severus
222–235	Alexander Severus
249–251	Decius
253–259	Valerian
259 (253)–268	Gallienus
268–270	Claudius II Gothicus
270–275	Aurelian
284–305	Diocletian
306–337	Constantine (sole emperor after 324)
337–361	Constantius II
361–363	Julian the Apostate
364–375	Valentinian I
364–378	Valens
379–395	Theodosius I

Division of the Empire The peace and unity Constantine established did not last long. Constantius II (r. 337–361 C.E.) won the struggle for succession after his death. Constantius's death, in turn, left the empire to his young cousin Julian (r. 361–363 C.E.), whom Christians called the Apostate because of his attempt to stamp out Christianity and restore paganism. Julian undertook a campaign against Persia to put a Roman on the throne of the Sassanids and end the Persian menace once and for all. He penetrated deep into Persia but was killed in battle. His death ended the expedition and the pagan revival.

The Germans in the West took advantage of the eastern campaign to attack along the Rhine and upper Danube Rivers. In addition, even greater trouble was brewing along the middle and upper Danube. (See Map 5–5.) The eastern Goths, known as the Ostrogoths, occupied that territory. They were being pushed hard by their western cousins, the Visigoths, who in turn had been driven from their home in the Ukraine by the fierce Huns, a nomadic people from central Asia. (See "Ammianus Marcellinus Describes the People Called Huns," page 157.)

Map 5–5 **THE EMPIRE'S NEIGHBORS** In the fourth century the Roman Empire was nearly surrounded by ever more threatening neighbors. The map shows who these so-called barbarians were and where they lived before their armed contact with the Romans.

The emperor Valentinian I (r. 364–375 C.E.) saw he could not defend the empire alone and appointed his brother Valens (r. 364–378 C.E.) as co-ruler. Valentinian made his own headquarters at Milan and spent the rest of his life fighting and defeating the Franks and the Alemanni in the West. Valens was given control of the East. The empire was once again divided in two. The two emperors maintained their own courts, and the halves of the empire became increasingly separate and different. Latin was the language of the West and Greek of the East.

In 376, the Visigoths, pursued by the Huns, won rights of settlement and material assistance within the empire from the eastern emperor Valens (r. 364–378) in exchange for defending the eastern frontier as *foederati*, or special allies of the empire. The Visigoths, however, did not keep their bargain with the Romans and plundered the Balkan provinces. Nor did the Romans comply. They treated the Visigoths cruelly, even forcing them to trade their children for dogs to eat. Valens attacked the Goths and died, along with most of his army, at Adrianople in Thrace in 378. Theodosius I (r. 379–395 C.E.), an able and experienced general, was named co-ruler in the East. By a combination of military and diplomatic skills, he pacified the Goths, giving them land and autonomy and enrolling many of them in his army. He made important military reforms, putting greater emphasis on the cavalry. Theodosius tried to unify the empire again, but his death in 395 left it divided and weak.

The Rural West The two parts of the empire went their different ways. The West became increasingly rural as barbarian invasions intensified. The *villa*, a fortified country estate, became the basic unit of life. There, *coloni* gave their services to the local magnate in return for economic assistance and protection from both barbarians and imperial officials. Many cities shrank to no more than tiny walled fortresses ruled by military commanders and bishops. The upper classes moved to the country and asserted an ever-greater independence from imperial authority. The failure of the central authority to maintain the roads and the constant danger from bands of robbers curtailed trade and communications, forcing greater self-reliance and a more primitive lifestyle.

The new world emerging in the West by the fifth century and afterwards was increasingly made up of isolated units of rural aristocrats and their dependent laborers. The only institution providing a high degree of unity was the Christian Church. The pattern for the early Middle Ages in the West was already formed.

The Byzantine East In the East the situation was different. Constantinople became the center of a vital and flourishing culture we call *Byzantine* that lasted until the fifteenth century. Because of its defensible location, the skill of its emperors, and the firmness and strength of its base in Asia Minor, it could deflect and repulse barbarian attacks. A strong navy allowed commerce to flourish in the eastern Mediterranean and, in good times, far beyond. Cities continued to prosper, and the emperors made their will good over the nobles in the countryside. The civilization of the Byzantine Empire was a unique combination of classical culture, the Christian religion, Roman law, and Eastern artistic influences. (See Chapter 6.)

While barbarians overran the West, the Roman Empire, in altered form, persisted in the East. While Rome shrank to an insignificant ecclesiastical town, Constantinople flourished as the seat of the empire, the "New Rome." Indeed, the Byzantines even called themselves "Romans." When we contemplate the decline and fall of the Roman Empire in the fourth and fifth centuries, we are speaking only of the West. A form of classical culture persisted in the Byzantine East for a thousand years more.

The Triumph of Christianity

The rise of Christianity to dominance in the empire was closely connected with the political and cultural experience of the third and fourth centuries. Political chaos and decentralization had religious and cultural consequences.

Religious Currents in the Empire In some provinces, native languages replaced Latin and Greek, sometimes even for official purposes. The classical tradition that had been the basis of imperial life became the exclusive possession of a small, educated aristocracy. In religion, the public cults had grown up in an urban environment and were largely political in character. As the importance of the cities diminished, so did the significance of their gods. People might still take comfort in the wor-

---

THE TRIUMPH OF CHRISTIANITY

ca. 4 B.C.E.	Jesus of Nazareth born
ca. 30 C.E.	Crucifixion of Jesus
64 C.E.	Fire at Rome: persecution by Nero
ca. 70–100 C.E.	Gospels written
ca. 250–260 C.E.	Severe persecutions by Decius and Valerian
303 C.E.	Persecution by Diocletian
311 C.E.	Galerius issues Edict of Toleration
312 C.E.	Battle of Milvian Bridge; conversion of Constantine to Christianity
325 C.E.	Council of Nicaea
395 C.E.	Christianity becomes official religion of Roman Empire

AMMIANUS MARCELLINUS DESCRIBES THE PEOPLE CALLED HUNS

Ammianus Marcellinus was born about 330 C.E. in Syria, where Greek was the language of his well-to-do family. After a military career, he lived in Rome and wrote an encyclopedic Latin history of the empire, covering the years 96 to 378 C.E., giving special emphasis to the difficulties of the fourth century. Here he describes the Huns, one of the barbarous peoples pressing on the frontiers. Like most Romans, he was appalled by these nomadic peoples. His account combines observation, hearsay, and prejudice, and it is not always easy to separate facts from fantasy.

How did the culture of the Huns differ from that of the Romans? How did their way of life give them an advantage against Rome? How was it disadvantageous? Which of the writer's statements do you think are factual?

The people called Huns, barely mentioned in ancient records, live beyond the sea of Azof, on the border of the Frozen Ocean, and are a race savage beyond all parallel. At the very moment of birth the cheeks of their infant children are deeply marked by an iron, in order that the hair, instead of growing at the proper season on their faces, may be hindered by the scars; accordingly the Huns grow up without beards, and without any beauty. They all have closely knit and strong limbs and plump necks; they are of great size, and low legged, so that you might fancy them two-legged beasts or the stout figures which are hewn out in a rude manner with an ax on the posts at the end of bridges.

They are certainly in the shape of men, however uncouth, and are so hardy that they neither require fire nor well-flavored food, but live on the roots of such herbs as they get in the fields, or on the half-raw flesh of any animal, which they merely warm rapidly by placing it between their own thighs and the backs of their horses.

They never shelter themselves under roofed houses, but avoid them, as people ordinarily avoid sepulchers as things not fit for common use. Nor is there even to be found among them a cabin thatched with reeds; but they wander about, roaming over the mountains and the woods, and accustom themselves to bear frost and hunger and thirst from their very cradles. . . .

There is not a person in the whole nation who cannot remain on his horse day and night. On horseback they buy and sell, they take their meat and drink, and there they recline on the narrow neck of their steed, and yield to sleep so deep as to indulge in every variety of dream.

And when any deliberation is to take place on any weighty matter, they all hold their common council on horseback. They are not under kingly authority, but are contented with the irregular government of their chiefs, and under their lead they force their way through all obstacles.

From Ammianus Marcellinus, *Res Gestae*, trans. by C. D. Yonge (London: George Bell and Son, 1862), pp. 312–314.

---

ship of the friendly, intimate deities of family, field, hearth, storehouse, and craft, but these gods were too petty to serve their needs in a confused and frightening world. The only universal worship was of the emperor, but he was far off, and obeisance to his cult was more a political than a religious act.

In the troubled fourth and fifth centuries, people sought powerful, personal deities who would bring them safety and prosperity in this world and immortality in the next. Paganism was open and tolerant. Many people worshipped new deities alongside the old and even intertwined elements of several to form a new amalgam by the device called **syncretism**.

Manichaeism was an especially potent rival of Christianity. Named for its founder, Mani, a Persian who lived in the third century C.E., this movement contained aspects of various religious traditions, including Zoroastrianism from Persia and both Judaism and Christianity. The Manichaeans pictured a world in which light and darkness, good and evil, were constantly at war. Good was spiritual and evil was material. Because human beings were made of matter, their bodies were a prison of evil and darkness, but they also contained an element of light and good. The "Father of Goodness" had sent Mani, among other prophets, to free humanity and gain its salvation. To achieve salvation, humans must want to reach the realm of light and abandon all physical desires. Manichaeans led an ascetic life and practiced a simple worship guided by a well-organized church. The movement reached its greatest strength in the fourth and fifth centuries, and some of its central ideas persisted into the Middle Ages.

Christianity had something in common with these cults and answered many of the same needs their devotees felt. None of them, however, attained Christianity's universality, and none appears to have given the early Christians as much competition as the ancient philosophies or the state religion.

Imperial Persecution By the third century, Christianity had taken firm hold in the eastern provinces and in Italy. It had not made much headway in the West, however. (See Map 5–6.) Christian apologists pointed out that Christians were good citizens who differed from others only in not worshipping the public gods. Until the middle of the third century, the emperors tacitly accepted this view, without granting official toleration. As times became bad and the Christians became more numerous and visible, that policy changed. Popular opinion blamed disasters, natural and military, on the Christians.

About 250, the emperor Decius (r. 249–251 C.E.) invoked the aid of the gods in his war against the Goths and required all citizens to worship the state gods publicly. True Christians could not obey, and Decius started a major persecution. Many Christians—even some bishops—yielded to threats and torture, but others held out and were killed. Valerian (r. 253–260 C.E.) resumed the persecutions, partly to confiscate the wealth of rich Christians. His successors, however, found other matters more pressing, and the persecution lapsed until the end of the century.

By the time of Diocletian, the increasing number of Christians included high officials. But hostility to the Christians had also grown on every level. Diocletian was not generous toward unorthodox intellectual or religious movements. His own effort to bolster imperial power with the aura of divinity boded ill for the church, and in 303 he launched the most serious persecution inflicted on the Christians in the Roman Empire. He confiscated church property and destroyed churches and their sacred books. He deprived upper-class Christians of public office and judicial rights, imprisoned clergy, and enslaved Christians of the lower classes. He fined anyone refusing to sacrifice to the public gods. A final decree required public sacrifices

MAP EXPLORATION

Interactive map: To explore this map further, go to
www.myhistorylab.com

(A) 200

Christian Areas, 200

(B) 200 – 400

Christian Areas, 200
Expansion, 200 – 400

(C) 400 – 600

Christian Areas, 400
Expansion, 400 – 600

Map 5–6 **THE SPREAD OF CHRISTIANITY** Christianity grew swiftly in the third, fourth, fifth, and sixth centuries—especially after the conversion of the emperors in the fourth century. By 600, on the eve of the birth of the new religion of Islam, Christianity was dominant throughout the Mediterranean world and most of western Europe.

and libations. The persecution horrified many pagans, and the plight and the demeanor of the martyrs aroused pity and sympathy.

Ancient states could not carry out a program of terror with the thoroughness of modern totalitarian governments, so the Christians and their church survived to enjoy what they must have considered a miraculous change of fortune. In 311, Galerius, who had been one of the most vigorous persecutors, was influenced, perhaps by his Christian wife, to issue the Edict of Toleration, permitting Christian worship.

The victory of Constantine and his emergence as sole ruler of the empire changed the condition of Christianity from a precariously tolerated sect to the religion the emperor favored. This put it on the path to becoming the official and only legal religion in the empire.

Emergence of Christianity as the State Religion

The sons of Constantine continued to favor the new religion, but the succession of Julian the Apostate in 360 posed a new threat. He was a devotee of traditional classical pagan culture and, as a believer in **Neoplatonism**, an opponent of Christianity. Neoplatonism was a religious philosophy, or a philosophical religion, whose connection with Platonic teachings was distant. Its chief formulator was Plotinus (205–270 C.E.), who tried to combine classical and rational philosophical speculation with the mystical spirit of his time. Plotinus's successors were bitter critics of Christianity, and their views influenced Julian. Though he refrained from persecution, he tried to undo the work of Constantine by withdrawing the privileges of the church, removing Christians from high offices, and introducing a new form of pagan worship. His reign, however, was short, and his work did not last.

In 394, Theodosius forbade the celebration of pagan cults and abolished the pagan religious calendar. At his death, Christianity was the official religion of the Roman Empire.

The establishment of Christianity as the state religion did not put an end to the troubles of the Christians and their church; instead, it created new ones and complicated some old ones. The favored position of the church attracted converts for the wrong reasons and diluted the moral excellence and spiritual fervor of its adherents. The problem of the relationship between church and state arose, presenting the possibility that religion would become subordinate to the state, as it had been in the classical world and in earlier civilizations. In the East, that largely happened.

In the West, the weakness of the emperors permitted church leaders to exercise remarkable independence. In 390, Ambrose, bishop of Milan, excommunicated Theodosius I for a massacre he had carried out, and the emperor did penance. This act provided an important precedent for future assertions of the church's autonomy and authority, but it did not end secular interference and influence in the church.

Arianism and the Council of Nicaea

Internal divisions proved to be even more troubling as new heresies emerged. Because they threatened the unity of an empire that was now Christian, they inevitably involved the emperor and the powers of the state. Before long, the world would see Christians persecuting other Christians with a zeal at least as great as the most fanatical pagans had displayed against them.

Among the many controversial views that arose, the most important and the most threatening was **Arianism**. A priest named Arius of Alexandria (ca. 280–336 C.E.) founded it. The issue creating difficulty was the relation of God the Father to God the Son. Arius argued that Jesus was a created being, unlike God the Father. He was, therefore, not made of the substance of God and was not eternal. "The Son has a beginning," he said, "but God is without beginning." For Arius, Jesus was neither fully man nor fully God, but something in between. Arius's view did away with the mysterious concept of the Trinity, the difficult doctrine that holds that God is three persons (the Father, the Son, and the Holy Spirit) and also one in substance and essence.

The Arian concept appeared simple, rational, and philosophically acceptable. To its ablest opponent, Athanasius, however, it had serious shortcomings. Athanasius (ca. 293–373 C.E.), later bishop of Alexandria, saw the Arian view as an impediment to any acceptable theory of salvation, to him the most important religious question. He adhered to the old Greek idea of salvation as involving the change of sinful mortality into divine immortality through the gift of "life." Only if Jesus were both fully human and fully God could the transformation of humanity to divinity have taken place in him and be transmitted by him to his disciples. "Christ was made man," he said, "that we might be made divine."

To deal with the controversy, Constantine called a council of Christian bishops at Nicaea, not far from Constantinople, in 325. For the emperor the question was essentially political, but for the disputants salvation was at stake. At Nicaea, Athanasius's view won out, became orthodox, and was embodied in the Nicene Creed. But Arianism persisted and spread. Some later emperors were either Arians or sympathetic to that view. Some of the most successful missionaries to the barbarians were Arians; as a result, many of the German tribes that overran the empire were Arians. The Christian emperors hoped to bring unity to their increasingly decentralized realms by imposing a single religion. Over time it did prove to be a unifying force, but it also introduced divisions where none had existed before.

▼ Arts and Letters in the Late Empire

The art and literature of the late empire reflect the confluence of pagan and Christian ideas and traditions and the conflict between them. Much of the literature is polemical and much of the art is propaganda.

A military revolution led by provincials whose origins were in the lower classes saved the empire from the chaos of the third century. They brought with them the fresh winds of cultural change, which blew out not only the dust of classical culture, but much of its substance as well. Yet the new ruling class was not interested in leveling; it wanted instead to establish itself as a new aristocracy. It thought of itself as effecting a great restoration rather than a revolution and sought to restore classical culture and absorb it. The comfort of Christianity tempered the confusion and uncertainty of the times. But the new ruling class also sought order and stability—ethical, literary, and artistic—in the classical tradition.

The Preservation of Classical Culture

One of the main needs and accomplishments of this period was the preservation of classical culture. Ways were discovered to make it available and useful to the newly arrived ruling class. Works of the great classical authors were reproduced in many copies and were transferred from perishable and inconvenient papyrus rolls to sturdier codices, bound volumes that were as easy to use as modern books. Scholars also digested long works like Livy's *History of Rome* into shorter versions, wrote learned commentaries, and compiled grammars. Original works by pagan writers of the late empire were neither numerous nor especially distinguished.

Christian Writers

The late empire, however, did see a great outpouring of Christian writings, including many examples of Christian apologetics, in poetry and prose, and sermons, hymns, and biblical commentaries. Christianity could also boast important scholars. Jerome (348–420 C.E.),

This late-Roman ivory plaque shows a scene from Christ's Passion. The art of the late empire was transitional between the classical past and the medieval future.   Crucifixion, carving, c. 420 A.D. (ivory). British Museum, London, UK/Bridgeman Art Library

thoroughly trained in classical Latin literature and rhetoric, produced a revised version of the Bible in Latin. Commonly called the **Vulgate**, it became the Bible the Catholic Church used. Probably the most important eastern scholar was Eusebius of Caesarea (ca. 260–340 C.E.). He wrote apologetics, an idealized biography of Constantine, and a valuable chronology of important events in the past. His most important contribution, however, was his *Ecclesiastical History*, an attempt to set forth the Christian view of history. He saw all of history as the working out of God's will. History, therefore, had a purpose and a direction, and Constantine's victory and the subsequent unity of empire and church were its culmination.

The closeness and also the complexity of the relationship between classical pagan culture and that of the Christianity of the late empire are nowhere better displayed than in the career and writings of Augustine (354–430 C.E.), bishop of Hippo in North Africa. He was born at Carthage and was trained as a teacher of rhetoric. His father was a pagan, but his mother was a Christian, and hers was ultimately the stronger influence. He passed through several intellectual way stations—skepticism and Neoplatonism among others—before his conversion to Christianity. His training and skill in pagan rhetoric and philosophy made him peerless among his contemporaries as a defender of Christianity and as a theologian.

His greatest works are his *Confessions*, an autobiography describing the road to his conversion, and *The City of God*. The latter was a response to the pagan charge that the abandonment of the old gods and the advent of Christianity caused the Visigoths' sack of Rome in 410. The optimistic view some Christians held that God's will worked its way in history and was easily comprehensible needed further support in the face of this calamity. Augustine sought to separate the fate of Christianity from that of the Roman Empire. He contrasted the secular world, the City of Man, with the spiritual, the City of God. The former was selfish, the latter unselfish; the former evil, the latter good.

Augustine argued that history was moving forward, in the spiritual sense, to the Day of Judgment, but there was no reason to expect improvement before then in the secular sphere. The fall of Rome was neither surprising nor important. All states, even a Christian Rome, were part of the City of Man and were therefore corrupt and mortal. Only the City of God was immortal, and it, consisting of all the saints on earth and in heaven, was untouched by earthly calamities.

Though the *Confessions* and *The City of God* are Augustine's most famous works, they emphasize only a part of his thought. His treatises *On the Trinity* and *On Christian Education* reveal the great skill with which he supported Christian belief with the learning, logic, and philosophy of the pagan classics. Augustine believed faith is essential and primary (a thoroughly Christian view), but it is not a substitute for reason (the foundation of classical thought). Instead, faith is the starting point for, and liberator of, human reason, which continues to be the means by which people can understand what faith reveals. His writings constantly reveal the presence of both Christian faith and pagan reason, as well as the tension between them, a legacy he left to the Middle Ages.

▼ The Problem of the Decline and Fall of the Empire in the West

Whether important to Augustine or not, the massive barbarian invasions of the fifth century put an end to effective imperial government in the West. For centuries people have speculated about the causes of the collapse of the ancient world. Every kind of reason has been put forward, and some suggestions seem to have nothing to do with reason at all. Exhaustion of the soil, plague, climatic change, and even poisoning by lead water pipes have been suggested as reasons for Rome's decline in population, vigor, and the capacity to defend itself. Some blame the slavery and a resulting failure to make advances in science and technology. Others blame excessive government interference in the economic life of the empire and still others the destruction of the urban middle class, the carrier of classical culture.

A simpler and more obvious explanation might begin with the observation that the growth of so mighty an empire as Rome's was by no means inevitable. Rome's greatness had come from conquests that provided the Romans with the means to expand still further, until there were not enough Romans to conquer and govern any more peoples and territory. When pressure from outsiders grew, the Romans lacked the resources to advance and defeat the enemy as in the past. The tenacity and success of their resistance for so long were remarkable. Without new conquests to provide the immense wealth needed to defend and maintain internal prosperity, the Romans finally yielded to unprecedented onslaughts by fierce and numerous attackers.

To blame the ancients and slavery for the failure to produce an industrial and economic revolution like that of the later Western world (one capable of producing wealth without taking it from another) is to stand the problem on its head. No one yet has a satisfactory explanation for those revolutions. So it is improper to blame any institution or society for not achieving what has been achieved only once in human history. Perhaps we would do well to think of the problem as did Edward

Gibbon, the author of the great eighteenth-century study of Rome's collapse and transformation:

The decline of Rome was the natural and inevitable effect of immoderate greatness. Prosperity ripened the principle of decay; the cause of the destruction multiplied with the extent of conquest; and, as soon as time or accident had removed the artificial supports, the stupendous fabric yielded to the pressure of its own weight. The story of the ruin is simple and obvious; and instead of inquiring why the Roman Empire was destroyed, we should rather be surprised that it had subsisted so long.[5]

In Perspective

Out of the civil wars and chaos that brought down the republic, Augustus brought unity, peace, order, and prosperity. As a result, he was regarded with almost religious awe and attained more military and political power than any Roman before him. He ruled firmly, but with moderation. He tried to limit military adventures and the costs they incurred. His public works encouraged trade and communications. He tried to restore and invigorate the old civic pride, and in this he had much success. He was less successful in promoting private morality based on family values. He patronized the arts to beautify Rome and glorify his reign. On his death, Augustus was able to pass on the regime to his family, the Julio-Claudians.

For almost two hundred years, with a few brief interruptions, the empire was generally prosperous, peaceful, and well run. But problems grew. Management of the many responsibilities the government assumed required the growth of a large bureaucracy that placed a heavy and increasing burden on the treasury, required higher taxes, and stifled both civic spirit and private enterprise. Pressure from barbarians on the frontiers required a large standing army, which led to further taxation.

In the late empire, Rome's rulers resorted to many devices for dealing with their problems. More and more, the emperors' rule and their safety depended on the loyalty of the army, so they courted the soldiers' favor with gifts. This only increased the burden of taxes; the rich and powerful found ways to avoid their obligations, increasing the load on everyone else. The government's control over the lives of its people became ever greater and the society more rigid as people tried to flee to escape the crushing load of taxes. Expedients were tried, including inflating the currency, fixing farmers to the soil as serfs or *coloni*, building walls to keep the barbarians out, and bribing barbarian tribes to fight for Rome

against other barbarians. Ultimately, all these measures failed. The Roman Empire in the west fell, leaving disunity, insecurity, disorder, and poverty. Like similar empires in the ancient world, it had been unable to sustain its "immoderate greatness."

REVIEW QUESTIONS

1. What solutions did Augustus provide for the political problems that had plagued the Roman Republic? Why was the Roman population willing to accept Augustus as head of the state?
2. How was the Roman Empire organized and why did it function smoothly? What role did the emperor play in maintaining political stability?
3. How did the literature in the Golden Age of Augustus differ from that of the Silver Age during the first and second centuries C.E.? How did the poetry of Vergil and Horace contribute to Augustus's rule?
4. Why did the Roman authorities persecute Christians? What were the more important reasons for Christianity's success?
5. What political, social, and economic problems beset Rome in the third and fourth centuries C.E.? How did Diocletian and Constantine deal with them? Were they effective in stemming the tide of decline and disintegration in the Roman Empire? What problems were they unable to solve?
6. What theories have scholars advanced to explain the decline and fall of the Roman Empire. What are the difficulties involved in explaining the fall? What explanation would you give?

SUGGESTED READINGS

W. Ball, *Rome in the East* (2000). A study of the eastern parts of the empire and how they interacted with the West.

A. A. Barrett, *Livia: First Lady of Imperial Rome* (2004). Biography of Augustus's powerful and controversial wife.

P. Brown, *The Rise of Western Christendom: Triumph and Diversity, 200–1000*, 2nd ed. (2003). A vivid picture of the spread of Christianity by a master of the field.

A. Ferrill, *The Fall of the Roman Empire, The Military Explanation* (1986). An interpretation that emphasizes the decline in the quality of the Roman army.

K. Galinsky, *Augustan Culture* (1996). A work that integrates art, literature, and politics.

E. Gibbon, *The History of the Decline and Fall of the Roman Empire*, 7 vols., ed. by J. B. Bury, 2nd ed. (1909–1914). A masterwork of the English language.

D. Johnston, *Roman Law in Context* (2000). Places Rome's law in the context of its economy and society.

D. Kagan, ed., *The End of the Roman Empire: Decline or Transformation*? 3rd ed. (1992). A collection of essays on the problems of the decline and fall of the Roman Empire.

C. Kelly, *Ruling the Later Roman Empire* (2004). A study of the complexities of Roman government in the last centuries of the empire.

[5]Edward Gibbon, *The History of the Decline and Fall of the Roman Empire*, 2nd ed., Vol. 4, ed. by J. B. Bury McThuen & Co. (London: 1909), pp. 173–174.

J. Lendon, *Empire of Honour: The Art of Government in the Roman World* (1997). A brilliant study that reveals how an aristocratic code of honor led the upper classes to cooperate in Roman rule.

R. W. Mathison, *Roman Aristocrats in Barbarian Gaul: Strategies for Survival* (1993). An unusual slant on the late empire.

S. Mattern, *Rome and the Enemy: Imperial Strategy in the Principate* (1999). A study of Rome's foreign and imperial policy under the Principate.

F. G. B. Millar, *The Emperor in the Roman World, 31 B.C.–A.D. 337* (1977). A study of Roman imperial government.

H. M. D. Parker, *A History of the Roman World from A.D. 138 to 337* (1969). A good survey.

D. S. Potter, *The Roman Empire at Bay: A.D. 180–395* (2004). An account of the challenges to Rome in the third and fourth centuries and how the Romans tried to meet them.

M. I. Rostovtzeff, *Social and Economic History of the Roman Empire*, 2nd ed. (1957). A masterpiece whose main thesis is much disputed.

V. Rudich, *Political Dissidence under Nero, The Price of Dissimulation* (1993). A brilliant exposition of the lives and thoughts of political dissidents in the early empire.

G. E. M. de Ste. Croix, *The Class Struggle in the Ancient World* (1981). An ambitious interpretation of all of classical civilization from a Marxist perspective.

R. Syme, *The Roman Revolution* (1960). A brilliant study of Augustus, his supporters, and their rise to power.

For additional learning resources related to this chapter, please go to www.myhistorylab.com

Ancient Warfare

The Causes of War

WAR HAS BEEN a persistent part of human experience since before the birth of civilization.[1] Organized warfare goes back to the Stone Age. There may be evidence of it as early as the late Paleolithic Age, but clearly it was a significant human activity by the Neolithic Age. The earliest civilizations of Egypt and Mesopotamia added powerful new elements to the character of warfare and were from the first occupied with war, as were later Bronze and Iron Age cultures all over the world.

The earliest literary work in the Western tradition, Homer's *Iliad*, describes a long, bitter war and the men who fought it. The Rigvedic hymns of the ancient culture of India tell of the warrior god Indra, who smashes the fortifications of his enemies. The earliest civilizations of China were established by armies armed with spears, composite bows, and war chariots. The evidence is plentiful that war is one of the oldest and most continuous activities of the human species.

Ancient philosophers like Plato and Aristotle took all this for granted. They believed men (they never thought of women in this context) were naturally acquisitive and aggressive, and that governments and laws existed to curb those tendencies. The ancient Greeks, wracked as they were by perpetual war, were eager to investigate its causes. Thucydides, writing at the end of the fifth century B.C.E., set forth with great care the quarrels between the Athenians and the Peloponnesians and told why they broke their treaty: "so that no one may ever have to seek the cause that led to the outbreak of so great a war among the Greeks." He provided a profound and helpful understanding of the causes of wars and of the motives of human beings in going to war. He understood war as the armed competition for power, but he thought that unusually wise and capable leaders could limit their own fears and desires—and those of their people—and could choose to gain and defend only so much power as was needed for their purposes.

In this struggle for power, whether for a rational sufficiency or in the insatiable drive for all the power there

is, Thucydides found that people go to war out of "fear, honor, and interest."[2] That trio of motives is illuminating in understanding the origins of wars throughout history. That fear and interest should move states to war will not surprise the modern reader, but that concern for honor should do so may seem strange. If we take honor to mean "fame," "glory," "renown," or "splendor," it may appear applicable to the premodern world alone. If, however, we understand its significance as "deference," "esteem," "just due," "regard," "respect," or "prestige," we will find it an important motive of nations in the modern world as well.

Wars are made by human beings who may choose different courses of action. Sometimes the decisions are made by a single individual or a small group, sometimes by a very large number. Their choices are always limited and affected by circumstances, and the closer they come to the outbreak of a war, the more limited the choices seem. Those who decide to make war always think they have good reason to fight. Although impersonal forces play a role, and the reasons publicly given are not necessarily the true ones, the reasons must be taken seriously, for "the conflicts between states which have usually led to war have normally arisen, not from any irrational and emotional drives, but from almost a superabundance of analytic rationality. . . . [I]n general men have fought during the past two hundred years neither because they are aggressive nor because they are acquisitive animals, but because they are reasoning ones: because they discern, or believe that they can discern, dangers before they become immediate, and thus the possibility of threats before they are made."[3]

At any time in history, there has been widespread agreement that some things are desirable and worth fighting for. Liberty, autonomy, the freedom to exercise one's religion, and the search for wealth have been among the most common through the ages. Fear of their opposites—slavery, subordination, religious suppression, and poverty—have probably been even greater causes of wars. All of them, however, depend on power, for the distribution of power determines who can and cannot impose his or her will on others. In one sense, there is no single cause

---

[1]Arther Ferrill, *The Origins of War* (London, Thames and Hudson, 1985), p. 13, says "organized warfare appeared at least by the end of the Paleolithic Age," but Richard A. Gabriel argues that true warfare did not come until the Bronze Age and the invention of the state and the social structure that came with it. No one, however, doubts that war is at least as old as civilization.

[2]1.75.3.

[3]Michael Howard, *The Lessons of History* (Yale University Press, New Haven, 1991), p. 81.

of war, but a myriad. But in another sense, there is only one cause: Wars have rarely happened by accident or because of honest misunderstandings; most of them have resulted from calculations about power, which is valued because it can provide security, reputation, and material advantage.

In the sixth century B.C.E., the Greek philosopher Heracleitus observed that "war is the father of all things." In 1968, Will and Ariel Durant calculated that, in the previous 3,421 years, only 268 were free of war. There have been none since, suggesting, in that respect, that little has changed in more than three millennia. The reasons that have led to war in the past seem not to have disappeared.

Human beings, organized into nations and states, continue to compete for a limited supply of desirable things, to seek honor and advantage, and to fear others. All too often, the result has been war.

War and Technology

The conduct of war is shaped at the deepest level by the character of the societies involved, their values, their needs, and their organization, but from the first, technology has played a vital role. Weapons and other necessities of war are the product of technological development, and war and technology have had a mutually stimulating effect from the earliest times as new technologies have helped shape the character of war, and the needs of armies have provoked technological advance.

FORTRESS WALLS

Jericho, built about 7000 B.C.E. in the Neolithic Age, already reveals the importance of warfare and the development of technology to deal with it. Jericho is surrounded by a stone wall 700 yards around, 10 feet thick, and 13 feet high, protected by a moat 10 feet deep and 30 feet wide. This barrier made the town a powerful fortress that could be defeated only by an enemy who could besiege it long enough to starve it out. Nobody would have undertaken the expense and effort to build such a structure unless war was a relatively common danger. Not too many years after the rise of civilization in Mesopotamia (ca. 3000 B.C.E.), fortified Sumerian cities appeared in the south. A thousand years later, the pharaohs of Dynasty 12 in Egypt devised a strategic defense system of fortresses on their southern frontier with Nubia. In early China, the towns had no walls because the surrounding plains lacked both trees and stone. During the Shang dynasty (ca. 1766–1050 B.C.E.), however, towns with walls made of beaten earth appeared. Once the techniques needed to build fortresses strong enough to withstand attack were mastered, kingdoms could expand into empires that could defend their conquered lands.

The history of warfare and military technology is a story of continued change caused by a permanent competition between defense and offense. In time, construction of fortified strongholds provoked new devices and techniques for besieging them. Excavations in Egypt

This mound marks the ancient city of Jericho. Thought by some to be the earliest Neolithic site in the Near East, it sprang up around an oasis about 7000 B.C.E. The thick stone walls and moat that surround it show it was meant to be a fortress that could resist sieges, affirming that warfare was common at least as early as the construction of this city. © Zev Radovan, Jerusalem, Israel and Mesopotamia have uncovered scaling ladders, battering rams, siege towers (some of them mobile), and mines burrowing under fortress walls. Catapults capable of hurling stones against an enemy's walls appear in Greece in the fourth century B.C.E.; the weapon was brought to greater perfection and power by the Romans centuries later. Alexander the Great and some of his Hellenistic successors became skillful at storming fortified cities with the aid of such technology, but throughout ancient history, success against a fortified place usually came as a result of starvation and surrender after a long siege. Not until the invention of gunpowder and powerful cannons did offensive technology overcome the defensive strength of fortification.

ARMY AGAINST ARMY

A different kind of warfare, of army against army in the open field, appeared as early as the Stone Age. Scholars disagree as to whether it came in the Paleolithic Age or emerged in Neolithic times, but we know that warriors used such weapons as wooden or stone clubs, spears and axes with sharpened stone heads, and simple bows with stone-tipped arrows. The discovery of metallurgy brought the Bronze Age to Mesopotamia, perhaps as early as 3500 B.C.E., providing armies with weapons that were sharper and sturdier than stone and with body armor and helmets that brought greater safety to warriors. The Mesopotamian rulers already had wealth, a sizable population, a civilized organization, and substantial fortress walls. Now, with bronze weapons, Mesopotamian rulers could expand their empires far beyond their early frontiers. When, not much later, the Bronze Age came to Egypt, its rulers, too, used the new technology to expand and defend their wealthy kingdom.

THE CHARIOT AND THE BOW

The next great revolution in warfare occurred with the inventions of the chariot and the composite bow. When these came together by about 1800 B.C.E., their users swept all before them, conquering both Egypt and Mesopotamia. The chariot was a light vehicle, a platform on two wheels pulled by a team of two or four horses that could move swiftly on a battlefield. It was strong enough to hold two men—a driver and a warrior—as it sped along on an open field. The wheels were of wood—not solid, but with spokes and a hub—and were attached to an axle; building them required great skill and experience. The warrior on the chariot wielded a new weapon: the composite bow, more powerful by far than anything that had come before it. Made of thin strips of wood glued together and fastened with animal tendons and horn, the bow was short and easy to use from a moving chariot. It could shoot a light arrow accurately

for 300 yards and penetrate the armor of the day at about 100. A man on a chariot on a flat enough field, using a composite bow with a quiver full of light arrows, could devastate an army of foot soldiers. "Circling at a distance of 100 or 200 yards from the herds of unarmored foot soldiers, a chariot crew—one to drive, one to shoot—might have transfixed six men a minute. Ten minutes' work by ten chariots would cause 500 casualties or more."[4]

For several centuries, beginning about 1800 B.C.E., peoples from the north using such weapons smashed into Mesopotamia and conquered the kingdoms they attacked. In India, the Aryans, who also spoke an Indo-European language, smashed the indigenous Indus civilization. In Egypt, the Hyksos, speakers of a Semitic language, conquered the northern kingdom. In China, the chariot-riding Shang dynasty established an aristocratic rule based on the new weapons. In Europe, the Mycenaean Greeks used chariots, although it is not clear if they had the composite bow and used the tactics that had brought such great success elsewhere.

The most sophisticated users of ancient military technology before Alexander the Great were the Assyrians. They had a wide range of devices for siege warfare and took them along on all their campaigns. As always, new weapons made of new materials with new techniques do not in themselves constitute a revolution in military affairs. To use them effectively, armies require organizations that can devise appropriate operational plans and train their soldiers in the needed skills and discipline.

The Assyrian annals suggest that by the eighth century B.C.E., their kings had turned their chariot forces into "a weapon of shock and terror, manipulated by the driver to charge at breakneck speed behind a team of perfectly schooled horses and used by the archer as a platform from which to launch a hail of arrows; squadrons of chariots, their drivers trained to act in mutual support, might have clashed much as armored vehicles have done in our time, success going to the side that could disable the larger opposing number, while the footmen unlucky or foolhardy enough to stand in their way would have been scattered like chaff."[5]

MOUNTED CAVALRY

In 612 B.C.E., the great Assyrian Empire fell before a coalition of opponents, but it had already been weakened by enemies who commanded a new military technique: mounted cavalry. Ironically, the Assyrians themselves may have been the first to develop the critical skills of riding astride a horse while keeping both hands free to shoot with a bow. The first peoples to use

[4]John Keegan, *A History of Warfare* (New York: Vintage Books, 1993), p. 166.
[5]Ibid., pp. 176–177.

This mosaic was found on a wall of the House of the Faun at Pompei. It is believed to be a copy of a painting by Philoxelus of Emtrea in the fourth century B.C.E. Alexander is the mounted hatless man on the left and King Darius wears a headdress as he stands on a chariot on the right.   Battle between Alexander the Great and King Dareios. House of the Faun, Pompeii VI 12, 2 Inv. 10020. Museo Archelogico Nazionale, Naples, Italy. Photograph © Erich Lessing/Art Resource, NY

the new cavalry technology to great effect were nomads from the steppes of northern Eurasia. About 690 B.C.E., a people the Greeks called Cimmerians flooded into Asia Minor on their warhorses, shaking the established order. Later in that century they were followed by another group of steppe nomads called the Scythians, who came from the Altay mountains in central Asia. The Scythians overthrew the Cimmerians and then joined with more settled peoples in the battles that destroyed the Assyrian Empire. This was the beginning of a series of attacks by horse-riding nomads from the steppes against the settled lands to their south that lasted for two millennia. In China no clear evidence exists for such attacks before the fourth century B.C.E., but it is possible that attacks from Mongolia and nearby areas may have brought down the western Chou dynasty in 771 B.C.E.

In the Middle East, the Babylonian Empire had succeeded the Assyrian but was soon replaced by the Persian Empire. The Persians had no other way of preventing the nomads' devastating raids than to pay other nomads to defend their frontiers, and the Chinese emperors did the same. The Chinese also developed a cavalry that carried the crossbow, more powerful than the composite bow.

Another device for defending against the invaders was the Great Wall of China, built during the Ch'in dynasty (256–206 B.C.E.) and designed to keep the ravaging horsemen out. But this, too, proved ineffective. Despite endless perturbations of the political and military relationships between grassland and plowland, peoples of the steppe enjoyed a consistent advantage because of their superior mobility and the cheapness of their military equipment. This produced a pattern of recurrent nomad conquests of civilized lands.[6]

IRON-WIELDING WARRIORS

Even as the chariot and the warhorse were having so great an impact on the nature of ancient warfare, a far more fundamental revolution in military affairs was under way. Bronze is an alloy of copper and tin, but the latter is a rather rare metal, so it was expensive. Horses also were costly to keep, so warfare that depended on bronze weapons and horses was necessarily limited to a relatively

[6]William H. McNeill, *The Pursuit of Power* (Chicago: University of Chicago Press, 1982), p. 16.

The Great Wall of China was originally built during the Ch'in dynasty (256–206 B.C.E.), but what we see today is the wall as it was completely rebuilt during the Ming dynasty (1368–1644 C.E.).   Paolo Koch/Photo Researchers, Inc.

small number of men. About 1400 B.C.E., however, in Asia Minor, someone discovered the technique of working iron to give it an edge so hard and durable that tools and weapons made of it were clearly superior to those of bronze. Iron, moreover, is far more abundant than the components of bronze, easier to work with, and much less expensive. For the first time, it became possible for common people to own and use metal. Now a much larger part of the population could own arms and armor, and "[o]rdinary farmers and herdsmen thereby achieved a new formidability in battle, and the narrowly aristocratic structure of society characteristic of the chariot age altered abruptly. A more democratic era dawned as iron-wielding invaders overthrew ruling elites that had based their power on a monopoly of chariotry."[7]

Within two centuries, the new technology spread over the Middle East and into Europe. A new round of invasions by iron-wielding warriors swept away kingdoms and empires and brought new peoples to power. The Assyrians, combining the bureaucratic organizational skills of Mesopotamian civilization with a warrior spirit and an ability to assimilate new techniques, achieved control of their own region with the aid of iron weapons, but many

indigenous rulers of civilized lands were subdued or swept away. In Europe, a Greek-speaking people we call the Mycenaeans had ruled the Greek peninsula and the Aegean Sea with a Bronze Age civilization similar to those of the Middle East. Between 1200 B.C.E. and 1100 B.C.E., however, the Mycenaeans were overthrown by a new wave of Greeks with iron weapons who obliterated the old civilization and brought a new culture based on new ways of fighting.

THE SHIELD AND THE PHALANX

The heart of this new Greek civilization, which is called *Hellenic*, was the city-state, or *polis*, hundreds of which came into being toward the end of the eighth century B.C.E. (See Chapter 2.) Their armies consisted of independent yeoman farmers who produced enough wealth to supply their own iron weapons and body armor, made cheap enough by the revolution in metallurgy. But again, these would have been of little value without organizational change. Now, a new way of warfare, which made infantry the dominant fighting force on land for centuries, permitted an alliance of poor Greek states to defeat the mighty and wealthy Persian Empire. The soldiers, wearing helmets, body armor,

[7]Ibid., p. 12.

and a heavy, large round shield for protection, carried short iron swords but used iron-tipped wooden pikes as their chief weapon. Arrayed in compact blocks called *phalanxes*, usually eight men deep, these freemen, well disciplined and highly motivated, defeated lesser infantries, archers, and cavalry. Adapted by the Macedonians under King Philip II and his son Alexander the Great, the *hoplite* phalanx remained the dominant infantry force until it was defeated by the Roman legion in the second century B.C.E.

TRIREME WARFARE

The Greeks also achieved supremacy at sea by improving an existing technological innovation and providing it with an effective operational plan. Oared galleys were known at Cyprus as early as about 1000 B.C.E., and the Phoenicians improved their speed and maneuverability by superimposing a second and then a third bank of rowers over the first to produce a ship the Greeks called a *trireme.* The Greeks added outriggers for the top rowers, and it is possible this permitted their rowers to use the full power of their strongest leg muscles by sliding back and forth as they rowed. At first, the main mode of *trireme* warfare was for one ship to come alongside another, grapple it, and send marines to board the enemy ship. In time, however, the Greeks placed a strong ram at the prow of each ship and learned how to row with great bursts of speed and to make sharp turns that allowed them to ram and disable their opponents by striking them in the side or rear. With such ships and tactics, the Greek *triremes* repeatedly sank fleets of the Egyptians and Phoenicians who rowed for the Persian Empire, thus gaining complete naval mastery.

The Macedonians came to dominate the Greek world, to conquer the Persian Empire, and to rule its successor states in the Hellenistic period (323–31 B.C.E.), but technological innovation in military affairs played only a small part in their success. Military victories came chiefly from the quality of their leaders, the number, spirit, and discipline of their troops, and the ability to combine infantry, cavalry, and light-armed troops to win battles. Alexander's engineers also brought unprecedented skill to the use of siege weapons.

ROMAN LEGIONS

The armies of the Roman Republic defeated Macedon in a series of wars in the third and second centuries B.C.E. and brought the entire Mediterranean world under Roman sway by the end of the second century. This conquest was achieved almost entirely by the power of the infantry. In time, the Roman army moved from the phalanx formation to a looser, more open order of battle based on the legion, which was divided into smaller, self-sufficient units. The Romans abandoned the pike as the chief infantry weapon, using instead the *pilum*, a heavy iron javelin that was thrown to cause disarray in the enemy line and permit the Romans to use their short double-edged swords at close quarters. In the imperial period, beginning especially in the third century of our era, nomadic barbarian tribes began applying the severe pressure on Rome's frontiers that would ultimately bring down the empire. Like the Chinese, the Romans built walls in some places to ease the burden of defending their extensive borders. In the empire's last years, the Romans began to use heavily armored horses ridden by knights in heavy armor, carrying lances and capable of charging an enemy with great force and effect. These armored cavalrymen, called *cataphracts* in Greek, would develop into a major new system of fighting in the Western Middle Ages, but they were too few to take a significant role in the final, futile defense of the empire.

How early is the evidence for warfare among human beings? What did Thucydides think war was about? For what purposes did he think people went to war? Is war a rational or irrational action? Can you think of any good reason for fighting a war? How did war and technology affect one another in the ancient world?

6

Late Antiquity and the Early Middle Ages: Creating a New European Society and Culture (476–1000)

KEY TOPICS

- The collapse of the Western Roman Empire and the resulting fusion of Roman and Germanic culture

- The Byzantine and Islamic empires and their impact on the West

- The role of the church in Western society during the early Middle Ages

- The political and economic features of Europe under the Franks

- The characteristics of feudal society

SCHOLARS INCREASINGLY VIEW the six centuries between 250 C.E. and 800 C.E. as a single world bounded by the Roman and Sassanian (Persian) empires, spreading from Rome to Baghdad. Embracing Late Antiquity and the early Middle Ages, this epoch saw the Western and Eastern (Byzantine) Empires of Rome alternately decline and recover, separate and mingle, while never succumbing culturally to barbarian and Muslim invaders. In the East, Rome's provinces were deeply penetrated by an enduring Iranian dynasty, the Sassanians, who came to power in Persia and Mesopotamia in the third century C.E., overthrowing the Parthians and creating a powerful empire. In doing so, they laid a sure foundation for a later Muslim empire in the Middle East. During the reign of the Sassanid king Khosro I Anushirvan (r. 530–579), a contemporary of the Byzantine emperor Justinian (r. 527–565), this new Persian Empire, like its Byzantine counterpart, attained its cultural and military peak. But decades of warfare exhausted both empires, and by the mid-eighth century, the Arab conquests had extended Muslim influence across the Middle East and North Africa into Europe and eventually as far as northern Spain.

Meanwhile, in Western Europe, the Merovingian and Carolingian Franks were weaving their own Germanic barbarian heritage together with Judeo-Christian religion, Roman language and law, and Greco-Byzantine administration and culture to create a Western civilization of their own. The reign of Charlemagne (r. 768–814) saw a modest renaissance of classical antiquity. The peculiar Western social and political forms that emerged at this time—the manor and feudalism—not only coped with unprecedented chaos, but proved also to be fertile seedbeds from which distinctive Western political institutions were in time to grow.

Late Antiquity The centuries before and after the fall of Rome (476) were thus a vibrant period of self-discovery and self-definition for all of the above peoples. Many scholars have called this period—between the end of the ancient world and the birth of the Middle Ages—**Late Antiquity** (250–800 C.E.). It witnessed a new appropriation of ancient history by Jews, Christians, Muslims, and pagan Germanic and eastern tribes, each of which competed for their roots in the past (from which they drew authority) and their place in the future (where they would exercise power). In the process, each appropriated the best features of the other. The Jews had long adopted the attractive myths of the ancient Mesopotamians and the Christians the biblical prophecies of the Jews, while the Muslims subordinated both the Jewish and Christian scriptures to God's final, seventh-century revelations to Muhammad, the last of the prophets. The Christian Franks, the most eclectic and enterprising of all, claimed an-

cestors among the ancient Trojans of Greek myth and Homer's *Iliad*. (See Chapter 2.)

In Late Antiquity, these various peoples and their religions borrowed from and bumped into each other for several centuries, as the ancient world evolved into the medieval. In government, religion, and language, as well as geography, the Christian West ultimately grew apart from the Byzantine East and the Islamic Arab world. Although divided by states and cultures that became increasingly rigid and competitive over time, the world these peoples inhabited between 250 C.E. and 800 C.E. was also a cohesive one, a world together as well as a world moving apart.

▼ On the Eve of the Frankish Ascendancy

As we have already seen, by the late third century, the Roman Empire had become too large for a single emperor to govern and was beginning to fail. (See Chapter 5.) The emperor Diocletian (r. 284–305) tried to strengthen the empire by dividing it between himself and a co-emperor. The result was a dual empire with an eastern and a western half, each with its own emperor and, eventually, imperial bureaucracy and army. A critical shift of the empire's resources and orientation to the eastern half accompanied these changes. In 284, Diocletian moved to Nicomedia (in modern Turkey), where he remained until the last two years of his reign. As imperial rule weakened in the West and strengthened in the East, it also became increasingly autocratic.

Diocletian's reign was followed by factional strife. His eventual successor, Constantine the Great (r. 306–337), briefly reunited the empire by conquest (his three sons and their successors would divide it again) and ruled as sole emperor of the eastern and western halves after 324. In that year, he moved the capital of the empire from Rome to Byzantium, an ancient Greek city that stood at the crossroads of the major sea and land routes between Europe and Asia Minor. Here, Constantine built the new city of Constantinople, which he dedicated in 330. As the imperial residence and the new administrative center of the empire, Constantinople gradually became a "new Rome." The "old" Rome, suffering from internal political and religious quarrels and geographically distant from the crucial military fronts in Syria and along the Danube River, declined in importance. The city of Rome and the Western empire were already in decline in the late third and fourth centuries, well before the barbarian invasions in the West began. Milan in northern Italy had replaced Rome as the imperial residence in 286. In 402, the seat of Western government would be moved to another northern Italian city, Ravenna, a seaport on the Adriatic that was protected on the landward side by impenetrable marshes. When the barbarian invasions of non-Roman Germanic and eastern peoples began in the late fourth century, the West was in political and economic disarray, and imperial power and prestige had shifted decisively to Constantinople and the East.

Germanic Migrations

The German tribes did not burst in on the West all of a sudden. They were at first a token and benign presence on the fringes of the empire and even within it. Before the massive migrations from the north and the east, Roman and Germanic cultures had commingled peacefully for centuries. The Romans had "imported" barbarians as servants, slaves, and soldiers. Barbarian soldiers commanded Roman legions.

Beginning in 376 with a great influx of Visigoths, or "west Goths," into the empire, this peaceful coexistence ended. The Visigoths, accomplished horsemen and fierce warriors, were themselves pushed into the empire by the emergence of a notoriously violent people, the Huns, from what is now Mongolia. The Visigoths ultimately reached southern Gaul and Spain. Soon to be Christianized, they won rights of settlement and material assistance within the empire from the Eastern emperor Valens (r. 364–378) in exchange for defending the eastern frontier as *foederati*, or the emperor's "special" allies. Instead of the promised assistance, however, the Visigoths received harsh treatment from their new allies. After repeated conflicts, the Visigoths rebelled and overwhelmed Valens at the Battle of Adrianople in 378. (See Chapter 5.)

Thereafter, the Romans passively permitted the settlement of barbarians within the heart of the Western empire. The Vandals crossed the Rhine in 406 and within three decades gained control of northwest Africa and much of the Mediterranean. The Burgundians, who came on the heels of the Vandals, settled in Gaul. Most important for subsequent Western history were the Franks, who settled northern and central Gaul, some along the seacoast (the Salian Franks) and others along the Rhine, Seine, and Loire Rivers (the Ripuarian Franks).

Why was there so little Roman resistance to these Germanic tribes, whose numbers—at most 100,000 people in the largest of them—were comparatively small? The invaders were successful because they came in rapid succession upon a badly overextended Western empire divided politically by ambitious military commanders and weakened by decades of famine, pestilence, and overtaxation. By the second half of the

fourth century, Roman frontiers had become too vast to manage. Efforts to do so by "barbarizing" the Roman army, that is, by recruiting many peasants into it and by making the Germanic tribes key Roman allies, only weakened it further. The Eastern empire retained enough wealth and vitality to field new armies or to buy off the invaders. The Western empire, in contrast, succumbed not only because of moral decay and materialism, but also because of a combination of military rivalry, political mismanagement, disease, and sheer poverty.

New Western Masters

In the early fifth century, Italy and the "eternal city" of Rome suffered devastating blows. In 410 the Visigoths, under Alaric (ca. 370–410), sacked Rome. In 452 the Huns, led by Attila—the "scourge of God"—invaded Italy. Rome was sacked still again, in 455—this time by the Vandals.

By the mid-fifth century, power in Western Europe had passed decisively from the hands of the Roman emperors to those of barbarian chieftains. In 476, the traditional date historians give for the fall of the Roman Empire, the barbarian Odovacer (ca. 434–493) deposed the last Western emperor Romulus Augustulus. The Eastern emperor Zeno (r. 474–491) recognized Odovacer's authority in the West, and Odovacer acknowledged Zeno as sole emperor, contenting himself to serve as Zeno's Western viceroy. In a later coup in 493, Theodoric (ca. 454–526), king of the Ostrogoths, or "east Goths," replaced Odovacer. Theodoric then governed with the full acceptance of the Roman people, the emperor in Constantinople, and the Christian Church.

By the end of the fifth century, the barbarians from west and east had saturated the Western empire. The Ostrogoths settled in Italy, the Franks in northern Gaul, the Burgundians in Provence, the Visigoths in southern Gaul and Spain, the Vandals in Africa and the western Mediterranean, and the Angles and Saxons in England. (See Map 6–1.)

These barbarian military victories did not, however, obliterate Roman culture; Western Europe's new masters were willing to learn from the people they had conquered. They admired Roman culture and had no desire to destroy it. Except in Britain and northern Gaul, Roman law, Roman government, and Latin, the Roman language, coexisted with the new Germanic institutions. In Italy under Theodoric, tribal custom gradually gave way to Roman law. Only the Vandals and the pagan Anglo-Saxons—and, after 466, the Visigoths—refused to profess at least titular obedience to the emperor in Constantinople.

The Visigoths, the Ostrogoths, and the Vandals had entered the West as Christians, which helped them accommodate to Roman culture. They were, however,

Map 6–1 **BARBARIAN MIGRATIONS INTO THE WEST IN THE FOURTH AND FIFTH CENTURIES**
The forceful intrusion of Germanic and non-Germanic barbarians into the Roman Empire from the last quarter of the fourth century through the fifth century made for a constantly changing pattern of movement and relations. The map shows the major routes taken by the usually unwelcome newcomers and the areas most deeply affected by the main groups.

Arians, followers of a version of Christianity that had been condemned as heresy at the **Council of Nicaea** in 325. Later, around 500, the Franks, who had settled in Gaul, would convert to the Nicene, or "Catholic," form of Christianity supported by the bishops of Rome. As we will see, the Franks ultimately dominated most of Western Europe, helping convert the Goths and other barbarians to Roman Christianity.

All things considered, a gradual interpenetration of two strong cultures—a creative tension—marked the period of the Germanic migrations. The stronger culture was the Roman, and it became dominant in a later fusion. Despite Western military defeat, the Goths and the Franks became far more romanized than the Romans were germanized. Latin language, Nicene Catholic Christianity, and eventually Roman law and government were to triumph in the West during the Middle Ages.

▼ The Byzantine Empire

As the Roman Empire in the West succumbed to Germanic and other barbarian invasions, imperial power shifted to the eastern part of the Roman Empire, whose center was the city of Constantinople or Byzantium (modern-day Istanbul). It remained the sole imperial capital until the eighth century, when Charlemagne revived the Western empire and reclaimed its imperial title. In historical usage, the term *Byzantine* indicates the Hellenistic Greek, Roman, and Judaic monotheistic elements that distinguish the culture of the East from the Latin West.

Between 324 and 1453, the Byzantine Empire passed from an early period of expansion and splendor to a time of sustained contraction and splintering and finally ended in catastrophic defeat. Historians divide its history into three distinct periods:

SALVIAN THE PRIEST COMPARES THE ROMANS AND THE BARBARIANS

Salvian, a Christian priest writing around 440, found the barbarians morally superior to the Romans—indeed, truer to Roman virtues than the Romans themselves, whose failings were all the more serious because they, unlike the barbarians, had knowledge of Christianity.

Does Salvian really believe the Germanic tribes are more moral than the Romans? Does he use different standards to judge the two groups? Is he trying to shame the Romans, and if so, why?

In what respects can our customs be preferred to those of the Goths and Vandals, or even compared with them? And first, to speak of affection and mutual charity, . . . almost all barbarians, at least those who are of one race and kin, love each other, while the Romans persecute each other. . . . The many are oppressed by the few, who regard public exactions as their own peculiar right, who carry on private traffic under the guise of collecting the taxes. . . . So the poor are despoiled, the widows sigh, the orphans are oppressed, until many of them, born of families not obscure, and liberally educated, flee to our enemies that they may no longer suffer the oppression of public persecution. They doubtless seek Roman humanity among the barbarians, because they cannot bear barbarian inhumanity among the Romans. And although they differ from the people to whom they flee in manner and in language; although they are unlike as regards the fetid odor of the barbarians' bodies and garments, yet they would rather endure a foreign civilization among the barbarians than cruel injustice among the Romans.

It is urged that if we Romans are wicked and corrupt, that the barbarians commit the same sins. . . . There is, however, this difference, that if the barbarians commit the same crimes as we, yet we sin more grievously. . . . All the barbarians . . . are pagans or heretics. The Saxon race is cruel, the Franks are faithless . . . the Huns are unchaste—in short there is vice in the life of all the barbarian peoples. But are their offenses as serious as [those of Christians]? Is the unchastity of the Hun so criminal as ours? Is the faithlessness of the Frank so blameworthy as ours?

From *Of God's Government*, in James Harvey Robinson, *Readings in European History*, Vol. 1 (Boston: Athenaeum, 1904), pp. 28–30.

1. From the rebuilding of Byzantium as Constantinople in 324 to the beginning of the Arab expansion and the spread of Islam in 632
2. From 632 to the conquest of Asia Minor by the Seljuk Turks in 1071, or, as some prefer, to the fall of Constantinople to the Western Crusaders in 1204
3. From 1071, or 1204, to the fall of Constantinople to the Ottoman Turks in 1453, the end of the empire in the East

The Reign of Justinian

In terms of territory, political power, and cultural achievement, the first period of Byzantine history (324–632) was far the greater. (See Map 6–2.) Its pinnacle was the reign of Emperor Justinian (r. 527–565) and his like-minded wife, Empress Theodora (d. 548). A strongman ruler who expected all his subjects, clergy and laity, high and low, to submit absolutely to his hierarchical control, Justinian spent, built, and destroyed on a grand scale. Theodora, the daughter of a circus bear trainer, had been an entertainer in her youth and, if Justinian's tell-all court historian, Procopius, is believed, a prostitute as well. Whatever her background, she possessed an intelligence and toughness that matched and might even have exceeded that of her husband. Theodora was a true co-ruler. In 532, after massive tax riots—the so-called Nika Revolt, named after the rebel's cry of "victory" (in Greek *Nika*)—rocked Constantinople threatening its

Map 6–2 **THE BYZANTINE EMPIRE AT THE TIME OF JUSTINIAN'S DEATH**   The inset shows the empire in 1025, before its losses to the Seljuk Turks.

destruction and the end of Justinian's reign, a panicked emperor contemplated abdication and flight. Theodora insisted that he reestablish his authority, which he did by ordering a bloodbath that left tens of thousands of protesters dead.

Cities During Justinian's thirty-eight-year reign, the empire's strength lay in its more than 1,500 cities. Constantinople, with perhaps 350,000 inhabitants, was the largest city and the cultural crossroads of Asian and European civilizations. The dominant provincial cities had populations of 50,000. A fifth-century record suggests the size and splendor of Constantinople at its peak: 5 imperial and 9 princely palaces; 8 public and 153 private baths; 4 public forums; 5 granaries; 2 theaters; 1 hippodrome; 322 streets; 4,388 substantial houses; 52 porticoes; 20 public and 120 private bakeries; and

14 churches.[1] The most popular entertainments were the theater, where, according to clerical critics, nudity and immorality were on display, and the chariot races at the Hippodrome.

Between the fourth and fifth centuries, urban councils of roughly two hundred members, known as *Decurions*, all local, wealthy landowners, governed the cities. Being the intellectual and economic elite of the empire, they were heavily taxed, which did not make them the emperor's most docile or loyal servants. By the sixth century, fidelity to the throne had become the coin of the realm, and special governors, lay and clerical, chosen from the landholding classes, replaced the *decurion* councils as more reliable instruments of the

[1]Cyril Mango, *Byzantium: The Empire of New Rome* (New York: Charles Scribner's Sons, 1980), p. 88.

emperor's sovereign will. As the sixth and seventh centuries saw the beginning of new barbarian invasions of the empire from the north and the east, such political tightening was imperative.

Law The imperial goal—as reflected in Justinian's policy of "one God, one empire, one religion"—was to centralize government by imposing legal and doctrinal conformity throughout. To this end, the emperor ordered a collation and revision of Roman law. Such a codification was long overdue because an enormous number of legal decrees, often contradictory, had been

Built during the reign of Justinian, Hagia Sophia (Church of Holy Wisdom) is a masterpiece of Byzantine and world architecture. After the Turkish conquest of Constantinople in 1453, Hagia Sophia was transformed into a mosque with four minarets, still visible today. Turkish Tourism and Information Office

piling up since the mid-second century, as the empire grew more complex and then more Christian and imperial rule became increasingly autocratic. What Justinian wanted was loyal and docile subjects guided by clear and enforceable laws.

The result was the *Corpus Juris Civilis*, or "body of civil law," a fourfold compilation undertaken by a committee of the most learned lawyers. The first compilation, known as the *Code*, appeared in 533 and revised imperial edicts issued since the reign of Hadrian (r. 117–138). A second compilation, the *Novellae*, or "new things," presented the decrees issued by Justinian and his immediate predecessors since 534. The third compilation, the *Digest*, gathered the major opinions of the old legal experts. The goal of the fourth compilation, the *Institutes*, was to put into the hands of young scholars a practical textbook that drew its lessons from the *Code* and the *Digest*. The *Code* was taught in the West by Irnerius at Bologna in Italy in the twelfth century (see Chapter 8), and beginning in the Renaissance (see Chapter 10), Justinian's *Code* laid the foundation for most subsequent European law. Because bringing subjects under the authority of a single sovereign was the fundamental feature of Roman law, rulers seeking to centralize their states especially benefited from Justinian's legal legacy.

Hagia Sophia Justinian was also a great builder. At his command and expense, fortifications, churches, monasteries, and palaces arose across the empire. His most famous and enduring monument in stone is the Church of Hagia Sophia (Holy Wisdom) completed in Constantinople in 537. Its key feature is a massive dome, 112 feet in diameter, which together with the church's many other windows, and open spaces, floods the nave with light and gives the interior a remarkable airiness and luminosity.

Reconquest in the West Justinian sought to reconquer the imperial provinces lost to the barbarians in the West. Beginning in 533, his armies overran the Vandal kingdom in North Africa and Sicily, the Ostrogothic kingdom in Italy, and part of Spain. But the price paid in blood and treasure was enormous, particularly in Italy, where prolonged resistance by the Ostrogoths did not end until 554. By Justinian's death, his empire was financially exhausted, and plague had ravaged the population of Constantinople and much of the East. Although Byzantine rule survived in Sicily and parts of southern Italy until the eleventh century, most of Justinian's Western and North African conquests were soon lost to Lombard invaders from north of the Alps and to the Muslim Arabs.

The Spread of Byzantine Christianity

In the late sixth and seventh centuries, nomadic, pagan tribes of Avars, Slavs, and Bulgars invaded and occupied the Balkan provinces of the eastern empire, threatening a "dark age" there. More than once, these fierce raiders menaced Constantinople itself. Yet after almost two centuries of intermittent warfare, the Slavs and Bulgars eventually converted to Eastern Orthodoxy or Byzantine Christianity. Hoping to build a cultural-linguistic firewall against menacing Franks from the West who had conquered the Avars and were attempting to convert his people to Roman Catholicism in Latin, a language they did not understand, the Slav Duke Rastislav of Moravia turned in the ninth century to Constantinople for help. In response, the emperor sent two learned missionaries to convert the Moravians: the brothers, priests, and future saints Constantine, later known as Cyril, and Methodius. In Moravia, the two created a new, Greek-based alphabet, which permitted the Slavs to create their own written language. That language gave the Christian gospels and Byzantine theology a lasting Slavic home. Later, after the Bulgars conquered and absorbed many of the Slavs, that alphabet was elevated to a broader script known as Cyrillic after St. Cyril. Known today as Old Church Slavonic, it has ever since been the international Slavic language through which Byzantine Christianity penetrated eastern Europe: Bohemia, much of the Balkans, Ukraine, and Kievan Russia. In prior centuries, the Byzantines had given Goths, Armenians, and Syrians similar native tools for accessing Byzantine culture and religion.

Persians and Muslims

During the reign of Emperor Heraclius (r. 610–641), the Byzantine Empire took a decidedly Eastern, as opposed to a Western Roman, direction. Heraclius spent his entire reign resisting Persian and Islamic invasions, the former successfully, the latter in vain. In 628 he defeated the Persian Sassanid king Chosroes and took back one of Western Christendom's great lost relics: a piece of Christ's Cross that Chosroes had carried off when he captured Jerusalem in 614. After 632, however, Islamic armies overran much of the empire, directly attacking Constantinople for the first time in the mid-670s. Not until Leo III of the Isaurian dynasty (r. 717–740) did the Byzantines succeed in repelling Arab armies and regaining most of Asia Minor, having lost forever Syria, Egypt, and North Africa. The setback was traumatic and forced a major restructuring of the diminished empire, creating a new system of provincial government under the direct authority of imperial generals. A major break with the old governance of the empire by local elites, the new system made possible a more disciplined and flexible use of military power in time of crisis. In the tenth century, a reinvigorated Byzantium went on the offensive, pushing back the Muslims in Armenia and northern Syria and conquering the Bulgar kingdom in the Balkans.

But like Justinian's conquests in the sixth century, these may have overtaxed the empire's strength; and in the eleventh century, Byzantine fortunes rapidly reversed. After inflicting a devastating defeat on the Byzantine

Empress Theodora and her attendants. The union of political and spiritual authority in the person of the empress is shown by the depiction on Theodora's mantle of three magi carrying gifts to the Virgin and Jesus. The Court of Empress Theodora. Byzantine early Christian mosaic. San Vitale, Ravenna, Italy Photograph © Scala/Art Resource, NY army at Manzikert in Armenia in 1071, Muslim Seljuk Turks overran most of Asia Minor, from which the Byzantines had drawn most of their tax revenue and troops. The empire never fully recovered, yet its end—which came when the Seljuks' cousins, the Ottoman Turks, captured Constantinople in 1453—was still almost four centuries away. In 1092, after two decades of steady Turkish advance, the Eastern emperor Alexius I Comnenus (r. 1081–1118) called for Western aid, which helped spark the First Crusade. It also heightened tensions between Latin West and Greek East and exposed the riches of Constantinople to predatory Western eyes. A century later (1204), the Fourth Crusade was diverted from Jerusalem to Constantinople, not, however, to rescue the city, but rather to inflict more damage on it and on the Byzantine Empire than all previous non-Christian invaders had done before. (See Chapter 7.) When the Byzantines eventually recovered the city in 1261, Byzantine power was a shadow of its former self, the empire was impoverished, and the Turks had become a constant threat.

▼ Islam and the Islamic World

A new drama began to unfold in the sixth century with the awakening of a rival far more dangerous to the West than the German tribes: the new faith of **Islam**. By the time of Muhammad's death (632), Islamic armies were beginning to absorb the attention and the resources of the emperors in Constantinople and the rulers in the West.

At first, the Muslims were both open and cautious. They borrowed and integrated elements of Persian and Greek culture into their own. The new religion of Islam adopted elements of Christian, Jewish, and Arab pagan religious beliefs and practices. Muslims tolerated religious minorities within the territories they conquered as long as those minorities recognized Islamic political rule, refrained from trying to convert Muslims, and paid their taxes. Nonetheless, the Muslims were keen to protect the purity and integrity of Islamic religion, language, and law from any corrupting foreign influence. Over time and after increased conflict with Eastern and Western Christians, this protective tendency grew stronger. Despite significant contacts and exchanges, Islamic culture did not take root as creatively in the West as barbarian and Byzantine cultures did, leaving Islam a strange and threatening religion to many Westerners.

Muhammad's Religion

Muhammad (570–632), an orphan, was raised by a family of modest means. As a youth, he worked as a merchant's assistant, traveling the major trade routes. When he was twenty-five, he married a wealthy widow from the city of Mecca, the religious and commercial center of Arabia.

Thereafter, himself a wealthy man, he became a kind of social activist, criticizing Meccan materialism, paganism, and unjust treatment of the poor and needy. At about age forty, a deep religious experience heightened his commitment to reform and it transformed his life. He began to receive revelations from the angel Gabriel, who recited God's word to him at irregular intervals. These revelations were collected after his death into the Islamic holy book, the **Qur'an** (literally, a "reciting"), which his followers compiled between 650 and 651. The basic message Muhammad received was a summons to all Arabs to submit to God's will. Followers of Muhammad's religion came to be called *Muslim* ("submissive" or "surrendering"); *Islam* itself, means "submission."

The message was not a new one. A long line of Jewish prophets going back to Noah had reiterated it. According to Muslims, however, this line ended with Muhammad, who, as the last of God's chosen prophets, became "the Prophet." The Qur'an also recognized Jesus Christ as a prophet but denied that he was God's co-eternal and co-equal son. Like Judaism, Islam was a monotheistic and theocentric religion, not a trinitarian one like Christianity.

Mecca was a major pagan pilgrimage site (the *Ka'ba*, which became Islam's holiest shrine, housed a sacred black meteorite that was originally a pagan object of worship). Muhammad's condemnation of idolatry and immorality threatened the trade that flowed from the pilgrims, enraging the merchants of the city. Persecuted for their attacks on traditional religion, Muhammad and his followers fled Mecca in 622 for Medina, 240 miles to the north. This event came to be known as the *Hegira* ("flight") and marks the beginning of the Islamic calendar.

In Medina, Muhammad organized his forces and drew throngs of devoted followers. He raided caravans going back and forth to Mecca. He also had his first conflicts with Medina's Jews, who were involved in trade with Mecca. By 624, he was able to conquer Mecca and make it the center of the new religion.

During these years the basic rules of Islamic practice evolved. True Muslims were expected (1) to be honest and modest in all their dealings and behavior; (2) to be unquestionably loyal to the Islamic community; (3) to abstain from pork and alcohol at all times; (4) to wash and pray facing Mecca five times a day; (5) to contribute to the support of the poor and needy; (6) to fast during daylight hours for one month each year; and (7) to make a pilgrimage to Mecca and visit the *Ka'ba* at least once in a lifetime. The last requirement reflects the degree to which Islam was an assimilationist religion: it "Islamicized" a major pagan religious practice.

Islam also permitted Muslim men to have up to four wives—provided they treated them all justly and gave each equal attention—and as many concubines as they wished. A husband could divorce a wife with a simple declaration, whereas, to divorce her husband, a wife had to show good cause before a religious judge. A wife was expected to be totally loyal and devoted to her husband and was allowed to show her face to no man but him. (See "Compare & Connect: The Battle of the Sexes in Christianity and Islam," page 180.)

In contrast to Christianity, Islam drew no rigid distinction between the clergy and the laity. A lay scholarly elite developed, however, and held moral authority within Islamic society in domestic and religious matters. This elite, known as the **ulema**, or "persons with correct knowledge," served a social function similar to that of a professional priesthood or rabbinate. Its members were men of great piety and obvious learning whose opinions came to have the force of law in Muslim society. They also saw that Muslim rulers adhered to the letter of the Qur'an.

Islamic Diversity

The success of Islam lay in its ability to unify and inspire tribal Arabs and other non-Jewish and non-Christian people. Islam also appealed to Arab pride, for it deemed Muhammad to be history's major religious figure and his followers to be God's chosen people.

As early as the seventh century, however, disputes arose among Muslims over the nature of Islamic society and authority within it that left permanent divisions. Disagreement over the true line of succession to Muhammad—the **caliphate**—was one source of discord. Another disagreement related to this was over doctrinal issues involving the extent to which Islam was an inclusive religion, open to sinners as well as to the virtuous. Several groups emerged from these disputes. The most radical was the Kharijites, whose leaders seceded from the camp of the caliph Ali (656–661) because Ali compromised with his enemies on a matter of principle. Righteous and judgmental, the Kharijites wanted all but the most rigorously virtuous Muslims excluded from the community of the faithful. In 661, a Kharijite assassinated Ali.

Another, more influential group was the **Shi'a**, or "partisans of Ali" (*Shi'at Ali*). The Shi'a looked on Ali and his descendants as the rightful successors of Muhammad not only by virtue of kinship, but also by the expressed will of the Prophet himself. To the Shi'a, Ali's assassination revealed the most basic truth of a devout Muslim life: A true *imam*, or "ruler," must expect to suffer unjustly even unto death in the world, and so, too, must his followers. A distinctive theology of martyrdom has ever since been a mark of Shi'a teaching. And the Shi'a, until modern times, have been an embattled minority within mainstream Islamic society.

A third group, which has been dominant for most of Islamic history, was the majority centrist **Sunnis** (followers of **sunna**, or "tradition"). Sunnis have always put loyalty to the community of Islam above all else and have spurned the exclusivism and purism of the Kharijites and the Shi'a.

A Muslim and a Christian play the *ud* or lute together, from a thirteenth-century *Book of Chants* in the Escorial Monastery of Madrid. Medieval Europe was deeply influenced by Arab–Islamic culture, transmitted particularly through Spain. Some of the many works in Arabic on musical theory were translated into Latin and Hebrew, but the main influence on music came from the arts of singing and playing spread by minstrels.   A Moor and a Christian playing the lute, miniature in a book of music from the "Cantigas" of Alphonso X "the Wise" (1221–1284). Thirteenth century (manuscript). Monastero de El Excorial, El Escorial, Spain/index/Bridgeman Art Library

The Battle of the Sexes in Christianity and Islam

IN EARLY CHRISTIANITY man and woman were viewed as one and the same offspring, Eve born of Adam, for which reason they were forever after drawn irresistibly to one another. What one did to the other, one also did to oneself, so tightly were they bound. And that bond between husband and wife made their relationship all the more caring and charitable.

Muhammad's role as a husband was by all accounts exemplary: a spouse who dealt shrewdly and fairly with his wives, a splendid model for his followers. In the teaching of the *Qur'an*, all conflict between husband and wife was to be resolved by talking and, that failing, by the husband's departure from the marital bed. Heeding the example of the Prophet and the teaching of the *Qur'an*, devout Muslim men viewed a husband's hitting a wife as a last resort in his disciplining of her. Yet, when a wife flagrantly disobeyed (*nashiz*) her husband, or, much worse, was unfaithful to him, hitting often became the husband's and society's first response.

QUESTIONS

1. How does the marriage bond differ in the Christian and Muslim faiths? What does it mean to Christians to say that husband and wife are one flesh? Is that also the way spouses are perceived in Islam?

2. How successful is male discipline of self and of wife in Islam? Is Christian marriage too egalitarian, and hence more vulnerable to failure?

3. If marriage is a mirror of a religion, what does it reveal Christianity and Islam to be?

I. Christian Marriage

St. John Chrysostom (347–407) elaborated the relationship between Christian spouses in his Homily on Christian Spouses: *"Wives, be subject to your husbands, as to the Lord . . . Husbands, love your wives as Christ loved the Church." (Ephesians 5:22–25)*

There is no relationship between human beings so close as that of husband and wife, if they are united as they ought to be . . . God did not fashion woman independently from man . . . nor did He enable woman to bear children without man . . . He made the one man Adam to be the origin of all mankind, both male and female, and made it impossible for men and women to be self-sufficient [without one another] . . .

The love of husband and wife is [thus] the force that wields society together . . . Why else would [God] say, "Wives, be subject to your husbands?" Because when harmony prevails, the children are raised well, the household is kept in order . . . and great benefits, both for families and for states result . . .

Having seen the amount of obedience necessary, hear now about the amount of love that is needed. [If] you want your wife to be obedient to you . . . then be responsible for the same providential care of her as Christ has for the Church. Even if you see her belittling you, or despising and mocking you . . . subject her to yourself through affection, kindness, and your great regard for her . . . One's partner for life, the mother of one's children, the source of one's every joy, should never be fettered with fear and threats, but with love and patience . . . What sort of satisfaction could a husband have, if he lives with his wife as if she were a slave and not a woman [there] by her own free will. [So] suffer anything for her sake, but never disgrace her, for Christ never did this with the Church . . .

A wife should never nag her husband [saying] "You lazy coward, you have no ambition! Look at our relatives and neighbors; they have plenty of money. Their wives have far more than I do." Let no wife say any such thing; she is her husband's body, and it is not for her to dictate to her head, but rather to submit and obey . . . Likewise, if a husband has a wife who behaves this way, he must never exercise his authority by insulting and abusing her.

Source: Don S. Browning et al., *Sex, Marriage, and Family in World Religions* (New York: Columbia University Press), pp. 106–108.

أماثل بلى هو ومن طوق الجماعة وجح النعامة اكذب من أي نعامة حين
محرف بالبيامة فرم ابن زيد رقم تبر السواط وانشاط انشاطة المعناط
وقال لها وبلك يادقان يا عجان بأعضة البعلاق والجار انعذبن في الخلوة

القاضي

لنعذبني وبسدبي في الجماعة نكبني وقد علم ان رحن يبين عليك ورنون البك
المثبل افم من قرة وايبس من قرة واخشن من ليفة وانتن من جيفة
وانقل من رضضه واقذ رمن حيطه وابرز من قرة وابو درمن قرة واجمرن

II. Muslim Marriage

Chroniclers Abu Hamid Al-Ghazali (1058–1111), Ihya'U-lum, 2:34–35 (eleventh century C.E.) elaborate the teaching of Qur'an 4:34: "Men are the protectors and maintainers of women because God has given [men] more strength . . . and because they support [women] from their means."

Treating women well and bearing their ill treatment [is] required for marriage . . . God said, "keep them good company." [Among] the last things the Messenger [Muhammad] recommended was to take care of your slaves. Do not burden them with things beyond their capacity, and observe God's exhortations relating to your wives, for they are like slaves in your hands. You took them in trust from God and made them your wives by His words . . .

One should know that treating one's wife well does not only mean not harming her; it also means to endure ill treatment and be patient when she gets angry and loses her temper, a [method] the Messenger used to forgive his wives who argued with him and turned away from him for the whole day . . .

'A'ishah [a wife of the Prophet] once got angry and said to the Prophet . . . "You, who claims to be the Prophet of God!" The Messenger of God smiled and tolerated her in the spirit of forgiveness and generosity . . . It is believed that the first love story in Islam was that of Prophet Muhammad and 'A'ishah. The Prophet used to say to his other wives: "Do not upset me by saying bad things about 'A'ishah, for she is the only woman in whose company I have received the revelation [of God]!" Anas [Ibn Malik, a ninth-century chronicler] reported that the Prophet was the most compassionate person in matters concerning women and children . . .

Respond to [as he did to women's] harshness by teasing, joking, and kidding them, for it is certain this softens women's hearts. The Prophet said, "The people with the most perfect faith are those with the best ethics and those who are the kindest toward their families." Umar [a companion of the Prophet and the second caliph of Islam] once said: "One should always be like a child with his family, but when they need him they should find [in him] a man."

Source: Browning, *Sex, Marriage, and Family*, pp. 190–91, 194–95.

181

Islamic Empires

Under Muhammad's first three successors—the caliphs Abu Bakr (r. 632–634), Umar (r. 634–644), and Uthman (r. 644–655)—Islam expanded by conquest throughout the southern and eastern Mediterranean, into territories mostly still held today by Islamic states. In the eighth century, Muslim armies occupied parts of Spain in the West and of India in the East, producing a truly vast empire. (See Map 6–3.) The capital of this empire moved, first, from Mecca to Damascus in Syria, and then, in 750, to Baghdad in Iraq after the Abbasid dynasty replaced the Umayyads in a struggle for the caliphate. Thereafter, the huge Muslim Empire gradually broke up into separate states, some with their own line of caliphs claiming to be the true successors of Muhammad.

The early Muslim conquests would not have been so rapid and thorough had the contemporary Byzantine and Persian empires not been exhausted by decades of war. The Muslims struck at both empires in the 630s, completely overrunning the Persian Empire by 651. Most of the inhabitants in Byzantine Syria and Palestine, although Christian, were Semites like the Arabs. Any religious unity they felt with the Byzantine Greeks may have been offset by hatred of the Byzantine army of occupation and by resentment of Constantinople's efforts to impose Greek "orthodox" beliefs on the Monophysite churches of Egypt and Syria. As a result, many Egyptian and Syrian Christians, hoping for deliverance from Byzantine oppression, appear to have welcomed the Islamic conquerors.

Although Islam gained converts from among the Christians in the Near East, North Africa, and Spain, its efforts to invade northern Europe were rebuffed. The ruler of the Franks, Charles Martel, defeated a raiding party of Arabs on the western frontier of Europe at Poitiers (today in central France) in 732. This victory and the failure to capture Constantinople ended any Arab effort to expand into Western or Central Europe.

The Western Debt to Islam

Arab invasions and their presence in the Mediterranean area during the early Middle Ages contributed both directly and indirectly to the formation of Western Europe. They did so indirectly by driving Western Europeans back onto their native tribal and inherited Judeo-Christian, Greco-Roman, and Byzantine resources, from which they created a Western culture of their own. Also, by diverting the attention and energies of the Byzantine Empire during the formative centuries, the Arabs may have prevented it from expanding into and reconquering Western Europe. That allowed two Germanic peoples to gain ascendancy: first, the Franks and then the Lombards, who invaded Italy in the sixth century and settled in the Po valley around the city of Milan.

Map 6–3 **MUSLIM CONQUESTS AND DOMINATION OF THE MEDITERRANEAN TO ABOUT 750 C.E.** The rapid spread of Islam (both as a religion and as a political-military power) is shown here. Within 125 years of Muhammad's rise, Muslims came to dominate Spain and all areas south and east of the Mediterranean.

Despite the hostility of the Christian West to the Islamic world, there was nonetheless much creative interchange between these two different cultures, and the West profited greatly and directly from it. At this time, Arab civilizations were the more advanced, enjoying their golden age, and they had much to teach a toddling West. Between the eighth and tenth centuries, Cordoba, the capital of Muslim Spain, was a model multicultural city embracing Arabs, Berbers from North Africa, Christian converts to Islam, and Jews. Cordoba was a conduit for the finest Arabian tableware, leather, silks, dyes, aromatic ointments, and perfumes into the West. The Arabs taught Western farmers how to irrigate fields and Western artisans how to tan leather and refine silk. The West also gained from its contacts with Arabic scholars. Thanks to the skills of Islamic scholars, ancient Greek works on astronomy, mathematics, and medicine became available in Latin translation to Westerners. Down to the sixteenth century, the basic gynecological and child-care manuals guiding the work of Western midwives and physicians were compilations made by the Baghdad physician Al-Razi (Rhazes), the philosopher and physician Ibn-Sina (Avicenna) (980–1037), and Ibn Rushd (known in the West as Averröes, 1126–1198), who was also Islam's greatest authority on Aristotle. Jewish scholars also thrived amid the intellectual culture Islamic scholars created. The greatest of them all, Moses Maimonides (1135–1204), wrote in both Arabic and Hebrew. The medieval Arabs also gave the West one of its most popular books: *The Arabian Nights*, poetic folk tales that are still read and imitated in the West.

▼ Western Society and the Developing Christian Church

Facing barbarian invasions from the north and east and a strong Islamic presence in the Mediterranean, the West found itself in decline during the fifth and sixth centuries. As trade waned, cities rapidly fell on hard times, depriving the West of centers for the exchange of goods and ideas that might enable it to look and live beyond itself.

In the seventh century, the Byzantine emperors, their hands full with the Islamic threat in the East, were unable to assert themselves in the West, leaving most of the region to the Franks and the Lombards. As a result, Western Europeans now had to rely on their native Greco-Roman, Judeo-Christian, and barbarian heritages as they put together a distinctive culture of their own. As Western shipping declined in the Mediterranean, urban populations that otherwise would have engaged in trade-related work left the cities for the countryside in ever greater numbers. There they found the employment and protection they sought on the estates of the great landholders, who, for their part, needed laborers and welcomed the new emigrants. (See "Feudal Society," page 196.)

While these social changes were occurring, one institution remained firmly entrenched and increasingly powerful within the declining cities of the waning Roman Empire: the Christian church. The church had long modeled its own structure on that of the imperial Roman administration. Like the imperial government, church government was centralized and hierarchical. Strategically placed "generals" (bishops) in European cities looked for spiritual direction to their leader, the bishop of Rome. As the Western empire crumbled, Roman governors withdrew and populations emigrated to the countryside, where the resulting vacuum of authority was filled by local bishops and cathedral chapters. The local cathedral became the center of urban life and the local bishop the highest authority for those who remained in the cities. In Rome, on a larger and more fateful scale, the pope took control of the city as the Western emperors gradually departed and died out. Left to its own devices, Western Europe soon discovered that the Christian church was its best repository of Roman administrative skills and classical culture.

Challenged by Rome's decline to become a major political force, the Christian church survived the period of Germanic and Islamic invasions as a somewhat spiritually weakened and compromised institution. Yet it remained a potent civilizing and unifying force. It had a religious message of providential purpose and individual worth that could give solace and meaning to life at its worst. It had a ritual of baptism and a creed, or statement of belief, that united people beyond the traditional barriers of social class, education, and gender. Alone in the West, the church retained an effective hierarchical administration, scattered throughout the old empire, staffed by the best educated minds in Europe and centered in emperor-less Rome.

Monastic Culture

Throughout late antiquity the Christian church gained the services of growing numbers of monks, who were not only loyal to its mission, but also objects of great popular respect. Monastic culture proved again and again to be the peculiar strength of the church during the Middle Ages.

The first monks were hermits who had withdrawn from society to pursue a more perfect way of life. Inspired by the Christian ideals, they led a life of complete self-denial in imitation of Christ. The popularity of monasticism began to grow as Roman persecution of Christians waned and Christianity became the favored religion of the empire during the fourth century. **Monasticism** replaced martyrdom as the most perfect way to imitate Christ and to confess one's faith.

Christians came to view monastic life—embracing, as it did, the biblical "counsels of perfection" (chastity, poverty, and obedience)—as the purest form of religious practice, going beyond the baptism and creed that identified ordinary believers. This view evolved during the Middle Ages into a belief in the general superiority of the clergy and in the church's mission over the laity and the state. That belief served the papacy in later confrontations with secular rulers.

Anthony of Egypt (ca. 251–356), the father of hermit monasticism, was inspired by Jesus' command in the Gospels to the rich young ruler: "If you will be perfect, sell all that you have, give it to the poor, and follow me" (Matthew 19:21). Anthony went into the desert to pray and work, setting an example followed by hundreds in Egypt, Syria, and Palestine in the fourth and fifth centuries.

Hermit monasticism was soon joined by the development of communal monasticism. In the first quarter of the fourth century, Pachomius (ca. 286–346) organized monks in southern Egypt into a highly regimented community in which monks shared a life of labor, order, and discipline enforced by a strict penal code. Such monastic communities grew to contain a thousand or more inhabitants. They were little "cities of God," trying to separate themselves from the collapsing Roman and the nominal Christian world. Basil the Great (329–379) popularized communal monasticism throughout the East, providing a less severe rule than Pachomius, one that directed monks into such worldly services as caring for orphans, widows, and the infirm in surrounding communities.

Athanasius (ca. 293–373) and Martin of Tours (ca. 315–399) introduced monasticism to the West. The teachings of John Cassian (ca. 360–435) and Jerome (ca. 340–420) then helped shape the basic values and practices of Western monasticism. The great organizer of Western monasticism, however, was Benedict of Nursia (ca. 480–547). In 529, he established a monastery at Monte Cassino, in Italy, founding the form of monasticism— Benedictine—that bears his name and quickly came to dominate in the West. It eventually replaced an Irish, non-Benedictine monasticism that was common until the 600s in the British Isles and Gaul.

Benedict wrote *Rule for Monasteries*, a sophisticated and comprehensive plan for every activity of the monks, even detailing the manner in which they were to sleep. His *Rule* opposed the severities of earlier monasticism that tortured the body and anguished the mind. Benedict insisted on good food and even some wine, adequate clothing, and proper amounts of sleep and relaxation. Periods of devotion (about four hours each day) were set aside for the "work of God." That is, regular prayers, liturgical activities, and study alternated with manual labor (farming). This program permitted not a moment's idleness and carefully nurtured the religious, intellectual, and physical well-being of the cloistered monks. The monastery was directed by an abbot, whose command the monks had to obey unquestioningly. (See "The Benedictine Order Sets Its Requirements for Entrance.")

Individual Benedictine monasteries remained autonomous until the later Middle Ages, when the Benedictines became a unified order of the church. During the early Middle Ages, Benedictine missionaries Christianized both England and Germany. Their disciplined organization and devotion to hard work made the Benedictines an economic and political power as well as a spiritual force wherever they settled.

The Doctrine of Papal Primacy

Constantine and his successors, especially the Eastern emperors, ruled religious life with an iron hand and consistently looked on the church as little more than a department of the state. Such political assumption of spiritual power involved the emperor directly in the church's affairs, allowing him to play the theologian and to summon councils to resolve its doctrinal quarrels. At first, state control of religion was also the rule in the West. Most of the early popes were mediocre and not very influential. To increase their influence, in the fifth and sixth centuries, they took advantage of imperial weakness and distraction to develop a new defense: the powerful weaponry of papal primacy. This doctrine raised the Roman pope, or pontiff, to unassailable supremacy within the church when it came to defining church doctrine. It also put him in a position to make important secular claims, paving the way to repeated conflicts between church and state, pope and emperor, throughout the Middle Ages.

Papal primacy was first asserted as a response to the decline of imperial Rome. It was also a response to the claims of the patriarchs of the Eastern church, who, after imperial power was transferred to Constantinople, looked on the bishop of Rome as an equal, but no superior. In 381, the ecumenical Council of Constantinople declared the bishop of Constantinople to be of first rank after the bishop of Rome "because Constantinople is the new Rome." In 451, the ecumenical Council of Chalcedon recognized Constantinople as having the same religious primacy in the East as Rome had possessed in the West. By the mid-sixth century, the bishop of Constantinople described himself in his correspondence as a "universal" patriarch.

Roman pontiffs, understandably jealous of such claims and resentful of the political interference of Eastern emperors, launched a counteroffensive. Pope Damasus I (r. 366–384)[2] took the first of several major steps in the rise of the Roman church when he declared a Roman **"apostolic" primacy**. Pointing to Jesus' words to Peter in the Gospel of Matthew (16:18) ("Thou art Peter, and upon this rock I will build my church"), he claimed himself and all other popes to be Peter's direct successors as the unique "rock" on which the Christian church was built. Pope Leo I (r. 440–461) took still another fateful

---

[2]Dates after popes' names are the years of each reign.

THE BENEDICTINE ORDER SETS ITS REQUIREMENTS FOR ENTRANCE

The religious life had great appeal in a time of political and social uncertainty. Entrance into a monastery was not, however, escapism. Much was demanded of the new monk, both during and after his probationary period, which is described here. Benedict's contribution was to prescribe a balanced blend of religious, physical, and intellectual activities within a well-structured community.

Why did the religious life have such great appeal at this time in history? Were there materialistic as well as spiritual reasons for entering a cloister? What are Benedict's reasons for not allowing a monk to change his mind and leave the cloister, once vows have been taken?

When anyone is newly come for the reformation of his life, let him not be granted an easy entrance, but, as the Apostle says, "Test the spirits to see whether they are from God." If the newcomer, therefore, perseveres in his knocking, and if it is seen after four or five days that he bears patiently the harsh treatment offered him and the difficulty of admission, and that he persists in his petition, then let entrance be granted him, and let him stay in the guest house for a few days.

After that let him live in the novitiate, where the novices study, eat, and sleep. A senior shall be assigned to them who is skilled in winning souls, to watch over them with the utmost care. Let him examine whether the novice is truly seeking God, and whether he is zealous for the Work of God, for obedience and for humiliations. Let the novice be told all the hard and rugged ways by which the journey to God is made.

If he promises stability and perseverance, then at the end of two months let this Rule be read through to him, and let him be addressed thus: "Here is the law under which you wish to fight. If you can observe it, enter; if you cannot, you are free to depart." If he still stands firm, let him be taken to the above-mentioned novitiate and again tested in all patience. And after the lapse of six months let the Rule be read to him, that he may know on what he is entering. And if he still remains firm, after four months let the same Rule be read to him again.

Then, having deliberated with himself, if he promises to keep it in its entirety and to observe everything that is commanded him, let him be received into the community. But let him understand that, according to the law of the Rule, from that day forward he may not leave the monastery nor withdraw his neck from under the yoke of the Rule which he was free to refuse or to accept during that prolonged deliberation.

Leonard J. Doyle, *St. Benedict's Rule for Monasteries* (Collegeville, MN: Liturgical Press, 1948), pp. 79–80.

step by assuming the title ***pontifex maximus***, or "supreme priest." He further proclaimed himself to be endowed with a "plentitude of power," thereby establishing the supremacy of the bishop of Rome over all other bishops. During Leo's reign, an imperial decree recognized his exclusive jurisdiction over the Western church. At the end of the fifth century, Pope Gelasius I (r. 492–496) proclaimed the authority of the clergy to be "more weighty" than the power of kings, because priests had charge of divine affairs and the means of salvation.

Events as well as ideology favored the papacy. As barbarian and Islamic invasions isolated the West by diverting the attention of the Byzantine empire, they also prevented both emperors and the Eastern patriarchs from interfering in the affairs of the Western church. Islam may even be said to have "saved" the Western church from Eastern domination. At the same time, the Franks became a new political ally of the church. Eastern episcopal competition with Rome ended as bishopric after bishopric fell to Islamic armies in the East. The power of the exarch of Ravenna—the Byzantine emperor's viceroy in the West—was eclipsed in the late sixth century by invading Lombards who conquered most of Italy. Thanks to Frankish prodding, the Lombards became Nicene Christians loyal to Rome and a new counterweight to Eastern power and influence in the West. In an unprecedented act, Pope Gregory I, "the Great" (r. 590–604), instead of looking for protection to the emperor in Constantinople, negotiated an independent peace treaty with the Lombards.

The Religious Division of Christendom

In both East and West, religious belief alternately served and undermined imperial political unity. Since the fifth century, the patriarch of Constantinople had blessed Byzantine emperors in that city (the "second Rome"), attesting the close ties between rulers and the Eastern church. In 391, Christianity became the official faith of the Eastern empire, while all other religions and sects were deemed "demented and insane."[3] Between the fourth and sixth centuries, the patriarchs of Constantinople, Alexandria, Antioch, and Jerusalem received generous endowments of land and gold from rich, pious donors, empowering the church to act as the state's welfare agency.

While Orthodox Christianity was the religion that mattered most, it was not the only religion in the empire with a significant following. Nor did Byzantine rulers view religion as merely a political tool. From time to time, Christian heresies also received imperial support. Moreover, with imperial encouragement, Christianity absorbed pagan religious practices and beliefs that were too deeply rooted in rural and urban cultures to be eradicated, thus turning local gods and their shrines into Christian saints and holy places. (See Encountering the Past, "Two Roman Festivals" in Chapter 4, page 112.)

The empire was also home, albeit inhospitably, to large numbers of Jews. Pagan Romans viewed Jews as narrow, dogmatic, and intolerant but tolerated Judaism as an ancient and acceptable form of worship. When Rome adopted Christianity, Jews continued to have legal protection as long as they did not attempt to convert Christians, build new synagogues, or try to hold certain official positions or enter some professions. Whereas the emperor most intent on religious conformity within the empire, Justinian, encouraged Jews to convert voluntarily, later emperors commanded them to be baptized and gave them tax breaks as incentives to become Christians. However, neither persuasion nor coercion succeeded in converting the empire's Jews.

The differences between Eastern and Western Christianity grew to be no less irreconcilable than those between Christians and Jews. One issue even divided Justinian and his wife Theodora. Whereas Justinian remained

A ninth-century Byzantine manuscript shows an iconoclast whiting out an image of Christ. The Iconoclastic Controversy was an important factor in the division of Christendom into separate Latin and Greek branches. State Historical Museum, Moscow

strictly orthodox in his Christian beliefs, Theodora supported a divisive Eastern teaching that the Council of Chalcedon in 451 had condemned as a heresy, namely, that Christ had a single, immortal nature and was not both eternal God and mortal man in one and the same person. In reaction to the Monophysite controversy, orthodox Christianity became even more determined to protect the sovereignty of God. This concern is apparent in Byzantine art, which portrays Christ as impassive and transcendent, as united in his personhood with God, not as a suffering mortal man. In the sixth century, despite imperial persecution, the Monophysites became a separate church in the East where many Christians still today adhere to it.

A similar dispute appeared in Eastern debates over the relationship among the members of the Trinity, specifically whether the Holy Spirit proceeded only from the Father, as the Nicene-Constantinopolitan Creed taught, or from the Father and the Son (filioque in Latin), an idea that became increasingly popular in the West and was eventually adopted by the Western church and inserted into its creed. These disputes, which appear trivial and are almost unintelligible to many people today, seemed vitally important to many Christians at the time. Eastern theologians argued that adding filioque to the creed not

[3]Mango, Byzantium, p. 88.

only diminished God's majesty by seeming to subordinate the Holy Spirit but also weakened a core Christian belief—the divine unity and dignity of all three persons of the Trinity. Some perceive here a hidden political concern, important in the East. By protecting the unity and majesty of God the Father, Eastern theology also safeguarded the unity and majesty of the emperor himself, from whom all power on earth was believed properly to flow. The idea of a divisible Godhead, no matter how abstract and subtle, was unacceptable to Eastern Christians and the imperial government because it also suggested the divisibility of imperial power, not a tenet for an emperor who closely associated himself with God.

Another major rift between the Christian East and West was over the veneration of images in worship. In 726, Emperor Leo III (r. 717–741) forbade the use of images and icons that portrayed Christ, the Virgin Mary, and the saints throughout Christendom. As their veneration had been commonplace for centuries, the decree came as a shock, especially to the West where it was rejected as heresy. **Iconoclasm**, as the change in policy was called, may have been a pretext to close monasteries and seize their lands because monks were among the most zealous defenders of the veneration of images. On the other hand, the emperor may have wished to accommodate Muslim sensitivities at a time when he was at war with the Arabs (Islam strictly forbade image worship). Be that as it may, the emperor's decree drove the popes into the camp of the Franks, where they found in Charlemagne an effective protector against the Byzantine world. (See page 000.) Although images were eventually restored in the Eastern churches, many masterpieces were lost during a near century of theology-inspired destruction.

A third difference between East and West was the Eastern emperors' pretension to absolute sovereignty, both secular and religious. Expressing their sense of sacred mission, the emperors presented themselves in the trappings of holiness and directly interfered in matters of church and religion, what is called **Caesaropapism**, or the emperor acting as if he were pope as well as caesar. To a degree unknown in the West, Eastern emperors appointed and manipulated the clergy, convening church councils and enforcing church decrees. By comparison, the West nurtured a distinction between church and state that became visible in the eleventh century.

The Eastern church also rejected several disputed requirements of Roman Christianity. It denied the existence of Purgatory, permitted lay divorce and remarriage, allowed priests, but not bishops, to marry, and conducted religious services in the languages that people in a given locality actually spoke (the so-called "vernacular" languages) instead of Greek and Latin. In these matters Eastern Christians gained opportunities and rights that Christians in the West would not enjoy, and then only in part, until the Protestant Reformation in the sixteenth century. (See Chapter 11.)

Having piled up over the centuries, these various differences ultimately resulted in a schism between the two churches in 1054. In that year a Western envoy of the pope, Cardinal Humbertus, visited the Patriarch of Constantinople, Michael Cerularius, in the hope of overcoming the differences that divided Christendom. The patriarch was not, however, welcoming. Relations between the two men quickly deteriorated, and cardinal and patriarch engaged in mutual recriminations and insults. Before leaving the city, Humbertus left a bull of excommunication on the altar of Hagia Sophia. In response, the patriarch proclaimed all Western popes to have been heretics since the sixth century! Nine hundred and eleven years would pass before this breach was repaired. In a belated ecumenical gesture in 1965, a Roman pope met with the patriarch of Constantinople to revoke the mutual condemnations of 1054.

▼ The Kingdom of the Franks: From Clovis to Charlemagne

A warrior chieftain, Clovis (ca. 466–511), who converted to Catholic Christianity around 496, founded the first Frankish dynasty, the Merovingians, named for Merovich, an early leader of one branch of the Franks. Clovis and his successors united the Salian and Ripuarian Franks, subdued the Arian Burgundians and Visigoths, and established the kingdom of the Franks within ancient Gaul, making the Franks and the Merovingian kings a significant force in Western Europe. The Franks themselves occupied a broad belt of territory that extended throughout modern France, Belgium, the Netherlands, and western Germany, and their loyalties remained strictly tribal and local.

Governing the Franks

In attempting to govern this sprawling kingdom, the Merovingians encountered what proved to be the most persistent problem of medieval political history—the competing claims of the "one" and the "many." On the one hand, the king struggled for a centralized government and transregional loyalty, and on the other, powerful local magnates strove to preserve their regional autonomy and traditions.

The Merovingian kings addressed this problem by making pacts with the landed nobility and by creating the royal office of counts. The counts were men without possessions to whom the king gave great lands in the expectation that they would be, as the landed aristocrats often were not, loyal officers of the kingdom. Like local aristocrats, however, the Merovingian counts also let their immediate self-interest gain the upper hand. Once established in office for a period of time, they, too, became ■ territorial rulers in their own right, so the

Frankish kingdom progressively fragmented into independent regions and tiny principalities. The Frankish custom of dividing the kingdom equally among the king's legitimate male heirs furthered this tendency.

Rather than purchasing allegiance and unity within the kingdom, the Merovingian largess simply occasioned the rise of competing magnates and petty tyrants, who became laws unto themselves within their regions. By the seventh century, the Frankish king was king in title only and had no effective executive power. Real power came to be concentrated in the office of the "mayor of the palace," spokesperson at the king's court for the great landowners of the three regions into which the Frankish kingdom was divided: Neustria, Austrasia, and Burgundy. Through this office, the Carolingian dynasty rose to power.

The Carolingians controlled the office of the mayor of the palace from the ascent to that post of Pepin I of Austrasia (d. 639) until 751, when, with the enterprising connivance of the pope, they simply seized the Frankish crown. Pepin II (d. 714) ruled in fact, if not in title, over the Frankish kingdom. His illegitimate son, Charles Martel ("the Hammer," d. 741), created a great cavalry by bestowing lands known as **benefices**, or **fiefs**, on powerful noblemen. In return, they agreed to be ready to serve as the king's army. It was such an army that defeated the Muslims at Poitiers in 732.

MAJOR POLITICAL AND RELIGIOUS DEVELOPMENTS OF THE EARLY MIDDLE AGES

313	Emperor Constantine issues the Edict of Milan
325	Council of Nicaea defines Christian doctrine
451	Council of Chalcedon further defines Christian doctrine
451–453	Europe invaded by the Huns under Attila
476	Odovacer deposes Western emperor and rules as king of the Romans
489–493	Theodoric establishes kingdom of Ostrogoths in Italy
529	Benedict founds monastery at Monte Cassino
533	Justinian codifies Roman law
533–554	Byzantines reconquer parts of the Western Empire
622	Muhammad's flight from Mecca (Hegira)
711	Muslim invasion of Spain
732	Charles Martel defeats Muslims at Poitiers
754	Pope Stephen II and Pepin III ally

The fiefs so generously bestowed by Charles Martel to create his army came in large part from landed property he usurped from the church. His alliance with the landed aristocracy in this grand manner permitted the Carolingians to have some measure of political success where the Merovingians had failed. The Carolingians created counts almost entirely from among the same landed nobility from which the Carolingians themselves had risen. The Merovingians, in contrast, had tried to compete directly with these great aristocrats by raising landless men to power. By playing to strength rather than challenging it, the Carolingians strengthened themselves, at least for the short term. The church, by this time dependent on the protection of the Franks against the Eastern emperor and the Lombards, could only suffer the loss of its lands in silence. Later, although they never returned them, the Franks partially compensated the church for these lands.

The Frankish Church The church came to play a large and enterprising role in the Frankish government. By Carolingian times, monasteries were a dominant force. Their intellectual achievements made them respected centers of culture. Their religious teaching and example imposed order on surrounding populations. Their relics and rituals made them magical shrines to which pilgrims came in great numbers. Also, thanks to their many gifts and internal discipline and industry, many had become profitable farms and landed estates, their abbots rich and powerful magnates. Already in Merovingian times, the higher clergy were employed along with counts as royal agents.

It was the policy of the Carolingians, perfected by Charles Martel and his successor, Pepin III ("the Short," d. 768), to use the church to pacify conquered neighboring tribes—Frisians, Thüringians, Bavarians, and especially the Franks' archenemies, the Saxons. Conversion to Nicene Christianity became an integral part of the successful annexation of conquered lands and people. The cavalry broke their bodies while the clergy won their hearts and minds. The Anglo-Saxon missionary Saint Boniface (born Wynfrith; 680?–754) was the most important cleric to serve Carolingian kings in this way. Christian bishops in missionary districts and elsewhere became lords, appointed by and subject to the king. In this ominous integration of secular and religious policy lay the seeds of the later investiture controversy of the eleventh and twelfth centuries. (See Chapter 7.)

The church served more than Carolingian territorial expansion. Pope Zacharias (r. 741–752) also sanctioned Pepin the Short's termination of the Merovingian dynasty and supported the Carolingian accession to outright kingship of the Franks. With the pope's public blessing, Pepin was proclaimed king by the nobility in council in 751; the last of the Merovingians, the puppet king Childeric III, was hustled off to a monastery and dynastic oblivion. According to legend, Saint Boniface first anointed Pepin, thereby investing Frankish rule from the start with a certain holiness.

Zacharias's successor, Pope Stephen II (r. 752–757), did not let Pepin forget the favor of his predecessor. In 753, when the Lombards besieged Rome, Pope Stephen crossed the Alps and appealed directly to Pepin to cast out the invaders and to guarantee papal claims to central Italy, largely dominated at this time by the Eastern emperor. As already noted, in 754 during the controversy over icons, the Franks and the church formed an alliance against the Lombards and the Eastern emperor. Carolingian kings became the protectors of the Catholic Church and thereby "kings by the grace of God." Pepin gained the title *patricius Romanorum*, "patrician of the Romans," a title first borne by the ruling families of Rome and heretofore applied to the representative of the Eastern emperor. In 755, the Franks defeated the Lombards and gave the pope the lands surrounding Rome, creating what came to be known as the **Papal States**.

In this period a fraudulent document appeared—the *Donation of Constantine* (written between 750 and 800)—that was enterprisingly designed to remind the Franks of the church's importance as the heir of Rome. Many believed it to be genuine until it was definitely exposed as a forgery in the fifteenth century by the humanist Lorenzo Valla. (See Chapter 10.)

The papacy had looked to the Franks for an ally strong enough to protect it from the Eastern emperors. It is an irony of history that the church found in the Carolingian dynasty a Western imperial government that drew almost as slight a boundary between state and church and between secular and religious policy as did Eastern emperors. Although Carolingian patronage was eminently preferable to Eastern domination for the popes, it proved in its own way to be no less constraining.

The Reign of Charlemagne (768–814)

Charlemagne, the son of Pepin the Short, continued the role of his father as papal protector in Italy and his policy of territorial conquest in the north. After decisively defeating King Desiderius and the Lombards of northern Italy in 774, Charlemagne took upon himself the title "King of the Lombards." He widened the frontiers of his kingdom further by subjugating surrounding pagan tribes, foremost among them the Saxons, whom the Franks brutally Christianized and dispersed in small groups throughout Frankish lands. The Muslims were chased beyond the Pyrenees, and the Avars (a tribe related to the Huns) were practically annihilated, bringing the Danubian plains into the Frankish orbit.

By the time of his death on January 28, 814, Charlemagne's kingdom embraced modern France, Belgium, Holland, Switzerland, almost the whole of western Germany, much of Italy, a portion of Spain, and the island of Corsica. (See Map 6–4, on page 190.)

The New Empire Encouraged by his ambitious advisers, Charlemagne came to harbor imperial designs. He desired to be not only king of all the Franks but a universal emperor as well. He had his sacred palace city, Aachen (in French, Aix-la-Chapelle) near the modern border between Germany and France, constructed in imitation of the courts of the ancient Roman and contemporary Eastern emperors. Although he permitted the church its independence, he looked after it with a

Interior of the Palace Chapel of Charlemagne, Aachen. French Government Tourist Office

Map 6–4 **THE EMPIRE OF CHARLEMAGNE TO 814** Building on the successes of his predecessors, Charlemagne greatly increased the Frankish domains. Such traditional enemies as the Saxons and the Lombards fell under his sway.

paternalism almost as great as that of any Eastern emperor. He used the church, above all, to promote social stability and hierarchical order throughout the kingdom—as an aid in the creation of a great Frankish Christian Empire. Frankish Christians were ceremoniously baptized, professed the Nicene Creed (with the *filioque* clause), and learned in church to revere Charlemagne.

The formation of a distinctive Carolingian Christendom was made clear in the 790s, when Charlemagne issued the so-called *Libri Carolini*. These documents attacked the Second Council of Nicaea, which, in what was actually a friendly gesture to the West, had met in 787 to formulate a new, more accommodating position for the Eastern church on the use of images. "No compromise" was Charlemagne's message to the East.

Charlemagne fulfilled his imperial pretensions on Christmas Day, 800, when Pope Leo III (r. 795–816) crowned him emperor in Rome. This event began what

would come to be known as the **Holy Roman Empire**, a revival of the old Roman Empire in the West, based in Germany after 870.

In 799, Pope Leo III had been imprisoned by the Roman aristocracy but escaped to the protection of Charlemagne, who restored him as pope. The fateful coronation of Charlemagne was thus, in part, an effort by the pope to enhance the church's stature and to gain some leverage over this powerful king. It was, however, no papal **coup d'état**; Charlemagne's control over the church remained as strong after as before the event. If the coronation benefited the church, as it certainly did, it also served Charlemagne's purposes.

Before his coronation, Charlemagne had been a minor Western potentate in the eyes of Eastern emperors. After the coronation, Eastern emperors reluctantly recognized his new imperial dignity, and Charlemagne even found it necessary to disclaim ambitions to rule as emperor over the East.

The New Emperor Charlemagne stood a majestic six feet three and a half inches tall—a fact confirmed when his tomb was opened and exact measurements of his remains were taken in 1861. He was restless, ever ready for a hunt. Informal and gregarious, he insisted on the presence of friends even when he bathed. He was widely known for his practical jokes, lusty good humor, and warm hospitality. Aachen was a festive palace city to which people and gifts came from all over the world. In 802, Charlemagne even received from the caliph of Baghdad, Harun-al-Rashid, a white elephant, whose transport across the Alps was as great a wonder as the creature itself.

Charlemagne had five official wives in succession, as well as many mistresses and concubines, and he sired numerous children. This connubial variety created special problems. His oldest son by his first marriage, Pepin, jealous of the attention shown by his father to the sons of his second wife and fearing the loss of paternal favor, joined noble enemies in a conspiracy against his father. He spent the rest of his life in confinement in a monastery after the plot was exposed.

Problems of Government Charlemagne governed his kingdom through counts, of whom there were perhaps as many as 250, strategically located within the administrative districts into which the kingdom was divided. Carolingian counts tended to be local magnates who possessed the armed might and the self-interest to enforce the will of a generous king. Counts had three main duties: to maintain a local army loyal to the king, to collect tribute and dues, and to administer justice throughout their districts.

This last responsibility a count undertook through a district law court known as the *mallus*. The *mallus* received testimony from witnesses familiar with the parties involved in a dispute or criminal case, much as a modern court does. Through such testimony, it sought to discover the character and believability of each side. On occasion, in difficult cases where the testimony was insufficient to determine guilt or innocence, recourse would be taken to judicial duels or to a variety of "divine" tests or ordeals. Among these was the length of time it took a defendant's hand to heal after immersion in boiling water. In another, a defendant was thrown with his hands and feet bound into a river or pond that a priest had blessed. If he floated, he was pronounced guilty, because the pure water had obviously rejected him; if, however, the water received him and he sank, he was deemed innocent and quickly retrieved.

In such ordeals God was believed to render a verdict. Once guilt had been made clear to the *mallus*, either by testimony or by ordeal, it assessed a monetary compensation to be paid to the injured party. This most popular way of settling grievances usually ended hostilities between individuals and families.

As in Merovingian times, many counts used their official position and new judicial powers to their own advantage and became little despots within their districts. As the strong became stronger, they also became more independent. They began to look on the land grants with which they were paid as hereditary possessions rather than generous royal donations—a development that began to fragment Charlemagne's kingdom. Charlemagne tried to oversee his overseers and improve local justice by creating special royal envoys. Known as ***missi dominici***, these were lay and clerical agents (counts, archbishops, and bishops) who made annual visits to districts other than their own. Yet their impact was marginal. Permanent provincial governors, bearing the title of prefect, duke, or margrave, were created in what was still another attempt to supervise the counts and organize the outlying regions of the kingdom. Yet as these governors became established in their areas, they proved no less corruptible than the others.

Charlemagne never solved the problem of creating a loyal bureaucracy. Ecclesiastical agents proved no better than secular ones in this regard. Landowning bishops had not only the same responsibilities, but also the same secular lifestyles and aspirations as the royal counts. Save for their attendance to the liturgy and to church prayers, they were largely indistinguishable from the lay nobility. *Capitularies*, or royal decrees, discouraged the more outrageous behavior of the clergy. However, Charlemagne also sensed, and rightly so as the Gregorian reform of the eleventh century would prove, that the emergence of a distinctive, reform-minded class of ecclesiastical landowners would be a danger to royal government. He purposefully treated his bishops as he treated his counts, that is, as vassals who served at the king's pleasure.

To be a Christian in this period was more a matter of ritual and doctrine (being baptized and reciting the creed) than of following rules for ethical behavior and social service. Both clergy and laity were more concerned with contests over the most basic kinds of social protections than with more elevated ethical issues. An important legislative achievement of Charlemagne's reign, for example, was to give a free vassal the right to break his oath of loyalty to his lord if the lord tried to kill him, reduce him to an unfree serf, withhold promised protection in time of need, or seduce his wife.

Alcuin and the Carolingian Renaissance Charlemagne accumulated great wealth in the form of loot and land from conquered tribes. He used part of this booty to attract Europe's best scholars to Aachen, where they developed court culture and education. By making scholarship materially as well as intellectually rewarding, Charlemagne attracted such scholars as Theodulf of Orleans, Angilbert, his own biographer Einhard, and the renowned Anglo-Saxon master Alcuin of York

(735–804). In 782, at almost fifty years of age, Alcuin became director of the king's palace school. He brought classical and Christian learning to Aachen in schools run by the monasteries. Alcuin was handsomely rewarded for his efforts with several monastic estates, including that of Saint Martin of Tours, the wealthiest in the kingdom.

Although Charlemagne also appreciated learning for its own sake, his grand palace school was not created simply for the love of classical scholarship. Charlemagne wanted to upgrade the administrative skills of the clerics and officials who staffed the royal bureaucracy. By preparing the sons of the nobility to run the religious and secular offices of the realm, court scholarship served kingdom building. The school provided basic instruction in the seven liberal arts, with special concentration on grammar, logic, rhetoric, and the basic mathematical arts. It therefore provided training in reading, writing, speaking, sound reasoning, and counting—the basic tools of bureaucracy.

Among the results of this intellectual activity was the appearance of a more accurate Latin in official documents and the development of a clear style of handwriting known as *Carolingian minuscule*. By making reading both easier and more pleasurable, Carolingian minuscule helped lay the foundations of subsequent Latin scholarship. It also increased lay literacy.

A modest renaissance of antiquity occurred in the palace school as scholars collected and preserved ancient manuscripts for a more curious posterity. Alcuin worked on a correct text of the Bible and made editions of the works of Gregory the Great and the monastic *Rule* of Saint Benedict. These scholarly activities aimed at concrete reforms and helped bring uniformity to church law and liturgy, educate the clergy, and improve monastic morals. Through personal correspondence and visitations, Alcuin created a genuine, if limited, community of scholars and clerics at court. He did much to infuse the highest administrative levels with a sense of comradeship and common purpose.

Breakup of the Carolingian Kingdom

In his last years, an ailing Charlemagne knew his empire was ungovernable. The seeds of dissolution lay in regionalism, that is, the determination of each region, no matter how small, to look first—and often only—to its own self-interest. Despite his skill and resolve, Charlemagne's realm became too fragmented among powerful regional magnates. Although they were his vassals, they were also landholders and lords in their own right. They knew their sovereignty lessened as Charlemagne's increased, and accordingly they became reluctant royal servants. In feudal society, a direct relationship existed between physical proximity to authority and loyalty to authority. Local people obeyed local lords more readily than they obeyed a glorious, but distant, king.

Charlemagne had been forced to recognize and even to enhance the power of regional magnates to gain needed financial and military support. But as in the Merovingian kingdom, the tail came increasingly also to wag the dog in the Carolingian.

Louis the Pious The Carolingian kings did not give up easily, however. Charlemagne's only surviving son and successor was Louis the Pious (r. 814–840), so-called because of his close alliance with the church and his promotion of puritanical reforms. Before his death, Charlemagne secured the imperial succession for Louis by raising him to "co-emperor" in a grand public ceremony. After Charlemagne's death, Louis no longer referred to himself as king of the Franks. He bore instead the single title of emperor. The assumption of this title reflected not only the Carolingian pretense to be an imperial dynasty, but also Louis's determination to unify his kingdom and raise its people above mere regional and tribal loyalties.

Unfortunately, Louis's own fertility joined with Salic, or Frankish, law and custom to prevent the attainment of this high goal. Louis had three sons by his first wife. According to Salic law, a ruler partitioned his kingdom equally among his surviving sons (Salic law forbade women to inherit the throne). Louis, who saw himself as an emperor and no mere king, recognized that a tripartite kingdom would hardly be an empire and acted early in his reign, in 817, to break this legal tradition. This he did by making his eldest son, Lothar (d. 855), co-regent and sole imperial heir by royal decree. To Lothar's brothers he gave important, but much lesser, *appanages*, or assigned hereditary lands; Pepin (d. 838) became king of Aquitaine, and Louis "the German" (d. 876) became king of Bavaria, over the eastern Franks.

In 823, Louis's second wife, Judith of Bavaria, bore him a fourth son, Charles, later called "the Bald" (d. 877). Mindful of Frankish law and custom, and determined her son should receive more than just a nominal inheritance, the queen incited the brothers Pepin and Louis against Lothar, who fled for refuge to the pope. More important, Judith was instrumental in persuading Louis to adhere to tradition and divide the kingdom equally among his four living sons. As their stepmother and the young Charles rose in their father's favor, the three brothers, fearing still further reversals, decided to act against their father. Supported by the pope, they joined forces and defeated their father in a battle near Colmar in 833.

As the bestower of crowns on emperors, the pope had an important stake in the preservation of the revived Western empire and the imperial title. Louis's belated agreement to an equal partition of his kingdom threatened to weaken the pope as well as the royal family. Therefore, the pope condemned Louis and restored Lothar to his original inheritance. But Lothar's regained

A Closer LOOK

A MULTICULTURAL BOOK COVER

CAROLINGIAN EDUCATION, ART, and architecture served royal efforts to unify the kingdom by fusing inherited Celtic-Germanic and Greco-Roman-Byzantine cultures. Charlemagne, his son, and grandsons decorated their churches with a variety of art forms, among them illuminated manuscripts, such as the bejeweled metalwork that became the binding of the *Lindau Gospels* (c. 870).

Precious stones are set on tiny pedestals to maximize the luster illuminating the crucified Christ from the gold background.

Art Resource/The Pierpont Morgan Library

The Christ seen here reflects early Christian art and Byzantine theology, which did not endow divinity with human suffering. So impassive is this Christ that he seems almost to smile on the cross. However, the surrounding panels show the angels in heaven and Christ's followers on earth writhing with grief.

To examine this image in an interactive fashion, please go to www.myhistorylab.com

PEARSON
myhistorylab

imperial dignity only stirred anew the resentments of his brothers, including his stepbrother, Charles, who joined in renewed warfare against him.

The Treaty of Verdun and Its Aftermath In 843, with the Treaty of Verdun, peace finally came to the surviving heirs of Louis the Pious. (Pepin had died in 838.) But this agreement also brought about the disaster that Louis had originally feared. The great Carolingian Empire was divided into three equal parts. Lothar received a middle section, known as Lotharingia, which embraced roughly modern Holland, Belgium, Switzerland, Alsace-Lorraine, and Italy. Charles the Bald acquired the western part of the kingdom, or roughly modern France. And Louis the German took the eastern part, or roughly modern Germany. (See Map 6–5.)

Although Lothar retained the imperial title, the universal empire of Charlemagne and Louis the Pious ceased to exist after Verdun. Not until the sixteenth century, with the election in 1519 of Charles I of Spain as Holy Roman Emperor Charles V (see Chapter 11), would the Western world again see a kingdom as vast as Charlemagne's.

The Treaty of Verdun proved to be only the beginning of Carolingian fragmentation. When Lothar died in 855, his middle kingdom was divided equally among his three surviving sons, the eldest of whom, Louis II,

retained Italy and the imperial title. This partition of the partition sealed the dissolution of the great empire of Charlemagne. Henceforth, Western Europe saw an eastern and a western Frankish kingdom—roughly Germany and France—at war over parts of the middle kingdom, a contest that continued into modern times.

In Italy the demise of the Carolingian emperors enhanced for the moment the power of the popes, who had become adept at filling vacuums. The popes were now strong enough to excommunicate weak emperors and override their wishes. In a major church crackdown on the polygyny of the Germans, Pope Nicholas I (r. 858–867) excommunicated Lothar II for divorcing his wife. After the death of the childless emperor Louis II in 875, Pope John VIII (r. 872–882) installed Charles the Bald as emperor against the express last wishes of Louis II.

When Charles the Bald died in 877, both the papal and the imperial thrones suffered defeat. They became pawns in the hands of powerful Italian and German magnates, respectively. The last Carolingian emperor died in 911. This internal political breakdown of the empire and the papacy coincided with new barbarian attacks. Neither pope nor emperor knew dignity and power again until a new Western imperial dynasty—the Saxons—attained dominance during the reign of Otto I (r. 962–973).

Map 6–5 **THE TREATY OF VERDUN, 843, AND THE TREATY OF MERSEN, 870** The Treaty of Verdun divided the kingdom of Louis the Pious among his three feuding children: Charles the Bald, Lothar, and Louis the German. After Lothar's death in 855, his lands and titles were divided among his three sons: Louis, Charles, and Lothar II. When Lothar II, who had received his father's northern kingdom, died in 870, Charles the Bald and Louis the German claimed the middle kingdom and divided it between themselves in the Treaty of Mersen.

Vikings, Magyars, and Muslims It is especially at this juncture in European history—the last quarter of the ninth and the first half of the tenth century—that we may speak with some justification of a "dark age." The late ninth and tenth centuries saw successive waves of Normans (North-men), better known as Vikings, from Scandinavia, **Magyars**, or Hungarians, the great horsemen from the eastern plains, and Muslims from the south. (See Map 6–6.) The political breakdown of the Carolingian Empire coincided with these new external threats, both probably set off by overpopulation and famine in northern and eastern Europe. The exploits of the Scandinavian peoples, or Vikings, who visited Europe, alternately as gregarious traders and savage raiders, have been preserved in Sagas and they reveal a cultural world filled with mythical gods and spirits. Taking to the sea in rugged longboats of doubled-hulled construction, they terrified their neighbors to the south, invading and occupying English and European coastal and river towns. In the 880s, the Vikings even penetrated to Aachen and besieged Paris.

In the ninth century, the Vikings turned York in northern England into a major trading post for their woolens, jewelry, and ornamental wares. Erik the Red made it to Greenland, and his son, Leif Erikson wintered in Newfoundland and may even have reached New England five hundred years before Columbus. In the eleventh century, Christian conversions and the English defeat of the Danes and Norwegians effectively restricted the Vikings to their Scandinavian homelands.

Magyars, the ancestors of the modern Hungarians, swept into Western Europe from the eastern plains, while Muslims made incursions across the Mediterranean from North Africa. The Franks built fortified towns and castles in strategic locations, and when they could, they bought off the invaders with grants of land and payments of silver. In the resulting turmoil, local populations became more dependent than ever on local strongmen for life, limb, and livelihood—the essential precondition for the maturation of feudal society.

Map 6–6 **VIKING, ISLAMIC, AND MAGYAR INVASIONS TO THE ELEVENTH CENTURY** Western Europe was sorely beset by new waves of outsiders from the ninth to the eleventh centuries. From north, east, and south, a stream of invading Vikings, Magyars, and Muslims brought the West at times to near collapse and, of course, gravely affected institutions within Europe.

This seventy-five-foot-long Viking burial ship from the early ninth century is decorated with beastly figures. It bore a dead queen, her servant, and assorted sacrificed animals to the afterlife. The bodies of the passengers were confined within a burial cabin at mid-ship surrounded with a treasure trove of jewels and tapestries. Dorling Kindersley Media Library. Universitets Oldsaksamling © Dorling Kindersley

▼ Feudal Society

The Middle Ages were characterized by a chronic absence of effective central government and the constant threat of famine, disease, and foreign invasion. In this state of affairs, the weaker sought the protection of the stronger, and the true lords and masters became those who could guarantee immediate security from violence and starvation. The term *feudal society* refers to the social, political, military, and economic system that emerged from these conditions.

The feudal society of the Middle Ages was dominated by warlords. What people needed most was the assurance that others could be depended on in time of dire need. Lesser men pledged themselves to powerful individuals—warlords or princes—recognizing them as personal superiors and promising them faithful service. Large warrior groups of vassals sprang up and ultimately developed into a prominent professional military class with its own code of knightly conduct. The result was a network of relationships based on mutual loyalty that enabled warlords to acquire armies and to rule over territory, whether or not they owned land or had a royal title. The emergence of these extensive military organizations—warlords and their groups of professional military vassals—was an adaptation to the absence of strong central government and the predominance of a noncommercial, rural economy.

Origins

Following the modern authority on the subject, the late French historian Marc Bloch, historians distinguish the cruder forms of feudal government that evolved during the early Middle Ages from the sophisticated institutional arrangements by which princes and kings consolidated their territories and established royal rule during the High Middle Ages (the so-called second feudal age).

The origins of feudal government can be found in the divisions and conflicts of Merovingian society. In the sixth and seventh centuries, it became customary for individual freemen who did not already belong to families or groups that could protect them to place themselves under the protection of more powerful freemen. In this way the latter built up armies and became local magnates, and the former solved the problem of simple survival. Freemen who so entrusted themselves to others came to be described as **vassals**, *vassi* or "those who serve," from which evolved the term *vassalage*, meaning the placement of oneself in the personal service of another who promises protection in return.

Landed nobles, like kings, tried to acquire as many such vassals as they could, because military strength in the early Middle Ages lay in numbers. Because it proved impossible to maintain these growing armies within the lord's own household (as was the original custom) or to support them by special monetary payments, the practice evolved of simply granting them land as a "tenement." Vassals were expected to dwell on these *benefices*, or

THE CAROLINGIAN DYNASTY (751–987)

751	Pepin III "the Short" becomes king of the Franks
755	Franks protect church against Lombards and create the Papal States
768–814	Charlemagne rules as king of the Franks
774	Charlemagne defeats Lombards in northern Italy
ca. 775	*Donation of Constantine* protests Frankish domination of church
800	Pope Leo III crowns Charlemagne emperor
814–840	Louis the Pious succeeds Charlemagne as emperor
843	Treaty of Verdun partitions the Carolingian Empire
911	Death of last Carolingian emperor
962	Saxons under Otto I firmly established as successors to Carolingians in Germany

MEDIEVAL COOKING

THE MENUS OF medieval Europeans seem, at first glance, similar to those of modern Europeans. As early as the twelfth century, the Italians were stuffing pasta and calling it ravioli and the French and the English baking meat pies and custards. Yet much in the medieval kitchen would be bizarre to a modern diner.

First, the priorities of the medieval cook were not those of a modern chef. Both artist and scientist, the medieval cook worried more about being "humorally" correct than about cooking food that tasted good. Medieval medical theory traced illness to imbalances among the four bodily humors (blood, black bile, yellow bile, and phlegm), each of which was generated by digested food and believed to contribute heat and moisture to the body. For instance, an excess of blood (considered hot and wet) would lead to a sanguine, or hot and wet, illness, whereas an excess of black bile might cause cold and dry suffering. The medieval cook had to choose ingredients that would maintain proper temperature and moisture levels in the diner by balancing the amounts of humors digested food would produce. The bad cook was thus one whose food caused humoral excess and illness. The bad cook added piquant spices to a roasted meat, causing a feverish abundance of hot and dry bile, whereas the good cook modulated hot spices with cold and wet seasonings, such as rosewater, to keep bile levels acceptable.

The medieval cook also attempted to delight the eye with extravagant and whimsical presentations, a passion inherited from the Romans. A simple recipe might add unusual colorings to gruel; more complex ones aimed for the surprising and even grotesque. An egg custard, for example, might be shaped into a giant egg, or cooked pieces of a chicken might be stuffed back into the feathered skin from which they had come and sewn shut. The bird would then be presented to the admiring diners in its natural state. Although such masterpieces were more available to a rich man than to a poor laborer, the village festivals of the rural poor could also inspire cooks to displays of food artistry. These folksy attempts to dress up food often took on the tone of a practical joke: One cookbook suggested sprinkling an animal's dried blood over stewed meat to make the diner believe the meat was raw or maggoty.[4]

Another characteristic of the poor person's diet was the absence of vegetables. Medieval peasants prized meat so highly that they scorned the greens growing around them. Most Europeans seem to have survived on a diet of mush and bread porridge, whipped together by boiling bread or meal in milk and coloring it with saffron, supplemented by an occasional egg. When meat was available, the country cook typically chopped it up, encased it within a thick pastry shell, and baked it under coals. Here, all in one, was the forerunner of the modern oven, the antecedent of the dessert pie, and the ancestor of modern dumplings and stuffed pastas.

Sources: *Food in the Middle Ages: A Book of Essays*, ed. by Melitta Weiss Adamson (New York: Greenwood Press, 1995); *Regional Cuisines of Medieval Europe: A Book of Essays*, ed. by Melitta Weiss Adamson (New York: Routledge, 2002); Terrence Scully, *The Art of Cookery in the Middle Ages* (Woodbridge, England: Boydell Press, 1995).

How were bad medieval cooks believed to make a diner ill? Give three examples of how a good medieval chef might please the diner.

[Top] The Lord of the Manor Dining. [Bottom] Kitchen Scene; Chopping Meat. From *The Luttrell Psalter*, by permission of The British Library (1000102.021).

[4]Melitta Weiss Adamson, "The Games Cooks Play," in *Food in the Middle Ages*, (New York: Greenwood Press, 1995), p. 184.

fiefs, and maintain horses, armor, and weapons in good order. Originally, vassals therefore were little more than gangs-in-waiting.

Vassalage and the Fief

Vassalage involved "fealty" to the lord. To swear **fealty** was to promise to refrain from any action that might in any way threaten the lord's well-being and to perform personal services for him on his request. Chief among the expected services was military duty as a mounted knight. This could involve a variety of activities: a short or long military expedition, escort duty, standing castle guard, or placing his own fortress at the lord's disposal, if the vassal had one. Continuous bargaining and bickering occurred over the terms of service. Limitations were placed on the number of days a lord could require services from a vassal. In France in the eleventh century, about forty days of service a year were considered sufficient. It also became possible for vassals to buy their way out of military service by a monetary payment, known as **scutage**. The lord, in turn, could use this payment to hire mercenaries, who often proved more efficient than contract-conscious vassals.

Beyond military duty, the vassal was also expected to advise his lord upon request and to sit as a member of his court when it was in session. The vassal also owed his lord financial assistance when his lord was in obvious need or distress, for example, if he were captured and needed to be ransomed or when he was outfitting himself for a crusade or a major military campaign. Also, gifts of money might be expected when the lord's daughters married or when his sons became knights.

Beginning with the reign of Louis the Pious (r. 814–840), bishops and abbots swore fealty to the king and received their offices from him as a *benefice*. The king formally "invested" these clerics in their offices during a special ceremony in which he presented them with a ring and a staff, the symbols of high spiritual office. Earlier, Louis's Frankish predecessors had confiscated church lands with only modest and belated compensation to the church. This practice was long a sore point with the church, and lay investiture of the clergy provoked a serious confrontation of church and state in the late tenth and eleventh centuries. At that time, reform-minded clergy rebelled against what they then believed to be a kind of involuntary clerical vassalage. Even reform-minded clerics, however, welcomed the king's grants of land and power to the clergy.

The lord's obligations to his vassals were specific. First, he was obligated to protect the vassal from physical harm and to stand as his advocate in public court. After fealty was sworn and homage paid, the lord provided for the vassal's physical maintenance by the bestowal of a *benefice,* or fief. The fief was simply the physical or material wherewithal to meet the vassal's military and other obligations. It could take the form of liquid wealth, as well as the more common grant of real property. There were so-called money fiefs, which empowered a vassal to receive regular payments from the lord's treasury. Such fiefs created potential conflicts because they made it possible for a nobleman in one land to acquire vassals among the nobility in another. Normally, the fief consisted of a landed estate of anywhere from a few to several thousand acres. It could also take the form of a castle.

In Carolingian times a *benefice,* or fief, varied in size from one or more small villas to several *mansi,* agricultural holdings of twenty-five to forty-eight acres. The king's vassals are known to have received benefices of at least 30 and as many as 200 such *mansi,* truly a vast estate. Royal vassalage with a *benefice* understandably came to be widely sought by the highest classes of Carolingian society. As a royal policy, however, it ultimately proved deadly to the king. Although Carolingian kings jealously guarded their rights over property granted in *benefice* to vassals, resident vassals could dispose of their *benefices* as they pleased. Vassals of the king, strengthened by his donations, in turn created their own vassals. These, in turn, created still further vassals of their own—vassals of vassals of vassals—in a pyramiding effect that fragmented land and authority from the highest to the lowest levels by the late ninth century.

Daily Life and Religion

The Humble Carolingian Manor The agrarian economy of the early Middle Ages was organized and controlled through village farms known as **manors**. On these, peasants labored as tenants for a lord, that is, a more powerful landowner who allotted them land and tenements in exchange for their services and a portion of their crops. The part of the land tended for the lord was the **demesne**, on average about one quarter to one third of the arable land. All crops grown there were harvested for the lord. The manor also included common meadows for grazing animals and forests reserved exclusively for the lord to hunt in.

Peasants were treated according to their personal status and the size of their tenements. A freeman, that is, a peasant with his own modest *allodial,* or hereditary property (property free from the claims of an overlord), became a serf by surrendering his property to a greater landowner—a lord—in exchange for protection and assistance. The freeman received his land back from the lord with a clear definition of his economic and legal rights. Although the land was no longer his property, he had full possession and use of it, and the number of services and amount of goods he was to supply to the lord were carefully spelled out.

Peasants who entered the service of a lord with little real property (perhaps only a few farm implements and animals) ended up as unfree serfs. Such serfs were far more vulnerable to the lord's demands, often spending up to three days a week working the lord's fields. Peasants who had nothing to offer a lord except their hands had the lowest status and were the least protected from excessive demands on their labor.

All classes of serfs were subject to various dues in kind: firewood in return for cutting the lord's wood, sheep for being allowed to graze their sheep on the lord's land, and the like. Thus the lord, who, for his part, furnished shacks and small plots of land from his vast domain, had at his disposal an army of servants of varying status who provided him with everything from eggs to boots. Weak serfs often fled to monasteries rather than continue their servitude. That many serfs were discontented is reflected in the high number of recorded escapes. An astrological calendar from the period even marks the days most favorable for escaping. Escaped serfs roamed as beggars and vagabonds, searching for better masters.

By the time of Charlemagne, the moldboard plow and the three-field system of land cultivation were coming into use. The **moldboard plow** cut deep into the soil, turning it to form a ridge, which provided a natural drainage system and permitted the deep planting of seeds. This made cultivation possible in the regions north of the Mediterranean, where soils were dense and waterlogged from heavy precipitation. The **three-field system** alternated fallow with planted fields each year, and this increased the amount of cultivated land by leaving only one third fallow in a given year. It also better adjusted crops to seasons. In fall, one field was planted with winter crops of wheat or rye, to be harvested in early summer. In late spring, a second field was planted with summer crops of oats, barley, and beans. The third field was left fallow, to be planted in its turn with winter and summer crops. The new summer crops, especially beans, restored nitrogen to the soil and helped increase yields. (See "Encountering the Past: Medieval Cooking," page 197.)

These developments made possible what has been called the "expansion of Europe within Europe." They permitted the old lands formerly occupied by barbarians to be cultivated and filled with farms and towns. This, in turn, led to major population growth in the north and ultimately a shift of political power from the Mediterranean to northern Europe.

The Cure of Carolingian Souls The lower clergy lived among, and were drawn from, peasant ranks. They fared hardly better than peasants in Carolingian times. As owners of the churches on their lands, the lords had the right to raise chosen serfs to the post of parish priest, placing them in charge of the churches on the lords' estates. Church law directed a lord to set a serf free before he entered the clergy. Lords, however, were reluctant to do this and risk thereby a possible later challenge to their jurisdiction over the ecclesiastical property with which the serf, as priest, was invested. Lords preferred a "serf priest," one who not only said the Mass on Sundays and

holidays, but who also continued to serve his lord during the week, waiting on the lord's table and tending his steeds. Like Charlemagne with his bishops, Frankish lords cultivated a docile parish clergy.

The ordinary people looked to religion for comfort and consolation. They especially associated religion with the major Christian holidays and festivals, such as Christmas and Easter. They baptized their children, attended mass, tried to learn the Lord's Prayer and the Apostles' Creed, and received the last rites from the priest as death approached. This was all probably done with more awe and simple faith than understanding. Because local priests on the manors were no better educated than their congregations, religious instruction in the meaning of Christian doctrine and practice remained at a bare minimum. The church sponsored street dramas in accordance with the church calendar. These were designed to teach onlookers the highlights of the Bible and church history and to instill basic Christian moral values.

People understandably became particularly attached in this period to the more tangible veneration of saints and relics. The Virgin Mary was also widely revered, although a true cult of Mary would not develop until the eleventh and twelfth centuries. Religious devotion to saints has been compared to subjection to powerful lords in the secular world. Both the saint and the lord were protectors whose honor the serfs were bound to defend and whose help in time of need they hoped to receive. Veneration of saints was also rooted in old tribal customs, to which the common folk were still attached. Indeed, Charlemagne enforced laws against witchcraft, sorcery, and the ritual sacrifice of animals by monks.

But religion also had an intrinsic appeal and special meaning to the masses of medieval men and women who found themselves burdened, fearful, and with little hope of material betterment on this side of eternity. Charlemagne shared many of the religious beliefs of his ordinary subjects. He collected and venerated relics, made pilgrimages to Rome, and frequented the Church of Saint Mary in Aachen several times a day. In his last will and testament, he directed that all but a fraction of his great treasure be spent to endow masses and prayers for his departed soul.

Fragmentation and Divided Loyalty

In addition to the fragmentation brought about by the multiplication of vassalage, effective occupation of land led gradually to claims of hereditary possession. Hereditary possession became a legally recognized principle in the ninth century and laid the basis for claims to real ownership. Fiefs given as royal donations became hereditary possessions and, over time, sometimes even the real property of the possessor.

Further, vassal obligations increased in still another way as enterprising freemen sought to accumulate as much land as possible. One man could become a vassal to several different lords. This development led in the ninth century to the "liege lord"—the one master the vassal must obey even against his other masters, should a direct conflict arise among them.

The problem of loyalty was reflected both in the literature of the period, with its praise of the virtues of honor and fidelity and in the ceremonial development of the very act of commendation by which a freeman became a vassal. In the mid-eighth century, an oath of fealty highlighted the ceremony. A vassal reinforced his promise of fidelity to the lord by swearing a special oath with his hand on a sacred relic or the Bible. In the tenth and eleventh centuries, paying homage to the lord involved not only swearing such an oath, but also placing the vassal's hands between the lord's and sealing the ceremony with a kiss.

As the centuries passed, personal loyalty and service became secondary to the acquisition of property. In developments that signaled the waning of feudal society in the tenth century, the fief came to overshadow fealty, the *benefice* became more important than vassalage, and freemen would swear allegiance to the highest bidder.

Feudal arrangements nonetheless provided stability throughout the early Middle Ages and aided the difficult process of political centralization during the High Middle Ages (c. 1000–1300). The genius of feudal government lay in its adaptability. Contracts of different kinds could be made with almost anybody, as circumstances required. The process embraced a wide spectrum of people, from the king at the top to the lowliest vassal in the remotest part of the kingdom. The foundations of the modern nation-state would emerge in France and England from the fine tuning of essentially feudal arrangements as kings sought to adapt their goal of centralized government to the reality of local power and control.

In Perspective

The centuries between 476 and 1000 saw both the decline of classical civilization and the birth of a new European civilization in the regions of what had been the Western Roman Empire. Beginning in the fifth century, barbarian invasions separated Western Europe culturally from much of its classical past. Although some important works and concepts survived from antiquity and the Church preserved major features of Roman government, the West would be recovering its classical heritage for centuries in "renaissances" that stretched into the sixteenth century. Out of the mixture of barbarian and surviving or recovered classical culture, a distinct Western culture was born. Aided and abetted by the Church, the Franks created a new imperial tradition and shaped basic Western political and social institutions for centuries to come.

The early Middle Ages also saw the emergence of a rift between Eastern and Western Christianity. Evolving from the initial division of the Roman Empire into eastern and western parts, this rift resulted in bitter conflict between popes and patriarchs.

During this period, the capital of the Byzantine Empire, Constantinople, far exceeded in population and culture any city of the West. Serving both as a buffer against Persian, Arab, and Turkish invasions of the West and as a major repository of classical learning and science for Western scholars, the Byzantine Empire did much to make possible the development of Western Europe as a distinctive political and cultural entity. Another cultural and religious rival of the West, Islam, also saw its golden age during these same centuries. Like the Byzantine world, the Muslim world preserved ancient scholarship and, especially through Muslim Spain, retransmitted it to the West. But despite examples of coexistence and even friendship, the cultures of the Western and Muslim worlds were too different and their people too estranged and suspicious of one another for them to become good neighbors.

The early Middle Ages were not centuries of great ambition in the West. It was a time when modest foundations were laid. Despite a semicommon religious culture, Western society remained more primitive and fragmented than probably anywhere else in the contemporary world. Two distinctive social institutions developed in response to these conditions: the manor and feudal bonds. The manor ensured that all would be fed and cared for; feudal bonds provided protection from outside predators. Western people were concerned primarily to satisfy basic needs; great cultural ambition would come later.

REVIEW QUESTIONS

1. What role did the church play in the West after the fall of the Roman Empire? Why did Christianity split into Eastern and Western branches?
2. What role did the nobility play during Charlemagne's rule? Why did Charlemagne encourage learning at his court? How could the Carolingian renaissance have been dangerous to Charlemagne's rule? Why did his empire break apart?
3. How and why was the history of the eastern half of the Roman empire so different from that of the western half? What role did emperors play in the Eastern Church?
4. What were the tenets of Islam, and how were the Muslims suddenly able to build an empire? How did Islamic civilization influence Western Europe?
5. How and why did feudal society begin? What were the essential ingredients of feudalism? How easy do you think it would be for modern society to slip back into a feudal pattern?

SUGGESTED READINGS

K. Armstrong, *Muhammad: A Biography of the Prophet* (1992). Substantial popular biography.

G. Barraclough, *The Origins of Modern Germany* (1963). Originally published in 1946 and still the best survey of medieval Germany.

R. Bartlett, *The Making of Europe* (1993). How migration and colonization created Europe.

G. W. Bowersock et al., *Interpreting Late Antiquity: Essays on the Postclassical World* (2001). Introductory essays presenting a unified interpretation of the centuries between 250 C.E. and 800 C.E.

P. Brown, *Augustine of Hippo: A Biography* (1967). Late antiquity seen through the biography of its greatest Christian thinker.

P. Brown et al. (eds.), *The Rise of Western Christendom: Triumph and Diversity* (1997). Sweeping, detailed summary.

Virginia Burrus, ed., *A Peoples' History of Christianity, II* (2005). Substantial and accessible.

R. Collins, *Charlemagne* (1998). Latest biography.

J. W. Currier, *Clovis, King of the Franks* (1997). Biography of founder of first Frankish dynasty.

F. L. Ganshof, *Feudalism* (1964). The most profound brief analysis of the subject.

P. Godman et al., eds., *Charlemagne's Heir: New Perspectives on Louis the Pious (814–40)* (1990). Latest research on the king whose divided kingdom set the boundaries of modern Europe.

S. Guthrie, *Arab Social Life in the Middle Ages* (1995). How Arab society holds itself together.

A. Hourani, *A History of the Arab Peoples* (1991). Comprehensive with overviews of the origins and early history of Islam.

B. Lewis, *The Middle East: A Brief History of the Last 2,000 Years* (1995). An authoritative overview.

R. McKitterick, ed., *Carolingian Culture: Emulation and Innovation* (1994). The culture from which western Europe was born.

R. J. Morrissey, *Charlemagne and France: A 1000 Years of Mythology* (2002). The European argument over who owns Charlemagne.

P. Riche, *The Carolingians: A Family Who Forged Europe* (1993). Readable account of the dynasty from start to finish.

P. Sawyer, *Kings and Vikings: Scandinavia and Europe A.D. 700–1100* (1994). Raiding Vikings and their impact on Europe.

W. Walther, *Woman in Islam* (1981). One hour spent with this book teaches more about the social import of Islam than days spent with others.

For additional learning resources related to this chapter, please go to www.myhistorylab.com

In medieval Europe, the traditional geocentric or earth-centered universe was usually depicted by concentric circles. In this popular German work on natural history, medicine, and science, Konrad von Megenberg (1309–1374) depicted the universe in a most unusual but effective manner. The seven known planets are contained within straight horizontal bands that separate the earth, below, from heaven, populated by the saints, above. Konrad von Megenberg. *Buch der Natur* (Book of Nature). Augsburg: Johannes Bämler, 1481. Rosenwald Collection. Courtesy of the Library of Congress. Rare Book and Special Collections Division.

7

The High Middle Ages: The Rise of European Empires and States (1000–1300)

▼ **Otto I and the Revival of the Empire**
Unifying Germany • Embracing the Church

▼ **The Reviving Catholic Church**
The Cluny Reform Movement • The Investiture Struggle: Gregory VII and Henry IV • The Crusades • The Pontificate of Innocent III (r. 1198–1216)

▼ **England and France: Hastings (1066) to Bouvines (1214)**
William the Conqueror • Henry II • Eleanor of Aquitaine and Court Culture • Popular Rebellion and Magna Carta • Philip II Augustus

▼ **France in the Thirteenth Century: The Reign of Louis IX**
Generosity Abroad • Order and Excellence at Home

▼ **The Hohenstaufen Empire (1152–1272)**
Frederick I Barbarossa • Henry VI and the Sicilian Connection • Otto IV and the Welf Interregnum • Frederick II • Romanesque and Gothic Architecture

▼ **In Perspective**

KEY TOPICS

• The revival of the Holy Roman Empire by a new German dynasty, the Saxons

• The emergence of a great reform movement in the church and the church's successful challenge to political domination by kings and emperors

• The development of strong national monarchies in England and France

• The fragmentation of Germany in the wake of a centuries-long struggle between the emperors of the Hohenstaufen dynasty and the papacy

THE HIGH MIDDLE Ages mark a period of political expansion and consolidation and of intellectual flowering and synthesis. The noted medievalist Joseph Strayer called it the age that saw "the full development of all the potentialities of medieval civilization."[1] Some even argue that as far as the development of Western institutions

[1]Joseph Strayer, *Western History in the Middle Ages—A Short History* (New York: Appleton-Century-Crofts, 1955).

is concerned, this was a more creative period than the later Italian Renaissance and the German Reformation.

The High Middle Ages saw the borders of Western Europe largely secured against foreign invaders. Although intermittent Muslim aggression continued well into the sixteenth century, fear of assault from without diminished. On the contrary, a striking change occurred during the late eleventh and the twelfth centuries. Western Europe, which had for so long been the prey of outsiders, became, through the Crusades and foreign trade, the feared hunter within both the eastern Byzantine and the Muslim worlds.

During the High Middle Ages, "national" monarchies emerged. Rulers in England and France successfully adapted feudal principles of government to create newly centralized political realms. At the same time, parliaments and popular assemblies emerged to secure the rights and customs of the privileged many—the nobility, the clergy, and propertied townspeople—against the desires of kings. In the process, the foundations of modern European states were laid. The Holy Roman Empire, however, proved the great exception to this centralizing trend: Despite a revival of the empire under the Ottonians (Otto I, the most powerful member of the Saxon imperial dynasty, and his immediate successors, Otto II and Otto III), the events of these centuries left it weak and fragmented until modern times.

The High Middle Ages also saw the Latin, or Western, church establish itself in concept and law as a spiritual authority independent of monarchical secular government, thus sowing the seeds of the distinctive Western separation of church and state. During the **investiture controversy**, a confrontation between popes and emperors that began in the late eleventh century and lasted through the twelfth, a reformed papacy overcame its long subservience to the Carolingian and Ottonian kings. In this struggle over the authority of rulers to designate bishops and other high clergy and to invest them with their symbols of authority, the papacy, under Gregory VII and his immediate successors, won out. It did so, however, by becoming itself a monarchy among the world's emerging monarchies, preparing the way for still more dangerous confrontations between popes and monarchs in the later Middle Ages. Some religious reformers later saw in the Gregorian papacy of the High Middle Ages the fall of the church from its spiritual mission as well as a declaration of its independence from secular power.

▼ Otto I and the Revival of the Empire

The fortunes of both the old empire and the papacy began to revive after the dark period of the late ninth century and the early tenth century. In 918, the Saxon Henry I ("the Fowler," d. 936), the strongest of the German dukes, became the first non-Frankish king of Germany.

Unifying Germany

Henry rebuilt royal power by forcibly combining the duchies of Swabia, Bavaria, Saxony, Franconia, and Lotharingia. He secured imperial borders by checking the invasions of the Hungarians and the Danes. Although much smaller than Charlemagne's empire, the German kingdom Henry created placed his son and successor Otto I (r. 936–973) in a strong territorial position.

The able Otto maneuvered his own kin into positions of power in Bavaria, Swabia, and Franconia. He refused to recognize each duchy as an independent hereditary entity, as the nobility increasingly expected, treating each instead as a subordinate member of a unified kingdom. In a truly imperial gesture in 951, he invaded Italy and proclaimed himself its king. In 955, he won his most magnificent victory by defeating the Hungarians at Lechfeld. That victory secured German borders against new barbarian attacks, further unified the German duchies, and earned Otto the well-deserved title "the Great." In defining the boundaries of Western Europe, Otto's conquest was comparable to Charles Martel's earlier triumph over the Saracens at Poitiers in 732.

Embracing the Church

As part of a careful rebuilding program, Otto, following the example of his predecessors, enlisted the church. Bishops and abbots—men who possessed a sense of universal empire, yet because they did not marry, could not found competitive dynasties—were made princes and agents of the king. Because these clergy, as royal bureaucrats, received great landholdings and immunity from local counts and dukes, they also found such vassalage to the king attractive. The medieval church did not become a great territorial power reluctantly. It appreciated the blessings of receiving while teaching the blessedness of giving.

In 961, Otto, who had long aspired to the imperial crown, responded to a call for help from Pope John XII (r. 955–964), who was then being bullied by an Italian enemy of the German king, Berengar of Friuli. In recompense for this rescue, Pope John crowned Otto emperor on February 2, 962. Otto, for his part, recognized the existence of the Papal States and proclaimed himself their special protector. Over time, such close cooperation between emperor and pope put the church more than ever under royal control. Its bishops and abbots became Otto's appointees and bureaucrats, and the pope reigned in Rome under the protection of the emperor's sword.

Pope John belatedly recognized the royal web in which the church was becoming entangled and joined the Italian opposition to the new emperor. This turnabout brought Otto's swift revenge. An ecclesiastical synod over which Otto presided deposed Pope John and proclaimed that henceforth no pope could take office without first swearing an oath of allegiance to the emperor. Under Otto I, popes ruled at the emperor's pleasure.

As these events reflect, Otto had shifted the royal focus from Germany to Italy. His successors—Otto II (r. 973–983) and Otto III (r. 983–1002)—became so preoccupied with running the affairs of Italy that their German base began to disintegrate, sacrificed to imperial dreams. They might have learned a lesson from the contemporary Capetian kings, the successor dynasty to the Carolingians in France. Those kings, perhaps more by circumstance than by design, pursued a different course than the Ottonians. They mended local fences and concentrated their limited resources on securing the royal domain, never neglecting it for the lure of foreign adventure.

The Ottonians, in contrast, reached far beyond their grasp when they tried to subdue Italy. As the briefly revived empire began to crumble in the first quarter of the eleventh century, the church, long unhappy with Carolingian and Ottonian domination, prepared to declare its independence and exact its own vengeance.

▼ The Reviving Catholic Church

During the late ninth and early tenth centuries, the clergy had become tools of kings and magnates, and the papacy a toy of Italian nobles. The Ottonians made bishops their servile princes and likewise dominated the papacy. The church was about to gain renewed respect and authority, however, thanks not only to the failing fortunes of the overextended Ottonian empire, but also to a new, determined force for reform within the church itself.

The Cluny Reform Movement

The great monastery in Cluny in east-central France gave birth to a monastic reform movement that won the support of secular lords and German kings. Here began the real Christianization of Europe. Surface belief and lip service to Christian values appear now to have penetrated more deeply into the lives of rulers and the laity, as both new, successful reform movements and the growth of heresy attest. This development enabled the church to challenge royal authority at both the episcopal and papal levels.

The reformers of Cluny were aided by widespread popular respect for the church that found expression in lay religious fervor and generous baronial patronage of religious houses. One reason so many people admired clerics and monks was that the church was medieval society's most democratic institution as far as lay participation was concerned. In the Middle Ages any man could theoretically rise to the position of pope, who was supposed to be elected by "the people and the clergy." All people were candidates for the church's grace and salvation. The church promised a better life to come to the great mass of ordinary people, who found the present one brutish and without hope.

Since the fall of the Roman Empire, popular support for the church had been especially inspired by the example set by monks. Monasteries provided an important alternative way of life for the religiously earnest in an age when most people had very few options. Monks remained the least secularized and most spiritual of the church's clergy. Their cultural achievements were widely admired, their relics and rituals were considered magical, and their high religious ideals and sacrifices were imitated by the laity.

The tenth and eleventh centuries saw an unprecedented boom in the construction of monasteries. William the Pious, duke of Aquitaine, founded Cluny in 910. It was a Benedictine monastery devoted to the strictest observance of Saint Benedict's *Rule for Monasteries*, with a special emphasis on liturgical purity. Although the reformers who emerged at Cluny were loosely organized and their demands not always consistent, they shared a determination to maintain a spiritual church. They absolutely rejected the subservience of the clergy, especially that of the German bishops, to royal authority. They taught that the pope in Rome was sole ruler over all the clergy.

No local secular rulers, the Cluniacs asserted, could have any control over their monasteries. And they further denounced the sins of the flesh of the "secular" parish clergy, who maintained concubines in a relationship akin to marriage. The Cluny reformers thus resolved to free the clergy from both kings and "wives"—to create an independent and chaste clergy. The church alone was to be the clergy's lord and spouse. Thus, the distinctive Western separation of church and state, and the celibacy of the Catholic clergy, both of which continue today, had their definitive origins in the Cluny reform movement.

Cluny rapidly became a center from which reformers were dispatched to other monasteries throughout France and Italy. Under its aggressive abbots, especially Saint Odo (r. 926–946), it grew to embrace almost fifteen hundred dependent cloisters, each devoted to monastic and church reform. In the latter half of the eleventh century, the Cluny reformers reached the summit of their influence when the papacy itself embraced their reform program.

The consecration of the Abbey of Cluny by Pope Urban II from a twelfth-century manuscript.   Bibliotheque Nationale Paris/Picture Desk, Inc./Kobal Collection

In the late ninth and early tenth centuries the proclamation of a series of church decrees, called the Peace of God, reflected the influence of the Cluny movement. Emerging from a cooperative venture between the clergy and the higher nobility, these decrees tried to lessen the endemic warfare of medieval society by threatening excommunication for all who, at any time, harmed members of such vulnerable groups as women, peasants, merchants, and the clergy. The Peace of God was subsequently reinforced by the Truce of God, a church order proclaiming that all men must abstain from violence and warfare during a certain part of each week (eventually from Wednesday night to Monday morning) and in all holy seasons.

Popes devoted to reforms like those urged by Cluny came to power during the reign of Emperor Henry III (r. 1039–1056). Pope Leo IX (r. 1049–1054) promoted regional synods to oppose *simony* (the selling of spiritual things, especially church offices) and clerical marriage (celibacy was not strictly enforced among the secular clergy until after the eleventh century). He also placed Cluniacs in key administrative posts in Rome. Imperial influence over the papacy, however, was still strong during Henry III's reign and provided a counterweight to the great aristocratic families that manipulated the elections of popes for their own gain. Before Leo IX's papacy, Henry had deposed three such popes, each a pawn of a Roman noble faction, and had installed a German bishop of his own choosing who ruled as Pope Clement II (r. 1046–1047).

Such high-handed practices ended soon after Henry III's death. During the turbulent minority of his successor, Henry IV (r. 1056–1106), reform popes began to assert themselves more openly. Pope Stephen IX (1057–1058) reigned without imperial ratification, contrary to the earlier declaration of Otto I. To prevent local factional control of papal elections, Pope Nicholas II (1059–1061) decreed in 1059 that a body of high church officials and advisers, known as the College of Cardinals, would henceforth choose the pope, establishing the procedures for papal succession that the Catholic Church still follows. With this action, the papacy declared its full independence from both local Italian and distant royal interference. Rulers continued nevertheless to have considerable indirect influence on the election of popes.

POPE GREGORY VII ASSERTS THE POWER OF THE POPE

Church reformers of the High Middle Ages vigorously asserted the power of the pope within the church and his rights against emperors and all others who might encroach on papal jurisdiction. Here is a statement of the basic principles of the Gregorian reformers, known as the Dictatus Papae *("The Sayings of the Pope"), which is attributed to Pope Gregory VII (1073–1085).*

In defining his powers as pope, on what authority does Pope Gregory base his authority? How many of his assertions are historically verifiable by actual events in church history? Can any of them be illustrated from Chapters 6 and 7? Compare Gregory's statements on papal power with those of Marsilius of Padua.

That the Roman Church was founded by God alone.

That the Roman Pontiff alone is rightly to be called universal.

That the Pope may depose the absent.

That for him alone it is lawful to enact new laws according to the needs of the time, to assemble together new congregations, to make an abbey of a canonry; and . . . to divide a rich bishopric and unite the poor ones.

That he alone may use the imperial insignia.

That the Pope is the only one whose feet are to be kissed by all princes.

That his name alone is to be recited in churches.

That his title is unique in the world.

That he may depose emperors.

That he may transfer bishops, if necessary, from one See to another.

That no synod may be called a general one without his order.

That no chapter or book may be regarded as canonical without his authority.

That no sentence of his may be retracted by any one; and that he, alone of all, can retract it.

That he himself may be judged by no one.

That the Roman Church has never erred, nor ever, by the witness of Scripture, shall err to all eternity.

That the Pope may absolve subjects of unjust men from their fealty.

From *Church and State through the Centuries: A Collection of Historic Documents*, trans. and ed. by S. Z. Ehler and John B. Morrall (New York: Biblo and Tannen, 1967), pp. 43–44. Reprinted by permission of Biblio-Moser Book Publishers.

Pope Nicholas II also embraced Cluny's strictures against simony and clerical concubinage and even struck his own political alliances with the Normans in Sicily and with France and Tuscany. His successor, Pope Alexander II (r. 1061–1073), was elected solely by the College of Cardinals, although not without a struggle.

The Investiture Struggle: Gregory VII and Henry IV

Alexander's successor was Pope Gregory VII (r. 1073–1085), a fierce advocate of Cluny's reforms who had entered the papal bureaucracy a quarter of a century earlier during the pontificate of Leo IX. (See "Pope Gregory VII Asserts the Power of the Pope.") It was he who put the church's declaration of independence to the test. Cluniacs had repeatedly inveighed against simony. Cardinal Humbert, a prominent reformer, argued that lay investiture of the clergy—that is, the appointment of bishops and other church officials by secular officials and rulers—was the worst form of this evil practice. In 1075, Pope Gregory embraced these arguments and condemned, under penalty of **excommunication**, lay investiture of clergy at any level. He had primarily in mind the emperor's well-established custom of installing bishops by presenting them with the ring and staff that symbolized the episcopal office.

After Gregory's ruling, emperors were no more able to install bishops than they were to install popes. As popes were elected by the College of Cardinals and were not raised up by kings or nobles, so bishops would henceforth be installed in their offices by high ecclesiastical authority empowered by the pope. The spiritual origins and allegiance of the episcopal office was thereby made clear.

Gregory's prohibition came as a jolt to royal authority. Since the days of Charlemagne, emperors had routinely passed out bishoprics to favored clergy. Bishops, who received royal estates, were the emperors' appointees and servants of the state. Henry IV's Carolingian and Ottonian predecessors had carefully nurtured the theocratic character of the empire in both concept and administrative bureaucracy. The church and religion had become integral parts of government.

Now the emperor, Henry IV, suddenly found himself ordered to secularize the empire by drawing a distinct line between the spheres of temporal and spiritual—royal and ecclesiastical—authority and jurisdiction. But if his key administrators were no longer to be his own carefully chosen and sworn servants, then was not his kingdom in jeopardy? Henry considered Gregory's action a direct challenge to his authority. The territorial princes, however, eager to see the emperor weakened, were quick to see the advantages of Gregory's ruling. If a weak emperor could not gain a bishop's ear, then a strong prince might, thus bringing the offices of the church into his orbit of power. In the hope of gaining an advantage over both the emperor and the clergy in their territory, the princes fully supported Gregory's edict.

The lines of battle were quickly drawn. Henry assembled his loyal German bishops at Worms in January 1076 and had them proclaim their independence from Gregory. Gregory promptly responded with the church's heavy artillery: He excommunicated Henry and absolved all of Henry's subjects from loyalty to him. This turn of events delighted the German princes, and Henry found himself facing a general revolt led by the duchy of Saxony. He had no recourse but to come to terms with Gregory. In a famous scene, Henry prostrated himself outside Gregory's castle retreat at Canossa on January 25, 1077. There he reportedly stood barefoot in the snow off and on for three days before the pope agreed to absolve him.

Papal power had at this moment reached a pinnacle. But Gregory's power, as he must have known when he restored Henry to power, was soon to be challenged.

Henry regrouped his forces, regained much of his power within the empire, and soon acted as if the humiliation at Canossa had never occurred. In March 1080, Gregory excommunicated Henry once again, but this time the action was ineffectual. (Historically, repeated excommunications of the same individual have proved to have diminishing returns.) In 1084, Henry, absolutely dominant, installed his own antipope, Clement III, and forced Gregory into exile, where he died the following year. It appeared as if the old practice of kings controlling popes had been restored—with a vengeance. Clement, however, was never recognized within the church, and Gregory's followers, who retained wide popular support, later regained power.

The settlement of the investiture controversy came in 1122 with the Concordat of Worms. Emperor Henry V (r. 1106–1125), having early abandoned his predecessors' practice of nominating popes and raising up antipopes, formally renounced his power to invest bishops with ring and staff. In exchange, Pope Calixtus II (r. 1119–1124) recognized the emperor's right to be present and to invest bishops with fiefs before and after their investment with ring and staff by the church. The old church-state back-scratching in this way continued, but now on different terms. The clergy received their offices and attendant religious powers solely from ecclesiastical authority and no longer from kings and emperors. Rulers continued to bestow lands and worldly goods on high clergy in the hope of influencing them. The Concordat of Worms thus made the clergy more independent, but not necessarily less worldly.

The Gregorian party may have won the independence of the clergy, but the price it paid was division among the feudal forces within the empire. The pope made himself strong by making imperial authority weak. In the end, those who profited most from the investiture controversy were the German princes.

The new Gregorian fence between temporal and spiritual power did not prevent kings and popes from being good neighbors if each was willing. Succeeding centuries, however, proved the aspirations of kings to be too often in conflict with those of popes for peaceful coexistence to endure. The most bitter clash between church and state was still to come. It would occur during the late thirteenth and early fourteenth centuries in the confrontation between Pope Boniface VIII and King Philip IV of France. (See Chapter 9.)

The Crusades

If an index of popular piety and support for the pope in the High Middle Ages is needed, the **Crusades** amply provide it. What the Cluny reform was to the clergy, the Crusades to the Holy Land were to the laity: an outlet for the heightened religious zeal, much of it fanatical, of the late eleventh and twelfth centuries.

Late in the eleventh century, the Byzantine Empire was under severe pressure from the Seljuk Turks, and the Eastern emperor, Alexius I Comnenus (r. 1081–1118), appealed for Western aid. At the Council of Clermont in 1095, Pope Urban II (r. 1088–1099) responded positively to that appeal, setting the First Crusade in motion. (See "Compare & Connect: Christian Jihad, Muslim Jihad," page 212.) This event has puzzled some historians, because the First Crusade was a risky venture. Yet the pope, the nobility, and Western society at large had much to gain by removing large numbers of nobility temporarily from Europe.

Too many idle, restless noble youths spent too great a part of their lives feuding with each other and raiding other people's lands. The pope saw that peace and tranquility might more easily be gained at home by sending these quarrelsome aristocrats abroad, 100,000 of whom marched off with the First Crusade. The nobility, in turn, saw that fortunes could be made in foreign wars. That was especially true for the younger sons of noblemen, who, in an age of growing population and shrinking landed wealth, saw in crusading the opportunity to become landowners. Pope Urban may well have believed that the Crusade would reconcile and reunite Western and Eastern Christianity.

Religion was not the only motive inspiring the Crusaders; hot blood and greed were no less strong. But unlike the later Crusades, which were undertaken for mercenary reasons, the early Crusades were inspired by genuine religious piety and carefully orchestrated by a revived papacy. Popes promised the first Crusaders a plenary indulgence should they die in battle. That was a complete remission of the temporal punishment due them for unrepented mortal sins, and hence a release from suffering for them in purgatory. In addition to this spiritual reward, the prospect of a Holy War against the Muslim infidel also propelled the Crusaders. Also, the sheer romance of a pilgrimage to the Holy Land played a role. All these motives combined to make the First Crusade a Christian success.

En route the Crusaders also began a general cleansing of Christendom that would intensify during the thirteenth-century papacy of Pope Innocent III. Accompanied by the new mendicant orders of Dominicans and Franciscans, Christian knights attempted to rid Europe of Jews as well as Muslims. Along the Crusaders' routes, especially in the Rhineland, Jewish communities were subjected to pogroms.

The First Victory The Eastern emperor welcomed Western aid against advancing Islamic armies. However, the Crusaders had not assembled merely to defend Europe's outermost borders against Muslim aggression. Their goal was to rescue the holy city of Jerusalem, which had been in the hands of the Muslims since the seventh century. To this end, three great armies—tens of thousands of Crusaders—gathered in France, Germany, and Italy and, taking different routes, reassembled in Constantinople in 1097. (See Map 7–1.)

The convergence of these spirited soldiers on the Eastern capital was a cultural shock that deepened antipathy toward the West. The Eastern emperor suspected their motives, and the common people, whose villages they plundered and suppressed, did not consider them to be Christian brothers in a common cause. Nonetheless, the Crusaders accomplished what no Byzantine army had been able to do. They soundly defeated one Muslim army after another in a steady advance toward Jerusalem, which they captured on July 15, 1099. The Crusaders owed their victory to superior military discipline and weaponry and were also helped by the deep political divisions within the Islamic world that prevented a unified Muslim resistance.

The victorious Crusaders divided conquered territories into the feudal states of Jerusalem, Edessa, and Antioch, which were apportioned to them as fiefs from the pope. Godfrey of Bouillon, leader of the French-German army, and after him his brother Baldwin, ruled over the kingdom of Jerusalem. The Crusaders, however, remained small islands within a great sea of Muslims, who looked on the Western invaders as savages to be slain or driven out. Once settled in the Holy Land, the Crusaders found themselves increasingly on the defensive. Now an occupying rather than a conquering army, they became obsessed with fortification, building castles and forts throughout the Holy Land, the ruins of which can still be seen today.

Once secure within their new enclaves, the Crusaders ceased to live off the land, as they had done since departing Europe, and increasingly relied on imports from home. As they developed the economic resources of their new possessions, the once fierce warriors were transformed into international traders and businessmen. The Knights Templar, originally a military-religious order, remade themselves into castle stewards and escorts for Western pilgrims going to and from the Holy Land. Through such endeavors, they became rich, ending up as wealthy bankers and moneylenders.

The Second and Third Crusades Native resistance broke the Crusaders' resolve around mid-century, and the forty-year-plus Latin presence in the East began to crumble. Edessa fell to Islamic armies in 1144. A Second Crusade, preached by Christendom's most eminent religious leader, the Cistercian monk Bernard of Clairvaux (1091–1153), attempted a rescue but met with dismal failure. In October 1187, Saladin (1138–1193), king of Egypt and Syria, reconquered Jerusalem. Save for a brief interlude in the thirteenth century, the holiest of cities remained thereafter in Islamic hands until the twentieth century.

THE CRUSADES

1095	Pope Urban II launches the First Crusade
1099	The Crusaders take Jerusalem
1147–1149	The Second Crusade
1187	Jerusalem retaken by the Muslims
1189–1192	Third Crusade
1202–1204	Fourth Crusade

MAP EXPLORATION

Interactive Map: To explore this map further, go to **www.myhistorylab.com**

Map 7–1 **THE EARLY CRUSADES** Routes and several leaders of the Crusades during the first century of the movement are shown. The names on this map do not exhaust the list of great nobles who went on the First Crusade. The even showier array of monarchs of the Second and Third Crusades still left the Crusades, on balance, ineffective in achieving their goals.

A Third Crusade in the twelfth century (1189–1192) attempted yet another rescue, led by the most powerful Western rulers: Hohenstaufen emperor Frederick Barbarossa, Richard the Lion-Hearted, the king of England, and Philip Augustus, the king of France. It became instead a tragicomic commentary on the passing of the original crusading spirit. Frederick Barbarossa drowned while fording a small stream, the Saleph River, near the end of his journey across Asia Minor. Richard the Lion-Hearted and Philip Augustus reached Palestine, only to shatter the Crusaders' unity and chances of victory by their intense personal rivalry. Philip Augustus returned to France and made war on Richard's continental territories. Richard, in turn, fell captive to the Emperor Henry VI while returning to England.

The English paid a handsome ransom for their adventurous king's release. Popular resentment of taxes levied for that ransom became part of the background of the revolt against the English monarchy that led to royal recognition of English freedoms in the Magna Carta of 1215.

The long-term results of the first three Crusades had little to do with their original purpose. Politically and religiously they were a failure. The Holy Land reverted as firmly as ever to Muslim hands. The Crusades had, however, been a safety valve for violence-prone Europeans. More importantly, they stimulated Western trade with the East, as Venetian, Pisan, and Genoan merchants followed the Crusaders across Byzantium to lucrative new markets. The need to resupply the

A Closer ▶ LOOK

EUROPEANS EMBRACE A BLACK SAINT

ST. MAURICE, PATRON saint of Magdeburg, Germany, was a third-century Egyptian Christian, who commanded the Egyptian legion of the Roman army in Gaul. In 286 C.E. he and his soldiers were executed for impiety after refusing to worship the Roman gods. Maurice's cult began in 515, and he became a favorite saint of Charlemagne and other pious, warring German kings.

Portrayed as a white man for centuries, St. Maurice first appeared as a black man in the mid-thirteenth century. In the era of the Crusades, rulers had their eyes on new possessions in the Orient, and an Eastern-looking patron saint (Maurice) seemed the perfect talisman as Western merchants and armies ventured forth to trade and conquer. At this time, artists also began to paint as a black man one of the three Magi who visited baby Jesus on his birthday. The name Maurice was close to the German word for black dye ("Mauro") and later Moors ("Mohren"). Progressively, the third-century saint was transformed into a black African. By the fifteenth and sixteenth centuries, his head adorned the coats-of-arms of leading Nuremberg families who traded in the Near East, among them the Tuchers, Nuremberg's great cloth merchants, and Albrecht Dürer, Germany's most famous Renaissance artist.

Note the exaggerated black African features, which Europeans apparently believed would win them more trust as they traded with and occupied Eastern lands.

Note also the simple suit of chain mail and the simplicity of the saint himself, which suggest that a living model, instead of the usual glorification of a saintly figure, may have posed for this realistic-looking hero.

To examine this image in an interactive fashion, please go to www.myhistorylab.com

Constantin Beyer

myhistorylab

Crusaders sail towards the Holy Land, from a twelfth-century gilded silver and enamel panel from the Pala d'Oro in the Basilica of St. Mark, Venice. The city-state of Venice, with its dominance of eastern Mediterranean shipping, profited enormously from the Crusades. Picture Desk, Inc./Kobal Collection

Christian settlements in the Near East also created new trade routes and reopened old ones long closed by Islamic supremacy over the Mediterranean.

The Fourth Crusade It is a commentary on both the degeneration of the original crusading ideal and the Crusaders' true historical importance that a Fourth Crusade transformed itself into a piratical, commercial venture controlled by the Venetians. In 1202, 30,000 Crusaders arrived in Venice to set sail for Egypt. When they could not pay the price of transport, the Venetians negotiated an alternative venture: the conquest of Zara, a rival Christian port on the Adriatic. As a shocked world watched, the Crusaders obliged the Venetians. Zara, however, proved to be only their first digression; in 1204, they besieged, captured, and sacked Constantinople itself.

This stunning event brought Venice new lands and maritime rights that assured its domination of the eastern Mediterranean. Constantinople was now the center for Western trade throughout the Near East. Although its capture embarrassed Pope Innocent III, the papacy was soon sharing the spoils, gleeful at the prospect of extending Roman Christianity to the East. A confidant of the pope became patriarch of Constantinople and launched a mission to win the Greeks and the Slavs to the Roman Church. Western control of Constantinople continued until 1261, when eastern emperor Michael Paleologus

(r. 1261–1282), helped by the Genoese, who envied their Venetian rival's windfall in the East, finally recaptured the city. This fifty-seven-year occupation of Constantinople did nothing to heal the political and religious divisions between East and West.

The Pontificate of Innocent III (r. 1198–1216)

Pope Innocent III was a papal monarch in the Gregorian tradition of papal independence from secular domination. He proclaimed and practiced as none before him the doctrine of the plenitude of papal power. In a famous statement, he likened the relationship of the pope to the emperor—or the church to the state—to that of the sun to the moon. As the moon received its light from the sun, so the emperor received his brilliance (that is, his crown) from the hand of the pope—an allusion to the famous precedent set on Christmas Day, 800, when Pope Leo III crowned Charlemagne.

Although this pretentious theory greatly exceeded Innocent's ability to practice it, he and his successors did not hesitate to act on the ambitions it reflected. When Philip II, the king of France, tried unlawfully to annul his marriage, Innocent placed France under interdict, suspending all church services save baptism and the last rites. The same punishment befell England with even greater force when King John refused to accept Innocent's nominee for archbishop of Canterbury. Later in the chapter it will be shown how Innocent also intervened frequently and forcefully in the political affairs of the Holy Roman Empire.

The New Papal Monarchy Innocent made the papacy a great secular power, with financial resources and a bureaucracy equal to those of contemporary monarchs. During his reign the papacy transformed itself, in effect, into an efficient ecclesio-commercial complex, which reformers would attack throughout the later Middle Ages. Innocent consolidated and expanded ecclesiastical taxes on the laity, the chief of which was "Peter's pence." In England, that tax, long a levy on all but the poorest houses, became a lump-sum payment by the English crown during Innocent's reign. Innocent also imposed an income tax of 2.5 percent on the clergy. *Annates* (the payment of a portion or all of the first year's income received by the holder of a new *benefice*) and fees for the *pallium* (an archbishop's symbol of office) became especially favored revenue-gathering devices.

Innocent also reserved to the pope the absolution of many sins and religious crimes, requiring those desirous of pardons or exemptions to bargain directly with Rome. It was a measure of the degree to which the papacy had embraced the new money economy, since it now employed Lombard merchants and bankers to collect the growing papal revenues.

Christian Jihad, Muslim Jihad

ON NOVEMBER 26, 1095, Pope Urban II summoned the First Crusade to the Holy Land, its mission to take back Jerusalem from the Muslims. In a seeming propaganda and smear campaign, Urban depicted Muslims as savages. Roughly four years later, July 15, 1099, Western Crusaders captured the holy city with overwhelming force and untold carnage.

Eighty-eight years later, October 2, 1187, the fabled Sultan of Egypt and Syria, Saladin, returned Jerusalem to the Muslim fold by defeating the Third Crusade. During his march to Jerusalem, he massacred captured members of the Christian military-religious orders of the Knights Templar and the Hospitallers, who were escorts and protectors of Christians journeying back and forth to the Holy Land.

QUESTIONS

1. Were the Christian Crusades, as the pope argued, a legitimate reclamation of the Christian Holy Land, or a preemptive Christian jihad?

2. Did Saladin's counteroffensive have stronger legal and moral grounds?

3. What role did religion play in the behavior of both sides?

I. Pope Urban II (r. 1088–1099) Preaches the First Crusade

When Pope Urban II summoned the First Crusade in a sermon at the Council of Clermont on November 26, 1095, he painted a savage picture of the Muslims who controlled Jerusalem. Urban also promised the Crusaders, who responded by the tens of thousands, remission of their unrepented sins and assurance of heaven. Robert the Monk is one of four witnesses who has left us a summary of the sermon.

From the confines of Jerusalem and the city of Constantinople a horrible tale has gone forth and very frequently has been brought to our ears, namely, that a race from the kingdom of the Persians [that is, the Seljuk Turks], an accursed race, a race utterly alienated from God, a generation forsooth which has not directed its heart and has not entrusted its spirit to God, has invaded the lands of those Christians and has depopulated them by the sword, pillage and fire; it has led away a part of the captives into its own country, and a part it has destroyed by cruel tortures; it has either entirely destroyed the churches of God or appropriated them for the rites of its own religion. They destroy the altars, after having defiled them with their uncleanness. They circumcise the Christians, and the blood of the circumcision they either spread upon the altars or pour into the vases of the baptismal font. When

they wish to torture people by a base death, they perforate their navels, and dragging forth the extremity of the intestines, bind it to a stake; then with flogging they lead the victim around until the viscera having gushed forth, the victim falls prostrate upon the ground. Others they bind to a post and pierce with arrows. Others they compel to extend their necks and then, attacking them with naked swords, attempt to cut through the neck with a single blow. What shall I say of the abominable rape of the women? The kingdom of the Greeks is now dismembered by them and deprived of territory so vast in extent that it can not be traversed in a march of two months. On whom therefore is the labor of avenging these wrongs and of recovering this territory incumbent, if not upon you? . . .

Jerusalem is the navel of the world; the land is fruitful above others, like another paradise of delights. This the Redeemer of the human race has made illustrious by His advent, has beautified by residence, has consecrated by suffering, has redeemed by death, has glorified by burial. This royal city, therefore, situated at the centre of the world, is now held captive by His enemies, and is in subjection to those who do not know God, to the worship of the heathens. She seeks therefore and desires to be liberated, and does not cease to implore you to come to her aid. From you especially she asks succor, because, as we have already said, God has conferred upon you above all nations great glory in arms.

Accordingly undertake this journey for the remission of your sins, with the assurance of the imperishable glory of the kingdom of heaven.

Source: Translations and reprints from *Original Sources of European History*, Vol. 1 (Philadelphia: Department of History, University of Pennsylvania, 1910), pp. 5–7.

II. Saladin (r. 1174–1193) Defeats the Third Crusade: The Report of an Eyewitness

[En route to liberating Jerusalem] Saladin sought out the Templars and Hospitallers . . . saying: 'I shall purify the land of these two impure races.' He ordered them to be beheaded, choosing to have them dead rather than in prison. With him [were] scholars and sufis [mystics] . . . devout men and ascetics, each begging to kill one of them . . . Saladin, his face joyful, sat on his dais [while] the unbelievers [Christians] showed black despair . . . There were some who slashed and cut [the Christians] cleanly, and were thanked for it. Some refused and failed to act . . . I [the eye-witness] saw the man who laughed scornfully as he slaughtered [the

Christians] . . . How much praise he won! [How great] the eternal rewards he secured by the blood he had shed . . .! How many ills did he cure by the ills he brought upon a Templar . . .! I saw how he killed unbelief to give life to Islam, and destroyed polytheism [i.e. Trinitarian Christianity] to build monotheism . . .

[Later, during the conquest of Jerusalem] the Franks [i.e. Crusaders] saw how violently the Muslims attacked [and] decided to ask for safe-conduct out of the city [agreeing to] hand Jerusalem over to Saladin . . . A deputation . . . asked for terms, but . . . Saladin refused to grant [them]. 'We shall deal with you,' he said, 'just as you dealt with the population of Jerusalem when you took it [from us] in 1099, with murder and enslavement and other such savageries . . .! Despairing of this approach, [one of the city's Christian leaders] said: 'Know, O Sultan, that there are many of us in this city . . . At the moment we are fighting [against you] half-hearted in the hope to be spared by you as you have spared others—this because of our horror of death and our love of life. However, if we see that death is inevitable . . . we shall kill our children and our wives, burn our possessions, so as not to leave you with . . . a single man or woman to enslave [and we will also raze the city]. Saladin took counsel with his advisers [and] agreed to give the Franks assurances of safety on the understanding that each man, rich and poor alike [would pay] the appropriate ransom.

Source: From "Chronicles of Imad Ad-Din and Ibn Al-Athir," in Francesco Gabrieli, ed. and trans., *Arab Historians of the Crusades* (Routledge & Kegan Paul: London, 1957), pp. 138–140; Carole Hillenbrand, *The Crusades: Islamic Perspectives* (Chicago: Fitzroy Dearborn Publishers, 1999), p. 554.

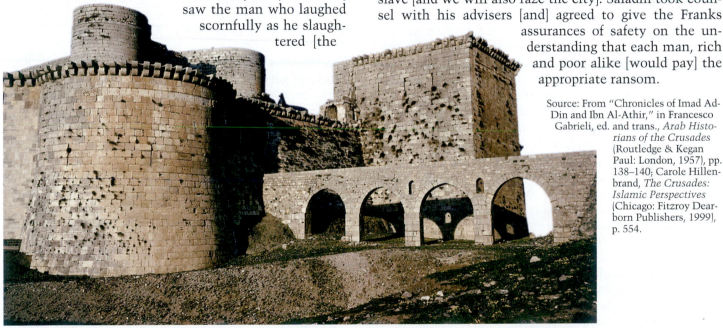

Krak des Chavaliers served as the headquarters of the Knights of St. John (Hospitallers) during the Crusades. This fortress is among the most notable surviving examples of medieval military architecture. Dorling Kindersley Media Library/Alistar Duncan © Dorling Kindersley

Crusades in France and the East Innocent's predilection for power politics also expressed itself in his use of the Crusade, the traditional weapon of the church against Islam, to suppress internal dissent and heresy. Heresy had grown under the influence of native religious reform movements that tried, often naively, to disassociate the church from the growing materialism of the age and to keep it pure of political scheming. Heresy also stemmed from anticlericalism fed by real clerical abuses that the laity could see for themselves, such as immorality, greed, and poor pastoral service.

The idealism of these movements was too extreme for the papacy. In 1209, Innocent launched a Crusade against the **Albigensians**, also known as Cathars, or "pure ones." These advocates of an ascetic, dualist religion were concentrated in the area of Albi in Languedoc in southern France, but they also had adherents among the laity in Italy and Spain. The Albigensians generally sought a pure and simple religious life, claiming to follow the model of the apostles of Jesus in the New Testament. Yet they denied the Old Testament and its God of wrath, as well as God's incarnation in Jesus Christ; despite certain Christian-influenced ideas, they were non-Christians. Their idea of a church was an invisible spiritual force, not a real-world institution.

The more radical Cathars opposed human procreation, because to reproduce corporeal bodies was to prolong the imprisonment of immortal souls in dying matter. They avoided it either through extreme sexual asceticism or the use of contraceptives (sponges and acidic ointments) and even abortion. The Cathars' strong dualism, however, also justified latitude in sexual behavior on the part of ordinary believers, this in the belief that the flesh and the spirit were so fundamentally different that it mattered little what the former did. It was in opposition to such beliefs that the church developed its strict social teachings condemning contraception and abortion.

The Crusades against the Albigensians were carried out by powerful noblemen from northern France. These great magnates, led by Simon de Montfort, were as much attracted by the great wealth of the area of Languedoc as they were moved by a Christian conscience to stamp out heresy. The Crusades also allowed the northerners to extend their political power into the south. This resulted in a succession of massacres and ended with a special Crusade led by King Louis VIII of France from 1225 to 1226, which destroyed the Albigensians as a political entity. Pope Gregory IX (r. 1227–1241) introduced the **Inquisition** into the region to complete the work of the Crusaders. This institution, a formal tribunal to detect and punish heresy, had been in use by the church since the mid-twelfth century as a way for bishops to maintain diocesan discipline. During Innocent's pontificate it became centralized in the papacy. Papal legates were dispatched to chosen regions to conduct interrogations, trials, and executions.

The Fourth Lateran Council Under Innocent's direction, the Fourth Lateran Council met in 1215 to formalize church discipline throughout the hierarchy, from pope to parish priest. The council enacted many important landmarks in ecclesiastical legislation. It gave full dogmatic sanction to the controversial doctrine of **transubstantiation**, according to which the bread and wine of the Lord's Supper become the true body and blood of Christ when consecrated by a priest in the sacrament of the Eucharist. This doctrine has been part of Catholic teaching ever since. It reflects the influence of the Cluniac monks and those of a new order, the Cistercians. During the twelfth century, these orders made the adoration of the Virgin Mary (the patron saint of the Cistercians) and the worship of Christ in the Eucharist the centerpieces of a reformed, christocentric piety. The doctrine of transubstantiation is an expression of the popularity of this piety. It also enhanced the power and authority of the clergy, because it specified that only they could perform the miracle of the Eucharist.

In addition, the council made annual confession and Easter communion mandatory for every adult Christian. This legislation formalized the sacrament of penance as the church's key instrument of religious education and discipline in the later Middle Ages.

Franciscans and Dominicans During his reign, Pope Innocent gave official sanction to two new monastic orders: the Franciscans and the Dominicans. No other action of the pope had more of an effect on spiritual life. Unlike other regular clergy, the members of these mendicant orders, known as *friars*, did not confine themselves to the cloister. They went out into the world to preach the church's mission and to combat heresy, begging or working to support themselves (hence the term *mendicant*).

Lay interest in spiritual devotion, especially among urban women, was particularly intense at the turn of the twelfth century. In addition to the heretical Albigensians, there were movements of **Waldensians**, Beguines, and Beghards, each of which stressed biblical simplicity in religion and a life of poverty in imitation of Christ. Such movements were especially active in Italy and France. Their heterodox teachings—teachings that, although not necessarily heretical, nonetheless challenged church orthodoxy—and the critical frame of mind they promoted caused the pope deep concern. Innocent feared they would inspire lay piety to turn militantly against the church. The Franciscan and Dominican orders, however, emerged from the same background of intense religiosity. By sanctioning them and thus keeping their followers within the confines of church organization, the pope provided a response to heterodox piety as well as an answer to lay criticism of the worldliness of the papal monarchy.

The Franciscan order was founded by Saint Francis of Assisi (1182–1226), the son of a rich Italian cloth merchant, who became disaffected with wealth and urged his followers to live a life of extreme poverty. Pope Innocent recognized the order in 1210, and its official rule was approved in 1223. The Dominican order, the Order of Preachers, was founded by Saint Dominic (1170–1221), a well-educated Spanish cleric, and was sanctioned in 1216. Both orders received special privileges from the pope and were solely under his jurisdiction. This special relationship with Rome gave the friars an independence from local clerical authority that bred resentment among some secular clergy.

Pope Gregory IX (r. 1227–1241) canonized Saint Francis only two years after Francis's death—a fitting honor for Francis and a stroke of genius by the pope. By bringing the age's most popular religious figure, one who had even miraculously received the *stigmata* (bleeding wounds like those of the crucified Jesus), so emphatically within the confines of the church, he enhanced papal authority over lay piety.

Two years after the canonization, however, Gregory canceled Saint Francis's own *Testament* as an authoritative rule for the Franciscan order. He did so because he found it to be an impractical guide for the order and because the unconventional nomadic life of strict poverty it advocated conflicted with papal plans to enlist the order as an arm of church policy. Most Franciscans themselves, under the leadership of moderates like Saint Bonaventure, general of the order between 1257 and 1274, also came to doubt the wisdom of extreme asceticism. During the thirteenth century, the main branch of the order progressively complied with papal wishes. In the fourteenth century, the pope condemned a radical branch, the Spiritual Franciscans, extreme followers of Saint Francis who considered him almost a new Messiah. In his condemnation, the pope declared absolute poverty a fictitious ideal that not even Christ endorsed.

The Dominicans, a less factious order, combated doctrinal error through visitations and preaching. They conformed new convents of **Beguines** (lay religious sisterhoods of single lay women in the Netherlands and Belgium; see Chapter 8) to the church's teaching, led the

Dominicans (top), and Franciscans (bottom). Unlike the other religious orders, the Dominicans and Franciscans did not live in cloisters but wandered about preaching and combating heresy. They depended for support on their own labor and the kindness of the laity. Cliche Bibliothèque Nationale de France, Paris

church's campaign against heretics in southern France, and staffed the offices of the Inquisition after Pope Gregory centralized it in 1223. The great Dominican theologian Thomas Aquinas (d. 1274) was canonized in 1322 for his efforts to synthesize faith and reason in an enduring definitive statement of Catholic belief. (See Chapter 8.)

The Dominicans and the Franciscans strengthened the church among the laity. Through the institution of so-called Third Orders, they provided ordinary men and women the opportunity to affiliate with the monastic life and pursue the high religious ideals of poverty, obedience, and chastity while remaining laypeople. Laity who joined such orders were known as **Tertiaries**. Such organizations helped keep lay piety orthodox and within the church during a period of heightened religiosity.

▼ England and France: Hastings (1066) to Bouvines (1214)

In 1066, the death of the childless Anglo-Saxon ruler Edward the Confessor (so named because of his reputation for piety) occasioned the most important change in English political life. Edward's mother was a Norman, giving the duke of Normandy a competitive, if not the best, hereditary claim to the English throne. Before his death, Edward, who was not a strong ruler, acknowledged that claim and even directed that his throne be given to William, the reigning duke of Normandy (d. 1087). Yet the Anglo-Saxon assembly, which customarily bestowed the royal power, had a mind of its own and vetoed Edward's last wishes, choosing instead Harold Godwinsson. This action triggered the swift conquest of England by the powerful Normans. William's forces defeated Harold's army at Hastings on October 14, 1066. Within weeks of the invasion William was crowned king of England in Westminster Abbey, both by right of heredity and by right of conquest.

William the Conqueror

Thereafter, William embarked on a twenty-year conquest that eventually made all of England his domain. Every landholder, whether large or small, was henceforth his vassal, holding land legally as a fief from the king. William organized his new English nation shrewdly. He established a strong monarchy whose power was not fragmented by independent territorial princes. He kept the Anglo-Saxon tax system and the practice of court writs (legal warnings) as a flexible form of central control over localities. And he took care not to destroy the Anglo-Saxon quasi-democratic tradition of frequent "parleying"—that is, the holding of conferences between the king and lesser powers who had vested interests in royal decisions.

The practice of parleying had been initially nurtured by Alfred the Great (r. 871–899). A strong and willful king who had forcibly unified England, Alfred cherished the advice of his councilors in the making of laws. His example was respected and emulated by Canute (r. 1016–1035), the Dane who restored order and brought unity to England after the civil wars that had engulfed the land during the reign of the incompetent Ethelred II (r. 978–1016). The new Norman king, William, although he thoroughly subjugated his noble vassals to the crown, maintained the tradition of parleying by consulting with them regularly about decisions of state. The result was a unique blending of the "one" and the "many," a balance between monarchical and parliamentary elements that has ever since been a feature of English government—although the English Parliament as we know it today did not formally develop as an institution until the late thirteenth century.

For administration and taxation purposes William commissioned a county-by-county survey of his new realm, a detailed accounting known as the **Domesday Book** (1080–1086). The title of the book may reflect the thoroughness and finality of the survey. As none would escape the doomsday judgment of God, so no property was overlooked by William's assessors.

Henry II

William's son, Henry I (r. 1100–1135), died without a male heir, throwing England into virtual anarchy until the accession of Henry II (r. 1154–1189). Son of the count of Anjou and Matilda, daughter of Henry I, Henry mounted the throne as head of the new Plantagenet dynasty, the family name of the Angevin (or Anjouan) line of kings who ruled England until the death of Richard III in 1485. Henry tried to recapture the efficiency and stability of his grandfather's regime, but in the process he steered the English monarchy rapidly toward an oppressive rule. Thanks to his inheritance from his father (Anjou) and his marriage to Eleanor of Aquitaine (ca. 1122–1204), Henry brought to the throne virtually the entire west coast of France.

The union with Eleanor created the Angevin, or English-French, Empire. Eleanor married Henry while

The *Battle of Hastings*. Detail of the *Bayeux Tapestry*, c. 1073–1083. Wool embroidery on linen, height 20" (50.7 cm). Centre Guillaume Le Conquerant. Detail of the Bayeux Tapestry-XIth century. By special permission of the City of Bayeux

THE GROWING POWER AND INFLUENCE OF THE CHURCH

910	Cluny founded by William the Pious
1059	Pope Nicholas II establishes College of Cardinals
1075	Pope Gregory VII condemns lay investiture of clergy under penalty of excommunication
1076	Emperor Henry IV excommunicated by Pope Gregory VII for defying ban on lay investiture
1077	Henry IV begs for and receives papal absolution in Canossa
1084	Henry IV installs an antipope and forces Gregory VII into exile
1095	Pope Urban II preaches the First Crusade at the Council of Clermont
1122	Concordat of Worms between Emperor Henry V and Pope Calixtus II ends investiture controversy
1209	Pope Innocent III launches Albigensian Crusade in southern France; excommunicates King John of England
1210	Pope Innocent III recognizes the Franciscan order
1215	Fourth Lateran Council sanctions doctrine of transubstantiation and mandates annual confession by all adult Christians

he was still the count of Anjou and not yet king of England. The marriage occurred eight weeks after the annulment of Eleanor's fifteen-year marriage to the ascetic French king Louis VII in March 1152. Although the annulment was granted on grounds of consanguinity (blood relationship), the true reason for the dissolution of the marriage was Louis's suspicion of her infidelity. According to rumor, Eleanor had been intimate with a cousin. The annulment was costly to Louis, who lost Aquitaine along with his wife. Eleanor and Henry had eight children, five of them sons, among them the future kings Richard the Lion-Hearted and John.

In addition to gaining control of most of the coast of France, Henry also conquered part of Ireland and made the king of Scotland his vassal. Louis VII saw a mortal threat to France in this English expansion. He responded by adopting what came to be a permanent French policy of containment and expulsion of the English from their continental holdings in France. This policy succeeded in the mid-fifteenth century, when English power on the Continent collapsed after the Hundred Years' War. (See Chapter 9.)

Eleanor of Aquitaine and Court Culture

Eleanor of Aquitaine was a powerful influence on both politics and culture in twelfth-century France and England. She accompanied her first husband, King Louis VII, on the Second Crusade, becoming an example for women of lesser stature, who were also then venturing in increasing numbers into war and business and other areas previously considered the province of men. After marrying Henry, she settled in Angers, the chief town of Anjou, where she sponsored troubadours and poets at her lively court. There the troubadour Bernart de Ventadorn composed in Eleanor's honor many of the most popular love songs of high medieval aristocratic society. Eleanor spent the years 1154 to 1170 as Henry's queen in England. She separated from Henry in 1170, partly because of his public philandering and cruel treatment of her, and took revenge on him by joining ex-husband Louis VII in provoking Henry's three surviving sons, who were unhappy with their inheritance, into an unsuccessful rebellion against their father in 1173. From 1179 until his death in 1189, Henry kept Eleanor under mild house arrest to prevent any further such mischief from her.

After her separation from Henry in 1170 and until her confinement in England, Eleanor lived in Poitiers with her daughter Marie, the countess of Champagne, and the two made the court of Poitiers a famous center for the literature of courtly love. This genre, with its thinly veiled eroticism, has been viewed as an attack on medieval ascetic values. Be that as it may, it was certainly a commentary on contemporary domestic life within the aristocracy. The troubadours hardly promoted promiscuity at court—the code of chivalry that guided relations between lords and their vassals condemned the seduction of the wife of one's lord as the most heinous offense, punishable in some places by castration or execution (or both). Rather, the troubadours, in a frank and entertaining way, satirized carnal love or depicted it with tragic irony, while praising the ennobling power of friendly, or "courteous," love. The most famous courtly literature was that of Chrétien de Troyes, whose stories of King Arthur and the Knights of the Round Table recounted the tragic story of Sir Lancelot's secret and illicit love for Arthur's wife, Guinevere.

Popular Rebellion and Magna Carta

As Henry II acquired new lands abroad, he became more autocratic at home. He forced his will on the clergy in the Constitutions of Clarendon (1164). These measures limited judicial appeals to Rome, subjected the clergy to the civil courts, and gave the king control over the election of bishops. The result was strong political resistance from both the nobility and the clergy. The archbishop of Canterbury, Thomas à Becket (1118?–1170), once Henry's compliant chancellor, broke openly with the king and fled to Louis VII. Becket's subsequent assassination in 1170 and his canonization by Pope Alexander III in 1172 helped focus popular resentment against the king's heavy-handed tactics. Two hundred years later, Geoffrey Chaucer, writing in an age made cynical by the Black Death and the Hundred Years' War, had the pilgrims of his *Canterbury Tales* journey to the shrine of Thomas à Becket. (See "Encountering the Past: Pilgrimages.")

Under Henry's successors, the brothers Richard I, the Lion-Hearted (r. 1189–1199), and John (r. 1199–1216), new burdensome taxation in support of unnecessary foreign Crusades and a failing war with France turned resistance into outright rebellion. In 1209, Pope Innocent III, in a dispute with King John over the pope's choice for archbishop of Canterbury, excommunicated the king and placed England under interdict. To extricate himself and keep his throne, John had to make humiliating concessions, even declaring England a fief of the pope. The last straw for the English, however, was the defeat of the king's forces by the French at Bouvines in 1214. With the full support of the clergy and the townspeople, English barons revolted against John. The popular rebellion ended with the king's grudging recognition of **Magna Carta**, or "Great Charter," in 1215.

The Magna Carta put limits on autocratic behavior of the kind exhibited by the Norman kings and Plantagenet kings. It also secured the rights of the privileged against the monarchy. In Magna Carta the privileged preserved their right to be represented at the highest levels of government in important matters like taxation. The monarchy, however, was also preserved and kept strong. This balancing act, which gave power to both sides, had always been the ideal of feudal government.

Political accident had more to do with Magna Carta than political genius. Nevertheless, the English did manage to avoid both a dissolution of the monarchy by the nobility and the abridgment of the rights of the nobility by the monarchy. Although King John continued to resist the Magna Carta in every way, and succeeding kings ignored it, Magna Carta nonetheless became a cornerstone of modern English law.

Philip II Augustus

The English struggle in the High Middle Ages had been to secure the rights of the privileged many, not the authority of the king. (The Plantagenets had unbroken rule in the male line from 1154–1485.) The French, by contrast, faced the opposite problem. In 987, noblemen chose Hugh Capet to succeed the last Carolingian ruler, replacing the Carolingian dynasty with the Capetian, a third Frankish dynasty that ruled France for twelve generations, until 1328. For two centuries thereafter, until the reign of Philip II Augustus (r. 1180–1223), powerful feudal princes contested Capetian rule, burying the principle of election.

During this period, after a rash attempt to challenge the more powerful French nobility before they had enough strength to do so, the Capetian kings concentrated their limited resources on securing the royal domain, their uncontested territory around Paris and the Ile-de-France to the northeast. Aggressively exercising their feudal rights,

A depiction of the murder of Saint Thomas à Becket in Canterbury Cathedral.
From the *Playfair Book of Hours*. The Murder of Saint Thomas Beckett. Playfair Book of Hours. Ms. L. 475–1918, fol. 176. French (Rouen), late 15th c. (CT9892). Victoria and Albert Museum, London, Great Britain/Art Resource, NY

PILGRIMAGES

A MEDIEVAL PILGRIMAGE WAS both a spiritual and a social event, and everyone, from king to peasant, might join it. For penitent Christians, a priest might impose a pilgrimage as a temporal "satisfaction" for their sins, a pious act that canceled the punishment that God meted out to sinners. Because travel to faraway shrines required self-sacrifice and posed dangers, the church considered pilgrimages especially pleasing to God. The pilgrims' destination was always the shrine and often the tomb of a saint, before whose remains and relics pilgrims gained both forgiveness for sins and the saint's friendship and protection. Saints' "bones" and the waters from springs, wells, and streams at the site were believed to cure the ills of body and mind, so pilgrims also came in search of miracles. Infertile women believed a pilgrimage could "open their womb," and parents took ill or crippled children on pilgrimage to beg for a cure. Some parents even carried dead infants, in desperate hope the saint would move God to restore their children's lives.[2]

The three great pilgrimage tombs were those of St. Peter in Rome, St. James in Santiago de Compostela in northern Spain, and Jesus in Jerusalem. Businesses sprang up along the pilgrim trails and at the shrines, providing transportation, shelter, and emergency services. Manuscript "guidebooks" described the routes to the shrines. For example, a mid-twelfth-century guide told pilgrims headed for Santiago de Compostela what to expect in southwestern France:

This is a desolate region . . . there is no bread, wine, meat, fish, water, or springs; villages are rare here. The sandy and flat land abounds none the less in honey, millet, panic-grass (fodder), and wild boars. If you . . . cross in summertime, guard your face diligently from the enormous flies [wasps and horseflies] that abound there. And if you do not watch your feet . . . you will rapidly sink up to the knees in the sea-sand.[3]

Pilgrimages were also often group "outings" that medieval people must have found diverting as well as edifying. Most pilgrims traveled with bands of friends, relatives, or neighbors. In the fourteenth century, the English poet Geoffrey Chaucer (ca. 1345–1400) wrote a famous work *The Canterbury Tales* about a group of pilgrims who were traveling to the shrine of St. Thomas à Becket (1118–1170), the martyred archbishop of Canterbury, and passed the time telling each other amusing stories.

Because the shrines were usually in or near great churches, pilgrimages also gave the best history and architecture lessons available in the Middle Ages. Thus, in Canterbury Cathedral, pilgrims could venerate Becket's relics, which were housed in a glittering jewel-encrusted shrine, and learn about the conflict that had led to the archbishop's murder in that same cathedral by the knights of King Henry II (r. 1154–1189).

Sources: Klaus Arnold, *Kind und Gesellschaft in Mittelalter und Renaissance* (MartinLurz, Munich Paderborn, 1980), pp. 30–31; Georges Duby, *The Age of the Cathedrals*, trans. by E. Levieux and B. Thompson (Chicago: University of Chicago Press, 1981), pp. 50–51; H. W. Janson and A. F. Janson, *History of Art* (New York: Prentice Hall, 1997), pp. 386–387; Compton Reeves, *Pleasures and Pastimes in Medieval England* (Oxford: Oxford University Press, 1998), pp. 174–175, 180.

List three reasons why people went on pilgrimages. Name the three great tombs to which pilgrims journeyed in the Middle Ages.

A thirteenth-century stained glass window depicts pilgrims traveling to Canterbury Cathedral. © Archivo Iconografico, S.A./CORBIS

[2]Klaus Arnold, *Kind und Gesellschaft in Mittelalter und Renaissance* (Munich: Paderborn, 1980), pp. 30–31.
[3]H. W. Janson and A. F. Janson, *History of Art* (New York: Prentice Hall, 1997), pp. 386–387.

French kings, especially after 1100, gained near absolute obedience from the noblemen in this area and established a solid base of power. By the reign of Philip II Augustus, Paris had become the center of French government and culture, and the Capetian dynasty a secure hereditary monarchy. Thereafter, the kings of France could impose their will on the French nobles, who were always in law, if not in political fact, the king's sworn vassals.

In an indirect way the Norman conquest of England helped stir France to unity and made it possible for the Capetian kings to establish a truly national monarchy. The duke of Normandy, who after 1066 was master of the whole of England, was also among the vassals of the French king in Paris. Capetian kings understandably watched with alarm as the power of their Norman vassal grew. Other powerful vassals of the king also watched with alarm. King Louis VI, the Fat (r. 1108–1137), entered an alliance with Flanders, traditionally a Norman enemy. King Louis VII (r. 1137–1180), assisted by a brilliant minister, Suger, abbot of St. Denis and famous for his patronage of Gothic architecture, found allies in the great northern French cities and used their wealth to build a royal army.

When he succeeded Louis VII as king, Philip II Augustus inherited financial resources and a skilled bureaucracy that put him in a strong position. He was able to resist the competition of the French nobility and the clergy and to focus on the contest with the English king. Confronted at the same time with an internal and an international struggle, he proved successful in both. His armies occupied all the English king's territories on the French coast except for Aquitaine. As a showdown with the English neared on the continent, however, Holy Roman Emperor Otto IV (r. 1198–1215) entered the fray on the side of the English, and the French found themselves assailed from both east and west. But when the international armies finally clashed at Bouvines in Flanders on July 27, 1214, in what history records as the first great European battle, the French won handily over the opposing Anglo-Flemish-German army. This victory unified France politically around the monarchy and thereby laid the foundation for French ascendancy in the later Middle Ages. The defeat so weakened Otto IV that he fell from power in Germany. (It also, as we have seen, sparked the rebellion in England that forced King John to accept Magna Carta.)

▼ France in the Thirteenth Century: The Reign of Louis IX

If Innocent III realized the fondest ambitions of medieval popes, Louis IX (r. 1226–1270), the grandson of Philip Augustus, embodied the medieval view of the perfect ruler. Coming to power after the French victory at Bouvines (1214), Louis inherited a unified and secure kingdom. Although he was endowed with a moral character that far exceeded that of his royal and papal contempo-

raries, he was also at times prey to naïveté. Not beset by the problems of sheer survival, and a reformer at heart, Louis found himself free to concentrate on what medieval people believed to be the business of civilization.

Generosity Abroad

Magnanimity in politics is not always a sign of strength, and Louis could be very magnanimous. Although in a strong position during negotiations for the Treaty of Paris (1259), which momentarily settled the dispute between France and England, he refused to take advantage of it to drive the English from their French possessions. Had he done so and ruthlessly confiscated English territories on the French coast, he might have lessened, if not averted altogether, the conflict underlying the Hundred Years' War, which began in the fourteenth century. Instead he surrendered disputed territory on the borders of Gascony to the English king, Henry III, and confirmed Henry's possession of the duchy of Aquitaine.

Although he occasionally chastised popes for their crude political ambitions, Louis remained neutral during the long struggle between the German Hohenstaufen emperor Frederick II and the papacy and his neutrality worked to the pope's advantage. Louis also remained neutral when his brother, Charles of Anjou, intervened in Italy and Sicily against the Hohenstaufens, again to the pope's advantage. Urged on by the pope and his noble supporters, Charles was crowned king of Sicily in Rome, and his subsequent defeat of the son and grandson of Frederick II ended the Hohenstaufen dynasty. For such service to the church, both by action and by inaction, the Capetian kings of the thirteenth century received many papal favors.

Order and Excellence at Home

Louis's greatest achievements lay at home. The efficient French bureaucracy, which his predecessors had used to exploit their subjects, became under Louis an instrument of order and fair play in local government. He sent forth royal commissioners (*enquêteurs*), reminiscent of Charlemagne's far less successful *missi dominici*. Their mission was to monitor the royal officials responsible for local governmental administration (especially the *baillis* and *prévôts*, whose offices had been created by his predecessor, Philip Augustus) and to ensure that justice would truly be meted out to all. These royal ambassadors were received as genuine tribunes of the people. Louis further abolished private wars and serfdom within his royal domain. He gave his subjects the judicial right of appeal from local to higher courts and made the tax system, by medieval standards, more equitable. The French people came to associate their king with justice; consequently, national feeling, the glue of nationhood, grew strong during his reign.

Respected by the kings of Europe and possessed of far greater moral authority than the pope, Louis became an arbiter among the world's powers. During his reign French society and culture became an example to all of Europe, a pattern that would continue into the modern period. Northern France became the showcase of monastic reform, chivalry, and Gothic art and architecture. Louis's reign also coincided with the golden age of Scholasticism, which saw the convergence of Europe's greatest thinkers on Paris, among them Saint Thomas Aquinas and Saint Bonaventure. (See Chapter 8.)

Louis's perfection remained, however, that of a medieval king. Like his father, Louis VIII (r. 1223–1226), who had taken part in the Albigensian Crusade, Louis was something of a religious fanatic. He sponsored the French Inquisition. He led two French Crusades against the Muslims, which, although inspired by the purest religious motives, proved to be personal disasters. During the first (1248–1254), Louis was captured and had to be ransomed out of Egypt. He died of a fever during the second in 1270. It was especially for this selfless, but also useless, service on behalf of the church that Louis later received the rare honor of sainthood. Probably not coincidentally, the church bestowed this honor when it was under pressure from a more powerful and less than "most Christian" French king, the ruthless Philip IV, "the Fair" (r. 1285–1314). (See Chapter 9.)

▼ The Hohenstaufen Empire (1152–1272)

During the twelfth and thirteenth centuries, stable governments developed in both England and France. In England Magna Carta balanced the rights of the nobility against the authority of the kings, and in France the reign of Philip II Augustus secured the authority of the king over the competitive claims of the nobility. During the reign of Louis IX, the French exercised international influence over politics and culture. The story within the Holy Roman Empire, which embraced Germany, Burgundy, and northern Italy by the mid-thirteenth century, was different. (See Map 7–2, page 222.) There, primarily because of the efforts of the Hohenstaufen dynasty to extend imperial power into southern Italy, disunity and blood feuding remained the order of the day for two centuries. It left as a legacy the fragmentation of Germany until the nineteenth century.

Frederick I Barbarossa

The investiture struggle had earlier weakened imperial authority. After the Concordat of Worms, the German princes were the supreme lay powers within the rich ecclesiastical territories and held a dominant influence over the appointment of the church's bishops.

The power of the emperor promised to return, however, with the accession to the throne of Frederick I Barbarossa (r. 1152–1190) of the Hohenstaufen dynasty, the strongest line of emperors yet to succeed the Ottonians. This new dynasty not only reestablished imperial authority but also started a new, deadlier phase in the contest between popes and emperors. Never have kings and popes despised and persecuted one another more than during the Hohenstaufen dynasty.

Frederick I confronted powerful feudal princes in Germany and Lombardy and a pope in Rome who still looked on the emperor as his creature. However, the incessant strife among the princes and the turmoil caused by the papacy's pretensions to great political power alienated many people. Such popular sentiment presented Frederick with an opportunity to recover imperial authority and he was shrewd enough to take advantage of it. Frederick especially took advantage of the contemporary revival of Roman law, which served him on two fronts. On one hand, it praised centralized authority, that of king or emperor, against the nobility; on the other, it stressed the secular origins of imperial power against the tradition of Roman election of the emperor and papal coronation of him, thus reducing papal involvement to a minimum.

From his base in Switzerland, Frederick attempted to hold his empire together by invoking feudal bonds. He was relatively successful in Germany, thanks largely to the fall from power and exile in 1180 of his strongest German rival, Henry the Lion (d. 1195), the duke of Saxony. Although he could not defeat the many German duchies, Frederick never missed an opportunity to remind each German ruler of his prescribed duties as one who held his land legally as a fief of the emperor. The Capetian kings of France had used the same tactic when they faced superior forces of the nobility.

Italian popes proved to be the greatest obstacle to Frederick's plans to revive his empire. In 1155, he restored Pope Adrian IV (r. 1154–1159) to power in Rome after a religious revolutionary had taken control of the city. For his efforts, Frederick won a coveted papal coronation—and strictly on his terms, not on those of the pope. Despite fierce resistance to him in Italy, led by Milan, the door to Italy had opened, and an imperial assembly sanctioned his claims to Italian lands.

As this challenge to royal authority was occurring, Cardinal Roland, a skilled lawyer, became Pope Alexander III (r. 1159–1181). In a clever effort to strengthen the papacy against growing imperial influence, the new pope had, while still a cardinal, negotiated an alliance between the papacy and the Norman kingdom of Sicily. Knowing him to be a capable foe, Frederick opposed his election as pope and backed a rival candidate after the election in a futile effort to undo it. Frederick now found himself at war with the pope, Milan, and Sicily.

Map 7–2   GERMANY AND ITALY IN THE MIDDLE AGES   Medieval
Germany and Italy were divided lands. The Holy Roman Empire
(Germany) embraced hundreds of independent territories that
the emperor ruled only in name. The papacy controlled the Rome
area and tried to enforce its will on Romagna. Under the Hohenstaufens (mid-twelfth to mid-thirteenth centuries), internal German divisions and papal conflict reached new heights; German
rulers sought to extend their power to southern Italy and Sicily.

By 1167, the combined forces of the
north Italian communes had driven Frederick back into Germany, and a decade later,
in 1176, Italian forces soundly defeated his
armies at Legnano. In the Peace of Constance in 1183, which ended the hostilities,
Frederick recognized the claims of the
Lombard cities to full rights of self-rule, a
great blow to his imperial plans.

Henry VI and the Sicilian Connection

Frederick's reign thus ended with stalemate
in Germany and defeat in Italy. At his death
in 1190, he was not a ruler equal in stature
to the kings of England and France. After
the Peace of Constance, he seems to have
accepted the reality of the empire's division
among the feudal princes of Germany.
However, in the last years of his reign he
seized an opportunity to gain control of
Sicily, then still a papal ally, and form a
new territorial base of power for future emperors. The opportunity arose when the
Norman ruler of the kingdom of Sicily,
William II (r. 1166–1189), sought an alliance
with Frederick that would free him to pursue a scheme to conquer Constantinople. In
1186, a fateful marriage occurred between
Frederick's son, the future Henry VI (r.
1190–1197), and Constance, the eventual
heiress to the kingdom of Sicily, which
promised to change the balance of imperial-
papal power.

It proved, however, to be but another
well-laid plan that went astray. The Sicilian
kingdom became a fatal distraction for succeeding Hohenstaufen kings, tempting
them to sacrifice their traditional territorial
base in northern Europe to dreams of imperialism. Equally disastrous for the Hohenstaufens, the union of the empire with
Sicily left Rome encircled, ensuring even
greater emmity from a papacy already thoroughly distrustful of the emperor.

When Henry VI became emperor in
1190, he thus faced a hostile papacy, German
princes more defiant than ever of the emperor, and an
England whose adventurous king, Richard the Lion-
Hearted, plotted against Henry VI with the old Hohenstaufen enemy, the exiled duke of Saxony, Henry the Lion.

It was into these circumstances that the future Emperor Frederick II was born in 1194. Heretofore the German princes had not recognized birth alone as

qualifying one for the imperial throne, although the off-spring of the emperor did have the inside track. To ensure baby Frederick's succession and stabilize his monarchy, Henry campaigned vigorously for recognition of the principle of hereditary succession. He won many German princes to his side by granting them what he asked for himself and his son: full hereditary rights to their own fiefs. Not surprisingly, the encircled papacy strongly opposed hereditary succession and joined dissident German princes against Henry.

Otto IV and the Welf Interregnum

Henry died in September 1197, leaving his son Frederick a ward of the pope. Henry's brother succeeded him as German king, but the Welf family, who were German rivals of the Hohenstaufens, put forth their own candidate, whom the English supported. The French, beginning a series of interventions in German affairs, stuck with the Hohenstaufens. The papacy supported first one side and then the other, depending on which seemed most to threaten it. The struggle for power threw Germany into anarchy and civil war.

The Welf candidate, Otto of Brunswick, outlasted his rival and was crowned Otto IV by his followers in Aachen in 1198, thereafter winning general recognition in Germany. In October 1209, Pope Innocent III (r. 1198–1216) boldly meddled in German politics by crowning Otto emperor in Rome. Playing one German dynasty against the other in an evident attempt to curb imperial power in Italy, while fully restoring papal power there, the pope had badly underestimated the ambition of the new German emperor. After his papal coronation, Otto proceeded to attack Sicily, an old imperial policy threatening to Rome. Four months after crowning Otto emperor, Pope Innocent excommunicated him.

Frederick II

Casting about for a counterweight to the treacherous Otto, the pope joined with the French, who had remained loyal to the Hohenstaufens. His new ally, French king Philip Augustus, impressed on Innocent that a solution to their mutual problem with Otto IV lay near at hand in the person of Innocent's ward: Frederick of Sicily, son of the late Hohenstaufen emperor Henry VI, who had now come of age. Unlike Otto, the young Frederick had an immediate hereditary claim to the imperial throne. In December 1212, with papal, French, and German support, Frederick was crowned king of the Romans in the German city of Mainz. Within a year and a half, Philip Augustus ended the reign of Otto IV on the battlefield of Bouvines, and three years later (1215), Frederick II was crowned emperor again, this time in the sacred imperial city of Aachen.

MAJOR POLITICAL EVENTS OF THE HIGH MIDDLE AGES	
955	Otto I defeats Hungarians at Lechfeld, securing Europe's eastern border
1066	Normans win the Battle of Hastings and assume English rule
1152	Frederick I Barbarossa becomes first Hohenstaufen emperor; reestablishes imperial authority
1154	Henry II assumes the English throne as the first Plantagenet or Angevin king
1164	Henry II forces the Constitutions of Clarendon on the English clergy
1170	Henry II's defiant archbishop, Thomas à Becket, assassinated
1176	Papal and other Italian armies defeat Frederick I at Legnano
1194	Birth of future Hohenstaufen ruler Frederick II, who becomes a ward of the pope
1198	Welf interregnum in the empire begins under Otto IV
1212	Frederick II crowned emperor in Mainz with papal, French, and German support
1214	French armies under Philip II Augustus defeat combined English and German forces at Bouvines in the first major European battle
1215	English barons revolt against King John and force the king's recognition of Magna Carta
1227	Frederick II excommunicated for the first of four times by the pope; conflict between Hohenstaufen dynasty and papacy begins
1250	Frederick II dies, having been defeated by the German princes with papal support
1257	German princes establish their own electoral college to elect future emperors

During his reign, Frederick effectively turned dreams of a unified Germany into a nightmare of disunity, assuring German fragmentation into modern times. Raised Sicilian and dreading travel beyond the Alps, Frederick spent only nine of his thirty-eight years as emperor in Germany, and six of those were before 1218. Although he pursued his royal interests in Germany, he did so mostly through representatives, seeming to desire only the imperial title for himself and his sons, and willing to give the German princes whatever they wanted to secure it. It was this eager compliance with their demands that laid the foundation for six centuries of German division. In 1220, he recognized the jurisdictional claims of the ecclesiastical princes of Germany, and twelve years later (1232) he extended the same recognition to the secular princes.

Ekkehard and Uta, ca. 1240–50. This famous noble pair founded Naumburg Cathedral in Germany in the middle of the thirteenth century and are exemplary studies of medieval nobility. © Achim Bednorz, Koln

mined to control Lombardy and Sicily, a policy that was anathema to the pope. The papacy came to view Frederick as the Antichrist, the biblical beast of the Apocalypse, whose persecution of the faithful signaled the end of the world.

The papacy won the long struggle that ensued, although its victory was arguably a Pyrrhic one. During this bitter contest, Pope Innocent IV (r. 1243–1254) launched the church into European politics on a massive scale, a policy that left the church vulnerable to criticism from both religious reformers and royal apologists. Pope Innocent organized the German princes against Frederick, who—thanks to Frederick's grand concessions—were a superior force and able to gain full control of Germany by the 1240s.

When Frederick died in 1250, the German monarchy died with him. The princes established their own informal electoral college in 1257, which thereafter controlled the succession. Through this institution, which the emperor recognized in 1356, the "king of the Romans" became a puppet of the princes, and one with firmly attached strings. The princes elected him directly, and his offspring had no hereditary right to succeed him. The last male Hohenstaufen was executed in 1268.

Independent princes henceforth controlled Germany while the imperial kingdom in Italy fell to local Italian magnates. The connection between Germany and Sicily ended forever, and the papal monarchy emerged as one of Europe's most formidable powers, soon to enter its most costly conflict of the Middle Ages with the new French and English monarchies. Internal division and the absence of a representative system of government persisted in Germany for six centuries. Even after Chancellor Bismarck created a new German empire in 1871, the legacy of the Hohenstaufen dynasty's defeat was still visible until the end of World War I.

Frederick's concessions amounted to an abdication of imperial power in Germany. Some view them as a kind of German Magna Carta in that they secured the rights of the German nobility for the forseeable future. But unlike the king of England within his realm, Frederick did little to secure the rights of the emperor in Germany. Whereas Magna Carta had the long-term consequence of promoting a balance of power between king and parliament, Frederick made the German princes little emperors within their respective realms. Centuries of petty absolutism, not parliamentary government, were the result.

Frederick's relations with the pope were equally disastrous, leading to his excommunication on four different occasions—the first in 1227 for refusing to finish a crusade he had begun at the pope's request. He was also deter-

Romanesque and Gothic Architecture

The High Middle Ages witnessed the peak of Romanesque art and the transition to the Gothic. Romanesque literally means "like Rome," and the art

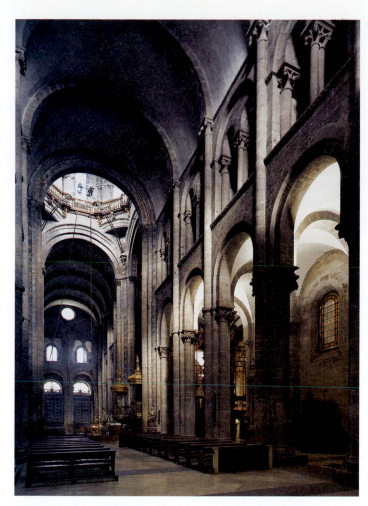

Transept, Cathedral of St. James Santiago de Compostela.
Achim Bednorz/© Achim Bednorz, Koln

Salisbury Cathedral, England.   © Christopher Cormack/CORBIS.

and architecture of the High Middle Ages embraced the classical style of ancient Rome. Romanesque churches are fortress-like. Rounded arches, thick stone walls, and heavy columns support their vaults or ceilings. In the early Middle Ages this architecture expressed the church's role as a refuge for the faithful and a new world power. Developed under the Carolingians and Ottonians, the Romanesque attained its perfection and predominated between 1050 and 1200.

Appearing first in mid-twelfth-century France, Gothic art and architecture evolved directly from the Romanesque. The term *Gothic* implies barbaric (although, in fact, Gothic art was not related in any way to the ancient Goths), and critics initially used it to condemn the new style. Gothic architecture, however, quickly silenced its critics. Its distinctive features are a ribbed, crisscrossed ceiling, with pointed arches in place of rounded ones, a clever construction technique that allows Gothic churches to soar far above their Romanesque predecessors. The greater weight on the walls was off-loaded by exterior "flying" buttresses built di-

rectly into them. With the walls thus shored up, they could be filled with wide expanses of stained glass windows that flooded the churches with colored light.

In Perspective

With its borders finally secured, Western Europe was free to develop its political institutions and cultural forms during the High Middle Ages. The map of Europe as we know it today began to take shape. England and France can be seen forming into modern nation-states, but within Germany and the Holy Roman Empire the story was different. There, imperial rule first revived (under the Ottonians) and then collapsed totally (under the Hohenstaufens). The consequences for Germany were ominous: Thereafter, it became Europe's most fractured land. On a local level, however, an effective organization of society from noble to serf emerged throughout Western Europe.

The major disruption of the period was an unprecedented conflict between former allies, church and state. During the investiture struggle and the period of the Crusades, the church became a powerful monarchy in its own right. For the first time, it competed with secular states on the latter's own terms, dethroning emperors, kings, and princes by excommunication and interdict. In doing so, it inadvertently laid the foundation for the Western doctrine of the separation of church and state.

Having succeeded so brilliantly in defending its spiritual authority against rulers, popes ventured boldly into the realm of secular politics as well, especially during the pontificates of Innocent III and Innocent IV. As the sad story of the Hohenstaufen dynasty attests, the popes had remarkable, if short-lived, success there also. But the church was to pay dearly for its successes, both spiritually and politically. Secularization of the papacy during the High Middle Ages left it vulnerable to the attacks of a new breed of unforgiving religious reformers, and the powerful monarchs of the later Middle Ages were to subject it to bold and vengeful bullying.

REVIEW QUESTIONS

1. How was the Saxon king Otto I able to consolidate political rule over the various German duchies and use the church to his advantage? Does he deserve the title "the Great"?

2. What were the main reasons for the Cluny reform movement? Why did it succeed? How did this reform movement influence the subsequent history of the medieval church?

3. Why did Pope Gregory VII and King Henry IV conflict over the issue of lay investiture? What was the outcome of the struggle? What did each side have at stake and how did the struggle affect the emperor's power in Germany?

4. The eighteenth-century French intellectual Voltaire said the Holy Roman Empire was neither holy, nor Roman, nor an empire. What did he mean? Do you agree with him?

5. What major development in western and eastern Europe encouraged the emergence of the Crusades? Why did the Crusaders fail to establish lasting political and religious control over the Holy Land? What were the political, religious, and economic results of the Crusades? Which do you consider most important and why?

6. What were some of the factors preventing German consolidation under the Hohenstaufens? Why did Germany remain in feudal chaos while France and England eventually coalesced into reasonably strong states?

SUGGESTED READINGS

J. W. Baldwin, *The Government of Philip Augustus* (1986). The standard work.

S. Flanagan, *Hildegard of Bingen, 1098–1179: A Visionary Life* (1998). Latest biography of a powerful religious woman.

S. D. Goitein, *Letters of Medieval Jewish Traders* (1973). Rare first-person accounts.

E. M. Hallam, *Capetian France 987–1328* (1980). Good on politics and heretics.

J. C. Holt, *Magna Carta*, 2nd ed. (1992). Succeeding generations interpret the famous document.

K. Leyser, *Medieval Germany and Its Neighbors, 900–1250* (1982). Basic and authoritative.

H. E. Mayer, *The Crusades*, trans. by John Gilligham (1972). The best one-volume account.

W. Melczer, *The Pilgrim's Guide to Santiago de Compostela* (1993). Do's and dont's, and what the medieval pilgrim might expect along the way.

C. Moriarity, ed., *The Voice of the Middle Ages: In Personal Letters, 1100–1500* (1989). Rare first-person accounts.

J. B. Morrall, *Political Thought in Medieval Times* (1962). Readable, elucidating account.

J. Riley-Smith, *The Oxford Illustrated History of the Crusades* (1995). Sweeping account.

C. Tyerman, *Fighting for Christendom* (2004). Brief and accessible.

For additional learning resources related to this chapter, please go to www.myhistorylab.com

myhistorylab

The livelihood of towns and castles depended on the labor of peasants in surrounding villages. Here a peasant family collects the September grape harvest from a vineyard outside a fortified castle in France in preparation for making wine.   The Granger Collection

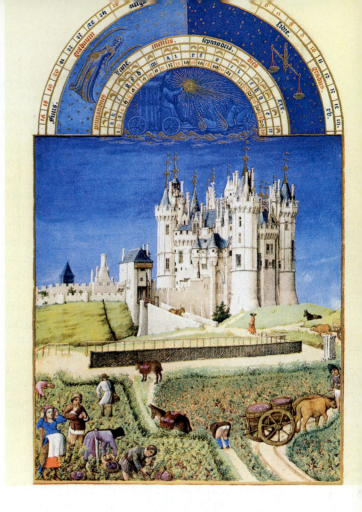

8

Medieval Society: Hierarchies, Towns, Universities, and Families (1000–1300)

KEY TOPICS

- The major groups composing medieval society

- The rise of towns and a new merchant class

- The founding of universities and educational curricula

- How women and children fared in the Middle Ages

BETWEEN THE TENTH and twelfth centuries, European agricultural production steadily improved, due to a warming climate and improved technology. With increased food supplies came something of a population explosion by the eleventh century. The recovery of the countryside, in turn, stimulated new migration into and trade with the long-dormant towns. Old towns revived and new ones arose. A rich and complex fabric of life developed, closely integrating town and countryside and allowing civilization to flourish in the twelfth and thirteenth centuries as it had not done in the West since the Roman Empire. Beginning with the Crusades, trade with distant towns and foreign lands also revived. With the rise of towns, a new merchant class, the ancestors of modern capitalists, came into being. Enormous numbers of skilled artisans and day workers, especially in the cloth-making industries, were the foundation of the new urban wealth.

Urban culture and education also flourished. The revival of trade with the East and contacts with Muslim intellectuals, particularly in Spain, made possible the recovery of ancient scholarship and science. Unlike the comparative dabbling in antiquity during Carolingian times, the twelfth century enjoyed a true renaissance of classical learning. Schools and curricula also broadened beyond the clergy during the twelfth century to educate lay men and some women, thereby greatly increasing literacy among laypeople and their role in government and culture.

In the mid-twelfth century in France, Gothic architecture began to replace the plain and ponderous Romanesque style preferred by fortress Europe during the vulnerable early Middle Ages. Its new grace and beauty—soaring arches, bold flying buttresses, dazzling light, and stained glass—were a testament to the vitality of humankind as well as to the glory of God in this unique period of human achievement.

▼ The Traditional Order of Life

In the art and literature of the Middle Ages, three basic social groups were represented: those who fought as mounted knights (the landed nobility), those who prayed (the clergy), and those who labored in fields and shops (the peasantry and village artisans). After the revival of towns in the eleventh century, a fourth social group emerged: long-distance traders and merchants. Like the peasantry, they also labored, but in ways strange to the traditional groups. They were freemen who often possessed great wealth, yet unlike the nobility and the clergy, they owned no land, and unlike the peasantry, they did not toil in fields and shops. Their rise to power caused an important crack in the old social order, for they drew behind them the leadership of the urban artisan groups that the new urban industries that grew up in the wake of the revival of trade had created. During the late Middle Ages, these new "middling classes" firmly established themselves, and their numbers have been enlarging ever since.

Nobles

As a distinctive social group, not all nobles were originally great men with large hereditary lands. Many rose from the ranks of feudal vassals or warrior knights. The successful vassal attained a special social and legal status based on his landed wealth (accumulated fiefs), his exercise of authority over others, and his distinctive social customs—all of which set him apart from others in medieval society. By the late Middle Ages, a distinguishable higher and lower nobility living in both town and country had evolved. The higher were the great landowners and territorial magnates, who had long been the dominant powers in their regions, while the lower were comprised of petty landlords, descendants of minor knights, newly rich merchants able to buy country estates, and wealthy farmers patiently risen from ancestral serfdom.

It was a special mark of the nobility that they lived off the labor of others. Basically lords of manors, the nobility of the early and High Middle Ages neither tilled the soil like the peasantry nor engaged in the commerce of merchants—activities considered beneath their dignity. The nobleman resided in a country mansion or, if he was particularly wealthy, a castle. Personal preference drew him to the countryside as much as the fact that his fiefs were usually rural manors.

Warriors Arms were the nobleman's profession; to wage war was his sole occupation and reason for living. In the eighth century, the adoption of stirrups made mounted warriors, or cavalry, indispensable to a successful army (stirrups permitted the rider to strike a blow without falling off the horse). Good horses (and a warrior needed several) and the accompanying armor and weaponry of horse warfare were expensive. Thus only those with means could pursue the life of a cavalryman. The nobleman's fief gave him the means to acquire the expensive military equipment that his rank required. He maintained that enviable position as he had gained it, by fighting for his chief.

The nobility accordingly celebrated the physical strength, courage, and constant activity of warfare. Warring gave them both new riches and an opportunity to gain honor and glory. Knights were paid a share in the plunder of victory, and in war everything became fair game. Special war wagons, designed to collect and transport booty, followed them into battle. Sadness greeted periods of peace, as they meant economic stagnation and boredom. Whereas the peasants and the townspeople counted peace the condition of their occupational success, the nobility despised it as unnatural to their profession.

They looked down on the peasantry as cowards who ran and hid during war. They held urban merchants, who amassed wealth by business methods strange to feudal society, in equal contempt, which increased as the affluence and political power of the townspeople grew. The nobility possessed as strong a sense of superiority over these "unwarlike" people as the clergy did over the general run of the laity.

A Closer LOOK

THE JOYS AND PAINS OF THE MEDIEVAL JOUST

THIS SCENE FROM a manuscript from c. 1300–1340 idealizes medieval noblewomen and the medieval joust. Revived in the late Middle Ages, jousts were frequently held in peacetime. They kept the warring skills of noblemen sharp and became popular entertainment. Only the nobility were legally allowed to joust, but over time, uncommon wealth enabled a persistent commoner to qualify.

Although jousts often led to mayhem and death, the intent was not to inflict bodily harm on one's opponent. To that end, the lances had blunt ends and the goal was to knock the crests or helmut ornamentation off the opponent's head. These crests, like body armor and shields, displayed the nobleman's valued coat-of-arms.

The helmet was especially designed to protect the face, while providing a thin window for visibility.

Missing from the illustration are the musicians and trumpeters who provided the hoopla that accompanied a joust. Also not depicted here are the nonparticipant knights who rode about on their chargers with noblewomen sitting sidesaddle at their backs with one hand firmly around the rider's waist, much as motorcycle couples do today.

Universitatsbibliothek Heidelberg.

To examine this image in an interactive fashion, please go to www.myhistorylab.com

PEARSON
myhistorylab

Knighthood The nobleman nurtured his sense of distinctiveness within medieval society by the chivalric ritual of dubbing to knighthood. This ceremonial entrance into the noble class became almost a religious sacrament. A bath of purification, confession, communion, and a prayer vigil preceded the ceremony. Thereafter, the priest blessed the knight's standard, lance, and sword. As prayers were chanted, the priest girded the knight with his sword and presented him his shield, enlisting him as much in the defense of the church as in the service of his lord. Dubbing raised the nobleman to a state as sacred in his sphere as clerical ordination made the priest in his. The comparison is legitimate: The clergy and the nobility were medieval society's privileged estates. The appointment of noblemen to high ecclesiastical office and their eager participation in the church's Crusades had strong ideological and social underpinnings as well as economic and political motives.

In the twelfth century, knighthood was legally restricted to men of high birth. This circumscription of noble ranks came in reaction to the growing wealth, political power, and successful social climbing of newly rich townspeople (mostly merchants), who formed a new urban patriciate that was increasingly competitive with the lower nobility. Kings remained free, however, to raise up knights at will and did not shrink from increasing royal revenues by selling noble titles to wealthy merchants. But the law was building fences—fortunately, with gates—between town and countryside in the High Middle Ages.

Sportsmen In peacetime, the nobility had two favorite amusements: hunting and tournaments. Where they could, noblemen progressively monopolized the rights to game, forbidding commoners from hunting in their "lord's'" forests. This practice built resentment among common people to the level of revolt. Free game, fishing, and access to wood were basic demands in the petitions of grievance and the revolts of the peasantry throughout the High and later Middle Ages.

Tournaments also sowed seeds of social disruption, but more within the ranks of the nobility itself. They were designed not only to keep men fit for war, but also to provide the excitement of war without the maiming and killing of prized vassals. But as regions competed fiercely with one another for victory and glory, even mock battles with blunted weapons proved to be deadly. Often, tournaments got out of hand, ending with bloodshed and animosity among the combatants. (The intense emotions and occasional violence that accompany interregional soccer in Europe today may be seen as a survival of this kind of rivalry.) The church came to oppose tournaments as occasions of pagan revelry and senseless violence. Kings and princes also turned against them as sources of division within their realms.

Henry II of England proscribed them in the twelfth century. They did not end in France until the mid-sixteenth century, after Henry II of France was mortally wounded by a shaft through his visor during a tournament celebrating his daughter's marriage. (See "Encountering the Past: Warrior Games.")

Courtly Love From the repeated assemblies in the courts of barons and kings, set codes of social conduct, or "courtesy," developed in noble circles. With the French leading the way, mannered behavior and court etiquette became almost as important as expertise on the battlefield. Knights became literate gentlemen, and lyric poets sang and moralized at court. The cultivation of a code of behavior and a special literature to eulogize it was not unrelated to problems within the social life of the nobility. Noblemen were notorious philanderers; their illegitimate children mingled openly with their legitimate offspring in their houses. The advent of courtesy was, in part, an effort to reform this situation.

Although the poetry of courtly love was sprinkled with frank eroticism and the beloved in these epics were married women pursued by those to whom they were not married, the poet usually recommended love at a distance, unconsummated by sexual intercourse. It was love without touching, a kind of sex without sex, and only as such was it ennobling. Court poets depicted those who succumbed to illicit carnal love as reaping at least as much suffering as joy.

Social Divisions No medieval social group was absolutely uniform—not the nobility, the clergy, the townspeople, or even the peasantry. Not only was the nobility a class apart; it also had strong social divisions within its own ranks. Noblemen formed a broad spectrum—from minor vassals without subordinate vassals to mighty barons, the principal vassals of a king or prince, who had many vassals of their own. Dignity and status within the nobility were directly related to the exercise of authority over others; a chief with many vassals obviously far excelled the small country nobleman who served another and was lord over none but himself.

Even among the domestic servants of the nobility, a social hierarchy developed according to assigned manorial duties. Although peasants in the eyes of the law, the chief stewards—charged with overseeing the operation of the lord's manor and the care and education of the noble children—became powerful "lords" within their "domains." Some freemen found the status of the steward enviable enough to surrender their own freedom and become domestic servants in the hope of attaining it. In time, the superiority of the higher ranks of domestic servants won legal recognition as medieval law adjusted to acknowledge the privileges of wealth and power at whatever level they appeared.

WARRIOR GAMES

IN THE MIDDLE Ages, the nobility—the warrior class—dominated society, and their favorite games grew out of their work, which was fighting. Boys of the warrior class learned to ride early. Some boys received horses and daggers at age two! At fourteen, they were given a man's sword and thereafter engaged in sports that prepared them for battle.

During the Middle Ages those war-preparing activities evolved into mock combats called *tournaments*. In peacetime, the warrior class continued to divert itself by such games amid a constant stream of poems, songs, and art that glorified war.

Peasants, townspeople, and clergy also engaged in warlike games and sports. Peasants and townspeople attended tournaments and imitated what they saw there; their children's toys (homemade lances, shields, and pikes) and games (mock combats, sheriffs and outlaws) reflected the tournament's influence.

Although there were famous clerical sportsmen and warriors, the clergy's "penchant for violence" was largely vicarious. The *Bayeaux Tapestry* (1070–1082), over two thirds of a football field long, with seventy-two scenes of blood-dripping medieval hunts and battles, was the brainstorm of a bishop, Odo of Bayeaux (ca. 1036–1097), half brother of William the Conqueror (r. 1066–1087). The aristocratic women who wove such tapestries might ride to the hunt and "ooh" and "ah" at tournaments but remained spectators, not participants, in the violent pastimes of the nobility.

More reflective of the contemplative life of the religious and of noblewomen were the indoor board games played in manor houses and cloisters. Two of many such games were "Tick, Tack, Toe" and "Fox and the Geese." The object of the latter game was to fill, or capture, the most holes, or spaces (geese), in the board with pebbles or fruit stones. Men and women of leisure, clerical and lay, also played chess and backgammon.

By the late fifteenth century, when changes in warfare had reduced the role of the mounted knight in battle, tournaments, like less bellicose games, were held for their own sake, merely as pastimes. At fairs, the horse races and mock combats of the tournament were now spread among ball games (early versions of rugby, soccer, and football), animal acts, puppet shows, juggling, and the like. Pieter Breughel's *Children's Games* (1560) depicts boys and girls engaged in seventy-eight different games. Some of them, such as jousting and wrestling, are adapted from the war preparation activities of the European nobility. Yet others are the kind of games children, like knights in earlier centuries preparing for real war, invented to escape boredom and idleness—hoops, leapfrog, blind man's bluff, marbles, golf, stilts, masquerades, tug-of-war, and jacks.

Source: John Marshall Carter, *Medieval Games: Sports and Recreations in Feudal Society* (New York: Greenwood Press, 1992), pp. 25, 30–33, 34, 69; ibid., "The Ludic Life of the Medieval Peasant: A Pictorial Essay," *Arete* III (1986): 169–187; J. T. Micklethwaite, "On the Indoor Games of School Boys in the Middle Ages," *Archeological Journal* (1892), pp. 319–328; Carter, "Ludic Life," p. 177; Steven Ozment, *Ancestors: The Loving Family in Old Europe* (Cambridge, MA: Harvard University Press, 2001), pp. 71–72.

Why did the medieval nobility play warlike games?

How did medieval women and children participate in these pastimes?

Breughel, *Children's Games.* Pieter the Elder Brueghel (1525–1569), "Children's Games," 1560. Oil on oakwood, 118 × 161 cm. Kunsthistoriches Museum, Vienna, Austria. Photo copyright Erich Lessing/Art Resource, NY

Lovers playing chess on an ivory mirror back, ca. 1300.
The Bridgeman Art Library International

In the late Middle Ages, the landed nobility suffered a steep economic and political decline. Climatic changes and agricultural failures created large famines, and the great plague (see Chapter 9) brought unprecedented population loss. Changing military tactics occasioned by the use of infantry and heavy artillery during the Hundred Years' War made the noble cavalry nearly obsolete. Also, the alliance of wealthy towns with kings challenged the nobility within their own domains. A waning of the landed nobility occurred after the fourteenth century when the effective possession of land and wealth counted more than lineage for membership in the highest social class. Still a shrinking nobility continued to dominate society down to the nineteenth century, and they have been with us ever since.

Clergy

Unlike the nobility and the peasantry, the clergy was an open estate. Although the clerical hierarchy reflected the social classes from which the clergy came, one was still a cleric by religious training and ordination, not by the circumstances of birth or military prowess.

Regular and Secular Clerics

There were two basic types of clerical vocation: the regular clergy and the secular clergy. The **regular clergy** was made up of the orders of monks who lived according to a special ascetic rule (*regula*) in cloisters separated from the world. They were the spiritual elite among the clergy, and theirs was not a way of life lightly entered. Canon law required that a man be at least twenty-one years old before making a final profession of the monastic vows of poverty, chastity, and obedience. The monks' personal sacrifices and high religious ideals made them much respected in high medieval society. This popularity was a major factor in the success of the Cluny reform movement and of the Crusades of the eleventh and twelfth centuries. (See Chapter 7.) The Crusades provided laypeople with a way to participate in the admired life of asceticism and prayer; in such holy pilgrimages they could imitate the suffering and perhaps even the death of Jesus, as the monks imitated his suffering and death by retreat from the world and severe self-denial.

Many monks (and also nuns, who increasingly embraced the vows of poverty, obedience, and chastity without a clerical rank) secluded themselves altogether. The regular clergy, however, were never completely cut off from the secular world. They maintained frequent contact with the laity through such charitable activities as feeding the destitute and tending the sick, through liberal arts instruction in monastic schools, through special pastoral commissions from the pope, and as supplemental preachers and confessors in parish churches during Lent and other peak religious seasons. It became the mark of the Dominican and Franciscan friars to live a common life according to a special rule and still to be active in a worldly ministry. Some monks, because of their learning and rhetorical skills, even rose to prominence as secretaries and private confessors to kings and queens.

The **secular clergy**, those who lived and worked directly among the laity in the world (*saeculum*), formed a vast hierarchy. At the top were the high prelates—the wealthy cardinals, archbishops, and bishops, who were drawn almost exclusively from the nobility—and below them the urban priests, the cathedral canons, and the court clerks. Finally, there was the great mass of poor parish priests, who were neither financially nor intellectually far above the common people they served. (The basic educational requirement was an ability to say the mass.) Until the Gregorian reform in the eleventh century, parish priests lived with women in a relationship akin to marriage, and the communities they served

Monks and nuns play a bat-and-ball game.   Bodleian Library, University of Oxford

accepted their concubines and children. Because of their relative poverty, priests often took second jobs as teachers, artisans, or farmers. Their parishioners also accepted and even admired this practice.

New Orders One of the results of the Gregorian reform was the creation of new religious orders aspiring to a life of poverty and self-sacrifice in imitation of Christ and the first apostles. The more important were the Canons Regular (founded 1050–1100), the Carthusians (founded 1084), the Cistercians (founded 1098), and the Praemonstratensians (founded 1121). Carthusians, Cistercians, and Praemonstratensians practiced extreme austerity in their quest to recapture the pure religious life of the early church.

Strictest of them all were the Carthusians. Members lived in isolation and fasted three days a week. They also devoted themselves to long periods of silence and even self-flagellation in their quest for perfect self-denial and conformity to Christ.

The Cistercians (from Citeaux in Burgundy) were a reform wing of the Benedictine order and were known as the "white monks," a reference to their all-white attire, symbolic of apostolic purity. (The Praemonstratensians also wore white.) They hoped to avoid the materialistic influences of urban society and maintain uncorrupted the original *Rule* of Saint Benedict, which their leaders believed Cluny was compromising. The Cistercians accordingly stressed anew the inner life and spiritual goals of monasticism. They located their houses in remote areas and denied themselves worldly comforts and distractions. Remarkably successful, the order could count three hundred chapter houses within a century of its founding, and many others imitated its more austere spirituality.

The Canons Regular were independent groups of secular clergy (and also earnest laity) who, in addition to serving laity in the world, adopted the *Rule* of Saint Augustine (a monastic guide dating from around the year 500) and practiced the ascetic virtues of regular clerics. There were monks who renounced exclusive withdrawal from the world. There were also priests who renounced exclusive involvement in it. By merging the life of the cloister with traditional clerical duties, the Canons Regular foreshadowed the mendicant friars of the thirteenth century—the Dominicans and the Franciscans, who combined the ascetic ideals of the cloister with an active ministry in the world.

The monasteries and nunneries of the established orders recruited candidates from among wealthy social groups. Crowding in these convents and the absence of patronage gave rise in the thirteenth century to lay satellite convents known as Beguine houses. These convents housed religiously earnest single women from the upper and middle social strata. In the German city of Cologne, one hundred such houses were established between 1250 and 1350, each with eight to twelve "sisters." Several of these convents fell prey to heresy. The church made the new religious orders of Dominicans and Franciscans responsible for "regularizing" such convents.

Prominence of the Clergy The clergy constituted a far greater proportion of medieval society than modern society. Estimates suggest that 1.5 percent of fourteenth-century Europe was in clerical garb. The clergy were concentrated in urban areas, especially in towns with universities and cathedrals, where, in addition to studying, they found work in a wide variety of religious services. Late-fourteenth-century England had one cleric for every seventy laypeople, and in counties with a cathedral or a university, the proportion rose to one cleric for every fifty laypeople.[1] In large university towns, the clergy might exceed 10 percent of the population.

Despite the moonlighting of poorer parish priests, the clergy as a whole, like the nobility, lived on the labor of others. Their income came from the regular collection of tithes and church taxes according to an elaborate system that evolved in the High and later Middle Ages. The church was, of course, a major landowner and regularly collected rents and fees. Monastic communities and high prelates amassed great fortunes; there was a popular saying that monastery granaries were always full. The immense secular power attached to high clerical posts can be seen in the intensity of the investiture struggle. (See Chapter 7.)

For most of the Middle Ages, the clergy were the "first estate," and theology was the queen of the sciences. How did the clergy achieve such prominence? Much of it was self-proclaimed. However, there was also popular respect and reverence for the clergy's role as a mediator between God and humanity. The priest brought the very Son of God down to earth when he celebrated the sacrament of the Eucharist; his absolution released penitents from punishment for mortal sin. It was improper for mere laypeople to sit in judgment on such a priest.

Theologians elaborated the distinction between the clergy and the laity to the clergy's benefit. The belief in the superior status of the clergy underlay the evolution of clerical privileges and immunities in both person and property. Secular rulers were not supposed to tax the clergy, who were holy persons, without special permission from the ecclesiastical authorities. Clerical crimes were under the jurisdiction of special ecclesiastical courts, not the secular courts. Because churches and monasteries were deemed holy places, they, too, were free from secular taxation and legal jurisdiction. Hunted criminals, lay and clerical, regularly sought asylum within them, disrupting the normal processes of law

---

[1] Denys Hay, *Europe in the Fourteenth and Fifteenth Centuries*, 2nd ed. (New York: Holt, Rinehart, 1966), pp. 58–59.

In this image of rustic labors, peasants clear ground, mow fields, plant seed, harvest grain, shear sheep, stomp grapes, and slaughter hogs, among other chores, while the lord of the manor hunts with his falcon in the fields as they work.   The Labors of the 12 Months. Pietro de Crescenzi, Le Rustican. Ms.340/603. France, c.1460. Location: Musée Condé, Chantilly, France. Giraudon/Art Resource, NY

The separation of church and state and the distinction between the clergy and the laity have persisted into modern times. After the fifteenth century, however, the clergy ceased to be the superior class they had been for so much of the Middle Ages. In both Protestant and Catholic lands, governments progressively subjected them to the basic responsibilities of citizenship.

Peasants

The largest and lowest social group in medieval society was the one on whose labor the welfare of all the others depended: the agrarian peasantry. Many peasants lived on and worked the manors of the nobility, the primitive cells of rural social life. All were to one degree or another dependent on their lords and were considered to be their property. The manor in Frankish times was a plot of land within a village, ranging from twelve to seventy-five acres in size, assigned to a certain member by a settled tribe or clan. This member and his family became lords of the land, and those who came to dwell there formed a smaller, self-sufficient community within a larger village. In the early Middle Ages, such manors consisted of the dwellings of the lord and his family, the huts of the peasants, agricultural sheds, and fields.

and order. When city officials violated this privilege, ecclesiastical authorities threatened excommunication and interdict. People feared this suspension of the church's sacraments, including Christian burial, almost as much as they feared the criminals to whom the church gave asylum.

By the late Middle Ages, townspeople increasingly resented the special immunities of the clergy. They complained that the clergy had greater privileges, yet fewer responsibilities, than all others who lived within the town walls. An early-sixteenth-century lampoon reflected what had by then become a widespread sentiment:

Priests, monks, and nuns
Are but a burden to the earth.
They have decided
That they will not become citizens.
That's why they're so greedy—
They stand firm against our city
And will swear no allegiance to it.
And we hear their fine excuses:
"It would cause us much toil and trouble
Should we pledge our troth as burghers."[2]

[2]Cited by S. Ozment, *The Reformation in the Cities* (New Haven, CT: Yale University Press, 1975), p. 36.

The Duties of Tenancy   The landowner or lord of the manor required a certain amount of produce (grain, eggs, and the like) and a certain number of services from the peasant families that came to dwell on and farm his land. The tenants were free to divide the labor as they wished and could keep what goods remained after the lord's levies were met. A powerful lord might own many such manors. Kings later based their military and tax assessments on the number of manors a vassal landlord owned. No set rules governed the size of manors. There were manors of a hundred acres or fewer and some of several thousand or more.

There were both servile and free manors. The tenants of the latter had originally been freemen known as *coloni*. (See Chapter 5.) Original inhabitants of the territory and petty landowners, they swapped their small possessions for a guarantee of security from a more powerful lord, who came in this way to possess their land. Unlike the pure serfdom of the servile manors, whose tenants had no original claim to a part of the land, the tenancy obligations on free manors tended to be limited, and the tenants' rights more carefully defined. It was a milder serfdom. Tenants of servile manors were, by comparison, far more vulnerable to the whims of their landlords. These two types of manors tended, however, to merge. The most common situation was the manor on which tenants of greater and lesser degrees of servitude dwelt together, their services to the lord defined by their personal status and local custom. In many regions free, self-governing peasant communities existed without any overlords and tenancy obligations.

The lord held both judicial and police powers. He owned and operated the machines that processed crops into food and drink. Marc Bloch, a modern authority on manorial society, has vividly depicted the duties of tenancy:

On certain days the tenant brings the lord's steward perhaps a few small silver coins or, more often, sheaves of grain harvested on his fields, chickens from his farmyard, cakes of wax from his beehives or from the swarms of the neighboring forest. At other times he works on the arable or the meadows of the demesne [the lord's plot of land in the manorial fields, between one-third and one-half of that available]. Or else we find him carting casks of wine or sacks of grain on behalf of the master to distant residences. His is the labour which repairs the walls or moats of the castle. If the master has guests the peasant strips his own bed to provide the necessary extra bedclothes. When the hunting season comes round, he feeds the pack. If war breaks out he does duty as a foot soldier or orderly, under the leadership of the reeve of the village.[3]

The lord also had the right to subject his tenants to exactions known as **banalities**. He could, for example, force them to breed their cows with his bull and to pay for the privilege, to grind their bread grains in his mill, to bake their bread in his oven, to make their wine in his wine press, to buy their beer from his brewery, and even to surrender to him the tongues or other choice parts of all animals slaughtered on his lands. The lord also collected a serf's best animal as an inheritance tax. Without the lord's permission, serfs could neither travel nor marry outside the manor in which they served.

The Life of a Serf Exploited as the serfs may appear to have been from a modern point of view, their status was far from chattel slavery. It was to the lord's advantage to keep his serfs healthy and happy; his welfare, like theirs, depended on a successful harvest. Serfs had their own dwellings and modest strips of land and lived by the produce of their own labor and organization. They could market for their own profit what surpluses might remain after the harvest. They were free to choose their spouses within the local village, although they needed the lord's permission to marry a wife or husband from another village. Serfs could pass their property (their dwellings and field strips) and worldly goods on to their children.

Peasants lived in timber-framed huts. Except for the higher domestic servants, they seldom ventured far beyond their own villages. The local priest often was their window on the world, and church festivals were their major communal entertainment.

Despite the social distinctions between free and servile serfs—and, within these groups, between those who owned plows and oxen and those who possessed only hoes—the common dependence on the soil forced close cooperation. The ratio of seed to grain yield was consistently poor; about two bushels of seed were required to produce six to ten bushels of grain in good times. There was rarely an abundance of bread and ale, the staple peasant foods. Two important American crops, potatoes and corn (maize), were unknown in Europe until the sixteenth century. Pork was the major source of protein, and every peasant household had its pigs. At slaughter time a family might also receive a little tough beef. Basically, however, everyone depended on the grain crops. When they failed or fell short, peasants went hungry unless their lord had surplus stores he was willing to share.

Changes in the Manor Two basic changes occurred in the evolution of the manor from the early to the later Middle Ages. The first was its fragmentation and the rise to dominance of the single-family holding. Such technological advances as the collar harness (ca. 800), the horseshoe (ca. 900), and the three-field system of crop rotation facilitated this development by making it easier for small family units to support themselves. As the lords parceled out their land to new tenants, their own plots became progressively smaller. This increase in tenants and decrease in the lord's fields brought about a corresponding reduction in the labor services exacted from the tenants. Also, the bringing of new fields into production increased individual holdings and modified labor services. In France, by the reign of Louis IX (r. 1226–1270), only a few days of labor a year were required, whereas in the time of Charlemagne (r. 768–814) peasants had worked the lords' fields several days a week.

As the single-family unit replaced the clan as the basic nuclear group, assessments of goods and services fell on individual fields and households, no longer on manors as a whole. Family farms replaced manorial units. The peasants' carefully nurtured communal life made possible a family's retention of its land and dwelling after the death of the head of the household. In this way, land and property remained in the possession of a single family from generation to generation.

The second change in the evolution of the manor was the conversion of the serf's dues into money payments, a change brought about by the revival of trade and the rise of the towns. This development, completed by the thirteenth century, permitted serfs to hold their land as rent-paying tenants and to overcome their servile status.

[3]Marc Bloch, *Feudal Society*, trans. by L. A. Manyon (Chicago: University of Chicago Press, 1968), p. 250.

Although tenants thereby gained more freedom, they were not necessarily better off materially. Whereas servile workers could have counted on the benevolent assistance of their landlords in hard times, rent-paying workers were left, by and large, to their own devices. Their independence caused some landlords to treat them with indifference and even resentment.

Lands and properties that generations of peasants had occupied as their own were always under the threat of the lord's claim to a prior right of inheritance and even outright usurpation. As their *demesnes* declined, the lords were increasingly tempted to encroach on such traditionally common lands. The peasantry fiercely resisted such efforts, instinctively clinging to the little they had. In many regions they organized to gain a voice in the choice of petty rural officials.

By the mid-fourteenth century, a declining nobility in England and France, faced with the ravages of the great plague and the Hundred Years' War, tried to turn back the historical clock by increasing taxes on the peasantry and restricting their migration into the cities. The peasantry responded with armed revolts. These revolts became the rural equivalents of the organization of medieval cities in sworn communes to protect their self-interests against powerful territorial rulers. The revolts of the agrarian peasantry, like those of the urban proletariat, were brutally crushed. They stand out at the end of the Middle Ages as violent testimony to the breakup of medieval society. As growing national sentiment would break its political unity and heretical movements would end its nominal religious unity, peasant revolts revealed the absence of medieval social unity.

▼ Towns and Townspeople

In the eleventh and twelfth centuries, towns held only about 5 percent of western Europe's population. By comparison to modern towns, they were small. Of Germany's 3,000 towns, for example, 2,800 had populations under 1,000. Only fifteen German towns exceeded 10,000. The largest, Cologne, had 30,000. In England, only London had more than 10,000. Paris was larger than London, but not by much. The largest European towns were in Italy; Florence approached 100,000 and Milan was not far behind. Italian towns were not feudally chartered, which accounts for their greater political independence. In the Middle Ages and now, cities and towns were where the action was. There one might find the whole of medieval society, including its most creative segments.

The Chartering of Towns

Feudal lords, both lay and clerical, originally dominated towns. The lords created the towns by granting charters to those who would agree to live and work within them. The charters guaranteed their safety and gave inhabitants a degree of independence unknown on the land. The purpose was originally to concentrate skilled laborers who could manufacture the finished goods lords and bishops wanted. In this way, manorial society actually created its urban challenger and weakened itself. Because the nobility longed for finished goods and luxuries from faraway places, noblemen prodded their serfs to become skilled craftspeople. By the eleventh century, skilled serfs began to pay their manorial dues in manufactured goods, rather than in field labor, eggs, chickens, and beans, as they had earlier done. In return for a fixed rent and proper subservience, serfs were also encouraged to move to the towns. There they gained special rights and privileges from the charters.

As towns grew and beckoned, serfs fled the countryside with their skills going directly to the new urban centers. There they found the freedom and profits that might lift an industrious craftsperson into higher social ranks. As this migration of serfs to the towns accelerated, the lords in the countryside offered them more favorable terms of tenure to keep them on the land. But serfs could not easily be kept down on the farms after they had discovered the opportunities of town life. In this way, the growth of towns improved the lot of serfs generally.

The Rise of Merchants

Not only did rural society give the towns their craftspeople and day laborers, the first merchants themselves may also have been enterprising serfs. Not a few long-distance traders were men who had nothing to lose and everything to gain by the enormous risks of foreign trade. They traveled together in armed caravans and convoys, buying goods and products as cheaply as possible at the source, and selling them for all they could get in Western ports. (See Map 8–1.)

At first, traditional social groups—nobility, clergy, and peasantry—considered the merchants an oddity. As late as the fifteenth century, we find the landed nobility still snubbing the urban patriciate. Such snobbery never died out among the older landed nobility, who looked down on the traders as men of poor breeding and character possessed of money they did not properly earn or deserve. Over time the powerful grew to respect the merchants, and the weak to imitate them, because wherever the merchants went, they left a trail of wealth behind.

Challenging the Old Lords

As they grew in wealth and numbers, merchants formed their own protective associations and were soon challenging traditional seigneurial authority. They especially wanted to end the tolls and tariffs regional authorities

MAP EXPLORATION

Interactive map: To explore this map further, go to **www.myhistorylab.com**

Map 8–1 **SOME MEDIEVAL TRADE ROUTES AND REGIONAL PRODUCTS**   The map shows some of the channels that came to be used in interregional commerce as well as the products traded by particular regions.

imposed on the surrounding countryside. Such regulations hampered the flow of commerce on which both merchant and craftsperson in the growing urban export industries depended. Wherever merchants settled in large numbers, they challenged the tolls, tariffs, and other petty restrictions on trade. Merchant guilds or protective associations also sprang up in the eleventh century and were followed in the twelfth century by those of craftspeople (drapers, haberdashers, furriers, hosiers, goldsmiths). Both quickly found themselves in conflict with the norms of a comparatively static agricultural society.

Merchants and craftspeople needed simple and uniform laws and a fluid government sympathetic to their new forms of business activity—not the fortress mentality of the lords of the countryside. The result was a struggle with the old nobility within and outside the towns. This conflict led towns in the High and later Middle Ages to form their own independent communes and to ally themselves with kings against the nobility in the countryside, a development that eventually rearranged the centers of power in medieval Europe and dissolved classic feudal government.

Because the merchants were so clearly the engine of the urban economy, small shopkeepers and artisans identified more with them than with the aloof royal lords and bishops who were the chartered town's original masters. Most townspeople found that the development of urban life to benefit merchants also best served their own interests. The merchants' way led to greater commercial freedom, fewer barriers to trade and business, and a more fluid urban life. The lesser nobility (the small knights) outside the towns also embraced the opportunities of the new mercantile economy. During the eleventh and twelfth centuries, the burgher upper class increased its economic strength and successfully challenged the old urban lords for control of the towns.

New Models of Government

With urban autonomy came new models of self-government. Around 1100, the old urban nobility and the new burgher upper class merged. It was a marriage between those wealthy by birth (inherited property) and those who made their fortunes in long-distance trade. From this new ruling class was born the aristocratic town council, which henceforth governed towns.

Enriching and complicating the situation, small artisans and craftspeople also slowly developed their own protective associations, or **guilds**, and began to gain a voice in government. The towns' ability to provide opportunities for the "little person" created the slogan, "Town air brings freedom." In the countryside the air one breathed still belonged to the lord of the land, but in the towns residents were treated as freemen. Within town walls, people thought of themselves as citizens with basic rights, not subjects liable to their masters' whim. Economic hardship certainly continued to exist among the lower urban groups, despite their basic legal and political freedoms, but social mobility was at least a possibility in the towns.

Keeping People in Their Places Traditional measures of success had great appeal within the towns. Despite their economic independence, the wealthiest urban groups admired and imitated the lifestyle of the old landed nobility. Although the latter treated the urban patriciate with disdain, successful merchants longed to live the noble, knightly life. They wanted coats of arms, castles, country estates, and the life of a gentleman or a lady on a great manor. This became particularly true in the later Middle Ages, when reliable bills of exchange and international regulation of trade, together with the maturation of merchant firms, allowed merchants to conduct their business by mail. Then only the young apprentices did a lot of traveling, to learn the business from the ground up. When merchants became rich enough to do so, they took their fortunes to the countryside.

Such social climbing disturbed city councils, and when merchants departed for the countryside, towns often lost out economically. A need to be socially distinguished and distinct pervaded urban society. The merchants were just the tip of the iceberg. Towns tried to control this need by defining grades of luxury in dress and residence for the various social groups and vocations. Overly conspicuous consumption was a kind of indecent exposure punishable by law. Such sumptuary laws restricted the types and amount of clothing one might wear (the length and width of fur pieces, for example) and how one might decorate one's dwelling architecturally. In this way, people were forced to dress and live according to their station in life. The intention of such laws was positive: to maintain social order and dampen social conflict by keeping everyone clearly and peacefully in their place.

Social Conflict and Protective Associations (Guilds)

Despite unified resistance to external domination, medieval towns were not internally harmonious social units. They were a collection of many selfish and competitive communities, each seeking to advance its own business and family interests. Conflict between haves and have-nots was inevitable, especially because medieval towns had little concept of social and economic equality. Theoretically, poor artisans could work their way up from lower social and vocational levels, and some lucky ones did. Yet those who had not done so were excluded from the city council. Only families of long standing in the town who owned property had full rights of citizenship and a direct say in the town's government at the highest levels. Government, in other words, was inbred and aristocratic.

Conflict also existed between the poorest workers in the export trades (usually the weavers and wool combers) and the economically better off and socially ascending independent workers and small shopkeepers. The better-off workers also had their differences with the merchants, whose export trade often brought competitive foreign goods into the city, so independent workers and small shopkeepers organized to restrict foreign trade to a minimum and corner the local market in certain items.

Over time, the formation of artisan guilds gave workers in the trades a direct voice in government. Ironically, the long-term effect of this gain limited the social mobility of the poorest artisans. The guilds gained representation on city councils, where, to discourage imports, they used their power to enforce quality standards and fair prices on local businesses. These actions tightly restricted guild membership, squeezing out poorer artisans and tradesmen. As a result, lesser merchants and artisans found their opportunities progressively limited. So rigid and exclusive did the dominant guilds become that they often stifled their own creativity and inflamed the journeymen whom they excluded from their ranks. Unrepresented artisans and craftspeople constituted a true urban proletariat prevented by law from forming their own guilds or entering existing ones. The efforts by guild-dominated governments to protect local craftspeople and industries tended to narrow trade and depress the economy for all.

Towns and Kings

By providing kings with the resources they needed to curb factious noblemen, towns became a major force in the transition from feudal societies to national governments. In many places kings and towns formally allied against the traditional lords of the land. A notable exception to this general development is England, where the towns joined with the barons against the oppressive monarchy of King John (r. 1199–1216), becoming part of the parliamentary opposition to the crown. But by the fifteenth century, kings and towns had also joined forces in England, so much so that Henry VII's (r. 1485–1509) support of towns brought him the title, the "burgher king."

Towns attracted kings and emperors for obvious reasons. They were a ready source of educated bureaucrats and lawyers who knew Roman law, the ultimate tool for running kingdoms and empires. Kings could also find money in the towns in great quantity, enabling them to hire their own armies instead of relying on the nobility. Towns had the human, financial, and technological resources to empower kings. By such alliances, towns won royal political recognition and guarantees for their constitutions. This proved somewhat easier to do in the stronger coastal areas than inland, where urban life remained less vigorous and territorial government was on the rise. In France, towns were integrated early into royal government. In Germany, they fell under ever tighter control by the princes. In Italy, uniquely, towns dominated the surrounding countryside, becoming genuine city-states during the Renaissance.

It was also in the towns' interest to have a strong monarch as their protector against despotic local lords and princes, who were always eager to integrate or engulf the towns within their expanding territories. Unlike a local magnate, a king tended to remain at a distance, allowing towns to exercise their precious autonomy. A king was thus the more desirable overlord. It was also an advantage for a town to conduct its long-distance trade in the name of a powerful monarch. This gave predators pause and improved official cooperation along the way. Such alliances profited both sides—kings and towns.

Between the eleventh and fourteenth centuries, towns had considerable freedom and autonomy. As in Roman times, they again became the flourishing centers of Western civilization. But after the fourteenth century, and even earlier in France and England, the towns, like the church before them, were steadily bent to the political will of kings and princes in most places. By the seventeenth century, few towns would be truly autonomous. Most had been integrated thoroughly into the larger purposes of the "state."

Jews in Christian Society

The major urban centers, particularly in France and Germany, attracted many Jews during the late twelfth and thirteenth centuries. Jews gathered there both by choice and for safety in the increasingly hostile Christian world. Mutually wary of one another, Christians and Jews limited direct contact with one another to exchanges between their merchants and scholars. The church expressly forbade Jews from hiring Christians in their businesses and from holding any public authority over them. Jews freely conducted their own small businesses, catering to private clients, both Christian and Jewish. The wealthier Jews became bankers to kings and popes. Jewish intellectual and religious culture, always elaborate and sophisticated, both dazzled and threatened Christians who viewed it from outside. These various factors—the separateness of Jews, their exceptional economic power, and their rich cultural strength—contributed to envy, suspicion, and distrust among many Christians, whose religious teaching held Jews responsible for the death of Christ.

Between the late twelfth and fourteenth centuries, Jews were exiled from France and persecuted elsewhere. Two factors lay behind this unprecedented surge in anti-Jewish sentiment. The first was a desire by kings to confiscate Jewish wealth and property and to eliminate the Jews as economic competitors with the monarchy. In the fourteenth century, French kings acted similarly against a wealthy Christian military order known as the Knights Templar. (See Chapters 7 and 9.) The church's increasing political vulnerability to the new dynastic monarchies also contributed to the surge in anti-Jewish sentiment. Faced with the loss of its political power, the church became more determined than ever to maintain its spiritual hegemony. Beginning with the Crusades and the creation of new mendicant orders, the church reasserted its claims to spiritual sovereignty over Europe, instigating campaigns against dissenters, heretics, witches, Jews, and infidels at home and abroad.

▼ Schools and Universities

In the twelfth century, Byzantine and Spanish Islamic scholars made it possible for the works of Aristotle on logic, the mathematical and astronomical writings of Euclid and Ptolemy, the basic works of Greek physicians and Arab mathematicians, and the larger texts of Roman law to circulate among Western scholars. Islamic scholars preserved these works and wrote extensive, thought-provoking commentaries on them, which were

Jonah is swallowed by a great fish in a scene from a thirteenth-century Hebrew Torah from Portugal, an example of the rich Jewish heritage of medieval Iberia.   Instituto da Biblioteca Nacional, Lisbon, Portugal/The Bridgeman Art Library

translated into Latin and made available to Western scholars and students. This renaissance of ancient knowledge produced an intellectual ferment that gave rise to Western universities.

University of Bologna

The first important Western university, established by Emperor Frederick I Barbarossa in 1158, was in Bologna. There we find the first formal organizations of students and masters and the first degree programs—the institutional foundations of the modern university. Originally, the term *university* meant simply a corporation of individuals (students and masters) who joined for their mutual protection from overarching episcopal authority (the local bishop oversaw the university) and from the local townspeople. Because townspeople then looked on students as foreigners without civil rights, such protective unions were necessary. They followed the model of an urban trade guild.

Bolognese students also "unionized" to guarantee fair rents and prices from their often reluctant hosts. And students demanded regular, high-quality teaching from their masters. In Italy, students actually hired their own teachers, set pay scales, and drew up desired lecture topics. Masters who did not keep their promises or live up to student expectations were boycotted. Price gouging by townspeople was met with the threat to move the university to another town. This could be done rather easily, because the university was not yet tied to a fixed physical plant. Students and masters moved freely from town to town as they chose. Such mobility gave them a unique independence from their surroundings.

Masters also formed their own protective associations and established procedures and standards for certification to teach within their ranks. The first academic degree was a certificate that licensed one to teach, a *licentia docendi.* It granted graduates in the liberal arts program—the program basic to all higher learning—as well as those in the higher professional sciences of med-

In this medieval school scene, a teacher and his wife, with switches, teach children their music lessons.   German Information Center

icine, theology, and law, "the right to teach anywhere" (*ius ibique docendi*).

Bologna was famous for the revival of Roman law. During the Frankish era and later, from the seventh to the eleventh centuries, only the most rudimentary manuals of Roman law had survived. With the growth of trade and towns in the late eleventh century, Western scholars had come into contact with the larger and more important parts of the *Corpus juris civilis* of Justinian, which had been lost during the intervening centuries. (See Chapter 6.) The study and dissemination of this recovered material was now undertaken in Bologna under the direction of Irnerius, a scholar who flourished in the early twelfth century. He and his students made authoritative commentaries, or *glosses*, on existing laws, based on their newly broadened knowledge of the *Corpus juris civilis*. Around 1140, a monk named Gratian, also a resident in Bologna, created the standard legal text in church, or canon, law, the *Concordance of Discordant Canons*, known simply as Gratian's *Decretum*.

As Bologna was the model for southern European universities (those of Spain, Italy, and southern France) and the study of law, so Paris became the model for northern European universities and the study of theology.

Oxford and Cambridge in England, and (much later) Heidelberg in Germany were among its imitators. All these universities required a foundation in the liberal arts for advanced study in the higher sciences of medicine, theology, and law. The **liberal arts** program consisted of the *trivium* (grammar, rhetoric, and logic) and the *quadrivium* (arithmetic, geometry, astronomy, and music), the language arts and the mathematical arts.

In this engraving, a teacher at the University of Paris leads fellow scholars in a discussion. As shown here, all of the students wore the scholar's cap and gown.
CORBIS/Bettmann

Cathedral Schools

Before the emergence of universities, the liberal arts were taught in cathedral and monastery schools to train the clergy. By the late eleventh and twelfth centuries, cathedral schools also began to provide lectures for nonclerical students, broadening their curricula to include training for purely secular vocations. In 1179, a papal decree obliged cathedrals to provide teachers at no cost for laity who wanted to learn.

After 1200, increasing numbers of future notaries and merchants who had no particular interest in becoming priests, but who needed Latin and related intellectual disciplines to fill their secular positions, studied side by side with aspiring priests in cathedral and monastery schools. By the thirteenth century, the demand for secretaries and notaries in growing urban and territorial governments and for literate personnel in the expanding merchant firms gave rise to schools for secular vocational preparation. With the appearance of these schools, the church began to lose its monopoly on higher education.

The most famous of the cathedral schools were those of Rheims and Chartres in France. Chartres won fame under the direction of such distinguished teachers as Fulbert, Saint Ivo, and Saint Bernard of Chartres (not to be confused with the more famous Saint Bernard of Clairvaux). Gerbert, later Pope Sylvester II (r. 999–1003), guided Rheims to greatness in the last quarter of the tenth century. Gerbert was filled with enthusiasm for knowledge and promoted both logical and rhetorical studies. He did much to raise the study of logic to preeminence within the liberal arts, despite his own preference for rhetoric.

University of Paris

The University of Paris grew institutionally out of the cathedral school of Notre Dame, among others. King Philip Augustus and Pope Innocent III gave the new university its charter in 1200. At Paris the college, or house system, originated. At first, a college was just a hospice providing room and board for poor students who could not rent rooms in town. But the educational life of the university quickly expanded into fixed structures and began to thrive on sure endowments.

In Paris, the most famous college was the Sorbonne, founded for theology students around 1257 by Robert de Sorbon, chaplain to

THOMAS AQUINAS PROVES THE EXISTENCE OF GOD

People in the Middle Ages saw continuity between Earth and heaven, the world of the living and the world of the dead. Intellectuals believed that reason and revelation, although different, were nonetheless connected. So reasoned argument could prove some of what the Bible revealed to faith. Thomas Aquinas, perhaps the greatest medieval theologian explicating orthodox Christian belief, here states his famous five arguments for the existence of God, which he believed any rational person would agree with.

Are these arguments persuasive? Which is the most persuasive, which is the least? Are they basically the same argument?

Is there a God?

REPLY: There are five ways in which one can prove that there is a God.

The FIRST . . . is based on change. Some things . . . are certainly in process of change: this we plainly see. Now anything in the process of change is being changed by something else. . . . Hence one is bound to arrive at some first cause of change not itself being changed by anything, and this is what everybody understands by God.

The SECOND way is based on the nature of causation. In the observable world causes are found to be ordered in series. . . . Such a series must however stop somewhere. . . . One is therefore forced to suppose some first cause, to which everyone gives the name "God."

The THIRD way is based on what need not be and on what must be. . . . Some . . . things . . . can be, but need not be for we find them springing up and dying away . . . Now everything cannot be like this [for then we must conclude that] once upon a time there was nothing. But if that were true there would be nothing even now, because some thing that does not exist can only be brought into being by something already existing. . . . One is forced therefore to suppose something which must be . . . [and] is itself the cause that other things must be.

The FOURTH way is based on the gradation observed in things. Some things are found to be more good, more true, more noble . . . and other things less [so]. But such comparative terms describe varying degrees of approximation to a superlative . . . [something that is] the truest and best and most noble of things. . . . There is something, therefore, which causes in all other things their being, their goodness, and whatever other perfection they have. And this we call "God."

The FIFTH way is based on the guidedness of nature. An orderedness of actions to an end is observed in all bodies obeying natural laws . . .; they truly tend to a goal and do not merely hit it by accident. . . . Everything in nature, therefore, is directed to its goal by someone with intelligence, and this we call "God."

Thomas Aquinas, *Summa Theologiae*, 1st ed. by Thomas Gilby (New York: Image Books, 1969), pp. 67–70.

the king. In Oxford and Cambridge, the colleges became the basic unit of student life and were indistinguishable from the university proper. By the end of the Middle Ages, such colleges tied universities to physical plants and fixed foundations. Their mobility was also forevermore restricted, as were their earlier autonomy and freedom.

As a group, Parisian students had power and prestige. They enjoyed royal protections and privileges that were denied to ordinary citizens. Many Parisian students were well-to-do, many of whom were spoiled and petulant.

They did not endear themselves to the townspeople, whom they considered inferior. The city's ordinances show that townspeople sometimes let their resentments lead to violence against students. City law forbade the beating of students. Only those students who had clearly committed serious crimes could be imprisoned. Only in self-defense might a citizen strike a student. Citizens had to testify against anyone seen abusing a student. University laws also required teachers to be carefully examined before being licensed to teach.

The Curriculum

Before the "renaissance" of the twelfth century, when many Greek and Arabic texts became available to Western scholars and students in Latin translations, the education available within cathedral and monastery schools had been limited. Students learned grammar, rhetoric, and elementary geometry and astronomy. They had the classical Latin grammars of Donatus and Priscian, Saint Augustine's treatise *On Christian Doctrine,* and Cassiodorus's treatise *On Divine and Secular Learning.* The writings of Boethius provided instruction in arithmetic and music and preserved the small body of Aristotle's works on logic then known in the West. After the textual finds of the early twelfth century, Western scholars possessed the whole of Aristotle's logic, the astronomy of Ptolemy, the writings of Euclid, and many Latin classics. By the mid-thirteenth century, almost all of Aristotle's works circulated in the West.

In the High Middle Ages, the learning process was basic. The assumption was that truth already existed; one did not have to go out and find it. Truth only had to be organized, elucidated, and defended. Such conviction made logic and dialectic the focus of education. Students wrote commentaries on authoritative texts, especially those of Aristotle and the Church Fathers. This method of study, based on logic and dialectic, was known as **Scholasticism**. It reigned supreme in all the faculties—in law and medicine as well as in philosophy and theology. Students read the traditional authorities in their field, formed short summaries of their teaching, disputed them with their peers, and then drew conclusions. Logic and dialectic dominated training in the arts because they were the tools that disciplined knowledge and thought. *Dialectic* is negative logical inquiry, the art of discovering a truth by finding the contradictions in arguments against it. Although seemingly abstract and boring, the reading and harmonizing of learned authorities in direct debate and disputation exhilarated students.

Few books existed for students and those available were expensive hand-copied works. Students could not leisurely master a subject in the quiet of a library as they do today. Instead they had to learn it in lecture, discussion, and debate. This required memorization and the ability to think on one's feet. Rhetoric, or persuasive argument, was the ultimate goal, an ability to eloquently defend the knowledge one had gained by logic and dialectic. Successful students became virtual encyclopedias.

Philosophy and Theology

Scholastics quarreled over the proper relationship between philosophy, by which they meant almost exclusively the writings of Aristotle, and theology, which they believed to be a "science" based on divine revelation. The problem between philosophy and theology arose because, in Christian eyes, Aristotle's writings contained heresy. Islamic commentators on Aristotle heightened the problem by embracing those heresies as true. Aristotle, for example, taught the eternality of the world, which called into question the Judeo-Christian teaching that God created the world in time, as the book of Genesis said. Aristotle also taught that intellect, or mind, was ultimately one, a seeming denial of human individuality and hence of Christian teaching about individual responsibility and personal immortality. Church authorities wanted the works of Aristotle and other ancient authorities to be submissive handmaidens to Christian truth.

Abelard When philosophers and theologians applied the logic and metaphysics of Aristotle to the interpretation of Christian revelation, many believed it posed a mortal threat to biblical truth and church authority. Few philosophers and theologians gained greater notoriety for such wrongful interpretation of the Scriptures than Peter Abelard (1079–1142). Possibly the brightest logician and dialectician of the High Middle Ages, Abelard was the first European scholar to gain a large student audience. No one promoted the new Aristotelian learning more boldly than he, nor did any other pay more dearly for it: Abelard ended his life not as an academic superstar, but in a monastery. His bold subjection of church teaching to Aristotelian logic and dialectic made him many powerful enemies at a time when there was no tenure to protect genius and free speech in schools and universities. Accused of multiple transgressions of church doctrine, he recounted in an autobiography the "calamities" that had befallen him over a lifetime because of his boldness.

His critics especially condemned him for his subjective interpretations of Scripture. He likened the trinitarian bonds among God the Father, the Son, and the Holy Spirit to sworn documents and covenants made among people. Rather than a God-begotten cosmic ransom of humankind from the Devil, Christ's crucifixion, he argued, redeemed Christians by virtue of its impact on their hearts and minds when they heard the story. Abelard's ethical teaching stressed intent over deed: The motives of the doer made an act good or evil, not the act itself. Inner feelings were thus more important for receiving divine forgiveness than the church's sacrament of penance administered by a priest.

Abelard's native genius and youthful disrespect for seniority and tradition gained him powerful enemies in high places. He gave those enemies the opportunity to strike him down when, in Paris, where he became Master of Students at Notre Dame, he seduced a bright, seventeen-year-old niece of a powerful canon, who hired him to be her tutor in his home. Her name was Héloïse and their passionate affair ended in public scandal, with Héloïse pregnant. Unable to marry officially (university teachers then had to be single and celibate), they wed secretly and placed their illegitimate child with Abelard's sister to raise. Intent on punishing Abelard and ending his career, the enraged uncle exposed their secret marriage and hired men to castrate Abelard.

In the aftermath of those terrible events, the lovers entered cloisters nearby Paris: Héloïse at Argentueil, Abelard at St. Denis. She continued to love Abelard and relive their passion in her mind, while Abelard became a self-condemning recluse, assuring Héloïse in his letters to her that his "love" had only been wretched desire. The famous philosopher ended his life as a platitudinous monk. In 1121, a church synod ordered all his writings to be burned. Another synod in 1140 condemned nineteen propositions from his philosophical and theological works as heresy. Retracting his teaching, Abelard lived out the remaining two years of his life in an obscure priory near Chalons. As for Héloïse, she lived another twenty years and gained renown for her positive efforts to reform the rules for the cloistered life of women, under which she had suffered. Their story is a revelation of both private and public life in the Middle Ages. It also shows how a powerful and demanding culture could shape and coerce universal human feelings.

▼ Women in Medieval Society

The image and the reality of medieval women are two different things. Male Christian clergy, whose ideal was a celibate life of chastity, poverty, and obedience, strongly influenced the image. Drawing on the Bible and classical medical, philosophical, and legal traditions predating Christianity, Christian thinkers depicted women as physically, mentally, and morally weaker than men.

On the basis of such assumptions, the religious life was led to be superior to marriage, and virgins and celibate widows were praised over wives. A wife was to be subject and obedient to her husband, who, as the stronger of the two, had a duty to protect and discipline her. This image of medieval woman suggests two basic options: to become either a subjugated housewife or a confined nun. In reality, most medieval women were neither.

Image and Status

Both within and outside Christianity, this image of women was contradicted. In chivalric romances and courtly love literature of the twelfth and thirteenth cen-

A fourteenth-century English manuscript shows women at their daily tasks: carrying jugs of milk from the sheep pen, feeding the chickens, carding and spinning wool. By permission of The British Library

turies, as in the contemporaneous cult of the Virgin Mary, women were put on pedestals and treated as superior to men in purity. If the church harbored misogynist sentiments, it also condemned them, as in the case of the late thirteenth century *Romance of the Rose* and other popular bawdy literature.

The learned churchman Peter Lombard (1100–1169), whose *Four Books of the Sentences* every theological student annotated, asked why Eve had been created from Adam's rib rather than from his head or his feet? The answer: God took Eve from Adam's side because she was meant neither to rule over man, nor to be man's slave, but rather to stand squarely at his side, as his companion and partner in mutual aid and trust. By such

SEPARATE AND APART in their respective cloisters, Abelard and Héloïse performed a lengthy postmortem on their tragic love affair in letters to one another. Therein, they show their open wounds and share completely different assessments of where their love led them. Unhappy in the cloister, Héloïse had only regret for what they had lost, while Abelard, having found his true self in the cloister, looked back on their relationship only with shame.

QUESTIONS

1. Did the expectations of contemporary religion and culture contribute to the tragedy of their love?

2. Did they have only themselves to blame?

3. Which of the two better understood the situation? Who, in the end, was the stronger?

I. Héloïse to Abelard

Why, after our conversion [and entrance into the cloisters], which you alone decreed, am I fallen into such neglect and oblivion that I am neither refreshed by your presence, nor comforted by a letter in your absence . . . When I was enjoying carnal pleasures with you, many were uncertain whether I did so from love or from desire. Now the end [result] shows the spirit [in which I acted]. I have forbidden myself all pleasures so that I might obey your will. I have reserved nothing for myself, save this one thing: to be entirely yours . . .

When we enjoyed the delights of love . . . we were spared divine wrath. But when we corrected the unlawful with the lawful [by marriage] and covered the filth of fornication with the honesty of marriage, the wrath of the Lord vehemently fell upon us . . . For men taken in the most flagrant adultery what you suffered [castration] would have been a proper punishment. But what others might merit by adultery, you incurred by a [proper] marriage. What an adulteress brings to her lover, your own wife brought to you! And this did not happen when we were still indulging our old pleasures, but when we were separated and living chaste lives apart . . .

So sweet to me were those delights of lovers that they can neither displease me nor pass from my memory. Whatever I am doing, they always come to mind. Not even when I am asleep do they spare me . . . [At] Mass, when prayer ought to be pure, the memory of those delights thoroughly captivate my wretched soul rather than heed my prayers. And although I ought to lament what I have done, I sigh rather for what I now have to forgo. Not only the things that we did, but the places and the times in which we did them are so fixed with you in my mind that I reenact them all . . . At times the thoughts of my mind are betrayed by the very motions of my body . . . 'O wretched person that I am, who shall deliver me from this body of death?' Would that I might truthfully add what follows: 'I thank God through Jesus Christ our Lord.'

II. Abelard to Héloïse

Héloïse, my lust sacrificed our bodies to such great infamy that no reverence for honor, nor for God, or for the days of our Lord's passion, or for any solemn thing whatsoever could I be stopped from wallowing in that filth . . . [and although you resisted] I made you consent. Wherefore most justly . . . of that part of my body have I been diminished wherein was the seat of my lust . . . God truly loved you [Héloïse], not I. My love . . . was lust, not love. I satisfied my wretched desires in you . . . So weep for your Savior, not for your seducer, for your Redeemer, not for your defiler, for the Lord who died for you, not for me, his servant, who is now truly free for the first time . . .

O how detestable a loss [it would have been] if, given over to carnal pleasure, you were to bring forth a few children . . . for the world, when you are now delivered of a numerous progeny [i.e. the young nuns who are Héloïse's wards in the cloister]. Nor would you then be more than a woman, you who now transcend even men, and have turned the curse of Eve into the blessing of Mary [by your chastity in the cloister]. O how indecent it would be for those holy hands of yours, which now turn the pages of sacred books, to serve the obscenities of womanly cares.

Source: *The Letters of Abelard and Heloise*, trans. by C. K. Scott Moncrieff (1942), pp. 59–61, 78, 81, 97–98, 100, 103.

Adam and Eve were not cast out of the Garden of Eden because of their sexual lust for one another but rather for their disobedience to God in eating the forbidden fruit from the Tree of Knowledge of Good and Evil. St. Augustine who, like Abelard, was known to exhibit a certain weakness for the charms of the opposite sex, taught that before their Fall, Adam and Eve had complete control over their libidos as opposed to their libidos having complete control over them. Their minds and hearts filled only with thoughts of God when, without any shame or self-indulgence, they engaged in sexual intercourse. Abelard and Heloise's sexual lust and shame serve as a commentary on fallen humankind, tracing back to Adam and Eve. This medieval depiction of Adam and Eve is courtesy of the Library of Congress, Rare Book and Special Collections Division insistence on the spiritual equality of men and women and their shared responsibility in marriage, the church to this extent also helped protect the dignity of women.

Germanic law treated women better than Roman law had done, recognizing basic rights that forbade their treatment as chattel. Unlike Roman women, who as teens married men much older than themselves, German women married husbands of similar age. Another practice unknown to the Romans was the groom's conveyance of a portion, or dowry (*dos*), to his bride, which became her own in the event of his death. All major Germanic law codes recognized the economic freedom of women: their right to inherit, administer, dispose of, and confer property and wealth on their children. They could also press charges in court against men for bodily injury and rape, whose punishment, depending on the circumstances, ranged from fines, flogging, and banishment to blinding, castration, and death.

Life Choices

The nunnery was an option for single women from the higher social classes. Entrance required a dowry and could be almost as expensive as a wedding, although usually cheaper. Within the nunnery, a woman could rise to a position of leadership as an abbess or a mother superior, exercising authority denied her in much of secular life. The nunneries of the established religious orders remained under male supervision, however, so that even abbesses had to answer to higher male authority.

In the ninth century, under the influence of Christianity, the Carolingians made monogamous marriage official policy. Heretofore they had practiced polygamy and concubinage and permitted divorce. The result was both a boon and a burden to women. On one hand, wives gained greater dignity and legal security. On the other hand, a wife's labor as household manager and bearer of children greatly increased. And the Carolingian wife was now also the sole object of her husband's wrath and pleasure. Such demands clearly took their toll. The mortality rates of Frankish women increased and their longevity decreased after the ninth century. Under such conditions, the cloister became an appealing refuge for women. However, the number of women in cloisters was never large. In late medieval England, no more than 3,500 women entered the cloister.

Working Women

Most medieval women were neither housewives nor nuns, but workers like their husbands. The evidence suggests that their husbands respected and loved them, per-

haps because they worked shoulder to shoulder with them in running the household and home-based businesses. Between the ages of ten and fifteen, girls were apprenticed and gained trade skills much as did boys. If they married, they often continued their trade, operating their bake or dress shops next to their husbands' businesses, or becoming assistants and partners in the shops of their husbands. Women appeared in virtually every "blue-collar" trade, from butcher to goldsmith, but mostly worked in the food and clothing industries. Women belonged to guilds, just like men, and they became craft masters. By the fifteenth century, townswomen increasingly had the opportunity to go to school and gain at least vernacular literacy.

Although women did not have as wide a range of vocations as men, the latter's vocational destinies were also fixed. Womens gender, however, excluded them from the learned professions of scholarship, medicine, and law. Women's freedom of movement within a profession was more often regulated than a man's and their wages for the same work were not as great. Still, women remained as prominent and as creative a part of workaday medieval society as men. Rare was the medieval woman who considered herself merely a wife.

▼ The Lives of Children

The image of medieval children and the reality of their lives were also two different things. Until recently, historians were inclined to believe that parents were emotionally distant from their children during the Middle Ages. Evidence of low esteem for children comes from a variety of sources.

Children as "Little Adults"

Some historians maintain that medieval art and sculpture rarely portray children as being different from adults. If, pictorially, children and adults look alike, does that mean that people in the Middle Ages were unaware that childhood was a separate period of life requiring special care and treatment? High infant and child mortality also existed, which, one theorizes, could only have discouraged parents from making a deep emotional investment in their children. Could a parent be deeply attached to a child who had a 30 to 50 percent chance of dying before age five?

During the Middle Ages, children also assumed adult responsibilities early in life. The children of peasants labored in the fields alongside their parents as soon as they could physically manage the work. Urban artisans and burghers sent their children out of their homes into apprenticeships in various crafts and trades be-

A scene of children at play, illustrating popular pastimes, toys and games: catching butterflies, spinning tops, toddling in a walker. Such scenes document the recognition of a child's world.   The Bridgeman Art Library International

tween the ages of eight and twelve. Could loving parents remove a child from the home at so tender an age? The canonical age for marriage, which was twelve for girls and fourteen for boys, is also evidence that children were expected to grow up fast, although few (mostly royalty) actually married at these ages.

The practice of infanticide is another striking suggestion of low esteem for children in ancient and early medieval times. According to the Roman historian Tacitus (ca. 55–120), the Romans exposed unwanted children, especially girls, at birth to regulate family size. The surviving children appear to have been given plenty of attention and affection. The Germanic tribes of medieval Europe, by contrast, had large families but tended to neglect their children by comparison to the Romans. Infanticide, particularly of girls, continued to be practiced in the early Middle Ages, if its condemnation in penance books and by church synods is any measure. The church also forbade parents to sleep with infants

and small children, less they suffocate them either by accident or design.

Among the German tribes, one paid a much lower compensatory fine (*wergild*) for injury to a child than to an adult—only one fifth of that for injuring an adult. The *wergild* for injury to a female child under fifteen was one half that for injury to a male child—an indication that female children were the least esteemed members of German tribal society. Mothers appear also to have nursed boys longer than they did girls, which favored boys' health and survival. A woman's *wergild*, however, increased eightfold between infancy and her childbearing years.[4]

[4]David Herlihy, "Medieval Children," in *Essays on Medieval Civilization*, ed. by B. K. Lackner and K. R. Phelp (Austin: University of Texas Press, 1978), pp. 109–131.

Childhood as a Special Stage

Despite such evidence of parental distance and neglect, there is another side to the story. Since the early Middle Ages, physicians and theologians had understood childhood to be a distinct and special stage of life. Isidore (560–636), bishop of Seville and a leading intellectual authority throughout the Middle Ages, distinguished six ages of life, the first four of which were infancy, childhood, adolescence, and youth.

According to the medical authorities, infancy proper extended from birth to anywhere between six months and two years and covered the period of speechlessness and suckling. The period thereafter, until age seven, was considered a higher level of infancy, marked by the beginning of a child's ability to speak and his or her weaning. At seven, when a child could think, act decisively, and speak clearly, childhood proper began. At this point a child could be reasoned with, profit from regular discipline, and begin to learn vocational skills. At seven a child was ready for schooling, private tutoring, or apprenticeship in a chosen craft or trade. Until physical growth was complete, which could extend to twenty-one years of age, the child or youth remained legally under the guardianship of parents or a surrogate authority.

There is evidence that high infant and child mortality, rather than distancing parents from their children, actually made them all the more precious to them. The medical authorities most respected during the Middle Ages—Hippocrates, Galen, and Soranus of Ephesus—dealt at length with postnatal care and childhood diseases. Both in learned and in popular medicine, sensible as well as fanciful cures existed for the leading killers of children (diarrhea, worms, pneumonia, and fever). When infants and children died, medieval parents can be found grieving as pitiably as modern parents do. In the art and literature of the Middle Ages, we find mothers baptizing dead infants and children, even carrying them to pilgrim shrines in the hope of miraculous revival. Examples also exist of parental mental illness and suicide brought on by the death of a child.[5]

Clear evidence of special attention being paid to children may be seen in children's toys and aids (walkers and potty chairs). Medieval authorities on child rearing widely condemned child abuse and urged moderation in disciplining and punishing children. In church art and drama, parents were urged to love their children as Mary loved Jesus. Early apprenticeships may also be seen as an expression of parental love and concern. In the Middle Ages, no parental responsibility was greater than that of equipping a child for useful and gainful work. Certainly, by the High Middle Ages if not earlier, children were widely viewed as special creatures with their own needs and rights.

In Perspective

During the High Middle Ages, the growth of Mediterranean trade revived old cities and caused the creation of new ones. The Crusades aided and abetted this development. Italian cities especially flourished during the late eleventh and twelfth centuries. Venice dominated Mediterranean trade and extended its political and economic influence throughout the Near East. It had its own safe ports as far away as Syria. As cities grew in population and became rich from successful trade, a new social group, the long-distance traders, rose to prominence. By marriage and political organization, these merchant families organized themselves into an unstoppable force. They successfully challenged the old nobility in and around the cities. A new elite of merchants gained control of city governments almost everywhere. They brought with them a policy of open trade and the blessings and problems of nascent capitalism. Artisans and small shopkeepers at the lower end of the economic spectrum aspired to follow their example, as new opportunities opened for all. The seeds of social conflict and of urban class struggle had been sown.

One positive result of the new wealth of towns was the patronage of education and culture, which was given an emphasis not experienced since Roman times. Western Europe's first universities appeared in the eleventh century, and universities steadily expanded over the next four centuries. There were twenty by 1300. Not only did Scholasticism flourish, but a new literature, art, and architecture reflected both a new human vitality and the reshaping of society and politics. For all of this, Western Europeans had no one to thank so much as the new class of merchants, whose greed, daring, and ambition made it all possible.

REVIEW QUESTIONS

1. How did the responsibilities of the nobility differ from those of the clergy and the peasantry during the High Middle Ages? What did each social class contribute to the stability of society?
2. What led to the revival of trade and the growth of towns in the twelfth century? What political and social conditions were essential for a revival of trade? How did towns change medieval society?

---

[5]Klaus Arnold, *Kind und Gesellschaft in Mittelater und Renaissance,* (Paderborn, Germany: 1980), pp. 31–37.

3. What were the strengths and weaknesses of higher education during the Middle Ages? What subjects made up the university curriculum?

4. What was the Scholastic program and method of study? Who were the main critics of Scholasticism and what were their complaints?

5. How would you assess the position of women in Germanic law and Roman law? What were the options and responsibilities for women in each social class? Were children viewed as small adults? What are our best sources for the study of parent–child relations?

SUGGESTED READINGS

E. Amt, ed., *Women's Lives in Medieval Europe: A Sourcebook* (1993). Outstanding collection of sources.

P. Aries, *Centuries of Childhood: A Social History of Family Life* (1962). Influential pioneer effort on the subject.

J. W. Baldwin, *The Scholastic Culture of the Middle Ages: 1000–1300* (1971). Good brief synthesis.

M. Black, *The Medieval Cookbook* (1992). Dishing it up in the Middle Ages.

M. T. Clanchy, *Abelard: A Medieval Life* (1998). The biography of the famous philosopher and seducer of Héloïse.

L. Grane, *Peter Abelard: Philosophy and Christianity in the Middle Ages* (1970).

B. A. Hanawalt, *Growing Up in Medieval London* (1993). Positive portrayal of parental and societal treatment of children.

D. Herlihy, *Women, Family, and Society in Medieval Europe: Historical Essays, 1978–91* (1995). A major historian's collected essays.

A. Hopkins, *Knights* (1990). Europe's warriors and models.

D. Krueger, ed., *Byzantine Christianity* (2006). A people's history of Christianity.

E. Male, *The Gothic Image: Religious Art in France in the Thirteenth Century* (1913). An enduring classic.

L. De Mause, ed., *The History of Childhood* (1974). Substantial essays on the inner as well as the material lives of children.

R. I. Moore, *The Formation of a Persecuting Society: Power and Deviance in Western Europe, 950–1250* (1987). A sympathetic look at heresy and dissent.

J. T. Noonan, *Contraception: A History of Its Treatment by the Catholic Theologians and Canonists* (1967). Fascinating account of medieval theologians' take on sex.

S. Ozment, *Ancestors: The Loving Family in Old Europe* (2001). A sympathetic look at families past.

S. Shahar, *The Fourth Estate: A History of Women in the Middle Ages* (1983). A comprehensive survey, making clear the great variety of women's work.

For additional learning resources related to this chapter, please go to www.myhistorylab.com

myhistorylab

The Invention of Printing in China and Europe

THE ABILITY TO put information and ideas on paper and to circulate them widely in multiple identical copies has been credited in the West with the rise of humanism, the Protestant Reformation, the modern state, and the scientific revolution. In truth, the message preceded the machinery: It was a preexisting desire to rule more effectively and to shape and control the course of events that brought the printing press into existence in both China and Europe. Before there was printing, rulers, religious leaders, and merchants longed to disperse their laws, scriptures, and wares more widely and efficiently among their subjects, followers, and customers.

To create the skilled agents and bureaucrats, leaders of state, church, and business cooperated in the sponsorship of schools and education, which spurred the growth of reading and writing among the middle and upper urban classes. Literacy, in turn, fueled the desire for easily accessible and reliable information. Literacy came more slowly to the lower social classes, because authorities feared too much knowledge in the hands of the uneducated or poorly educated would only fan the fires of discontent. To the many who remained illiterate after the invention of printing, information was conveyed carefully in oral and pictorial form. Printed official statements were designed to be read to, as well as read by, people; and religious leaders put images and pictures in the hands of simple folk, hoping to content them with saints and charms.

Resources and Technology: Paper and Ink

Among the indispensable materials of the print revolution were sizable supplies of durable, inexpensive paper and a reliable ink. As early as the Shang period (1766–1122 B.C.E.), a water-based soot and gum ink was used across Asia. (Europe would not have such an ink until the early Middle Ages.) Also in the Shang period, official seals and stamps used to authenticate documents were made by carving bronze, jade, ivory, gold, and stone in a reverse direction (that is, in a mirror form, to prevent the print from appearing backward).

Similar seals appeared in ancient Mesopotamia and Egypt, but only for religious use—not for the affairs of daily secular life. Later, more easily carved clay or wax seals reproduced characters on silk or bamboo surfaces.

Silk in the East and parchment in the West had been early, but very expensive, print media. Bamboo and wood were cheaper, but neither was suited to large-scale printing.

A step forward occurred in the second century B.C.E. when the Chinese invented a crude paper from hemp fibers, which was previously used only for wrappings. Three centuries later (105 C.E.), an imperial eunuch named Ts'ia Lun combined tree bark, hemp, rags, and old fishnets into a superior and reliable paper. A better blend of mulberry bark, fishnets, and natural fibers became the standard paper mixture. By the Tang period (618–907), high-quality paper manufacturing had become a major industry.

In the eighth century, the improved Chinese recipe began to make its way west, after Chinese prisoners taught their Arab captors how to make paper. By the ninth century, Samarkand in Russian Turkestan had become the leading supplier of paper in the East. A century later, Baghdad and Damascus shipped fine paper to Egypt and Europe. Italy became a major Western manufacturer in the thirteenth century followed by Nuremberg, Germany, in the late fourteenth.

Early Printing Techniques

By the seventh century C.E., multiple copies of the *Confucian Scriptures* were made by taking paper rubbings from stone and metal engravings, a direct prelude to block printing. At this time in the West, the arts of engraving, and particularly of coin casting (by hammering hot alloy on an anvil that bore a carved design), took the first steps toward printing with movable type.

The invention of printing occurred much earlier in the East than in the West. The Chinese invented *block printing* (that is, printing with carved wooden blocks) in the eighth century, almost six hundred years before the technique appeared in Europe (1395). The Chinese also far outpaced the West in printing with *movable type* (that is, with individual characters or letters that could

The Diamond Sutra. This Chinese translation of a Sanskrit Buddhist work was printed in 868 and found at Dunhuang. It is the earliest dated piece of block printing yet discovered. Dorling Kindersley Media Library. The image depicts the frontispiece to the world's earliest dated printed book, the Chinese translation of the Buddhist text the Diamond Sutra. This consists of a scroll, over sixteen feet long, made up of a long series of printed pages. Printed in China in 868 C.E., it was found in the Dunhuang Caves in 1907, in the North Western province of Gansu. Image taken from The Diamond Sutra. Originally published/produced in China, 11th May, 868. (c) British Library Board. All Rights Reserved (Picture number 1022251.611). © Dorling Kindersley.

be arranged by hand to make a page)—a technique invented by Pi Scheng in the 1040s, four hundred years before Johann Gutenberg set up the first Western press in Mainz, Germany (around 1450).

Block printing used hard wood (preferably from pear or jujube trees), whose surface was glazed with a filler (glue, wax, or clay). A paper copy of what one wanted to duplicate (be it a drawn image, a written sentence, or both) was placed face down on a wet glaze covering the block and the characters cut into it. The process accommodated any artistic style while allowing text and illustration to coexist harmoniously on a page. Once carved, the block was inked and mild pressure applied, allowing a great many copies to be made before it wore out.

The first movable type was ceramic. The printer set each character or piece in an iron form and arranged them on an iron baking plate filled with heated resin and wax, which, when cooled, created a tight page. After the print run was finished, the plate was heated again to melt the wax and free the type for new settings. Ceramic and later metal type was fragile and left uneven impressions, and metal type was expensive as well and did not hold water-based Chinese inks.

Carved wooden type did not have these problems and therefore became the preferred tool. Set in a wooden frame and tightened with wooden wedges, the readied page was inked up and an impression made, just as in printing with carved wooden blocks. Cutting a complete set of type or font required much time and effort because of the complexity and enormity of Chinese script. To do the latter justice, a busy press required 10,000 individual characters, and that number could increase several-fold, depending on the project.

Printing Comes of Age

In 952, after a quarter century of preparation, a standardized Chinese text, unblemished by any scribal errors, was printed for the first time on a large scale. That text, the *Confucian Classics*, was an epochal event in the history of printing. The main reading of the elite, these famous scrolls became the basis of the entry exam for a government office. In awakening people to the power of printing, the *Confucian Classics* may be compared to the publication of Gutenberg's Latin Bible.

The Sung period (960–1278) saw the first sustained flowering of block printing. Still today among the Chinese the phrase "Sung style" connotes high quality. Three monumental publications stand out: the *Standard Histories* of previous Chinese dynasties, serially appearing between 994 and 1063; the *Buddhist Scriptures* in scrolls up to sixty feet and longer, requiring 130,000 carved wooden blocks (971–983); and the *Daoist Scriptures* (early eleventh century). For the literate, but not necessarily highly educated, numerous how-to books on medical, botanical, and agricultural topics became available. Printed paper money also appeared for the first time in copper-poor Szechwan during the Sung.

There is no certain evidence that printing was a complete gift of the Far East to the West. Although some scholars believe Chinese block printing accompanied playing cards through the Islamic world and into Europe, the actual connecting links have not yet been demonstrated. So although there was a definite paper trail from East to West, Europe appears to have developed its own inks and invented its own block and movable type printing presses independently.[1]

Indeed in the East and the West, different writing systems would favor distinct forms of printing. In China, carved wooden blocks suited an ideographic script that required a seemingly boundless number of characters. Each ideograph, or character, expressed a complete concept. In contrast, European writing was based on a very small phonetic alphabet. Each letter could express meaning only when connected to other letters, forming words. For such a system, movable metal type worked far better than carved wooden blocks. So although China mastered movable type printing earlier than the West, the enormous number of characters required by the Chinese language made movable type impractical.

Ironically, the simpler machinery of block printing did greater justice to China's more intricate and complex script, whereas Europe's far simpler script required the more complex machinery of movable type. Today the Chinese still face the problem of storing and retrieving their rich language in digitized form, "the space-age equivalent of movable type." In telecommunications, they prefer faxes, "the modern-day equivalent of the block print."[2]

Society and Printing

In neither the East nor the West do the availability of essential material resources (wood, ink, and paper) and the development of new technologies sufficiently explain the advent of printing. Cultural and emotional factors played an equally large role. In China, the religious and moral demands of Buddhists, Taoists, and Confucians lay behind the invention of block printing. For Buddhists, copying and disseminating their sacred writings had always been a traditional path of salvation. Taoists, who wanted to hang protective charms or seals around their necks, printed sacred messages blessed by their priests that were up to four inches wide. These were apparently the first block prints. Confucianists, too, lobbied for standardized printed copies of their texts, which they had for centuries duplicated by crude rubbings from stone-carved originals.

In Europe, the major religious orders (Augustinians, Dominicans, and Franciscans) and popular lay religious movements (Waldensians, Lollards, and Hussites) joined with humanists to promote the printing of standardized, orthodox editions of the Bible and other religious writings. As the numbers of literate laity steadily grew, the demand for cheap, practical reading material (calendars, newssheets, and how-to pamphlets) also rapidly increased. By 1500, fifty years after Gutenberg's invention, two hundred printing presses operated throughout Europe, sixty of them in German cities. Just as in China, the large print runs of the new presses tended to be religious or moral subjects in the early years: Latin Bibles and religious books, indulgences and Protestant pamphlets, along with decorated playing cards often bearing moral messages.

With the printing press came the first copyright laws. Knowledge had previously been considered "free." The great majority of medieval scholars and writers were clergy, who lived by the church or other patronage and whose knowledge was deemed a gift of God to be shared freely with all. After the printing press, however, a new sense of intellectual property emerged. In Europe, primitive protective laws took the form of a ruler's "privilege," by

---

[1]Carter, *Invention of Printing in China*, pp. 143, 150, 182.

[2]Twitchett, *Printing and Publishing in Medieval China*, p. 86.

A European Printshop. This sixteenth-century woodcut shows typesetting and printing underway in an early printshop. Printing made it possible to reproduce exactly and in quantity both text and illustrations, leading to the distribution of scientific and technical information on a scale unimaginable in the pre-print world. *Courtesy of the Library of Congress*

which a ruler pledged to punish the pirating of a particular work within his or her realm over a limited period of time. Such measures had clear limits: More than half of the books published during the first century of print in the West were pirated editions, a situation that would not change significantly until the eighteenth century.

Government censorship laws also ran apace with the growth of printing. The clergy of Cologne, Germany, issued the first prohibition of heretical books in 1479. In 1485, the church banned the works of the heretics John Wycliffe and John Huss throughout Europe, and two years later the pope promulgated the first bull against any and all books "harmful to the faith." In 1521, Emperor Charles V banned Martin Luther's works throughout the Holy Roman Empire, along with their author. In 1527, the first publisher was hanged for printing a banned book of Luther's. And in 1559, the pope established the *Index of Forbidden Books*, which still exists.

Printing stimulated numerous new ancillary trades. In addition to the proliferation of bookstores and the rise of traveling booksellers, who carried flyers from town to town promoting particular works, there were new specialized stationery shops, ink and inkstone stores, bookshelf and reading-table makers, and businesses manufacturing brushes and other printing tools. The new print industry also brought social and economic upheaval to city and countryside when, like modern corporations relocating factories to underdeveloped countries, it went in search of cheaper labor by moving presses out of guild-dominated cities and into the freer marketplace of the countryside.

For society's authorities, the new numbers of literate citizens and subjects made changes and reforms both easier and more difficult. As a tool of propaganda, the print-ing press remained a two-edged sword. On the one hand, it gave authorities the means to propagandize more effectively than ever. On the other hand, the new literate public found itself in an unprecedented position to recognize deceit, challenge tradition, and expose injustice.

Sources: Thomas F. Carter, *The Invention of Printing in China and Its Spread Westward* (1928); Elisabeth L. Eisensrein, *The Printing Press as an Agent of Change*, I–II (1979); Rudolf Hirsch, *Printing, Selling and Reading 1450–1550* (Wiesbaden: Harrassowitz, 1967); Constance R. Miller, *Technical and Cultural Prerequisites for the Invention of Printing in China and the West* (Chinese Materials Center, 1983). Denis Twitchett, *Printing and Publishing in Medieval China* (New York: Frederic C. Beil, 1983).

Why did the invention of printing occur earlier in the East than in the West? Did the West inherit all of its knowledge of printing from the East? What are the differences between the Chinese and European writing systems? What problems do these systems create for printing? Why might one Chinese scholar prefer to send another Chinese scholar a fax rather than an e-mail? What was the impact of printing on Chinese and European societies?

A procession of flagellants at Tournai in Flanders in 1349, marching with the crucified Christ and scourging themselves in imitation of his suffering. © ARPL/HIP/The Image Works

9

The Late Middle Ages: Social and Political Breakdown (1300–1453)

▼ **The Black Death**
Preconditions and Causes of the Plague • Popular Remedies • Social and Economic Consequences • New Conflicts and Opportunities

▼ **The Hundred Years' War and the Rise of National Sentiment**
The Causes of the War • Progress of the War

▼ **Ecclesiastical Breakdown and Revival: The Late Medieval Church**
The Thirteenth-Century Papacy • Boniface VIII and Philip the Fair • The Avignon Papacy (1309–1377) • John Wycliffe and John Huss • The Great Schism (1378–1417) and the Conciliar Movement to 1449

▼ **Medieval Russia**
Politics and Society • Mongol Rule (1243–1480)

▼ **In Perspective**

KEY TOPICS

• The effects of the bubonic plague on population and society

• The Hundred Years' War between England and France

• The growing power of secular rulers over the papacy

• Schism, heresy, and reform of the church

T HE LATE MIDDLE Ages saw almost unprecedented political, social, and ecclesiastical calamity. Bubonic plague, known to contemporaries as the Black Death, swept over almost all of Europe between 1348 and 1350 leaving as much as two fifths of the population dead and transforming many pious Christians into believers in the omnipotence of death. France and England grappled with each other in a bitter conflict known as the Hundred Years' War (1337–1453), an exercise in seemingly willful self-destruction that was made even more terrible in its later stages by the introduction of gunpowder and the invention of heavy artillery. A schism emerged within the church, which lasted thirty-nine years (1378–1417) and led, by 1409, to the election of three competing popes and colleges of cardinals. In 1453, the Turks marched seemingly invincibly through Constantinople and toward the West. As their political and religious institutions buckled, disease, bandits, and wolves ravaged their cities, and Islamic armies gathered at their borders, Europeans beheld what seemed to be the imminent total collapse of Western civilization.

It was against this background that such scholars as Marsilius of Padua, William of Ockham, and Lorenzo Valla produced lasting criticisms of medieval assumptions about the nature of God, humankind, and society. Kings worked through parliaments and clergy through councils to limit the pope's temporal power. The notion, derived from Roman law, that a secular ruler is accountable to the body he or she governs had already found expression in documents like the Magna Carta. It came increasingly to carry the force of accepted principle, and conciliarists, who advocated the judicial superiority of church councils over popes, now sought to extend it to papal accountability to the church.

Viewed in terms of their three great calamities—war, plague, and schism—the fourteenth and fifteenth centuries were years in which politics resisted wisdom, nature strained mercy, and the church was less than faithful to its flock.

▼ The Black Death

The virulent plague known as the Black Death struck fourteenth-century Europe when it was already suffering from overpopulation and malnutrition.

Preconditions and Causes of the Plague

In the fourteenth century, nine tenths of the population worked the land. The three-field system of crop production increased the amount of arable land and with it the food supply. As that supply grew, however, so did the population. It is estimated that Europe's population doubled between the years 1000 and 1300 and began thereafter to outstrip food production. There were now more people than there was food to feed them or jobs to employ them, and the average European faced the probability of extreme hunger at least once during his or her expected thirty-five-year life span.

Between 1315 and 1317, crop failures produced the greatest famine of the Middle Ages. Densely populated urban areas such as the industrial towns of the Netherlands suffered greatly. Decades of overpopulation, economic depression, famine, and bad health progressively weakened Europe's population and made it highly vul-

nerable to a virulent bubonic plague that struck with full force in 1348.

The **Black Death**, so called by contemporaries because of the way it discolored the body, followed the trade routes from Asia into Europe. Rats, or more precisely, the fleas the rats bore, on ships from the Black Sea area most likely brought it to Western Europe. Appearing in Constantinople in 1346 and Sicily in late 1347, it entered Europe through the ports of Venice, Genoa, and Pisa in 1348. From there it swept rapidly through Spain and southern France and into northern Europe. Areas that lay outside the major trade routes, like Bohemia, appear to have remained virtually unaffected. Bubonic plague made numerous reappearances in succeeding decades. (See Map 9–1.)

Popular Remedies

The plague often reached a victim's lungs during the course of the disease. From the lungs, the victim's sneezing and wheezing spread it from person to person. Physicians had little understanding of these processes, so even the most rudimentary preventive measures against the disease were lacking. Contemporaries could neither explain the plague nor defend themselves against it. To them, the Black Death was a catastrophe with no apparent explanation and against which there was no known defense. Throughout much of Western Europe, it inspired an obsession with death and dying and a deep pessimism that endured long after the plague years. (See "Encountering the Past: Dealing with Death," page 261.)

Popular wisdom held that a corruption in the atmosphere caused the disease. Some blamed poisonous fumes released by earthquakes. Many wore aromatic amulets as a remedy. According to the contemporary observations of Giovanni Boccaccio, an Italian who recorded the reactions in his *Decameron* (1353), some sought a remedy in moderation and a temperate life, others gave themselves over entirely to their passions (sexual promiscuity ran high within the stricken areas), and still others, "the most sound, perhaps, in judgment," chose flight and seclusion as the best medicine.

One extreme reaction was processions of flagellants, religious fanatics who beat themselves in ritual penance, believing such action would bring divine intervention. The terror the flagellants created—and their dirty, bleeding bodies may have spread the disease—became so socially disruptive and threatening that the church finally outlawed such processions.

In some places, Jews were cast as scapegoats. Centuries of Christian propaganda had bred hatred toward Jews, as had their role as society's moneylenders. Pogroms occurred in several cities, sometimes incited by the flagellants.

MAP EXPLORATION

Interactive map: To explore this map further, go to www.myhistorylab.com

Map 9–1 **SPREAD OF THE BLACK DEATH** Apparently introduced by seaborne rats from Black Sea areas where plague-infested rodents had long been known, the Black Death brought huge human, social, and economic consequences. One of the lower estimates of Europeans dying is 25 million. The map charts the plague's spread in the mid-fourteenth century. Generally following trade routes, the plague reached Scandinavia by 1350, and some believe it then went on to Iceland and even Greenland. Areas off the main trade routes were largely spared.

The Prince of the World, a sandstone sculpture, vividly portrays the transitory nature of life. When viewers look behind the attractive young prince, they discover his beauty to be only skin deep. His body, like every human body, is filled with death, here symbolized by worms and flesh-eating frogs. A serpect spirals up his left leg and enters his back, an allusion to the biblical teaching that the wages of sin are death.   Stadt Nürnberg

Social and Economic Consequences

Whole villages vanished in the wake of the plague. Among the social and economic consequences of such high depopulation were a shrunken labor supply and a decline in the value of the estates of the nobility.

Farms Decline   As the number of farm laborers decreased, wages increased and those of skilled artisans soared. Many serfs chose to commute their labor services into money payments and pursue more interesting and rewarding jobs in skilled craft industries in the cities. Agricultural prices fell because of waning demand, and the price of luxury and manufactured goods—the work of skilled artisans—rose. The noble landholders suffered the greatest decline in power. They were forced to pay more for finished products and for farm labor, while receiving a smaller return on their agricultural produce. Everywhere rents declined after the plague.

Peasants Revolt   To recoup their losses, some landowners converted arable land to sheep pasture, substituting more profitable wool production for labor-intensive grains. Others abandoned the farms, leasing them to the highest bidder. Landowners also sought to reverse their misfortune by new repressive legislation that forced peasants to stay on their farms while freezing their wages at low levels. In 1351, the English Parliament passed a Statute of Laborers, which limited wages to pre-plague levels and restricted the ability of peasants to leave their masters' land. Opposition to such legislation sparked the English peasants' revolt in 1381. In France the direct tax on the peasantry, the **taille**, was increased, and opposition to it helped ignite the French peasant uprising known as the Jacquerie.

Cities Rebound   Although the plague hit urban populations hard, the cities and their skilled industries came in time to prosper from its effects. Cities had always protected their own interests, passing legislation as they grew to regulate competition from rural areas and to control immigration. After the plague, the reach of such laws extended beyond the cities to include the surrounding lands of nobles and landlords, many of whom now peacefully integrated into urban life.

The omnipresence of death also whetted the appetite for goods that only skilled industries could produce. Expensive clothes and jewelry, furs from the north, and silks from the south were in great demand in

DEALING WITH DEATH

DEATH WAS ALL too familiar in the late Middle Ages, and not just in the time of the plague, when both princes and the simple folk buried their children in the same communal pits. In popular art and literature, the living and the dead embraced in the "Dance of Death," reminding rich and poor, young and old, of their mortality. In the fourteenth century, death divided the Middle Ages from the Renaissance: On one side of the divide was an overpopulated medieval society devastated by the four horsemen of the Apocalypse, while on the other side, a newly disciplined Renaissance society learned to forestall famine, plague, war, and conquest, by abstinence, late marriage, birth control, and diplomacy.

Yet death rates in the past were three times those of the modern West and life expectancy only half as long. Life was a progressive dying, and death a promise of everlasting life. In sixteenth-century Florence, fully a third of newborns died in infancy. In seventeenth-century England, infant mortality was 2 percent on the day of birth, 4 percent at the first week, 9 percent by the first month, and 13 percent at the end of the first year.

Almost everyone by their teens and adulthood suffered from some chronic illness (tuberculosis), debilitating condition (arthritis, gout), or life-threatening infection (streptococci) that pitted them in a personal battle with death.

In Renaissance Italy, Lorenzo de' Medici, duke of Urbino (d. 1519), was plagued with leg ulcers and syphilis in his early twenties. At twenty-five, he received a head wound that was treated by trephination, or by boring holes in his skull. He also developed an abscessed foot that never healed. At twenty-six, he fell prey to chills, fever, diarrhea, vomiting, joint pains, and

A caricature of physicians (early sixteenth century). A physician carries a uroscope (for collecting and examining urine; discolored urine signaled an immediate need for bleeding. The physician/surgeon wears surgical shoes and his assistant carries a flail—a comment on the risks of medical services. Hacker Art Books Inc.

anorexia, and was dead at twenty-seven. His physicians identified the cause of death as a catarrhal phlegm, or tuberculosis, that caused "suffocation of the heart."

In Reformation Germany, at thirty-nine, Elector Frederick III the Wise of Saxony (d. 1525), Luther's protector, spent the last year of his life enclosed in his favorite residence. When his strength permitted, he rolled about the castle on a specially made stool with wheels. Cursed with kidney stones, he died from a septic infection and kidney failure when the stones became too many and too large to pass through his urethra. An autopsy discovered stones "almost two finger joints long and spiked."

Those who suffered from such afflictions found themselves, in the words of a sixteenth-century merchant, "between God and the physicians," a precarious position for the chronically ill in any age. The clergy and the physicians profited greatly from the age's great mortality. People feared both dying and dying out of God's grace. Together, the physician and the priest prepared the way to a good temporal death, while the priest guided the dead through purgatory and into heaven, assisted by the laity's purchase of indulgences and commemorative masses. Like the physicians' bleedings and herbal remedies, the church's sacraments and commemorations both exploited and eased the feared passage into eternity that every Christian soul had to make.

Source: Bruce Gordon and Peter Marshall, eds. *The Place of the Dead: Death and Remembrance in Late Medieval and Early Modern Europe* (Cambridge: Cambridge University Press, 2008), chaps. 2, 14; Ann C. Carmichael, "The Health Status of Florentines in the Fifteenth Century," in M. Tetel et al., eds. *Life and Death in Fifteenth-Century Florence* (Durham: Duke University Press, 1989), chap. 3.

How do illness and death shape history and culture?

How effective were the physicians and the clergy in the face of everyday afflictions? Why did people bother with them?

This illustration from the *Canon of Medicine* by the Persian physician and philosopher Avicenna (980–1037), whose Arabic name was Ibn Sina, shows him visiting the homes of rich patients. In the High Middle Ages, the *Canon of Medicine* was the standard medical textbook in the Middle East and Europe.
Biblioteca Universitaria, Bologna, Italy. Scala/Art Resource, NY

the decades after the plague. Initially this new demand could not be met. The basic unit of urban industry, the master and his apprentices (usually one or two), purposely kept its numbers low, jealously guarding its privileges. The first wave of plague turned this already restricted supply of skilled artisans into a shortage almost overnight. As a result, the prices of manufactured and luxury items rose to new heights, which, in turn, encouraged workers to migrate from the countryside to the city and learn the skills of artisans. Townspeople profited coming and going. As wealth poured into the cities and per capita income rose, the prices of agricultural products from the countryside, now less in demand, declined.

The church also gained and lost. It suffered as a landholder and was politically weakened, yet it also received new revenues from the vastly increased demand for religious services for the dead and the dying, along with new gifts and bequests.

New Conflicts and Opportunities

By increasing the importance of skilled artisans, the plague contributed to new social conflicts within the cities. The economic and political power of local arti-

sans and trade guilds grew steadily in the late Middle Ages, along with the demand for their goods and services. The merchant and patrician classes found it increasingly difficult to maintain their traditional dominance and grudgingly gave guild masters a voice in city government. As the guilds won political power, they encouraged restrictive legislation to protect local industries. The restrictions, in turn, caused conflict between master artisans, who wanted to keep their numbers low and expand their industries at a snail's pace, and the many journeymen, who were eager to rise to the rank of master. To the long-existing conflict between the guilds and the ruling urban patriciate was now added one within the guilds themselves.

Also, after 1350, the results of the plague put two traditional "containers" of monarchy—the landed nobility and the church—on the defensive. Kings now exploited growing national sentiment in an effort to centralize their governments and economies. At the same time, the battles of the Hundred Years' War demonstrated the military superiority of paid professional armies over the traditional noble cavalry, thus bringing the latter's future role into question. The plague also killed many members of the clergy—perhaps one third of the German clergy fell victim as they dutifully ministered to the sick and dying. This reduction in clerical ranks occurred in the same century that saw the pope move from Rome to Avignon in southeast France (1309–1377) and the Great Schism (1378–1417) divide the Church into warring factions.

▼ The Hundred Years' War and the Rise of National Sentiment

Medieval governments were by no means all-powerful and secure. The rivalry of petty lords kept localities in turmoil, and dynastic rivalries could plunge entire lands into war, especially when power was being transferred to a new ruler—and woe to the ruling dynasty that failed to produce a male heir.

To field the armies and collect the revenues that made their existence possible, late medieval rulers depended on carefully negotiated alliances among a wide range of lesser powers. Like kings and queens in earlier centuries, they, too, practiced the art of feudal government, but on a grander scale and with greater sophistication. To maintain the order they required, the Norman kings of England and the Capetian kings of France fine-tuned traditional feudal relationships by stressing the duties of lesser to higher powers and the unquestioning loyalty noble vassals owed to the king. The result was a degree of centralized royal power unseen before in these lands and a growing national consciousness that together equipped both France and England for international warfare.

The Causes of the War

The conflict that came to be known as the Hundred Years' War began in May 1337 and lasted until October 1453. The English king Edward III (r. 1327–1377), the grandson of Philip the Fair of France (r. 1285–1314), may have started the war by asserting a claim to the French throne after the French king Charles IV (r. 1322–1328), the last of Philip the Fair's surviving sons, died without a male heir. The French barons had no intention of placing the then fifteen-year-old Edward on the French throne. They chose instead the first cousin of Charles IV, Philip VI of Valois (r. 1328–1350), the first of a new French dynasty that would rule into the sixteenth century.

But there was, of course, more to the war than just an English king's assertion of a claim to the French throne. England and France were then emergent territorial powers in too close proximity to one another. Edward was actually a vassal of Philip VI, holding several sizable French territories as fiefs from the king of France, a relationship that went back to the days of the Norman conquest. English possession of any French land was repugnant to the French because it threatened the royal policy of centralization. England and France also quarreled over control of Flanders, which, although a French fief, was subject to political influence from England because its principal industry, the manufacture of cloth, depended on supplies of imported English wool. Compounding these frictions was a long history of prejudice and animosity between the French and English people, who constantly confronted one another on the high seas and in ports. Taken together, these various factors made the Hundred Years' War a struggle for national identity as well as for control of territory.

French Weakness   France had three times the population of England, was far the wealthier of the two countries, and fought on its own soil. Yet, for most of the conflict, until after 1415, the major battles ended in often stunning English victories. (See Map 9–2, page 264.) The primary reason for these French failures was internal disunity caused by endemic social conflicts. Unlike England, fourteenth-century France was still struggling to make the transition from a splintered feudal society to a centralized "modern" state.

Desperate to raise money for the war, French kings resorted to such financial policies as depreciating the currency and borrowing heavily from Italian bankers, which aggravated internal conflicts. In 1355, in a bid to secure funds, the king turned to the **Estates General**, a representative council of townspeople, clergy, and nobles. Although it levied taxes at the king's request, its independent members also exploited the king's plight to broaden their own regional sovereignty, thereby deepening territorial divisions.

France's defeats also reflected English military superiority. The English infantry was more disciplined than the French, and English archers carried a formidable weapon, the longbow, capable of firing six arrows a minute with enough force to pierce an inch of wood or the armor of a knight at two hundred yards.

Edward III pays homage to his feudal lord Philip VI of France. Legally, Edward was a vassal of the king of France.   Archives Snark International/Art Resource, NY

MAP EXPLORATION

Interactive map: To explore this map further, go to **www.myhistorylab.com**

ENGLAND
London
Crécy
Rouen
Paris
Orléans
FRANCE
Poitiers
Lyons
Bordeaux
150 MI.
150 KM.
(A) 1328
Under English Influence

ENGLAND
London
Calais 1347
Crécy 1346
Rouen
Paris
Orléans
FRANCE
Poitiers 1356
Lyons
Bordeaux
150 MI.
150 KM.
(B) 1360
Under English Influence

ENGLAND
London
Southampton
Calais
North Sea
Rhine R.
FLANDERS
BRABANT
LIMBURG
Brussels
HAINAULT
Agincourt 1415
LUXEMBOURG
PICARDY
Rouen
English Channel
CHANNEL ISLANDS
NORMANDY
Seine R.
Reims
Marne R.
Paris
CHAMPAGNE
Brétigny
Troyes
Orléans
BRITTANY
Loire R.
DUCHY OF BURGUNDY
Nevers
FRANCHE-COMTÉ
POITOU
Bourges
FRANCE
AUVERGNE
Rhône R.
DAUPHINÉ
(C) 1429
Under English Influence
Boundary of France, 1453
Bordeaux
AQUITAINE
Garonne R.
Avignon
PROVENCE
ARMAGNAC
Toulouse
Marseilles
NAVARRE
150 MILES
150 KILOMETERS
ARAGON
Mediterranean Sea

Map 9–2   **THE HUNDRED YEARS' WAR**
The Hundred Years' War went on intermittently from the late 1330s until 1453. These maps show the remarkable English territorial gains up to the sudden and decisive turning of the tide of battle in favor of the French by the forces of Joan of Arc in 1429.

Finally, French weakness during the Hundred Years' War was due, in no small degree, to the comparative mediocrity of its royal leadership. English kings were far shrewder.

Progress of the War

The war had three major stages of development, each ending with a seemingly decisive victory by one or the other side.

The Conflict During the Reign of Edward III   In the first stage of the war, Edward embargoed English wool to Flanders, sparking urban rebellions by merchants and the trade guilds. Inspired by a rich merchant, Jacob van Artevelde, the Flemish cities, led by Ghent, revolted against the French and in 1340 signed an alliance with England acknowledging Edward as king of France. On June 23 of that same year, in the first great battle of the war, Edward defeated the French fleet in the Bay of Sluys, but his subsequent effort to invade France by way of Flanders failed.

In 1346, Edward attacked Normandy and, after a series of easy victories that culminated at the Battle of Crécy, seized the port of Calais (which the English would retain until 1558). Exhaustion of both sides and the onset of the Black Death forced a truce in late 1347, as the war entered a brief lull. In 1356, near Poitiers, the English won their greatest victory, routing France's noble cavalry and taking the French king, John II the Good (r. 1350–1364), captive back to England. A complete breakdown of political order in France followed.

Power in France now lay with the Estates General. Led by the powerful merchants of Paris under Etienne Marcel, that body took advantage of royal weakness, demanding and receiving rights similar to those the Magna Carta had granted to the English privileged classes. Yet, unlike the English Parliament, which represented the interests of a comparatively unified English nobility, the French Estates General was too divided to be an instrument for effective government.

To secure their rights, the French privileged classes forced the peasantry to pay ever-increasing taxes and to repair their war-damaged properties without compensation. This bullying became more than the peasants could bear, and they rose up in several regions in a series of bloody rebellions known as the **Jacquerie** in 1358 (after the peasant revolutionary popularly known as Jacques Bonhomme, or "simple Jack"). The nobility quickly put down the revolt, matching the rebels atrocity for atrocity.

On May 9, 1360, another milestone of the war was reached when England forced the Peace of Brétigny-Calais on the French. This agreement declared an end to Edward's vassalage to the king of France and affirmed his sovereignty over English territories in France (including Gascony, Guyenne, Poitou, and Calais). France

also agreed to pay a ransom of 3 million gold crowns to win King John the Good's release. In return, Edward simply renounced his claim to the French throne.

Such a partition was unrealistic, and sober observers on both sides knew it could not last. France struck back in the late 1360s and, by the time of Edward's death in 1377, had beaten the English back to coastal enclaves and the territory around Bordeaux.

French Defeat and the Treaty of Troyes   After Edward's death the English war effort lessened, partly because of domestic problems within England. During the reign of Richard II (r. 1377–1399), England had its own version of the Jacquerie. In June 1381, long-oppressed peasants and artisans joined in a great revolt of the underprivileged classes under the leadership of John Ball, a secular priest, and Wat Tyler, a journeyman. As in France, the revolt was brutally crushed within the year, but it left the country divided for decades.

England recommenced the war under Henry V (r. 1413–1422), who took advantage of internal French turmoil created by the rise to power of the duchy of Burgundy. With France deeply divided, Henry V struck hard in Normandy. Happy to see the rest of France besieged, the Burgundians foolishly watched from the sidelines while Henry's army routed the French at Agincourt on October 25, 1415. In the years thereafter, belatedly recognizing that the defeat of France would leave them easy prey for the English, the Burgundians closed ranks with French royal forces. The renewed French unity, loose as it was, promised to bring eventual victory over the English, but it was shattered in September 1419 when the duke of Burgundy was assassinated. The duke's son and heir, determined to avenge his father's death, joined forces with the English.

France now became Henry V's for the taking—at least in the short run. The Treaty of Troyes in 1420 disinherited the legitimate heir to the French throne and proclaimed Henry V the successor to the French king, Charles VI. When Henry and Charles died within months of one another in 1422, the infant Henry VI of England was proclaimed in Paris to be king of both France and England. The dream of Edward III that had set the war in motion—to make the ruler of England the ruler also of France—seemed to have been realized.

The son of Charles VI went into retreat in Bourges, where, on the death of his father, he became Charles VII to most of the French people, who ignored the Treaty of Troyes. Displaying unprecedented national feeling inspired by the remarkable Joan of Arc, they soon rallied to his cause and united in an ultimately victorious coalition.

Joan of Arc and the War's Conclusion   Joan of Arc (1412–1431), a peasant from Domrémy in Lorraine in eastern France, presented herself to Charles VII in March

A contemporary portrait of Joan of Arc (1412–1431).   Anonymous, 15th century. "Joan of Arc." Franco-Flemish miniature. Archives Nationales, Paris, France. Photograph copyright Bridgeman-Giraudon/Art Resource, NY

Within a few months of the liberation of Orléans, Charles VII received his crown in Rheims, ending the nine-year "disinheritance" prescribed by the Treaty of Troyes. The king now forgot his liberator as quickly as he had embraced her. When the Burgundians captured Joan in May 1430, he might have secured her release but did little to help her. The Burgundians and the English wanted her publicly discredited, believing this would also discredit Charles VII and demoralize French resistance. She was turned over to the Inquisition in English-held Rouen. The inquisitors there broke the courageous "Maid of Orléans" after ten weeks of interrogation, and she was executed as a relapsed heretic on May 30, 1431. Twenty-five years later, in 1456, Charles reopened her trial, as the French state and church moved to get on history's side. She was now declared innocent of all the charges against her. In 1920, the Roman Catholic Church declared her a saint.

In 1435, the duke of Burgundy made peace with Charles, allowing France to force the English back. By 1453, when the war ended, the English held only their coastal enclave of Calais.

The Hundred Years' War, with sixty-eight years of nominal peace and forty-four of hot war, had lasting political and social consequences. It devastated France, but it also awakened French nationalism and hastened

1429, declaring that the King of Heaven had called her to deliver besieged Orléans from the English. Charles was skeptical, but being in retreat from what seemed to be a hopeless war, he was also willing to try anything to reverse French fortunes. The deliverance of Orléans, a city key to the control of the territory south of the Loire River, would be a godsend. Charles's desperation overcame his skepticism, and he gave Joan his leave.

Circumstances worked perfectly to her advantage. The English force, already exhausted by a six-month siege, was at the point of withdrawal when Joan arrived with fresh French troops. After repulsing the English from Orléans, the French enjoyed a succession of victories they popularly attributed to Joan. She did deserve much of this credit, but not because she was a military genius. She rather gave the French something military experts could not: an enraged sense of national identity and destiny.

THE HUNDRED YEARS' WAR (1337–1453)

1340	English victory at Bay of Sluys
1346	English victory at Crécy and seizure of Calais
1347	Black Death strikes
1356	English victory at Poitiers
1358	Jacquerie disrupts France
1360	Peace of Brétigny-Calais recognizes English holdings in France
1381	English peasants revolt
1415	English victory at Agincourt
1420	Treaty of Troyes recognizes the English king as heir to the French throne
1422	Henry VI proclaimed king of both England and France
1429	Joan of Arc leads French to victory at Orléans
1431	Joan of Arc executed as a heretic
1453	War ends; English retain only Calais

the transition there from a feudal monarchy to a centralized state. It saw Burgundy become a major European political power. It also encouraged the English, in response to the seesawing allegiance of the Netherlands throughout the conflict, to develop their own clothing industry and foreign markets. In both France and England, the burden of the on-again, off-again war fell most heavily on the peasantry, who were forced to support it with taxes and services.

▼ Ecclesiastical Breakdown and Revival: The Late Medieval Church

At first glance, the popes may appear to have been in a favorable position in the latter thirteenth century. Frederick II had been vanquished and imperial pressure on Rome had been removed. (See Chapter 8.) The French king, Louis IX, was an enthusiastic supporter of the church, as evidenced by his two disastrous Crusades, which won him sainthood. Although it lasted only seven years, a reunion of the Eastern church with Rome was proclaimed by the Council of Lyons in 1274, when the Western church took advantage of Byzantine emperor Michael VII Palaeologus's (r. 1261–1282) request for aid against the Turks. But despite these positive events, the church's position was less favorable than it appeared.

The Thirteenth-Century Papacy

As early as the reign of Pope Innocent III (r. 1198–1216), when papal power reached its height, there were ominous developments. Innocent had elaborated the doctrine of papal **plenitude of power** and on that authority had declared saints, disposed of *benefices*, and created a centralized papal monarchy with a clearly political mission. Innocent's transformation of the papacy into a great secular power weakened the church spiritually even as it strengthened it politically. Thereafter, the church as a papal monarchy increasingly parted company with the church as the "body of the faithful." It was against this perceived "papal church" and in the name of the "true Christian church" that both reformers and heretics protested until the Protestant Reformation.

What Innocent began, his successors perfected. Under Urban IV (r. 1261–1264), the papacy established its own law court, the *Rota Romana*, which tightened and centralized the church's legal proceedings. The latter half of the thirteenth century saw an elaboration of the system of clerical taxation; what had begun in the twelfth century as an emergency measure to raise funds for the Crusades became a fixed institution. In the same period, papal power to determine appointments to many major and minor church offices—the "reserva-

tion of *benefices*"—was greatly broadened. The thirteenth-century papacy became a powerful political institution governed by its own law and courts, serviced by an efficient international bureaucracy, and preoccupied with secular goals.

Papal centralization of the church undermined both diocesan authority and popular support. Rome's interests, not local needs, came to control church appointments, policies, and discipline. Discontented lower clergy appealed to the higher authority of Rome against the discipline of local bishops. In the second half of the thirteenth century, bishops and abbots protested such undercutting of their power. To its critics, the church in Rome was hardly more than a legalized, "fiscalized," bureaucratic institution. As early as the late twelfth century, heretical movements of Cathars and Waldensians had appealed to the biblical ideal of simplicity and separation from the world. Other reformers who were unquestionably loyal to the church, such as Saint Francis of Assisi, also protested perceived materialism in official religion.

Political Fragmentation More than internal religious disunity was undermining the thirteenth-century church. The demise of imperial power meant the papacy in Rome was no longer the leader of anti-imperial (Guelf, or propapal) sentiment in Italy. Instead of being the center of Italian resistance to the emperor, popes now found themselves on the defensive against their old allies. That was the ironic price the papacy paid to vanquish the Hohenstaufens.

Rulers with a stake in Italian politics now directed the intrigue formerly aimed at the emperor toward the College of Cardinals. For example, Charles of Anjou, the French king of Naples and Sicily (r. 1266–1285), managed to create a French-Sicilian faction within the college. Such efforts to control the decisions of the college led Pope Gregory X (r. 1271–1276) to establish the practice of sequestering the cardinals immediately upon the death of the pope. The purpose of this so-called conclave of cardinals was to minimize political influence on the election of new popes, but the college became so politicized that it proved to be of little avail.

In 1294, such a conclave, in frustration after a deadlock of more than two years, chose a saintly, but inept, hermit as Pope Celestine V. Celestine abdicated under suspicious circumstances after only a few weeks in office. He also died under suspicious circumstances; his successor's critics later argued that the powers behind the papal throne had murdered him to ensure the survival of the papal office. Celestine's tragicomic reign shocked the Cardinals into electing his opposite, Pope Boniface VIII (r. 1294–1303), a nobleman and a skilled politician. His pontificate, however, would mark the beginning of the end of papal pretensions to great-power status.

JOAN OF ARC REFUSES TO RECANT HER BELIEFS

Joan of Arc, threatened with torture, refused to recant her beliefs and instead defended the instructions she had received from the voices that spoke to her. Here is a part of her self-defense from the contemporary trial record.

Do the judges appear to have made up their minds about Joan in advance? How does this judicial process, which was based on intensive interrogation of the accused, differ from a trial today? Why was Joan deemed heretical and not insane when she acknowledged hearing voices?

On Wednesday, May 9th of the same year [1431], Joan was brought into the great tower of the castle of Rouen before us the said judges and in the presence of the reverend father, lord abbot of St. Cormeille de Compiegne, of masters Jean de Châtillon and Guillaume Erart, doctors of sacred theology, of André Marguerie and Nicolas de Venderos, archdeacons of the church of Rouen, of William Haiton, bachelor of theology, Aubert Morel, licentiate in canon law, Nicolas Loiseleur, canon of the cathedral of Rouen, and master Jean Massieu.

And Joan was required and admonished to speak the truth on many different points contained in her trial which she had denied or to which she had given false replies, whereas we possessed certain information, proofs, and vehement presumptions upon them. Many of the points were read and explained to her, and she was told that if she did not confess them truthfully she would be put to the torture, the instruments of which were shown to her all ready in the tower. There were also present by our instruction men ready to put her to the torture in order to restore her to the way and knowledge of truth, and by this means to procure the salvation of her body and soul which by her lying inventions she exposed to such grave perils.

To which the said Joan answered in this manner: "Truly if you were to tear me limb from limb and separate my soul from my body, I would not tell you anything more and if I did say anything, I should afterwards declare that you had compelled me to say it by force." Then she said that on Holy Cross Day last she received comfort from St. Gabriel, she firmly believes it was St. Gabriel. She knew by her voices whether she should submit to the Church, since the clergy were pressing her hard to submit. Her voices told her that if she desired Our Lord to aid her, she must wait upon Him in all her doings. She said that Our Lord has always been the master of her doings, and the Enemy never had power over them. She asked her voices if she would be burned and they answered that she must wait upon God, and He would aid her.

W. P. Barrett, *The Trial of Jeanne D'Arc* (New York: Gotham House, 1932), pp. 303–304.

Boniface VIII and Philip the Fair

Boniface came to rule when England and France were maturing as nation-states. In England, a long tradition of consultation between the king and powerful members of English society evolved into formal parliaments during the reigns of Henry III (r. 1216–1272) and Edward I (r. 1272–1307), and these meetings helped create a unified kingdom. The reign of the French king Philip IV the Fair (r. 1285–1314) saw France become an efficient, centralized monarchy. Philip was no Saint Louis, but a ruthless politician. He was determined to end England's continental holdings, control wealthy Flanders, and establish French hegemony within the Holy Roman Empire.

Boniface had the further misfortune of bringing to the papal throne memories of the way earlier popes had brought kings and emperors to their knees. Painfully he was to discover that the papal monarchy of the early thirteenth century was no match for the new political powers of the late thirteenth century.

The Royal Challenge to Papal Authority France and England were on the brink of all-out war when Boniface became pope in 1294. Only Edward I's preoccupation with rebellion in Scotland, which the French encouraged, prevented him from invading France and starting the Hundred Years' War a half century earlier than it did start. As both countries mobilized for war, they used the pretext of preparing for a Crusade to tax the clergy heavily. In 1215, Pope Innocent III had decreed that the clergy were to pay no taxes to rulers without papal consent. Viewing English and French taxation of the clergy as an assault on traditional clerical rights, Boniface took a strong stand against it. On February 5, 1296, he issued a bull, *Clericis laicos*, which forbade lay taxation of the clergy without papal approval and revoked all previous papal dispensations in this regard.

In England, Edward I retaliated by denying the clergy the right to be heard in royal court, in effect removing from them the protection of the king. But Philip the Fair struck back with a vengeance: In August 1296, he forbade the exportation of money from France to Rome, thereby denying the papacy the revenues it needed to operate. Boniface had no choice but to come to terms quickly with Philip. He conceded Philip the right to tax the French clergy "during an emergency," and, not coincidentally, he canonized Louis IX in the same year.

Boniface was then also under siege by powerful Italian enemies, whom Philip did not fail to patronize. A noble family (the Colonnas), rivals of Boniface's family (the Gaetani) and radical followers of Saint Francis of Assisi (the Spiritual Franciscans), were seeking to invalidate Boniface's election as pope on the grounds that Celestine V had been forced to resign the office. Charges of heresy, simony, and even the murder of Celestine were hurled against Boniface.

Boniface's fortunes appeared to revive in 1300, a "Jubilee year." During such a year, all Catholics who visited Rome and fulfilled certain conditions had the penalties for their unrepented sins remitted. Tens of thousands of pilgrims flocked to Rome, and Boniface, heady with this display of popular religiosity, reinserted himself into international politics. He championed Scottish resistance to England, for which he received a firm rebuke from an outraged Edward I and from Parliament.

But once again a confrontation with the king of France proved the more costly. Philip seemed to be eager for another fight with the pope. He arrested Boniface's Parisian legate, Bernard Saisset, the bishop of Pamiers and also a powerful secular lord, whose independence Philip had opposed. Accused of heresy and treason, Saisset was tried and convicted in the king's court. Thereafter, Philip demanded that Boniface recognize the process against Saisset, something Boniface could do only if he was prepared to surrender his jurisdiction over the French episco-

Pope Boniface VIII (r. 1294–1303), depicted here, opposed the taxation of the clergy by the kings of France and England and issued one of the strongest declarations of papal authority over rulers, the bull *Unam Sanctam*. This statue is in the Museo Civico, Bologna, Italy. Statue of Pope Boniface VIII. Museo Civico, Bologna. Scala/Art Resource, NY

pate. Boniface could not sidestep this challenge, and he acted swiftly to champion Saisset as a defender of clerical political independence within France. He demanded Saisset's unconditional release, revoked all previous agreements with Philip regarding clerical taxation, and ordered the French bishops to convene in Rome within a year. A bull, *Ausculta fili*, or "Listen, My Son," was sent to Philip

Who Runs the World:
Priests or Princes?

IN ONE OF the boldest papal bulls in the history of Christianity, Pope Boniface VIII declared the temporal authority of rulers to be subject to papal authority. Behind that ideology lay a long, bitter dispute between the papacy and the kings of France and England. Despite the strained scholastic arguments from each side's apologists, the issue was paramount and kingdoms were at stake. The debaters were Giles of Rome, a philosopher and papal adviser, and John of Paris, a French Dominican and Aristotle expert. Quoting ecclesiastical authorities, Giles defended a papal theocracy, while John made the royal case for secular authority.

QUESTIONS

1. Are the arguments pro and con logical and transparent?

2. How is history invoked to support their positions?

3. Which of the two seems to have the better authorities behind his arguments?

I. Giles of Rome, *On Ecclesiastical Power* (1301)

Hugh of St. Victor ... declares that the spiritual power has to institute the earthly power and to judge it if it has not been good ... We can clearly prove from the order of the universe that the church is set above nations and kingdoms [Jeremias 1:10] ... It is the law of divinity that the lowest are led to the highest through intermediaries ... At Romans 13 ... the Apostle, having said that there is no power except from God, immediately added: "And those that are, are ordained of God." If then there are two swords [governments], one spiritual, the other temporal, as can be gathered from the words of the Gospel, "Behold, here are two swords" (Luke 22:38), [to which] the Lord at once added, "It is enough" because these two swords suffice for the church, [then] it follows that these two swords, these two powers and authorities, are [both] from God, since there is no power except from God. But, therefore they must be rightly ordered since, what is from God must be ordered. [And] they would not be so ordered unless one sword was led by the other and one was under the other since, as Dionysius said, the law of divinity which God gave to all created things requires this ... Therefore the temporal sword, as being inferior, is led by the spiritual sword, as being superior, and the one is set below the other as an inferior below a superior.

It may be said that kings and princes ought to be subject spiritually but not temporally ... But those who speak thus have not grasped the force of the argument. For if kings and princes were only spiritually subject to the church, one sword would not be below the other, nor temporalities below spiritualities; there would be no order in the powers, the lowest would not be led to the highest through intermediaries. If they *are* ordered, the temporal sword must be below the spiritual, and [royal] kingdoms below the vicar of Christ, and that by law ... [then] the vicar of Christ must hold dominion over temporal affairs.

II. John of Paris, *Treatise on Royal and Papal Power* (1302–1303)

It is easy to see which is first in dignity, the kingship or the priesthood ... A kingdom is ordered to this end, that an assembled multitude may live virtuously ... and it is further ordered to a higher end which is the enjoyment of God; and responsibility for this end belongs to Christ, whose ministers and vicars are the priests. Therefore, the priestly power is of greater dignity than the secular and this is commonly conceded ...

But if the priest is greater in himself than the prince and is greater in dignity, it does not follow that he is greater in all respects. For the lesser secular power is not related to the greater spiritual power as having its origin from it or being derived from it as the power of a proconsul is related to that of the emperor, which is greater in all respects since the power of the former is derived from the latter. The relationship is rather like that of a head of a household to a general of armies, since one is not derived from the other but both from a superior power. And so the secular power is greater than the spiritual in some things, namely in temporal affairs, and in such affairs it is not subject to the spiritual power in any way because it does not have its origin from it, but rather both have their origin immediately from the one supreme power, namely, the divine. Accordingly the inferior power is not subject to the superior in all things, but only in those where the supreme power has subordinated it to the greater. [For example] a teacher of literature or an instructor in morals directs the members of a household to a very noble end: the knowledge of truth. [That] end is more noble than [that] of a doctor who is concerned with a lower end, namely, the health of bodies. But who would say therefore that the doctor should be subjected to the teacher in preparing his medicines . . .? Therefore, the priest is greater than the prince in spiritual affairs and, on the other hand, the prince is greater in temporal affairs.

Source: Brian Tierney, *The Crisis of Church and State 1050–1300* (Toronto: Toronto University Press, 1996) pp. 198–199 [Giles of Rome], 209–209 [John of Paris].

Papal ring: gold with an engraving on each side and set with a square stone.
Dorling Kindersley Media Library. Geoff Dann © The British Museum

in December 1301, pointedly informing him that "God has set popes over kings and kingdoms."

***Unam Sanctam* (1302)** Philip unleashed a ruthless antipapal campaign. Two royal apologists, Pierre Dubois and John of Paris, refuted papal claims to the right to intervene in temporal matters. Increasingly placed on the defensive, Boniface made a last-ditch stand against state control of national churches. On November 18, 1302, he issued the bull *Unam Sanctam*. This famous statement of papal power declared that temporal authority was "subject" to the spiritual power of the church. On its face a bold assertion, *Unam Sanctam* was, in truth, the desperate act of a besieged papacy. (See "Compare & Connect: Who Runs the World: Priests or Princes?" pages 270–271.)

After *Unam Sanctam*, the French and the Colonnas moved against Boniface with force. Philip's chief minister, Guillaume de Nogaret, denounced Boniface to the French clergy as a heretic and common criminal. In mid-August 1303, his army surprised the pope at his retreat in Anagni, beat him up, and almost executed him before an aroused populace returned him safely to Rome. The ordeal, however, proved to be too much, and Boniface died in October 1303.

Boniface's immediate successor, Benedict XI (r. 1303–1304), excommunicated Nogaret for his deed, but there was to be no lasting papal retaliation. Benedict's successor, Clement V (r. 1305–1314), was forced into French subservience. A former archbishop of Bordeaux, Clement declared that *Unam Sanctam* should not be understood as in any way diminishing French royal authority. He released Nogaret from excommunication and pliantly condemned the Knights Templars, whose treasure Philip thereafter seized.

In 1309, Clement moved the papal court to Avignon, an imperial city on the southeastern border of France. Situated on land that belonged to the pope, the city maintained its independence from the French king. In 1311, Clement made it his permanent residence, to escape both a Rome ridden with strife after the confrontation between Boniface and Philip and further pressure from Philip. There the papacy would remain until 1377.

After Boniface's humiliation, popes never again seriously threatened kings and emperors, despite continuing papal excommunications and political intrigue. The relationship between church and state now tilted in favor of the state, and the control of religion fell into the hands of powerful monarchies. Ecclesiastical authority would become subordinate to larger secular political policies.

The Avignon Papacy (1309–1377)

The Avignon papacy was in appearance, although not always in fact, under strong French influence. Under Clement V, the French dominated the College of Cardinals, testing the papacy's agility both politically and economically. Finding itself cut off from its Roman estates, the papacy had to innovate to get needed funds. Clement expanded papal taxes, especially the practice of collecting *annates*, the first year's revenue of a church office, or *benefice*, bestowed by the pope. Clement VI (r. 1342–1352) began the practice of selling *indulgences*, or pardons, for unrepented sins. To make the purchase of indulgences more compelling, church doctrine on purgatory—a place of punishment where souls would atone for venial sins—also developed enterprisingly during this period. By the fifteenth century, the church had extended indulgences to cover the souls of people already dead, allowing the living to buy a reduced sentence in purgatory for their deceased loved ones. Such practices contributed to the Avignon papacy's reputation for materialism and political scheming and gave reformers new ammunition.

Pope John XXII Pope John XXII (r. 1316–1334), the most powerful Avignon pope, tried to restore papal independence and to return to Italy. This goal led him into war with the Visconti, the powerful ruling family of Milan, and a costly contest with Emperor Louis IV (r. 1314–1347). John had challenged Louis's election as emperor in 1314 in favor of the rival Habsburg candidate. The result was a minor replay of the confrontation between Philip the Fair and Boniface VIII. When John obstinately and without legal justification refused to recognize Louis's election, the emperor declared him deposed and put in his place an antipope. As Philip the Fair had also done, Louis enlisted the support of the Spiritual Franciscans, whose views on absolute poverty John had condemned as heretical. Two outstanding pamphleteers wrote lasting tracts for the royal cause: William of Ockham, whom John excommunicated in 1328, and Marsilius of Padua (ca. 1290–1342), whose teaching John declared heretical in 1327.

In his *Defender of Peace* (1324), Marsilius of Padua stressed the independent origins and autonomy of secular government. Clergy were subjected to the strictest apostolic ideals and confined to purely spiritual functions, and all power of coercive judgment was denied the pope. Marsilius argued that spiritual crimes must await an eternal punishment. Transgressions of divine law, over which the pope had jurisdiction, were to be punished in the next life, not in the present one, unless the secular ruler declared a divine law also a secular law. This assertion directly challenged the power of the pope to excommunicate rulers and place countries under interdict. The *Defender of Peace* depicted the pope as a subordinate member of a society over which the emperor ruled supreme and in which temporal peace was the highest good.

John XXII made the papacy a sophisticated international agency and adroitly adjusted it to the growing European money economy. The more the **Curia**, or papal court, mastered the latter, however, the more vulnerable it became to criticism. Under John's successor, Benedict

XII (r. 1334–1342), the papacy became entrenched in Avignon. Seemingly forgetting Rome altogether, Benedict began to build the great Palace of the Popes and attempted to reform both papal government and the religious life. His high-living French successor, Clement VI (r, 1342–1352), placed papal policy in lockstep with the French. In this period the cardinals became barely more than lobbyists for policies their secular patrons favored.

National Opposition to the Avignon Papacy As Avignon's fiscal tentacles probed new areas, monarchies took strong action to protect their interests. The latter half of the fourteenth century saw legislation restricting papal jurisdiction and taxation in France, England, and Germany. In England, where the Avignon papacy was identified with the French enemy after the outbreak of the Hundred Years' War, Parliament passed statutes that restricted payments and appeals to Rome and the pope's power to make high ecclesiastical appointments several times between 1351 and 1393.

In France, the so-called Gallican, or French, liberties regulated ecclesiastical appointments and taxation.

These national rights over religion had long been exercised in fact, and the church legally acknowledged them in the *Pragmatic Sanction of Bourges* in 1438. This agreement recognized the right of the French church to elect its own clergy without papal interference, prohibited the payment of *annates* to Rome, and limited the right of appeals from French courts to the Curia in Rome. In German and Swiss cities in the fourteenth and fifteenth centuries, local governments also limited and even overturned traditional clerical privileges and immunities.

John Wycliffe and John Huss

The popular lay religious movements that most successfully assailed the late medieval church were the **Lollards** in England and the **Hussites** in Bohemia. The Lollards looked to the writings of John Wycliffe (d. 1384) to justify their demands, while moderate and extreme Hussites turned to those of John Huss (d. 1415), although both Wycliffe and Huss would have disclaimed the extremists who revolted in their names.

A portrayal of John Huss as he was led to the stake at Constance. After his execution, his bones and ashes were scattered in the Rhine River to prevent his followers from claiming them as relics. This pen-and-ink drawing is from Ulrich von Richenthal's *Chronicle of the Council of Constance* (ca. 1450).   CORBIS/Bettmann

Wycliffe was an Oxford theologian and a philosopher of high standing. His work initially served the anticlerical policies of the English government. He became within England what William of Ockham and Marsilius of Padua had been for Emperor Louis IV: a major intellectual spokesman for the rights of royalty against the secular pretensions of popes. After 1350, English kings greatly reduced the power of the Avignon papacy to make ecclesiastical appointments and to collect taxes within England, a position that Wycliffe strongly supported. His views on clerical poverty followed original Franciscan ideals and, more by accident than by design, gave justification to government restriction and even confiscation of church properties within England. Wycliffe argued that the clergy "ought to be content with food and clothing."

Wycliffe also maintained that personal merit, not rank and office, was the true basis of religious authority. This was a dangerous teaching, because it raised allegedly pious laypeople above allegedly corrupt ecclesiastics, regardless of the latter's official stature. It thus threatened secular as well as ecclesiastical dominion and jurisdiction. At his posthumous condemnation by the pope, Wycliffe was accused of the ancient heresy of **Donatism**—the teaching that the efficacy of the church's sacraments did not only lie in their true performance but also depended on the moral character of the clergy who administered them. Wycliffe also anticipated certain Protestant criticisms of the medieval church by challenging papal infallibility, the sale of indulgences, the authority of Scripture, and the dogma of transubstantiation.

The Lollards, English advocates of Wycliffe's teaching, like the Waldensians, preached in the vernacular, disseminated translations of Holy Scripture, and championed clerical poverty. At first, they came from every social class. Lollards were especially prominent among the groups that had something tangible to gain from confiscating clerical properties (the nobility and the gentry) or that had suffered most under the current church system (the lower clergy and the poor people). After the English peasants' revolt in 1381, an uprising filled with egalitarian notions that could find support in Wycliffe's teaching, Lollardy was officially viewed as subversive. Opposed by an alliance of church and crown, it became a capital offense in England by 1401.

Heresy was less easily brought to heel in Bohemia, where it coalesced with a strong national movement. The University of Prague, founded in 1348, became the center for both Czech nationalism and a religious reform movement. The latter began within the bounds of orthodoxy. It was led by local intellectuals and preachers, the most famous of whom was John Huss, the rector of the university after 1403.

The Czech reformers supported vernacular translations of the Bible and were critical of traditional ceremonies and allegedly superstitious practices, particularly those relating to the sacrament of the Eucharist. They advocated lay communion with cup as well as bread, which was traditionally reserved only for the clergy as a sign of the clergy's spiritual superiority over the laity. Hussites taught that bread and wine remained bread and wine after priestly consecration, and they questioned the validity of sacraments performed by priests in mortal sin.

Wycliffe's teaching appears early to have influenced the movement. Regular traffic between England and Bohemia had existed since the marriage in 1381 of Anne of Bohemia to King Richard II. Czech students studied at Oxford and returned with Wycliffe's writings.

Huss became the leader of the pro-Wycliffe faction at the University of Prague. In 1410, his activities brought about his excommunication, and Prague was placed under papal interdict. In 1414, Huss won an audience with the newly assembled Council of Constance. He journeyed to the council eagerly under a safe-conduct pass from Emperor Sigismund (r. 1410–1437), naïvely believing he would convince his strongest critics of the truth of his teaching. Within weeks of his arrival in early November 1414, he was accused of heresy and imprisoned. He died at the stake on July 6, 1415, and was followed there less than a year later by his colleague Jerome of Prague.

The reaction in Bohemia to the execution of these national heroes was fierce revolt. Militant Hussites, the Taborites, set out to transform Bohemia by force into a religious and social paradise under the military leadership of John Ziska. After a decade of belligerent protest, the Hussites won significant religious reforms and control over the Bohemian church from the Council of Basel.

The Great Schism (1378–1417) and the Conciliar Movement to 1449

Pope Gregory XI (r. 1370–1378) reestablished the papacy in Rome in January 1377, ending what had come to be known as the "Babylonian Captivity" of the church in Avignon, a reference to the biblical bondage of the Israelites. The return to Rome proved to be short lived, however.

Urban VI and Clement VII On Gregory's death, the cardinals, in Rome, elected an Italian archbishop as Pope Urban VI (r. 1378–1389), who immediately announced his intention to reform the Curia. The cardinals, most of whom were French, responded by calling for the return of the papacy to Avignon. The French king, Charles V (r. 1364–1380), wanting to keep the papacy within the sphere of French influence, lent his support to what came to be known as the **Great Schism**.

On September 20, 1378, five months after Urban's election, thirteen cardinals, all but one of whom was French, formed their own conclave and elected Pope

Clement VII (r. 1378–1397), a cousin of the French king. They insisted they had voted for Urban in fear of their lives, surrounded by a Roman mob demanding the election of an Italian pope. Be that as it may, the papacy now became a "two-headed thing" and a scandal to Christendom. Allegiance to the two papal courts divided along political lines. England and its allies (the Holy Roman Empire, Hungary, Bohemia, and Poland) acknowledged Urban VI, whereas France and those in its orbit (Naples, Scotland, Castile, and Aragon) supported Clement VII. Subsequent church history has, however, recognized the Roman line of popes as legitimate.

Two approaches were initially taken to end the schism. One tried to win the mutual cession of both popes, thereby clearing the way for the election of a new pope. The other sought to secure the resignation

Justice in the late Middle Ages. Depicted are the most common forms of corporal and capital punishment in Europe in the late Middle Ages and the Renaissance. At top: burning, hanging, drowning. At center: blinding, quartering, the wheel, cutting of hair (a mark of great shame for a freeman). At bottom: thrashing, decapitation, amputation of hand (for thieves). *Herzog August Bibliothek*

of the one in favor of the other. Both approaches proved fruitless. Each pope considered himself fully legitimate, and too much was at stake for either to make a magnanimous concession. One way remained: the deposition of both popes by a special council of the church.

Conciliar Theory of Church Government Legally, only a pope could convene a church council, but the competing popes were not inclined to summon a council they knew would depose them. Also, the deposition of a legitimate pope against his will by a council of the church was as serious as the deposition of a monarch by a representative assembly.

The correctness of a conciliar deposition of a pope was thus debated a full thirty years before any direct action was taken. Advocates of **conciliar theory** sought to fashion a church in which a representative council could effectively regulate the actions of the pope. The conciliarists defined the church as the whole body of the faithful, of which the elected head, the pope, was only one part. And the pope's sole purpose was to maintain the unity and well-being of the church—something the schismatic popes were far from doing. The conciliarists further argued that a council of the church acted with greater authority than the pope alone. In the eyes of the pope(s), such a concept of the church threatened both its political and its religious unity.

The Council of Pisa (1409–1410) On the basis of the arguments of the conciliarists, cardinals representing both popes convened a council on their own authority in Pisa in 1409, deposed both the Roman and the Avignon popes, and elected a new pope, Alexander V. To the council's consternation, neither pope accepted its action, and Christendom suddenly faced the spectacle of three contending popes. Although most of Latin Christendom accepted Alexander and his Pisan successor John XXIII (r. 1410–1415), the popes of Rome and Avignon refused to step down.

The Council of Constance (1414–1417) The intolerable situation ended when Emperor Sigismund prevailed on John XXIII to summon a new council in Constance in 1414, which the Roman pope Gregory XII also recognized. In a famous declaration entitled *Sacrosancta*, the council asserted its supremacy and elected a new pope, Martin V (r. 1417–1431), after the three contending popes had either resigned or been deposed. The council then made provisions for regular meetings of church councils, within five, then seven, and thereafter every ten years.

The Council of Basel (r. 1431–1449) Conciliar government of the church peaked at the Council of Basel, when the council directly negotiated church doctrine with heretics. In 1432, the Hussites of Bohemia presented the *Four Articles of Prague* to the council as a basis for negotiations. This document contained requests for (1) giving the laity the Eucharist with cup as well as bread; (2) free, itinerant preaching; (3) the exclusion of the clergy from holding secular offices and owning property; and (4) just punishment of clergy who commit mortal sins.

In November 1433, an agreement among the emperor, the council, and the Hussites gave the Bohemians jurisdiction over their church similar to what the French and the English held. Three of the four Prague articles were conceded: communion with cup, free preaching by ordained clergy, and similar punishment of clergy and laity for mortal sins.

The end of the Hussite wars and the new reform legislation curtailing the pope's powers of appointment and taxation were the high points of the Council of Basel and ominous signs of what lay ahead for the church. The exercise of such power by a council did not please the pope, and in 1438, he upstaged the Council of Basel by negotiating a reunion with the Eastern church. Although the agreement, signed in Florence in 1439, was short lived, it restored papal prestige and signaled the demise of the conciliar movement. Having overreached itself, the Council of Basel collapsed in 1449. A decade later, Pope Pius II (r. 1458–1464) issued the papal bull *Execrabilis* (1460) condemning appeals to councils as "erroneous and abominable" and "completely null and void."

Consequences A major consequence of the conciliar movement was the devolving of greater religious responsibility onto the laity and secular governments. Without effective papal authority and leadership, secular control of national or territorial churches increased. Kings asserted their power over the church in England and France. In German, Swiss, and Italian cities, magistrates and city councils reformed and regulated religious life. The High Renaissance could not reverse this development. On the contrary, as the papacy became a limited, Italian territorial regime, national control of the church ran apace. Perceived as just one among several Italian states, the Papal States could now be opposed as much on the grounds of "national" policy as for religious reasons.

A Closer LOOK

THE ENCAMPMENT OF THE IMPERIAL ARMY

THIS FIFTEENTH-CENTURY scene, drawn by a skilled and imaginative artist, depicts an imperial Habsburg army. Because every army marches on its stomach, the wagons carrying provisions make up the inner circle, which is protected by a wider circle of war wagons.

The cavalry is either mustering for a foray or returning from one.

A face appears to be looking out of a window on the scene below. Could this be a crude depiction of God gazing down from the heavens? Or is it the artist's signature? Most likely it is graffiti added later by an opportunist seeking a bit of fame.

The provision wagons are empty because the tents, weapons, clothing, food, and cooking pots they carry have been unloaded. In the middle, standing around the towering black and gold Habsburg flag, are the commanders, their staff, and perhaps the emperor himself (speaking to a rider).

Kunstsammlungen der Fursten zu Waldburg-Wolfegg

Armed soldiers man a gate as scouts enter with a captive whose hands are bound. To the right of the gate, a mother with two small children and another beggar seek alms.

Workers and soldiers play games of cards and dice, while outside the barrier is danger, death, and desolation: Wolves gnaw at dead horses.

To examine this image in an interactive fashion, please go to www.myhistorylab.com

PEARSON myhistorylab

▼ Medieval Russia

In the late tenth century, Prince Vladimir of Kiev (r. 980–1015), then Russia's dominant city, received delegations of Muslims, Roman Catholics, Jews, and Greek Orthodox Christians, each of which hoped to persuade the Russians to embrace their religion. Vladimir chose Greek Orthodoxy, which became the religion of Russia, adding strong cultural bonds to the close commercial ties that had long linked Russia to the Byzantine Empire.

Politics and Society

Vladimir's successor, Yaroslav the Wise (r. 1016–1054), developed Kiev into a magnificent political and cultural center, with architecture rivaling that of Constantino- ple. He also pursued contacts with the West in an unsuccessful effort to counter the political influence of the Byzantine emperors. After his death, rivalry among their princes slowly divided Russians into three cultural groups: the Great Russians, the White Russians, and the Little Russians (Ukrainians). Autonomous principalities also challenged Kiev's dominance, and it became just one of several national centers. Government in the principalities combined monarchy (the prince), aristocracy (the prince's council of noblemen), and democracy (a popular assembly of all free adult males). The broadest social division was between freemen and slaves. Freemen included the clergy, army officers, **boyars** (wealthy landowners), townspeople, and peasants. Slaves were mostly prisoners of war. Debtors working off their debts made up a large, semifree, group.

Genghis Khan holding an audience. This Persian miniature shows the great conqueror and founder of the Mongol empire with members of his army and entourage as well as an apparent supplicant (lower right).   Picture Desk, Inc./Kobal Collection

Mongol Rule (1243–1480)

In the thirteenth century, Mongol, or Tatar, armies swept through China, much of the Islamic world, and Russia. These were steppe peoples with strongholds in the south, whence they raided the north, devastating Russia and compelling the obedience of Moscow for a while. Ghengis Khan (1155–1227) invaded Russia in 1223, and Kiev fell to his grandson Batu Khan in 1240. Russian cities became dependent, tribute-paying principalities of the segment of the Mongol Empire known as the *Golden Horde* (the Tatar words for the color of Batu Khan's tent). Geographically, the Golden Horde included the steppe region of what is today southern Russia and its capital at Sarai on the lower Volga. The conquerors stationed their own officials in all the principal Russian towns to oversee taxation and the conscription of Russians into Tatar armies. The Mongols filled their harems with Russian women and sold Russians who resisted into slavery in foreign lands. Russian women—under the influence of Islam, which became the religion of the Golden Horde—began to wear veils and lead more secluded lives. This forced integration of Mongol and Russian created further cultural divisions between Russia and the West. The Mongols, however, left Russian political and religious institutions largely intact and, thanks to their far-flung trade, brought most Russians greater prosperity. Princes of Moscow collected tribute for their overlords and grew wealthy under Mongol rule. As that rule weakened, the Moscow princes took control of the territory surrounding the city in what was called "the gathering of the Russian Land." Gradually the principality of Moscow expanded through land purchases, colonization, and conquest. In 1380, Grand Duke Dimitri of Moscow (r. 1350–1389) defeated Tatar forces at Kulikov Meadow, a victory that marked the beginning of the decline of the Mongol hegemony. Another century would pass, however, before Ivan III, the Great (d. 1505), would bring all of northern Russia under Moscow's control and end Mongol rule (1480). Moscow replaced Kiev as the political and religious center of Russia. After Constantinople fell to the Turks in 1453, the city became, in Russian eyes, the "third Rome."

In Perspective

Plague, war, and schism convulsed much of late medieval Europe throughout the fourteenth and into the fifteenth centuries. Two fifths of the population, particularly along the major trade routes, died from plague in the fourteenth century. War and famine continued to take untold numbers after the plague had passed. Revolts erupted in town and countryside as ordinary people attempted to defend their traditional communal rights and privileges against the new autocratic territorial regimes. Even God's house seemed to be in shambles in 1409, when three popes came to rule simultaneously.

There is, however, another side to the late Middle Ages. By the end of the fifteenth century, the population losses were rapidly being made up. Between 1300 and 1500, education had become far more accessible, especially to lay people. The number of universities increased from twenty to seventy, and the rise in the number of residential colleges was even more impressive, especially in France, where sixty-three were built. The fourteenth century saw the birth of humanism, and the fifteenth century gave us the printing press. Most impressive were the artistic and cultural achievements of the Italian Renaissance during the fifteenth century. The later Middle Ages were thus a period of growth and creativity, as well as one of waning and decline.

REVIEW QUESTIONS

1. What were the underlying and precipitating causes of the Hundred Years' War? What advantages did each side have? Why were the French finally able to drive the English almost entirely out of France?

2. What were the causes of the Black Death, and why did it spread so quickly throughout Western Europe? Where was it most virulent? How did it affect European society? How important do you think disease is in changing the course of history?

3. Why did Pope Boniface VIII quarrel with King Philip the Fair? Why was Boniface so impotent in the conflict? How had political conditions changed since the reign of Pope Innocent III in the late twelfth century, and what did that mean for the papacy?

4. How did the church change from 1200 to 1450? What was its response to the growing power of monarchs? How great an influence did the church have on secular events?

5. What was the Avignon papacy, and why did it occur? How did it affect the papacy? What relationship did it have to the Great Schism? How did the church become divided and how was it reunited? Why was the conciliar movement a setback for the papacy?

6. Why were kings in the late thirteenth and early fourteenth centuries able to control the church more than the church could control the kings? How did kings attack the church during this period?

SUGGESTED READINGS

C. Allmand, *The Hundred Years' War: England and France at War, c. 1300–c. 1450* (1988). Overview of the war's development and consequences.

P. R. Backscheider et al., eds., *A Journal of the Plague Year* (1992). The Black Death at ground level.

R. Barber, ed., *The Pastons: Letters of a Family in the War of the Roses* (1984). Rare revelations of English family life in an age of crisis.

E. H. Gillett et al., *Life and Times of John Huss: The Bohemian Reformation of the Fifteenth Century* (2001). The latest biography.

J. Huizinga, *The Waning of the Middle Ages: A Study of the Forms of Life, Thought, and Art in France and the Netherlands in the Dawn of the Renaissance* (1924). Exaggerated but engrossing study of mentality at the end of the Middle Ages.

P. Kahn et al., *Secret History of the Mongols: The Origins of Ghingis Kahn* (1998). Introduction to the greatest Mongol ruler.

S. Ozment, *The Age of Reform, 1250–1550* (1980). Highlights of late medieval intellectual and religious history.

E. Perroy, *The Hundred Years' War*, trans. by W. B. Wells (1965). Still the most comprehensive one-volume account.

M. Spinka, *John Huss's Concept of the Church* (1966). Lucid account of Hussite theology.

W. R. Trask, ed. and trans., *Joan of Arc in Her Own Words* (1996). Joan's interrogation and self-defense.

P. Ziegler, *The Black Death* (1969). Highly readable account.

For additional learning resources related to this chapter, please go to www.myhistorylab.com

PEARSON **myhistorylab**

10

Renaissance and Discovery

KEY TOPICS

• **The politics, culture, and art of the Italian Renaissance**

• **Political struggle and foreign intervention in Italy**

• **The powerful new monarchies of northern Europe**

• **The thought and culture of the northern Renaissance**

IF THE LATE Middle Ages saw unprecedented chaos, it also witnessed a rebirth that would continue into the seventeenth century. Two modern Dutch scholars have employed the same word (*Herfsttij*, or "harvesttide") with different connotations to describe the period. Johan Huizinga has used the word to mean a "waning" or "decline," and Heiko Oberman has used it to mean a "harvest." If something was dying away, some ripe fruit was also being gathered and seed grain was being sown. The late Middle Ages was a time of creative fragmentation.

By the late fifteenth century, Europe was recovering well from two of the three crises of the late Middle Ages: the demographic and the political. The great losses in population were being replenished, and able monarchs and rulers were imposing a new political order. However, a solution to the religious crisis would have to await the Reformation and Counter-Reformation of the sixteenth century.

Although the opposite would be true in the sixteenth and seventeenth centuries, the city-states of Italy survived the century and a half between 1300 and 1450 better than the territorial states of northern Europe. This was due to Italy's strategic location between East and West and its lucrative Eurasian trade. Great wealth gave rulers and merchants the ability to work their will on both society and culture. They became patrons of government, education, and the arts, always as much for their own self-aggrandizement as out of benevolence, for whether a patron was a family, a firm, a government, or the church, endowments enhanced their reputation and power. The result of such patronage was a cultural Renaissance in Italian cities unmatched elsewhere.

With the fall of Constantinople to the Turks in 1453, Italy's once unlimited trading empire began to shrink. City-state soon turned against city-state, and by the 1490s, French armies invaded Italy. Within a quarter century, Italy's great Renaissance had peaked.

The fifteenth century also saw an unprecedented scholarly renaissance. Italian and northern humanists made a full recovery of classical knowledge and languages and set in motion educational reforms and cultural changes that would spread throughout Europe in the fifteenth and sixteenth centuries. In the process the Italian humanists invented, for all practical purposes, critical historical scholarship, while exploiting a new fifteenth-century invention, the "divine art" of printing with movable type.

In this period the vernacular—the local language—began to take its place alongside Latin, the international language, as a widely used literary and political means of communication. In addition, European states progressively superseded the church as the community of highest allegiance, as patriotism and incipient nationalism seized hearts and minds as strongly as religion. Nations henceforth "transcended" themselves not by journeys to Rome, but by competitive voyages to the Far East and the Americas, as the age of global exploration opened.

For Europe, the late fifteenth and sixteenth centuries were a period of unprecedented expansion and experimentation. Permanent colonies were established within the Americas, and the exploitation of the New World's human and mineral resources began. Imported American gold and silver spurred scientific invention and a new weapons industry. The new bullion also helped create the international traffic in African slaves as rival African tribes eagerly sold their captives to the Portuguese. Transported in ever-increasing numbers, these slaves worked the mines and plantations of the New World as replacements for American natives, whose population declined precipitously following the conquest.

The period also saw social engineering and political planning on a large scale, as newly centralized governments began to put long-range economic policies into practice, a development that came to be called mercantilism.

▼ The Renaissance in Italy (1375–1527)

A nineteenth-century Swiss historian famously described the Renaissance as the "prototype of the modern world." In his *Civilization of the Renaissance in Italy* (1860), Jacob Burckhardt argued that the revival of ancient learning in fourteenth- and fifteenth-century Italy gave rise to new secular and scientific values. This was the period in which people began to adopt a rational and statistical approach to reality and to rediscover the worth and creativity of the individual. The result, in Burckhardt's words, was the gradual release of the "full, whole nature of man."

Most scholars today find Burckhardt's description exaggerated and accuse him of overlooking the continuity between the Middle Ages and the Renaissance. His critics especially point to the still strongly Christian character of Renaissance humanism. Earlier "renaissances," such as that of the twelfth century, had also seen the revival of the ancient classics, new interest in the Latin language and Greek science, and an appreciation of the worth and creativity of individuals.

Despite the exaggeration and bias of Burckhardt's portrayal, most scholars agree that the **Renaissance** (which means "rebirth" in French) was a time of transition from medieval to modern times. Medieval Europe, especially before the twelfth century, had been a fragmented feudal society with an agricultural economy, and the church largely dominated its thought and culture. Renaissance Europe, especially after the fourteenth century, was characterized by growing national consciousness and political centralization, an urban economy based on organized commerce and capitalism, and growing lay and secular control of thought and culture, including religion.

Italy between 1375 and 1527, a century and a half of cultural creativity, most strikingly reveals the distinctive features of the Renaissance. Two events coincide with the beginning of this period: the deaths of Petrarch, considered the "father" of humanism, in 1374 and that of Giovanni Boccaccio, author of the *Decameron*, in 1375. Thereafter, Florentine humanist culture spread throughout Italy and into northern Europe. Scholars have coined the term *civic humanism* to describe this apparent coalescence of humanism and civic reform.

This creative expansion, however, appeared to reach an abrupt end in 1527, when Spanish-imperial soldiers looted and torched Rome, recalling Rome's sacking by the Visigoths and Vandals in antiquity. At this time, French king Francis I and the Holy Roman Emperor Charles V had made Italy the battleground for their mutual dynastic claims to Burgundy and parts of Italy. Pope Clement VIII (r. 1523–1534) had incurred the emperor's wrath by taking the side of the French. However, the infamous sack of Rome in 1527 appears to have been less the result of a breach of papal loyalty than of the anger and boredom of

Spanish-imperial soldiers poorly provisioned and paid by the emperor. Their looting and sacking have since marked the beginning of the end of the cultured Italian Renaissance.

The Italian City-State

Renaissance society first took distinctive shape within the merchant cities of late medieval Italy. Italy had always had a cultural advantage over the rest of Europe because its geography made it the natural gateway between East and West. Venice, Genoa, and Pisa had traded uninterruptedly with the Near East throughout the Middle Ages, maintaining vibrant urban societies by virtue of such trade. When commerce revived on a large scale in the eleventh century, Italian merchants had quickly mastered the business skills of organization, bookkeeping, scouting new markets, and securing monopolies. During the thirteenth and fourteenth centuries, trade-rich cities became powerful city-states, dominating the political and economic life of the surrounding countryside. By the fifteenth century, the great Italian cities were the bankers for much of Europe.

Growth of City-States The endemic warfare between pope and emperor and the Guelf (propapal) and Ghibelline (proimperial) factions assisted the growth of Italian cities and urban culture. Either of these factions might successfully have subdued the cities had they permitted each other to concentrate on doing so. Instead, they chose to weaken one another, which strengthened the merchant oligarchies of the cities. Unlike the great cities of northern Europe, which kings and territorial princes dominated, the great Italian cities remained free to expand on their own. Becoming independent states, they absorbed the surrounding countryside, assimilating the local nobility in a unique urban meld of old and new rich. Five such major competitive states evolved: the duchy of Milan the republics of Florence and Venice, the Papal States, and the kingdom of Naples. (See Map 10–1.)

Social strife and competition for political power became so intense within the cities that most evolved into despotisms just to survive. A notable exception was Venice, which was ruled by a successful merchant oligarchy. The Venetian government operated through a patrician senate of three hundred members and a ruthless judicial body. The latter, known as the Council of Ten, was quick to anticipate and suppress all rival groups.

Social Class and Conflict Florence was the most striking example of social division and anarchy. Four distinguishable social groups existed within the city. There was the old rich, or *grandi*, the nobles and merchants who traditionally ruled the city. The emergent newly rich merchant class, capitalists and bankers

MAP EXPLORATION

Interactive map: To explore this map further, go to www.myhistorylab.com

Duchy of Milan
Republic of Genoa
Republic of Florence
Republic of Venice
Papal States
Kingdom of Naples

Map 10–1 **RENAISSANCE ITALY** The city-states of Renaissance Italy were self-contained principalities whose internal strife was monitored by their despots and whose external aggression was long successfully controlled by treaty.

known as the *popolo grosso*, or "fat people," formed a second group. In the late thirteenth and early fourteenth centuries, they began to challenge the old rich for political powers. Then there were the middle-burgher ranks of guild masters, shop owners, and professionals, the smaller businesspeople who, in Florence, as elsewhere, tended to side with the new rich against the conservative policies of the old rich. Finally, there was the

Florentine women doing needlework, spinning, and weaving. These activities took up much of a woman's time and contributed to the elegance of dress for which Florentine men and women were famed. *Palazzo Schifanoia, Ferrara. Alinari/Art Resource, NY*

popolo minuto, or the "little people," the lower economic classes. In 1457, one third of the population of Florence, about 30,000 people, was officially listed as paupers, that is, as having no wealth at all.

These social divisions produced conflict at every level of society, to which was added the ever-present fear of foreign intrigue. In 1378, a great uprising of the poor, known as the Ciompi Revolt, occurred. It resulted from a combination of three factors that made life unbearable for those at the bottom of society: the feuding between the old rich and the new rich; the social anarchy created when the Black Death cut the city's population almost in half; and the collapse of the great banking houses of Bardi and Peruzzi, which left the poor more vulnerable than ever. The Ciompi Revolt established a chaotic four-year reign of power by the lower Florentine classes. True stability did not return to Florence until the ascent to power of the Florentine banker and statesman, Cosimo de' Medici (1389–1464) in 1434.

Despotism and Diplomacy Cosimo de' Medici was the wealthiest Florentine and a natural statesman. He controlled the city internally from behind the scenes, manipulating the constitution and influencing elections.

A council, first of six and later of eight members, known as the *Signoria,* governed the city. These men were chosen from the most powerful guilds, namely, those representing the major clothing industries (cloth, wool, fur, and silk) and such other groups as bankers, judges, and doctors. Through informal, cordial relations with the electors, Cosimo was able to keep councilors loyal to him in the *Signoria.* From his position as the head of the Office of Public Debt, he favored congenial factions. His grandson, Lorenzo the Magnificent (1449–1492; r. 1478–1492), ruled Florence in almost totalitarian fashion during the last, chaotic quarter of the fifteenth century. The assassination of his brother in 1478 by a rival family, the Pazzi, who had long plotted with the pope against the Medicis, made Lorenzo a cautious and determined ruler.

Despotism elsewhere was even less subtle. To prevent internal social conflict and foreign intrigue from paralyzing their cities, the dominant groups cooperated to install hired strongmen, or despots. Known as a *podestà,* the despot's sole purpose was to maintain law and order. He held executive, military, and judicial authority, and his mandate was direct and simple: to permit, by whatever means required, the normal flow of business activity without which neither the old rich and new rich, nor the poor of a city, could long survive, much less prosper. Because despots could not count on the loyalty of the divided populace, they operated through mercenary armies obtained through military brokers known as **condottieri**.

It was a hazardous job. Not only was a despot subject to dismissal by the oligarchies that hired him, he was also a popular object of assassination attempts. The spoils of success, however, were great. In Milan, it was as despots that the Visconti family came to power in 1278 and the Sforza family in 1450, both ruling without constitutional restraints or serious political competition.

Mercifully, the political turbulence and warfare of the times also gave birth to the art of diplomacy. Through their diplomats, the various city-states stayed abreast of foreign military developments and, when shrewd enough, gained power and advantage over their enemies without actually going to war. Most city-states established resident embassies in the fifteenth century for that very purpose. Their ambassadors not only represented them in ceremonies and at negotiations, they also became their watchful eyes and ears at rival courts.

Whether within the comparatively tranquil republic of Venice, the strong-arm democracy of Florence, or the undisguised despotism of Milan, the disciplined Italian city proved a congenial climate for an unprecedented flowering of thought and culture. Italian Renaissance culture was promoted as vigorously by despots as by republicans and as enthusiastically by secularized popes as by the more spiritually minded. Such widespread support occurred because the main requirement for patronage of the arts and letters was the one thing that Italian cities of the High Renaissance had in abundance: great wealth.

Humanism

Scholars still debate the meaning of the term *humanism.* Some see the Italian Renaissance as Burckhardt did, as the birth of modernity, driven by an un-Christian philosophy that stressed the dignity of humankind, individualism, and secular values. Others argue that the humanists were actually the champions of Catholic Christianity, opposing the pagan teaching of Aristotle and the Scholasticism his writings nurtured. For still others, humanism was a neutral form of historical scholarship adopted to promote above all a sense of civic responsibility and political liberty.

A leading scholar, Paul O. Kristeller, accused all of the above of dealing more with the secondary effects of humanism than with its essence. Humanism was not a philosophy or a value system, but an educational program built on rhetoric and scholarship for their own sake.

Each of these definitions has some truth. **Humanism** was the scholarly study of the Latin and Greek classics and of the ancient Church Fathers, both for its own sake and in the hope of reviving respected ancient norms and values. Humanists advocated the ***studia humanitatis***, a liberal arts program of study embracing grammar, rhetoric, poetry, history, politics, and moral philosophy. Not only were these subjects considered a joy in themselves, they also celebrated the dignity of humankind and prepared people for a life of virtuous action. The Florentine Leonardo Bruni (ca. 1370–1444) first gave the name *humanitas*, or "humanity," to the learning that resulted from such scholarly pursuits. Bruni was a star student of Manuel Chrysoloras (ca. 1355–1415), the Byzantine scholar who opened the world of Greek scholarship to Italian humanists when he taught at Florence between 1397 and 1403.

The first humanists were orators and poets. They wrote original literature in both classical and vernacular languages, inspired by and modeled on the newly discovered works of the ancients. They also taught rhetoric within the universities. When humanists were not employed as teachers of rhetoric, princely and papal courts sought their talents as secretaries, speechwriters, and diplomats.

The study of classical and Christian antiquity had existed before the Italian Renaissance. There were memorable recoveries of ancient civilization during the Carolingian renaissance of the ninth century, within the cathedral school of Chartres in the twelfth century, during the great Aristotelian revival in Paris in the thirteenth century, and among the Augustinians in the early fourteenth century. These precedents, however, only partially compare with the achievements of the Italian Renaissance of the fourteenth and fifteenth centuries. The latter was far more secular and lay-dominated, had much broader interests, was blessed with far more recovered manuscripts, and its scholars possessed far superior technical skills than those who had delivered the earlier "rebirths" of antiquity.

Unlike their Scholastic rivals, humanists were less bound to recent tradition; nor did they focus all their attention on summarizing and comparing the views of recognized authorities. Their most respected sources were classical and biblical, not medieval philosophers and theologians. Avidly searching out manuscript collections, Italian humanists made the full riches of Greek and Latin antiquity available to contemporary scholars. So great was their achievement that there is a kernel of truth in their assertion that the period between themselves and classical civilization was a "dark middle age."

Petrarch, Dante, and Boccaccio   Francesco Petrarch (1304–1374) was the "father of humanism." He left the legal profession to pursue letters and poetry. Most of his life was spent in and around Avignon. He was involved in a popular revolt in Rome (1347–1349) and, in his later years, he served the Visconti family in Milan.

Petrarch celebrated ancient Rome in his *Letters to the Ancient Dead*, fancied personal letters to Cicero, Livy, Vergil, and Horace. He also wrote a Latin epic poem (*Africa*, a poetic historical tribute to the Roman general Scipio Africanus) and biographies of famous Roman men (*Lives of Illustrious Men*). His most famous contemporary work was a collection of highly introspective love sonnets to a certain Laura, a married woman he admired romantically from a safe distance.

His critical textual studies, elitism, and contempt for the learning of the Scholastics were features many later humanists also shared. As with many later humanists, Classical and Christian values coexist uneasily in his work. Medieval Christian values can be seen in his imagined dialogues with Saint Augustine and in tracts he wrote to defend the personal immortality of the soul against the Aristotelians.

Petrarch was, however, far more secular in orientation than his famous near-contemporary Dante

THE RENAISSANCE GARDEN

IN THE MIDDLE Ages and early Renaissance, few possessions were as prized, or as vital, as a garden. Within that enclosed space grew both ornamental and medicinal flowers and herbs. The more common kitchen garden existed in every manor, castle, monastery, guildhall, and small household. In addition to their large, elaborate gardens, the rich also had orchards and vineyards to grow the fruit from which they made sweet drinks and wine. Behind their shops and guildhalls, apothecaries and barber-surgeons cultivated the curative flowers and herbs from which they concocted the medicines of their trades. Beyond manor and guildhall walls, small householders and cottagers hoed the small, narrow plots behind their houses in which they grew the basic herbs and vegetables of their diet. Although the grandeur and variety of a garden reflected the prestige of its owner, every garden's main purpose was to serve the immediate needs of the household.

Versatility and pungency distinguished the most popular flowers and herbs. The violet was

A wealthy man oversees apple picking at harvest time in a fifteenth-century French orchard. In the town below, individual house gardens can be seen. Protective fences, made of woven sticks, keep out predatory animals. In the right foreground, a boar can be seen overturning an apple barrel. The British Library

admired for its beauty, fragrance, and utility. Medieval people put violets in baths, oils, and syrups, prizing its soft scent and healing power as well as its ability to color, flavor, and garnish dishes. Nonetheless, subtlety and delicacy were not as important to the medieval palate as they are to ours. An herb or flower was only as good as its impact on the senses. Potent scents and flavors were loved for their ability to bring an otherwise starchy and lackluster meal to life. Fruit, although it was the main ingredient for sweet drinks, rarely appeared on a medieval plate, and vegetables were only slightly more common. Cabbage, lentils, peas, beans, onions, leeks, beets, and parsnips were the most often served vegetables at the medieval table, made palatable by heavy application of the sharpest and bitterest spices.

Beyond its practical function as a source of food and medicine, the medieval garden was a space of social and religious significance. In Christian history, gardens represented sacred places on earth. During the Middle Ages and early Renaissance, it was not the sprawling paradise of the Garden of Eden that captured the imagination, but rather the closed garden of the Bible's Song of Songs (4:12): "A garden enclosed is my sister, my spouse; a spring shut up, a fountain sealed." Such sensuous imagery symbolized the soul's union with God, Christ's union with the Catholic Church, and the bond of love between a man and a woman.

Although enclosed behind walls, fences, or hedges to protect them as vital food sources, gardens were also the private places of dreamers and lovers. Pleasure gardens bloomed around the homes of the wealthy. There, amid grottoes and fountains, lovers breathed the warm scents of roses and lilies and pursued the romantic trysts popularized in court poetry. The stories of courtly love were cautionary as well as titillating, for as the catechism reminded every medieval Christian, the garden was also a place of temptation and lost innocence.

What kinds of gardens existed in the Middle Ages and early Renaissance? How did religion give meaning to gardens?

Teresa McClean, *Medieval English Gardens* (New York: Viking Press, 1980), pp. 64, 133; Marilyn Stokstad and Jerry Stannard, *Gardens of the Middle Ages* (Lawrence, KS: Spencer Museum, 1983), pp. 19–21, 61.

Alighieri (1265–1321), whose *Vita Nuova* and *Divine Comedy* form, with Petrarch's sonnets, the cornerstones of Italian vernacular literature. Petrarch's student and friend Giovanni Boccaccio (1313–1375) was also a pioneer of humanist studies. His *Decameron*—one hundred often bawdy tales told by three men and seven women in a safe country retreat away from the plague that ravaged Florence in 1348 (see Chapter 9)—is both a stinging social commentary (it exposes sexual and economic misconduct) and a sympathetic look at human behavior. An avid collector of manuscripts, Boccaccio also assembled an encyclopedia of Greek and Roman mythology.

Educational Reforms and Goals Humanists delighted in taking their mastery of ancient languages directly to the past, refusing to be slaves to later tradition. Such an attitude not only made them innovative educators, but also kept them constantly in search of new sources of information. In the search, they assembled magnificent manuscript collections, treating them as potent medicines for the ills of contemporary society, and capable of enlightening the minds of any who would immerse themselves in them.

The goal of humanist studies was wisdom eloquently spoken, both knowledge of the good and the ability to move others to desire it. Learning was not meant to remain abstract and unpracticed. "It is better to will the good than to know the truth," Petrarch taught, and it became a motto of many later humanists, who, like Petrarch, believed learning ennobled people. Pietro Paolo Vergerio (1349–1420), the author of the most influential Renaissance tract on education (*On the Morals That Befit a Free Man*), left a classic summary of the humanist concept of a liberal education:

We call those studies liberal which are worthy of a free man; those studies by which we attain and practice virtue and wisdom; that education which calls forth, trains, and develops those highest gifts of body and mind which ennoble men and which are rightly judged to rank next in dignity to virtue only, for to a vulgar temper, gain and pleasure are the one aim of existence, to a lofty nature, moral worth and fame.[1]

The ideal of a useful education and well-rounded people inspired far-reaching reforms in traditional education. The Roman orator Quintilian's (ca. 35–100) *Education of the Orator*, the complete text of which was discovered in 1416, became the basic classical guide for the humanist revision of the traditional curriculum. Vittorino da Feltre (d. 1446) exemplified the ideals of humanist teaching. Not only did he have his students read the difficult works of Pliny, Ptolemy, Terence, Plautus, Livy, and Plutarch, he also subjected them to vigorous physical exercise and games. Still another contemporary educator, Guarino da Verona (d. 1460), the rector of the

[1]Cited by De Lamar Jensen, *Renaissance Europe: Age of Recovery and Reconciliation* (Lexington, MA: D. C. Health, 1981), p. 111.

new University of Ferrara and another student of Greek scholar Manuel Chrysoloras, streamlined the study of classical languages.

Despite the grinding scholarly process of acquiring ancient knowledge, humanistic studies were not confined to the classroom. As Baldassare Castiglione's (1478–1529) *Book of the Courtier* illustrates, the rediscovered knowledge of the past was both a model and a challenge to the present. Written as a practical guide for the nobility at the court of Urbino, a small duchy in central Italy, it embodies the highest ideals of Italian humanism. The successful courtier is said to be one who knows how to integrate knowledge of ancient languages and history with athletic, military, and musical skills, while at the same time practicing good manners and exhibiting a high moral character.

Privileged, educated noblewomen also promoted the new education and culture at royal courts. Among them was Christine de Pisan (1363?–1434), the Italian-born daughter of the physician and astrologer of French king Charles V. She became an expert in classical, French, and Italian languages and literature. Married at fifteen and the widowed mother of three at twenty-seven, she wrote lyric poetry to support herself and was much read throughout the courts of Europe. Her most famous work, *The Treasure of the City of Ladies*, is a chronicle of the accomplishments of the great women of history. (See "Christine de Pisan Instructs Women on How to Handle Their Husbands," page 288.)

The Florentine "Academy" and the Revival of Platonism Of all the important recoveries of the past made during the Italian Renaissance, none stands out more than the revival of Greek studies—especially the works of Plato—in fifteenth-century Florence. Many factors combined to bring this revival about. A foundation, already mentioned above, was laid in 1397 when the city invited Manuel Chrysoloras to come from Constantinople to promote Greek learning. A half century later (1439), the ecumenical Council of Ferrara-Florence, convened to negotiate the reunion of the Eastern and Western churches, opened the door for many Greek scholars and manuscripts to pour into the West. After the fall of Constantinople to the Turks in 1453, many Greek scholars fled to Florence for refuge. This was the background against which the Florentine Platonic Academy evolved under the patronage of Cosimo de' Medici and the supervision of Marsilio Ficino (1433–1499) and Pico della Mirandola (1463–1494).

Renaissance thinkers were especially attracted to the Platonic tradition and to those Church Fathers who tried to synthesize Platonic philosophy with Christian teaching. The so-called Florentine Academy was actually not a formal school, but an informal gathering of influential Florentine humanists devoted to the revival of the works of Plato and the Neoplatonists: Plotinus, Proclus,

CHRISTINE DE PISAN INSTRUCTS WOMEN ON HOW TO HANDLE THEIR HUSBANDS

Renowned Renaissance noblewoman Christine de Pisan has the modern reputation of being perhaps the first feminist, and her book, The Treasure of the City of Ladies *(also known as* The Book of Three Virtues*), has been described as the Renaissance woman's survival manual. Here she gives advice to the wives of artisans.*

How does Christine de Pisan's image of husband and wife compare with other medieval views? Would the church question her advice? As a noblewoman commenting on the married life of artisans, does her high social standing influence her advice? Would she give similar advice to women of her own social class?

All wives of artisans should be very painstaking and diligent if they wish to have the necessities of life. They should encourage their husbands or their workmen to get to work early in the morning and work until late. . . . [And] the wife herself should [also] be involved in the work to the extent that she knows all about it, so that she may know how to oversee his workers if her husband is absent, and to reprove them if they do not do well. . . . And when customers come to her husband and try to drive a hard bargain, she ought to warn him solicitously to take care that he does not make a bad deal. She should advise him to be chary of giving too much credit if he does not know precisely where and to whom it is going, for in this way many come to poverty. . . .

In addition, she ought to keep her husband's love as much as she can, to this end: that he will stay at home more willingly and that he may not have any reason to join the foolish crowds of other young men in taverns and indulge in unnecessary and extravagant expense, as many tradesmen do, especially in Paris. By treating him kindly she should protect him as well as she can from this. It is said that three things drive a man from his home: a quarrelsome wife, a smoking fireplace, and a leaking roof. She too ought to stay at home gladly and not go off every day traipsing hither and yon gossiping with

Christine de Pisan, who has the modern reputation of being the first European feminist, presents her internationally famous book *The Treasure of the City of Ladies*, also known as *The Book of Three Virtues*, to Isabella of Bavaria amid her ladies in waiting. Historical Picture Archive/CORBIS/Bettmann

the neighbours and visiting her chums to find out what everyone is doing. That is done by slovenly housewives roaming about the town in groups. Nor should she go off on these pilgrimages got up for no good reason and involving a lot of needless expense.

Porphyry, and Dionysius the Areopagite. To this end, Ficino edited and published the complete works of Plato.

The appeal of **Platonism** lay in its flattering view of human nature. It distinguished between an eternal sphere of being and the perishable world in which humans actually lived. Human reason was believed to have preexisted in this pristine world and still to commune with it, a theory supported by human knowledge of eternal mathematical and moral truths.

Strong Platonic influence is evident in Pico's *Oration on the Dignity of Man*, perhaps the most famous Renaissance statement on the nature of humankind. (See "Compare & Connect: Is the "Renaissance Man" a Myth?" page 290.) Pico wrote the *Oration* as an introduction to his pretentious collection of nine hundred theses. Published in Rome in December 1486, the theses were intended to serve as the basis for a public debate on all of life's important topics. The *Oration* drew on Platonic teaching to depict humans as the only creatures in the world who possessed the freedom to be whatever they chose, able at will to rise to the height of angels or just as quickly to wallow with pigs.

Critical Work of the Humanists: Lorenzo Valla Because they were guided by scholarly ideals of philological accuracy and historical truth, the humanists could become critics of tradition even when that was not their intention. Dispassionate critical scholarship shook long-standing foundations, not the least of which were those of the medieval church.

The work of Lorenzo Valla (1406–1457), author of the standard Renaissance text on Latin philology, the *Elegances of the Latin Language* (1444), reveals the explosive character of the new learning. Although a good Catholic, Valla became a hero to later Protestant reformers. His popularity among them stemmed from his exposé of the *Donation of Constantine* (see Chapter 6) and his defense of predestination against the advocates of free will.

The fraudulent *Donation*, written in the eighth century, purported to be a grant of vast territories that the Roman emperor Constantine (r. 307–337) donated to the pope. Valla did not intend the exposé of the *Donation* to have the devastating force that Protestants later attributed to it. He only proved in a careful, scholarly way what others had long suspected. Using textual analysis and historical logic, Valla demonstrated that the document was filled with anachronistic terms, such as *fief*, and contained information that could not have existed in a fourth-century document. In the same dispassionate way, he also pointed out errors in the Latin Vulgate, still the authorized version of the Bible for the Western church.

Such discoveries did not make Valla any less loyal to the church, nor did they prevent his faithful fulfillment of the office of apostolic secretary in Rome under Pope Nicholas V (r. 1447–1455). Nonetheless, historical humanistic criticism of this type also served those less loyal to the medieval church. Young humanists formed the first identifiable group of Martin Luther's supporters.

Civic Humanism A basic humanist criticism of Scholastic education was that much of its content was useless. Education, humanists believed, should promote individual virtue and public service, hence the designation, **civic humanism**. The most striking examples of this were found in Florence, where three humanists served as chancellors of the city: Coluccio Salutati (1331–1406), Leonardo Bruni (ca. 1370–1444), and Poggio Bracciolini (1380–1459). Each used his rhetorical skills to rally the Florentines against the aggression of Naples and Milan. Bruni and Poggio wrote adulatory histories of the city. Another accomplished humanist scholar, Leon Battista Alberti (1402–1472), was a noted Florentine architect and builder. However, many modern scholars doubt that humanistic scholarship really accounted for such civic activity and rather view the three famous humanist chancellors of Florence as men who simply wanted to exercise power.

Toward the end of the Renaissance, many humanists became cliquish and snobbish, an intellectual elite more concerned with narrow scholarly interests and writing pure, classical Latin than with revitalizing civic and social life. In reaction to this elitist trend, the humanist historians Niccolò Machiavelli (1469–1527) and Francesco Guicciardini (1483–1540) wrote in Italian and made contemporary history their primary source and subject matter. Here, arguably, we can see the two sides of humanism: deep scholarship and practical politics.

Renaissance Art

In Renaissance Italy, as in Reformation Europe, the values and interests of the laity were no longer subordinated to those of the clergy. In education, culture, and religion, the laity assumed a leading role and established models for the clergy to emulate. This development was due in part to the church's loss of international power during the great crises of the late Middle Ages. The rise of national sentiment and the emergence of national bureaucracies staffed by laymen, not clerics, and the rapid growth of lay education over the fourteenth and fifteenth centuries also encouraged it. Medieval Christian values were adjusted to a more this-worldly spirit.

This new perspective on life is prominent in the painting and sculpture of the High Renaissance (1450–1527), when art and sculpture reached their full maturity. Whereas medieval art tended to be abstract and formulaic, Renaissance art emphatically embraced the natural world and human emotions. Renaissance artists gave their works a rational, even mathematical, order—perfect symmetry and proportionality reflecting a belief in the harmony of the universe.

COMPARE AND CONNECT

Is the "Renaissance Man" a Myth?

AS SEVERAL ILLUSTRATIONS in this chapter attest, the great artists of the Renaissance (Raphael, Leonardo da Vinci, Albrecht Dürer) romanticized their human subjects and made them larger than life. Not only was the iconic "Renaissance man" perfectly proportioned physically, he was also effective in what he undertook, endowed with the divine freedom and power to be and to do whatever he chose.

QUESTIONS

1. Who or what are Pico's and Dürer's glorified humans? Is the vaunted "Renaissance Man" real or fictional?

2. What is one to make of an era fixated on the perfect body and mind?

3. Is Martin Luther's rejoinder (the bondage of the human will) truer to life, or religious misanthropy?

I. Pico della Mirandola, *Oration on the Dignity of Man* (ca. 1486)

One of the most eloquent descriptions of the Renaissance image of human beings comes from the Italian humanist Pico della Mirandola (1463–1494). In his famed Oration on the Dignity of Man *(ca. 1486), Pico describes humans as free to become whatever they choose.*

Pico's "Renaissance Man" stands in stark contrast to the devout Christian pilgrim of the Middle Ages. The latter found himself always at the crossroads of heaven and hell, in constant fear of sin, death, and the devil, regularly confessing his sins and receiving forgiveness in an unending penitential cycle. Had the Middle Ages misjudged human nature? Was there a great transformation in human nature between the Middle Ages and the Renaissance?

The best of artisans [God] ordained that that creature (man) to whom He had been able to give nothing proper to himself should have joint possession of whatever had been peculiar to each of the different kinds of being. He therefore took man as a creature of indeterminate nature and, assigning him a place in the middle of the world, addressed him thus: "Neither a fixed abode nor a form that is thine alone nor any function peculiar to thyself have we given thee, Adam, to the end that according to thy longing and according to thy judgment thou mayest have and possess what abode, what form, and what functions thou thyself shalt desire. The nature of all other beings is limited and constrained within the bounds of laws prescribed by Us. Thou, constrained by no limits, in accordance with thine own free will, in whose hand We have placed thee, shall ordain for thyself the limits of thy nature. We have set thee at the world's center that thou mayest from thence more easily observe whatever is in the world. We have made thee neither of heaven nor of earth, neither mortal nor immortal, so that with freedom of choice and with honor, as though the maker and molder of thyself, thou mayest fashion thyself in whatever shape thou shalt prefer. Thou shalt have the power to degenerate into the lower forms of life, which are brutish. Thou shalt have the power, out of thy soul's judgment, to be reborn into the higher forms, which are divine." O supreme generosity of God the Father, O highest and most marvelous felicity of man! To him it is granted to have whatever he chooses, to be whatever he wills.

Source: Giovanni Pico della Mirandola, *Oration on the Dignity of Man*, in *The Renaissance Philosophy of Man*, ed. by E. Cassirer et al. (Chicago: Phoenix Books, 1961), pp. 224–225.

II. Albrecht Dürer

In 1500, Albrecht Dürer, then 28, painted the most famous self-portrait of the European Renaissance and Reformation, one that celebrated his own beauty and genius by imposing his face on a portrayal of Christ, a work of art that has been called "the birth of the modern artist."

Fourteen years later (1514), on the occasion of his mother's death, Dürer engraved another famous image of himself, only now as a man in deep depression, or melancholy, his mind darkened and his creativity throttled.

In this self-portrait he is neither effective nor handsome, much less heroic and divine, not a self-portrait of a Renaissance man.

Albrecht Dürer (1471–1528). *Self-portrait at Age 28 with Fur Coat.* 1500. Oil on wood, 67 × 49 cm. Alte Pinakothek, Munich, Germany. Photograph © Scala/Art Resource, NY

Albrecht Dürer. *Melencolia I.* 1514. Engraving. 23.8 × 18.9 cm. Courtesy of the Library of Congress.

III. Martin Luther, *The Bondage of the Will* (1525)

The greater challenge to the Renaissance man came from Martin Luther, who met his "Pico" in the northern humanist Desiderius Erasmus. Like Pico, Erasmus, flying in the face of Reformation theology, conceived free will to be "a power of the human will by which a man may apply himself to those things that lead to eternal salvation, or turn away from the same." Of such thinking, Luther made short-shift.

It is in the highest degree wholesome and necessary for a Christian to know whether or not his will has anything to do in matters pertaining to salvation . . . We need to have in mind a clear-cut distinction between God's power and ours and God's work and ours, if we would live a godly life . . . The will, be it God's or man's, does what it does, good or bad, under no compulsion, but just as it wants or pleases, as if totally free . . . Wise men know what experience of life proves, that no man's purposes ever go forward as planned, but events overtake all men contrary to their expectation. . . Who among us always lives and behaves as he should? But duty and doctrine are not therefore condemned, rather they condemn us.

God has promised His grace to the humbled, that is, to those who mourn over and despair of themselves. But a man cannot be thoroughly humbled till he realizes that his salvation is utterly beyond his own powers, counsels, efforts, will and works, and depends absolutely on the will, counsel, pleasure, and work of Another: GOD ALONE. As long as he is persuaded that he can make even the smallest contribution to his salvation, he . . . does not utterly despair of himself, and so is not humbled before God, but plans for himself a position, an occasion, a work, which shall bring him final salvation. But he who [no longer] doubts that his destiny depends entirely only on the will of God . . . waits for God to work in him, and such a man is very near to grace for his salvation. So if we want to drop this term ("free will") altogether, which would be the safest and most Christian thing to do, we may, still in good faith, teach people to use it to credit man with 'free will' in respect not of what is above him, but of what is below him . . . However, with regard to God and in all that bears on salvation or damnation, he has no 'free will' but is a captive, prisoner and bond-slave, either to the will of God, or to the will of Satan.

Source: Martin Luther, *On the Bondage of the Will*, ed. by J. I Packer and O. R. Johnston (Westwood, NJ: Fleming H. Fevell Co., 1957), pp. 79, 81, 83, 87, 100, 104, 107, 137.

Combining the painterly qualities of all the Renaissance masters, Raphael created scenes of tender beauty and subjects sublime in both flesh and spirit.   Musée du Louvre, Paris/Giraudon, Paris/SuperStock

Renaissance artists were helped by the development of new technical skills during the fifteenth century. In addition to the availability of oil paints, two special techniques gave them an edge: the use of shading to enhance naturalness (**chiaroscuro**) and the adjustment of the size of figures to give the viewer a feeling of continuity with the painting (*linear perspective*). These techniques enabled the artist to portray space realistically and to paint a more natural world. The result, compared to their flat Byzantine and Gothic counterparts, was a three-dimensional canvas filled with energy and life.

Giotto (1266–1336), the father of Renaissance painting, signaled the new direction. An admirer of Saint Francis of Assisi, whose love of nature he shared, Giotto painted a more natural world. Though still filled with religious seriousness, his work was no longer an abstract and unnatural depiction of the world. The painter Masaccio (1401–1428) and the sculptor Donatello (1386–1466) also portrayed the world around them literally and naturally. The great masters of the High

Renaissance, Leonardo da Vinci (1452–1519), Raphael (1483–1520), and Michelangelo Buonarroti (1475–1564), reached the heights of such painting.

Leonardo da Vinci   A true master of many skills, Leonardo exhibited the Renaissance ideal of the universal person. One of the greatest painters of all time, he also advised Italian princes and the French king Francis I (r. 1515–1547) on military engineering. He advocated scientific experimentation, dissected corpses to learn anatomy, and was a self-taught botanist. His inventive mind foresaw such modern machines as airplanes and submarines. The variety of his interests was so great that it could shorten his attention span. His great skill in conveying inner moods through complex facial expression is apparent not only in his most famous painting, the *Mona Lisa,* but in his self-portrait as well.

Raphael   A man of great kindness and a painter of great sensitivity, Raphael was loved by his contemporaries as much for his person as for his work. He is most famous for his tender madonnas and the great fresco in the Vatican, *The School of Athens,* a virtually perfect example of Renaissance technique. It depicts Plato and Aristotle surrounded by other great philosophers and scientists of antiquity who bear the features of Raphael's famous contemporaries.

Michelangelo   The melancholy genius Michelangelo also excelled in a variety of arts and crafts. His eighteen-foot sculpture of David, which long stood majestically in the great square of Florence, is a perfect example of Renaissance devotion to harmony, symmetry, and proportion, all serving the glorification of the human form. Four different popes commissioned works by Michelangelo. The frescoes in the Vatican's Sistine Chapel are the most famous, painted during the pontificate of Pope Julius II (r. 1503–1513), who also set Michelangelo to work on his own magnificent tomb. The Sistine frescoes originally covered 10,000 square feet and involved 343 figures, over half of which exceeded ten feet in height, but it is their originality and perfection as works of art that impress one most. This labor of love and piety took four years to complete.

His later works are more complex and suggest deep personal changes. They mark, artistically and philosophically, the passing of High Renaissance painting and the advent of a new style known as **mannerism**, which reached its peak in the late sixteenth and early seventeenth centuries. A reaction to the simplicity and symmetry of High Renaissance art, which also had a parallel in contemporary music and literature, mannerism made room for the strange and the abnormal, giving freer reign to the individual perceptions and feelings of the artist, who now felt free to paint, compose, or write in a "mannered," or "affected," way. Tintoretto (d. 1594) and El Greco (d. 1614) are mannerism's supreme representatives.

LEONARDO PLOTS THE PERFECT MAN

VITRUVIAN MAN BY Leonardo da Vinci, c. 1490. The name "Vitruvian" is taken from that of a first-century C.E. Roman architect and engineer, Marcus Pollio Vitruvius, who used squares and circles to demonstrate the human body's symmetry and proportionality. According to Vitruvius:

And just as the human body yields a circular outline, so too a square figure may be found from it. For if we measure the distance from the soles of the feet to the top of the head, and then apply that measure to the outstretched arms, the breadth will be found to be the same as the height.

Leonardo, like most artists of his time, shared this classical ideal of human perfection even in his gloomiest etchings and paintings. With few exceptions, the great painters of the age wanted to portray men and women in a more than human beauty and glory. Even the rabbits of the German painter Albrecht Dürer, who shared this ideal, were superior to any rabbit one might see in the wild.

If a man be placed flat on his back, with his hands and feet extended, and a pair of compasses centered at his navel, the fingers and toes of his two hands and feet will touch the circumference of a circle described therefrom.

CORBIS/Bettmann

To examine this image in an interactive fashion, please go to www.myhistorylab.com

PEARSON
myhistorylab

Marilyn Stokstad and David Cateforis, *Art History* (New York: Pearson, 2005), p. 651.

Michelangelo's Scene from the Last Judgment. The High Italian Renaissance obsession with the beefy, pumped up, heroic body finds expression in this detail of a fresco in Michelangelo's rendering of the *Last Judgment* in the Sistine Chapel.   Nippon Television Network Corporation

MAJOR POLITICAL EVENTS OF THE ITALIAN RENAISSANCE (1375–1527)

1378–1382	The Ciompi Revolt in Florence
1434	Medici rule in Florence established by Cosimo de' Medici
1454–1455	Treaty of Lodi allies Milan, Naples, and Florence (in effect until 1494)
1494	Charles VIII of France invades Italy
1494–1498	Savonarola controls Florence
1495	League of Venice unites Venice, Milan, the Papal States, the Holy Roman Empire, and Spain against France
1499	Louis XII invades Milan (the second French invasion of Italy)
1500	The Borgias conquer Romagna
1512–1513	The Holy League (Pope Julius II, Ferdinand of Aragon, Emperor Maximilian, and Venice) defeats the French
1513	Machiavelli writes *The Prince*
1515	Francis I leads the third French invasion of Italy
1516	Concordat of Bologna between France and the papacy
1527	Sack of Rome by imperial soldiers

Slavery in the Renaissance

Throughout Renaissance Italy, slavery flourished as extravagantly as art and culture. A thriving western slave market existed as early as the twelfth century, when the Spanish sold Muslim slaves captured in raids and war to wealthy Italians and other buyers. Contemporaries looked on such slavery as a merciful act, since their captors would otherwise have killed the captives. In addition to widespread household or domestic slavery, collective plantation slavery, following East Asian models, also developed in the eastern Mediterranean during the High Middle Ages. In the savannas of Sudan and the Venetian estates on the islands of Cyprus and Crete, gangs of slaves cut sugarcane, setting the model for later slave plantations in the Mediterranean and the New World.

After the Black Death (1348–1350) reduced the supply of laborers everywhere in Western Europe, the demand for slaves soared. Slaves were imported from Africa, the Balkans, Constantinople, Cyprus, Crete, and the lands surrounding the Black Sea. Taken randomly from conquered people, they consisted of many races: Tatars, Circassians, Greeks, Russians, Georgians, and Iranians as well as Asians and Africans. According to one source, "By the end of the fourteenth century, there was hardly a well-to-do household in Tuscany without at least one slave: brides brought them [to their marriages] as part of their dowry, doctors accepted them from their patients in lieu of fees—and it was not unusual to find them even in the service of a priest."[2]

Owners had complete dominion over their slaves; in Italian law, this meant the "[power] to have, hold, sell, alienate, exchange, enjoy, rent or unrent, dispose of in [their] will[s], judge soul and body, and do with in perpetuity whatsoever may please [them] and [their] heirs and no man may gainsay [them]."[3] A strong, young, healthy slave cost the equivalent of the wages paid a free servant over several years. Considering the lifetime of free service thereafter, slaves were well worth the price.

[2]Iris Origo, *The Merchant of Prato: Francesco di Marco Datini, 1335–1410* (New York: David Godine, 1986), pp. 90–91.
[3]Origo, *The Merchant of Prato*, p. 209.

Tatars and Africans appear to have been the worst treated, but as in ancient Greece and Rome, slaves at this time were generally accepted as family members and integrated into households. Not a few women slaves became mothers of their masters' children. Fathers often adopted children of such unions and raised them as their legitimate heirs. It was also in the interest of their owners to keep slaves healthy and happy; otherwise they would be of little use and even become a threat. Slaves nonetheless remained a foreign and suspected presence in Italian society; they were, as all knew, uprooted and resentful people.

▼ Italy's Political Decline: The French Invasions (1494–1527)

As a land of autonomous city-states, Italy had always relied on internal cooperation for its peace and safety from foreign invasion—especially by the Turks. Such cooperation was maintained during the second half of the fifteenth century, thanks to a political alliance known as the Treaty of Lodi (1454–1455). Its terms brought Milan and Naples, long traditional enemies, into the alliance with Florence. These three stood together for decades against Venice, which frequently joined the Papal States to maintain an internal balance of power. However, when a foreign enemy threatened Italy, the five states could also present a united front.

Around 1490, after the rise to power of the Milanese despot Ludovico il Moro, hostilities between Milan and Naples resumed. The peace that the Treaty of Lodi made possible ended in 1494 when Naples, supported by Florence and the Borgia Pope Alexander VI (r. 1492–1503), threatened Milan. Ludovico made a fatal response to these new political alignments: He appealed to the French for aid. French kings had ruled Naples from 1266 to 1442 before being driven out by Duke Alfonso of Sicily. Breaking a wise Italian rule, Ludovico invited the French to reenter Italy and revive their dynastic claim to Naples. In his haste to check rival Naples, Ludovico did not recognize sufficiently that France also had dynastic claims to Milan. Nor did he foresee how insatiable the French appetite for new territory would become once French armies had crossed the Alps and encamped in Italy.

Charles VIII's March Through Italy

The French king Louis XI had resisted the temptation to invade Italy while nonetheless keeping French dynastic claims in Italy alive. His successor, Charles VIII (r. 1483–1498), an eager youth in his twenties, responded to Ludovico's call with lightning speed. Within five months, he had crossed the Alps (August 1494) and raced as conqueror through Florence and the Papal States into Naples.

As Charles approached Florence, its Florentine ruler, Piero de' Medici, who was allied with Naples against Milan, tried to placate the French king by handing over Pisa and other Florentine possessions. Such appeasement only brought about Piero's exile by a citizenry that was being revolutionized by a radical Dominican preacher named Girolamo Savonarola (1452–1498). Savonarola convinced the fearful Florentines that the French king's arrival was a long-delayed and fully justified divine vengeance on their immorality.

That allowed Charles to enter Florence without resistance. Between Savonarola's fatal flattery and the payment of a large ransom, the city escaped destruction. After Charles's departure, Savonarola exercised virtual rule over Florence for four years. In the end, the Florentines proved not to be the stuff theocracies are made of. Savonarola's moral rigor and antipapal policies made it impossible for him to survive indefinitely in Italy. After the Italian cities reunited and ousted the French invader, whom Savonarola had praised as a godsend, Savonarola's days were numbered. In May 1498, he was imprisoned and executed.

Charles's lightning march through Italy also struck terror in non-Italian hearts. Ferdinand of Aragon (r. 1479–1516), who had hoped to expand his own possessions in Italy from his base in Sicily, now found himself vulnerable to a French-Italian axis. In response he created a new counteralliance—the League of Venice. Formed in March 1495, the League brought Venice, the Papal States, and Emperor Maximilian I (r. 1493–1519) together with Ferdinand against the French. The stage was now set for a conflict between France and Spain that would not end until 1559.

Ludovico il Moro meanwhile recognized that he had sown the wind. Having desired a French invasion only as long as it weakened his enemies, he now saw a whirlwind of events he had himself created threaten Milan. In reaction, he joined the League of Venice, which was now strong enough to send Charles into retreat and to end the menace he posed to Italy.

Pope Alexander VI and the Borgia Family

The French returned to Italy under Charles's successor, Louis XII (r. 1498–1515). This time a new Italian ally, the Borgia pope, Alexander VI, assisted them. Probably the most corrupt pope who ever sat on the papal throne, he openly promoted the political careers of Cesare and Lucrezia Borgia, the children he had had before he became pope. He placed papal policy in tandem with the efforts of his powerful family to secure a political base in Romagna in north central Italy.

In Romagna, several principalities had fallen away from the church during the Avignon papacy. Venice, the pope's ally within the League of Venice, continued to contest the Papal States for their loyalty. Seeing that a French alliance would allow him to reestablish control over the region, Alexander took steps to secure French favor. He annulled Louis XII's marriage to Charles VIII's sister so Louis could marry Charles's widow, Anne of Brittany—a popular political move designed to keep Brittany French. The pope also bestowed a cardinal's hat on the archbishop of Rouen, Louis's favorite cleric. Most important, Alexander agreed to abandon the League of Venice, a withdrawal of support that made the league too weak to resist a French reconquest of Milan. In exchange, Cesare Borgia received the sister of the king of Navarre, Charlotte d'Albret, in marriage, a union that enhanced Borgia military strength. Cesare also received land grants from Louis XII and the promise of French military aid in Romagna.

All in all it was a scandalous trade-off, but one that made it possible for both the French king and the pope to realize their ambitions within Italy. Louis invaded Milan in August 1499. Ludovico il Moro, who had originally opened the Pandora's box of French invasion, spent his last years languishing in a French prison. In 1500, Louis and Ferdinand of Aragon divided Naples between them, and the pope and Cesare Borgia conquered the cities of Romagna without opposition. Alexander's victorious son was given the title "duke of Romagna."

Pope Julius II

Cardinal Giuliano della Rovere, a strong opponent of the Borgia family, succeeded Alexander VI as Pope Julius II (r. 1503–1513). He suppressed the Borgias and placed their newly conquered lands in Romagna under papal jurisdiction. Julius raised the Renaissance papacy to its peak of military prowess and diplomatic intrigue, gaining him the title of "warrior pope." Shocked, as were other contemporaries, by this thoroughly secular papacy, the humanist Erasmus (1466?–1536), who had witnessed in disbelief a bullfight in the papal palace during a visit to Rome, wrote a popular anonymous satire entitled *Julius Excluded from Heaven*. This humorous account purported to describe the pope's unsuccessful efforts to convince Saint Peter that he was worthy of admission to heaven.

Assisted by his powerful allies, Pope Julius drove the Venetians out of Romagna in 1509 and fully secured the Papal States. Having realized this long-sought papal goal, Julius turned to the second major undertaking of his pontificate: ridding Italy of his former ally, the French invader. Julius, Ferdinand of Aragon, and Venice formed a second Holy League in October 1511 and were joined by Emperor Maximilian I and the Swiss. In 1512, the league had the French in full retreat, and the Swiss defeated them in 1513 at Novara.

The French were nothing if not persistent. They invaded Italy a third time under Louis's successor, Fran-

cis I (r. 1515–1547). This time French armies massacred Swiss soldiers of the Holy League at Marignano in September 1515, avenging the earlier defeat at Novara. The victory won the Concordat of Bologna from the pope in August 1516, an agreement that gave the French king control over the French clergy in exchange for French recognition of the pope's superiority over church councils and his right to collect annates in France. This concordat helped keep France Catholic after the outbreak of the Protestant Reformation, but the new French entry into Italy set the stage for the first of four major wars with Spain in the first half of the sixteenth century: the Habsburg-Valois wars, none of which France won.

Niccolò Machiavelli

The foreign invasions made a shambles of Italy. The same period that saw Italy's cultural peak in the work of Leonardo, Raphael, and Michelangelo also witnessed Italy's political tragedy. One who watched as French, Spanish, and German armies wreaked havoc on Italy was Niccolò Machiavelli (1469–1527). The more he saw, the more convinced he became that Italian political unity and independence were ends that justified any means.

A humanist and a careful student of ancient Rome, Machiavelli was impressed by the way Roman rulers and citizens had then defended their homeland. They possessed *virtù*, the ability to act decisively and heroically for the good of their country. Stories of ancient Roman patriotism and self-sacrifice were Machiavelli's favorites, and he lamented the absence of such traits among his compatriots. Such romanticizing of the Roman past exaggerated both ancient virtue and contemporary failings. His Florentine contemporary, Francesco Guicciardini (1483–1540), a more sober historian less given to idealizing antiquity, wrote truer chronicles of Florentine and Italian history.

Machiavelli also held republican ideals, which he did not want to see vanish from Italy. He believed a strong and determined people could struggle successfully with fortune. He scolded the Italian people for the self-destruction their own internal feuding was causing. He wanted an end to that behavior above all, so a reunited Italy could drive all foreign armies out.

His fellow citizens were not up to such a challenge. The juxtaposition of what Machiavelli believed the ancient Romans had been, with the failure of his contemporaries to attain such high ideals, made him the famous cynic whose name—in the epithet "Machiavellian"—has become synonymous with ruthless political expediency. Only a strongman, he concluded, could impose order on so divided and selfish a people; the salvation of Italy required, for the present, cunning dictators.

Santi di Tito's portrait of Machiavelli, perhaps the most famous Italian political theorist, who advised Renaissance princes to practice artful deception and inspire fear in their subjects if they wished to be successful. Scala/Art Resource, NY

It has been argued that Machiavelli wrote *The Prince* in 1513 as a cynical satire on the way rulers actually do behave and not as a serious recommendation of unprincipled despotic rule. To take his advocacy of tyranny literally, it is argued, contradicts both his earlier works and his own strong family tradition of republican service. But Machiavelli seems to have been in earnest when he advised rulers to discover the advantages of fraud and brutality, at least as a temporary means to the higher end of a unified Italy. He apparently hoped to see a strong ruler emerge from the Medici family, which had captured the papacy in 1513 with the pontificate of Leo X (r. 1513–1521). At the same time, the Medici family retained control over the powerful territorial state of Florence. The situation was similar to that of Machiavelli's hero Cesare Borgia and his father Pope Alexander VI, who had earlier brought factious Romagna to heel by combining secular family goals with religious policy. *The Prince* was pointedly dedicated to Lorenzo de' Medici, duke of Urbino and grandson of Lorenzo the Magnificent.

Whatever Machiavelli's hopes may have been, the Medicis were not destined to be Italy's deliverers. The second Medici pope, Clement VII (r. 1523–1534), watched helplessly as the army of Emperor Charles V sacked Rome in 1527, also the year of Machiavelli's death.

▼ Revival of Monarchy in Northern Europe

After 1450, the emergence of truly sovereign rulers set in motion a shift from divided feudal monarchy to unified national monarchies. Dynastic and chivalric ideals of feudal monarchy did not, however, vanish. Territorial princes remained on the scene and representative bodies persisted and even grew in influence. Still, in the late fifteenth and early sixteenth centuries, the old problem of the one and the many was now progressively decided in favor of national monarchs.

The feudal monarchy of the High Middle Ages was characterized by the division of the basic powers of government between the king and his semiautonomous vassals. The nobility and the towns then acted with varying degrees of unity and success through evolving representative assemblies, such as the English Parliament, the French Estates General, and the Spanish *Cortés*, to thwart the centralization of royal power into a united nation. But after the Hundred Years' War and the Great Schism in the church, the nobility and the clergy were in decline and less able to block growing national monarchies.

The increasingly important towns now began to ally with the king. Loyal, business-wise townspeople, not the nobility and the clergy, increasingly staffed royal offices and became the king's lawyers, bookkeepers, military tacticians, and foreign diplomats. This new alliance between king and town broke the bonds of feudal society and made possible the rise of sovereign states.

In a sovereign state, the powers of taxation, war making, and law enforcement no longer belong to semiautonomous vassals but are concentrated in the monarch and exercised by his or her chosen agents. Taxes, wars, and laws become national, rather than merely regional, matters. Only as monarchs became able to act independently of the nobility and representative assemblies could they overcome the decentralization that impeded nation building. Ferdinand and Isabella of Spain rarely called the *Cortés* into session. The French Estates General met irregularly, mostly in time of crisis, but was never essential to royal governance. Henry VII (r. 1485–1509) of England managed to raise revenues without going begging to Parliament, which had voted him customs revenues for life in 1485. Brilliant theorists, from Marsilius of Padua in the fourteenth century to Machiavelli in the fifteenth to Jean Bodin (1530–1596) in the sixteenth, emphatically defended the sovereign rights of monarchy.

The many were, of course, never totally subjugated to the one. But in the last half of the fifteenth century, rulers demonstrated that the law was their creature. They appointed civil servants whose vision was no longer merely local or regional. In Castile they were the *corregidores,* in England the justices of the peace, and in France bailiffs operating through well-drilled lieutenants. These royal ministers and agents could become closely attached to the localities they administered in the ruler's name, and regions were able to secure congenial royal appointments. Throughout England, for example, local magnates served as representatives of the Tudor dynasty that seized the throne in 1485. Nonetheless, these new executives remained royal executives, bureaucrats whose outlook was now "national" and whose loyalty was to the "state."

Monarchies also began to create standing national armies in the fifteenth century. The noble cavalry receded as the infantry and the artillery became the backbone of royal armies. Mercenary soldiers were recruited from Switzerland and Germany to form the major part of the "king's army." Professional soldiers who fought for pay and booty proved far more efficient than feudal vassals who fought simply for honor's sake. Monarchs who failed to meet their payrolls, however, now faced a new danger of mutiny and banditry by foreign troops.

The growing cost of warfare in the fifteenth and sixteenth centuries increased the monarch's need for new national sources of income. The great obstacle was the stubborn belief of the highest social classes that they were immune from government taxation. The nobility guarded their properties and traditional rights and despised taxation as an insult and a humiliation. Royal revenues accordingly had to grow at the expense of those least able to resist and least able to pay.

The monarchs had several options when it came to raising money. As feudal lords, they could collect rents from their royal domains. They could also levy national taxes on basic food and clothing, such as the salt tax (*gabelle*) in France and the 10 percent sales tax (*alcabala*) on commercial transactions in Spain. The rulers could also levy direct taxes on the peasantry, which they did through agreeable representative assemblies of the privileged classes in which the peasantry did not sit. The *taille,* which the French kings independently determined from year to year after the Estates General was suspended in 1484, was such a tax. Innovative fund-raising devices in the fifteenth century included the sale of public offices and the issuance of high-interest government bonds. Rulers still did not levy taxes on the powerful nobility, but instead, they borrowed from rich nobles and the great bankers of Italy and Germany. In money matters, the privileged classes remained as much the kings' creditors and competitors as their subjects.

France

Charles VII (r. 1422–1461) was a king made great by those who served him. His ministers created a permanent professional army, which—thanks initially to the inspiration of Joan of Arc—drove the English out of France. In addition, the enterprise of an independent merchant banker named Jacques Coeur helped develop a strong economy, diplomatic corps, and national administration during Charles's reign. These sturdy tools in turn enabled Charles's son and successor, the ruthless Louis XI (r. 1461–1483), to make France a great power.

French nation building had two political cornerstones in the fifteenth century. The first was the collapse of the English Empire in France following the Hundred Years' War. The second was the defeat of Charles the Bold (r. 1467–1477) and his duchy of Burgundy. Perhaps Europe's strongest political power in the mid-fifteenth century, Burgundy aspired to dwarf both France and the Holy Roman Empire as the leader of a dominant middle kingdom, which it might have done had not the continental powers joined to prevent it. When Charles the Bold died in defeat in a battle at Nancy in 1477, the dream of a Burgundian Empire died with him. Louis XI and Habsburg emperor Maximilian I divided the conquered Burgundian lands between them, with the treaty-wise Habsburgs getting the better part. The dissolution of Burgundy ended its constant intrigue against the French king and left Louis XI free to secure the monarchy. Between the newly acquired Burgundian lands and his own inheritance the king was able to end his reign with a kingdom almost twice the size of that he had inherited. Louis successfully harnessed the nobility, expanded the trade and industry that Jacques Cœur so carefully had nurtured, created a national postal system, and even established a lucrative silk industry.

A strong nation is a two-edged sword. Because Louis's successors inherited a secure and efficient government, they felt free to pursue what proved ultimately to be a bad foreign policy. Conquests in Italy in the 1490s and a long series of losing wars with the Habsburgs in the first half of the sixteenth century left France, by the mid-sixteenth century, once again a defeated nation almost as divided as it had been during the Hundred Years' War.

Spain

Both Castile and Aragon had been poorly ruled and divided kingdoms in the mid-fifteenth century, but the union of Isabella of Castile (r. 1474–1504) and Ferdinand of Aragon (r. 1479–1516) changed that situation. The two future sovereigns married in 1469, despite strong protests from neighboring Portugal and France, both of which foresaw the formidable European power the marriage would create. Castile was by far the richer and more populous of the two, having an estimated 5 million inhabitants to Aragon's population of under 1 million. Castile was also distinguished by its lucrative sheep-farming industry, run by a government-backed organization called the *Mesta*, another example of a developing centralized economic planning. Although the marriage of Ferdinand and Isabella dynastically united the two kingdoms, they remained constitutionally separated. Each retained its respective government agencies—separate laws, armies, coinage, and taxation—and cultural traditions.

Ferdinand and Isabella could do together what neither was able to accomplish alone: subdue their realms, secure their borders, venture abroad militarily, and Christianize the whole of Spain. Between 1482 and 1492 they conquered the Moors in Granada. Naples became a Spanish possession in 1504. By 1512, Ferdinand had secured his northern borders by conquering the kingdom of Navarre. Internally, the Spanish king and queen won the allegiance of the *Hermandad,* a powerful league of cities and towns that served them against stubborn noble landowners. The crown also extended its authority over the wealthy chivalric orders, further limiting the power of the nobility.

Spain had long been remarkable among European lands as a place where three religions—Islam, Judaism, and Christianity—coexisted with a certain degree of toleration. That toleration was to end dramatically under Ferdinand and Isabella, who made Spain the prime exemplar of state-controlled religion.

Ferdinand and Isabella exercised almost total control over the Spanish church as they placed religion in the service of national unity. They appointed the higher clergy and the officers of the Inquisition. The latter, run by Tomás de Torquemada (d. 1498), Isabella's confessor, was a key national agency established in 1479 to monitor the activity of converted Jews (*conversos*) and Muslims (*Moriscos*) in Spain. In 1492, the Jews were exiled and their properties confiscated. In 1502, nonconverting Moors in Granada were driven into exile by Cardinal Francisco Jiménez de Cisneros (1437–1517), under whom Spanish spiritual life was successfully conformed. This was a major reason why Spain remained a loyal Catholic country throughout the sixteenth century and provided a secure base of operation for the European Counter-Reformation.

Despite a certain internal narrowness, Ferdinand and Isabella were rulers with wide horizons. They contracted anti-French marriage alliances that came to determine a large part of European history in the sixteenth century. In 1496, their eldest daughter, Joanna, later known as "the Mad," married Archduke Philip, the son of Emperor Maximilian I. The fruit of this union, Charles I, was the first to rule over a united Spain; because of his inheritance and election as emperor in 1519, his empire almost equaled in size that of Charlemagne. A second daughter, Catherine of Aragon, wed Arthur, the son of the English king Henry VII. After Arthur's premature death, she was betrothed to his brother, the future King Henry VIII (r. 1509–1547), whom she married eight years later, in 1509. The failure of this marriage became the key factor in the emergence of the Anglican church and the English Reformation.

The new power of Spain was also revealed in Ferdinand and Isabella's promotion of overseas exploration. They sponsored the Genoese adventurer Christopher Columbus (1451–1506), who arrived at the islands of the Caribbean while sailing west in search of a shorter route to the spice markets of the Far East. This patronage led to the creation of the Spanish Empire in Mexico and Peru, whose gold and silver mines helped make Spain Europe's dominant power in the sixteenth century.

England

The latter half of the fifteenth century was a period of especially difficult political trial for the English. Following the Hundred Years' War, civil warfare broke out between two rival branches of the royal family: the House of York and the House of Lancaster. The roots of the war lay in succession irregularities after the forced deposition of the erratic king Richard II (r. 1377–1399). This conflict, known to us today as the Wars of the Roses (because York's symbol, according to legend, was a white rose and Lancaster's a red rose), kept England in turmoil from 1455 to 1485.

The duke of York and his supporters in the prosperous southern towns challenged the Lancastrian monarchy of Henry VI (r. 1422–1461). In 1461, Edward IV (r. 1461–1483), son of the duke of York, seized power and instituted a strong-arm rule that lasted more than twenty years; it was only briefly interrupted, in 1470–1471, by Henry VI's short-lived restoration. Assisted by able ministers, Edward effectively increased the power and finances of the monarchy.

His brother, Richard III (r. 1483–1485), usurped the throne from Edward's son, and after Richard's death, the new Tudor dynasty portrayed him as an unprincipled villain who had also murdered Edward's sons in the Tower of London to secure his hold on the throne. Shakespeare's *Richard III* is the best-known version of this characterization—unjust according to some. Be that as it may, Richard's reign saw the growth of support for the exiled Lancastrian Henry Tudor, who returned to England to defeat Richard on Bosworth Field in August 1485.

Henry Tudor ruled as Henry VII (r. 1485–1509), the first of the new Tudor dynasty that would dominate England throughout the sixteenth century. To bring the rival royal families together and to make the hereditary claim of his offspring to the throne uncontestable, Henry married Edward IV's daughter, Elizabeth of York.

He succeeded in disciplining the English nobility through a special instrument of the royal will known as the Court of Star Chamber. Created with the sanction of Parliament in 1487, the court was intended to end the perversion of English justice by "over-mighty subjects," that is, powerful nobles who used intimidation and bribery to win favorable verdicts in court cases. In the Court of Star Chamber, the king's councilors sat as judges, and such tactics did not sway them. The result was a more equitable court system.

It was also a court more amenable to the royal will. Henry shrewdly used English law to further the ends of the monarchy. He managed to confiscate lands and fortunes of nobles with such success that he was able to govern without dependence on Parliament for royal funds, always a cornerstone of a strong monarchy. In these ways, Henry began to shape a monarchy that would develop into one of early modern Europe's most exemplary governments during the reign of his granddaughter, Elizabeth I (r. 1558–1603).

The Holy Roman Empire

Germany and Italy were the striking exceptions to the steady development of politically centralized lands in the last half of the fifteenth century. Unlike England, France, and Spain, the Holy Roman Empire saw the many thoroughly repulse the one. In Germany, territorial rulers and cities resisted every effort at national consolidation and unity. As in Carolingian times, rulers continued to partition their kingdoms, however small, among their sons. By the late fifteenth century, Germany was hopelessly divided into some three hundred autonomous political entities.

The princes and the cities did work together to create the machinery of law and order, if not of union, within the divided empire. Emperor Charles IV (r. 1346–1378) and the major German territorial rulers reached an agreement in 1356 known as the **Golden Bull**. It established a seven-member electoral college consisting of the archbishops of Mainz, Trier, and Cologne; the duke of Saxony; the margrave of Brandenburg; the count Palatine; and the king of Bohemia. This group also functioned as an administrative body. They elected the emperor and, in cooperation with him, provided what transregional unity and administration existed.

The figure of the emperor gave the empire a single ruler in law if not in fact. The conditions of his rule and the extent of his powers over his subjects, especially the seven electors, were renegotiated with every imperial election. Therefore, the rights of the many (the princes) were always balanced against the power of the one (the emperor).

In the fifteenth century, an effort was made to control incessant feuding by the creation of an imperial diet known as the *Reichstag*. This was a national assembly

This portrait of Katharina, by Albrecht Dürer, provides evidence of African slavery in Europe during the sixteenth century. Katharina was in the service of one João Bradao, a Portuguese economic minister living in Antwerp, then the financial center of Europe. Dürer became friends with Bradao during his stay in the Low Countries in the winter of 1520–1521. Albrecht Dürer (1471–1528), *Portrait of the Moorish Woman Katharina*. Drawing. Uffizi Florence, Italy. Photograph © Foto Marburg/Art Resource, NY

of the seven electors, the nonelectoral princes, and representatives from the sixty-five imperial free cities. The cities were the weakest of the three bodies represented in the diet. During such an assembly in Worms in 1495, the members won from Emperor Maximilian I an imperial ban on private warfare, the creation of a Supreme Court of Justice to enforce internal peace, and an imperial Council of Regency to coordinate imperial and internal German policy. The emperor only grudgingly conceded the latter because it gave the princes a share in executive power.

These reforms were still a poor substitute for true national unity. In the sixteenth and seventeenth centuries, the territorial princes became virtually sovereign rulers in their various domains. Such disunity aided religious dissent and conflict. It was in the cities and territories of still feudal, fractionalized, backward Germany that the Protestant Reformation broke out in the sixteenth century.

▼ The Northern Renaissance

The scholarly works of northern humanists created a climate favorable to religious and educational reforms on the eve of the Reformation. Northern humanism was initially stimulated by the importation of Italian learning through such varied intermediaries as students who had studied in Italy, merchants who traded there, and the Brothers of the Common Life. This last was an influential lay religious movement that began in the Netherlands and permitted men and women to live a shared religious life without making formal vows of poverty, chastity, and obedience.

The northern humanists, however, developed their own distinctive culture. They tended to come from more diverse social backgrounds and to be more devoted to religious reforms than their Italian counterparts. They were also more willing to write for lay audiences as well as for a narrow intelligentsia. Thanks to the invention of printing with movable type, it became possible for humanists to convey their educational ideals to laypeople and clerics alike. Printing gave new power and influence to elites in both church and state, who now could popularize their viewpoints freely and widely.

The Printing Press

A variety of forces converged in the fourteenth and fifteenth centuries to give rise to the invention of the printing press. Since the days of Charlemagne, kings and princes had encouraged schools and literacy to help provide educated bureaucrats to staff the offices of their kingdoms. Without people who could read, think critically, and write reliable reports, no kingdom, large or small, could be properly governed. By the fifteenth century, a new literate lay public had been created, thanks to the enormous expansion of schools and universities during the late Middle Ages.

The invention of a cheap way to manufacture paper also helped make books economical and broaden their content. Manuscript books had been inscribed on vellum, a cumbersome and expensive medium (170 calfskins or 300 sheepskins were required to make a single vellum Bible.) Single-sheet woodcuts had long been printed. The process involved carving words and pictures on a block of wood, inking it, and then stamping out as many copies as possible before the wood deteriorated. The end product was much like a cheap modern poster.

In response to the demand for books that the expansion of lay education and literacy created, Johann Gutenberg (d. 1468) invented printing with movable type in the mid-fifteenth century in the German city of Mainz, the center of printing for the whole of Western Europe. Thereafter, books were rapidly and handsomely produced on topics both profound and practical and were intended for ordinary lay readers, scholars, and clerics alike. Especially popular in the early decades of print were books of piety and religion, calendars and almanacs, and how-to books (for example, on childrearing, making brandies and liquors, curing animals, and farming).

The new technology proved enormously profitable to printers, whose numbers exploded. By 1500, within just fifty years of Gutenberg's press, printing presses operated in at least sixty German cities and in more than two hundred cities throughout Europe. The printing press was a boon to the careers of humanists, who now gained international audiences.

Literacy deeply affected people everywhere, nurturing self-esteem and a critical frame of mind. By standardizing texts, the print revolution made anyone who could read an instant authority. Rulers in church and state now had to deal with a less credulous

The printing press made possible the diffusion of Renaissance learning, but no book stimulated thought more at this time than did the Bible. With Gutenberg's publication of a printed Bible in 1454, scholars gained access to a dependable, standardized text, so Scripture could be discussed and debated as never before.
This item is reproduced by permission of The Huntington Library, San Marino, California

and less docile laity. Print was also a powerful tool for political and religious propaganda. Kings could now indoctrinate people as never before, and clergymen found themselves able to mass-produce both indulgences and pamphlets. (See "The West & The World: The Invention of Printing in China and Europe," on page 252.)

Erasmus

The far-reaching influence of Desiderius Erasmus (1466?–1536), the most famous northern humanist, illustrates the impact of the printing press. Through his printed works, Erasmus gained fame both as an educational and as a religious reformer. A lifelong Catholic, Erasmus, through his life and work, made clear that many loyal Catholics wanted major reforms in the church long before the Reformation made them a reality.

When patronage was scarce (authors received no royalties and had to rely on private patrons for their livelihood), Erasmus earned his living by tutoring well-to-do youths. He prepared short Latin dialogues for his students, intended to teach them how to speak and live well, inculcating good manners and language by internalizing what they read.

These dialogues were entitled *Colloquies*. In consecutive editions, they grew in number and length, including anticlerical dialogues and satires on religious dogmatism and superstition. Erasmus also collected ancient and contemporary proverbs, which appeared under the title *Adages*. Beginning with 800 examples, the final edition included more than 5,000. Among the locutions the *Adages* popularized are such common expressions as "Leave no stone unturned" and "Where there is smoke, there is fire."

Erasmus aspired to unite classical ideals of humanity and civic virtue with the Christian ideals of love and piety. He believed disciplined study of the classics and the Bible, if begun early enough, was the best way to reform individuals and society. He summarized his own beliefs with the phrase *philosophia Christi*, a simple, ethical piety in imitation of Christ. He set this ideal in stark contrast to what he believed to be the dogmatic, ceremonial, and bullying religious practices of the later Middle Ages. What most offended him about the Scholastics, both the old authorities of the Middle Ages and the new Protestant ones, was their letting dogma and argument overshadow Christian piety and practice.

Erasmus was a true idealist, who expected more from people than the age's theologians believed them capable of doing. To promote what he deemed to be the essence of Christianity, he made ancient Christian sources available in their original versions, believing that if people would only imbibe the pure sources of the faith, they would recover the moral and religious health the New Testament promises. To this end, Erasmus edited the works of the Church Fathers and produced a

Greek edition of the New Testament (1516), later adding a new Latin translation of the latter (1519). Martin Luther used both of those works when he translated the New Testament into German in 1522.

These various enterprises did not please the church authorities. They remained unhappy with Erasmus's "improvements" on the Vulgate, Christendom's Bible for over a thousand years, and his popular anticlerical writings. At one point in the mid-sixteenth century, all of Erasmus's works were on the church's *Index of Forbidden Books*. Luther also condemned Erasmus for his views on the freedom of human will. Still, Erasmus's works put sturdy tools of reform in the hands of both Protestant and Catholic reformers. Already in the 1520s, there was a popular saying: "Erasmus laid the egg that Luther hatched."

Humanism and Reform

In Germany, England, France, and Spain, humanism stirred both educational and religious reform.

Germany   Rudolf Agricola (1443–1485), the "father of German humanism," spent ten years in Italy and introduced Italian learning to Germany when he returned. Conrad Celtis (d. 1508), the first German poet laureate, and Ulrich von Hutten (1488–1523), a fiery knight, gave German humanism a nationalist coloring hostile to non-German cultures, particularly Roman culture. Von Hutten especially illustrates the union of humanism, German nationalism, and Luther's religious reform. A poet who admired Erasmus, he attacked indulgences and published an edition of Valla's exposé of the *Donation of Constantine*. He died in 1523, the victim of a hopeless knights' revolt against the princes.

The controversy that brought von Hutten onto the historical stage and unified reform-minded German humanists was the Reuchlin affair. Johann Reuchlin (1455–1522) was Europe's foremost Christian authority on Hebrew and Jewish learning. He wrote the first reliable Hebrew grammar by a Christian scholar and was attracted to Jewish mysticism. Around 1506, supported by the Dominican order in Cologne, a Christian who had converted from Judaism began a movement to suppress Jewish writings. When this man, whose name was Pfefferkorn, attacked Reuchlin, many German humanists, in the name of academic freedom and good scholarship—not for any pro-Jewish sentiment—rushed to Reuchlin's defense. The controversy lasted for years and produced one of the great satires of the period, the *Letters of Obscure Men* (1515), a merciless satire of monks and Scholastics to which von Hutten contributed. When Martin Luther came under attack in 1517 for his famous ninety-five theses against indulgences, many German humanists saw a repetition of the Scholastic attack on Reuchlin and rushed to his side.

England Italian learning came to England by way of English scholars and merchants and visiting Italian prelates. Lectures by William Grocyn (d. 1519) and Thomas Linacre (d. 1524) at Oxford and those of Erasmus at Cambridge marked the scholarly maturation of English humanism. John Colet (1467–1519), dean of Saint Paul's Cathedral, patronized humanist studies for the young and promoted religious reform.

Thomas More (1478–1535), a close friend of Erasmus, is the best-known English humanist. His *Utopia* (1516), a conservative criticism of contemporary society, rivals the plays of Shakespeare as the most read sixteenth-century English work. *Utopia* depicted an imaginary society based on reason and tolerance that overcame social and political injustice by holding all property and goods in common and requiring everyone to earn their bread by their own work.

More became one of Henry VIII's most trusted diplomats. His repudiation of the Act of Supremacy (1534), which made the king of England head of the English church in place of the pope (see Chapter 11), and his refusal to recognize the king's marriage to Anne Boleyn, however, led to his execution in July 1535. Although More remained Catholic, humanism in England, as also in Germany, helped prepare the way for the English Reformation.

France The French invasions of Italy made it possible for Italian learning to penetrate France, stirring both educational and religious reform. Guillaume Budé (1468–1540), an accomplished Greek scholar, and Jacques Lefèvre d'Etaples (1454–1536), a biblical authority, were the leaders of French humanism. Lefèvre's scholarly works exemplified the new critical scholarship and influenced Martin Luther. Guillaume Briçonnet (1470–1533), the bishop of Meaux, and Marguerite d'Angoulême (1492–1549), sister of King Francis I, the future queen of Navarre, and a successful spiritual writer in her own right, cultivated a generation of young reform-minded humanists. The future Protestant reformer John Calvin was a product of this native reform circle.

Spain Whereas in England, France, and Germany humanism prepared the way for Protestant reforms, in Spain it entered the service of the Catholic Church. Here the key figure was Francisco Jiménez de Cisneros (1437–1517), a confessor to Queen Isabella and, after 1508, the "Grand Inquisitor"—a position that allowed him to enforce the strictest religious orthodoxy. Jiménez founded the University of Alcalá near Madrid in 1509, printed a Greek edition of the New Testament, and translated many religious tracts designed to reform clerical life and better direct lay piety. His great achievement, taking fifteen years to complete, was the *Complutensian Polyglot Bible,* a six-volume work that placed the Hebrew, Greek, and Latin versions of the Bible in parallel columns. Such scholarly projects and internal church reforms joined with the repressive measures of Ferdinand and Isabella to keep Spain strictly Catholic throughout the Age of Reformation.

▼ Voyages of Discovery and the New Empires in the West and East

The discovery of the Americas dramatically expanded the horizons of Europeans, both geographically and intellectually. Knowledge of the New World's inhabitants and the exploitation of its mineral and human wealth set new cultural and economic forces in motion throughout Western Europe.

Beginning with the voyages of the Portuguese and Spanish in the fifteenth century, commercial supremacy progressively shifted from the Mediterranean and Baltic seas to the Atlantic seaboard, setting the stage for global expansion. (See Map 10–2, page 304.)

The Portuguese Chart the Course

Seventy-seven years before Columbus, who sailed under the flag of Spain, set foot in the Americas, Prince Henry "the Navigator" (1394–1460), brother of the king of Portugal, captured the North African Muslim city of Ceuta. His motives were mercenary and religious, both a quest for gold and spices and the pious work of saving the souls of Muslims and pagans who had no knowledge of Christ. Thus began the Portuguese exploration of the African coast, first in search of gold and slaves, and then by century's end, of a sea route around Africa to Asia's spice markets. Pepper and cloves topped the list of spices, as they both preserved and enhanced the dull diet of most Europeans. Initially the catch of raiders, African slaves were soon taken by Portuguese traders in direct commerce with tribal chiefs, who readily swapped captives for horses, grain, and finished goods (cloth and brassware). Over the second half of the fifteenth century, Portuguese ships delivered 150,000 slaves to Europe.

Before there was a sea route to the East, Europeans could only get spices through the Venetians, who bought or bartered them from Muslim merchants in Egypt and the Ottoman Empire. The Portuguese resolved to beat this powerful Venetian-Muslim monopoly by sailing directly to the source. Overland routes to India and China had long existed, but their transit had become too difficult and unprofitable by the fifteenth century. The route by sea posed a different obstacle and risk: fear of the unknown, making the first voyages of exploration slow and tentative. Venturing down the African coast, the

VOYAGES OF DISCOVERY

Portuguese Claims
Spanish Claims
Line of Demarcation, 1494

Map 10–2 EUROPEAN VOYAGES OF DISCOVERY AND THE COLONIAL CLAIMS OF SPAIN AND PORTUGAL IN THE FIFTEENTH AND SIXTEENTH CENTURIES   The map dramatizes Europe's global expansion in the fifteenth and sixteenth centuries.

Portuguese ships were turned out into the deep ocean by every protruding cape, and the farther out they sailed to round them, the greater the sailors' fear that the winds would not return them to land. Each cape rounded became a victory and a lesson, giving the crews the skills they needed to cross the oceans to the Americas and East Asia.

In addition to spice markets, the voyagers also gained new allies against Western Europe's archenemies, the Muslims. In 1455, a self-interested pope granted the Portuguese explorers all the spoils of war—land, goods, and slaves—from the coast of Guinea in West Africa to the Indies in East Asia. The church expected exploration to lead to mass conversions, a Christian coup as well as a mercantile advantage. The explorers also kept an eye out for a legendary Eastern Christian ruler known as Prester John.

Bartholomew Dias (ca. 1450–1500) pioneered the eastern Portuguese Empire after safely rounding the Cape of Good Hope at the tip of Africa in 1487. A decade later, in 1498, Vasco da Gama (1469–1525) stood on the shores of India. When he returned to Portugal, he carried a cargo of spices worth sixty times the cost of the voyage. Later, the Portuguese established colonies in Goa and Calcutta on the coast of India, whence they challenged the Arabs and the Venetians for control of the spice trade.

The Portuguese had concentrated their explorations on the Indian Ocean. The Spanish turned west, believing they could find a shorter route to the East Indies by sailing across the Atlantic. Instead, Christopher Columbus (1451–1506) discovered the Americas.

The Spanish Voyages of Columbus

Thirty-three days after departing the Canary Islands, on October 12, 1492, Columbus landed in San Salvador (Watlings Island) in the eastern Bahamas. Thinking he was in the East Indies, he mistook his first landfall as an outer island of Japan. The error was understandable given the information he relied on, namely, Marco Polo's thirteenth-century account of his years in China and Martin Behaim's spherical map of the presumed world. That map showed only ocean and Cipangu (Japan) between the west coast of Europe and the east coast of Asia. (See Martin Behaim's map, page 306.) Not until his third voyage to the Caribbean in 1498 did Columbus realize that Cuba was not Japan and South America was not China.

Naked, friendly natives met Columbus and his crew on the beaches of the New World. They were Taino Indians, who spoke a variant of a language known as Arawak. Believing the island on which he landed to be the East Indies, Columbus called these people Indians, a name that stuck with Europeans even after they realized he had actually discovered a new continent. The natives' generosity amazed Columbus, as they freely gave his men all the corn, yams, and sexual favors they desired. "They

never say no," Columbus marveled. He also observed how easily the Spanish could enslave them.

On the heels of Columbus, Amerigo Vespucci (1451–1512), after whom America is named, and Ferdinand Magellan (1480–1521) explored the coastline of South America. Their travels proved that the new lands Columbus had discovered were an entirely unknown continent that opened on the still greater Pacific Ocean. Magellan, who was continuing the search for a westward route to the Indies, made it all the way around South America and across the Pacific to the Philippines, where he was killed in a skirmish with the inhabitants. The remnants of his squadron eventually sailed on to Spain, making them the first sailors to circumnavigate the globe.

Intended and Unintended Consequences   Columbus's first voyage marked the beginning of more than three centuries of a vast Spanish empire in the Americas. What began as voyages of discovery became expeditions of conquest, not unlike the warfare Christian Aragon and Castile waged against Islamic Moors. Those wars had just ended in 1492, and their conclusion imbued the early Spanish explorers with a zeal for conquering and converting non-Christian peoples.

Much to the benefit of Spain, the voyages of discovery created Europe's largest and longest surviving trading bloc and spurred other European countries to undertake their own colonial ventures. The wealth extracted from its American possessions financed Spain's commanding role in the religious and political wars of the sixteenth and seventeenth centuries, while fueling a Europe-wide economic expansion.

European expansion also had a profound biological impact. Europeans introduced numerous new species of fruits, vegetables, and animals into the Americas and brought American species back to Europe. European expansion also spread European diseases. Vast numbers of Native Americans died from measles and smallpox epidemics, while Europeans died from a virulent form of syphilis that may have originated in the Americas.

For the Native Americans, the voyages of discovery were the beginning of a long history of conquest, disease, and slave labor they could neither evade nor survive. In both South and North America, Spanish rule left a lasting imprint of Roman Catholicism, economic dependency, and hierarchical social structure, all still visible today. (See Chapter 18.)

The Spanish Empire in the New World

When the first Spanish explorers arrived, the Aztec Empire dominated Mesoamerica, which stretches from Central Mexico to Guatemala, and the Inca Empire dominated Andean South America. Both were rich, and their conquest promised the Spanish the possibility of acquiring large quantities of gold.

What Columbus knew of the world in 1492 was contained in this map by the Nuremberg geographer Martin Behaim, creator of the first spherical globe of the earth. The ocean section of Behaim's globe is reproduced here. Departing the Canary Islands (in the second section from the right), Columbus expected his first major landfall to be Japan (Cipangu, in the second section from the left). When he landed at San Salvador, he thought he was on the outer island of Japan. Thus, when he arrived in Cuba, he thought he was in Japan. From *Admiral of the Ocean Sea* by Samuel Eliot Morison. Copyright © 1942 by Samuel Eliot Morison; Copyright © renewed 1970 by Samuel Eliot Morison. By permission of Little, Brown and Company, (Inc.)

The Aztecs in Mexico The forebears of the Aztecs had arrived in the Valley of Mexico early in the twelfth century, where they lived as a subservient people. In 1428, however, they began a period of imperial expansion. By the time of Spanish conquest, the Aztecs ruled almost all of central Mexico from their capital Tenochtitlán (modern-day Mexico City). The Aztecs demanded heavy tribute in goods and labor from their subjects and, believing the gods must literally be fed with human blood to guarantee sunshine and fertility, they also took thousands of captives each year for human sacrifice. These policies bred resentment and fear among the subject peoples.

In 1519, Hernán Cortés (1485–1547) landed in Mexico with about five hundred men and a few horses. He opened communication with Moctezuma II (1466–1520), the Aztec emperor. Moctezuma may initially have believed Cortés to be the god Quetzalcoatl, who, according to legend, had been driven away centuries earlier but had promised to return. Whatever the reason, Moctezuma hesitated to confront Cortés, attempting at first to appease him with gold, which only whetted Spanish appetites. Cortés forged alliances with the Aztecs' subject peoples, most importantly, with Tlaxcala, an independent state and traditional enemy of the Aztecs. His forces then marched on Tenochtitlán, where Moctezuma welcomed him. Cortés soon seized Moctezuma, who died in unexplained circumstances. The Aztecs' wary acceptance of the Spaniards turned to open hostility. The Spaniards were driven from Tenochtitlán and were nearly wiped out, but they returned and laid siege to the city. The Aztecs, under their last ruler, Cuauhtemoc (ca. 1495–1525), resisted fiercely but were finally defeated in 1521. Cortés razed Tenochtitlán, building his own capital over its ruins, and proclaimed the Aztec Empire to be New Spain.

Armored Spanish soldiers, under the command of Pedro de Alvarado (d. 1541) and bearing crossbows, engage unprotected and crudely armed Aztecs, who are nonetheless portrayed as larger than life by Spanish artist Diego Duran (sixteenth century). Codex Duran: Pedro de Alvarado (c. 1485–1541), companion-at-arms of Hernando Cortés (1845–1547) besieged by Aztec warriors (vellum) by Diego Duran (16th Century), Codex Duran, Historia De Las Indias (16th century). Biblioteca Nacional, Madrid, Spain. The Bridgeman Art Library International Ltd.

The Incas in Peru   The second great Native American civilization the Spanish conquered was that of the Incas in the highlands of Peru. Like the Aztecs, the Incas also began to expand rapidly in the fifteenth century and, by the time of the Spanish conquest, controlled an enormous empire. Unlike the Aztecs, who extracted tribute from their subject peoples, the Incas compelled their subjects to work for the state on a regular basis.

In 1532, largely inspired by Cortés's example in Mexico, Francisco Pizarro (c. 1478–1541) landed on the western coast of South America with about two hundred men to take on the Inca Empire. Pizarro lured Atahualpa (ca. 1500–1533), the Inca ruler, into a conference and then seized him, killing hundreds of Atahualpa's followers in the process. The imprisoned Atahualpa tried to ransom himself with a hoard of gold, but instead of releasing him, Pizarro executed him in 1533. The Spaniards then captured Cuzco, the Inca capital, but Inca resistance did not end until the 1570s.

The conquests of Mexico and Peru are among the most dramatic and brutal events in modern history. Small military forces armed with advanced weapons subdued, in a remarkably brief time, two powerful peoples. The spread of European diseases, especially smallpox, among the Native Americans also aided the conquest. But beyond the drama and bloodshed, these conquests, as well as those of other Native American peoples, marked a fundamental turning point. Whole civilizations with long histories and enormous social, architectural, and technological achievements were destroyed. Native American cultures endured, accommodating themselves to European dominance, but there was never any doubt about which culture had the upper hand. In that sense, the Spanish conquests of the early sixteenth century marked the beginning of the transformation of South America into Latin America.

The Church in Spanish America

Roman Catholic priests had accompanied the earliest explorers and the conquerors of the Native Americans. Steeped with the social and religious ideals of Christian humanism, these first clergy members believed they could foster Erasmus's concept of the "philosophy of Christ" in the New World. They were filled with zeal not only to convert the inhabitants to Christianity, but also to bring to them European learning and civilization.

Tension, however, existed between the early Spanish conquerors and the mendicant friars who sought to minister to the Native Americans. Without conquest, the church could not convert the Native Americans, but the priests often deplored the harsh conditions imposed on the native peoples. By far the most effective and outspoken clerical critic of the Spanish conquerors was Bartolomé de Las Casas (1474–1566), a Dominican. He contended that conquest was not necessary for conversion. One result of his campaign was new royal regulations to protect the Indians after 1550.

Another result of Las Casas's criticism was the emergence of the "Black Legend," according to which all Spanish treatment of the Native Americans was unprincipled and inhumane. (See "A Defense of American Natives," page 308.) Those who created this view of Spanish behavior drew heavily on Las Casas's writings. Although substantially true, the "Black Legend" exaggerated the case against Spain. Certainly the rulers of the native empires— as the Aztec demands for sacrificial victims attest—had often themselves been exceedingly cruel to their subjects.

By the end of the sixteenth century, the church in Spanish America had become largely an institution upholding the colonial status quo. Although individual priests defended the communal rights of Indian peoples, the colonial church prospered as the Spanish elite prospered by exploiting the resources and peoples of the New World. The church became a great landowner through crown grants and bequests from Catholics who died in the New World. The monasteries took on an economic as well as a spiritual life of their own. Whatever its concern for the spiritual welfare of the Native Americans, the church remained one of the indications that Spanish

A DEFENSE OF AMERICAN NATIVES

Bartolomé de Las Casas (1474–1566), a Dominican missionary to the New World, describes the native people of the islands of the Caribbean and their systematic slaughter by the Spanish.

Is Las Casas romanticizing the American natives? Does he truly respect their native culture and beliefs?

This infinite multitude of people was so created by God that they were without fraud . . . or malice. . . . Toward the Spaniards whom they serve, patient, meek, and peaceful, [they] lay aside all contentious and tumultuous thoughts, and live without any hatred or desire of revenge. The people are most delicate and tender, enjoying such a feeble constitution of body as does not permit them to endure labour. . . . The[ir] nation [the West Indies] is very poor and indigent, possessing little, and by reason that they gape not after temporal goods, [being] neither proud nor ambitious. Their diet is such that the most holy hermit cannot feed more sparingly in the wildernesse. They go naked . . . and a poor shag mantle . . . is their greatest and their warmest covering. They lie upon mats; only those who have larger fortunes lie upon a kind of net which is tied at the four corners and so fasten'd to the roof, which the Indians in their natural language call *Hamecks* [hammocks]. They are of a very apprehensive and docile wit, and capable of all good learning, and very apt to receive our Religion, which when they have but once tasted [it], they are carried [off] with a very ardent and zealous desire to make further progress in it; so that I have heard divers Spaniards confess that they had nothing else to hinder them from enjoying heaven, but the ignorance of the true God.

To these quiet Lambs, endued with such blessed qualities, came the Spaniards like most cruel Tygres, Wolves, and Lions . . . for these forty years, minding nothing else but the slaughter of these unfortunate wretches . . . [whom] they have so cruelly and inhumanely butchered, [so] that of three millions of people which Hispaniola [modern Haiti and the Dominican Republic] itself did contain, there are left remaining alive scarce three hundred persons. And the island of Cuba . . . lies wholly desert, untilled and ruined. The islands of St. John and Jamaica lie waste and desolate. The Lycayan islands neighboring to the north upon Cuba and Hispaniola . . . are now totally unpeopled and destroyed; the inhabitants thereof amounting to above 500,000 souls, partly killed, and partly forced away to work in other places. . . . Other islands there were near the island of St. John, more than thirty in number, which were totally made desert. All which islands . . . lie now altogether solitary without any people or inhabitant.

Bartolomé de Las Casas, *The Tears of the Indians*, trans. by John Phillips (1656), from reprint of original edition (Stanford, CA: Academic Reprints, n.d.), pp. 2–4.

America was a conquered world. Those who spoke for the church did not challenge Spanish domination or any but the most extreme modes of Spanish economic exploitation. By the end of the colonial era in the late eighteenth century, the Roman Catholic Church had become one of the most conservative forces in Latin America.

The Economy of Exploitation

From the beginning, both the Native Americans and their lands were drawn into the Atlantic economy and the world of competitive European commercialism. For the Indians of Latin America and, somewhat later, the black peoples of Africa, that drive for gain meant forced labor.

The colonial economy of Latin America had three major components: mining, agriculture, and shipping. Each involved labor, servitude, and the intertwining of the New World economy with that of Spain.

Mining   The early *conquistadores*, or "conquerors," were primarily interested in gold, but by the mid-sixteenth century, silver mining provided the chief source of metallic wealth. The great mining centers were Potosí in Peru and somewhat smaller sites in northern Mexico. The Spanish crown received one fifth (the *quinto*) of all mining revenues. For this reason, the crown maintained a monopoly over the production and sale of mercury, required in the silver-smelting process. Exploring for silver continued throughout the colonial era. Its production by forced labor for the benefit of Spaniards and the Spanish crown epitomized the wholly extractive economy that stood at the foundation of colonial life.

Agriculture The major rural and agricultural institution of the Spanish colonies was the **hacienda**, a large landed estate owned by persons originally born in Spain (*peninsulares*) or persons of Spanish descent born in America (*creoles*). Laborers on the *hacienda* were usually subject in some legal way to the owner and were rarely free to move from working for one landowner to another.

The *hacienda* economy produced two major products: foodstuffs for mining areas and urban centers and leather goods used in mining machinery. Both farming and ranching were subordinate to the mining economy.

In the West Indies, the basic agricultural unit was the plantation. In Cuba, Hispaniola, Puerto Rico, and other islands, the labor of black slaves from Africa produced sugar to supply an almost insatiable demand for the product in Europe.

A final major area of economic activity in the Spanish colonies was urban service occupations, including government offices, the legal profession, and shipping. Those who worked in these occupations were either *peninsulares* or *creoles*, with the former dominating more often than not.

Labor Servitude All of this extractive and exploitive economic activity required labor, and the Spanish in the New World decided early that the native population would supply it. A series of social devices was used to draw them into the new economic life the Spanish imposed.

The first of these was the **encomienda**, a formal grant of the right to the labor of a specific number of Indians, usually a few hundred, but sometimes thousands, for a particular period of time. The *encomienda* was in decline by the mid-sixteenth century because the Spanish monarchs feared its holders might become too powerful. There were also humanitarian objections to this particular kind of exploitation of the Indians.

The passing of the *encomienda* led to a new arrangement of labor servitude: the *repartimiento*. This device required adult male Indians to devote a certain number of days of labor annually to Spanish economic enterprises. In the mines of Peru, the *repartimiento* was known as the *mita*, the Inca term for their labor tax. *Repartimiento* service was often harsh, and some Indians did not survive their stint. The limitation on labor time led some Spanish managers to abuse their workers on the assumption that fresh workers would soon replace them.

The eventual shortage of workers and the crown's pressure against extreme versions of forced labor led to the use of free labor. The freedom, however, was more in appearance than reality. Free Indian laborers were required to purchase goods from the landowner or mine owner, to whom they became forever indebted. This form of exploitation, known as *debt peonage*, continued in Latin America long after the nineteenth-century wars of liberation.

Black slavery was the final mode of forced or subservient labor in the New World. Both the Spanish and the Portuguese had earlier used African slaves in Europe. The sugar plantations of the West Indies and Brazil now became the major center of black slavery.

The conquest, the forced labor of the economy of exploitation, and the introduction of European diseases had devastating demographic consequences for the Native Americans. For centuries, Europeans had lived in a far more complex human and animal environment than Native Americans did. They had frequent contact with different ethnic and racial groups and with a variety of domestic animals. Such interaction helped them develop strong immune systems that enabled them to survive measles, smallpox, and typhoid. Native Americans, by contrast, grew up in a simpler and more sterile environment and were defenseless against these diseases. Within a generation, the native population of New Spain (Mexico) was reduced to an estimated 8 percent of its numbers, from 25 million to 2 million.

The Impact on Europe

Among contemporary European intellectuals, Columbus's discovery increased skepticism about the wisdom of the ancients. If traditional knowledge about the world had been so wrong geographically, how trustworthy was it on other matters? For many, Columbus's discovery demonstrated the folly of relying on any fixed body of presumed authoritative knowledge. Both in Europe and in the New World, there were those who condemned the explorers' treatment of American natives, as more was learned about their cruelty. (See "Montaigne on 'Cannibals' in Foreign Lands," page 310.) Three centuries later, however, on the third centenary of Columbus's discovery (1792), the great thinkers of the age lionized Columbus for having opened up new possibilities for civilization and morality. By establishing new commercial contacts among different peoples of the world, Columbus was said to have made cooperation, civility, and peace among them indispensable. Enlightenment thinkers drew parallels between the discovery of America and the invention of the printing press—both portrayed as world-historical events opening new eras in communication and globalization, an early multicultural experiment.[4]

[4]Cf. Anthony Pagden, "The Impact of the New World on the Old: The History of an Idea," *Renaissance and Modern Studies* 30 (1986): pp. 1–11.

MONTAIGNE ON "CANNIBALS" IN FOREIGN LANDS

The French philosopher Michel de Montaigne (1533–1592) had seen a Brazilian native in Rouen in 1562, who was alleged to be a cannibal. The experience gave rise to an essay on the subject of what constitutes a "savage." Montaigne concluded that no people on earth were more barbarous than Europeans, who take natives of other lands captive.

Is Montaigne romanticizing the New World natives? Is he being too hard on Europeans? Had the Aztecs or Incas had the ability to discover and occupy Europe, would they have enslaved and exploited Europeans?

Now, to return to my subject, I think there is nothing barbarous and savage in that nation [Brazil], from what I have been told . . . Each man calls barbarism whatever is not his own practice; for indeed it seems we have no other test of truth and reason than the example and pattern of the opinions and customs of the country we live in. There [we] always [find] the perfect religion, the perfect government, the perfect and accomplished manners in all things. Those [foreign] people are wild, just as we call wild the fruits that Nature has produced by herself and in her normal course; where really it is those that we have changed artificially and led astray from the common order that we should rather call wild. The former retain alive and vigorous their genuine virtues and properties, which we have debased in the latter by adapting them to gratify our corrupted taste. And yet for all that, the savor and delicacy of some uncultivated fruits of those countries is quite as excellent, even to our taste, as that of our own. It is not reasonable that [our human] art should win the place of honor over our great and powerful mother Nature. We have so overloaded the beauty and richness of her works by our inventions that we have quite smoth-ered her. Yet wherever her purity shines forth, she wonderfully puts to shame our vain and frivolous attempts: "Ivy comes readier without our care;/In lonely caves the arbutus grows more fair;/No art with artless bird song can compare."[1] All our efforts cannot even succeed in reproducing the nest of the tiniest little bird, its contexture, its beauty and convenience; or even the web of the puny spider. All things, says Plato,[2] are produced by nature, by fortune, or by art; the greatest and most beautiful by one or the other of the first two, the least and most imperfect by the last.

These nations, then, seem to me "barbarous" in this sense, that they have been fashioned very little by the human mind, and are still very close to their original naturalness. The laws of nature still rule them, very little corrupted by ours; and they are in such a state of purity that I am sometimes vexed that they were unknown earlier, in the days when there were men able to judge them better than we.

[1]Propertius 1.11.10.
[2]Laws 10.

From *The Complete Essays of Montaigne*, trans. by Donald M. Frame (Stanford, CA: Stanford University Press, 1958), pp. 153–154.

On the material side, the influx of spices and precious metals into Europe from the new Portuguese and Spanish Empires was a mixed blessing. It contributed to a steady rise in prices during the sixteenth century that created an inflation rate estimated at 2 percent a year. The new supply of bullion from the Americas joined with enlarged European production to increase greatly the amount of coinage in circulation, and this increase, in turn, fed inflation. Fortunately, the increase in prices was by and large spread over a long period and was not sudden. Prices doubled in Spain by 1550, quadrupled by 1600. In Luther's Wittenberg in Germany, the cost of basic food and clothing increased almost 100 percent between 1519 and 1540. Generally, wages and rents remained well behind the rise in prices.

The new wealth enabled governments and private entrepreneurs to sponsor basic research and expansion in the printing, shipping, mining, textile, and weapons industries. There is also evidence of large-scale government planning in such ventures as the French silk industry and the Habsburg-Fugger development of mines in Austria and Hungary.

In the thirteenth and fourteenth centuries, capitalist institutions and practices had already begun to develop in the rich Italian cities (for example, the Florentine banking houses of Bardi and Peruzzi). Those who owned the means of production, either privately or corporately, were clearly distinguished from the workers who operated them. Wherever possible, entrepreneurs created monopolies in basic goods. High interest was charged on loans—actual, if not legal, usury. The "capitalist" virtues of thrift, industry, and orderly planning were everywhere in evidence—all intended to permit the free and efficient accumulation of wealth.

The late fifteenth and the sixteenth centuries saw the maturation of this type of capitalism together with its attendant social problems. The Medicis of Florence grew rich as bankers of the pope, as did the Fuggers of Augsburg, who bankrolled Habsburg rulers. The Fuggers lent Charles I of Spain more than 500,000 florins to buy his election as the Holy Roman Emperor in 1519 and boasted they had created the emperor. The new wealth and industrial expansion also raised the expectations of the poor and the ambitious and heightened the reactionary tendencies of the wealthy. This effect, in turn, aggravated the traditional social divisions between the clergy and the laity, the urban patriciate and the guilds, and the landed nobility and the agrarian peasantry.

These divisions indirectly prepared the way for the Reformation as well, by making many people critical of traditional institutions and open to new ideas—especially those that seemed to promise greater freedom and a chance at a better life.

In Perspective

As it recovered from national wars during the late Middle Ages, Europe saw the establishment of permanent centralized states and regional governments. The foundations of modern France, Spain, England, Germany, and Italy were laid at this time. As rulers imposed their will on regions outside their immediate domains, the "one" progressively took control of the "many," and previously divided lands came together as nations.

Thanks to the work of Byzantine and Islamic scholars, ancient Greek science and scholarship found its way into the West in these centuries. Europeans had been separated from their classical cultural heritage for almost eight centuries. No other world civilization had experienced such a disjunction from its cultural past. The discovery of classical civilization occasioned a rebirth of intellectual and artistic activity in both southern and northern Europe. One result was the splendor of the Italian Renaissance, whose scholarship, painting, and sculpture remain among Western Europe's most impressive achievements.

Ancient learning was not the only discovery of the era. New political unity spurred both royal greed and national ambition. By the late fifteenth century, Europeans were in a position to venture far away to the shores of Africa, the southern and eastern coasts of Asia, and the New World of the Americas. European discovery was not the only outcome of these voyages: The exploitation of the peoples and lands of the New World revealed a dark side of Western civilization. Some penalties were paid even then. The influx of New World gold and silver created new human and economic problems on the European mainland. Some Europeans even began to question their civilization's traditional values.

REVIEW QUESTIONS

1. What was Jacob Burckhardt's interpretation of the Renaissance? What criticisms have been leveled against it? What did the term mean in the context of fifteenth- and sixteenth-century Italy?
2. How would you define Renaissance humanism? In what ways was the Renaissance a break with the Middle Ages, and in what ways did it owe its existence to medieval civilization?
3. Who were some of the famous literary and artistic figures of the Italian Renaissance? What did they have in common that might be described as "the spirit of the Renaissance"?
4. Why did the French invade Italy in 1494? How did this event trigger Italy's political decline? How did the actions of Pope Julius II and the ideas of Niccolò Machiavelli signify a new era in Italian civilization?
5. A common assumption is that creative work proceeds best in periods of calm and peace. Given the combination of political instability and cultural productivity in Renaissance Italy, do you think this assumption is valid?
6. How did the Renaissance in the north differ from the Italian Renaissance? In what ways was Erasmus the embodiment of the northern Renaissance?
7. What factors led to the voyages of discovery? Why were the Portuguese interested in finding a route to the East? Why did Columbus sail west across the Atlantic in 1492?

SUGGESTED READINGS

D. Abulafia, *The Discovery of Mankind: Atlantic Encounters in the Age of Columbus* (2008). The latest telling of the European invasion of the New World.

L. B. Alberti, *The Family in Renaissance Florence*, trans. by R. N. Watkins (1962). A contemporary humanist, who never married, explains how a family should behave.

K. Atchity, ed., *The Renaissance Reader* (1996). The Renaissance in its own words.

H. Baron, *The Crisis of the Early Italian Renaissance*, Vols. 1 and 2 (1966). A major work on the civic dimension of Italian humanism.

G. A. Brucker, *Giovanni and Lusanna: Love and Marriage in Renaissance Florence* (1986). Love in the Renaissance shown to be more Bergman than Fellini.

J. Burckhardt, *The Civilization of the Renaissance in Italy* (1958). Modern edition of an old nineteenth-century classic that still has as many defenders as detractors.

R. E. Conrad, *Children of God's Fire: A Documentary History of Black Slavery in Brazil* (1983). Not for the squeamish.

L. Hanke, *Bartholomé de Las Casas: An Interpretation of His Life and Writings* (1951). Biography of the great Dominican critic of Spanish exploitation of Native Americans.

J. Hankins, *Plato in the Renaissance* (1992). A magisterial study of how Plato was read and interpreted by Renaissance scholars.

D. Herlihy and C. Klapisch-Zuber, *Tuscans and Their Families* (1985). Important work based on unique demographic data that give the reader a new appreciation of quantitative history.

J. C. Hutchison, *Albrecht Dürer: A Biography* (1990).

L. Martines, *Power and Imagination: City States in Renaissance Italy* (1980). Stimulating account of cultural and political history.

S. E. Morrison, *Admiral of the Ocean Sea: A Life of Christopher Columbus* (1946). Still the best Columbus read.

E. Panofsky, *Meaning in the Visual Arts* (1955). Eloquent treatment of Renaissance art.

J. H. Parry, *The Age of Reconnaissance* (1964). A comprehensive account of exploration in the years 1450 to 1650.

I. A. Richter, ed., *The Notebooks of Leonardo da Vinci* (1985). The master in his own words.

A. Wheatcroft, *The Habsburgs* (1995). The dynasty that ruled the center of late medieval and early modern Europe.

C. C. Willard, *Christine de Pizan* (1984). Demonstration of what an educated woman could accomplish in the Renaissance.

For additional learning resources related to this chapter, please go to www.myhistorylab.com

Painted on the eve of the Reformation, Matthias Grunewald's (ca. 1480–1528) *Crucifixion* shows a Christ who takes all the sins of the world into his own body, as his mother, Mary Magdalene, and John the Baptist share the pain of his afflictions.   Musée Unterlinden, Colmar, France/SuperStock

11

The Age of Reformation

KEY TOPICS

- **The social and religious background of the Reformation**

- **Martin Luther's challenge to the church and the course of the Reformation in Germany**

- **The Reformation in Switzerland, France, and England**

- **Transitions in family life between medieval and modern times**

IN THE SECOND decade of the sixteenth century, a long-building, powerful religious movement began in Saxony in Germany and spread rapidly throughout northern Europe, deeply affecting society and politics, as well as the spiritual lives of men and women. Attacking what they believed to be burdensome superstitions that robbed people of both their money and their peace of mind, Protestant reformers led a broad revolt against the medieval church. In a short time, hundreds of thousands of people from all social classes set aside the beliefs of centuries and adopted a more simplified religious practice.

The Protestant Reformation challenged aspects of the Renaissance, especially its tendency to follow classical sources in glorifying human nature and its loyalty to traditional religion. Protestants were more impressed by the human potential for evil than by the inclination to do good. They encouraged parents, teachers, and magistrates to be firm disciplinarians, but they also embraced many Renaissance values, especially educational reforms and the training of students in ancient languages. Like the Italian humanists, the Protestant reformers prized the tools that allowed them to go directly to the original sources. For the reformers, however, this meant the study of the Hebrew and Greek scriptures, enabling them to root their challenges to traditional authority and institutions in biblical antiquity.

▼ Society and Religion

The Protestant **Reformation** occurred at a time of sharp conflict between the emerging nation-states of Europe bent on conformity and centralization within their realms and the self-governing towns and villages long accustomed to running their own affairs. Since the late fourteenth century, the territorial ruler's law and custom had progressively overridden local law and custom almost everywhere. The towns remained keenly sensitive to the loss of traditional rights and freedoms. Many townspeople and village folk perceived in the religious revolt an ally in their struggle to remain politically free and independent.

Social and Political Conflict

The Reformation broke out first in the free imperial cities of Germany and Switzerland, and the basic tenets of Lutheran and Zwinglian Protestantism remained visible in subsequent Protestant movements. There were about sixty-five free imperial cities, each a small kingdom unto itself. Most had Protestant movements but with mixed success and duration. Some quickly turned Protestant and remained so. Some were Protestant only for a short time. Still others developed mixed confessions. Frowning on sectarianism and aggressive proselytizing, they made it possible for Catholics and Protestants to live side by side with appropriate barriers between them.

A seeming life-and-death struggle with higher princely or royal authority was not the only conflict late medieval cities were experiencing. They also coped with deep social and political divisions. Certain groups favored the Reformation more than others. In many places, guilds whose members were economically prospering and socially rising were in the forefront of the Reformation. The printers' guild is a prominent example. Its members were literate, sophisticated about the world, and belonged to a rapidly growing industry. They also had an economic stake in fanning religious conflict with Protestant propaganda, which many, of course, also sincerely believed. Guilds with a history of opposition to reigning governmental authority also stood out among early Protestant supporters, regardless of education level. Evidence also suggests that people who felt pushed around and bullied by either local or distant authority—a guild by an autocratic local government, or a city or region by a powerful prince or king—often perceived an ally in the Protestant movement.

Social and political experience naturally influenced religious change in town and countryside. A Protestant sermon or pamphlet praising religious freedom seemed directly relevant, for example, to the townspeople of German and Swiss cities who faced incorporation into the territory of a powerful local prince, who looked on them as his subjects rather than as free citizens. When Martin Luther and his followers, who wrote, preached, and sang about a priesthood of all believers, scorned the authority of ecclesiastical landlords and ridiculed papal laws as arbitrary human inventions, they touched political as well as religious nerves. This was also true in the villages and in the towns. Like city dwellers, the peasants on the land also heard in the Protestant sermon and pamphlet a promise of political liberation, even a degree of social betterment. More than the townspeople, the peasants found their traditional liberties—from fishing and hunting rights to representation at local diets—progressively being chipped away by the secular and ecclesiastical landlords of the age.

Popular Religious Movements and Criticism of the Church

The Protestant Reformation could also not have occurred without the monumental challenges to the medieval church during its "exile" in Avignon, the Great Schism, the Conciliar period, and the Renaissance papacy. For sizable numbers of people in future Protestant lands, the medieval church had ceased to provide a viable foundation for religious piety. Many intellectuals and laypeople felt a sense of spiritual crisis. At the Diet of Worms in 1521 (see page 320), the German nobility presented the emperor with a list of 102 "oppressive [church] burdens and abuses" said to be corrupting the care of German souls. Between the secular pretensions of the papacy and the dry teaching of Scholastic theologians, laity and clerics alike began to seek a more heartfelt, idealistic, and—often, in the eyes of the pope—heretical religious piety. The late Middle Ages were marked by independent lay and clerical efforts to reform local religious practice and by widespread experimentation with new religious forms.

A variety of factors contributed to the growing lay criticism of the church. Urban laypeople were increasingly knowledgeable about the world around them and about the rulers who controlled their lives. They traveled widely—as soldiers, pilgrims, explorers, and traders. New postal systems and the printing press increased the information at their disposal. A new age of books and libraries raised literacy and heightened curiosity. Laypeople were able to shape the cultural life of their communities.

From the Albigensians, Waldensians, Beguines, and Beghards in the thirteenth century to the Lollards and Hussites in the fifteenth, lay religious movements shared a common goal of religious simplicity in the imitation of Jesus. Almost everywhere, the laity was inspired by ideals of apostolic poverty in religion. A simple religion of love and self-sacrifice like that of Jesus and the first disciples seemed to be the ideal. To that end, the laity sought a more egalitarian church—one that gave the members as well as the head of the church a voice—and also a more spiritual church—one that lived manifestly according to its New Testament model.

The Modern Devotion   One of the more constructive lay religious movements in northern Europe on the eve of the Reformation was that of the Brothers of the Common Life, also known as the Modern Devotion, a kind of boarding school for reform-minded laity. The brothers fostered religious life outside formal church offices and apart from formal religious vows—a lay religious life of prayer and study without surrendering the world. Centered at Zwolle and Deventer in the Netherlands, the brother and (less numerous) sister houses of the Modern Devotion spread rapidly throughout northern Europe and influenced parts of southern Europe as well. In these houses clerics and laity shared a common life, stressing individual piety and practical religion. Lay members were not expected to take special religious vows or to wear a special religious dress, nor did they abandon their ordinary secular vocations.

The brothers were also educators. They worked as copyists, sponsored many religious and some classical publications, ran hospices for poor students, and conducted schools for the young—especially boys preparing for the priesthood or a monastic vocation. As youths, the future philosopher Nicholas of Cusa, the humanist and Hebraist Johannes Reuchlin, and Desiderius Erasmus, the proclaimed "prince of the humanists," were looked after by these brothers. Erasmus later formulated his own "philosophy of Christ" after what he had learned there. Thomas à Kempis (d. 1471) summarized the philosophy of the brothers in what became the most popular religious book of the period, the *Imitation of Christ*. This semimystical guide to the inner life was intended primarily for monks and nuns but was also widely read by laity who wanted to pursue the ascetic life.

The Modern Devotion has been seen as the source of humanist, Protestant, and Catholic reform movements in the sixteenth century. Some scholars, however, believe it represented an individualistic approach to religion, indifferent and even hostile to the sacramental piety of the church and papal authority. It was, in truth, a conservative movement. The brothers retained the old clerical doctrines and values but placed them within the new framework of an active common life. Their practices clearly met a need for a more personal piety and a more informed religious life. Their movement appeared at a time when the laity was demanding good preaching in the **vernacular** and taking the initiative to endow special funds for preaching in cities and towns to ensure it.

Lay Control over Religious Life   On the eve of the Reformation, Rome's international network of church offices, which had unified Europe religiously during the Middle Ages, was falling apart in many areas. This collapse was hurried along by a growing sense of regional identity, an increasingly competent local secular administration, and a newly emerging nationalism. The long-entrenched *benefice* system of the medieval church had permitted important ecclesiastical posts to be sold to the highest bidders and had often failed to enforce the requirement that priests and bishops had to live in their parishes and dioceses. Such a system threatened a vibrant, lay spiritual life. The substitutes hired by nonresident holders of *benefices* frequently lived elsewhere, preferably in Rome. They milked the revenues of their offices, performed their clerical chores mechanically, if they did them at all, and had neither firsthand knowledge of, nor much sympathy for, local spiritual needs and problems. Rare was the late medieval German town that did not have complaints about the maladministration, concubinage, or financial greed of its clergy—especially the higher clergy (bishops, abbots, and prelates).

Communities loudly protested the financial and spiritual abuses of the medieval church long before Luther published his famous summary of economic grievances in a treatise entitled *Address to the Christian Nobility of the German Nation* (1520). The sale of indulgences, in particular, had been repeatedly attacked before Luther came on the scene. On the eve of the Reformation, this practice had expanded to permit people to buy release from time in purgatory for both themselves and their deceased loved ones. Rulers and magistrates had little objection to their sale and might even encourage it, as long as a generous portion of the income the sales generated remained in the local coffers. Yet when an indulgence was offered primarily for the benefit of distant interests, as with the sale of indulgences to raise money for a new Saint Peter's basilica in Rome that Luther protested, resistance arose also for strictly financial reasons: their sale drained away local revenues.

The sale of indulgences would not end until rulers found new ways to profit from religion and the laity discovered more effective remedies for religious anxiety. The Reformation provided the former by sanctioning the secular dissolution of monasteries and the confiscation of ecclesiastical properties. It promised the latter in its new theology of justification by faith in God and a life of self-sacrificial service to one's neighbor.

City governments also undertook to improve local religious life on the eve of the Reformation by endowing preacherships. These positions, supported by *benefices*, made possible the hiring of well-trained pastors who provided regular preaching and pastoral care beyond the performance of the Mass. These preacherships often became platforms for Protestants.

Magistrates also carefully restricted the growth of ecclesiastical properties and clerical privileges. During the Middle Ages, canon and civil law had recognized special clerical rights in both property and person. Because they were holy places of "sacral peace" and asylum, churches and monasteries were exempted from the taxes and laws that affected others. Law also deemed it inappropriate for holy persons (clergy) to burden themselves with such "dirty jobs" as military service, compulsory labor, standing watch at city gates, and other ordinary civic obligations. Nor was it thought right that the laity should sit in judgment on those who were their shepherds and intermediaries with God. The clergy, accordingly, came to enjoy an immunity from the jurisdiction of civil courts.

Already on the eve of the Reformation, measures were passed to restrict these clerical privileges and to end their abuses. Governments grew tired of church interference in what to them were strictly secular political spheres of competence and authority. Secular authorities accordingly began to scrutinize the church's acquisition of new properties, finding ways to get around its right of asylum when it interrupted the administration of justice, and generally bringing the clergy under local tax codes.

▼ Martin Luther and the German Reformation to 1525

Unlike England and France, late medieval Germany lacked the political unity to enforce "national" religious reforms during the late Middle Ages. There were no lasting Statutes of Provisors and Praemunire, as in England, nor a Pragmatic Sanction of Bourges, as in France, limiting papal jurisdiction and taxation on a national scale. What had happened on a unified national level in England and France occurred only locally and piecemeal within German territories and towns. As popular resentment of clerical immunities and ecclesiastical abuses spread among German cities and towns, an unorganized "national" opposition to Rome formed. German humanists had long given voice to such criticism, and by 1517 it was pervasive enough to

provide a solid foundation for Martin Luther's protest of indulgences and the theology that legitimated them.

The son of a successful Thüringian miner, Luther (1483–1546) was educated in Mansfeld, Magdeburg (where the Brothers of the Common Life had been his teachers) and Eisenach. Between 1501 and 1505, he attended the University of Erfurt, where the nominalist teachings of William of Ockham and Gabriel Biel (d. 1495) prevailed. (See Chapter 8.) After receiving his master-of-arts degree in 1505, Luther registered with the law faculty in accordance with his parents' wishes. But he never began the study of law. To the disappointment of his family, he instead entered the Order of the Hermits of Saint Augustine in Erfurt on July 17, 1505. That decision had apparently been building for some time and was resolved during a lightning storm in which a young Luther, terrified and crying out to Saint Anne for assistance (she was the patron saint of travelers in distress), promised to enter a monastery if he escaped death.

Ordained in 1507, Luther pursued a traditional course of study. In 1510, he journeyed to Rome on the business of his order, finding there justification for the many criticisms of the church he had heard in Germany. In 1511, he moved to the Augustinian monastery in Wittenberg, where he earned his doctorate in theology in 1512, thereafter, to become a leader within the monastery, the new university, and the spiritual life of the city.

Justification by Faith Alone

Luther was especially plagued by the disproportion between his own sense of sinfulness and the perfect righteousness God required for salvation, according to traditional church teaching. Luther came to despise the phrase "righteousness of God," because it demanded of him a perfection neither he nor any other human being could attain. His insight into the meaning of "justification by faith alone" (*sola fide*) was a gradual process between 1513 and 1518. The righteousness that God demands, he concluded, did not result from charitable acts and religious ceremonies but was given in full measure to any and all who believe in and trust Jesus Christ as their perfect righteousness satisfying to God.

The medieval church had always taught that salvation was a joint venture, a combination of divine mercy and human good works, what God alone could do and what man was expected to do in return. Luther also believed that faith without charitable service to one's neighbor was dead. The Christian did not fulfill all the due obligations of a Christian life by simply saying, "I believe," and thereafter did as he pleased. The issue was not whether good works should be done, but how those works should be regarded. It was unbiblical, Luther argued, to treat works as contributing to one's eternal salvation, something only an almighty God could bestow. He also believed that the church's conditioning of salvation on

A Closer LOOK

A SAINT AT PEACE IN THE GRASP OF TEMPTATION

MARTIN SCHONGAUER (c. 1430–1491), the best engraver in the Upper Rhine, portrays the devil's temptation of St. Anthony in the wilderness as a robust physical attack by demons rather than the traditional melancholic introspection.

Unlike the saint, the demons look perplexed and disbelieving, as their every thrust fails to penetrate.

Although the demons are all over him, Anthony remains untouched. The artist's remarkably distinct lines keep saint and demons apart, reinforcing the saint's inner peace and serenity.

National Gallery of Art, Washington, DC

This rendering of faith as serenity amid the most brutal assault anticipates Martin Luther's great hymn of the Reformation: "A Mighty Fortress Is Our God," in which it is said that "one little word" (belief in Christ) slays the devil and his minions.

To examine this image in an interactive fashion, please go to www.myhistorylab.com

PEARSON
myhistorylab

good works left many Christians only counting their merits and demerits, unable to act selflessly, and struggling to maintain inner peace of mind.

Good works were expected over a lifetime, Luther taught, but not because they earned salvation. The believer who is bound to Christ by faith already possesses God's perfect righteousness. It is this knowledge of faith that sets narcissistic souls free to serve their neighbors selflessly. Such service is ethical, not soteriological—a good work, not a saving work. Inspired by the security faith conveys, such works belong to one's neighbor, who needs help, not to God in heaven, who has everything. God is pleased when those who believe in him do good works, and he expects his people always to do them, but he does not take those works into account when he is merciful and bestows eternal life, which would make God a puppet of man.

The Attack on Indulgences

An **indulgence** was a remission of the temporal penalty imposed on penitents by priests as a "work of satisfaction" for their confessed mortal sins. According to medieval theology, after the priest absolved a penitent of guilt for sin, the penitent still remained under an eternal penalty, a punishment God justly imposed. Priestly absolution, however, was said to transform this eternal penalty into a temporal penalty, a manageable "work of satisfaction" a penitent might perform here and now by

prayers, fasting, almsgiving, retreats, and/or pilgrimages. Penitents who defaulted on such prescribed works of satisfaction could expect to suffer for them in purgatory for an indefinite period of time before entering heaven.

Indulgences were originally given to Crusaders who could not complete their penances because they had fallen in battle. By the late Middle Ages, indulgences had become an aid to laypeople made genuinely anxious by their fear of a future suffering in purgatory for neglected penances or unrepented sins. In 1343, Pope Clement VI (r. 1342–1352) proclaimed the existence of a "treasury of merit," an infinite reservoir of good works in the church's possession that could be dispensed at the pope's discretion. On the basis of this alleged treasury, the church sold "letters of indulgence," which made good on the works of satisfaction owed by penitents. In 1476, Pope Sixtus IV (r. 1471–1484) extended indulgences to the unrepented sins of all Christians in purgatory.

By Luther's time, indulgences were regularly dispensed for small cash payments, modest sums that were regarded as a good work of almsgiving. Indulgence preachers presented them to the laity as remitting not only their own future punishments, but also those of dead relatives presumed still to be suffering in purgatory.

In 1517, Pope Leo X (r. 1513–1521) revived a plenary Jubilee Indulgence that had first been issued by Pope Julius II (r. 1503–1513), the proceeds of which were to rebuild St. Peter's Basilica in Rome. Such an indulgence promised for-

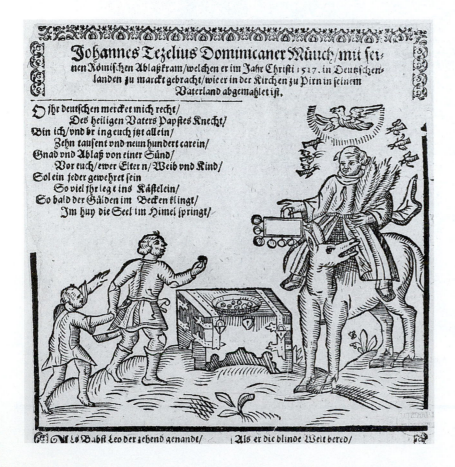

A contemporary caricature depicts John Tetzel, the famous indulgence preacher. The last lines of the jingle read, "As soon as gold in the basin rings, right then the soul to Heaven springs." It was Tetzel's preaching that spurred Luther to publish his ninety-five theses.   Courtesy Stiftung Lutherge-denkstaten in Sachsen-Anhalt/Lutherhalle, Wittenberg giveness of all outstanding unrepented sins upon the completion of certain acts. That indulgence was subsequently preached on the borders of Saxony in the territories of the future Archbishop Albrecht of Mainz, who was much in need of revenues because of the large debts he had incurred to gain a papal dispensation to hold three ecclesiastical appointments at one and the same time.

The selling of the indulgence became a joint venture by Albrecht, the Augsburg banking house of Fugger, and Pope Leo X, with half the proceeds going to the pope and half to Albrecht and his creditors. The famous indulgence preacher John Tetzel (d. 1519) was enlisted to preach the indulgence in Albrecht's territories. A seasoned professional, he knew how to stir ordinary people to action. As he exhorted on one occasion,

Don't you hear the voices of your dead parents and other relatives crying out, "Have mercy on us, for we suffer great punishment and pain. From this you could release us with a few alms. . . . We have created you, fed you, cared for you, and left you our temporal goods. Why do you treat us so cruelly and leave us to suffer in the flames, when it takes only a little to save us?"[1]

When Luther posted his ninety-five theses against indulgences on the door of Castle Church in Wittenberg (October 31, 1517), he protested especially the impression Tetzel created that indulgences remitted sins and released unrepentant sinners from punishment in purgatory. Luther believed these claims went far beyond the traditional practice and seemed to make salvation something that could be bought and sold.

Election of Charles V

The ninety-five theses were embraced by Nuremberg humanists, who translated and widely circulated them. This made Luther a central figure in an already organized national German cultural movement against foreign influence and competition, particularly on the part of the Italians. In October, he was summoned before the general of the Dominican order in Augsburg to answer for his criticism of the church. Yet as sanctions were being prepared against him, Emperor Maximilian I died (January 12, 1519)—a fortunate event for the budding Reformation, because it turned attention away from heresy in Saxony to the contest for a new emperor.

In that contest, the pope backed the French king, Francis I. However, Charles I of Spain, a youth of nineteen, successfully succeeded his grandfather as Emperor Charles V. (See Map 11–1, page 320.) Charles was blessed by both the long tradition of the Habsburg imperial rule and a massive Fugger campaign chest that secured the votes of the seven imperial **electors**. The most prominent among the seven was Frederick the Wise, Luther's lord and protector. Frederick took great pride in

[1]*Die Reformation in Augenzeugen berichten*, ed. by Helmar Junghaus (Düsseldorf: Karl Rauch Verlag, 1967), p. 44.

his new University of Wittenberg, and he was not about to let any harm come to his famous court preacher.

In exchange for their votes, the electors wrung new concessions from the Spanish favorable to the Germans. Before becoming emperor, Charles I agreed to revive the German-based Imperial Supreme Court and the Council of Regency and also promised to consult with a diet of the empire on all major domestic and foreign affairs affecting the empire. These measures also helped the development of the Reformation by preventing unilateral imperial action against the Germans.

Luther's Excommunication and the Diet of Worms

In the same month in which Charles was elected emperor, Luther debated the Ingolstadt professor John Eck in Leipzig (June 27, 1519). During this contest, Luther challenged the infallibility of the pope and the inerrancy of church councils, appealing, for the first time, to the

AETHERNA IPSE SVAE MENTIS SIMVLACHRA LVTHERVS
EXPRIMIT·AT VVLTVS CERA LVCAE OCCIDVOS·

M·D·XX·

In 1520, Luther's first portrait, shown here, depicted him as a tough, steely-eyed monk. Afraid that this portrayal might convey defiance rather than reform to Emperor Charles V, Elector Frederick the Wise of Saxony, Luther's protector, ordered court painter Lucas Cranach to soften the image. The result was a Luther placed within a traditional monk's niche reading an open Bible, a reformer, unlike the one depicted here, who was prepared to listen as well as to instruct.   Martin Luther as a monk, 1521. © Foto Marburg/Art Resource, NY

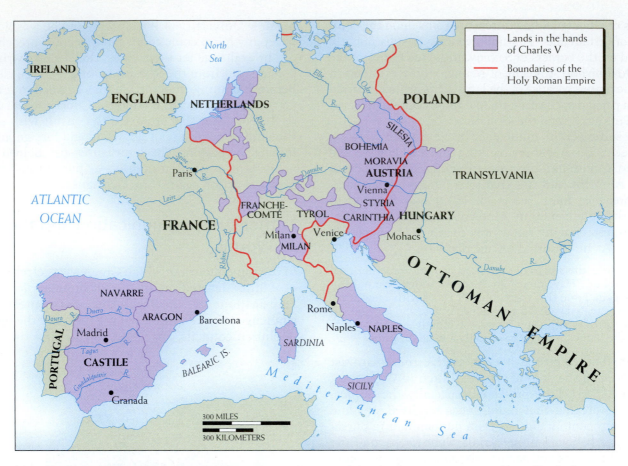

Map 11–1   **THE EMPIRE OF CHARLES V**   Dynastic marriages and simple chance concentrated into Charles's hands rule over the lands shown here, plus Spain's overseas possessions. Crowns and titles rained down on him; his election in 1519 as emperor gave him new distractions and responsibilities.

sovereign authority of Scripture alone. He burned all his bridges to the old church when he further defended certain teachings of John Huss, who had been condemned to death for heresy at the Council of Constance.

In 1520, Luther signaled his new direction with three famous pamphlets. The *Address to the Christian Nobility of the German Nation* urged the German princes to force reforms on the Roman church, especially to curtail its political and economic power in Germany. The *Babylonian Captivity of the Church* attacked the traditional seven sacraments, arguing that only two, baptism and the Eucharist, were unquestionably biblical, and it exalted the authority of Scripture, church councils, and secular princes over that of the pope. The eloquent *Freedom of a Christian* summarized the new teaching of salvation by faith alone.

On June 15, 1520, Leo's papal bull *Exsurge Domine* ("Arise, O Lord") condemned Luther for heresy and gave him sixty days to retract. The final bull of excommunication was issued on January 3, 1521.

In April 1521, Luther presented his views before the Diet of Worms, over which the newly elected Emperor Charles V presided. Ordered to recant, Luther declared that to do so would be to act against Scripture, reason, and his

conscience. On May 26, 1521, he was placed under the imperial ban, which made him an "outlaw" to secular as well as religious authority. For his own protection, friends disguised and hid him in Wartburg Castle at the instruction of Elector Frederick. There, he spent almost a year, from April 1521 to March 1522. During his stay, he translated the New Testament into German using Erasmus's new Greek text and Latin translation, while overseeing by correspondence the first steps of the Reformation in Wittenberg.

Imperial Distractions: War with France and the Turks

The Reformation was greatly helped in these early years by the emperor's war with France and the advance of the Ottoman Turks into eastern Europe. Against both adversaries Charles V, who remained a Spanish king with dynastic responsibilities in Spain and Austria, needed loyal German troops, to which end he sought friendly relations with the German princes. Between 1521 and 1559, Spain (the Habsburg dynasty) and France (the Valois dynasty) fought four major wars over disputed territories within Italy and along their respective borders.

Thus preoccupied, the emperor agreed through his representatives at the German Diet of Speyer (1526) that each German territory was free to enforce the Edict of Worms (1521) against Luther "so as to be able to answer in good conscience to God and the emperor." That concession in effect gave the German princes, who five years earlier had refused to publish the emperor's condemnation of Luther, territorial sovereignty in religious matters. It also bought the Reformation time to put down deep roots in Germany and Switzerland. In addition, Speyer proved to be a true precedent for the final settlement of the religious conflict in the empire. Later, the Peace of Augsburg (1555) would enshrine regional princely control over religion in imperial law.

How the Reformation Spread

In the late 1520s and 1530s, the Reformation passed from the free hands of the theologians and pamphleteers into the firmer ones of the magistrates and princes. In many cities, the latter quickly mandated new religious reforms. Many rulers had themselves worked for decades to bring about basic church reforms, and they welcomed Lutheran preachers as new allies. Reform now ceased to be merely slogans and was transformed into laws all townspeople had to obey.

The elector of Saxony and the prince of Hesse, the two most powerful German Protestant rulers, led the politicization of religious reform within their territories. Like the urban magistrates, the German princes recognized the political and economic opportunities offered them by the demise of the Roman Catholic Church in their lands. Soon they were pushing Protestant faith and politics onto their neighbors. In the 1530s, German Protestant lands formed a powerful defensive alliance, the Schmaldkaldic League, and prepared for war with the Catholic emperor.

The Peasants' Revolt

In its first decade, the Reformation suffered more from internal division than from imperial interference. By 1525, Luther had become almost as much an object of protest within Germany as was the pope. Original allies, sympathizers, and fellow travelers increasingly declared their independence from Wittenberg.

Like the German humanists, the German peasantry also had at first believed Luther to be an ally. Since the late fifteenth century, the peasantry had opposed the efforts of their secular and ecclesiastical lords to override their traditional laws and customs and to subject them to new territorial regulations and taxes. Peasant leaders, several of whom had been Lutherans, saw in Luther's teaching about Christian freedom and his criticism of monastic landowners a point of view close to their own. They openly solicited

The punishment of a peasant leader in a village near Heilbronn. After the defeat of rebellious peasants in and around the city of Heilbronn, Jacob Rorbach, a well-to-do peasant leader from a nearby village, was tied to a stake and slowly roasted to death.
Courtesy of the Library of Congress

Luther's support of their alleged "Christian" political and economic rights, including a revolutionary demand of release from serfdom.

Luther had initially sympathized with the peasants, condemning the tyranny of the princes and urging them to meet the just demands of the peasants. Lutheran pamphleteers made Karsthans (Hans with a hoe), the burly, hard-working peasant who earned his bread by the sweat of his brow, a model of the honest life God wanted all people to live. The Lutherans, however, were not social revolutionaries and they saw no hope for their movement if it became intertwined with a peasant revolution. When the peasants revolted against their landlords in 1524–1525, invoking Luther's name, Luther predictably condemned them as "un-Christian" and urged the princes to crush the revolt mercilessly. Tens of thousands of peasants (estimates run between 70,000 and 100,000) died by the time the revolt was suppressed.

For Luther, the freedom of the Christian lay in inner spiritual release from guilt and anxiety, not in revolutionary politics. Had the reformers joined the peasants' revolt, Luther would have contradicted his own teaching and likely shared the fate of former Lutherans who died as leaders of peasant revolts. In that scenario the

A Raw Deal for the Common Man, or His Just Desserts?

BEGINNING IN THE late fifteenth century, German feudal lords, both secular and ecclesiastical, increased labor and crop quotas on their peasant tenants, while restricting their freedoms and overriding their customary laws as well. In 1525 massive revolts occurred in southern Germany, in what became the largest social uprising before the French Revolution. Among those responding directly to the revolt were two highly respected authorities: Wittenberg theologian Martin Luther and Nuremberg artist Albrecht Dürer.

QUESTIONS

1. What is there in Luther's religious teaching that might have led the peasants to think he would support their revolt? What personal interest might he have had in turning them his way? What does he advise them to do to address their grievances properly?

2. Does Dürer's 1527 sketch of a "Memorial to the Peasants' Revolt," depicting a peasant sitting atop a chicken coop with a sword thrust through his back, suggest a greater sympathy for the peasants? Or can it be read as agreement with Luther that the peasants received their just desserts for rebelling against lawful authority?

3. Does Dürer's monument support or condemn the rebellious peasants?

I. Martin Luther, *An Admonition to Peace* (1525)

ON STOPPING THE WAR

This matter is great and perilous, concerning both the kingdom of God and the kingdom of the world; if this rebellion gets the upper hand, both kingdoms will be destroyed and there will be neither world government nor Word of God; there will rather result the permanent destruction of all of Germany, therefore, it is necessary . . . to speak boldly . . . Since there is nothing Christian on either side and nothing Christian is at issue between you . . . let yourselves be advised and attack these matters with justice, not with force or strife, and do not start an endless bloodshed in Germany!

We have no one on earth to thank for this mischievous rebellion, except you lords and princes, especially you blind bishops and mad priests and monks . . . In your government you do nothing but flay and rob your subjects in order that you may lead a life of splendor and pride, until the poor common folk can bear it no longer . . .

[As for] the peasants, they must take the name and title of a people who fight because they will not and ought not endure wrong or evil, according to the teaching of nature. You should have <u>that</u> name, and let the name of Christ alone . . . [As for your so-called 'Christian' demands for] freedom of game, birds, fish, wood, forests, labor services, tithes, imposts, excises, and release from the death tax, these I leave to the lawyers, for they are things that do not concern a Christian who is a martyr on this earth . . . Let the name of Christian alone and act in some other name, as men and women who want human and natural rights.

Sources: *A Sincere Admonition to Peace*, cited by Ozment, *Age of Reform*, p. 283 [first paragraph]; cited by Steven Ozment, *The Age of Reform* (New Haven, CT:, Yale University Press, 1980), pp. 280–282, [second and third paragraphs].

II. Martin Luther, *Against the Robbing and Murdering Peasants* (1525)

FINAL WORDS

[The princes] should have no mercy on obstinate, hardened, blinded peasants who refuse to listen to reason. Let everyone, as he is able, strike, hew, stab, and slay, as though among mad dogs, so that by doing so he may show mercy to those [non-rebelling peasants] who have been ruined, put to flight, and led astray by these rebelling peasants [so that] peace and safety may return . . .

Source: Ozment, *The Age of Reform*, p. 284.

III. *An Open Letter Concerning the Hard Book Against the Peasants* (1525)

FINAL WORDS

Suppose I were to break into a man's house, rape his wife and daughters, break open his coffers, take his money, set a sword to his breast and say: 'If you will not put up with this, I shall run you through, for you are a godless wretch.' Then if a crowd gathered and were about to kill me for doing this, or if the judge ordered my head off, suppose I were to cry out: 'But Christ teaches that you are to be merciful and not kill me.' What would people say then? Well, that is exactly what my peasants and their advocates are doing now. The kingdom of this world is nothing else than the servant of God's wrath upon the wicked and it is a real precursor of hell and everlasting death. It should not be merciful, but strict, severe, and wrathful in the fulfillment of its works and duty. Its tool is not a wreath or roses or a flower of love, but a naked sword.

From the start I had two fears. If the peasants became lords, the devil would become abbot; if these tyrants became lords, the devil's dam would become abbess. Therefore I wanted to do two things: quiet the peasants and instruct the lords. The peasants were unwilling, and now they have their reward. The lords will not hear, and they shall have their reward also.

Sources: An Open Letter Concerning the Hard Book Against the peasants, cited by Ozment, Age of Reform, p. 286-287 [first paragraph]; Ozment, *The Age of Reform*, p. 287, [second and third paragraph].

IV. Albrecht Dürer, *Memorial to the Peasants' Revolt* (1527)

Dürer's "Memorial to the Peasants," drawn in 1527, the year before his death, appeared in a book devoted to 'perspective in art.' Fearing that Protestant iconoclasm (destruction of icons) and the coming of religious wars would remove decorative art from the churches, his book was to be a primer for artists who in the aftermath of such destruction would have to learn the art of painting all over again. The sketch shows a peasant sitting atop a chicken coop with a sword thrust through his back, the classic iconography of betrayal.

At this time Dürer's peers, friends, and associates condemned the Peasants' Revolt as strongly as Luther. During the war Dürer painted portraits of the Fuggers, the great merchant family the peasants despised, and also Margrave Casimir of Brandenburg-Ansbach, a brutal slayer of peasants and Anabaptists. Within this context might Dürer's slain rebellious peasant, like Luther's, have gotten his just due?

Source: Joseph Leo Koerner, *The Moment of Self-Portraiture in Renaissance Art* (Chicago: Chicago University Press, 1993), p. 235.

10.

The caption reads: "He who wants to commemorate his victory over the rebellious peasants might use to that end a structure such as I portray here." Illustration Foto Marburg/Art Resource, N.Y.

German Reformation would not have survived beyond the 1520s. Still, many critics believe that Luther's decision ended the promise of the Reformation as a social and moral force in history.

▼ The Reformation Elsewhere

Although the German Reformation was the first, Switzerland and France had their own independent church reform movements almost simultaneously with Germany's. From them developed new churches as prominent and lasting as the Lutheran.

A Catholic Portrayal of Martin Luther Tempting Christ (1547). Reformation propaganda often portrayed the pope as the Antichrist or the devil. Here Catholic propaganda turns the tables on the Protestant reformers by portraying a figure of Martin Luther as the devil (note the monstrous feet and tail under his academic robes). Re-creating the biblical scene of Christ being tempted by the devil in the wilderness, the figure of Luther asks Christ to transform stone into bread, to which temptation Christ responds by saying that humans do not live by bread alone. Versucung Christi, 1547, Gemälde, Bonn, Rheinisches Landesmuseum, Inv. Nr. 58.3

Zwingli and the Swiss Reformation

Switzerland was a loose confederacy of thirteen autonomous *cantons,* or states, and their allied areas. (See Map 11–2.) Some cantons became Protestant, some remained Catholic, and a few others managed to effect a compromise. There were two main preconditions of the Swiss Reformation. First was the growth of national sentiment occasioned by popular opposition to foreign mercenary service. (Providing mercenaries for Europe's warring nations was a major source of Switzerland's livelihood.) Second was a desire for church reform that had persisted in Switzerland since the councils of Constance (1414–1417) and Basel (1431–1449).

The Reformation in Zurich   Ulrich Zwingli (1484–1531), the leader of the Swiss Reformation, had been humanistically educated. He credited Erasmus over Luther with having set him on the path to reform. He served as a chaplain with Swiss mercenaries who were on the losing side in the disastrous Battle of Marignano in Italy in 1515. Thereafter he became an eloquent critic of Swiss mercenary service, believing it threatened both the political sovereignty and the moral fiber of the Swiss confederacy. By 1518, Zwingli was also widely known for his opposition to the sale of indulgences and to religious superstition.

In 1519, he competed for the post of people's priest in the main church of Zurich. His candidacy was initially questioned after he acknowledged fornicating with a barber's daughter, who had since delivered a child. Zwingli successfully minimized the affair, claiming the woman in question had been a skilled seducer, and denying any paternity as she had had affairs with other men as well. Zwingli's conduct was not so scandalous to contemporaries, who sympathized with the plight of a celibate clergy. One of Zwingli's first acts as a reformer was to petition for an end to clerical celibacy and for the right of clergy legally to marry, a practice accepted in all Protestant lands.

From his new position as people's priest in Zurich, Zwingli engineered the Swiss Reformation. In March 1522, he was party to the breaking of the Lenten fast—then an act of protest analogous to burning one's national flag today. Zwingli's reform guideline was simple and effective: Whatever lacked literal support in Scripture was to be neither believed nor practiced. As had also happened with Luther, that test soon raised questions about such honored traditional teachings and practices as fasting, transubstantiation, the worship of saints, pilgrimages, purgatory, clerical celibacy, and certain sacraments. A disputation held on January 29, 1523, concluded with the city government's sanction of Zwingli's Scripture test. (See "Zwingli Lists the Errors of the Roman Church," page 326.) Thereafter Zurich became the center of the Swiss Reformation. The new regime imposed a harsh discipline that made the city one of the first examples of puritanical Protestantism.

Map 11–2 **THE SWISS CONFEDERATION** Although nominally still a part of the Holy Roman Empire, Switzerland grew from a loose defensive union of the central "forest cantons" in the thirteenth century into a fiercely independent association of regions with different languages, histories, and, finally, religions.

The Marburg Colloquy Landgrave Philip of Hesse (1504–1567) sought to unite Swiss and German Protestants in a mutual defense pact. However, Luther's and Zwingli's bitter theological differences, especially over the nature of Christ's presence in the Eucharist, spoiled his efforts. Zwingli favored a symbolic interpretation of Christ's words, "This is my body." Christ, he argued, was spiritually, not bodily, present in the bread and wine of the Eucharist. Luther, to the contrary, insisted that Christ's human nature was such that it shared the properties of his divine nature. Hence, where Christ was spiritually present, he could also be bodily present, for such was his special human nature. Luther wanted no part of an abstract, spiritualized Christ, while Zwingli feared Luther was still mired in medieval sacramental theology.

Philip of Hesse brought the two Protestant leaders together in his castle in Marburg in early October 1529, to work out their differences. However, the effort proved to be in vain. Luther left thinking Zwingli a dangerous fanatic, forevermore to paint him black. Although cooperation between the two Protestant sides did not cease altogether, the disagreement splintered the Protestant movement theologically and politically.

Separate defense leagues formed, and semi-Zwinglian theological views came to be embodied in the non-Lutheran *Tetrapolitan Confession* prepared by the Strasbourg reformers Martin Bucer and Caspar Hedio in 1530.

Swiss Civil Wars As the Swiss cantons divided themselves between Protestantism and Catholicism, civil wars erupted. There were two major battles, both at Kappel, one in June 1529 and a second in October 1531. The first ended in a Protestant victory, which forced the Catholic cantons to break their foreign alliances and to recognize the rights of Swiss Protestants. After the second battle, Zwingli lay wounded on the battlefield, and when discovered, he was unceremoniously executed, his remains thereafter hacked into pieces and scattered to the four winds so his followers would have no relics to console and inspire them. The subsequent treaty confirmed the right of each canton to determine its own religion. Heinrich Bullinger (1504–1575), Zwingli's protégé and later son-in-law, became the new leader of the Swiss Reformation and guided its development into an established religion, eventually to merge with Calvinism.

ZWINGLI LISTS THE ERRORS OF THE ROMAN CHURCH

▦

Prior to the first Zurich Disputation (1523), which effectually introduced the Protestant Reformation in Zurich, the reformer Zwingli prepared such a summary of the errors of the Roman Church known as the Sixty-Seven Articles. *Here are some of them.*

How do Zwingli's basic religious views compare with those of Martin Luther?

All who consider other teachings equal to or higher than the Gospel err, and they do not know what the Gospel is.

In the faith rests our salvation, and in unbelief our damnation; for all truth is clear in Christ.

In the Gospel one learns that human doctrines and decrees do not aid in salvation.

That Christ, having sacrificed himself once, is to eternity a certain and valid sacrifice for the sins of all faithful, wherefrom it follows that the Mass is not a sacrifice, but is a remembrance of the sacrifice and assurance of the salvation which Christ has given us.

That God desires to give us all things in his name, whence it follows that outside of this life we need no [intercession of the saints or any] mediator except himself.

That no Christian is bound to do those things which God has not decreed, therefore one may eat at all times all food, where from one learns that the decree about cheese and butter is a Roman swindle.

That no special person can impose the ban upon anyone, but the Church, that is, the congregation of those among whom the one to be banned dwells, together with their watchman, i.e., the pastor.

All that the spiritual so-called state [i.e., the papal church] claims to have of power and protection belongs to the lay [i.e., the secular magistracy], if they wish to be Christians.

Greater offence I know not than that one does not allow priests to have wives, but permits them to hire prostitutes.

Christ has borne all our pains and labor. Hence whoever assigns to works of penance what belongs to Christ errs and slanders God.

The true divine Scriptures know naught about purgatory after this life.

The Scriptures know no priests except those who proclaim the word of God.

Ulrich Zwingli (1484–1531), *Selected Works*, ed. by Samuel M. Jackson (Philadelphia: University of Pennsylvania Press, 1972), pp. 111–117.

Anabaptists and Radical Protestants

The moderate pace and seemingly low ethical results of the Lutheran and Zwinglian reformations discontented many people, among them some of the original followers of Luther and Zwingli. These were devout fundamentalist Protestants who desired a more rapid and thorough implementation of Apostolic Christianity. They accused the reform movements that went before them of having gone only halfway. The most important of these radical groups were the **Anabaptists**, the sixteenth-century ancestors of the modern Mennonites and Amish. The Anabaptists were especially distinguished by their rejection of infant baptism and their insistence on only adult baptism, as was the case with Jesus, who was baptized as an adult. (The term *Anabaptism* derives from the Greek word meaning "to rebaptize.") Only a thoughtful consenting adult, able to understand the Scriptures and what the biblical way of life required, could enter the covenant of faith.

Although Luther and Zwingli also taught that believers must believe for themselves (Luther called it the "priesthood of all believers"), they retained the historical practice of infant baptism, despite the absence of any clear biblical mandate. They argued that the congregation "believed for the infant," stood in his or her place, and pledged to raise the baptized infant in the faith. Here, the communal nature and responsibility of the church was deemed to be more basic to Christianity than the radical individualism the Anabaptists asserted.

Conrad Grebel and the Swiss Brethren Conrad Grebel (1498–1526), with whom Anabaptism originated, performed the first adult rebaptism in Zurich in January 1525. Initially a co-worker of Zwingli's and an even greater biblical literalist, Grebel broke openly with him.

In a religious disputation in October 1523, Zwingli supported the city government's plea for a peaceful, gradual removal of resented traditional religious practices—not the rush to perfection the Anabaptists demand.

The alternative of the Swiss Brethren, as Grebel's group came to be called, was embodied in the *Schleitheim Confession* of 1527. This document distinguished Anabaptists not only by their practice of adult baptism, but also by their pacifism, refusal to swear oaths, and nonparticipation in the offices of secular government. By both choice and coercion, Anabaptists physically separated from established society to form a more perfect communion modeled on the first Christians. Because of the close connection between religious and civic life in the sixteenth century, the political authorities also viewed such separatism as a threat to basic social bonds, even as a form of sedition.

The Anabaptist Reign in Münster At first, Anabaptism drew adherents from all social classes. As Lutherans and Zwinglians joined with Catholics in opposition and persecuted them within the cities, however, a more rural, agrarian class came to make up the great majority of Anabaptists. In 1529, rebaptism became a capital offense within the Holy Roman Empire. At least 1,000 and perhaps as many as 5,000 men and women were executed for rebaptizing themselves as adults between 1525 and 1618.

Brutal measures were universally applied against nonconformists after Anabaptist extremists came to power in the German city of Münster in 1534–1535. Led by two Dutch emigrants, a baker, Jan Matthys of Haarlem, and a tailor, Jan Beukelsz of Leiden, the Anabaptists in Münster forced Lutherans and Catholics in the city either to convert or to emigrate. After their departure, the city was blockaded by besieging armies. Under such pressures, Münster was transformed into an Old Testament theocracy, replete with charismatic leaders and the practice of polygamy. The latter was implemented as a measure of social control to deal with the many recently widowed and deserted women left behind in the city. Women opposed to the practice were allowed to leave polygymous marriages.

These developments shocked the outside world, and Protestant and Catholic armies united to crush the radicals. The skeletons of their leaders long hung in public view as a warning to all who would so offend traditional Christian sensitivities. After this episode, moderate, pacifistic Anabaptism became the norm among most nonconformists. Menno Simons (1496–1561), the founder of the Mennonites, set an example of non-provocative separatist Anabaptism, which became the historical form in which Anabaptist sects survived down to the present.

Spiritualists Another diverse and highly individualistic group of Protestant dissenters was the Spiritualists. These were mostly isolated individuals distinguished by their disdain for external, institutional religion. They believed the only religious authority was the Spirit of God, which spoke not in some past revelation, but here and now in the heart and mind of every listening individual. Among them were several renegade Lutherans. Thomas Müntzer (d. 1525), who had close contacts with Anabaptist leaders in Germany and Switzerland, died as a leader of a peasants' revolt in Frankenhausen, Germany. Sebastian Franck (d. 1541), a critic of all dogmatic religion, proclaimed the religious autonomy and freedom of every individual soul. Caspar Schwenckfeld (d. 1561) was a prolific writer and wanderer after whom the Schwenckfeldian Church is named.

Antitrinitarians A final group of persecuted radical Protestants also destined for prominence in the modern world was the Antitrinitarians. These were exponents of a commonsense, rational, and ethical religion. Prominent among them were the Spaniard Michael Servetus (1511–1553), executed in 1553 in Geneva at the encouragement of John Calvin for "blasphemies against the Holy Trinity." The Italians, Lelio (d. 1562) and Faustus Sozzini (d. 1604), the founders of Socinianism, also stand out. These thinkers were the strongest opponents of Calvinism, especially its belief in original sin and **predestination**, and have a deserved reputation as defenders of religious toleration.

John Calvin and the Genevan Reformation

In the second half of the sixteenth century, Calvinism replaced Lutheranism as the dominant Protestant force in Europe. Calvinism was the religious ideology that inspired or accompanied massive political resistance in France, the Netherlands, and Scotland. During the reign of Elector Frederick III (r. 1559–1576) Calvinism established itself within the geographical region of the Palatinate, the German state in the Rhineland in which the Thirty Years' War, the worst of the wars of religion, would break out in 1618. Calvinists believed strongly in both divine predestination and the individual's responsibility to reorder society according to God's plan. They were determined to transform society so men and women lived their lives externally as they professed to believe internally and were presumably destined to live eternally.

The namesake of Calvinism and its perfect embodiment, John Calvin (1509–1564), was born into a well-to-do French family, the son of the secretary to the bishop of Noyon. At age twelve, he received church *benefices* that financed the best possible education at Parisian colleges and a law degree. In the 1520s, he identified with the French reform party. Although he would finally reject this group as ineffectual compromisers, its members contributed much to his intellectual preparation as a religious reformer.

A portrait of the young John Calvin. Bibliothèque Publique et Universitaire, Geneva

It was probably in the spring of 1534 that Calvin experienced that conversion to Protestantism by which he said his "long stubborn heart" was "made teachable" by God. His own hard experience became a personal model of reform by which he would measure the recalcitrant citizenry of Geneva. His mature theology stressed the sovereignty of God's will over all creation and the necessity of humankind's conformity to it. In May 1534, he dramatically surrendered the *benefices* that had educated him and joined the budding Reformation in Geneva.

Political Revolt and Religious Reform in Geneva
Whereas in Saxony religious reform paved the way for a political revolution against the emperor, in Geneva a political revolution against the local prince-bishop laid the foundation for the religious change. Genevans revolted against their resident prince-bishop in the late 1520s, and the city council assumed his legal and political powers in 1527.

In late 1533, the Protestant city of Bern dispatched two reformers to Geneva: Guillaume Farel (1489–1565) and Antoine Froment (1508–1581). In the summer of 1535, after much internal turmoil, the Protestants triumphed, and the traditional Mass and other religious practices were removed. On May 21, 1536, Geneva voted officially to adopt the Reformation: "to live according to the Gospel and the Word of God . . . without any more Masses, statues, idols, or other papal abuses."

Calvin arrived in Geneva after these events, in July 1536. He was actually en route to a scholarly refuge in Strasbourg, in flight from the persecution of Protestants in France, when warring between France and Spain forced him to turn sharply south to Geneva. Farel persuaded him to stay in the city and assist the Reformation, threatening Calvin with divine vengeance if he turned away from this task.

Calvin drew up articles for the governance of the new church, as well as a catechism to guide and discipline the people. Both were presented for approval to the city councils in early 1537. Because of the strong measures they proposed to govern Geneva's moral life, many suspected the reformers were intent on creating a "new papacy." Opponents feared Calvin and Farel were going too far too fast. Geneva's powerful Protestant ally, Bern, which had adopted a more moderate Protestant reform, pressured Geneva's magistrates to restore traditional religious ceremonies and holidays that Calvin and Farel had abolished. When the reformers opposed these actions, they were exiled from the city.

Calvin went to Strasbourg, a model Protestant city, where he became pastor to French exiles and wrote biblical commentaries. He also produced a second edition of his masterful *Institutes of the Christian Religion*, which many consider the definitive theological statement of the Protestant faith. Most importantly, he learned from the Strasbourg reformer Martin Bucer how to achieve his goals.

Calvin's Geneva In 1540, Geneva elected officials both favorable to Calvin and determined to establish full Genevan political and religious independence from Bern. They knew Calvin would be a valuable ally in that undertaking and invited him to return. This he did in September 1540, never to leave the city again. Within months of his return, the city implemented new ecclesiastical ordinances that provided for cooperation between the magistrates and the clergy in matters of internal discipline.

Following the Strasbourg model, the Genevan Church was organized into four offices: (1) pastors, of whom there were five; (2) teachers or doctors to instruct the populace in, and to defend, true doctrine; (3) elders, a group of twelve laypeople chosen by and from the Genevan councils and empowered to "oversee the life of everybody"; and (4) deacons to dispense church goods and services to the poor and the sick.

The controversial doctrine of predestination was at the center of Calvin's theology as justification by faith was at Luther's. Both doctrines have been criticized,

Luther's for seeming to deny the believer's need to do good works and Calvin's for seeming to deny the existence of human free will. Luther believed works were a mark of a true Christian, even though they did not make him such or save him. Calvin did not discuss predestination until the end of his great theological work, the *Institutes of the Christian Religion*. Explaining why he delayed its discussion, he described predestination as a doctrine only for mature Christians. Whereas it offended nonbelievers, true Christians might take consolation from it. For true believers, predestination recognized that the world and all who dwell in it are in God's hands from eternity to eternity, regardless of all else. When the world seems utterly godless and the devil to be its only lord, the true Christian takes consolation from the knowledge that his present life and future destiny are determined irrevocably by a loving and ever-lasting God. By believing that, and living as the Bible instructed them to do, Calvinists found consoling, presumptive evidence that they were among God's elect.

Possessed of such assurance, Calvinists turned their energies to transforming society spiritually and morally. Faith, Calvin taught, did not sit idly in the mind but conformed one's every action to God's law. The "elect" should at least live in a manifestly God-pleasing way if they are truly God's "elect." In the attempted realization of that goal, Calvin spared no effort. The consistory, or Geneva's regulatory court, became his instrument of power. Composed of the elders and the pastors and presided over by one of the city's chief magistrates that body implemented the strictest moral discipline.

Among the personal conflicts in Geneva that gave Calvin the reputation of a stern moralist, none proved more damaging than his role in the capture and execution in 1553 of the Spanish physician and amateur theologian Michael Servetus, who had already been condemned by the Inquisition for heresy. He died at the stake in Protestant Geneva for denying the doctrine of the Trinity, a subject on which he had written a book scandalous to church authorities.

After 1555, Geneva became home to thousands of exiled Protestants who had been driven out of France, England, and Scotland. Refugees numbering more than 5,000, most of them utterly loyal to Calvin, made up more than one third of Geneva's population. All of Geneva's magistrates were now devout Calvinists, greatly strengthening Calvin's position in the city.

To the thousands of persecuted Protestants who flocked to Geneva in mid-century, the city was a beacon and a refuge, Europe's only free city. During Calvin's lifetime, Geneva also gained the reputation of being a "woman's paradise" because its laws severely punished men who beat their wives, behavior deemed unbefitting a true Calvinist Christian.

▼ Political Consolidation of the Lutheran Reformation

By 1530, the Reformation was in Europe to stay. It would, however, take several decades and major attempts to eradicate it, before all would recognize this fact. With the political triumph of Lutheranism in the empire by the 1550s, Protestant movements elsewhere gained a new lease on life.

The Diet of Augsburg

Charles V devoted most of his first decade as emperor to the pursuit of politics and military campaigns outside the empire, particularly in Spain and Italy. In 1530, he returned to the empire to direct the Diet of Augsburg. This assembly of Protestant and Catholic representatives had been called to address the growing religious division within the empire in the wake of the Reformation's success. With its terms dictated by the Catholic emperor, the diet adjourned with a blunt and unrealistic order to all Lutherans to revert to Catholicism.

The Reformation was by this time too firmly established for that to occur. In February 1531, the Lutherans responded with the formation of their own defensive alliance, the Schmalkaldic League. The league took as its banner the **Augsburg Confession**, a moderate statement of Protestant beliefs that had been spurned by the emperor at the Diet of Augsburg. In 1538, Luther drew up a more strongly worded Protestant confession known as the *Schmalkaldic Articles*. Under the leadership of Landgrave Philip of Hesse and Elector John Frederick of Saxony, the league achieved a stalemate with the emperor, who was again distracted by renewed war with France and the ever-resilient Turks.

The Expansion of the Reformation

In the 1530s, German Lutherans formed regional consistories, judicial bodies composed of theologians and lawyers, which oversaw and administered the new Protestant churches and replaced the old Catholic episcopates. Educational reforms provided for compulsory primary education, schools for girls, a humanist revision of the traditional curriculum, and instruction of the laity in the new religion.

The Reformation also entrenched itself elsewhere. Introduced into Denmark by King Christian II (r. 1513–1523), Lutheranism thrived there under Frederick I (r. 1523–1533), who joined the Schmalkaldic League. Under Christian III (r. 1536–1559), Lutheranism became the official state religion.

In Sweden, King Gustavus Vasa (r. 1523–1560), supported by a Swedish nobility greedy for church lands, embraced Lutheranism, confiscated church property, and subjected the clergy to royal authority at the Diet of Vesteras (1527).

In politically splintered Poland, Lutherans, Anabaptists, Calvinists, and even Antitrinitarians found room to practice their beliefs. Primarily because of the absence of a central political authority, Poland became a model of religious pluralism and toleration in the second half of the sixteenth century.

Reaction Against Protestants

Charles V made abortive efforts in 1540–1541 to enforce a compromise between Protestants and Catholics. As these and other conciliar efforts failed, he turned to a military solution. In 1547, imperial armies crushed the Protestant Schmalkaldic League, defeating and capturing John Frederick of Saxony and Philip of Hesse.

The emperor established puppet rulers in Saxony and Hesse and issued an imperial law mandating that Protestants everywhere readopt old Catholic beliefs and practices. Protestants were granted a few cosmetic concessions, for example, clerical marriage (with papal approval of individual cases) and communion in both bread and wine. Many Protestant leaders went into exile. In Germany, the city of Magdeburg became a refuge for persecuted Protestants and the center of Lutheran resistance.

The Peace of Augsburg

The Reformation was too entrenched by 1547 to be ended even by brute force. Maurice of Saxony, handpicked by Charles V to rule Saxony, had recognized the inevitable and shifted his allegiance to the Lutherans. Confronted by fierce resistance and weary from three decades of war, the emperor was forced to relent. After a defeat by Protestant armies in 1552, Charles reinstated the Protestant leaders and guaranteed Lutherans religious freedoms in the Peace of Passau (August 1552). With this declaration, he effectively surrendered his lifelong quest for European religious unity.

The Peace of Augsburg in September 1555 made the division of Christendom permanent. This agreement recognized in law what had already been well established in practice: *Cuius regio, eius religio,* meaning the ruler of a land would determine its religion. Lutherans were permitted to retain all church lands forcibly seized before 1552. An "ecclesiastical reservation" was added, however, that was intended to prevent high Catholic prelates who converted to Protestantism from taking their lands, titles, and privileges with them. People discontented with the religion of their region were permitted to migrate to another.

The Peace of Augsburg did not extend official recognition to Calvinism and Anabaptism as legal forms of Christian belief and practice. Anabaptists had long adjusted to such exclusion by forming their own separatist communities. Calvinists, however, were not separatists. They remained determined to secure the right to worship publicly as they pleased, and to shape society according to their own religious convictions. While Anabaptists retreated and Lutherans enjoyed the security of an established religion, Calvinists organized to lead national revolutions throughout northern Europe in the second half of the sixteenth century.

▼ The English Reformation to 1553

Late medieval England had a well-earned reputation for maintaining the rights of the crown against the pope. Edward I (r. 1272–1307) had rejected efforts by Pope Boniface VIII to prevent secular taxation of the clergy. Statutes of Provisors and Praemunire passed in the mid-fourteenth century laid a foundation for curtailing payments and judicial appeals to Rome rejecting papal appointments in England. Lollardy, humanism, and widespread anticlerical sentiments prepared the way for Protestant ideas, which entered England in the early sixteenth century.

The Preconditions of Reform

In the early 1520s, future English reformers met in Cambridge to discuss Lutheran writings smuggled into England by merchants and scholars. One of these future reformers was William Tyndale (ca. 1492–1536), who translated the New Testament into English in 1524–1525 while in Germany. Printed in Cologne and Worms, Tyndale's New Testament began to circulate in England in 1526.

Cardinal Thomas Wolsey (ca. 1475–1530), the chief minister of King Henry VIII (r. 1509–1547), and Sir Thomas More (1478–1535), Wolsey's successor, guided royal opposition to incipient English Protestantism. The king himself defended the seven sacraments against Luther, receiving as a reward the title "Defender of the Faith" from Pope Leo X. Following Luther's intemperate reply to Henry's amateur theological attack, More wrote a lengthy *Response to Luther* in 1523.

The King's Affair

Lollardy and humanism may have provided some native seeds for religious reform, but it was Henry's unhappy marriage to Catherine of Aragon (d. 1536) and obsession to get a male heir that broke the soil and allowed the seeds to take root. In 1509, Henry had married Catherine, the daughter of Ferdinand and Isabella of Spain and the aunt of Emperor Charles V. By 1527, the union had produced only one surviving child, a daughter, Mary. Although women could inherit the throne, Henry fretted over the political consequences of leaving only a female heir. In this period, people believed it unnatural for women to rule over men. At best a woman ruler foreshadowed a contested reign, at worst turmoil and revolution. By the end of the century, Elizabeth's strong rule would expose such fears as greatly exaggerated.

Henry came even to believe that God had cursed his union with Catherine, who had many miscarriages and stillbirths. The reason lay in Catherine's previous marriage to Henry's brother Arthur. After Arthur's premature death, Henry's father, Henry VII, betrothed her to Henry to keep the English alliance with Spain intact. The two were wed in 1509, a few days before Henry VIII received his crown. Because marriage to the wife of one's brother was prohibited by both canon and biblical law (see Leviticus 18:16, 20:21), the marriage had required a special dispensation from Pope Julius II.

By 1527, Henry was also thoroughly enamored of Anne Boleyn, one of Catherine's ladies-in-waiting. He determined to put Catherine aside and take Anne as his wife. This he could not do in Catholic England, however, without a papal annulment of the marriage to Catherine. Therein lay a special problem. 1527 was also the year when imperial soldiers fighting in Italy mutinied and sacked Rome. Pope Clement VII was then a prisoner of Emperor Charles V, who also happened to be Catherine's nephew, and he was not about to encourage the pope to annul the royal marriage. Even if such coercion had not existed, it would have been virtually impossible for the pope to grant an annulment of a marriage that not only had survived for eighteen years but had also been made possible in the first place by a special papal dispensation.

Cardinal Wolsey, who aspired to become pope, was placed in charge of securing the royal annulment. Lord Chancellor since 1515 and papal legate-at-large since 1518, Wolsey had long been Henry's heavy and the object of much popular resentment. When he failed to secure the annulment through no fault of his own, he was dismissed in disgrace in 1529. Thomas Cranmer (1489–1556) and Thomas Cromwell (1485–1540), both of whom harbored Lutheran sympathies, thereafter became the king's closest advisers. Finding the way to a papal annulment closed, Henry's new advisers struck a different course: Why not simply declare the king supreme in English spiritual affairs as he was in English temporal affairs? Then the king could settle the king's affair himself.

The "Reformation Parliament"

In 1529, Parliament convened for what would be a seven-year session that earned it the title of the "Reformation Parliament." During this period, it passed a flood of legislation that harassed, and finally placed royal reins on, the clergy. In so doing, it established a precedent that would remain a feature of English government: Whenever fundamental changes are made in religion, the monarch must consult with and work through Parliament. In January 1531, the Convocation (a legislative assembly representing the English clergy) publicly recognized Henry as head of the church in England "as far as the law of Christ allows." In 1532, Parliament published official grievances against the church, ranging from alleged indifference to the needs of the laity to an excessive number of religious holidays. In the same year, Parliament passed the Submission of the Clergy, which effectively placed canon law under royal control and thereby the clergy under royal jurisdiction.

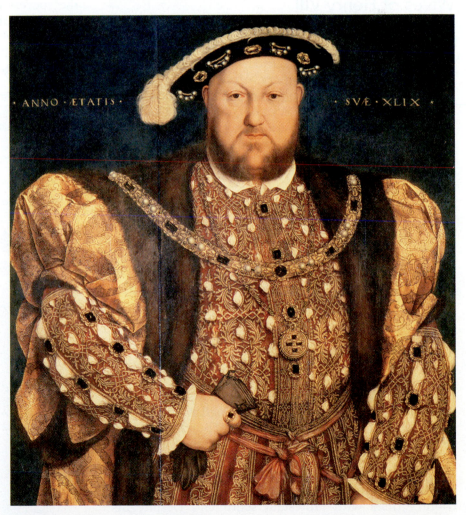

Hans Holbein the Younger (1497–1543) was the most famous portrait painter of the Reformation. Here he portrays a seemingly almighty Henry VIII. © Scala / Art Resource

In January 1533, Henry wed the pregnant Anne Boleyn, with Thomas Cranmer officiating. In February 1533, Parliament made the king the highest court of appeal for all English subjects. In March 1533, Cranmer became archbishop of Canterbury and led the Convocation in invalidating the king's marriage to Catherine. In 1534, Parliament ended all payments by the English clergy and laity to Rome and gave Henry sole jurisdiction over high ecclesiastical appointments. The Act of Succession in the same year made Anne Boleyn's children legitimate heirs to the throne, and the **Act of Supremacy** declared Henry "the only supreme head in earth of the Church of England."

When Thomas More and John Fisher, bishop of Rochester, refused to recognize the Act of Succession and the Act of Supremacy, Henry had them executed, making clear his determination to have his way regardless of the cost. In 1536 and 1538, Parliament dissolved England's monasteries and nunneries.

Wives of Henry VIII

Henry's domestic life lacked the consistency of his political life. In 1536, Anne Boleyn was executed for alleged treason and adultery, and her daughter Elizabeth, like Elizabeth's half sister Mary before her, was declared illegitimate by her father. Henry had four more marriages. His third wife, Jane Seymour, died in 1537 shortly after giving birth to the future Edward VI. Henry wed Anne of Cleves sight unseen on the advice of Cromwell, the purpose being to create by the marriage an alliance with the Protestant princes of Germany. Neither the alliance nor the marriage proved worth the trouble; the marriage was annulled by Parliament, and Cromwell was dismissed and executed. Catherine Howard, Henry's fifth wife, was beheaded for adultery in 1542. His last wife, Catherine Parr, a patron of humanists and reformers, for whom Henry was the third husband, survived him to marry still a fourth time—obviously she was a match for the English king.

The King's Religious Conservatism

Henry's boldness in politics and domestic affairs did not extend to religion. True, because of Henry's actions, the pope had ceased to be head of the English church and English Bibles were placed in English churches, but despite the break with Rome, Henry remained decidedly conservative in his religious beliefs. With the Ten Articles of 1536, he made only mild concessions to Protestant tenets. Otherwise Catholic doctrine was maintained in a country filled with Protestant sentiment. Despite his many wives and amorous adventures, Henry forbade the English clergy to marry and threatened to execute clergy who were caught twice in concubinage.

Angered by the growing popularity of Protestant views, even among his chief advisers, Henry struck directly at them in the Six Articles of 1539. These reaffirmed transubstantiation, denied the Eucharistic cup to the laity, declared celibate vows inviolable, provided for private Masses, and ordered the continuation of oral confession. Protestants referred to the articles as the "whip with six stings," a clear warning from the king that religious reform would not race ahead in England during his reign. Although William Tyndale's English New Testament grew into the Coverdale Bible (1535) and the Great Bible (1539), and the latter was mandated for every English parish, England had to await Henry's death before it could become a genuinely Protestant country.

The Protestant Reformation under Edward VI

When Henry died in 1547, his son and successor, Edward VI (d. 1553), was only ten years old. Edward reigned under the successive regencies of Edward Seymour, who became the duke of Somerset (1547–1550), and the earl of Warwick, who became known as the duke of Northumberland (1550–1553). During this time, England enacted Protestant Reformation. The new king and Somerset cor-

---

MAIN EVENTS OF THE ENGLISH REFORMATION	
1529	Reformation Parliament convenes
1532	Parliament passes the Submission of the Clergy
1533	Henry VIII weds Anne Boleyn; Convocation invalidates marriage to Catherine of Aragon
1534	Act of Succession makes Anne Boleyn's children legitimate heirs to the English throne
1534	Act of Supremacy declares Henry VIII "the only supreme head of the Church of England"
1535	Thomas More executed for opposition to Acts of Succession and Supremacy
1535	Publication of Coverdale Bible
1539	Henry VIII imposes the Six Articles
1547	Edward VI succeeds to the throne under protectorships of Somerset and Northumberland
1549	First Act of Uniformity imposes *Book of Common Prayer* on English churches
1553–1558	Mary Tudor restores Catholic doctrine
1558–1603	Elizabeth I fashions an Anglican religious settlement

responded directly with John Calvin. During Somerset's regency, Henry's Six Articles and laws against Protestant heresy were repealed, and clerical marriage and communion with cup were sanctioned.

In 1547, the chantries, places where endowed Masses had traditionally been said for the dead, were dissolved. In 1549, the Act of Uniformity imposed Thomas Cranmer's *Book of Common Prayer* on all English churches. Images and altars were removed from the churches in 1550. After Charles V's victory over the German princes in 1547, German Protestant leaders had fled to England for refuge. Several of these refugees, with Martin Bucer prominent among them, now directly assisted the completion of the English Reformation.

The Second Act of Uniformity, passed in 1552, imposed a revised *Book of Common Prayer* on all English churches. A forty-two-article confession of faith, also written by Thomas Cranmer, set forth a moderate Protestant doctrine. It taught justification by faith and the supremacy of Holy Scripture, denied transubstantiation (although not the real presence), and recognized only two sacraments.

All these changes were short-lived, however. In 1553, Catherine of Aragon's daughter succeeded Edward (who had died in his teens) to the throne as Mary I (d. 1558) and restored Catholic doctrine and practice with a single-mindedness rivaling that of her father. It was not until the reign of Anne Boleyn's daughter, Elizabeth I (r. 1558–1603), that England worked out a lasting religious settlement.

▼ Catholic Reform and Counter-Reformation

The Protestant Reformation did not take the medieval church completely by surprise. There were many internal criticisms and efforts at reform before there was a Counter-Reformation in reaction to Protestant successes.

Sources of Catholic Reform

Before the Reformation began, ambitious proposals had been made for church reform. But sixteenth-century popes, ever mindful of how the councils of Constance and Basel had stripped the pope of his traditional powers, squelched such efforts to change the laws and institutions of the church.

Despite such papal foot-dragging, the old church was not without its reformers. Many new religious orders also sprang up in the sixteenth century to lead a broad revival of piety within the church. The first of these orders was the Theatines, founded in 1524 to groom devout and reform-minded leaders at the higher levels of the church hierarchy. One of the co-founders was Bishop Gian Pietro Carafa, who would be Pope Paul IV (r. 1555–1559). Another new order, whose mission pointed in the opposite direction, was the Capuchins. Recognized by the pope in 1528, they sought to return to the original ideals of Saint Francis and became popular among the ordinary people to whom they directed their ministry. The Somaschi, who became active in the mid-1520s, and the Barnabites, founded in 1530, worked to repair the moral, spiritual, and physical damage done to people in war-torn Italy.

For women, there was the influential new order of Ursulines. Founded in 1535, it established convents in Italy and France for the religious education of girls from all social classes. Another new order, the Oratorians, officially recognized in 1575, was an elite group of clerics devoted to the promotion of religious literature and church music. Among their members was the great hymnist and musician Giovanni Perluigi da Palestrina (1526–1594).

In addition to these lay and clerical movements, the mystical piety of medieval monasticism was revived and popularized by two Spanish mystics, Saint Teresa of Avila (1515–1582) and Saint John of the Cross (1542–1591).

Ignatius of Loyola and the Jesuits

Of the various reform groups, none was more instrumental in the success of the Counter-Reformation than the Society of Jesus, the new order of Jesuits. Organized by Ignatius of Loyola in the 1530s, the church recognized it in 1540. The society grew within a century from its original ten members to more than 15,000 members scattered throughout the world, with thriving missions in India, Japan, and the Americas.

The founder of the Jesuits, Ignatius of Loyola (1491–1556), was a heroic figure. A dashing courtier and *soldiero* in his youth, he began his spiritual pilgrimage in 1521 after he had been seriously wounded during a battle with the French. During a lengthy and painful convalescence, he passed the time by reading Christian classics. So impressed was he with the heroic self-sacrifice of the church's saints and their methods of overcoming mental anguish and pain that he underwent a profound religious conversion. Henceforth, he, too, would serve the church as a soldier of Christ.

After recuperating, Ignatius applied the lessons he had learned during his convalescence to a program of religious and moral self-discipline that came to be embodied in the *Spiritual Exercises.* This psychologically perceptive devotional guide contained mental and emotional exercises designed to teach one absolute spiritual self-mastery over one's feelings. It taught that a person could shape his or her own behavior—even create a new religious self—through disciplined study and regular practice.

Whereas in Jesuit eyes Protestants had distinguished themselves by disobedience and religious

MAP EXPLORATION

Interactive map: To explore this map further, go to **www.myhistorylab.com**

Legend:
- Lutheran
- Anglican
- Calvinist Control or Influence
- Anabaptist
- Roman Catholic
- Eastern Border of Western Christianity

300 MILES
300 KILOMETERS

Map 11–3   THE RELIGIOUS SITUATION ABOUT 1560   By 1560, Luther, Zwingli, and Loyola were dead, Calvin was near the end of his life, the English break from Rome was complete, and the last session of the Council of Trent was about to assemble. This map shows "religious geography" of western Europe at the time.

innovation, the exercises of Ignatius were intended to teach good Catholics to deny themselves and submit without question to higher church authority and spiritual direction. Perfect discipline and self-control were the essential conditions of such obedience. To these were added the enthusiasm of traditional spirituality and mysticism and uncompromising loyalty to the church's cause. This potent combination helped counter the Reformation and win many Protestants

back to the Catholic fold, especially in Austria and parts of Germany. (See Map 11–3.)

The Council of Trent (1545–1563)

The broad success of the Reformation and the insistence of the Emperor Charles V forced Pope Paul III (r. 1534–1549) to call a general council of the church to

...ctrine. In anticipation, the pope ap-...ommission, chaired by Caspar Con-... a leading liberal theologian. His ...to the pope in February 1537, was so critical of the fiscal practices and simony of the papal Curia that Paul attempted unsuccessfully to suppress its publication, while Protestants circulated it as justification of their criticism.

The long-delayed council of the church met in 1545 in the imperial city of Trent in northern Italy. There were three sessions, spread over eighteen years, with long interruptions due to war, plague, and imperial and papal politics. The council met from 1545 to 1547, from 1551 to 1552, and from 1562 to 1563, a period that spanned the reigns of four different popes.

Unlike the general councils of the fifteenth century, Trent was strictly under the pope's control, with high Italian prelates prominent in the proceedings. At its final session in 1562, more than three quarters of the council fathers were Italians. Voting was limited to the high levels of the clergy; university theologians, the lower clergy, and the laity did not share in the council's decisions.

The council's most important reforms concerned internal church discipline. Steps were taken to curtail the selling of church offices and other religious goods. Many bishops who resided in Rome were forced to move to their dioceses. Trent strengthened the authority of local bishops so they could effectively discipline popular religious practices. The bishops were also subjected to new rules that required them to be highly visible by preaching regularly and conducting annual visitations of their diocesan parishes. Parish priests were required to be neatly dressed, better educated, strictly celibate, and active among their parishioners. To train priests, Trent also called for a seminary in every diocese.

Not a single doctrinal concession was made to the Protestants, however. Instead, the Council of Trent reaffirmed the traditional Scholastic education of the clergy; the role of good works in salvation; the authority of tradition; the seven sacraments; transubstantiation; the withholding of the Eucharistic cup from the laity; clerical celibacy; purgatory; the veneration of saints, relics, and sacred images; and indulgences. The council resolved medieval Scholastic quarrels in favor of the theology of Saint Thomas Aquinas, further enhancing his authority within the church. Thereafter, the church offered its strongest resistance to groups like the Jansenists, who endorsed the medieval Augustinian tradition, a source of alternative Catholic, as well as many Protestant, doctrines.

Rulers initially resisted Trent's reform decrees, fearing a revival of papal political power and new confessional conflicts within their lands. Over time, however, and with the pope's assurances that religious reforms were his sole intent, the new legislation took hold, and parish life revived under a devout and better trained clergy.

▼ The Social Significance of the Reformation in Western Europe

The Lutheran, Zwinglian, and Calvinist reformers all sought to work within the framework of reigning political power. Luther, Zwingli, and Calvin saw themselves and their followers as subject to definite civic responsibilities and obligations. Their political conservatism has led scholars to characterize them as "magisterial reformers," meaning not only that they were the leaders of the major Protestant movements, but also that they succeeded by the force of the magistrate's sword. Some have argued that this willingness to resort to coercion led the reformers to compromise their principles. They themselves, however, never contemplated reform outside or against the societies of which they were

PROTESTANT REFORMATION AND CATHOLIC REFORM ON THE CONTINENT

1517	Luther posts ninety-five theses against indulgences
1519	Charles I of Spain elected Holy Roman Emperor (as Charles V)
1519	Luther challenges authority of pope and inerrancy of church councils at Leipzig Debate
1521	Papal bull excommunicates Luther for heresy
1521	Diet of Worms condemns Luther
1521–1522	Luther translates the New Testament into German
1524–1525	Peasants' revolt in Germany
1527	The *Schleitheim Confession* of the Anabaptists
1529	Marburg Colloquy between Luther and Zwingli
1530	Diet of Augsburg fails to settle religious differences
1531	Formation of Protestant Schmalkaldic League
1534–1535	Anabaptists assume political power in Münster
1536	Calvin arrives in Geneva
1540	Jesuits, founded by Ignatius of Loyola, recognized as order by pope
1546	Luther dies
1547	Armies of Charles V crush Schmalkaldic League
1555	Peace of Augsburg recognizes rights of Lutherans to worship as they please
1545–1563	Council of Trent institutes reforms and responds to the Reformation

members. They wanted reform to take shape within reigning laws and institutions. They thus remained highly sensitive to what was politically and socially possible in their age. Some scholars believe the reformers were so cautious that they changed late medieval society very little and actually encouraged acceptance of the sociopolitical status quo.

The Revolution in Religious Practices and Institutions

The Reformation may have been politically conservative, but by the end of the sixteenth century, it had brought about radical changes in traditional religious practices and institutions in those lands where it succeeded.

Religion in Fifteenth-Century Life In the fifteenth century, on the streets of the great cities of Europe that later turned Protestant (for example, Zurich, Strasbourg, Nuremberg, and Geneva), the clergy and the religious were everywhere. They made up six to eight percent of the urban population, and they exercised considerable political as well as spiritual power. They legislated and taxed, they tried cases in special church courts, and they enforced their laws with threats of excommunication.

The church calendar regulated daily life. About one third of the year was given over to some kind of religious observance or celebration. There were frequent periods of fasting. On almost a hundred days out of the year, a pious Christian could not, without special dispensation, eat eggs, butter, animal fat, or meat.

Monasteries, and especially nunneries, were prominent and influential institutions. The children of society's most powerful citizens resided there. Local aristocrats identified with particular churches and chapels, whose walls recorded their lineage and proclaimed their generosity. On the streets, friars begged alms from passersby. In the churches, the Mass and liturgy were read entirely in Latin. Images of saints were regularly displayed, and on certain holidays their relics were paraded about and venerated.

Local religious shrines enjoyed a booming business. Pilgrims gathered there by the hundreds—even thousands—many sick and dying, all in search of a cure or a miracle, but also for diversion and entertainment. Several times during the year, special preachers arrived in the city to sell letters of indulgence.

Many clergy walked the streets with concubines and children, although they were sworn to celibacy and forbidden to marry. The church tolerated such relationships upon payment of penitential fines.

People everywhere complained about the clergy's exemption from taxation and also often from the civil criminal code. People also grumbled about having to support church offices whose occupants actually lived and worked elsewhere, turning the cure of souls over to poorly trained and paid substitutes. Townspeople expressed concern that the church had too much influence over education and culture.

Religion in Sixteenth-Century Life In these same cities, after the Reformation had firmly established itself, few changes in politics and society were evident. The same aristocratic families governed as before, and the rich generally got richer and the poor poorer. Overall numbers of clergy fell by two thirds, and religious holidays shrank by one third. Cloisters were nearly gone, and many that remained were transformed into hospices for the sick and poor or into educational institutions, their endowments turned over to these new purposes. A few cloisters remained for devout old monks and nuns who could not be pensioned off or lacked families and friends to care for them. These remaining cloisters died out with their present inhabitants, since no new religious were allowed to enter.

The churches, were reduced in number by at least one third, and worship was conducted almost completely in the vernacular. In some, particularly those in Zwinglian cities, the walls were stripped bare and whitewashed to make sure the congregation meditated only on God's word. The laity observed no obligatory fasts. Indulgence preachers no longer appeared. Local shrines were closed down, and anyone found openly venerating saints, relics, and images was subject to fine and punishment.

Copies of Luther's translation of the New Testament (1522) or, more often, excerpts from it could be found in private homes, and the new clergy encouraged meditation on the Bible. The clergy could marry, and most did. They paid taxes and were punished for their crimes in civil courts. Committees composed of roughly equal numbers of laity and clergy, over whose decisions secular magistrates had the last word, regulated domestic moral life.

Not all Protestant clergy remained enthusiastic about this new lay authority in religion. And the laity was also ambivalent about certain aspects of the Reformation. Over half of the original converts returned to the Catholic fold before the end of the sixteenth century. Whereas one half of Europe could be counted in the Protestant camp in the mid-sixteenth century, only one fifth would be there by the mid-seventeenth century.[2]

The Reformation and Education

Another major cultural achievement of the Reformation was its implementation of many of the educational reforms of humanism in new Protestant schools and universities. Many Protestant reformers in Germany, France,

---

[2]Geoffrey Parker, *Europe in Crisis, 1598–1648* (Ithaca, NY: Cornell University Press, 1979), p. 50.

and England were humanists. And even when their views on church doctrine and human nature separated them from the humanist movement, the Protestant reformers continued to share a common opposition to Scholasticism and a belief in the unity of wisdom, eloquence, and action. The humanist program of studies, providing the language skills to deal authoritatively with original sources, proved to be a more appropriate tool for the elaboration of Protestant doctrine than it did for Scholastic dialectic, which remained ascendant in the Counter-Reformation.

The Catholic counter-reformers recognized the close connections between humanism and the Reformation. Ignatius of Loyola observed how the new learning had been embraced by and served the Protestant cause. In his *Spiritual Exercises*, he insisted that when the Bible and the Church Fathers were read directly, they be read under the guidance of the authoritative Scholastic theologians: Peter Lombard, Bonaventure, and Thomas Aquinas. Aquinas especially, Ignatius argued, being "of more recent date," had the clearest understanding of what Scripture and the Fathers meant and, therefore, he should guide the study of the past.

When, in August 1518, Philip Melanchthon (1497–1560), "the praeceptor of Germany," a young humanist and professor of Greek, arrived at the University of Wittenberg, his first act was to reform the curriculum on the humanist model. In his inaugural address, entitled *On Improving the Studies of the Young*, Melanchthon presented himself as a defender of good letters and classical studies against "barbarians who practice barbarous arts." By the latter, he meant the Scholastic theologians of the later Middle Ages, whose methods of seeking to reconcile the views of conflicting authorities by disputation had, he believed, undermined both good

Brothers and Sisters. While away from home at law school in Padua, Italy, nineteen-year-old Paul Behaim, Jr., wrote in July 1577 to his older sisters Magdalena (twenty-two) and Sabina (twenty-one) to complain about the infrequency of their writing to him. Typical of sibling relations in every age, the letter is affectionate and joking. The sisters were then at home with their widowed mother and busy with the many chores of the self-sufficient sixteenth-century domestic household—especially, at this time of the year, gardening. Because of their alleged neglect Paul teasingly tells them they must now do "penance" by making him two new shirts, as his were embarrassingly tattered. He indicated in the left margin the exact collar length (A) and style (B) he wishes the shirts to be. Sewing for the household was another regular domestic chore for burgher and patrician women not working in trades outside the home. But Magdalena and Sabina went even further to "cover" their brother: They also allowed him to receive income (to be repaid in the future) from their own paternal inheritances so he might finish his legal education, on the successful completion of which the whole family depended for its future success. German National Museum, Nuremberg, Germany, Behaim-Archiv Fasz, 106 letters and sound biblical doctrine. Melanchthon saw Scholastic dominance in the universities as breeding contempt for the Greek language and learning and encouraging neglect of the study of mathematics, sacred studies, and oratory. He urged the careful study of history, poetry, and other humanist disciplines.

Together, Luther and Melanchthon restructured the University of Wittenberg's curriculum. Commentaries on Lombard's *Sentences* were dropped, as was canon law. Straightforward historical study replaced old Scholastic lectures on Aristotle. Students read primary sources directly, rather than by way of accepted Scholastic commentators. Candidates for theological degrees defended the new doctrine on the basis of their own study of the Bible. New chairs of Greek and Hebrew were created.

In Geneva, John Calvin and his successor, Theodore Beza, founded the Genevan Academy, which later evolved into the University of Geneva. That institution, created primarily to train Calvinist ministers, pursued ideals similar to those set forth by Luther and Melanchthon. Calvinist refugees who studied there later carried Protestant educational reforms to France, Scotland, England, and the New World. Through such efforts, many educated people acquired a working knowledge of Greek and Hebrew in the sixteenth and seventeenth centuries.

Some famous contemporaries decried what they saw as a narrowing of the original humanist program as Protestants took it over. Erasmus, for example, came to fear the Reformation as a threat to the liberal arts and good learning. Sebastian Franck pointed to parallels between Luther's and Zwingli's debates over Christ's presence in the Eucharist and such old Scholastic disputations as that over the Immaculate Conception of the Virgin.

Humanist culture and learning nonetheless remained indebted to the Reformation. The Protestant endorsement of the humanist program of studies remained as significant for the humanist movement as the latter had been for the Reformation. Protestant schools and universities consolidated and preserved for the modern world many of the basic pedagogical achievements of humanism. There, the *studia humanitatis,* although often as little more than a handmaiden to theological doctrine, found a permanent home, one that remained hospitable even in the heyday of conservative Protestantism.

The Reformation and the Changing Role of Women

The Protestant reformers favored clerical marriage and opposed monasticism and the celibate life. From this position, they challenged the medieval tendency alternately to degrade women as temptresses (following the model of Eve) and to exalt them as virgins (following the model of Mary). Protestants opposed the popular anti-woman and antimarriage literature of the Middle Ages. They praised woman in her own right, but especially in her biblical vocation as mother and housewife. Although wives remained subject to their husbands, new laws gave them greater security and protection.

Relief of sexual frustration and a remedy for fornication were prominent in Protestant arguments for universal marriage. But the reformers also viewed their wives as indispensable companions in their work, and this not solely because they took domestic cares off their husbands' minds. Luther, who married in 1525 at the age of forty-two, wrote the following of women:

Imagine what it would be like without women. The home, cities, economic life, and government would virtually disappear. Men cannot do without women. Even if it were possible for men to beget and bear children, they still could not do without women.[3]

John Calvin wrote this at the death of his wife:

I have been bereaved of the best companion of my life, of one who, had it been so ordered, would not only have been the willing sharer of my indigence, but even of my death. During her life she was the faithful helper of my ministry.[4]

Such tributes were intended to counter Catholic criticism of clerical marriage as a distraction of the clergy from their ministry. They were an expression of the high value Protestants placed on marriage and family life. In opposition to the celibate ideal of the Middle Ages, Protestants stressed, as no religious movement before them had ever done, the sacredness of home and family.

The ideal of the companionate marriage—that is, of husband and wife as co-workers in a special God-ordained community of the family, sharing authority equally within the household—led to an expansion of the grounds for divorce in Protestant lands as early as the 1520s. Women gained an equal right with men to divorce and remarry in good conscience—unlike the situation in Catholicism, where only a separation from bed and table, not divorce and remarriage, was permitted a couple in a failed marriage. The reformers were more willing to permit divorce and remarriage on grounds of adultery and abandonment than were secular magistrates, who feared liberal divorce laws would lead to social upheaval.

Typical of reforms and revolutions in their early stages, Protestant doctrines emboldened women as well as men. Renegade nuns wrote exposés of the nun-

[3]*Luther's Works*, Vol. 54: *Table Talk*, ed. and trans. by Theodore G. Tappert (Philadelphia: Fortress Press, 1967), p. 161.

[4]*Letters of John Calvin*, Vol. 2, trans. by J. Bonnet (Edinburgh: T. Constable, 1858), p. 216; E. G. Schwiebert, *Luther and His Times* (St. Louis, MO: Concordia, 1950), pp. 226–227, 266–268, 581–602; Steven Ozment, *Protestants: The Birth of a Revolution* (New York: Doubleday, 1992), pp. 17, 154, 159–162.

nery in the name of Christian freedom and justification by faith, declaring the nunnery was no special woman's place at all and that supervisory male clergy (who alone could hear the nuns' confessions and administer sacraments to them) made their lives as unpleasant and burdensome as any abusive husband. Women in the higher classes, who enjoyed new social and political freedoms during the Renaissance, found in Protestant theology a religious complement to their greater independence in other walks of life. Some cloistered noblewomen, however, protested the closing of nunneries, arguing that the cloister provided them a more interesting and independent way of life than they would have known in the secular world.

Because Protestants wanted women to become pious housewives, they encouraged the education of girls to literacy in the vernacular, with the expectation that they would thereafter model their lives on the Bible. However, women also found biblical passages that made clear their equality to men in the presence of God. Education also gave some women roles as independent authors on behalf of the Reformation. Although small advances from a modern perspective, these were also steps toward the emancipation of women.

▼ Family Life in Early Modern Europe

Changes in the timing and duration of marriage, family size, and infant and child care suggest that family life was under a variety of social and economic pressures in the sixteenth and seventeenth centuries.

Later Marriages

Between 1500 and 1800, men and women in Western Europe married at later ages than they had in previous centuries: men in their mid- to late-twenties, and women in their early- to mid-twenties. The canonical, or church-sanctioned, age for marriage remained fourteen for men and twelve for women. The church also recognized as valid free, private exchanges of vows between a man and a woman for whom no impediment to marriage existed. After the Reformation, which condemned such clandestine unions, both Protestants and Catholics required parental consent and public vows in church before a marriage could be deemed fully licit.

Late marriage in the West reflected the difficulty couples had supporting themselves independently. It simply took the average couple a longer time than before to prepare themselves materially for marriage. In the sixteenth century, one in five women never married, and these, combined with the estimated 15 percent who were unmarried widows, constituted a large unmarried female population. A later marriage was also a shorter marriage; in an age when few people lived into their sixties, couples who married in their thirties spent less time together than couples who married in their twenties. Also, because women who bore children for the first time at advanced ages had higher mortality rates, late marriage meant more frequent remarriage for men. As the rapid growth of orphanages and foundling homes between 1600 and 1800 makes clear, delayed marriage increased premarital sex and the number of illegitimate children.

Arranged Marriages

Marriage tended to be "arranged" in the sense that the parents met and discussed the terms of the marriage before the prospective bride and bridegroom became directly party to the preparations. The wealth and social standing of the bride and the bridegroom, however, were not the only things considered when youth married. By the fifteenth century, it was usual for the future bride and bridegroom to have known each other and to have had some prior relationship. Also, parents respected the couple's emotional feeling for one another. Parents did not force total strangers to live together, and children had a legal right to resist a coerced marriage, which was by definition invalid. The best marriage was one desired by both the bride and groom and their families.

Family Size

The Western European family was conjugal, or nuclear, consisting of a father and a mother and two to four children who survived into adulthood. This nuclear family lived within a larger household, including in-laws, servants, laborers, and boarders. The average husband and wife had six to seven children, a new birth about every two years. Of these, an estimated one third died by age five, and one half by their teens. Rare was the family, at any social level, that did not experience child death.

Birth Control

Artificial birth control (sponges, acidic ointments) has existed since antiquity. The church's condemnation of *coitus interruptus* (male withdrawal before ejaculation) during the thirteenth and fourteenth centuries suggests the existence of a contraceptive mentality, that is, a conscious, regular effort at birth control. Early birth control measures, when applied, were not very effective, and for both historical and moral reasons, the church opposed them. According to Saint Thomas Aquinas, a moral act

Encountering THE Past

TABLE MANNERS

PLEASURE AT TABLE in the sixteenth century was considered a matter of self-control. The well-dressed table taught the lessons of life as well as offered its bread. Neatness and order showed respect, respect ensured attentiveness, and attentiveness made for learning. The union of pleasure and discipline at mealtime was believed to inculcate in the young the traits that would keep them free and safe in an unforgiving world. Here is how Hans Sachs, a sixteenth-century father, expected children to behave:

Listen you children who are going to table.
Wash your hands and cut your nails.
Do not sit at the head of the table;
This is reserved for the father of the house.
Do not commence eating until a blessing has
    been said.
Dine in God's name
And permit the eldest to begin first.
Proceed in a disciplined manner.
Do not snort or smack like a pig.
Do not reach violently for bread,
Lest you may knock over a glass.
Do not cut bread on your chest,
Or conceal pieces of bread or pastry under
    your hands.
Do not tear pieces for your plate with your
    teeth.
Do not stir food around on your plate
Or linger over it.
Do not fill your spoon too full.

Rushing through your meal is bad manners.
Do not reach for more food
While your mouth is still full,
Nor talk with your mouth full.
Be moderate; do not fall upon your plate like
    an animal.
Be the last to cut your meat and break your fish.
Chew your food with your mouth closed.
Do not lick the corners of your mouth like a
    dog.
Do not hover greedily over your food.
Wipe your mouth before you drink,
So that you do not grease up your wine.
Drink politely and avoid coughing into your cup.
Do not belch or cry out.
With drink be most prudent.
Sit smartly, undisturbed, humble . . .
Do not stare at a person
As if you were watching him eat.
Do not elbow the person sitting next to you.
Sit up straight; be a model of gracefulness.
Do not rock back and forth on the bench,
Lest you let loose a stink.
Do not kick your feet under the table.
Guard yourself against all shameful
Words, gossip, ridicule, and laughter . . .
If sexual play occurs at table,
Pretend you do not see it.
Never start a quarrel,
Quarreling at table is most despicable.
Say nothing that might offend another.
Do not blow your nose
Or do other shocking things.
Do not pick your nose.
If you must pick your teeth, be discreet about it.
Never scratch your head
(This goes for girls and women too);
Or fish out lice.
Let no one wipe his mouth on the table cloth,
Or lay his head in his hands.
Do not lean back against the wall
Until the meal is finished.
Silently praise and thank God
For the food he has graciously provided. . . .

Source: Trans. by S. Ozment, from S. Ozment, *When Fathers Ruled: Family Life in Reformation Europe* (Cambridge, MA: Harvard University Press, 1983), pp. 142–43.

A Family Meal. In Max Geisberg, *The German Single-Leaf Woodcuts, III: 1500–1550*, rev. and ed. by W. L. Strauss (New York: Hacker Art Books, 1974). Used by permission of Hacker Art Books.

How do table manners prepare a child for life? Has table etiquette changed since the sixteenth century?

must aid and abet, never frustrate, nature's goal, and the natural end of sex was the birth of children and their godly rearing within the bounds of holy matrimony and the community of the church.

Wet Nursing

The church allied with the physicians of early modern Europe on another intimate family matter. Both condemned women who hired wet nurses to suckle their newborn children. The practice was popular among upper-class women and reflected their social standing. It appears to have increased the risk of infant mortality by exposing infants to a strange and shared milk supply from women who were often not as healthy as the infants' own mothers and lived under less sanitary conditions. Nursing was distasteful to some upper-class women, whose husbands also preferred that they not do it. Among women, vanity and convenience appear to have been motives for hiring a wet nurse, while for husbands, even more was at stake. Because the church forbade lactating women from indulging in sexual intercourse, a nursing wife could become a reluctant lover. Nursing also had a contraceptive effect (about 75 percent effective). Some women prolonged nursing their children to delay a new pregnancy, and some husbands cooperated in this form of family planning. For other husbands, however, especially noblemen and royalty who desired an abundance of male heirs, nursing seemed to rob them of offspring and jeopardize their patrimony—hence their support of hired wet nurses.

Loving Families?

The traditional Western European family had features that seem cold and distant. Children between the ages of eight and thirteen were routinely sent from their homes into apprenticeships, school, or employment in the homes and businesses of relatives, friends, and occasionally strangers. The emotional ties between spouses also seem to have been as tenuous as those between parents and children. Widowers and widows often married again within a few months of their spouses' deaths, and marriages with extreme difference in age between partners suggest limited affection.

In response to modern-day criticism, an early modern parent might well have asked: "What greater love can parents have for their children than to equip them well for a worldly vocation?" A well-apprenticed child was a self-supporting child, and hence a child with a future. In light of the comparatively primitive living conditions, contemporaries also appreciated the purely utilitarian and humane side of marriage and understood when widowers and widows quickly remarried. Marriages with extreme disparity in age, however, were no

more the norm in early modern Europe than the practice of wet nursing, and they received just as much criticism and ridicule.

▼ Literary Imagination in Transition

Alongside the political and cultural changes brought about by the new religious systems of the Reformation (Lutheranism, Calvinism, and Puritanism) and Catholic Reform, medieval outlooks and religious values continued to be debated, embraced, and rejected into the seventeenth century. Major literary figures of the post-Reformation period had elements of both the old and the new in their own new transitional works. Two who stand out are Miguel de Cervantes Saavedra (1547–1616), writing in still deeply Catholic Spain, and William Shakespeare (1564–1616), who wrote in newly Anglican England.

Miguel de Cervantes Saavedra: Rejection of Idealism

Spanish literature of the sixteenth and seventeenth centuries reflects the peculiar religious and political history of Spain in this period. Traditional Catholic teaching was a major influence on Spanish life. Since the joint reign of Ferdinand and Isabella (1479–1504), the church had received the unqualified support of the reigning political power. Although there was religious reform in Spain, and genuine Protestant groups were persecuted for "Lutheranism," a Protestant Reformation never occurred there, thanks largely to the entrenched power of the church and the Inquisition.

A second influence on Spanish literature was the aggressive piety of Spanish rulers. Their intertwining of Catholic piety and political power underlay a third influence: preoccupation with medieval chivalric virtues, in particular, questions of honor and loyalty. The novels and plays of the period almost invariably focus on a special test of character, bordering on the heroic, that threatens honor and reputation. In this regard, Spanish literature remained more Catholic and medieval than that of England and France, where major Protestant movements had occurred. Two of the most important Spanish writers of this period became priests (the dramatists Lope de Vega and Pedro Calderón de la Barca). The writer generally acknowledged to be Spain's greatest, Cervantes, was preoccupied in his work with the strengths and weaknesses of traditional religious idealism.

Cervantes (1547–1616) had only a smattering of formal education. He educated himself by wide reading in popular literature and immersion in the "school of life." As a young man, he worked in Rome for a Spanish cardinal. As a soldier, he was decorated for gallantry in the Battle of Lepanto against the Turks (1571). He also spent five years as a slave in Algiers after his ship was pirated in 1575. Later, while working as a tax collector, he was imprisoned several times for padding his accounts, and it was in prison that he began, in 1603, to write his most famous work, *Don Quixote.*

The first part of *Don Quixote* appeared in 1605. The intent of this work seems to have been to satirize the chivalric romances then popular in Spain. But Cervantes could not conceal his deep affection for the character he created as an object of ridicule. The work is satire only on the surface and appeals as much to philosophers and theologians as to students of Spanish literature. Cervantes presented Don Quixote as a none-too-stable middle-aged man. Driven mad by reading too many chivalric romances, he had come to believe he was an aspiring knight who had to prove his worthiness by brave deeds. To this end, he donned a rusty suit of armor and chose for his inspiration an unworthy peasant girl (Dulcinea), whom he fancied to be a noble lady to whom he could, with honor, dedicate his life.

Don Quixote's foil—Sancho Panza, a clever, worldly wise peasant who serves as Quixote's squire—watches with bemused skepticism as his lord does battle with a windmill (which he has mistaken for a dragon) and repeatedly makes a fool of himself as he gallops across the countryside. The story ends tragically with Don Quixote's humiliating defeat at the hand of a well-meaning friend who, disguised as a knight, bested Quixote in combat and forced him to renounce his quest for knighthood. Don Quixote did not, however, come to his senses but rather returned to his village to die a brokenhearted old man.

Throughout the novel, Cervantes juxtaposes the down-to-earth realism of Sancho Panza with the old-fashioned religious idealism of Don Quixote. The reader perceives that Cervantes admired the one as much as the other and meant to portray both as representing attitudes necessary for a happy life.

William Shakespeare: Dramatist of the Age

There is much less factual knowledge about Shakespeare (1564–1616) than we would expect of the greatest playwright in the English language. He married at the early age of eighteen, in 1582, and he and his wife, Anne Hathaway, were the parents of three children (including twins) by 1585. He apparently worked as a schoolteacher for a time and in this capacity gained his broad knowledge of Renaissance literature. His own reading and enthusiasm for the learning of his day are manifest in the many literary allusions that appear in his plays.

Shakespeare lived the life of a country gentleman. There is none of the Puritan distress over worldliness in his work. He took the new commercialism and the bawdy pleasures of the Elizabethan Age in stride and with amusement. He was a radical neither in politics nor religion. The few allusions in his works to the Puritans seem more critical than complimentary.

That Shakespeare was interested in politics is apparent from his historical plays and the references to contemporary political events that fill all his plays. He viewed government through the character of the individual ruler, whether Richard III or Elizabeth Tudor, rather than in terms of ideal systems or social goals. By modern standards, he was a political conservative, accepting the social rankings and the power structure of his day and demonstrating unquestioned patriotism.

Shakespeare knew the theater as one who participated in every phase of its life—as a playwright, an actor, and part owner of a theater. He was a member and principal writer of a famous company of actors known as the King's Men. Between 1590 and 1610, many of his plays were performed at court, where he moved with comfort and received enthusiastic royal patronage.

Elizabethan drama was already a distinctive form when Shakespeare began writing. Unlike French drama of the seventeenth century, which was dominated by classical models, English drama developed in the sixteenth and seventeenth centuries as a blending of many forms: classical comedies and tragedies, medieval morality plays, and contemporary Italian short stories.

Two contemporaries, Thomas Kyd and Christopher Marlowe, influenced Shakespeare's tragedies. Kyd (1558–1594) wrote the first dramatic version of *Hamlet.* The tragedies of Marlowe (1564–1593) set a model for character, poetry, and style that only Shakespeare among the English playwrights of the period surpassed. Shakespeare synthesized the best past and current achievements. A keen student of human motivation and passion, he had a unique talent for getting into people's minds.

Shakespeare wrote histories, comedies, and tragedies. *Richard III* (1593), an early play, stands out among the histories, although some scholars view the picture it presents of Richard as an unprincipled villain as "Tudor propaganda." Shakespeare's comedies, although not attaining the heights of his tragedies, surpass his history plays in originality.

Shakespeare's tragedies are considered his unique achievement. Four of these were written within a three-year period: *Hamlet* (1603), *Othello* (1604), *King Lear* (1605), and *Macbeth* (1606). The most original of the tragedies, *Romeo and Juliet* (1597), transformed an old popular story into a moving drama of "star-cross'd lovers." Both Romeo and Juliet, denied a marriage by their warring families, die tragic deaths. Romeo, believing Juliet to be dead when she has merely taken a sleeping potion, poisons himself. When Juliet awakes to find Romeo dead, she kills herself with his dagger.

Shakespeare's works struck universal human themes, many of which were deeply rooted in contemporary religious traditions. His plays were immensely popular with both the playgoers and the play readers of Elizabethan England. Still today, the works of no other dramatist from his age are performed in theaters or on film more regularly than his.

In Perspective

During the early Middle Ages, Christendom had been divided into Western and Eastern churches with irreconcilable theological differences. When, in 1517, Martin Luther posted ninety-five theses questioning the selling of indulgences and the traditional sacrament of penance that lay behind them, he created a division within Western Christendom itself—an internal division between Protestants and Catholics.

The Lutheran protest came at a time of political and social discontent with the church. Not only princes and magistrates but many ordinary people as well resented traditional clerical rights and privileges. The clergy were exempted from many secular laws and taxes while remaining powerful landowners whose personal lifestyles were not all that different from those of the laity. Spiritual and secular protest combined to make the Protestant Reformation a successful assault on the old church. In town after town and region after region within Protestant lands, the major institutions and practices of traditional piety were transformed.

It soon became clear, however, that the division would not stop with the Lutherans. Making Scripture the only arbiter in religion had opened a Pandora's box. People proved to have different ideas about what Scripture taught. Indeed, there seemed to be as many points of view as there were readers. Rapidly, the Reformation created Lutheran, Zwinglian, Anabaptist, Spiritualist, Calvinist, and Anglican versions of biblical religion—a splintering of Protestantism that has endured and increased until today.

Catholics had been pursuing reform before the Reformation broke out in Germany, although without papal enthusiasm and certainly not along clear Protestant lines. When major reforms finally came in the Catholic Church around the mid-sixteenth century, they were doctrinally reactionary, but administratively and spiritually flexible. The church enforced strict obedience and conformity to its teaching, but it also provided the laity with a better educated and disciplined clergy. For laity who wanted a deeper and more individual piety, experimentation with proven spiritual practices was now permitted. By century's end, such measures had countered, and in some areas even spectacularly reversed, Protestant gains.

After the Reformation, pluralism steadily became a fact of Western religious life. It did so at first only by sheer force, since no one religious body was then prepared to concede the validity of alternative Christian beliefs and practices. During the sixteenth and seventeenth centuries, only those groups that fought doggedly for their faith gained the right to practice it freely. Despite these struggles, religious pluralism endured. Never again would there be only a Catholic Christian Church in Europe.

REVIEW QUESTIONS

1. What problems in the church contributed to the Protestant Reformation? Why was the church unable to suppress dissent as it had earlier?
2. What were the basic similarities and differences between the ideas of Luther and Zwingli? Between Luther and Calvin? How did the differences tend to affect the success of the Protestant movement?
3. Why did the Reformation begin in Germany? What political factors contributed to its success there as opposed to in France, Spain, or Italy?
4. What was the Catholic Counter-Reformation? What reforms did the Council of Trent introduce? Was the Protestant Reformation healthy for the Catholic Church?
5. Why did Henry VIII break with Rome? Was the "new" church he established really Protestant? How did the English church change under his successors?
6. How did the Reformation affect women in the sixteenth and seventeenth centuries? How did relations between men and women, family size, and child care change during this period?

SUGGESTED READINGS

H. Bloom, *Shakespeare: The Invention of the Human* (1998). An analysis of the greatest writer in the English language.

T. A. Brady, Jr. ed., *Handbook of European History: Late Middle Ages, Renaissance, Reformation* (1995). Essays summarizing recent research on aspects of the Reformation.

P. Collinson, *The Reformation* (2004). Portrays the Reformation as creating religious pluralism and civil liberty despite itself.

E. Duffy, *The Stripping of the Altars: Traditional Religion in England, 1400–1580* (1992). Strongest of recent arguments that popular piety survived the Reformation in England.

M. Duran, *Cervantes* (1974). Detailed biography.

B. S. Gregory, *Salvation at Stake: Christian Martyrdom in Early Modern Europe* (1999). Massive, enthralling study of religion.

R. Houlbrooke, *English Family Life, 1450–1716. An Anthology from Diaries* (1988). A rich collection of documents illustrating family relationships.

J. C. Hutchison, *Albrecht Dürer: A Biography* (1990). An art historian chronicles both the life and work of the artist.

H. Jedin, *A History of the Council of Trent*, Vols. 1 and 2 (1957–1961). Still the gold standard.

P. Johnston and R. W. Scribner, *The Reformation in Germany and Switzerland* (1993). Reformation from the bottom up.

D. MacColloch, *The Reformation* (2004). Finds old Catholics and non-Protestant Evangelicals to be the forerunners of modern religion.

H. A. Oberman, *Luther: Man between God and the Devil* (1989). Perhaps the best account of Luther's life, by a Dutch master.

J. O'Malley, *The First Jesuits* (1993). Detailed account of the creation of the Society of Jesus and its original purposes.

S. Ozment, *The Age of Reform, 1250–1550: An Intellectual and Religious History of Late Medieval and Reformation Europe* (1980). A broad survey of major religious ideas and beliefs.

B. Roberts, *Through the Keyhole: Dutch Child-Rearing Practices in the 17th and 18th Centuries* (1998). A study of three elite families.

Q. Skinner, *The Foundations of Modern Political Thought II: The Age of Reformation* (1978). A comprehensive survey that treats every political thinker and tract.

D. Starkey, *Elizabeth: The Struggle for the Throne* (2000). Complex, riveting account by a sympathetic historian.

L. Stone, *The Family, Sex, and Marriage in England 1500–1800* (1977). Controversial but enduring in many respects.

G. Strauss, ed. and trans., *Manifestations of Discontent in Germany on the Eve of the Reformation* (1971). Rich collection of both rural and urban sources.

F. Wendel, *Calvin: The Origins and Development of His Religious Thought*, trans. by P. Mairet (1963). The best treatment of Calvin's theology.

H. Wunder, *He Is the Sun, She Is the Moon: A History of Women in Early Modern Germany* (1998). A model of gender history.

For additional learning resources related to this chapter, please go to www.myhistorylab.com

myhistorylab

The massacre of worshipping Protestants at Vassy, France (March 1, 1562), which began the French wars of religion. An engraving by an unidentified seventeenth-century artist.   The Granger Collection

12

The Age of Religious Wars

▼ **Renewed Religious Struggle**

▼ **The French Wars of Religion (1562–1598)**
Appeal of Calvinism • Catherine de Médicis and the Guises • The Rise to Power of Henry of Navarre
• The Edict of Nantes

▼ **Imperial Spain and Philip II (r. 1556–1598)**
Pillars of Spanish Power • The Revolt in the Netherlands

▼ **England and Spain (1553–1603)**
Mary I (r. 1553–1558) • Elizabeth I (r. 1558–1603)

▼ **The Thirty Years' War (1618–1648)**
Preconditions for War • Four Periods of War • The Treaty of Westphalia

▼ **In Perspective**

THE LATE SIXTEENTH and the first half of the seventeenth centuries are described as the Age of Religious Wars because of the bloody conflict of Protestants and Catholics across Europe. Both genuine religious conflict and bitter dynastic rivalries fueled the wars. In France, the Netherlands, England, and Scotland in the second half of the sixteenth century, Calvinists fought Catholic rulers for the right to govern their own territories and to practice their chosen religion openly. In the first half of the seventeenth century, Lutherans, Calvinists, and Catholics marched against one another in central and northern Europe during the Thirty Years' War. By the mid-seventeenth century, English Puritans had successfully revolted against the Stuart monarchy and the Anglican Church. (See Chapter 13.)

▼ Renewed Religious Struggle

During the first half of the sixteenth century, religious conflict had been confined to central Europe and was primarily a struggle by Lutherans and Zwinglians to secure rights and freedoms for themselves. In the second half of the century, the focus shifted to Western Europe—to France, the Netherlands, England, and Scotland—and became a struggle by Calvinists for recognition. After the Peace of Augsburg (1555) and acceptance of the principle that a region's ruler determined its religion (*cuius regio, eius religio*), Lutheranism became a legal religion in the Holy Roman Empire. The Peace of Augsburg did not, however, extend recognition to non-Lutheran Protestants. Anabaptists and other sectarians continued to be scorned as heretics and anarchists, and Calvinists were not strong enough to gain legal standing.

Outside the empire, the struggle for religious freedom had intensified in most countries. After the Council of Trent adjourned in 1563, Catholics began a Jesuit-led international counteroffensive against Protestants. At the time of John Calvin's death in 1564, Geneva had become both a refuge for Europe's persecuted Protestants and an international school for Protestant resistance, producing leaders equal to the new Catholic challenge.

Genevan Calvinism and Catholicism as revived by the Council of Trent were two equally dogmatic, aggressive, and irreconcilable church systems. Calvinists may have looked like "new papists" to critics when they dominated cities like Geneva. Yet when, as minorities, they found their civil and religious rights denied, they became firebrands and revolutionaries. Calvinism adopted an organization that magnified regional and local religious authority. Boards of **presbyters**, or elders, represented the individual congregations of Calvinists, directly shaping policy.

By contrast, the **Counter-Reformation** sponsored a centralized episcopal church system hierarchically arranged from pope to parish priest and stressing unquestioning obedience to the person at the top. The high clergy—the pope and his bishops—not the synods of local churches, were supreme. Calvinism proved attractive to proponents of political decentralization who opposed such hierarchical rule, in principle, whereas the Roman Catholic Church, an institution also devoted to one head and one law, found absolute monarchy congenial.

The opposition between the two religions may be seen in their respective art and architecture. The Catholic Counter-Reformation found the baroque style congenial. A successor to mannerism, **baroque** presented life in a grandiose, three-dimensional display of raw energy. The great baroque artists Peter Paul Rubens (1571–1640) and Gianlorenzo Bernini (1598–1680) were Catholics. By contrast, the works of prominent Protestant artists were restrained, as can be seen in the gentle, searching portraits of the Dutch Mennonite, Rembrandt van Rijn (1606–1669). (See the juxtaposition of Bavarian Catholic and Palatine Calvinist churches.)

As religious wars engulfed Europe, the intellectuals perceived the wisdom of religious pluralism and toleration more quickly than did the politicians. A new skepticism, relativism, and individualism in religion became respectable in the sixteenth and seventeenth centuries. (See Chapter 14.) Sebastian Castellio's (1515–1563) pithy

censure of John Calvin for his role in the execution of the Antitrinitarian Michael Servetus summarized a growing sentiment: "To kill a man is not to defend a doctrine, but to kill a man."[1] The French essayist Michel de Montaigne (1533–1592) asked in scorn of the dogmatic mind, "What do I know?" The Lutheran Valentin Weigel (1533–1588), surveying a half century of religious strife in Germany, advised people to look within themselves for religious truth and no longer to churches and creeds.

Such skeptical views gained currency in larger political circles only at the cost of painful experience. Religious strife and civil war were best held in check where rulers tended to subordinate theological doctrine to political unity, urging tolerance, moderation, and compromise—even indifference—in religious matters. Rulers of this kind came to be known as *politiques*, and the most successful among them was Elizabeth I of England. By contrast, Mary I of England, Philip II of Spain, and Oliver Cromwell, all of whom took their religion with the utmost seriousness and refused any compromise, did not, in the end, achieve their political goals.

The wars of religion were both internal national conflicts and truly international wars. Catholic and Protestant subjects struggled against one another for control of the crown of France, the Netherlands, and England. The Catholic governments of France and Spain conspired and finally sent armies against Protestant regimes in England and the Netherlands. The outbreak of the Thirty Years' War in 1618 made the international dimension of the religious conflict especially clear; before it ended in 1648, the war drew every major European nation directly or indirectly into its deadly net.

▼ The French Wars of Religion (1562–1598)

French Protestants are known as **Huguenots**, a term derived from Besançon Hugues, the leader of Geneva's political revolt against the House of Savoy in the 1520s, which had been a prelude to that city's Calvinist Reformation. Huguenots were already under surveillance in France in the early 1520s when Lutheran writings and doctrines began to circulate in Paris. The capture of the French king Francis I by the forces of Emperor Charles V at the Battle of Pavia in 1525 provided a motive for the first wave of Protestant persecution in France. The French government hoped thereby to pacify the Habsburg victor, a fierce opponent of German Protestants, and to win their king's swift release.

A second major crackdown came a decade later. When Protestants plastered Paris and other cities with anti-Catholic placards on October 18, 1534, mass arrests

[1]*Contra libellum Calvini* (N.P., 1562), p. E2a.

A Closer ▶ LOOK

BAROQUE AND PLAIN CHURCH: ARCHITECTURAL REFLECTIONS OF BELIEF

CONTRAST AN eighteenth-century Catholic baroque church in Ottobeuren, Bavaria, and a seventeenth-century Calvinist plain church in the Palatinate. The Catholic church pops with sculptures, paintings, and ornamentation, while the Calvinist church has been stripped of every possible decoration.

Decorated altars dominate the interior of the Catholic church and make the sacrifice of the Eucharist in the Mass the center of worship. The intent is to inspire worshippers to self-transcendence.

Vanni/Art Resource, NY

The open Bible and raised pulpit dominate the Protestant church. The intent is to keep worshippers' attention on God's word and their own immortal souls and to prevent any form of decoration from distracting them.

To examine this image in an interactive fashion, please go to www.myhistorylab.com

German National Museum, Nuremberg, Germany

of suspected Protestants followed. The government retaliation drove John Calvin and other members of the French reform party into exile. In 1540, the Edict of Fontainebleau subjected French Protestants to the Inquisition. Henry II (r. 1547–1559) established new measures against Protestants in the Edict of Chateaubriand in 1551. Save for a few brief interludes, the French monarchy remained a staunch foe of the Protestants until the ascension to the throne of Henry IV of Navarre in 1589.

The Habsburg-Valois wars (see Chapter 11) had ended with the Treaty of Cateau-Cambrésis in 1559, after which Europe experienced a moment of peace. The same year, however, marked the beginning of internal French conflict and a shift of the European balance of power away from France to Spain. The shift began with an accident. During a tournament held to celebrate the marriage of his thirteen-year-old daughter to Philip II, the son of Charles V and heir to the Spanish Habsburg lands, the French king, Henry II, was mortally wounded when a lance pierced his visor. This unforeseen event brought to the throne his sickly fifteen-year-old son, Francis II, who died after reigning only a year (1559–1560). With the monarchy weakened, three powerful families saw their chance to control France and began to compete for the young king's ear: the Bourbons, whose power lay in the south and west; the Montmorency-Chatillons, who controlled the center of France; and the strongest among them, the Guises, who were dominant in eastern France.

The Guises had little trouble establishing firm control over the young king. Francis, duke of Guise, had been Henry II's general and his brothers, Charles and Louis, were cardinals of the church. Mary Stuart, Queen of Scots, the eighteen-year-old widow of Francis II, was their niece. Throughout the latter half of the sixteenth century, the name "Guise" remained interchangeable with militant, reactionary Catholicism.

The Bourbon and Montmorency-Chatillon families, in contrast, developed strong Huguenot sympathies, largely for political reasons. The Bourbon Louis I, prince of Condé (d. 1569), and the Montmorency-Chatillon admiral Gaspard de Coligny (1519–1572) became the political leaders of the French Protestant resistance. They collaborated early in an abortive plot to kidnap Francis II from his Guise advisers in the Conspiracy of Amboise in 1560. Calvin, who considered such tactics a disgrace to the Reformation, condemned this conspiracy.

Appeal of Calvinism

Often for different reasons, ambitious aristocrats and discontented townspeople joined Calvinist churches in opposing the Guise-dominated French monarchy. In 1561, more than 2,000 Huguenot congregations existed throughout France. Yet Huguenots were a majority of the population in only two regions: Dauphiné and Languedoc. Although they made up only about one fifteenth of the population, Huguenots held important geographic areas and were heavily represented among the more powerful segments of French society. A good two fifths of the French aristocracy became Huguenots. Many apparently hoped to establish within France a principle of territorial sovereignty akin to what the Peace of Augsburg had secured within the Holy Roman Empire. Calvinism thus served the forces of political decentralization.

John Calvin and Theodore Beza sought to advance their cause by currying favor with powerful aristocrats. Beza converted Jeanne d'Albert, the mother of the future Henry IV. The prince of Condé was apparently converted in 1558 under the influence of his Calvinist wife. For many aristocrats—Condé probably among them—Calvinist religious convictions proved useful to their political goals.

The military organization of Condé and Coligny progressively merged with the religious organization of the French Huguenot churches, creating a potent combination that benefited both political and religious dissidents. Calvinism justified and inspired political resistance, while the resistance made Calvinism a viable religion in Catholic France. Each side had much to gain from the other. The confluence of secular and religious motives, although beneficial to aristocratic resistance and the Calvinist religion alike, cast suspicion on the religious appeal of Calvinism. Clearly, religious conviction was neither the only, nor always the main, reason for becoming a Calvinist in France in the second half of the sixteenth century.

Catherine de Médicis and the Guises

Following Francis II's death in 1560, the queen mother, Catherine de Médicis (1519–1589) became regent for her minor son, Charles IX (r. 1560–1574). At a meeting in Poissy, she tried unsuccessfully to reconcile the Protestant and Catholic factions. Fearing the power and guile of the Guises, Catherine, whose first concern was always to preserve the monarchy, sought allies among the Protestants. In 1562, after conversations with Beza and Coligny, she issued the January Edict, which granted Protestants freedom to worship publicly outside towns—although only privately within them—and to hold synods. In March 1562, this royal toleration came to an abrupt end when the duke of Guise surprised a Protestant congregation at Vassy in Champagne and massacred many worshippers. That event marked the beginning of the French wars of religion.

Had Condé and the Huguenot armies rushed immediately to the queen's side after this attack, Protestants might well have secured an alliance with the crown. The queen mother's fear of Guise power was great. Condé's hesitation, however, placed the young king and the

Catherine de Médicis (1519–1589) exercised power in France during the reigns of her three sons, Francis II (r. 1559–1560), Charles IX (r. 1560–1574), and Henry III (r. 1574–1589). *Getty Images, Inc.–Liaison*

queen mother, against their deepest wishes, under firm Guise control. Cooperation with the Guises became the only alternative to capitulation to the Protestants.

The Peace of Saint-Germain-en-Laye

During the first French war of religion, fought between April 1562 and March 1563, the duke of Guise was assassinated. It was a measure of the international character of the struggle in France that troops from Hesse and the Palatinate fought alongside the Huguenots. A brief resumption of hostilities in 1567–1568 was followed by the bloodiest of all the conflicts, between September 1568 and August 1570. In this period, Condé was killed, and Huguenot leadership passed to Coligny. This was actually a blessing in disguise for the Protestants, because Coligny was far the better military strategist. In the peace of Saint-Germain-en-Laye (1570), which ended the third war, the crown, acknowledging the power of the Protestant nobility, granted the Huguenots religious freedoms within their territories and the right to fortify their cities.

Perpetually caught between fanatical Huguenot and Guise extremes, Queen Catherine had always sought to balance one side against the other. Like the Guises, she wanted a Catholic France, but she feared a Guise-dominated monarchy. After the Peace of Saint-Germain-en-Laye, the crown tilted manifestly toward the Bourbon faction and the Huguenots, and Coligny became Charles IX's most trusted adviser. Unknown to the king, Catherine began to plot with the Guises against the ascendant Protestants. As she had earlier sought Protestant support when Guise power threatened to subdue the monarchy, she now sought Guise support as Protestant influence grew.

There was reason for Catherine to fear Coligny's hold on the king. Louis of Nassau, the leader of Protestant resistance to Philip II in the Netherlands, had gained Coligny's ear. Coligny used his influence to win the king of France over to a planned French invasion of the Netherlands to support the Dutch Protestants. This would have placed France squarely on a collision course with mighty Spain. Catherine recognized far better than her son that France stood little chance in such a contest. News of the stunning Spanish victory over the Turks at Lepanto in October 1571 had sobered Catherine and her advisors.

The Saint Bartholomew's Day Massacre

When Catherine lent her support to the infamous Saint Bartholomew's Day Massacre of Protestants, she did so out of a far less reasoned judgment. Her decision appears to have been made in near panic. On August 22, 1572, four days after the Huguenot Henry of Navarre had married the king's sister, Marguerite of Valois—still another sign of growing Protestant power—Coligny was struck down, although not killed, by an assassin's bullet. Catherine had apparently been party to this Guise plot to eliminate Coligny. After its failure, she feared both the king's reaction to her complicity with the Guises and Coligny's response. Catherine convinced Charles that a Huguenot coup was afoot, inspired by Coligny, and that only the swift execution of Protestant leaders could save the crown from a Protestant attack on Paris.

On Saint Bartholomew's Day, August 24, 1572, Coligny and 3,000 fellow Huguenots were butchered in Paris. Within three days coordinated attacks across France killed an estimated 20,000 Huguenots. It is a date that has ever since lived in infamy for Protestants.

Pope Gregory XIII and Philip II of Spain reportedly greeted the news of the Protestant massacre with special religious celebrations. Philip had good reason to rejoice. By throwing France into civil war, the massacre ended any planned French opposition to his efforts to subdue his rebellious subjects in the Netherlands. But the massacre of thousands of Protestants also gave the discerning Catholic world cause for new alarm. The event changed the nature of the struggle between Protestants and Catholics both within and beyond the borders of France. It was thereafter no longer an internal contest between Guise and Bourbon factions for French political influence, nor was it simply a Huguenot campaign to win basic religious freedoms. Henceforth, in Protestant eyes, it became an international struggle for sheer survival against an adversary whose cruelty justified any means of resistance.

Protestant Resistance Theory Only as Protestants faced suppression and sure defeat did they begin to sanction active political resistance. At first, they tried to practice the biblical precept of obedient subjection to worldly authority (Romans 13:1). Luther had only grudgingly approved resistance to the emperor after the Diet of Augsburg in 1530. In 1550, Lutherans in Magdeburg had published an influential defense of the right of lower authorities to oppose the emperor's order that all Lutherans return to the Catholic fold.

Calvin, who never faced the specter of total political defeat after his return to Geneva in September 1540, had always condemned willful disobedience and rebellion against lawfully constituted governments as unChristian. Yet he also taught that lower magistrates, as part of the lawfully constituted government, had the right and duty to oppose tyrannical higher authority.

The exiled Scots reformer John Knox (1513–1572), who had seen Mary of Guise, the Regent of Scotland, and Mary I of England crush his cause, laid the groundwork for later Calvinist resistance. In his famous *First Blast of the Trumpet against the Terrible Regiment of Women* (1558), he declared that the removal of a heathen tyrant was not only permissible, but also a Christian duty. He had the Catholic queen of England in mind.

After the great massacre of French Protestants on Saint Bartholomew's Day 1572, Calvinists everywhere came to appreciate the need for an active defense of their religious rights. Classical Huguenot theories of resistance appeared in three major works of the 1570s. The first was the *Franco-Gallia* of François Hotman (1573), a humanist argument that the representative Estates General of France historically held higher authority than the French king. The second was Theodore Beza's *On the Right of Magistrates over Their Subjects* (1574), which, going beyond Calvin's views, justified the correction and even the overthrow of tyrannical rulers by lower authorities. (See "Theodore Beza Defends the Right to Resist Tyranny.") Finally, Philippe du Plessis Mornay's *Defense of Liberty against Tyrants* (1579) admonished princes, nobles, and magistrates beneath the king, as guardians of the rights of the body politic, to take up arms against tyranny in other lands.

The Rise to Power of Henry of Navarre

Henry III (r. 1574–1589) was the last of Henry II's sons to wear the French crown. He found the monarchy wedged between a radical Catholic League, formed in 1576 by Henry of Guise, and vengeful Huguenots. Neither group would have been reluctant to assassinate a ruler they considered heretical and a tyrant. Like the queen mother, Henry sought to steer a middle course. In this effort, he received support from a growing body of neutral Catholics and Huguenots, who put the political survival of France above its religious unity. Such *politiques* were prepared to compromise religious creeds to save the nation.

The Peace of Beaulieu in May 1576 granted the Huguenots almost complete religious and civil freedom. France, however, was not ready then for such sweeping toleration. Within seven months of the Peace, the Catholic League forced Henry to return to the illusory quest for absolute religious unity in France. In October 1577, the king truncated the Peace of Beaulieu and once again limited areas of permitted Huguenot worship. Thereafter, Huguenot and Catholic factions returned to their accustomed anarchical military solutions. The Protestants were led by Henry of Navarre, a legal heir to the French throne by virtue of his descent in a direct male line from St. Louis IX (d. 1270).

In the mid-1580s, the Catholic League, with Spanish support, became dominant in Paris. In what came to be known as the Day of the Barricades, Henry III attempted to rout the league with a surprise attack in 1588. The effort failed, and the king had to flee Paris. Forced by his weakened position into unkingly guerrilla tactics, and also emboldened by news of the English victory over the Spanish Armada in 1588, Henry had both the duke and the cardinal of Guise assassinated. These murders sent France reeling once again. Led by still another Guise brother, the Catholic League reacted with a fury that matched the earlier Huguenot response to the Massacre of Saint Bartholomew's Day. The king was now forced to strike an alliance with the Protestant Henry of Navarre in April 1589.

As the two Henrys prepared to attack the Guise stronghold of Paris, however, an enraged Dominican friar killed Henry III. Thereupon, the Bourbon Huguenot Henry of Navarre succeeded the childless Valois king to the French throne as Henry IV (r. 1589–1610). Pope Sixtus V and Philip II were aghast at the sudden prospect of a Protestant France. They had always wanted France to be religiously Catholic and politically weak, and they now acted to achieve that end. Spain rushed troops to support the besieged Catholic League. Philip II apparently even hoped to place his eldest daughter, Isabella, the granddaughter of Henry II and Catherine de Médicis, on the French throne.

Direct Spanish intervention in the affairs of France seemed only to strengthen Henry IV's grasp on the crown. The French people viewed his right to hereditary succession more seriously than his Protestantism. Henry was also widely liked. Notoriously informal in dress and manner—which made him especially popular with the soldiers—Henry also had the wit and charm to neutralize the strongest enemy in a face-to-face confrontation. He came to the throne as a *politique*, long weary with religious

THEODORE BEZA DEFENDS THE RIGHT TO RESIST TYRANNY

One of the oldest problems in political and social theory has been that of knowing when resistance to repression in matters of conscience is justified. Since Luther's day, Protestant reformers, although accused by their Catholic critics of fomenting social division and revolution, had urged their followers to strict obedience to established political authority. After the 1572 massacre of Saint Bartholomew's Day, however, Protestant pampheteers urged Protestants to resist tyrants and persecutors with armed force. Here, in 1574, Theodore Beza points out the obligation of rulers to their subjects and the latter's right to resist rulers who fail to meet the conditions of their office.

It is apparent that there is a mutual obligation between the king and the officers of a kingdom; that the government of the kingdom is not in the hands of the king in its entirety, but only the sovereign degree; that each of the officers has a share in accord with his degree; and that there are definite conditions on either side. If these conditions are not observed by the inferior officers, it is the part of the sovereign to dismiss and punish them. . . . If the king, hereditary or elective, clearly goes back on the conditions without which he would not have been recognized and acknowledged, can there be any doubt that the lesser magistrates of the kingdom, of the cities, and of the provinces, the administration of which they have received from the sovereignty itself, are free of their oath, at least to the extent that they are entitled to resist flagrant oppression of the realm which they swore to defend and protect according to their office and their particular jurisdiction? . . .

We must now speak of the third class of subjects, which though admittedly subject to the sovereign in a certain respect, is, in another respect, and in cases of necessity the protector of the rights of the sovereignty itself, and is established to hold the sovereign to his duty, and even, if need be, to constrain and punish him. . . . The people is prior to all the magistrates, and does not exist for them, but they for it. . . . Whenever law and equity prevailed, nations neither created nor accepted kings except upon definite conditions. From this it follows that when kings flagrantly violate these terms, these who have the power to give them their authority have no less power to deprive them of it.

Hotman, Beza, and Mornay, trans. and ed. by Julian H. Franklin, *Constitutionalism and Resistance in the Sixteenth Century: Three Treatises* (New York: Pegasus, 1969), pp. 111–114.

strife and fully prepared to place political peace above absolute religious unity. He believed a royal policy of tolerant Catholicism would be the best way to achieve such peace. On July 25, 1593, he publicly abandoned the Protestant faith and embraced the traditional and majority religion of his country. "Paris is worth a Mass," he is reported to have said.

It was, in fact, a decision he had made only after a long period of personal agonizing. The Huguenots were horrified, and Pope Clement VIII was skeptical of Henry's sincerity, but most of the French church and people, having known internal strife too long, rallied to his side. By 1596, the Catholic League was dispersed, its ties with Spain were broken, and the wars of religion in France, to all intents, had ground to a close.

The Edict of Nantes

On April 13, 1598, Henry IV's famous Edict of Nantes proclaimed a formal religious settlement. The following month, on May 2, 1598, the Treaty of Vervins ended hostilities between France and Spain.

In 1591, Henry IV had already assured the Huguenots of at least qualified religious freedoms. The Edict of Nantes made good that promise. It recognized minority religious rights within what was to remain an officially Catholic country. This religious truce—and it was never more than that—granted the Huguenots, who by this time numbered well over a million, freedom of public worship, the right of assembly, admission to public offices and universities, and permission to maintain

Henry IV of France (r. 1589–1610) on horseback, painted in 1594. Réunion des Musées Nationaux/Art Resource, NY

fortified towns. They were to exercise most of the new freedoms, however, within their own towns and territories. Concession of the right to fortify their towns revealed the continuing distrust between French Protestants and Catholics. As significant as it was, the edict only transformed a long hot war between irreconcilable enemies into a long cold war. To its critics, it had only created a state within a state.

A Catholic fanatic assassinated Henry IV in May 1610. Although he is best remembered for the Edict of Nantes, Henry IV's political and economic policies were equally important. They laid the foundations for the transformation of France into the absolute state it would become under Cardinal Richelieu and Louis XIV. (See Chapter 13.) Ironically, in pursuit of the political and religious unity that had escaped Henry IV, Louis XIV, calling for "one king, one law, one faith," would revoke the Edict of Nantes in 1685, an action that forced France and Europe to learn again by bitter experience the hard lessons of the wars of religion.

▼ Imperial Spain and Philip II (r. 1556–1598)

Pillars of Spanish Power

Until the English defeated the mighty Spanish Armada in 1588, no one person stood larger in the second half of the sixteenth century than Philip II of Spain. Philip was heir to the intensely Catholic and militarily supreme western Habsburg kingdom. His father, Charles V, had

given the eastern Habsburg lands of Austria, Bohemia, and Hungary to Philip's uncle, the emperor Ferdinand I (r. 1558–1564). These lands, together with the imperial title, remained in the possession of the Austrian branch of the family until 1918.

New World Riches Populous and wealthy Castile gave Philip a solid home base. The regular arrival in Seville of bullion from the Spanish colonies in the New World provided additional wealth. In the 1540s, great silver mines had been opened in Potosí in present-day Bolivia and in Zacatecas in Mexico. These provided the great sums needed to pay the king's bankers and mercenaries. He nonetheless never managed to erase the debts his father left or to finance his own foreign adventures fully. He later contributed to the bankruptcy of the Fuggers when, at the end of his life, he defaulted on his enormous debts.

Increased Population The new American wealth brought dramatic social change to the peoples of Europe during the second half of the sixteenth century. As Europe became richer, it was also becoming more populous. In the economically and politically active towns of France, England, and the Netherlands, populations had tripled and quadrupled by the early seventeenth century. Europe's population exceeded 70 million by 1600.

The combination of increased wealth and population triggered inflation. A steady 2-percent-a-year rise in prices in much of Europe had serious cumulative effects by the mid-sixteenth century. There were more people and more coinage in circulation than before, but less food and fewer jobs; wages stagnated while prices doubled and tripled in much of Europe.

This was especially the case in Spain. Because the new wealth was concentrated in the hands of a few, the traditional gap between the haves—the propertied, privileged, and educated classes—and the have-nots widened. Nowhere did the unprivileged suffer more than in Spain, where the Castilian peasantry, the backbone of Philip II's great empire, became the most heavily taxed people of Europe. Those whose labor contributed most to making possible Spanish hegemony in Europe in the second half of the sixteenth century prospered least from it.

Efficient Bureaucracy and Military A subjugated peasantry and wealth from the New World were not the only pillars of Spanish strength. Philip II shrewdly organized the lesser nobility into a loyal and efficient national bureaucracy. A reclusive man, he managed his kingdom by pen and paper rather than by personal presence. He was also a learned and pious Catholic, although some popes suspected he used religion as much for political as for devotional purposes. That he was a generous patron of the arts and culture can be seen in his unique retreat outside Madrid, the Escorial, a combination palace, church, tomb, and monastery. Philip also knew personal sorrows: His mad and treacherous son, Don Carlos, died under suspicious circumstances in 1568—some contemporaries suspected that Philip had him quietly executed—only three months before the death of his queen.

Supremacy in the Mediterranean During the first half of Philip's reign, attention focused almost exclusively on the Mediterranean and the Turkish threat. By history, geography, and choice, Spain had traditionally been Catholic Europe's champion against Islam. During the 1560s, the Turks advanced deep into Austria, and their fleets dominated the Mediterranean. Between 1568 and 1570, armies under Philip's half brother, Don John of Austria (1547–1578), the illegitimate son of Charles V, suppressed and dispersed the Moors in Granada.

In May 1571, a Holy League of Spain, Venice, Genoa, and the pope, again under Don John's command, formed to check Turkish belligerence in the Mediterranean. In the largest naval battle of the sixteenth century, Don John's fleet engaged the Ottoman navy under Ali Pasha off Lepanto in the Gulf of Corinth on October 7, 1571. Before the engagement ended, over a third of the Turkish fleet had been sunk or captured, and 30,000 Turks had died. However, the resilient Ottomans still maintained their base in Cyprus and would soon rebuild their fleet and regain control of the eastern Mediterranean. For the moment, however, the Mediterranean belonged to Spain, and the Europeans were left to fight each other. Philip's armies also suppressed resistance in neighboring Portugal, when Philip inherited the throne of that kingdom in 1580. The union with Portugal not only enhanced Spanish sea power, but it also brought Portugal's overseas empire in Africa, India, and Brazil into the Spanish orbit.

The Revolt in the Netherlands

The spectacular Spanish military success in southern Europe was not repeated in northern Europe. When Philip attempted to impose his will within the Netherlands and on England and France, he learned the lessons of defeat. The resistance of the Netherlands especially proved the undoing of Spanish dreams of world empire. (See Map 12–1, page 354.)

Cardinal Granvelle The Netherlands was the richest area not only of Philip's Hapsburg kingdom, but of Europe as well. In 1559, Philip departed the Netherlands for Spain, never again to return. His half sister, Margaret of Parma, assisted by a special council of state, became regent in his place. The council was headed by the extremely able Antoine Perrenot (1517–1586), known after 1561 as Cardinal Granvelle, who hoped to check Protestant gains by internal church reforms. He planned to break down the traditional local autonomy of the seventeen Netherlands provinces by stages and establish in its place a centralized royal government directed from Madrid. A politically docile and religiously uniform country was the goal.

The merchant towns of the Netherlands were, however, Europe's most independent; many, like magnificent Antwerp, were also Calvinist strongholds. By tradition and habit, the people of the Netherlands were far more disposed to variety and toleration than to obedient conformity and hierarchical order. Two members of the council of state led a stubborn opposition to the

Map 12–1 **THE NETHERLANDS DURING THE REFORMATION** The northern and southern provinces of the Netherlands. The former, the United Provinces, were mostly Protestant in the second half of the sixteenth century; the southern Spanish Netherlands made peace with Spain and remained largely Catholic.

Spanish overlords, who now attempted to reimpose their traditional rule with a vengeance. They were the Count of Egmont (1522–1568) and William of Nassau, the Prince of Orange (1533–1584), known as "the Silent" because of his small circle of confidants.

Like other successful rulers in this period, William of Orange placed the political autonomy and well-being of the Netherlands above religious creeds. He personally was successively a confessed Catholic, Lutheran, and Calvinist. In 1561, he married Anne of Saxony, the daughter of the Lutheran elector Maurice and the granddaughter of the late landgrave Philip of Hesse. He maintained his Catholic practices until 1567, the year he turned Lutheran. After the Saint Bartholomew's Day

Massacre (1572), Orange (as he was called) became an avowed Calvinist.

In 1561, Cardinal Granvelle proceeded with his planned ecclesiastical reorganization of the Netherlands. It was intended to tighten the control of the Catholic hierarchy over the country and to accelerate its consolidation as a Spanish ward. Organizing the Dutch nobility in opposition, Orange and Egmont succeeded in gaining Granvelle's removal from office in 1564. Aristocratic control of the country after Granvelle's departure, however, proved woefully inefficient. Popular unrest grew, especially among urban artisans, who joined the congregations of radical Calvinist preachers in large numbers.

The Compromise The year 1564 also saw the first fusion of political and religious opposition to Regent Margaret's government. This opposition resulted from Philip II's unwise insistence on trying to enforce the decrees of the Council of Trent throughout the Netherlands. William of Orange's younger brother, Louis of Nassau, who had been raised a Lutheran, led the opposition with support from the Calvinist-inclined lesser nobility and townspeople. A national covenant called the *Compromise* was drawn up, a solemn pledge to resist the decrees of Trent and the Inquisition. Grievances were loudly and persistently voiced. When Regent Margaret's government spurned the protesters as "beggars" in 1566, Calvinists rioted throughout the country. Louis called for aid from French Huguenots and German Lutherans, and a full-scale rebellion against the Spanish regency appeared imminent.

The Duke of Alba The rebellion failed to materialize, however, because the higher nobility of the Netherlands would not support it. Their shock at Calvinist iconoclasm and anarchy was as great as their resentment of Granvelle's more subtle repression. Philip, determined to make an example of the Protestant rebels, dispatched the duke of Alba to suppress the revolt. His army of 10,000 journeyed northward from Milan in 1567 in a show of combined Spanish and papal might. A special tribunal, known to the Spanish as the Council of Troubles and among the Netherlanders as the Council of Blood, reigned over the land. Before Alba's reign of terror ended, the counts of Egmont and Horn and several thousand suspected heretics were publicly executed.

The Spanish levied new taxes, forcing the Netherlands to pay for the suppression of its own revolt. One, the "tenth penny," a 10 percent sales tax, met such resistance from merchants and artisans that it could not be collected in some areas even after reduction to 3 percent. Combined persecution and taxation sent tens of thousands fleeing from the Netherlands during Alba's six-year rule, a man more hated than Granvelle or the radical Calvinists had ever been.

Resistance and Unification William of Orange was an exile in Germany during these turbulent years. He now emerged as the leader of a broad movement for the independence of the Netherlands from Spain. The northern, Calvinist-inclined provinces of Holland, Zeeland, and Utrecht, of which Orange was the *Stadholder*, or governor, became his base. As in France, political resistance in the Netherlands gained both organization and inspiration by merging with Calvinism.

The early victories of the resistance attest to the popular character of the revolt. A case in point is the capture of the port city of Brill by the "Sea Beggars," an international group of anti-Spanish exiles and criminals, among them many Englishmen. William of Orange did not hesitate to enlist their services. Their brazen piracy, however, had forced Queen Elizabeth to disassociate herself from them and to bar their ships from English ports. In 1572, the Beggars captured Brill and other seaports in Zeeland and Holland. Mixing with the native population, they quickly sparked rebellions against Alba in town after town and spread

The Milch Cow, a sixteenth-century satirical painting depicting the Netherlands as a cow in whom all the great powers of Europe have an interest. Elizabeth of England is feeding her (England had long-standing commercial ties with Flanders); Philip II of Spain is attempting to ride her (Spain was trying to reassert its control over the entire area); William of Orange is trying to milk her (he was the leader of the anti-Spanish rebellion); and the king of France holds her tail (France hoped to profit from the rebellion at Spain's expense). The "Milch Cow." Rijksmuseum, Amsterdam the resistance southward. In 1574, the people of Leiden heroically resisted a long Spanish siege. The Dutch opened the dikes and flooded their country to repulse the hated Spanish. The faltering Alba had by that time ceded power to Don Luis de Requesens, who replaced him as commander of the Spanish forces in the Netherlands in November 1573.

The Pacification of Ghent The greatest atrocity of the war came after Requesens's death in 1576. Spanish mercenaries, leaderless and unpaid, ran amok in Antwerp on November 4, 1576, leaving 7,000 people dead in the streets. The event came to be known as the Spanish Fury.

These atrocities accomplished in just four days what neither religion nor patriotism had previously been able to do. The ten largely Catholic southern provinces (what is roughly modern Belgium) now came together with the seven largely Protestant northern provinces (what is roughly the modern Netherlands) in unified opposition to Spain. This union, known as the Pacification of Ghent, was accomplished on November 8, 1576. It declared internal regional sovereignty in matters of religion, a key clause that permitted political cooperation among the signatories, who were not agreed over religion. It was a Netherlands version of the territorial settlement of religious differences brought about in the Holy Roman Empire in 1555 by the Peace of Augsburg. Four provinces initially held out, but they soon made the resistance unanimous by joining the all-embracing Union of Brussels in January 1577. For the next two years, the Spanish faced a unified and determined Netherlands.

Don John, the victor over the Turks at Lepanto in 1571, had taken command of Spanish land forces in November 1576. He now experienced his first defeat. Confronted by unified Netherlands' resistance, he signed the humiliating Perpetual Edict in February 1577, which provided for the removal of all Spanish troops from the Netherlands within twenty days. The withdrawal gave the country to William of Orange and effectively ended, for the time being, whatever plans Philip may have had for using the Netherlands as a staging area for an invasion of England.

The Union of Arras and the Union of Utrecht The Spanish, however, were nothing if not persistent. Don John and Alexander Farnese of Parma, the Regent Margaret's son, revived Spanish power in the southern provinces, where fear of Calvinist extremism had moved the leaders to break the Union of Brussels. In January 1579, the southern provinces formed the Union of Arras and soon made peace with Spain. These provinces later served the cause of the Counter-Reformation. The northern provinces responded by forming the Union of Utrecht.

Netherlands Independence Seizing what now appeared to be a last opportunity to break the back of Netherlands' resistance, Philip II declared William of Orange an outlaw and placed a bounty of 25,000 crowns on his head. The act predictably stiffened the resistance of the northern provinces. In a famous defiant speech to the Estates General of Holland in December 1580, known as the Apology, Orange publicly denounced Philip as a heathen tyrant whom the Netherlands need no longer obey.

On July 22, 1581, the member provinces of the Union of Utrecht met in The Hague and formally declared Philip no longer their ruler. They turned instead to the French duke of Alençon, the youngest son of Catherine de Médicis. The southern provinces had also earlier looked to him as a possible middle way between Spanish and Calvinist overlordship. All the northern provinces save Holland and Zeeland (which distrusted him almost as much as they did Philip II) accepted Alençon as their "sovereign" but with the clear understanding that he would be only a titular ruler. Yet Alençon, an ambitious failure, saw this as his one chance at greatness. When he rashly attempted to take actual control of the provinces in 1583, he was deposed and returned to France.

Spanish efforts to reconquer the Netherlands continued into the 1580s. William of Orange, assassinated in July 1584, was succeeded by his seventeen-year-old son, Maurice (1567–1625), who, with the assistance of England and France, continued the Dutch resistance. Fortunately for the Netherlands, Philip II began now to meddle directly in French and English affairs. He signed a secret treaty with the Guises (the Treaty of Joinville in December 1584) and sent armies under Alexander Farnese into France in 1590. Hostilities with the English, who openly aided the Dutch rebels, also increased. Gradually, they built to a climax in 1588, when Philip's great Armada was defeated in the English Channel.

These new fronts overextended Spain's resources, thus strengthening the Netherlands. Spanish preoccupation with France and England now permitted the northern provinces to drive out all Spanish soldiers by 1593. In 1596, France and England formally recognized their independence. Peace was not, however, concluded with Spain until 1609, when the Twelve Years' Truce gave the northern provinces virtual independence. Full recognition came with the Peace of Westphalia in 1648.

▼ England and Spain (1553–1603)

Before Edward VI died in 1553, he agreed to a device to make Lady Jane Grey, the teenage daughter of a powerful Protestant nobleman and the granddaughter, on her mother's side, of Henry VIII's younger sister Mary, his successor in place of the Catholic Mary Tudor

(r. 1553–1558). Yet popular support for the principle of hereditary monarchy was too strong to deprive Mary of her rightful rule. Uprisings in London and elsewhere led to Jane Grey's removal from the throne within days of her crowning, and she was eventually beheaded.

Mary I (r. 1553–1558)

Once enthroned, Mary proceeded to act even beyond the worst fears of the Protestants. In 1554, she entered a highly unpopular political marriage with Philip (later Philip II) of Spain, a symbol of militant Catholicism to English Protestants. At his direction, she pursued a foreign policy that in 1558 cost England its last enclave on the Continent, Calais.

Mary's domestic measures were equally shocking to the English people and even more divisive. During her reign, Parliament repealed the Protestant statutes of Edward and reverted to the Catholic religious practice of her father, Henry VIII. The great Protestant leaders of the Edwardian Age—John Hooper, Hugh Latimer, and Thomas Cranmer—were executed for heresy. Hundreds of Protestants either joined them in martyrdom (287 were burned at the stake during Mary's reign) or fled to the Continent. These "Marian exiles" settled in Ger-

Portrait of Mary I (r. 1553–1558), Queen of England. Queen Mary I, 1554 (oil on panel) by Sir Anthonis Mor (Antonio Moro) (1517/20 - 76/7). Prado, Madrid, Spain/Bridgeman Art Library

many and Switzerland, especially in Frankfurt, Strasbourg, and Geneva. (John Knox, the future leader of the Reformation in Scotland, was prominent among them.) There they waited for the time when a Protestant counteroffensive could be launched in their homelands. They were also exposed to Protestant religious beliefs more radical than any set forth during Edward VI's reign. Many of these exiles later held positions in the Church of England during Elizabeth I's reign.

Elizabeth I (r. 1558–1603)

Mary's successor was her half sister, Elizabeth I, the daughter of Henry VIII and Anne Boleyn. Elizabeth had remarkable and enduring successes in both domestic and foreign policy. Assisted by a shrewd adviser, Sir William Cecil (1520–1598), she built a true kingdom on the ruins of Mary's reign. Between 1559 and 1603, she and Cecil guided a religious settlement through Parliament that prevented religious differences from tearing England apart in the sixteenth century. A ruler who subordinated religious to political unity, Elizabeth merged a centralized episcopal system that she firmly controlled with broadly defined Protestant doctrine and traditional Catholic ritual. The resulting Anglican Church contained inflexible religious extremes for decades.

In 1559, an Act of Supremacy passed Parliament, repealing all the anti-Protestant legislation of Mary Tudor and asserting Elizabeth's right as "supreme governor" over both spiritual and temporal affairs. In the same year, the Act of Uniformity mandated for every English parish a revised version of the second *Book of Common Prayer* (1552). In 1563, the issuance of the **Thirty-Nine Articles**, a revision of Thomas Cranmer's original forty-two, made a moderate Protestantism the official religion within the Church of England.

Catholic and Protestant Extremists Elizabeth hoped to avoid both Catholic and Protestant extremism by pursuing a middle way. Her first archbishop of Canterbury, Matthew Parker (d. 1575), represented this ideal. Elizabeth could not prevent the emergence of subversive Catholic and Protestant zealots, however. When she ascended the throne, Catholics were in the majority in England. The extremists among them, encouraged by the Jesuits, plotted against her. The Spanish, piqued both by Elizabeth's Protestant sympathies and by her refusal to take Philip II's hand in marriage, encouraged and later directly assisted Catholic radicals. Elizabeth deliberately remained unmarried throughout her reign, using the possibility of a royal marriage to her diplomatic advantage.

Catholic extremists hoped eventually to replace Elizabeth with Mary Stuart, Queen of Scots. Unlike Elizabeth, who had been declared illegitimate during the reign of her father, Mary Stuart had an unblemished

A Great Debate Over Religious Tolerance

ON OCTOBER 27, 1553, the Spanish physician and amateur theologian Michael Servetus died at the stake in Geneva for alleged "blasphemies against the Holy Trinity." A bold and confident man, he had also incurred the wrath of Rome before badgering John Calvin in Geneva on theological issues. In the wake of Sevetus's execution, Calvin was much criticized for fighting heresy with capital punishment. In 1544, he came to his own defense in a tract entitled *Defense of the Orthodox Faith in the Holy Trinity Against the Monstrous Errors of Michael Servetus of Spain.* Thereafter, Sebastian Castellio, an accomplished humanist and former rector of the *college* in Geneva, whom Calvin had driven out of the city years earlier, began a series of writings against Calvin. One of his titles, *Whether Heretics Should Be Punished By the Sword of the Magistrates*, was an anonymous anthology on religious toleration that included a supporting excerpt from John Calvin himself! Writing over the years under several pseudonyms, Castellio excerpted statements from Calvin's works and put them in a sustained "debate" with his own liberal point of view.

QUESTIONS

1. Why does Calvin believe that heresy deserves capital punishment?

2. What are Castellio's best rebuttal arguments?

3. Why does Castellio write under pseudonyms?

I

CALVIN: Kings are duty bound to defend the doctrine of piety.

CASTELLIO: [Yes, but] to kill a man is not to defend doctrine, but rather to kill a man . . .

CALVIN: What of today? The majority of people have lost all sense of shame and openly mock God. They burst as boldly into God's awesome mysteries as pigs poke their snouts into costly storehouses.

CASTELLIO: Calvin appears to be criticizing himself. For truly the awesome mysteries of God are the Trinity, predestination, and election. But this man [Calvin] speaks so assuredly about these matters that one would think he was in Paradise. So thorny is his own teaching about the Trinity . . . that by his own curiosity he weakens and makes doubtful the consciences of the simple. He has taught so crudely about predestination that innumerable men have been seduced into a security as great as that which existed before the Flood . . .
Tell me, in brief, what you think about predestination.

CALVIN: I have been taught the following about predestination: All men are not created in an equal state. Rather in eternity, God, by inevitable decree, determined in advance those whom he would save and those whom he would damn to destruction. Those whom he has deemed worthy of salvation have been chosen by his mercy without consideration of their worthiness. And those given damnation, he shuts off from life by a just and irreprehensible, albeit incomprehensible, judgment.

CASTELLIO: So you maintain that certain men are created by God already marked for damnation so that they cannot be saved?

CALVIN: Precisely.

CASTELLIO: But what if they *should* obey God? Would they not then be saved?

CALVIN: They would then be saved. However, they are not able to obey God, because God excludes them from the knowledge of his name and the spirit of his justification so that they can and will do only evil and are inclined only to every kind of sin.

CASTELLIO: Hence, they have that inclination [to sin] from God's creation and predestination?

CALVIN: They have it so, just as surely as God has created the wolf with the inclination to eat sheep!

CASTELLIO: Therefore they have been damned and rejected by God even before they existed?

CALVIN: Exactly.

CASTELLIO: But are they not damned for their sins?

CALVIN: Indeed so. Those who were destined to that [damned] lot are completely worthy of it.

CASTELLIO: When were they worthy of it?

CALVIN: When they were destined to it?

CASTELLIO: Then they have 'been' before they 'are'. Do you see what you are saying?!

CALVIN: I don't understand.

CASTELLIO: If they were worthy, then they 'were.' For to be worthy is to be. And if you concede that they have been damned before they are, then they have 'been' before they were.

CALVIN: God elects the foolish things of the world to confound the wise.

CASTELLIO: Calvin and his kind reject the foolish things of the world so that they may exalt the wise [themselves]. Hence, they admit hardly anyone into . . . their circle who is not accomplished in sciences and languages . . . If Christ himself came to them, he would certainly be turned away if he spoke no Latin . . .

[But] Christ wishes to be judged by common sense and refers the matters of the gospel to human judgment . . . He would never have employed such analogies had he wished to deprive us of our common sense. And who would have believed him had he taught things repugnant to nature and contradictory to human experience . . .? What kind of master would he have been, had he said to the woman who cried out to him and washed his feet with her hair: "O woman, whatever your sin, it was done by God's decree!

Source: Steven Ozment, *Mysticism and Dissent: Religious Ideology and Social Protest in the Sixteenth Century* (New Haven, CT: Yale University Press), pp. 171–179.

Queen Elizabeth I of England (r. 1558–1603) served as an example of religious tolerance during her reign. Despite her Protestant sympathies, she steered clear of both Catholic and Protestant extremism and, despite proven cases of Catholic treason and even attempted regicide, she executed fewer Catholics during her forty-five years on the throne than Mary Tudor had executed Protestants during her brief five-year reign.   Courtesy of the Library of Congress, Rare Book and Special Collections Division

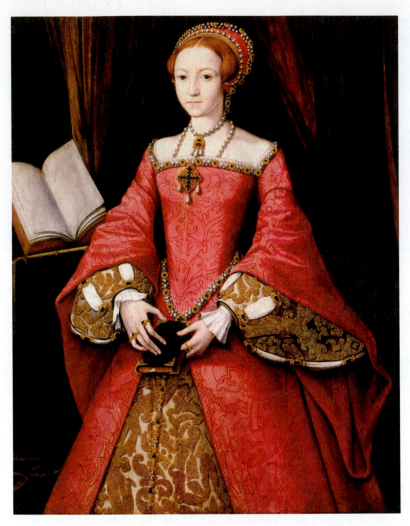

An idealized likeness of Elizabeth Tudor when she was a princess, attributed to Flemish court painter L. B. Teerling, ca. 1551. The painting shows her blazing red hair and alludes to her learning by the addition of books.
UNKNOWN, formerly attributed to William Scrots. Elizabeth I, when Princess (1533–1603). The Royal Collection © 2002, Her Majesty Queen Elizabeth II

claim to the throne by way of her grandmother Margaret, the sister of Henry VIII. Elizabeth acted swiftly against Catholic assassination plots, rarely letting her emotions override her political instincts. Despite proven cases of Catholic treason and even attempted regicide, she executed fewer Catholics during her forty-five years on the throne than Mary Tudor had executed Protestants during her brief five-year reign.

Elizabeth showed little mercy, however, to any who threatened the unity of her rule. She dealt cautiously with the Puritans, who were Protestants working within the national church to "purify" it of every vestige of "popery" and to make its Protestant doctrine more precise. The Puritans had two special grievances against her reign:

1. The retention of Catholic ceremony and vestments within the Church of England, which made it appear to the casual observer that no Reformation had occurred

2. The continuation of the episcopal system of church governance, which conceived the English church to be theologically the true successor to Rome, while placing it politically under the firm hand of the queen and her compliant archbishop

Sixteenth-century Puritans were not true separatists. They enjoyed popular support and were led by widely respected men like Thomas Cartwright (d. 1603). They worked through Parliament to create an alternative national church of semiautonomous congregations governed by representative presbyteries (hence, **Presbyterians**), following the model of Calvin and Geneva. Elizabeth dealt firmly, but subtly, with them, conceding nothing that lessened the hierarchical unity of the Church of England and her control over it.

The more extreme Puritans wanted every congregation to be autonomous, a law unto itself, with neither higher episcopal nor presbyterian control. They came to be known as **Congregationalists**. Elizabeth and her second archbishop of Canterbury, John Whitgift (d. 1604), refused to tolerate this group, whose views on independence they found patently subversive. The Conventicle Act of 1593 gave such separatists the option either to conform to the practices of the Church of England or face exile or death.

Deterioration of Relations with Spain A series of events led inexorably to war between England and Spain, despite the sincere desires of both Philip II and Elizabeth to avoid a confrontation. In 1567, the Spanish duke of Alba marched his mighty army into the Netherlands, which was, from the English point of view, simply a convenient staging area for a Spanish invasion of England. Pope Pius V (r. 1566–1572), who favored a military conquest of Protestant England, "excommunicated" Elizabeth for heresy in 1570. This mischievous act encouraged both internal resistance and international intrigue against the queen. Two years later, as noted earlier, the piratical sea beggars, many of whom were Englishmen, occupied the port of Brill in the Netherlands and aroused the surrounding countryside against the Spanish.

Following Don John's demonstration of Spain's awesome sea power at Lepanto in 1571, England signed a mutual defense pact with France. Also in the 1570s, Elizabeth's famous seamen John Hawkins (1532–1595) and Sir Francis Drake (1545?–1596) began to prey regularly on Spanish shipping in the Americas. Drake's circumnavigation of the globe between 1577 and 1580 was one in a series of dramatic demonstrations of English ascendancy on the high seas.

After the Saint Bartholomew's Day Massacre, Elizabeth was the only protector of Protestants in France and the Netherlands. In 1585, she signed the Treaty of Nonsuch, which provided English soldiers and cavalry to the

GOING TO THE THEATER

THE MODERN ENGLISH stage play originated in the religious dramas that educated and entertained medieval Europeans for centuries before Shakespeare's birth in 1564. Teaching a lesson as well as telling a suspenseful story, these dramas were known as *morality plays* and typically were presented in the countryside by roving bands of players under church supervision. The medieval theater usually consisted of a small circular field for the actors, ringed by earthen mounds for the spectators. The circular stage was divided into four quadrants, each with its own tent at the four points of the compass: heaven at the east, evil at the north, worldly rulers at the west, and good characters at the south.

Each player emerged from his tent in turn to speak his lines, then went back in to await his next appearance. This format was a way of shifting scenes and a forerunner of the custom in modern theaters of ending a scene by lowering a curtain.

In England in the fifteenth century, as the urban population grew, ambitious promoters moved their productions into the courtyards of inns. London, the seat of the royal court, became the center of English theatrical life.

This sheltered, urban setting gave theater companies several advantages. Audiences were larger, and the inns could be easily renovated to provide permanent stages and more complex sets. The enclosed courtyards also made it easier to keep out nonpaying crashers, the greatest enemies of the new showmen—capitalists who produced and often wrote the plays and had to make a living from them.

Several of London's more scrupulous clergymen decried another advantage of the combined inn and theater—the opportunity it gave for sexual license. By the sixteenth century, the allegorical moralizing of the medieval country theater had evolved into the ribald, worldly entertainment of the London stage. Going to the theater was now more like being part of a festival than listening to a sermon. The workmen and young women who comprised much of the audience found it convenient to hire rooms in which they might romance one another during or after the performance.

London's theater world reached full maturity in the late sixteenth and early seventeenth centuries. The Rose and The Globe theaters, where many of Shakespeare's plays were presented, were built in the 1590s on the south bank of the River Thames, reachable only by water taxis. During Shakespeare's heyday, some 40,000 waterboys were said to ferry customers to these theaters. Performances by troupes of adult males or boys (women were banned from the stage) were often rowdy affairs, the crowds egged on both by the witty repartee on stage and the food and beer sold in the pit.

What were the basic elements and purpose of the medieval stage, and what was carried over from it to the Elizabethan theater?

Sources: E. K. Chambers, *The Elizabethan Stage*, Vols. I–IV (Oxford: Oxford University Press, 1923); Lawrence M. Clopper, *Drama, Play, and Game: English Festive Culture in the Medieval and Early Modern Period* (Chicago: Chicago University Press, 2001); F. E. Halliday, *Shakespeare in His Age* (New York: Duckworth, 1956).

A seventeenth-century sketch of the Swan Theater, which stood near Shakespeare's Globe Theater on the south bank of the Thames.   The Bridgeman Art Library

Netherlands. Funds that had previously been funneled covertly to support Henry of Navarre's army in France now flowed openly.

Mary, Queen of Scots

These events made a tinderbox of English–Spanish relations. The spark that finally touched it off was Elizabeth's execution of Mary, Queen of Scots (1542–1587).

Mary Stuart was the daughter of King James V of Scotland and Mary of Guise and had resided in France from the time she was six years old. This thoroughly French and Catholic queen had returned to Scotland after the death of her husband, the French king Francis II, in 1561. There she found a successful, fervent Protestant Reformation legally sanctioned the year before by the Treaty of Edinburgh (1560). As hereditary heir to the throne of Scotland, Mary remained queen by divine and human right and the Protestants who controlled her realm did not intimidate her. She established an international French court culture, the gaiety and sophistication of which impressed many Protestant nobles whose religion often made their lives exceedingly dour.

The ever-vigilant Scottish reformer John Knox watched Mary closely. He fumed publicly and always with effect against the queen's private Mass and other Catholic practices, which Scottish law made a capital offense for everyone else. Knox won support in his role of watchdog from Elizabeth and Cecil. Elizabeth personally despised Knox and never forgave him for writing the *First Blast of the Trumpet against the Terrible Regiment of Women*, a work aimed at provoking a revolt against Mary Tudor but, unfortunately for Knox, published in the year of Elizabeth's ascent to the throne. Elizabeth and Cecil tolerated Knox because they knew he would never permit Scotland to succumb to young Mary's French and Catholic ways.

In 1568, a public scandal forced Mary's abdication and flight to her cousin Elizabeth in England. Mary's reputed lover, the earl of Bothwell, was, with cause, suspected of having killed her legal husband, Lord Darnley. When a packed court acquitted Bothwell, he subsequently married Mary. The outraged reaction from Protestant nobles forced Mary to surrender the throne to her one-year-old son, the future James VI of Scotland and, later, Elizabeth's successor as King James I of England. Because of Mary's clear claim to the English throne, she was an international symbol of a possible Catholic England and consumed by the desire to be England's queen. For this reason, her presence in England, where she resided under house arrest for nineteen years, was a constant discomfort to Elizabeth.

In 1583, Elizabeth's vigilant secretary, Sir Francis Walsingham, uncovered a plot against Elizabeth involving the Spanish ambassador Bernardino de Mendoza. After Mendoza's deportation in January 1584, popular antipathy toward Spain and support for Protestant resistance in France and the Netherlands became massive throughout England.

In 1586, Walsingham uncovered still another plot against Elizabeth, the so-called Babington plot, after Anthony Babington, who was caught seeking Spanish support for an attempt on the queen's life. This time he had uncontestable proof of Mary's complicity. Elizabeth believed the execution of a sovereign, even a dethroned sovereign, weakened royalty everywhere. She was also aware of the outcry that Mary's execution would create throughout the Catholic world, and she sincerely wanted peace with English Catholics. Yet she really had no choice in the matter and consented to Mary's execution, which took place on February 18, 1587. This event dashed all Catholic hopes for a bloodless reconversion of Protestant England. After the execution of the Catholic queen of Scotland, Pope Sixtus V (r. 1585–1590), who feared Spanish domination almost as much as he abhorred English Protestantism, could no longer withhold public support for a Spanish invasion of England. Philip II ordered his Armada to make ready.

The Armada

In the spring of 1587, Sir Francis Drake shelled the port of Cádiz, inflicting heavy damages on Spanish ships and stores and interrupting Spain's war preparations. After "singeing the beard of Spain's king," as he put it, Drake raided the coast of Portugal, further incapacitating the Spanish. These strikes forced the Spanish to postpone their invasion of England until 1588.

On May 30 of that year, 130 ships bearing 25,000 sailors and soldiers under the command of the duke of Medina-Sidonia set sail for England. In the end, however, the English won a stunning victory. The invasion barges that were to transport Spanish soldiers from the galleons onto English shores were prevented from leaving Calais and Dunkirk. The swifter English and Netherlands' ships, helped by what came to be known as an "English wind," dispersed the waiting Spanish fleet, over one third of which never returned to Spain.

The news of the Armada's defeat gave heart to Protestant resistance everywhere. Although Spain continued to win impressive victories in the 1590s, it never fully recovered. Spanish soldiers faced unified and inspired French, English, and Dutch armies. By the time of Philip's death on September 13, 1598, his forces had been rebuffed on all fronts. His seventeenth-century successors were all inferior leaders who never knew responsibilities equal to his, nor did Spain ever again know such imperial grandeur. The French soon dominated the Continent, and in the New World the Dutch and the English whittled away at Spain's overseas empire.

Elizabeth died on March 23, 1603, leaving behind her a strong nation poised to expand into a global empire.

▼ The Thirty Years' War (1618–1648)

The Thirty Years' War in the Holy Roman Empire was the last and most destructive of the wars of religion. Religious and political differences had long set Catholics against Protestants and Calvinists against Lutherans. What made the Thirty Years' War so devastating was the entrenched hatred of the various sides and their seeming determina-

tion to sacrifice all for their religious beliefs. When the hostilities ended in 1648, the peace terms shaped the map of northern Europe much as we know it today.

Preconditions for War

Fragmented Germany In the second half of the six-teenth century, Germany was an almost ungovernable land of about 360 autonomous political entities. (See Map 12–2.) There were independent secular principalities

Map 12–2 **GERMANY IN 1547** Mid-sixteenth-century Germany was an almost ungovernable land of about 360 autonomous political en-tities. Originally "Map of Germany Showing Its Great Division/Fragmentation in the 16th Century" from Hajo Holborn, *A History of Germany: The Reformation*, Copyright © 1982 by Princeton University Press. Reprinted by permission of Princeton University Press.

(duchies, landgraviates, and marches), ecclesiastical principalities (archbishoprics, bishoprics, and abbeys), numerous free cities, and knights ruling small areas from castles. The Peace of Augsburg (1555) had given each of them significant sovereignty within its own borders. Each levied its own tolls and tariffs and coined its own money, which made land travel and trade between the various regions difficult to impossible. Many of these little lands also had great-power pretensions. As the seventeenth century opened, Germany was decentralized and fragmented; it was not a unified nation like Spain, England, or even strife-filled France.

Because of its central location, Germany had always been Europe's highway for merchants and traders going north, south, east, and west. Europe's rulers pressed in on Germany both because of trade and because some held lands or legal privileges within certain German principalities. German princes, in their turn, looked to import and export markets beyond German borders and opposed efforts to consolidate the Holy Roman Empire, lest their territorial rights, confirmed by the Peace of Augsburg, be overturned. German princes were not loath to turn to Catholic France or to the kings of Denmark and Sweden for allies against the Habsburg emperor.

After the Council of Trent, Protestants in the empire suspected the existence of an imperial and papal conspiracy to re-create the Catholic Europe of pre-Reformation times. The imperial diet, which the German princes controlled, demanded strict observance of the constitutional rights of Germans, as set forth in agreements with the emperor since the mid-fourteenth century. In the late sixteenth century, the emperor ruled only to the degree to which he was prepared to use force of arms against his subjects.

Religious Division Religious conflict accentuated the international and internal political divisions. (See Map 12–3.) During this period, the population within the Holy Roman Empire was about equally divided between Catholics and Protestants, the latter having perhaps a slight numerical edge by 1600. The terms of the Peace of Augsburg had attempted to freeze the territorial holdings of the Lutherans and the Catholics (the so-called *ecclesiastical reservation*). In the intervening years, however, the Lutherans had gained and kept political control in some Catholic areas, as had the Catholics in a few previously Lutheran areas. Such territorial reversals, or the threat of them, only increased the suspicion and antipathy between the two sides.

The Lutherans had been far more successful in securing their rights to worship in Catholic lands than the Catholics had been in securing such rights in Lutheran lands. The Catholic rulers, who were in a weakened position after the Reformation, had made,

but resented, concessions to Protestant communities within their territories. With the passage of time, they demanded that all ecclesiastical princes, electors, archbishops, bishops, and abbots who had deserted the Catholic for the Protestant side be immediately deprived of their religious offices and that their ecclesiastical holdings be promptly returned to Catholic control in accordance with the ecclesiastical reservation. However, the Lutherans and, even more so, the Calvinists in the Palatinate ignored this stipulation at every opportunity.

There was also religious strife in the empire between liberal and conservative Lutherans and between Lutherans and the growing numbers of Calvinists. The last half of the sixteenth century was a time of warring Protestant factions within German universities. And in addition to the heightened religious strife, a new scientific and material culture was becoming ascendant in intellectual and political circles, increasing the anxiety of religious people of all persuasions.

Calvinism and the Palatinate As elsewhere in Europe, Calvinism was the political and religious leaven within the Holy Roman Empire on the eve of the Thirty Years' War. Unrecognized as a legal religion by the Peace of Augsburg, it gained a strong foothold within the empire when Frederick III (r. 1559–1576), a devout convert to Calvinism, became Elector Palatine (ruler within the Palatinate; see Map 12–3) and made it the official religion of his domain. Heidelberg became a German Geneva in the 1560s: both a great intellectual center of Calvinism and a staging area for Calvinist penetration into the empire. By 1609, Palatine Calvinists headed a Protestant defensive alliance that received support from Spain's sixteenth-century enemies: England, France, and the Netherlands.

The Lutherans came to fear the Calvinists almost as much as they did the Catholics. By their bold missionary forays into the empire, Palatine Calvinists seemed to the Lutherans to threaten the Peace of Augsburg—and hence the legal foundation of the Lutheran states. Also, outspoken Calvinist criticism of the doctrine of Christ's real presence in the Eucharist shocked the more religiously conservative Lutherans. The Elector Palatine once expressed his disbelief in transubstantiation by publicly shredding the host and mocking it as a "fine God." To Lutherans, such religious disrespect disgraced the Reformation as well as the elector.

Maximilian of Bavaria and the Catholic League If the Calvinists were active within the Holy Roman Empire, so also were their Catholic counterparts, the Jesuits. Staunchly Catholic Bavaria, supported by Spain, became militarily and ideologically for the Counter-Reformation what the Palatinate was for

MAP EXPLORATION

Interactive map: To explore this map further, go to www.myhistorylab.com

Map 12–3 **RELIGIOUS DIVISIONS ABOUT 1600** By 1600, few could seriously expect Christians to return to a uniform religious allegiance. In Spain and southern Italy, Catholicism remained relatively unchallenged, but note the existence elsewhere of large religious minorities, both Catholic and Protestant.

Protestantism. From Bavaria, the Jesuits launched successful missions throughout the empire, winning such major cities as Strasbourg and Osnabrück back to the Catholic fold by 1600. In 1609, Maximilian I, duke of Bavaria (r. 1597–1651), organized a Catholic league to counter a new Protestant alliance that had been formed in the same year under the leadership of Calvinist Elector Palatine, Frederick IV (r. 1583–1610). When the league fielded a great army under the command of Count Johann von Tilly, the stage was set, both internally and internationally, for the worst of the religious wars, the Thirty Years' War. (See Map 12–4, page 366.)

Four Periods of War

The war went through four distinguishable periods. During its course, it drew in every major Western European nation—at least diplomatically and financially if not by direct military intervention. The four periods were the Bohemian (1618–1625); the Danish (1625–1629); the Swedish (1630–1635); and the Swedish-French (1635–1648).

The Bohemian Period The war broke out in Bohemia after the ascent to the Bohemian throne in 1618 of the Habsburg Ferdinand, archduke of Styria, who was

Map 12–4 **THE HOLY ROMAN EMPIRE ABOUT 1618** On the eve of the Thirty Years' War, the Holy Roman Empire was politically and religiously fragmented, as revealed by this somewhat simplified map. Lutherans dominated the north and Catholics the south; Calvinists controlled the United Provinces and the Palatinate and were important in Switzerland and Brandenburg.

also heir to the imperial throne. Educated by the Jesuits and a fervent Catholic, Ferdinand was determined to restore the traditional faith to the eastern Habsburg lands (Austria, Bohemia, and Hungary).

No sooner had Ferdinand become king of Bohemia than he revoked the religious freedoms of Bohemian Protestants. In force since 1575, these freedoms had even been recently broadened by Emperor Rudolf II (r. 1576–1612) in his Letter of Majesty in 1609. The Protestant nobility in Prague responded to Ferdinand's act in May 1618 by throwing his regents out the window of the

royal palace. The event has ever since been known as the "defenestration of Prague." (The three officials fell fifty feet into a dry moat that, fortunately, was padded with manure, which cushioned their fall and spared their lives.) In the following year Ferdinand became Holy Roman Emperor as Ferdinand II (r. 1619–1637), by the unanimous vote of the seven electors. The Bohemians, however, defiantly deposed him in Prague and declared the Calvinist elector Palatine, Frederick V (r. 1616–1623), their king.

What had begun as a revolt of the Protestant nobility against an unpopular king of Bohemia escalated into

Bohemian protesters throw three of Emperor Ferdinand II's agents out of windows at Hradschin Castle in Prague to protest his revocation of Protestant freedoms.   Bildarchiv Preussischer Kulturbesitz/Art Resource, NY

an international war. Spain sent troops to Ferdinand, who found more motivated allies in Maximilian of Bavaria and the Lutheran elector John George I of Saxony (r. 1611–1656). The latter had their own agendas. Maximilian wanted to wrest the electoral title from his distant Palatine cousin, while John George saw a sure route to territorial gain by joining in an easy victory over the weaker elector Palatine. This was not the only time politics and greed would overshadow religion during the long conflict, although Lutheran-Calvinist religious animosity also overrode a common Protestantism.

Ferdinand's army under Tilly routed Frederick V's troops at the Battle of White Mountain in 1620. By 1622, Ferdinand had not only subdued and re-Catholicized Bohemia but conquered the Palatinate as well. Meanwhile, Maximilian of Bavaria pressed the conflict into northwestern Germany, laying claim to land as he went.

The Danish Period   These events raised new fears that a reconquest and re-Catholicization of the empire now loomed, which was precisely Ferdinand II's design. The Lutheran king Christian IV (r. 1588–1648) of Denmark, who already held territory within the empire as the duke of Holstein, was eager to extend Danish influence over the coastal towns of the North Sea. With English, French, and Dutch encouragement, he picked up the Protestant banner of resistance, opening the Danish period of the conflict (1625–1629). Entering Germany with his army in 1626, he was, however, quickly humiliated by Maximilian and forced to retreat into Denmark.

As military success made Maximilian stronger and an untrustworthy ally, Emperor Ferdinand sought a more pliant tool for his policies in Albrecht of Wallenstein (1583–1634), a powerful mercenary. Another opportunistic Protestant, Wallenstein had gained a great deal of territory by joining Ferdinand during the conquest of Bohemia. A brilliant and ruthless military strategist, Wallenstein carried Ferdinand's campaign into Denmark. By 1628, he commanded a crack army of more than 100,000 men and also became a law unto himself, completely outside of the emperor's control.

Wallenstein, however, had so broken Protestant resistance that Ferdinand could issue the Edict of Restitution in 1629, reasserting the Catholic safeguards of the Peace of Augsburg (1555). It reaffirmed the illegality of Calvinism—a completely unrealistic move by 1629—and it ordered the return of all church lands the Lutherans had acquired since 1552, an equally unrealistic goal despite its legal basis. Compliance would have involved the return of no fewer than sixteen bishoprics and twenty-eight cities and towns to Catholic allegiance. The new edict struck panic in the hearts of Protestants and Habsburg opponents everywhere.

The Swedish Period   Gustavus Adolphus II of Sweden (r. 1611–1632), a deeply pious king of a unified Lutheran nation, became the new leader of Protestant forces within the empire, opening the Swedish period of the war (1630–1635). He was controlled by two interested bystanders: (1) the French minister Cardinal Richelieu (1585–1642), whose foreign policy was to protect

French interests by keeping the Habsburg armies tied down in Germany, and (2) the Dutch, who had not forgotten Spanish Habsburg rule in the sixteenth century. In alliance with the electors of Brandenburg and Saxony, the Swedish king won a smashing victory at Breitenfeld in 1630—one that reversed the course of the war so dramatically that it has been regarded as the most decisive engagement of the long conflict.

One of the reasons for the overwhelming Swedish victory at Breitenfeld was the military genius of Gustavus Adolphus. The Swedish king brought a new mobility to warfare by having both his infantry and his cavalry employ fire-and-charge tactics. At six deep, his infantry squares were smaller than the traditional ones, yet he filled them with equal numbers of musketeers and pikemen. His cavalry also alternated pistol shots with charges with the sword. His artillery was lighter and more mobile in battle. Each unit of his army—infantry, cavalry, and artillery—had both defensive and offensive capability and could quickly change from one to the other.

Gustavus Adolphus died at the hands of Wallenstein's forces during the Battle of Lützen (November 1632)—a costly engagement for both sides that created a brief standstill. Ferdinand had long resented Wallenstein's independence, although he was the major factor in imperial success. In 1634, Ferdinand had Wallenstein assassinated. By that time, not only had the great general served his purpose for the emperor, but, ever opportunistic, he was openly trying to strike bargains with the Protestants for his services. The episode is a telling commentary on this war without honor. Despite the deep religious motivations, greed and political gain were the real forces at work in the Thirty Years' War. Even allies that owed one another their success were not above treating each other as mortal enemies.

In the Peace of Prague in 1635, the German Protestant states, led by Saxony, reached a compromise with Ferdinand. France and the Netherlands, however, continued to support Sweden. Desiring to maximize their investment in the war, they refused to join the agreement. Their resistance to settlement plunged the war into its fourth and most devastating phase.

The Swedish-French Period The French openly entered the war in 1635, sending men and munitions as well as financial subsidies. Thereafter, the war dragged on for thirteen years, with French, Swedish, and Spanish soldiers looting the length and breadth of Germany—warring, it seemed, simply for the sake of warfare itself. The Germans, long weary of the devastation, were too disunited to repulse the foreign armies; they simply suffered. By the time peace talks began at Münster and Osnabrück in Westphalia in 1644, the war had killed an estimated one third of the German population. It has been called the worst European catastrophe since the Black Death of the fourteenth century.

The Treaty of Westphalia

The Treaty of Westphalia in 1648 ended all hostilities within the Holy Roman Empire. It was the first general peace in Europe after a war unprecedented for its number of warring parties. (See Map 12–5.) Written not in Latin, but in French, henceforth to become the international diplomatic language, the treaty rescinded Ferdinand's Edict of Restitution and reasserted the major feature of the religious settlement of the Peace of Augsburg ninety-three years earlier: The ruler of a land determines the official religion of that land. The treaty also gave the Calvinists their long-sought legal recognition. The independence of the Swiss Confederacy and the United Provinces of the Netherlands, long recognized in fact, was now proclaimed in law. Bavaria became an elector state, Brandenburg-Prussia emerged as the most powerful northern German state, and the other German princes became supreme over their principalities. Yet, as guarantors of the treaty, Sweden and France found many opportunities to meddle in German affairs until the century's end—France for reasons of considerable territorial gain. Because the treaty broadened the legal status of Protestantism, the pope opposed it altogether, but he had no power to prevent it.

France and Spain remained at war outside the empire until 1659, when French victories forced the humiliating Treaty of the Pyrenees on the Spanish. Thereafter France became Europe's dominant power, and Habsburg Spain never recovered. (See Chapter 13.)

By confirming the territorial sovereignty of Germany's many political entities, the Treaty of Westphalia perpetuated German division and political weakness into the modern period. Only two German states attained any international significance during the seventeenth century: Austria and Brandenburg-Prussia. The petty regionalism within the empire also reflected on a small scale the drift of larger European politics. In the seventeenth century, distinctive nation-states, each with their own political, cultural, and religious identity, reached maturity and firmly established the competitive nationalism of the modern world.

In Perspective

Religion and politics played major roles in each of the great conflicts of the Age of Religious Wars—the internal struggle in France, Spain's unsuccessful effort to subdue the Netherlands, England's successful resistance to Spain, and the intervention of virtually every major European power in the hapless Holy Roman Empire during the first half of the seventeenth century. Each conflict involved parties and armies of different religious persuasions in a life-or-death political struggle.

Swedish Dominions
Brandenburg Prussia
Spanish Monarchy
Austria Habsburg
Church Lands
Boundary of the Empire

ATLANTIC OCEAN

SCOTLAND
Edinburgh
Belfast
IRELAND
Dublin
Cork
York
ENGLAND
WALES
Bristol
London
Plymouth

Bergen
Christiania
Stavanger
NORWAY
KINGDOM OF DENMARK AND NORWAY

SWEDEN
Stockholm
Copenhagen
DENMARK
SCHLESWIG
HOLSTEIN

North Sea
Baltic Sea

Finland
Stolbova
Reval
ESTONIA
INGRIA
Novgorod
Pskov
LIVONIA
Riga
COURLAND
Memel
LITHUANIA
Minsk
Vitebsk
Smolensk

RUSSIA
Moscow
Chernigov

POLAND
Warsaw
Danzig
Posen
EAST PRUSSIA
BRANDENBURG
Cracow

VOLHYNIA
PODOLIA
Lemberg

UNITED PROVINCES
SPANISH NETH.
Brussels
HESSE
MINOR GERMAN STATES
SAXONY
SILESIA
Breslau
Prague
BOHEMIA
MORAVIA
Pressburg
AUSTRIA
Vienna
BAVARIA
FRANCHE COMTÉ
SWITZ.

France
Rouen
Reims
Paris
Orléans
Tours
Nantes
Bordeaux
Lyons
FRANCE
SAVOY
PIEDMONT
AVIGNON
LANGUEDOC
Toulouse
Marseilles

Barcelona
Saragossa
ARAGON
Madrid
Toledo
SPAIN
CASTILE
Leon
Navarre
Burgos
Salamanca
PORTUGAL
Oporto
Lisbon
Cordoba
Granada
Seville
Cadiz
Tangier (PORT.)
Ceuta (SP.)
FEZ & MOROCCO

CROATIA
HABSBURG
Budapest
HUNGARY
SLAVONIA
Belgrade
BOSNIA
MONTE-NEGRO
SERBIA
Spalato
Cattaro (VEN.)
RAGUSA
ALBANIA
BULGARIA
Bucharest
WALLACHIA
TRANSYLVANIA
MOLDAVIA
Jassi
BESSARABIA
JEDISAN
CRIMEA

OTTOMAN EMPIRE

Black Sea
Constantinople
Scutari
Adrianople
RUMELIA
Salonica
Smyrna
Athens
MOREA
LESBOS
CHIOS
NAXOS
CYPRUS
RHODES
CRETE (VEN.)

Adriatic Sea
VENICE
Venice
Bologna
PAPAL STATES
Rome
ITALY
TUSCANY
LUCCA
Genoa
Milan
MILAN
Capua
Naples
Bari
KINGDOM OF TWO SICILIES
CORSICA (GENOA)
SARDINIA (SP.)
BALEARIC ISLANDS

Mediterranean Sea
Algiers
Tunis
ALGERIA

400 MILES
400 KILOMETERS

Map 12–5   **EUROPE IN 1648**   At the end of the Thirty Years' War, Spain still had extensive possessions. Austria and Brandenburg-Prussia were rising powers, the independence of the United Provinces and Switzerland was recognized, and Sweden had footholds in northern Germany.

369

The wars ended with the recognition of minority religious rights and a guarantee of the traditional boundaries of political sovereignty. In France, the Edict of Nantes (1598) brought peace by granting Huguenots basic religious and civil freedoms and by recognizing their towns and territories. With the departure of the Spanish, peace and sovereignty also came to the Netherlands, guaranteed initially by the Twelve Years' Truce (1609) and secured fully by the Peace of Westphalia (1648). The conflict between England and Spain ended with the removal of the Spanish threat to English sovereignty in politics and religion, which resulted from the execution of Mary, Queen of Scots (1587) and the English victory over the Armada (1588). In the Holy Roman Empire, peace came with the reaffirmation of the political principle of the Peace of Augsburg (1555), as the Peace of Westphalia brought the Thirty Years' War to an end by again recognizing the sovereignty of rulers within their lands and their right to determine the religious beliefs of their subjects. Europe at mid-century had real, if brief, peace.

REVIEW QUESTIONS

1. How did politics shape the religious positions of the French leaders? What led to the Saint Bartholomew's Day Massacre, and what did it achieve?

2. How did Spain gain a position of dominance in the sixteenth century? What were Philip II's successes and failures?

3. Henry of Navarre (Henry IV of France), Elizabeth I, and William of Orange were all *politiques*. What does that term mean and why does it apply to these three rulers?

4. What led to the establishment of the Anglican Church in England? Why did Mary I fail? What was Elizabeth I's settlement, and why was it difficult to impose on England? Who were her detractors and what were their criticisms?

5. Why was the Thirty Years' War fought? Was politics or religion more important in determining the outcome of the war? What were the main terms of the Treaty of Westphalia in 1648?

6. Why has the Thirty Years' War been called the outstanding example in European history of meaningless conflict? Was it really such? Were the results worth the cost of the war?

SUGGESTED READINGS

F. Braudel, *The Mediterranean and the Mediterranean World in the Age of Philip the Second*, Vols. 1 and 2 (1976). Widely acclaimed "big picture" by a master historian.

N. Z. Davis, *Society and Culture in Early Modern France* (1975). Essays on popular culture.

R. Dunn, *The Age of Religious Wars, 1559–1689* (1979). Excellent brief survey of every major conflict.

J. H. Franklin, ed. and trans., *Constitutionalism and Resistance in the Sixteenth Century: Three Treatises by Hotman, Beza, and Mornay* (1969). Three defenders of the right to resist tyranny.

J. Guy, *Tudor England* (1990). The standard history and a good synthesis of recent scholarship.

D. Loades, *Mary Tudor* (1989). Authoritative and good storytelling.

G. Mattingly, *The Armada* (1959). A masterpiece resembling a novel in style.

J. E. Neale, *The Age of Catherine de Médicis* (1962). Short, concise summary.

A. Soman, ed., *The Massacre of St. Bartholomew's Day: Reappraisals and Documents* (1974). Essays from an international symposium on the anniversary of the massacre.

C. Wedgwood, *William the Silent* (1944). Eloquent political biography of William of Orange.

A. B. Weir, *The Life of Elizabeth I* (1998). Detailed portrayal of a successful ruler.

J. Wormald, *Mary, Queen of Scots: A Study in Failure* (1991). Mary portrayed as out of touch with her country and her times.

For additional learning resources related to this chapter, please go to www.myhistorylab.com

myhistorylab

Peter the Great (r. 1682–1725), seeking to make Russia a military power after West European models reorganized the country's political, social, and economic structures. He also radically changed the relationship of the Russian Church to the Russian state. His reign saw Russia enter fully into European power politics. *The Apotheosis of Tsar Peter the Great 1672–1725* by unknown artist, 1710. Historical Museum, Moscow, Russia/E.T. Archive

13

European State Consolidation in the Seventeenth and Eighteenth Centuries

▼ **The Netherlands: Golden Age to Decline**
Urban Prosperity • Economic Decline

▼ **Two Models of European Political Development**

▼ **Constitutional Crisis and Settlement in Stuart England**
James I • Charles I • The Long Parliament and Civil War • Oliver Cromwell and the Puritan Republic • Charles II and the Restoration of the Monarchy • The "Glorious Revolution" • The Age of Walpole

▼ **Rise of Absolute Monarchy in France: The World of Louis XIV**
Years of Personal Rule • Versailles • King by Divine Right • Louis's Early Wars • Louis's Repressive Religious Policies • Louis's Later Wars • France After Louis XIV

▼ **Central and Eastern Europe**
Poland: Absence of Strong Central Authority • The Habsburg Empire and the Pragmatic Sanction • Prussia and the Hohenzollerns

▼ **Russia Enters the European Political Arena**
The Romanov Dynasty • Peter the Great • Russian Expansion in the Baltic: The Great Northern War

▼ **The Ottoman Empire**
Religious Toleration and Ottoman Government • The End of Ottoman Expansion

▼ **In Perspective**

KEY TOPICS

• **The Dutch Golden Age**

• **The divergent political paths of Britain and France: Parliamentary supremacy and royal absolutism**

• **Poland's failure to establish a strong central government**

• **The Habsburg efforts to preserve their holdings**

• **The emergence of Prussia and Russia as major powers**

• **Power and decline of the Ottoman Empire**

BETWEEN THE EARLY seventeenth and the mid-twentieth centuries, no region so dominated other parts of the world politically, militarily, and economically as Europe. Such had not been the case before that date and would not be the case after World War II. However, for approximately three and a half centuries, Europe became the chief driving force in one world historical development after another. This era of European dominance, which appears quite temporary in the larger scope of history, also coincided with a shift in power within Europe itself from the Mediterranean, where Spain and Portugal had taken the lead in the conquest and early exploitation of the Americas, to the states of northwest and later north-central Europe.

During the seventeenth and early eighteenth centuries, certain states in northern Europe organized themselves politically so as to be able to dominate Europe and later to influence and even govern other large areas of the world through military might and economic strength. Even within the region of northern Europe, there occurred a sorting out of influence among political states with some successfully establishing long-term positions of dominance and others passing from the scene after relatively brief periods of either military or economic strength.

By the mid-eighteenth century, five major states had come to dominate European politics and would continue to do so until at least World War I. They were Great Britain, France, Austria, Prussia, and Russia. Through their military strength, economic development, and, in some cases, colonial empires, they would affect virtually every other world civilization. Within Europe, these states established their dominance at the expense of Spain, Portugal, the United Provinces of the Netherlands, Poland, Sweden, and the Ottoman Empire. Equally essential to their rise was the weakness of the Holy Roman Empire after the Peace of Westphalia (1648).

In western Europe, Britain and France emerged as the dominant powers. This development represented a shift of influence away from Spain and the United Netherlands. Both of the latter countries had been powerful and important during the sixteenth and seventeenth centuries, but they became politically and militarily marginal during the eighteenth century. Neither, however, disappeared from the map, and both retained considerable economic vitality and influence. Spanish power declined after the War of the Spanish Succession. The case of the Netherlands was more complicated.

▼ The Netherlands: Golden Age to Decline

The seven provinces that became the United Provinces of the Netherlands emerged as a nation after revolting against Spain in 1572. During the seventeenth century, the Dutch engaged in a series of naval wars with England. Then, in 1672, the armies of Louis XIV invaded the Netherlands. Prince William III of Orange (1650–1702), the grandson of William the Silent (1533–1584) and the hereditary chief executive, or *stadtholder*, of Holland, the most important of the provinces, rallied the Dutch and eventually led the entire European coalition against France. As a part of that strategy, he answered the invitation of Protestant English aristocrats in 1688 to assume, along with his wife Mary, the English throne.

During both the seventeenth and eighteenth centuries, the political and economic life of the Netherlands differed from that of the rest of Europe. The other major nations pursued paths toward strong central government, generally under monarchies, as with France, or in the case of England, under a strong parliamentary system. By contrast, the Netherlands was formally a republic. Each of the provinces retained considerable authority, and the central government, embodied in the States General that met in the Hague, exercised its authority through a kind of ongoing negotiation with the provinces. Prosperous and populous Holland dominated the States General. The Dutch deeply distrusted monarchy and the ambitions of the House of Orange. Nonetheless, when confronted with major military challenges, the Dutch would permit the House of Orange and, most notably, William III to assume dominant leadership. These political arrangements proved highly resilient and allowed the republic to establish itself permanently in the European state system during the seventeenth century. When William died in 1702 and the wars with France ended in 1714, the Dutch reverted to their republican structures.

Although the provinces making up the Netherlands were traditionally identified with the Protestant cause in Europe, toleration marked Dutch religious life. The Calvinist Reformed Church was the official church of the nation, but it was not an established church. There was always a significant number of Roman Catholics and Protestants who did not belong to the Reformed Church. The country also became a haven for Jews. Consequently, while governments in other European states attempted to impose a single religion on their people or tore themselves apart in religious conflict, in the Netherlands peoples of differing religious faiths lived together peacefully.

Urban Prosperity

Beyond the climate of religious toleration, what most amazed seventeenth-century contemporaries about the Dutch Republic was its economic prosperity. Its remarkable economic achievement was built on the foundations of high urban consolidation, transformed agriculture, extensive trade and finance, and an overseas commercial empire.

In the Netherlands, more people lived in cities than in any other area of Europe. Key transformations in Dutch farming that served as the model for the rest of Europe made this urban transformation possible. During the seventeenth century, the Dutch drained and reclaimed land from the sea, which they used for highly profitable farming. Because Dutch shipping provided a steady supply of cheap grain, Dutch farmers themselves could produce more profitable dairy products and beef and cultivate cash products such as tulip bulbs.

Dutch fishermen dominated the market for herring and supplied much of the continent's dried fish. The Dutch also supplied textiles to many parts of Europe. Dutch ships appeared in harbors all over the continent, with their captains purchasing goods that they then transported and resold at a profit to other nations. The overseas trades also supported a vast shipbuilding and ship supply industry. The most advanced financial system of the day supported all of this trade, commerce, and manufacturing.

The final foundation of Dutch prosperity was a seaborne empire. Dutch traders established a major presence in East Asia, particularly in spice-producing areas of Java, the Moluccas, and Sri Lanka. The vehicle for this penetration was the Dutch East India Company (chartered in 1602). The company eventually displaced Portuguese dominance in the spice trade of East Asia and for many years prevented English traders from establishing a major presence there. Initially, the Dutch had only wanted commercial dominance of the spice trade, but in time, they moved toward producing the spices themselves, which required them to control many of the islands that now constitute Indonesia. The Netherlands remained the colonial master of this region until after World War II.

Economic Decline

The decline in political influence of the United Provinces of the Netherlands occurred in the eighteenth century. After the death of William III of Britain in 1702, the provinces prevented the emergence of another strong *stadtholder*. Unified political leadership therefore vanished. Naval supremacy slowly but steadily passed to the British. The fishing industry declined, and the Dutch lost their technological superiority in shipbuilding. Countries between which Dutch ships had once carried goods now traded directly with each other.

Similar stagnation overtook the Dutch domestic industries. The disunity of the provinces hastened this economic decline and prevented action that might have halted it.

What saved the United Provinces from becoming completely insignificant in European affairs was their continued financial dominance. Well past the middle of the eighteenth century, Dutch banks continued to finance European trade, and the Amsterdam stock exchange remained an important financial institution.

The technologically advanced fleet of the Dutch East India Company, shown here at anchor in Amsterdam, linked the Netherlands' economy with that of southeast Asia. Andries van Eertvelt (1590–1652), *The Return to Amsterdam of the Fleet of the Dutch East India Company in 1599*. Oil on copper. Johnny van Haeften Gallery, London, UK. The Bridgeman Art Library

▼ Two Models of European Political Development

The United Netherlands, like Venice and the Swiss cantons, was a republic governed without a monarch. Elsewhere in Europe monarchy of two fundamentally different patterns predominated in response to the military challenges of international conflict.

The two models became known as *parliamentary monarchy* and **political absolutism**. England embodied the first, and France, the second. Neither model was inevitable for either country, but each resulted from the historical developments and political personalities that molded each nation during the seventeenth century.

The political forces that led to the creation of these two models had arisen from military concerns. During the second half of the sixteenth century, changes in military organization, weapons, and tactics sharply increased the cost of warfare. Because their traditional sources of income could not finance these growing expenses, in addition to the other costs of government, monarchs sought new revenues. Only monarchies that succeeded in building a secure financial base that was not deeply dependent on the support of noble estates, diets, or assemblies achieved absolute rule. The French monarchy succeeded in this effort, whereas the English monarchy failed. That success and failure led to the two models of government—*absolutism* in France and **parliamentary monarchy** in England—that shaped subsequent political development in Europe.

The divergent developments of England and France in the seventeenth century would have surprised most people in 1600. It was not inevitable that the English monarchy would have to govern through Parliament or that the French monarchy would avoid dealing with national political institutions that could significantly limit its authority. The Stuart kings of England aspired to the autocracy Louis XIV achieved, and some English political philosophers eloquently defended the **divine right of kings** and absolute rule. At the beginning of the seventeenth century, the English monarchy was strong. Queen Elizabeth, after a reign of almost forty-five years (1558–1603), was much revered. Parliament met only when the monarch summoned it to provide financial support. France, however, was emerging from the turmoil of its religious wars. The strife of that conflict had torn French society apart. The monarchy was relatively weak. Henry IV, who had become king in 1589, pursued a policy of religious toleration. The French nobles had significant military forces at their disposal and in the middle of the seventeenth century rebelled against the king. These conditions would change dramatically in both nations by the late seventeenth century.

▼ Constitutional Crisis and Settlement in Stuart England

James I

In 1603 James VI, the son of Mary Stuart, Queen of Scots, who had been King of Scotland since 1567, succeeded without opposition or incident the childless Elizabeth I as James I of England. He also inherited a large royal debt and a fiercely divided church. A strong believer in the divine right of kings, he expected to rule with a minimum of consultation beyond his own royal court.

Parliament met only when the monarch summoned it, which James hoped to do rarely. In place of parliamentarily approved revenues, James developed other sources of income, largely by levying new custom duties known as *impositions*. Members of Parliament regarded this as an affront to their authority over the royal purse, but they did not seek a serious confrontation. Rather, throughout James's reign they wrangled and negotiated.

The religious problem also festered under James. Since the days of Elizabeth, **Puritans** within the Church of England had sought to eliminate elaborate religious ceremonies and replace the hierarchical episcopal system of church governance under bishops appointed by the king with a more representative Presbyterian form like that of the Calvinist churches in Scotland and on the Continent. At the Hampton Court Conference of January 1604, James rebuffed the Puritans and firmly declared his intention to maintain and even enhance the Anglican episcopacy. Thereafter, both sides had deep suspicions of the other. (See "King James I Defends Popular Recreation against the Puritans.")

Religious dissenters began to leave England. In 1620, Puritan separatists founded Plymouth Colony on Cape Cod Bay in North America, preferring flight from England to Anglican conformity. Later in the 1620s, a larger, better financed group of Puritans left England to found the Massachusetts Bay Colony. In each case, the colonists believed that reformation would or could not go far enough in England and that only in America could they worship freely and organize a truly reformed church.

James's court became a center of scandal and corruption. He governed by favorites, of whom the most influential was the duke of Buckingham, whom rumor made the king's homosexual lover. Buckingham controlled royal patronage and openly sold peerages and titles to the highest bidders—a practice that angered the nobility because it cheapened their rank. There had always been court favorites, but seldom before had a single person so controlled access to the monarch.

James's foreign policy roused further opposition and doubt about his Protestant loyalty. In 1604, he concluded a much-needed peace with Spain, England's longtime adversary. The war had been ruinously ex-

KING JAMES I DEFENDS POPULAR RECREATION AGAINST THE PURITANS

The English Puritans believed in strict observance of the Sabbath, disapproving any sports, games, or general social conviviality on Sunday. James I thought these strictures prevented many Roman Catholics from joining the Church of England. In 1618, he ordered the clergy of the Church of England to read the Book of Sports from their pulpits. In this declaration, he permitted people to engage in certain sports and games after church services. His hope was to allow innocent recreations on Sunday while encouraging people to attend the Church of England. Despite the king's good intentions, the order offended the Puritans. The clergy resisted his order and he had to withdraw it.

What motives of state might have led James I to issue this declaration? How does he attempt to make it favorable to the Church of England? Why might so many clergy have refused to read this statement to their congregations?

With our own ears we heard the general complaint of our people, that they were barred from all lawful recreation and exercise upon the Sunday's afternoon, after the ending of all divine service, which cannot but produce two evils: the one the hindering of the conversion of many [Roman Catholic subjects], whom their priests will take occasion hereby to vex, persuading them that no honest mirth or recreation is lawful or tolerable in our religion, which cannot but breed a great discontentment in our people's hearts, especially as such as are peradventure upon the point of turning [to the Church of England]: the other inconvenience is, that this prohibition barreth the common and meaner sort of people from using such exercises as may make their bodies more able for war, when we or our successors shall have occasion to use them; and in place thereof sets up filthy tipplings and drunkenness, and breeds a number of idle and discontented speeches in their ale-houses. For when shall the common people have leave to exercise, if not upon the Sundays and holy days, seeing they must apply their labor and win their living in all working days? . . .

[A]s for our good people's lawful recreation, our pleasure likewise is, that after the end of divine service our good people be not disturbed, . . . or discouraged from any lawful recreation, such as dancing, either men or women; archery for men, leaping, vaulting, or any other such harmless recreation, or from having of Hay-games, Whitsun-ales, and Morris-dances; and the setting up of May-poles and other sports therewith used; . . . but withal we do here account still as prohibited all unlawful games to be used upon Sundays only, as bear and bull-baitings . . . and at all times in the meaner sort of people by law prohibited, bowling.

And likewise we bar from this benefit and liberty all such known as recusants [Roman Catholics], either men or women, as will abstain from coming to church or divine service, being therefore unworthy of any lawful recreation after the said service, that will not first come to the church and serve God; prohibiting in like sort the said recreations to any that, though [they] conform in religion [i.e., members of the Church of England], are not present in the church at the service of God, before their going to the said recreations.

From Henry Bettenson, ed., *Documents of the Christian Church*, 2nd ed. (London: Oxford University Press, 1963), pp. 400–403. By permission of Oxford University Press.

pensive, but his subjects considered the peace a sign of pro-Catholic sentiment. James's unsuccessful attempt to relax penal laws against Catholics further increased suspicions, as did his wise hesitancy in 1618 to rush English troops to the aid of German Protestants at the outbreak of the Thirty Years' War. His failed efforts to arrange a marriage between his son Charles and a Spanish princess, and then Charles's marriage in 1625 to Henrietta Marie, the Catholic daughter of Henry IV of France, further increased religious concern. In 1624,

Encountering the Past

EARLY CONTROVERSY OVER TOBACCO AND SMOKING

SMOKING TODAY IS widely condemned throughout the West, but the controversy over tobacco goes back to the earliest European encounter with the plant, which was native to the Americas.

Christopher Columbus on his first voyage in 1492 saw Native Americans smoking tobacco. Later, the first Spanish missionaries associated smoking with pagan religious practices and tried to stop Native Americans from using tobacco. Once tobacco reached Europe in the late sixteenth century, more opposition to smoking arose (although—ironically—some physicians thought it might cure diseases of the lungs and internal organs). As early as 1610, Sir Francis Bacon (1561–1626) noted that smokers found it difficult to stop smoking. The Christian clergy throughout Europe denounced smoking as immoral, and Muslim clerics condemned the practice as contrary to Islam when it spread to the Ottoman Empire. Nonetheless, smoking tobacco in pipes became popular.

The chief British critic of the new practice was none other than King James I (r. 1603–1625). While he defended Sunday sports against Puritan critics who believed any amusements on the Sabbath were sinful, he detested smoking. In 1604, he published his *Counterblaste to Tobacco* in which he declared, "Have you not reason then to be ashamed, and to forbear this filthy novelty . . .? In your abuse thereof sinning against God, harming yourselves in person . . . and taking thereby the marks . . . of vanity upon you. . . . A custom loathsome to the eye, hateful to the nose, harmful to the brain, dangerous to the lungs, and the black stinking fume thereof, nearest resembling the horrible Stygian smoke of the pit that is bottomless."[1]

To discourage smoking, James's government put a high tax on tobacco. Yet when a brisk trade in smuggled tobacco developed, the government decided to lower the tax to a level where people would not seek to evade it. In 1614, James created a royal monopoly to import tobacco into England, which created a steady government revenue that the increasingly unpopular king badly needed. James, like governments to the present day, may also have regarded this policy as a tax on sin. By 1619, James approved the incorporation of a company of clay pipe makers in London, and 40,000 pounds of tobacco arrived from Virginia the next year. Other European governments would also find tobacco a significant source of tax revenue. Often they would tax tobacco and at the same time attempt to regulate its use, especially among the young.

Which groups in Europe in the sixteenth and seventeenth centuries opposed the habit of smoking tobacco?

Why did the English government under King James I modify its opposition to tobacco?

[1]*A Counterblaste to Tobacco* (1604), reprinted by the Rodale Press, London, 1954, p. 36.

Practically from the moment of its introduction into Europe tobacco smoking was controversial. Here a court jester is portrayed as exhaling rabbits from a pipe as three pipe-smoking gentlemen look on.
© Christel Gerstenberg/Corbis

shortly before James's death, England again went to war against Spain, largely in response to parliamentary pressures.

Charles I

Parliament had favored the war with Spain but would not adequately finance it because its members distrusted the monarchy. Unable to gain adequate funds from Parliament, Charles I (r. 1625–1649), like his father, resorted to extraparliamentary measures. These included levying new tariffs and duties, attempting to collect discontinued taxes, and subjecting English property owners to a so-called forced loan (a tax theoretically to be repaid) and then imprisoning those who refused to pay. All these actions, as well as quartering troops in private homes, challenged local political influence of nobles and landowners.

King CHARLES *the* FIRST *in the* HOUSE *of* COMMONS, *demanding the* FIVE *impeached* MEMBERS *to be delivered up to his* AUTHORITY.

One of the key moments in the conflict between Charles I and Parliament occurred in January 1642 when Charles personally arrived at the House of Commons intent on arresting five members who had been responsible for opposing him. They had already escaped. Thereafter Charles departed London to raise his army. The event was subsequently often portrayed in English art. The present illustration is from an eighteenth-century engraving.
The Granger Collection, New York

When Parliament met in 1628, its members would grant new funds only if Charles recognized the Petition of Right. This document required that henceforth there should be no forced loans or taxation without the consent of Parliament, that no freeman should be imprisoned without due cause, and that troops should not be billeted in private homes. Charles agreed to the petition, but whether he would keep his word was doubtful. The next year after further disputes, Charles dissolved Parliament and did not recall it until 1640.

Years of Personal Rule To conserve his limited resources, Charles made peace with France in 1629 and Spain in 1630, again rousing fears that he was too friendly to Roman Catholic powers. To allow Charles to rule without renegotiating financial arrangements with Parliament, his chief adviser Thomas Wentworth (1593–1641; after 1640, earl of Strafford), imposed strict efficiency and administrative centralization in the government and exploited every legal fund-raising device, enforcing previously neglected laws and extending existing taxes into new areas.

Charles might have ruled indefinitely without Parliament had not his religious policies provoked war with Scotland. James I had allowed a wide variety of religious observances in England, Scotland, and Ireland; by contrast, Charles hoped to impose religious conformity at least within England and Scotland. In 1637, Charles and his high-church Archbishop William Laud (1573–1645), against the opposition of both the English Puritans and the Presbyterian Scots, tried to impose on Scotland the English episcopal system and a prayer book almost identical to the Anglican Book of Common Prayer.

The Scots rebelled, and Charles, with insufficient resources for war, was forced in 1640 to call Parliament. It refused even to consider funds for war until the king agreed to redress a long list of political and religious grievances. The king, in response, immediately dissolved that Parliament—hence its name, the Short Parliament (April–May 1640). When the Scots defeated an English army at the Battle of Newburn in the summer of 1640, Charles reconvened Parliament—this time on its terms—for a long and fateful duration.

The Long Parliament and Civil War

The landowners and the merchant classes represented in Parliament had long resented the king's financial measures and paternalistic rule. The Puritans in Parliament resented his religious policies and distrusted the influence of his Roman Catholic wife. What became known as the Long Parliament (1640–1660) thus acted with widespread support and general unanimity when it convened in November 1640.

The House of Commons impeached both Strafford and Laud. Both were executed—Strafford in 1641, Laud in 1645. Parliament abolished the courts that had enforced royal policy and prohibited the levying of new taxes without its consent. Finally, Parliament resolved that no more than three years should elapse between its meetings and that the king could not dissolve it without its own consent.

Parliament, however, was sharply divided over religion. Both moderate Puritans (the Presbyterians) and more extreme Puritans (the Independents) wanted to abolish bishops and the Book of Common Prayer. Yet religious conservatives in both houses of Parliament were determined to preserve the Church of England in its current form.

These divisions intensified in October 1641, when Parliament was asked to raise funds for an army to suppress the rebellion in Scotland. Charles's opponents argued that he could not be trusted with an army and that Parliament should become the commander-in-chief of English armed forces. In January 1642, Charles invaded Parliament, intending to arrest certain of his opponents, but they escaped. The king then left London and began to raise an army. Shocked, a majority of the House of Commons passed the Militia Ordinance, which gave Parliament authority to raise an army of its own. The die was now cast. For the next four years (1642–1646), civil war engulfed England with the king's supporters known as Cavaliers and the parliamentary opposition as Roundheads.

Oliver Cromwell and the Puritan Republic

Two factors led finally to Parliament's victory. The first was an alliance with Scotland in 1643 that committed Parliament to a Presbyterian system of church government. The second was the reorganization of the parliamentary army under Oliver Cromwell (1599–1658), a country squire of iron discipline and strong, independent religious sentiment. Cromwell and his "godly men" were willing to tolerate an established majority church, but only if it permitted Protestant dissenters to worship outside it.

Defeated militarily by June 1645, Charles for the next several years tried to take advantage of divisions within Parliament, but Cromwell and his army foiled him. Members who might have been sympathetic to the monarch were expelled from Parliament in December 1648. After a trial by a special court, Charles was executed on January 30, 1649, as a public criminal. Parliament then abolished the monarchy, the House of Lords, and the Anglican Church.

From 1649 to 1660, England became officially a Puritan republic, although Cromwell dominated it. His army brutally conquered Scotland and Ireland, where his radically Protestant army carried out numerous atrocities against Irish Catholics. As a national leader, however, Cromwell, proved to be no politician. When in 1653, the House of Commons wanted to disband his expensive army of 50,000 men, Cromwell instead disbanded Parliament. He ruled thereafter as Lord Protector.

Oliver Cromwell's New Model Army defeated the royalists in the English Civil War. After the execution of Charles I in 1649, Cromwell dominated the short-lived English republic, conquered Ireland and Scotland, and ruled as Lord Protector from 1653 until his death in 1658.   Dorling Kindersley Media Library. The Wallace Collection, London

Cromwell's military dictatorship, however, proved no more effective than Charles's rule and became just as harsh and hated. People deeply resented his Puritan prohibitions of drunkenness, theatergoing, and dancing. Political liberty vanished in the name of religious conformity. When Cromwell died in 1658, the English were ready by 1660 to restore both the Anglican Church and the monarchy.

Charles II and the Restoration of the Monarchy

After negotiations with the army, Charles II (r. 1660–1685) returned to England amid great rejoicing. A man of considerable charm and political skill, Charles set a refreshing new tone after eleven years of somber Puritanism. England returned to the status quo of 1642, with a hereditary monarch, a Parliament of Lords and Commons that met only when the king summoned it, and the Anglican Church, with its bishops and prayer book, supreme in religion.

The king, however, had secret Catholic sympathies and favored religious toleration. He wanted to allow loyal Catholics and Puritans to worship freely. Yet ultraroyalists in Parliament between 1661 and 1665, through a series of laws known as the Clarendon Code, excluded

ENGLAND IN THE SEVENTEENTH CENTURY

1603	James VI of Scotland becomes James I of England
1604	Hampton Court conference
1611	Publication of the authorized, or King James, version of the English Bible
1625	Charles I becomes English monarch
1628	Petition of Right
1629	Charles I dissolves Parliament and embarks on eleven years of personal rule
1640	April–May, Short Parliament; November, Long Parliament convenes
1642	Outbreak of the Civil War
1645	Charles I defeated at Naseby
1648	Pride's Purge
1649	Charles I executed
1649–1660	Various attempts at a Puritan Commonwealth
1660	Charles II restored to the English throne
1670	Secret Treaty of Dover between France and England
1672	Parliament passes the Test Act
1678	Popish Plot
1685	James II becomes king of England
1688	"Glorious Revolution"
1689	William and Mary proclaimed English monarchs
1701	Acts of Settlement provides for Hanoverian succession
1702–1714	Reign of Queen Anne, the last of the Stuarts
1707	Act of Union between England and Scotland
1713	Treaty of Utrecht ends the War of the Spanish Succession
1714	George I becomes king of Great Britain and establishes the Hanoverian dynasty
1721–1742	Robert Walpole dominates British politics
1727	George II becomes king of Great Britain

Roman Catholics, Presbyterians, and Independents from the official religious and political life of the nation.

In 1670 by the Treaty of Dover, England and France formally allied against the Dutch, their chief commercial competitor. In a secret portion of this treaty, Charles pledged to announce his conversion to Catholicism as soon as conditions in England permitted this to happen. In return for this announcement (which Charles never made), Louis XIV promised to pay Charles a substantial subsidy. In an attempt to unite the English people behind the war with Holland, and as a sign of good faith to Louis XIV, Charles is-

sued a Declaration of Indulgence in 1672, suspending all laws against Roman Catholics and non-Anglican Protestants. Parliament refused to fund the war, however, until Charles rescinded the measure. After he did so, Parliament passed the Test Act requiring all civil and military officials of the crown to swear an oath against the doctrine of transubstantiation—which no loyal Roman Catholic could honestly do. Parliament had aimed the Test Act largely at the king's brother, James, duke of York, heir to the throne and a recent, devout convert to Catholicism.

In 1678, a notorious liar named Titus Oates swore before a magistrate that Charles's Catholic wife, through her physician, was plotting with Jesuits and Irishmen to kill the king so James could assume the throne. Parliament believed Oates. In the ensuing hysteria, known as the Popish Plot, several innocent people were tried and executed. Riding the crest of anti-Catholic sentiment and led by the earl of Shaftesbury (1621–1683), opposition members of Parliament, called Whigs, made an unsuccessful effort to exclude James from succession to the throne.

More suspicious than ever of Parliament, Charles II turned again to increased customs duties and the assistance of Louis XIV for extra income. By these means, he was able to rule from 1681 to 1685 without recalling Parliament. In those years, Charles drove Shaftesbury into exile, executed several Whig leaders for treason, and bullied local corporations into electing members of Parliament submissive to the royal will. When Charles died in 1685 (after a deathbed conversion to Catholicism), he left James the prospect of a Parliament filled with royal friends.

The "Glorious Revolution"

When James II (r. 1685–1688) became king, he immediately demanded the repeal of the Test Act. When Parliament balked, he dissolved it and proceeded to appoint Catholics to high positions in both his court and the army. In 1687, he issued another Declaration of Indulgence suspending all religious tests and permitting free worship. In June 1688, James imprisoned seven Anglican bishops who had refused to publicize his suspension of laws against the Catholics. Each of these actions represented a direct royal attack on the local authority of nobles, landowners, the church, and other corporate bodies whose members believed they possessed particular legal privileges. James not only sought to aid his fellow Roman Catholics but also to pursue absolutist policies similar to those of Louis XIV whom he deeply admired.

The English had hoped that James would be succeeded by Mary (r. 1689–1694), his Protestant eldest daughter. She was the wife of William III of Orange, the leader of European opposition to Louis XIV. But on June 20, James II's Catholic second wife gave birth to a son. There was now a Catholic male heir to the throne. The Parliamentary opposition invited William to invade

England to preserve its "traditional liberties," that is, the Anglican Church and parliamentary government.

William of Orange arrived with his army in November 1688 and was received with considerable popular support. James fled to France, and Parliament, in 1689, proclaimed William III and Mary II the new monarchs, thus completing the "**Glorious Revolution**." William and Mary, in turn, recognized a Bill of Rights that limited the powers of the monarchy and guaranteed the civil liberties of the English privileged classes. Henceforth, England's monarchs would be subject to law and would rule by the consent of Parliament, which was to be called into session every three years. The Bill of Rights also prohibited Roman Catholics from occupying the English throne. The Toleration Act of 1689 permitted worship by all Protestants and outlawed only Roman Catholics and those who denied the Christian doctrine of the Trinity. It did not, however, extend full political rights to persons outside the Church of England.

As will be seen more fully in the next chapter, in 1690 John Locke published his *Second Treatise of Civil Government*, which defended the idea that government resided in the consent of the governed. This view directly opposed Tory support for absolutism as well as absolutist political thought on the continent. (See "Compare & Connect: The Debate over the Origin and Character of Political Authority," pages 386–387.)

The Revolution of 1688 has traditionally been seen as a relatively peaceful event. Recent scholarship, however, has disclosed considerable resistance in both Scotland and Ireland, which resulted in significant loss of life. Conversely events in England itself now appear driven not only by the long recognized actions of the political elite, but also by a genuinely popular resistance to James II. Furthermore, the political results of the revolution went well beyond the assertion of parliamentary authority. In one area of government policy after another the reign of William and Mary marked important new departures for Britain. These included not only the aforementioned embrace of moderate religious toleration, but also a turn to policies favoring more modern economic activity resembling that of the Netherlands and a redirection of foreign policy toward direct opposition to France whereas both Charles II and James II had sought to imitate French absolutism and to pursue close relationships with Louis XIV.

The parliamentary measure closing this century of strife was the Act of Settlement (1701), which provided for the English crown to go to the Protestant House of Hanover in Germany if Queen Anne (r. 1702–1714), the second daughter of James II and the heir to the childless William III, died without issue. Thus, at Anne's death in 1714, the Elector of Hanover became King George I of Great Britain (r. 1714–1727) since England and Scotland had been combined in an Act of Union in 1707.

The Age of Walpole

George I almost immediately confronted a challenge to his title. James Edward Stuart (1688–1766), the Catholic son of James II, landed in Scotland in December 1715, but met defeat less than two months later.

Despite the victory over the Stuart pretender, the political situation after 1715 remained in flux until Sir Robert Walpole (1676–1745) took over the helm of government. Walpole's ascendancy from 1721 to 1742 was based on royal support, his ability to handle the House of Commons, and his

Sir Robert Walpole (1676–1745), far left, is shown talking with the Speaker of the House of Commons. Walpole, who dominated British political life from 1721 to 1742, is considered the first prime minister of Britain. Mansell/TimePix/Getty Images, Inc.

control of government patronage. Walpole maintained peace abroad and promoted the status quo at home. Britain's foreign trade spread from New England to India. Because the central government refrained from interfering with the local political influence of nobles and other landowners, they were willing to serve as local government administrators, judges, and military commanders, and to collect and pay the taxes to support a powerful military force, particularly a strong navy. As a result, Great Britain became not only a European power of the first order but eventually a world power as well.

The power of the British monarchs and their ministers had real limits. Parliament could not wholly ignore popular pressure. Even with the extensive use of patronage, many members of Parliament maintained independent views. Newspapers and public debate flourished. Free speech could be exercised, as could freedom of association. There was no large standing army. There existed significant religious toleration. Walpole's enemies could and did openly oppose his policies, which would not have been possible on the Continent. Consequently, the English state combined considerable military power with both religious and political liberty. British political life became the model for all progressive Europeans who questioned the absolutist political developments of the Continent. Furthermore, many of the political values that had emerged in the British Isles during the seventeenth century also took deep root among their North American colonies.

▼ Rise of Absolute Monarchy in France: The World of Louis XIV

Historians once portrayed Louis XIV's reign (r. 1643–1715) as a time when the French monarchy exerted far-reaching, direct control of the nation at all levels. A somewhat different picture has now emerged.

The French monarchy, which had faced numerous challenges from strong, well-armed nobles and discontented Protestants during the first half of the seventeenth century, only gradually achieved the firm authority for which it became renowned later in the century. The groundwork for Louis XIV's absolutism had been laid by two powerful chief ministers, Cardinal Richelieu (1585–1642) under Louis XIII (r. 1610–1643), and then by Cardinal Mazarin (1602–1661). Both Richelieu and Mazarin attempted to impose direct royal administration on France. Richelieu had also circumscribed many of the political privileges Henry IV had extended to French Protestants in the Edict of Nantes (1598). The centralizing policies of Richelieu and then of Mazarin, however, finally provoked a series of widespread rebellions among French nobles between 1649 and 1652 known as the **Fronde** (after the slingshots used by street boys).

Though unsuccessful, these rebellions convinced Louis XIV and his advisors that heavy-handed policies could endanger the throne. Thereafter Louis would concentrate unprecedented authority in the monarchy, but he would be more subtle than his predecessors. His genius was to make the monarchy the most important and powerful political institution in France while also assuring the nobles and other wealthy groups of their social standing and influence on the local level. Rather than destroying existing local social and political institutions, Louis largely worked through them. Nevertheless, the king was clearly the senior partner in the relationship.

Years of Personal Rule

On the death of Mazarin in 1661, Louis XIV assumed personal control of the government at the age of twenty-three. He appointed no single chief minister. Rebellious nobles would now be challenging the king directly; they could not claim to be resisting only a bad minister.

Louis XIV of France came to symbolize absolute monarchy though such government was not as absolute as the term implied. This state portrait was intended to convey the grandeur of the king and of his authority. The portrait was brought into royal council meetings when the king himself was absent. Hyacinthe Rigaud (1659–1743), *Portrait of Louis XIV*. Louvre, Paris, France. Dorling Kindersley Media Library/Max Alexander. © Dorling Kindersley, courtesy of l'Etablissement public du musée et du domaine national de Versailles

Louis devoted enormous personal energy to his political tasks. He ruled through councils that controlled foreign affairs, the army, domestic administration, and economic regulations. Each day he spent hours with the ministers of these councils, whom he chose from families long in royal service or from among people just beginning to rise in the social structure. Unlike the more ancient noble families, the latter had no real or potential power bases in the provinces and depended solely on the king for their standing in both government and society.

Louis made sure, however, that the nobility and other major social groups would benefit from the growth of his own authority. Although he controlled foreign affairs and limited the influence of noble institutions on the monarchy, he never tried to abolish those institutions or limit their local authority. The crown, for example, usually conferred informally with regional judicial bodies, called **parlements**, before making rulings that would affect them. Likewise, the crown would rarely enact economic regulations without consulting local opinion. Louis did, however, clash with the Parlement of Paris, which had the right to register royal laws. In 1673, he curtailed its power by requiring it to register laws before raising any questions about them. Many regional parlements and other authorities, however, had long resented the power of that Parisian body and thus supported the monarch.

Versailles

Louis and his advisors became masters of propaganda and political image creation. Louis never missed an opportunity to impress the grandeur of his crown on the French people but most especially on the French nobility. He did so by the manipulation of symbols. For example, when the *dauphin* (the heir to the French throne) was born in 1662, Louis appeared for the celebration dressed as a Roman emperor. He also dominated the nobility by demonstrating that he could outspend them and create a greater social display than the strongest nobles in the land.

The central element of the image of the monarchy was the palace of Versailles, which, when completed, was the largest secular structure in Europe. More than any other monarch of the day, Louis XIV used the physical setting of his court to exert political control. Versailles, built between 1676 and 1708 on the outskirts of Paris, became Louis's permanent residence after 1682. It was a temple to royalty, designed and decorated to proclaim the glory of the Sun King, as Louis was known. A spectacular estate with magnificent fountains and gardens, it housed thousands of the more important nobles, royal officials, and servants. The stables alone could hold 12,000 horses. Some nobles paid for their own residence at the palace, thus depleting their resources; others required royal patronage to remain in residence. In either case they became dependent on the monarch. Although it consumed over half Louis's annual revenues, Versailles paid significant political dividends.

Because Louis ruled personally, he was himself the chief source of favors and patronage in France. To emphasize his prominence, he organized life at court around every aspect of his own daily routine. Elaborate etiquette governed every detail of life at Versailles. Moments near the king were important to most court nobles because they were effectively excluded from the real business of government. The king's rising and dressing were times of rare intimacy, when nobles could whisper their special requests in his ear. Fortunate nobles held his night candle when he went to his bed.

Some nobles, of course, avoided Versailles. They managed their estates and cultivated their local influence. Many others were simply too poor to cut a figure at court. All the nobility understood, however, that Louis, unlike Richelieu and Mazarin, would not threaten their local social standing. Louis supported France's traditional social structure and the social privileges of the nobility. Yet even the most powerful nobles knew they could strike only a modest figure when compared to the Sun King.

King by Divine Right

An important source for Louis's concept of royal authority was his devout tutor, the political theorist Bishop Jacques-Bénigne Bossuet (1627–1704). Bossuet defended what he called the "divine right of kings" and cited examples of Old Testament rulers divinely appointed by and answerable only to God. Medieval popes had insisted that only God could judge a pope; so Bossuet argued that only God could judge the king. Although kings might be duty bound to reflect God's will in their rule, yet as God's regents on earth they could not be bound to the dictates of mere nobles and parliaments. Such assumptions lay behind Louis XIV's alleged declaration: *"L'état, c'est moi"* ("I am the state"). (See "Compare & Connect: The Debate over the Origin and Character of Political Authority," pages 386–387.)

Despite these claims, Louis's rule did not exert the oppressive control over the daily lives of his subjects that police states would do in the nineteenth and twentieth centuries. His absolutism functioned primarily in the classic areas of European state action—the making of war and peace, the regulation of religion, and the oversight of economic activity. Even at the height of his power, local institutions, some controlled by townspeople and others by nobles, retained their administrative authority. The king and his ministers supported the social and financial privileges of these local elites. In contrast to the Stuart kings of England, however, Louis firmly prevented them from interfering with his authority on the national level. This system would endure until a financial crisis demoralized the French monarchy in the 1780s.

A Closer LOOK

VERSAILLES

LOUIS XIV CONSTRUCTED his great palace at Versailles, as painted here in 1668 by Pierre Patel the Elder (1605–1676), to demonstrate the new centralized power he sought to embody in the French monarchy.

The central building is the hunting lodge his father Louis XIII had built earlier in the century. Its interior and that of the wings added to it were decorated with themes from mythology presenting Louis XIV as the "Sun King" around whom all his kingdom revolved.

The outer wings, extending from the front of the central structure, housed governmental offices.

The gardens and ponds behind the main structure were the sites of elaborate entertainment, concerts, and fireworks.

Pierre Patel, *Perspective View of Versailles.* Chateaux de Versailles et de Trianon, Versailles, France. Photo copyright Bridgeman-Giraudon/ Art Resource, NY

To examine this image in an interactive fashion, please go to www.myhistorylab.com

Louis's Early Wars

By the late 1660s, France was superior to any other European nation in population, administrative bureaucracy, army, and national unity. Because of the economic policies of Jean-Baptiste Colbert (1619–1683), his most brilliant minister, Louis could afford to raise and maintain a large and powerful army. His enemies and some later historians claimed that Louis wished to dominate all of Europe, but it would appear that his chief military and foreign policy goal was to achieve secure international boundaries for France. He was particularly concerned to secure its northern borders along the Spanish Netherlands, the Franche-Comté, Alsace, and Lorraine from which foreign armies had invaded France and could easily do so again. Louis was also determined to frustrate Habsburg ambitions that endangered France and, as part of that goal, sought to secure his southern borders toward Spain. Whether reacting to external events or pursuing his own ambitions, Louis's pursuit of French interests threatened and terrified neighboring states and led them to form coalitions against France.

FRANCE FROM LOUIS XIV TO CARDINAL FLEURY

Year	Event
1643	Louis ascends the French throne at the age of five
1643–1661	Cardinal Mazarin directs the French government
1648	Peace of Westphalia
1649–1652	The *Fronde* revolt
1653	The pope declares Jansenism a heresy
1660	Papal ban on Jansenists enforced in France
1661	Louis commences personal rule
1667–1668	War of Devolution
1670	Secret Treaty of Dover between France and Great Britain
1672–1679	French war against the Netherlands
1685	Louis revokes the Edict of Nantes
1688–1697	War of the League of Augsburg
1701	Outbreak of the War of the Spanish Succession
1713	Treaty of Utrecht between France and Great Britain
1714	Treaty of Rastatt between France and the Empire and Holland
1715	Death of Louis XIV
1715–1720	Regency of the duke of Orléans in France
1720	Mississippi Bubble bursts in France
1726–1743	Cardinal Fleury serves as Louis XV's chief minister

The early wars of Louis XIV included conflicts with Spain and the United Netherlands. The first was the War of the Devolution in which Louis supported the alleged right of his first wife, Marie Thérèse, to inherit the Spanish Netherlands. He contended that through complex legal arrangements they should have "devolved" upon her, hence the name of the war. In 1667, Louis's armies invaded Flanders and the Franche-Comté. He was repulsed by the Triple Alliance of England, Sweden, and the United Provinces. By the Treaty of Aix-la-Chapelle (1668), he gained control of certain towns bordering the Spanish Netherlands. (See Map 13–1.)

In 1670, with the secret Treaty of Dover, England and France became allies against the Dutch. Louis invaded the Netherlands again in 1672. The Prince of Orange, the future William III of England, forged an alliance with the Holy Roman Emperor, Spain, Lorraine, and Brandenburg against Louis, now regarded as a menace to the whole of western Europe, Catholic and Protestant alike. The war ended inconclusively with the Peace of Nijmwegen, signed with different parties in successive years (1678, 1679). France gained more territory, including the Franche-Comté.

Louis's Repressive Religious Policies

Like Richelieu before him, Louis believed that political unity and stability required religious conformity. To that end he carried out repressive actions against both Roman Catholics and Protestants.

Suppression of the Jansenists The French crown and the French Roman Catholic church had long jealously guarded their ecclesiastical independence or "Gallican Liberties" from papal authority in Rome. However, after the conversion to Roman Catholicism of Henry IV in 1593, the Jesuits, fiercely loyal to the authority of the Pope, had monopolized the education of French upper-class men, and their devout students promoted the religious reforms and doctrines of the Council of Trent. As a measure of their success, Jesuits served as confessors to Henry IV, Louis XIII, and Louis XIV.

A Roman Catholic religious movement known as *Jansenism* arose in the 1630s in opposition to the theology and the political influence of the Jesuits. Jansenists adhered to the teachings of St. Augustine (354–430) that had also influenced many Protestant doctrines. Serious and uncompromising, they particularly opposed Jesuit teachings about free will. They believed with Augustine that original sin had so corrupted humankind that individuals could by their own effort do nothing good nor contribute anything to their own salvation. The namesake of the movement, Cornelius Jansen (d. 1638), was a Flemish theologian and the bishop of Ypres. His posthumously published *Augustinus* (1640) assailed Jesuit teaching on grace and salvation as morally lax.

MAP EXPLORATION

Interactive map: To explore this map further, go to www.myhistorylab.com

THE EARLY WARS OF LOUIS XIV, 1667–1697

Treaty of Aix-la-Chapelle, 1668
▢ To France

Treaty of Nijmwegen, 1678–1679
▢ To France
▢ To Spain

Treaty of Ryswick, 1697
▢ To France
▬ Boundary of France, 1648

Map 13–1 THE FIRST THREE WARS OF LOUIS XIV This map shows the territorial changes resulting from Louis XIV's first three major wars (1667–1697).

Jansenism made considerable progress among prominent families in Paris. They were opposed to the Jesuits and supported Jansenist religious communities such as the convent at Port-Royal outside Paris. Jansenists, whose Augustinian theology resembled Calvinism, were known to live extremely pious and morally austere lives. In these respects, though firm Roman Catholics, they resembled English Puritans. Also, like the Puritans, the Jansenists became associated with opposition to royal authority, and families of Jansenist sympathies had been involved in the *Fronde*.

COMPARE AND CONNECT

The Debate over the Origin and Character of Political Authority

DURING THE SECOND half of the seventeenth century a profound dispute occurred among European political philosophers over the origin and character of political authority. Some political philosophers, here illustrated by the French bishop Jacques-Bénigne Bossuet, contended that monarchs governed absolutely by virtue of authority derived from God. Other philosophers, here illustrated by the English writer John Locke, contended that political authority originated in the consent of the governed and that such authority was inherently limited in its scope.

QUESTIONS

1. Why might Bossuet have wished to make such extravagant claims for absolute royal power? How might these claims be transferred to any form of government?

2. How does Bossuet's argument for absolute royal authority lead also to the need for a single uniform religion in France?

3. Why does Locke find an absolute monarch in conflict with his subjects and they with him?

4. How do Locke's views serve to provide a foundation for parliamentary government?

5. How might subjects governed according to Bossuet's and Locke's principles relate differently to their monarchs and to the officials of monarchs administering their local communities?

I. Bishop Bossuet Defends the Divine Right of Kings

The revolutions of the seventeenth century caused many to fear anarchy far more than tyranny, among them the influential French bishop Jacques-Bénigne Bossuet (1627–1704), the leader of French Catholicism in the second half of the seventeenth century. Louis XIV made him court preacher and tutor to his son, for whom Bossuet wrote a celebrated universal history. In the following excerpt, Bossuet defends the divine right and absolute power of kings. He depicts kings as embracing in their person the whole body of the state and the will of the people they govern and, as such, as being immune from judgment by any mere mortal.

The royal power is absolute. . . . The prince need render account of his acts to no one. "I counsel thee to keep the king's commandment, and that in regard of the oath of God. Be not hasty to go out of his sight; stand not on an evil thing for he doeth whatsoever pleaseth him. Where the word of a king is, there is power; and who may say unto him, What doest thou? Whoso keepeth the commandment shall feel no evil thing" [Eccles. 8:2–5]. Without this absolute authority the king could neither do good nor repress evil. It is necessary that his power be such that no one can hope

to escape him, and finally, the only protection of individuals against the public authority should be their innocence. This confirms the teaching of St. Paul: "Wilt thou then not be afraid of the power? Do that which is good" [Rom. 13:3].

God is infinite, God is all. The prince, as prince, is not regarded as a private person: he is a public personage, all the state is in him; the will of all the people is included in his. As all perfection and all strength are united in God, so all the power of individuals is united in the person of the prince. What grandeur that a single man should embody so much! . . .

Behold an immense people united in a single person; behold this holy power, paternal and absolute; behold the secret cause which governs the whole body of the state, contained in a single head: you see the image of God in the king, and you have the idea of royal majesty. God is holiness itself, goodness itself, and power itself. In these things lies the majesty of God. In the image of these things lies the majesty of the prince.

Source: From *Politics Drawn from the Very Words of Holy Scripture*, as quoted in James Harvey Robinson, ed., *Readings in European History*, Vol. 2 (Boston: Athenaeum, 1906), pp. 275–276.

II. John Locke Denounces the Idea of Absolute Monarchy

John Locke (1632–1704) was the most important English philosopher of the late seventeenth century. As will be seen in Chapter 14 he wrote on a wide variety of subjects including both political philosophy and religious toleration. In 1690 he published his second Treatise of Civil Government. *In this work he defended limitations on government and rooted political authority in the consent of the governed. He drafted the treatise in the late 1670s in response to Tory assertions of absolute monarchy set forth by supporters of Charles II. The treatise was published in the wake of the Revolution of 1688 and was read at the time as a justification of that event. Locke's thought would almost a century later influence the American Declaration of Independence. In the passages below Locke explains that under absolute monarchy citizens must submit to an authority from which they can make no appeal. Consequently, there is a necessary conflict between citizens and the absolute monarchy. It was to escape such conflict and to secure property and liberty that human beings had left the state of nature to found civil society.*

Man being born . . . with a title to perfect freedom, and an uncontrolled enjoyment of all the rights and privileges of the law of nature, equally with any other man, or number of men in the world, hath by nature a power, not only to preserve his property, that is, his life, liberty and estate, against the injuries and attempts of other men; but to judge of, and punish the breaches of that law in others, as he is persuaded the offence deserve . . . [T]here and there only is political society, where every one of the members hath quitted this natural power, resigned it up into the hands of the community in all cases that excludes him not from appealing for protection to the law established by it. And thus all private judgment of every particular member being excluded, the community comes to be umpire, by settled standing rules, indifferent, and the same to all parties; and by men hav-

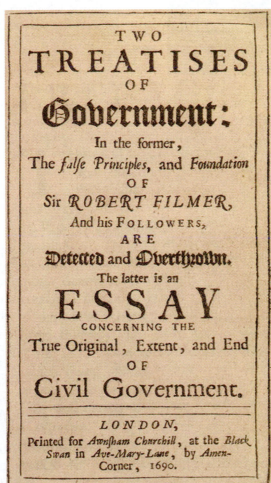

Title page from *Two Treatises of Government* by John Locke, London, 1690.   Courtesy of the Library of Congress (Rosenwald Collection, Rare Book and Special Collections Division)

ing authority from the community, for the execution of those rules, decides all the differences that may happen between any members of that society concerning any matter of right . . .

Whenever therefore any number of men are so united into one society, as to quit every one his executive power of the law of nature, and to resign it to the public, there and there only is a political, or civil society. . . .

Hence it is evident, that absolute monarchy, which by some men is counted the only government in the world, is indeed inconsistent with civil society, and so can be no form of civil government at all; for the end of civil society, being to avoid, and remedy those inconveniencies of the state of nature, which necessarily follow from every man's being judge in his own case, by setting up a known authority, to which every one of that society may appeal upon any injury received, or controversy that may arise, and which every one of the society ought to obey; whereever any persons are, who have not such an authority to appeal to, for the decision of any difference between them, there those persons are still in the state of nature; and so is every absolute prince, in respect of those who are under his dominion.

For he being supposed to have all, both legislative and executive power in himself alone, there is no judge to be found, no appeal lies open to any one, who may fairly, and indifferently, and with authority decide, and from whose decision relief and redress may be expected of any injury or inconveniency, that may be suffered from the prince, or by his order: so that such a man, however intitled, czar, or grand seignior, or how you please, is as much in the state of nature, with all under his dominion, as he is with the rest of mankind: for where-ever any two men are, who have no standing rule, and common judge to appeal to on earth, for the determination of controversies of right betwixt them, there they are still in the state of nature, and under all the inconveniencies of it . . .

Source: John Locke, *Of Civil Government,* paragraphs 87, 89, 90, 91 in *Two Treatises of Government,* a new ed. (London: 1824), pp. 179–183.

Françoise d'Aubigne, Madame de Maintenon (1635–1719), a mistress to Louis XIV, secretly married him after his first wife's death. The deeply pious Maintenon influenced Louis's policy to make Roman Catholicism France's only religion.   Pierre Mignard (1612–1695), *Portrait of Francoise d'Aubigne, Marquise de Maintenon (1635–1719), mistress and second wife of Louis XIV*, c. 1694. Oil on canvas, 128 × 97 cm. Inv.: MV 3637. Chateaux de Versailles et de Trianon, Versailles. Bridgeman-Giraudon/Art Resource, NY

On May 31, 1653, Pope Innocent X declared heretical five Jansenist theological propositions on grace and salvation. In 1656, the pope banned Jansen's *Augustinus*. In 1660, Louis permitted the papal bull banning Jansenism to be enforced in France. He also eventually closed down the Port-Royal community. Thereafter, Jansenists either retracted their views or went underground. In 1713, Pope Clement XI issued the bull *Unigenitus*, which again extensively condemned Jansenist teaching. The now aged Louis XIV ordered the French church to accept the bull despite internal ecclesiastical opposition.

The theological issues surrounding Jansenism were complex. By persecuting the Jansenists, however, Louis XIV turned his back on the long tradition of protecting the Gallican Liberties of the French Church and fostered within the French Church a core of opposition to royal authority. This had long-term political significance. During the eighteenth century after the death of Louis XIV, the Parlement of Paris and other French judicial bodies would reassert their authority in opposition to the monarchy. These courts were sympathetic to the Jansenists because of their common resis-

tance to royal authority. Jansenism, because of its austere morality, then also came to embody a set of religious and moral values that contrasted with what eighteenth-century public opinion saw as the corruption of the mid-eighteenth-century French royal court.

Revocation of the Edict of Nantes   After the Edict of Nantes in 1598, relations between the Catholic majority (nine tenths of the French population) and the Protestant minority had remained hostile. There were about 1.75 million Huguenots in France in the 1660s (out of an overall population of around 18 million), but their numbers were declining. The French Catholic church had long supported their persecution as both pious and patriotic.

After the Peace of Nijmwegen, Louis launched a methodical campaign against the Huguenots in an effort to unify France religiously. He was also influenced in this policy by his mistress who became his second wife Madame de Maintenon (1635–1719), a deeply pious Catholic who drew Louis toward a much more devout religious observance. Louis hounded Huguenots out of public life, banning them from government office and excluding them from such professions as printing and medicine. He used financial incentives to encourage them to convert to Catholicism. In 1681, he bullied them by quartering troops in their towns. Finally, in October 1685, Louis revoked the Edict of Nantes, and extensive religious repression followed. Protestant churches and schools were closed, Protestant ministers exiled, nonconverting laity were condemned to be galley slaves, and Protestant children were baptized by Catholic priests. (See "Louis XIV Revokes the Edict of Nantes.")

The revocation was a major blunder. Henceforth, Protestants across Europe considered Louis a fanatic who must be resisted at all costs. More than a quarter million people, many of whom were highly skilled, left France. They formed new communities abroad and joined the resistance to Louis in England, Germany, Holland, and the New World. As a result of the revocation of the Edict of Nantes and the ongoing persecution of Jansenists, France became a symbol of religious repression in contrast to England's reputation for moderate, if not complete, religious toleration.

Louis's Later Wars

The League of Augsburg and the Nine Years' War
After the Treaty of Nijmwegen in 1678–1679, Louis maintained his army at full strength and restlessly probed beyond his borders. In 1681 his forces occupied the free city of Strasbourg on the Rhine River, prompting new defensive coalitions to form against him. One of these, the League of Augsburg, grew to include England, Spain, Sweden, the United Provinces, and the major German states. It also had the support of the

LOUIS XIV REVOKES THE EDICT OF NANTES

Believing a country could not be governed by one king and one law unless it was also under one religious system, Louis XIV stunned much of Europe in October 1685, by revoking the Edict of Nantes, which had protected the religious freedoms and civil rights of French Protestants since 1598. Years of serious, often violent, persecution of French Protestants followed this revocation. Consequently, after 1685 in the minds of many Europeans political absolutism was associated with intolerance and religious persecution. Paradoxically, Pope Innocent XI (1676–1689) opposed Louis XIV's revocation of the Edict of Nantes because he understood that this act and other aspects of Louis's ecclesiastical policy were intended as political measures to allow his government to dominate the Roman Catholic Church in France.

Compare this document to the one on page 396 in which the elector of Brandenburg welcomes displaced French Protestants into his domains.

What specific actions does this declaration order against Protestants? Does it offer any incentives for Protestants to convert to Catholicism? How does this declaration compare with the English Test Act?

Art. 1. Know that we . . . with our certain knowledge, full power and royal authority, have by this present, perpetual and irrevocable edict, suppressed and revoked the edict of the aforesaid king our grandfather, given at Nantes in the month of April, 1598, in all its extent . . . together with all the concessions made by [this] and other edicts, declarations, and decrees, to the people of the so-called Reformed religion, of whatever nature they be . . . and in consequence we desire . . . that all the temples of the people of the aforesaid so-called Reformed religion situated in our kingdom . . . should be demolished forthwith.

Art. 2. We forbid our subjects of the so-called Reformed religion to assemble any more for public worship of the above-mentioned religion. . . .

Art. 3. We likewise forbid all lords, of whatever rank they may be, to carry out heretical services in houses and fiefs . . . the penalty for . . . the said worship being confiscation of their body and possessions.

Art. 4. We order all ministers of the aforesaid so-called Reformed religion who do not wish to be converted and to embrace the Catholic, Apostolic, and Roman religion, to depart from our kingdom and the lands subject to us within fifteen days from the publication of our present edict . . . on pain of the galleys.

Art. 5. We desire that those among the said [Reformed] ministers who shall be converted [to the Catholic religion] shall continue to enjoy during their life, and their wives shall enjoy after their death as long as they remain widows, the same exemptions from taxation and billeting of soldiers, which they enjoyed while they fulfilled the function of ministers. . . .

Art. 8. With regard to children who shall be born to those of the aforesaid so-called Reformed religion, we desire that they be baptized by their parish priests. We command the fathers and mothers to send them to the churches for that purpose, on penalty of a fine of 500 livres or more if they fail to do so; and afterwards, the children shall be brought up in the Catholic, Apostolic, and Roman religion. . . .

Art. 10. All our subjects of the so-called Reformed religion, with their wives and children, are to be strongly and repeatedly prohibited from leaving our aforesaid kingdom . . . or of taking out . . . their possessions and effects. . . .

The members of the so-called Reformed religion, while awaiting God's pleasure to enlighten them like the others, can live in the towns and districts of our kingdom . . . and continue their occupation there, and enjoy their possessions . . . on condition . . . that they do not make public profession of [their religion].

S. Z. Ehler and John B. Morrall, eds. and trans., *Church and State Through the Centuries: A Collection of Historic Documents* (New York: Biblo and Tannen, 1967), pp. 209–213. Reprinted by permission of Biblo and Tannen Booksellers and Publishers.

Map 13–2 **EUROPE IN 1714** The War of the Spanish Succession ended a year before the death of Louis XIV. The Bourbons had secured the Spanish throne, but Spain had forfeited its possessions in Flanders and Italy.

Habsburg emperor Leopold I (r. 1658–1705). Between 1689 and 1697, the League and France battled each other in the Nine Years' War, while England and France struggled to control North America.

The Peace of Ryswick, signed in September 1697, which ended the war, secured Holland's borders and thwarted Louis's expansion into Germany.

War of the Spanish Succession On November 1, 1700, the last Habsburg king of Spain, Charles II (r. 1665–1700), died without direct heirs. Before his death, negotiations had begun among the nations involved to partition his inheritance in a way that would preserve the existing balance of power. Charles II, however, left his entire inheritance to Louis's grandson Philip of Anjou, who became Philip V of Spain (r. 1700–1746).

Spain and the vast trade with its American empire appeared to have fallen to France. In September 1701, England, Holland, and the Holy Roman Empire formed the Grand Alliance to preserve the balance of power by once and for all securing Flanders as a neutral barrier between Holland and France and by gaining for the emperor, who was also a Habsburg, his fair share of the Spanish inheritance. Louis soon increased the political stakes by recognizing the Stuart claim to the English throne.

In 1701 the War of the Spanish Succession (1701–1714) began, and it soon enveloped western Europe. France for the first time in Louis's reign went to war with inadequate finances, a poorly equipped army, and mediocre generals. The English, in contrast, had advanced weaponry (flintlock rifles, paper cartridges, and ring bayonets) and superior tactics (thin, maneuverable troop columns rather than the traditional deep ones). John Churchill, the Duke of Marlborough (1650–1722), bested Louis's soldiers in every major engagement, although French arms triumphed in Spain. After 1709 the war became a bloody stalemate.

France finally made peace with England at Utrecht in July 1713, and with Holland and the emperor at Rastatt in March 1714. Philip V remained king of Spain, but England got Gibraltar and the island of Minorca, making it a Mediterranean power. (See Map 13–2.) Louis also recognized the right of the House of Hanover to the English throne.

France After Louis XIV

Despite its military reverses in the War of the Spanish Succession, France remained a great power. It was less strong in 1715 than in 1680, but it still possessed the largest European population, an advanced, if troubled, economy, and the administrative structure bequeathed it by Louis XIV. Moreover, even if France and its resources had been drained by the last of Louis's wars, the other major states of Europe were similarly debilitated.

The impending collapse of John Law's bank triggered a financial panic throughout France. Desperate investors, such as those shown here in the city of Rennes, sought to exchange their paper currency for gold and silver before the banks' supply of precious metals was exhausted.   Collection Musée de Bretagne, Rennes

Louis XIV was succeeded by his five-year-old great-grandson Louis XV (r. 1715–1774). The young boy's uncle, the duke of Orléans, became regent and remained so until his death in 1720. The regency, marked by financial and moral scandals, further undermined the faltering prestige of the monarchy.

John Law and the Mississippi Bubble   The duke of Orléans was a gambler, and for a time he turned over the financial management of the kingdom to John Law (1671–1729), a Scottish mathematician and fellow gambler. Law believed an increase in the paper-money supply would stimulate France's economic recovery. With the permission of the regent, he established a bank in Paris that issued paper money. Law then organized a monopoly, called the Mississippi Company, on trading privileges with the French colony of Louisiana in North America.

The Mississippi Company also took over the management of the French national debt. The company issued shares of its own stock in exchange for government bonds, which had fallen sharply in value. To redeem large quantities of bonds, Law encouraged speculation in the Mississippi Company stock. In 1719, the price of the stock rose handsomely. Smart investors, however, took their profits by selling their stock in exchange for paper money from Law's bank, which they then sought to exchange for gold. The bank, however, lacked enough gold to redeem all the paper money brought to it.

In February 1720, all gold payments were halted in France. Soon thereafter, Law himself fled the country. The Mississippi Bubble, as the affair was called, had burst. The fiasco brought disgrace on the government that had sponsored Law. The Mississippi Company was later reorganized and functioned profitably, but fear of paper money and speculation marked French economic life for decades.

Renewed Authority of the Parlements   The duke of Orléans made a second decision that also lessened the power of the monarchy. He attempted to draw the French nobility once again into the decision-making processes of the government. He set up a system of councils on which nobles were to serve along with bureaucrats. The years of idle noble domestication at Versailles, however, had worked too well, and the nobility seemed to lack both the talent and the desire to govern. The experiment failed. Despite this failure, the great French nobles did not surrender their ancient ambition to assert their rights, privileges, and local influence over those of the monarchy. The chief feature of eighteenth-century French political life was the attempt of the nobility to use its authority to limit the power of the monarchy. The most effective instrument in this process was the previously mentioned *parlements*, or courts dominated by the nobility.

The duke of Orléans reversed the previously noted policy of Louis XIV and formally approved the reinstitution of the full power of the Parlement of Paris to allow

Under Louis XV (r. 1715–1774) France suffered major defeats in Europe and around the world and lost most of its North American empire. Louis himself was an ineffective ruler, and during his reign, the monarchy encountered numerous challenges from the French aristocracy. CORBIS/Bettmann

or disallow laws. Moreover, throughout the eighteenth century that and other local *parlements* also succeeded in identifying their authority and resistance to the monarchy with wider public opinion. This situation meant that until the revolution in 1789, the *parlements* became natural centers not only for aristocratic, but also for popular resistance to royal authority. In a vast transformation from the days of Louis XIV, the *parlements* rather than the monarchy would come to be seen as more nearly representing the nation.

By 1726, the general political direction of the nation had come under the authority of Cardinal Fleury (1653–1743). He worked to maintain the authority of the monarchy, including ongoing repression of the Jansenists, while continuing to preserve the local interests of the French nobility. Like Walpole in Britain, he pursued economic prosperity at home and peace abroad. Again like Walpole, after 1740, Fleury could not prevent France from entering a worldwide colonial conflict. (See Chapter 17.)

▼ Central and Eastern Europe

Central and eastern Europe were economically much less advanced than western Europe. Except for the Baltic ports, the economy was agrarian. There were fewer cities and many more large estates worked by serfs. The states

in this region did not possess overseas empires; nor did they engage in extensive overseas trade of any kind, except for supplying grain to western Europe—grain, more often than not, carried on western European ships.

During the sixteenth and early seventeenth centuries, the political authorities in this region, which lay largely east of the Elbe River, were weak. The almost constant warfare of the seventeenth century had led to a habit of temporary and shifting political loyalties with princes and aristocracies of small states refusing to subordinate themselves to central monarchical authorities.

During the last half of the seventeenth century, however, three strong dynasties, whose rulers aspired to the absolutism then being constructed in France, emerged in central and eastern Europe. After the Peace of Westphalia in 1648, the Austrian Habsburgs recognized the basic weakness of the position of the Holy Roman Emperor and started to consolidate their power outside Germany. At the same time, Prussia under the Hohenzollern dynasty emerged as a factor in north German politics and as a major challenger to the Habsburg domination of Germany. Most important, Russia under the Romanov dynasty at the opening of the eighteenth century became a military and naval power of the first order. These three monarchies would dominate central and eastern Europe until the close of World War I in 1918. By contrast, Poland during the eighteenth century became the single most conspicuous example in Europe of a land that failed to establish a viable centralized government.

Poland: Absence of Strong Central Authority

In no other part of Europe was the failure to maintain a competitive political position as complete as in Poland. In 1683 King John III Sobieski (r. 1674–1696) had led a Polish army to rescue Vienna from a Turkish siege. Following that spectacular effort, however, Poland became a byword for the dangers of aristocratic independence.

The Polish monarchy was elective, but the deep distrust and divisions among the nobility usually prevented their electing a king from among themselves. Sobieski was a notable exception. Most of the Polish monarchs were foreigners and the tools of foreign powers. The Polish nobles did have a central legislative body called the **Sejm**, or diet. It included only nobles and specifically excluded representatives from corporate bodies, such as the towns. The diet, however, had a practice known as the *liberum veto*, whereby the staunch opposition of any single member, who might have been bribed by a foreign power, could require the body to disband. Such opposition, termed "exploding the diet," was most often the work of a group of dissatisfied nobles rather than of one person. Nonetheless, the requirement of unanimity was a major stumbling block

In 1683 the Ottomans laid siege to Vienna. Only the arrival of Polish forces under King John III Sobieski (r. 1674–1696) saved the Habsburg capital.   Dagli Orti/Picture Desk, Inc./Kobal Collection

to effective government. The price of this noble liberty would eventually be the disappearance of Poland from the map of Europe in the late eighteenth century.

The Habsburg Empire and the Pragmatic Sanction

The close of the Thirty Years' War marked a fundamental turning point in the history of the Austrian Habsburgs. Previously, in alliance with their Spanish cousins, they had hoped to bring all of Germany under their control and back to the Catholic fold. In this they had failed, and the decline of Spanish power meant that the Austrian Habsburgs were on their own. (See Map 13–3, page 394.)

After 1648, the Habsburg family retained a firm hold on the title of Holy Roman Emperor, but the power of the emperor depended less on the force of arms than on the cooperation he could elicit from the various political bodies in the empire. These included large German units (such as Saxony, Hanover, Bavaria, and Brandenburg) and scores of small German cities, bishoprics, principalities, and territories of independent knights. While establishing their new dominance among the German states, the Habsburgs also began to consolidate their power and influence within their hereditary possessions outside the Holy Roman Empire, which included the Crown of Saint Wenceslas, encompassing the kingdom of Bohemia (in the modern Czech Republic) and the duchies of Moravia

and Silesia; and the Crown of Saint Stephen, which ruled Hungary, Croatia, and Transylvania. Much of Hungary was only liberated from the Turks at the end of the seventeenth century (1699).

Through the Treaty of Rastatt in 1714, the Habsburgs further extended their domains, receiving the former Spanish (thereafter Austrian) Netherlands and Lombardy in northern Italy. Thereafter, the Habsburgs' power and influence would be based primarily on their territories outside of Germany.

In each of their many territories the Habsburgs ruled by virtue of a different title—king, archduke, duke—and they needed the cooperation of the local nobility, which was not always forthcoming. They repeatedly had to bargain with nobles in one part of Europe to maintain their position in another. Their domains were so geographically diverse and the people who lived in them of so many different languages and customs that almost no grounds existed on which to unify them politically. Even Roman Catholicism proved ineffective as a common bond, particularly in Hungary, where many Magyar nobles were Calvinist and seemed ever ready to rebel. Over the years the Habsburg rulers established various central councils to chart common policies for their far-flung domains. Virtually all of these bodies, however, dealt with only a portion of the Habsburg holdings.

Despite these internal difficulties, Leopold I (r. 1658–1705) managed to resist the advances of the

Map 13–3   THE AUSTRIAN HABSBURG EMPIRE, 1521–1772   The empire had three main units—Austria, Bohemia, and Hungary. Expansion was mainly eastward: eastern Hungary from the Ottomans (seventeenth century) and Galicia from Poland (1772). Meantime, Silesia was lost after 1740, but the Habsburgs remained Holy Roman Emperors.

Ottoman Empire into central Europe, which included a siege of Vienna in 1683, and to thwart the aggression of Louis XIV. He achieved Ottoman recognition of his sovereignty over Hungary in 1699 and extended his territorial holdings over much of the Balkan Peninsula and western Romania. These conquests allowed the Habsburgs to hope to develop Mediterranean trade through the port of Trieste on the northern coast of the Adriatic Sea and helped compensate for their loss of effective power over the Holy Roman Empire. Strength in the East gave them greater political leverage in Germany. Joseph I (r. 1705–1711) continued Leopold's policies.

When Charles VI (r. 1711–1740) succeeded Joseph, a new problem was added to the chronic one of territorial diversity. He had no male heir, and there was only the weakest of precedents for a female ruler of the Habsburg domains. Charles feared that on his death the Austrian Habsburg lands might fall prey to the surrounding powers, as had those of the Spanish Habsburgs in 1700. He was determined to prevent that disaster and to provide his domains with the semblance of legal unity. To those ends, he devoted most of his reign to seeking the approval of his family, the estates of his realms, and the major foreign powers for a document called the ***Pragmatic Sanction***.

This instrument provided the legal basis for a single line of inheritance within the Habsburg dynasty through Charles VI's daughter Maria Theresa (r. 1740–1780). Other members of the Habsburg family recognized her as the rightful heir. After extracting various

AUSTRIA AND PRUSSIA IN THE LATE SEVENTEENTH AND EARLY EIGHTEENTH CENTURIES	
1640–1688	Reign of Frederick William, the Great Elector
1658–1705	Leopold I rules Austria and resists the Turkish invasions
1683	Turkish siege of Vienna
1688–1713	Reign of Frederick I of Prussia
1699	Peace treaty between Turks and Habsburgs
1711–1740	Charles VI rules Austria and secures agreement to the Pragmatic Sanction
1713–1740	Frederick William I builds up the military power of Prussia
1740	Maria Theresa succeeds to the Habsburg throne
1740	Frederick II violates the Pragmatic Sanction by invading Silesia

concessions from Charles, the nobles of the various Habsburg domains and the other European rulers also recognized her. Consequently, when Charles VI died in October 1740, he believed that he had secured legal unity for the Habsburg Empire and a safe succession for his daughter. He had indeed established a permanent line of succession and the basis for future legal bonds within the Habsburg holdings. Despite the Pragmatic Sanction, however, his failure to provide his daughter with a strong army or a full treasury left her inheritance open to foreign aggression. Less than two months after his death, the fragility of the foreign agreements became apparent. In December 1740, Frederick II of Prussia invaded the Habsburg province of Silesia in eastern Germany. Maria Theresa had to fight for her inheritance.

Prussia and the Hohenzollerns

The rise of Prussia occurred within the German power vacuum created by the Peace of Westphalia. It is the story of the extraordinary Hohenzollern family, which had ruled Brandenburg since 1417. Through inheritance the family had acquired the duchy of Cleves, and the counties of Mark and Ravensburg in 1614, East Prussia in 1618, and Pomerania in 1648. (See Map 13–4.) Except for Pomerania, none of these lands shared a border with Brandenburg. East Prussia lay inside Poland and outside the authority of the Holy Roman Emperor. All of the territories lacked good natural resources, and many of them were devastated during the Thirty Years' War. Still, by the late seventeenth century, the geographically scattered Hohenzollern holdings represented a block of territory within the Holy Roman Empire, second in size only to that of the Habsburgs.

The person who began to forge these areas into a modern state was Frederick William (r. 1640–1688), who became known as the Great Elector. He established himself and his successors as the central uniting power by breaking the local noble estates, organizing a royal bureaucracy, and building a strong army. (See "The Great Elector Welcomes Protestant Refugees from France," page 396.)

Between 1655 and 1660, Sweden and Poland fought each other across the Great Elector's holdings in Pomerania and East Prussia. Frederick William had neither an adequate army nor the tax revenues to confront this threat. In 1655, the Brandenburg estates refused to grant him new taxes; however, he proceeded to collect them by military force. In 1659, a different grant of taxes, originally made in 1653, elapsed; Frederick William continued to collect them as well as those he had imposed by his own authority. He used the money to build an army, which allowed him to continue to enforce his will without the approval of the nobility. Similar coercion took place against the nobles in his other territories.

There was, however, a political and social trade-off between the Elector and his various nobles. In exchange for their obedience to the Hohenzollerns, the **Junkers**, or German noble landlords, received the right to demand obedience from their serfs. Frederick William also tended to choose as the local administrators of the tax structure men who would normally have been members of the

Map 13–4 **EXPANSION OF BRANDEBURG-PRUSSIA** In the seventeenth century Brandenburg-Prussia expanded mainly by acquiring dynastic titles in geographically separated lands. In the eighteenth century it expanded through aggression to the east, seizing Silesia in 1740 and various parts of Poland in 1772, 1793, and 1795.

THE GREAT ELECTOR WELCOMES PROTESTANT REFUGEES FROM FRANCE

The Hohenzollern dynasty of Brandenburg–Prussia pursued a policy of religious toleration. The family itself was Calvinist, whereas most of its subjects were Lutherans. When Louis XIV of France revoked the Edict of Nantes in 1685, Frederick William, the Great Elector, seized the opportunity to invite French Protestants into his realms. As his proclamation indicates, he wanted to attract persons with productive skills who could aid the economic development of his domains.

In reading this document, do you believe religious or economic concerns more nearly led the elector of Brandenburg to welcome the French Protestants? What specific privileges did the elector extend to them? To what extent were these privileges a welcoming measure, and to what extent were they inducements to emigrate to Brandenburg? In what kind of economic activity does the elector expect the French refugees to engage?

We, Friedrich Wilhelm, by Grace of God Margrave of Brandenburg . . . Do hereby proclaim and make known to all and sundry that since the cruel persecutions and rigorous ill-treatment in which Our co-religionists of the Evangelical-Reformed faith have for some time past been subjected in the Kingdom of France, have caused many families to remove themselves and to betake themselves out of the said Kingdom into other lands, We now . . . have been moved graciously to offer them through this Edict . . . a secure and free refuge in all Our Lands and Provinces. . . .

Since Our Lands are not only well and amply endowed with all things necessary to support life, but also very well-suited to the reestablishment of all kinds of manufactures and trade and traffic by land and water, We permit, indeed, to those settling therein free choice to establish themselves where it is most convenient for their profession and way of living. . . .

The personal property which they bring with them, including merchandise and other wares, is to be totally exempt from any taxes, customs dues, licenses, or other imposts of any description, and not detained in any way. . . .

As soon as these Our French co-religionists of the Evangelical-Reformed faith have settled in any town or village, they shall be admitted to the domiciliary rights and craft freedoms customary there, gratis and without payments of any fee; and shall be entitled to the benefits, rights, and privileges enjoyed by Our other, native, subjects, residing there. . . .

Not only are those who wish to establish manufacture of cloth, stuffs, hats, or other objects in which they are skilled to enjoy all necessary freedoms, privileges and facilities, but also provision is to be made for them to be assisted and helped as far as possible with money and anything else which they need to realize their intention. . . .

Those who settle in the country and wish to maintain themselves by agriculture are to be given a certain plot of land to bring under cultivation and provided with whatever they need to establish themselves initially. . . .

From C. A. Macartney, ed., *The Habsburg and Hohenzollern Dynasties in the Seventeenth and Eighteenth Centuries* (New York: Walker, 1970), pp. 270–273.

noble branch of the old parliament. He thus co-opted potential opponents into his service. The taxes fell most heavily on the backs of the peasants and the urban classes. As the years passed, *Junkers* increasingly dominated the army officer corps, and this situation became even more pronounced during the eighteenth century. All officials and army officers took an oath of loyalty directly to the

Elector. The army and the Elector thus came to embody the otherwise absent unity of the state. The army made Prussia a valuable potential ally.

Yet even with the considerable accomplishments of the Great Elector, the house of Hohenzollern did not possess a crown. The achievement of a royal title was one of the few state-building accomplishments of Frederick I (r. 1688–1713). This son of the Great Elector was the least "Prussian" of his family during these crucial years. He built palaces, founded Halle University (1694), patronized the arts, and lived luxuriously. In the War of the Spanish Succession, he put his army at the disposal of the Habsburg Holy Roman Emperor Leopold I. In exchange, the emperor permitted Frederick to assume the title of "King in Prussia" in 1701.

His successor, Frederick William I (r. 1713–1740), was both the most eccentric monarch to rule the Hohenzollern domains and one of the most effective. He organized the bureaucracy along military lines. The discipline that he applied to the army was fanatical. The Prussian military grew from about 39,000 in 1713 to over 80,000 in 1740, making it the third or fourth largest army in Europe. Prussia's population, in contrast, ranked thirteenth in size. Separate laws applied to the army and to civilians. Laws, customs, and royal attention made the officer corps the highest social class of the state. Military service thus attracted the sons of *Junkers*. In this fashion the army, the *Junker* nobility, and the monarchy became forged into a single political entity. Military priorities and values dominated Prussian government, society, and daily life as in no other state in Europe. It has often been said that whereas other states possessed armies, the Prussian army possessed its state.

Although Frederick William I built the best army in Europe, he avoided conflict. His army was a symbol of Prussian power and unity, not an instrument for foreign adventures or aggression. At his death in 1740, he passed to his son Frederick II later known as Frederick the Great (r. 1740–1786), this superb military machine, but not the wisdom to refrain from using it. Almost immediately on coming to the throne, Frederick II upset the Pragmatic Sanction and invaded Silesia. He thus crystallized the Austrian-Prussian rivalry for the control of Germany that would dominate central European affairs for over a century.

▼ Russia Enters the European Political Arena

The emergence of Russia in the late seventeenth century as an active European power was a wholly new factor in European politics. Previously, Russia had been considered part of Europe only by courtesy. Before 1673, it did not send permanent ambassadors to western Europe, though it had sent various diplomatic missions since the fifteenth century. Geographically and politically, it lay on the periphery. Hemmed in by Sweden on the Baltic and by the Ottoman Empire on the Black Sea, Russia had no warm-water ports. Its chief outlet for trade to the West was Archangel on the White Sea, which was ice free for only part of the year.

The Romanov Dynasty

The reign of Ivan IV (r. 1533–1584), later known as Ivan the Terrible, had commenced well but ended badly. About midway in his reign he underwent a personality change that led him to move from a program of sensible reform of law, government, and the army toward violent personal tyranny. A period known as the "Time of Troubles" followed upon his death. In 1613, hoping to end the uncertainty, an assembly of nobles elected as tsar a seventeen-year-old boy named Michael Romanov (r. 1613–1645). Thus began the dynasty that ruled Russia until 1917.

Michael Romanov and his two successors, Aleksei (r. 1654–1676) and Theodore II (r. 1676–1682), brought stability and modest bureaucratic centralization to Russia. The country remained, however, weak and impoverished. After years of turmoil, the *boyars*, the old nobility, still largely controlled the bureaucracy. Furthermore, the government and the tsars faced the danger of mutiny from the *streltsy*, or guards of the Moscow garrison.

Peter the Great

In 1682, another boy—ten years old at the time—ascended the fragile Russian throne as co-ruler with his half brother. His name was Peter (r. 1682–1725), and Russia would never be the same after him. He and the sickly Ivan V had come to power on the shoulders of the *streltsy*, who expected to be rewarded for their support. Violence and bloodshed had surrounded the disputed succession. Matters became even more confused when the boys' sister, Sophia, was named regent. Peter's followers overthrew her in 1689. From that date onward, Peter ruled personally, although in theory he shared the crown until Ivan died in 1696. The dangers and turmoil of his youth convinced Peter of two things: First, the power of the tsar must be made secure from the jealousy of the *boyars* and the greed of the *streltsy*; second, Russian military power must be increased. In both respects, he self-consciously resembled Louis XIV of France, who had experienced the turmoil of the *Fronde* during his youth and resolved to establish a strong monarchy safe from the nobility and defended by a powerful army.

Northwestern Europe, particularly the military resources of the maritime powers, fascinated Peter I, who eventually became known as Peter the Great. In 1697, he made a famous visit in transparent disguise to western Europe. There he dined and talked with the great and the powerful, who considered this almost seven-foot-tall ruler crude. He spent his happiest moments on the trip inspecting shipyards, docks, and the manufacture of military hardware in England and the Netherlands. An imitator of the first order, Peter returned to Moscow determined to copy what he had seen abroad, for he knew warfare would be necessary to make Russia a great power. Yet he understood his goal would require him to confront the long-standing power and traditions of the Russian nobles.

Taming the *Streltsy* and *Boyars*

In 1698, while Peter was abroad, the *streltsy* had rebelled. On his return, Peter brutally suppressed the revolt with private tortures and public executions, in which Peter's own ministers took part. Approximately a thousand of the rebels were put to death, and their corpses remained on public display to discourage disloyalty.

The new military establishment that Peter built would serve the tsar and not itself. He introduced effective and ruthless policies of conscription, drafting an unprecedented 130,000 soldiers during the first decade of the eighteenth century and almost 300,000 troops by the end of his reign. He had adopted policies for the officer corps and general military discipline patterned on those of West European armies.

Peter also made a sustained attack on the *boyars* and their attachment to traditional Russian culture. After his European journey, he personally shaved the long beards of the court *boyars* and sheared off the customary long hand-covering sleeves of their shirts and coats, which had made them the butt of jokes among other European courts. Peter became highly skilled at balancing one group off against another while never completely excluding any as he set about to organize Russian government and military forces along the lines of the more powerful European states.

Developing a Navy

In the mid-1690s, Peter oversaw the construction of ships to protect his interests in the Black Sea against the Ottoman Empire. In 1695, he began a war with the Ottomans and captured Azov on the Black Sea in 1696.[1] Part of the reason for Peter's trip to western Europe in 1697 was to learn how to build still better warships, this time for combat on the Baltic. The construction of a Baltic fleet was essential in Peter's struggles with Sweden that over the years accounted for many of his major steps toward westernizing his realm.

Russian Expansion in the Baltic: The Great Northern War

Following the end of the Thirty Years' War in 1648, Sweden had consolidated its control of the Baltic, thus preventing Russian possession of a port on that sea and permitting Polish and German access to the sea only on Swedish terms. The Swedes also had one of the better armies in Europe. Sweden's economy, however, based

primarily on the export of iron, was not strong enough to ensure continued political success.

In 1697, Charles XII (r. 1697–1718) came to the Swedish throne. He was headstrong, to say the least, and perhaps insane. In 1700, Peter the Great began a drive to the west against Swedish territory to gain a foothold on the Baltic. In the resulting Great Northern War (1700–1721), Charles XII led a vigorous and often brilliant campaign, defeating the Russians at the Battle of Narva (1700). As the conflict dragged on, however, Peter was able to strengthen his forces. By 1709, he decisively defeated the Swedes at the Battle of Poltava in Ukraine. Thereafter, the Swedes could maintain only a holding action against their enemies. Charles himself sought refuge in Turkey and did not return to Sweden until 1714. He was killed under uncertain circumstances four years later while fighting the Danes in Norway. When the Great Northern War came to a close in 1721, the Peace of Nystad confirmed the Russian conquest of Estonia, Livonia, and part of Finland. Henceforth, Russia possessed ice-free ports and a permanent influence on European affairs.

Founding St. Petersburg

At one point, the domestic and foreign policies of Peter the Great intersected. This was at the site on the Gulf of Finland where he founded his new capital city of St. Petersburg in 1703. There he built government structures and compelled the *boyars* to construct town houses. He thus imitated those European monarchs who had copied Louis XIV by constructing smaller versions of Versailles. The founding of St. Petersburg went beyond establishing a central imperial court, however; it symbolized a new Western orientation of Russia and Peter's determination to hold his position on the Baltic coast. Moreover, he and his successors employed architects from western Europe for many of the most prominent buildings in and around the city. Consequently, St. Petersburg looked different from the old capital Moscow and other Russian cities.

The Case of Peter's Son Aleksei

Peter's son Aleksei had been born to his first wife whom he had divorced in 1698. Peter was jealous of the young man, who had never demonstrated strong intelligence or ambition. (See "Peter the Great Tells His Son to Acquire Military Skills," page 399.) By 1716, Peter was becoming convinced that his opponents looked to Aleksei as a focus for their possible sedition while Russia remained at war with Sweden. There was some truth to these concerns because the next year Aleksei went to Vienna where he attempted to enter into a vague conspiracy with the Habsburg emperor Charles VI. Compromised by this trip, Aleksei then returned to Russia surrounded by rumors and suspicions.

Peter, who was investigating official corruption, realized his son might become a rallying point for those he accused. Early in 1718, when Aleksei reappeared in St. Petersburg, the tsar began to look into his son's

---

[1]Although Peter had to return Azov to the Ottomans in 1711, its recapture became a goal of Russian foreign policy. See Chapter 18.

PETER THE GREAT TELLS HIS SON TO ACQUIRE MILITARY SKILLS

■■

Enormous hostility existed between Peter the Great and his son Aleksei. Peter believed his son was not prepared to inherit the throne. In October 1715, he composed a long letter to Aleksei in which he berated him for refusing to take military matters seriously. The letter indicates how an early eighteenth-century ruler saw the conduct of warfare as a fundamental part of the role of a monarch. Peter also points to Louis XIV of France as a role model. Peter and Aleksei did not reach an agreement. Aleksei died under mysterious circumstances in 1718, with Peter possibly responsible for his death.

How did Peter use the recent war with Sweden to argue for the necessity of his son acquiring military skills? What concept of leadership does Peter attempt to communicate to his son? Why did Peter see military prowess as the most important ability in a ruler?

You cannot be ignorant of what is known to all the world, to what degree our people groaned under the oppression of the Swede before the beginning of the present war. . . . You know what it has cost us in the beginning of this war . . . to make ourselves experienced in the art of war, and to put a stop to those advantages which our implacable enemies obtained over us. . . .

But you even will not so much as hear warlike exercises mentioned: though it was by them that we broke through that obscurity in which we were involved, and that we make ourselves known to nations, whose esteem we share at present.

I do not exhort you to make war without lawful reasons: I only desire you to apply yourself to learn the art of it: for it is impossible to govern well without knowing the rules and discipline of it, was it for no other end than for the defense of the country. . . .

You mistake, if you think it is enough for a prince to have good generals to act under his order. Everyone looks upon the head; they study its inclinations and conform themselves to them: all the world own this. . . .

You have no inclination to learn war. You do not apply yourself to it, and consequently you will never learn it: And how then can you command others, and judge of the reward which those deserve who do their duty, or punish others who fail of it? You will do nothing, nor judge of anything but by the assent and help of others, like a young bird that holds up his bill to be fed. . . .

If you think there are some, whose affairs do not fail of success, though they do not go to war themselves; it is true: But they do not go themselves, yet they have an inclination for it, and understand it.

For instance, the late King of France did not always take the field in person; but it is known to what degree he loved war, and what glorious exploits he performed in it, which make his campaigns to be called the theatre and school of the world. His inclinations were not confined solely to military affairs, he also loved mechanics, manufacture and other establishment, which rendered his kingdom more flourishing than any other whatsoever.

From Friedrich C. Weber, *The Present State of Russia* (London, 1722), 2, pp. 97–100; P. F. Riley, *The Global Experience*, 3rd ed., Vol. 2, © 1998. Reprinted by permission of Prentice Hall, Inc., Upper Saddle River, NJ.

Peter the Great built St. Petersburg on the Gulf of Finland to provide Russia with better contact with western Europe. He moved Russia's capital there from Moscow in 1712. This is an eighteenth-century view of the city. The Granger Collection

Vue des bords de la Neva en descendant la riviere entre le Palais d'hyver de Sa Majesté Imperiale & les batimens de l'Academie des Sciences

RISE OF RUSSIAN POWER

1533–1584	Reign of Ivan the Terrible
1584–1613	"Time of Troubles"
1613	Michael Romanov becomes tsar
1682	Peter the Great, age ten, becomes tsar
1689	Peter assumes personal rule
1696	Russia captures Azov on the Black Sea from the Turks
1697	European tour of Peter the Great
1698	Peter returns to Russia to put down the revolt of the *streltsy*
1700	The Great Northern War opens between Russia and Sweden; Russia defeated at Narva by Swedish army of Charles XII
1703	St. Petersburg founded
1709	Russia defeats Sweden at the Battle of Poltava
1718	Charles XII of Sweden dies
1718	Aleksei, son of Peter the Great, dies in prison under mysterious circumstances
1721	Peace of Nystad ends the Great Northern War
1721	Peter establishes a synod for the Russian church
1722	Peter issues the Table of Ranks
1725	Peter dies, leaving an uncertain succession

relationships with Charles VI. Peter discovered that had Aleksei and Charles VI succeeded in organizing a conspiracy, many Russian nobles, officials, and churchmen might have joined them. During this six-month investigation, Peter personally interrogated Aleksei, who was eventually condemned to death and died under mysterious circumstances on June 26, 1718.

Reforms of Peter the Great's Final Years The interrogations surrounding Aleksei had revealed greater degrees of court opposition than Peter had suspected. Recognizing he could not eliminate his opponents the way he had attacked the *streltsy* in 1698, Peter undertook radical administrative reforms designed to bring the nobility and the Russian Orthodox Church more closely under the authority of persons loyal to the tsar.

Administrative Colleges In December 1717, while his son was returning to Russia, Peter reorganized his domestic administration to sustain his own personal authority and to fight rampant corruption. To achieve this goal, Peter looked to Swedish institutions called *colleges*—bureaus of several persons operating according to written instructions rather than departments headed by a single minister. He created eight of these colleges to oversee matters such as the collection of taxes, foreign relations, war, and economic affairs. Each college was to receive advice from a foreigner. Peter divided the members of these colleges between nobles and persons he was certain would be personally loyal to himself.

Table of Ranks Peter made another major administrative reform with important consequences when in 1722 he published a **Table of Ranks**, which was intended to draw the nobility into state service. That table equated a person's social position and privileges with his rank in the bureaucracy or the military, rather than with his lineage among the traditional landed nobility, many of whom continued to resent the changes Peter had introduced into Russia. Peter thus made the social standing of individual *boyars* a function of their willingness to serve the central state.

Achieving Secular Control of the Church Peter also moved to suppress the independence of the Russian Orthodox Church where some bishops and clergy had displayed sympathy for the tsar's son. In 1721, Peter simply abolished the position of *patriarch*, the bishop who had been head of the church. In its place he established a government department called the *Holy Synod*, which consisted of several bishops headed by a layman, called the *procurator general*. This body would govern the church in accordance with the tsar's secular requirements. This ecclesiastical reorganization was the most radical transformation of a traditional institution in Peter's reign.

For all the numerous decisive actions Peter had taken since 1718, he still had not settled on a successor. Consequently, when he died in 1725, there was no clear line of succession to the throne. For more than thirty years, soldiers and nobles again determined who ruled Russia. Peter had laid the foundations of a modern Russia, but not the foundations of a stable state.

▼ The Ottoman Empire

On the southeastern borders of Europe and surrounding the southern and eastern shores of the Mediterranean Sea lay the Ottoman Empire. Throughout the sixteenth and seventeenth centuries, Europeans had found themselves in frequent conflict with this empire in the Mediterranean, the Balkans, around the Black Sea, along the borders of Russia, and as far west as Vienna. As Ottoman authority gradually receded during the eighteenth century, the European states on the empire's borders sought to extend their own influence at its expense.

Now that it no longer exists, it is difficult to realize the enormous importance and geographical magnitude of the Ottoman Empire, although its final demise has affected Europe and the United States since the outbreak of the First World War. Governing a remarkably diverse collection of peoples that ranged from Baghdad westward across the Arabian peninsula, Anatolia, the Balkan peninsula, and across North Africa from Egypt to Algiers, the **Ottoman Empire** was the largest and most stable political entity to arise in or near Europe following the collapse of the Roman Empire. (See Map 13–5, page 403.) It had achieved this power between the eleventh and early sixteenth centuries as Ottoman tribes migrated westward from the steppes of Asia. In 1453, they conquered Constantinople, thus putting an end to the Byzantine Empire.

Religious Toleration and Ottoman Government

The Ottoman Empire was the dominant political power in the Muslim world after 1516, when it administered the holy cities of Mecca and Medina as well as Jerusalem, and arranged the safety of Muslim pilgrimages to Mecca. Yet its population was exceedingly diverse ethnically, linguistically, and religiously with significant numbers of Orthodox and Roman Catholic Christians and, after the late fifteenth century, thousands of Jews from Spain.

The Ottomans extended far more religious toleration to their subjects than existed anywhere in Europe. The Ottoman sultans governed their empire through units, called **millets**, of officially recognized religious communities. Various laws and regulations applied to the persons who belonged to a particular millet rather than to a particular administrative territory. Non-Islamic persons in the empire, known as *dhimmis*, or followers of religions tolerated by law, could practice their religion and manage their internal community affairs through their own religious officials but were second-class citizens generally unable to rise in the service of the empire. *Dhimmis* paid a special poll tax (*jizyah*), could not serve in the military, and were prohibited from wearing certain colors. Their residences and places of worship could not be as large as those of Muslims. Over the years, however, they often attained economic success because they possessed the highest level of commercial skills in the empire. Because the Ottomans discouraged their various peoples from interacting with each other, the Islamic population rarely acquired these and other skills from their non-Islamic neighbors. Thus, for example, when the Ottomans negotiated with European powers, their Greek subjects almost invariably served as the interpreters.

The Ottoman dynasty also kept itself separated from the most powerful families of the empire by recruiting military leaders and administrative officers from groups whom the sultans believed would be personally loyal to them. For example, through a practice known as the *devshirme*, the Ottomans, until the end of the seventeenth century, recruited their most elite troops from Christian communities usually in the Balkans. Christian boys so recruited were raised as

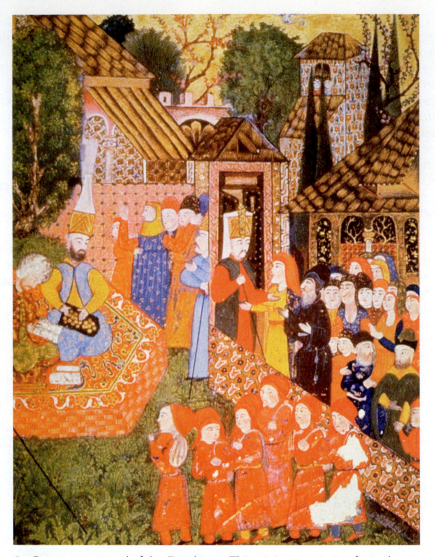

An Ottoman portrayal of the *Devshirme*. This miniature painting from about 1558 depicts the recruiting of young Christian children for the Sultan's elite Janissary corps.   Arifi, "Suleymanname," Topkapi Palace Museum, II 1517, fol. 31b, photograph courtesy of Talat Halman.

Muslims and organized into elite military units, the most famous of which were infantry troops called *Janissaries*. It was thought these troops would be extremely loyal to the sultan and the state because they owed their life and status to the sultan. As a result of this policy, entry into the elite military organizations and advancement in the administrative structures of the empire remained generally closed to the native Islamic population and most especially to members of the most elite Islamic families. Instead, in addition to the army, thousands of persons usually from the outer regions of the empire, who were technically slaves of the sultan, filled government posts and achieved major political influence and status. Thus, in contrast to Eu-

rope, few people from the socially leading families gained military, administrative, or political experience in the central institutions of the empire but remained primarily linked to local government in provincial cities. Paradoxically, many people in the Ottoman Empire believed it was better to be a favored slave of the sultan than a free subject.

The Role of the Ulama   Again in contrast to the long-standing tension between church and state in Europe, Islamic religious authorities played a significant and enduring role in the political, legal, and administrative life of the Ottoman Empire. The dynasty saw itself as one of the chief protectors of Islamic law (*Shari'a*) and

Map 13–5 **THE OTTOMAN EMPIRE IN THE LATE SEVENTEENTH CENTURY** By the 1680s the Ottoman Empire had reached its maximum extent, but the Ottoman failure to capture Vienna in 1683 marked the beginning of a long and inexorable decline that ended with the empire's collapse after World War I.

the Sunni traditions of Islam as well as its holy places. Islamic scholars, or *Ulama*, dominated not only Ottoman religious institutions, but also schools and courts of law. There essentially existed a trade-off between Ottoman political and religious authorities. The sultan and his administrative officials would consult these Islamic scholars for advice with regard to how their policies and the behavior of their subjects accorded with Islamic law and the Qur'an. In turn, the Ulama would support the Ottoman state while the latter deferred to their judgments. This situation would prove a key factor in the fate of the Ottoman Empire. From the late seventeenth century onward, the Ulama urged the sultans to conform to traditional life even as the empire confronted a rapid-

ly changing and modernizing Europe. The Janissaries also resisted changes that might undermine their own privileged status.

The End of Ottoman Expansion

From the fifteenth century onward, the Ottoman Empire had tried to push further westward into Europe. Even after its naval defeat in 1571 at the Battle of Lepanto, the empire retained control of the eastern Mediterranean and the lands bordering it. Still determined to move toward the west, the Ottomans made their deepest military invasion into Europe in 1683, when they unsuccessfully besieged Vienna. Although that defeat proved to be decisive, many observers at the time thought it the result only of an overreach of power by the Ottomans rather than as a symptom of a deeper decline, which was actually the case.

Gradually, from the seventeenth century onward, the authority of the grand vizier, the major political figure after the sultan, began to grow. This development meant that more and more authority lay with the administrative and military bureaucracy. Rivalries for power among army leaders and nobles, as well as their flagrant efforts to enrich themselves, weakened the effectiveness of the government. About the same time local elites in the various provincial cities of the empire began to assert their own influence. They did not as much reject imperial authority but instead quietly renegotiated its conditions. For example, in the outer European provinces, such as Transylvania, Wallachia, and Moldavia (all parts of modern Romania), the empire depended on the goodwill of local rulers, who paid tribute but never submitted fully to imperial authority. The same was true in Egypt, Algeria, Tunisia, and elsewhere.

External factors also accounted for both the blocking of Ottoman expansion in the late seventeenth century and then its slow decline thereafter. During the European Middle Ages, the Islamic world had far outdistanced Europe in learning, science, and military prowess. From the fifteenth century onward, however, Europeans had begun to make rapid advances in technology, wealth, and scientific knowledge. For example, they designed ships for the difficult waters of the Atlantic and thus eventually opened trade routes to the East around Africa and reached the Americas. As trade expanded, Europeans achieved new commercial skills, founded trading posts in South Asia, established the plantation economies and precious metal mines of the Americas, and became much wealthier. By the seventeenth century, Europeans, particularly the Dutch and Portuguese, imported directly from Asia or America commodities such as spices, sugar, and coffee that they had previously acquired through the Ottoman Empire. By sailing around the Cape of Good Hope in Africa, the Europeans literally circumnavigated the Middle East, which could not match the quantity of raw goods and commodities available in South Asia. During the same decades, Europeans developed greater military and naval power and new weapons.

The Ottoman defeats at Lepanto and Vienna had occurred at the outer limits of their expansion. Then, however, during the 1690s, the Ottomans unsuccessfully fought a league of European states including Austria, Venice, Malta, Poland, and Tuscany, joined by Russia, which, as we have already seen, was emerging as a new aggressive power to the north. In early 1699, the defeated Ottomans negotiated the Treaty of Carlowitz, which required them to surrender significant territory lying not at the edges, but at the heart of their empire in Europe, including most of Hungary, to the Habsburgs. This treaty meant not only the loss of territory but also of the revenue the Ottomans had long drawn from those regions. From this time onward, Russia and the Ottomans would duel for control of regions around the Black Sea with Russia achieving ever greater success by the close of the eighteenth century.

Despite these defeats, the Ottomans remained deeply inward looking, continuing to regard themselves as superior to the once underdeveloped European West. Virtually no works of the new European science were translated into Arabic or Ottoman Turkish. Few Ottoman subjects traveled in Europe. The Ottoman leaders, isolated from both their own leading Muslim subjects and from Europe, failed to understand what was occurring far beyond their immediate borders, especially European advances in military technology. When during the eighteenth century the Ottoman Empire began to recognize the new situation, it tended to borrow European technology and import foreign advisers, thus failing to develop its own infrastructure. Moreover, the powerful influence of the Ulama worked against imitation of Christian Europe. Although traditionally opposed to significant interaction with non-Muslims, they did eventually allow non-Muslim teachers into the empire and approved alliances with non-Muslim powers. But the Ulama limited such relationships. For example, in the middle of the eighteenth century, the Ulama persuaded the sultan to close a school of technology and to abandon a printing press he had opened. This influence by Muslim religious teachers occurred just as governments, such as that of Peter the Great, and secular intellectuals across Europe, through the influence of the Enlightenment (see Chapter 17), were increasingly diminishing the influence of the Christian churches in political and economic affairs. Consequently, European intellectuals began to view the once feared Ottoman Empire as a declining power and Islam as a backward-looking religion.

In Perspective

By the second quarter of the eighteenth century, the major European powers were not yet nation-states in which the citizens felt themselves united by a shared sense of community, culture, language, and history. Rather, they were monarchies in which the personality of the ruler and the personal relationships of the great noble families continued to exercise considerable influence over public affairs. The monarchs, except in Great Britain, had generally succeeded in making their power greater than that of the nobility. The power of the aristocracy and its capacity to resist or obstruct the policies of the monarch were not destroyed, however.

In Britain, of course, the nobility had tamed the monarchy, but even there tension between nobles and monarchs would continue throughout the rest of the century.

In foreign affairs, the new arrangement of military and diplomatic power established early in the century prepared the way for two long conflicts. The first was a commercial rivalry for trade and the overseas empire between France and Great Britain. During the reign of Louis XIV, these two nations had collided over the French bid for dominance in Europe. During the eighteenth century, they would duel for control of commerce on other continents. The second arena of warfare would arise in central Europe, where Austria and Prussia fought for the leadership of the German states.

Behind these international conflicts and the domestic rivalry of monarchs and nobles, however, the society of eighteenth-century Europe began to change. The character and the structures of the societies over which the monarchs ruled were beginning to take on some features associated with the modern age. These economic and social developments would eventually transform the life of Europe to a degree beside which the state building of the early eighteenth-century monarchs paled. Parallel to that economic advance, Europeans came to have new knowledge and understanding of nature.

REVIEW QUESTIONS

1. What were the sources of Dutch prosperity and why did the Netherlands decline in the eighteenth century? Why did England and France develop different systems of government and religious policies?

2. Why did the English king and Parliament quarrel in the 1640s? What were the most important issues behind the war between them, and who bears more responsibility for it? What was the Glorious Revolution, and why did it take place? What role did religion play in seventeenth-century English politics? Do you think the victory of Parliament over the monarchy in England inevitable?

3. Why did France become an absolute monarchy? How did Louis XIV consolidate his monarchy? What limits were there on his authority? What was Louis's religious policy? What were the goals of his foreign policy? How did he use ceremony and his royal court to strengthen his authority? What features of French government might Europeans outside of France have feared?

4. How were the Hohenzollerns able to forge their diverse landholdings into the state of Prussia? Who were the major personalities involved in this process and what were their individual contributions? Why was the military so important in Prussia? What major problems did the Habsburgs face and how did they seek to resolve them? Which family, the Hohenzollerns or the Habsburgs, was more successful and why?

5. How and why did Russia emerge as a great power but Poland did not? How were Peter the Great's domestic reforms related to his military ambitions? What were his methods of reform? How did family conflict influence his later policies? Was Peter a successful ruler? In what respects might one regard Peter as an imitator of Louis XIV?

6. What were the strengths and weaknesses of the Ottoman Empire? How did the Ottomans deal with religious minorities? Why did the Empire discourage interaction between its subjects and people from Europe? How did its failure to adapt to modern technology undermine its power?

SUGGESTED READINGS

W. Beik, *Louis XIV and Absolutism: A Brief Study with Documents* (2000). An excellent collection by a major scholar of absolutism.

T. Blanning, *The Pursuit of Glory: Europe 1648–1815* (2007). The best recent synthesis of the emergence of the modern European state system.

J. Brewer, *The Sinews of Power: War, Money and the English State, 1688–1783* (1989). An important study of the financial basis of English power.

P. Burke, *The Fabrication of Louis XIV* (1992). Examines how Louis XIV used art to forge his public image.

C. Clark, *The Rise and Downfall of Prussia 1600–1947* (2006). A stunning survey.

P. Collinson, *The Religion of Protestants: The Church in English Society, 1559–1625* (1982). Remains the best introduction to Puritanism.

R. Cust, *Charles I* (2007). The definitive biography.

N. Davis, *God's Playground: A History of Poland: The Origins to 1795* (2005). The recent revision of a classic survey.

J. De Vries and A. van der Woude, *The First Modern Economy* (1997). Compares Holland to other European nations.

P. G. Dwyer, *The Rise of Prussia 1700–1830* (2002). An excellent collection of essays.

S. Faroqhi, *The Ottoman Empire and the World Around It* (2006). Emphasizes the various interactions of the empire with both Asian and European powers.

R. I. Frost, *The Northern Wars: War, State and Society in Northeastern Europe, 1558–1721* (2000). A survey of an often neglected subject.

D. Goffman, *The Ottoman Empire and Early Modern Europe* (2002). An accessible introduction to a complex subject.

T. Harris, *Restoration: Charles II and His Kingdom, 1660–1685* (2006). A major exploration of the tumultuous years of the restoration of the English monarchy after the civil war.

L. Hughes, *Russia in the Age of Peter the Great* (2000). A major overview of the history and society of Peter's time.

C. Imber, *The Ottoman Empire, 1300–1650: The Structure of Power* (2003). A sweeping analysis based on a broad range of sources.

C. J. Ingrao, *The Habsburg Monarchy, 1618–1815* (2000). The best recent survey.

J. I. Israel, *The Dutch Republic: Its Rise, Greatness, and Fall, 1477–1806* (1995). The major work of the subject.

M. Kishlansky, *A Monarchy Transformed: Britain, 1603–1714* (1996). An important overview.

J. A. Lynn, *The Wars of Louis XIV* (1999). The best recent treatment.

J. Lukowski and H. Zawadzki, *A Concise History of Poland* (2006). A straightforward survey.

D. McKay, *The Great Elector: Frederick William of Brandenburg–Prussia* (2001). An account of the origins of Prussian power.

P. K. Monod, *The Power of Kings: Monarchy and Religion in Europe, 1589–1715* (1999). An important and innovative examination of the roots of royal authority as early modern Europe became modern Europe.

G. Parker, *The Military Revolution: Military Innovation and the Rise of the West (1500–1800)* (1988). A classic work on the impact of military matters on the emergence of centralized monarchies.

H. Phillips, *Church and Culture in Seventeenth-Century France* (1997). A clear examination of the major religious issues confronting France and their relationship to the larger culture.

S. Pincus, *England's Glorious Revolution 1688–1689: A Brief History with Documents* (2005). A useful collection by an outstanding historian of the subject.

G. Treasure, *Louis XIV* (2001). The best, most accessible recent study.

For additional learning resources related to this chapter, please go to www.myhistorylab.com

The great Dutch artist Rembrandt van Rijn (1606–1669) recorded the contemporary life of the United Provinces of the Netherlands during its golden age. The new sciences including medicine made much progress in the Netherlands, which was a center for publishing and instrument making and known for its religious toleration. *The Anatomy Lesson of Dr. Tulp* (1632) presents the dissection of a cadaver of an executed criminal by the noted Dutch physician Dr. Nicolass Tulp who stands on the right surrounded by other members of the Amsterdam guild of surgeons. Such dissections were a controversial part of new emerging medical education with only one a year permitted in Amsterdam. The dramatic use of light and darkness is characteristic of the painting of the baroque style. Rembrandt van Rijn (1606–1669). *The Anatomy Lesson of Dr. Tulp.* Mauritshuis, The Hague, The Netherlands. SCALA/Art Resource, NY

14

New Directions in Thought and Culture in the Sixteenth and Seventeenth Centuries

▼ **The Scientific Revolution**
Nicolaus Copernicus Rejects an Earth-Centered Universe • Tycho Brahe and Johannes Kepler Make New Scientific Observations • Galileo Galilei Argues for a Universe of Mathematical Laws • Isaac Newton Discovers the Laws of Gravitation

▼ **Philosophy Responds to Changing Science**
Nature as Mechanism • Francis Bacon: The Empirical Method • René Descartes: The Method of Rational Deduction • Thomas Hobbes: Apologist for Absolute Government • John Locke: Defender of Moderate Liberty and Toleration

▼ **The New Institutions of Expanding Natural Knowledge**

▼ **Women in the World of the Scientific Revolution**

▼ **The New Science and Religious Faith**
The Case of Galileo • Blaise Pascal: Reason and Faith • The English Approach to Science and Religion

▼ **Continuing Superstition**
Witch Hunts and Panic • Village Origins • Influence of the Clergy • Who Were the Witches? • End of the Witch Hunts

▼ **Baroque Art**

▼ **In Perspective**

THE SIXTEENTH AND seventeenth centuries witnessed a sweeping change in the scientific view of the universe. An earth-centered picture gave way to one in which the earth was only another planet orbiting about the sun. The sun itself became one of millions of stars. This transformation of humankind's perception of its

407

place in the larger scheme of things led to a profound rethinking of moral and religious matters, as well as of scientific theory. Faith and reason needed new modes of reconciliation, as did faith and science. The new ideas and methods of science, usually termed *natural philosophy* at the time, challenged those modes of thought associated with late medieval times: Scholasticism and Aristotelian philosophy.

The impact of the new science that explored the realm of the stars through the newly invented telescope and the world of microorganisms through the newly invented microscope must be viewed in the context of two other factors that simultaneously challenged traditional modes of European thought and culture in the sixteenth and seventeenth centuries. The first of these was the Reformation, which permanently divided the religious unity of central and western Europe and fostered decades of warfare and theological dispute. Although by no means a complete break with medieval thought, the theology of the Reformation did question many ideas associated with medieval Christianity and society. The second factor was the cultural impact of Europe's encounter with the New World of the Americas. The interaction with the Americas meant that Europeans directly or indirectly acquired knowledge of new peoples, plants, and animals wholly different from their own and about which Europeans in neither ancient nor medieval times had any information. Consequently, new uncertainties and unfamiliar vistas confronted many Europeans as they considered their souls, geographical knowledge, and physical nature.

Side by side with this new knowledge and science, however, came a new wave of superstition and persecution. The changing world of religion, politics, and knowledge also created profound fear and anxiety among both the simple and the learned, resulting in the worst witch hunts in European history.

▼ The Scientific Revolution

The process that established the new view of the universe is normally termed the **scientific revolution**. The revolution-in-science metaphor must be used carefully, however. Not everything associated with the "new" science was necessarily new. Sixteenth- and seventeenth-century natural philosophers were often reexamining and rethinking theories and data from the ancient world and the late Middle Ages. Moreover, the word *revolution* normally denotes rapid, collective political change involving many people. The scientific revolution was not rapid. It was a complex movement with many false starts and brilliant people suggesting wrong as well as useful ideas. Nor did it involve more than a few hundred people who labored in widely separated

studies and crude laboratories located in Poland, Italy, Denmark, Bohemia, France, and Great Britain. Furthermore, the achievements of the new science were not simply the function of isolated brilliant scientific minds. The leading figures of the scientific revolution often drew on the aid of artisans and craftspeople to help them construct new instruments for experimentation and to carry out those experiments. Thus, the scientific revolution involved older knowledge as well as new discoveries. Additionally, because the practice of science involves social activity as well as knowledge, the revolution also saw the establishment of new social institutions to support the emerging scientific enterprise.

Natural knowledge was only in the process of becoming science as we know it today during the era of the scientific revolution. In fact the word *scientist*, which was only coined in the 1830s, did not yet exist in the seventeenth century, nor did anything resembling the modern scientific career. Individuals devoted to natural philosophy might work in universities or in the court of a prince or even in their own homes and workshops. Only in the second half of the seventeenth century did formal societies and academies devoted to the pursuit of natural philosophy come into existence. Even then the entire process of the pursuit of natural knowledge was a largely informal one.

Yet by the close of the seventeenth century, the new scientific concepts and the methods of their construction were so impressive that they set the standard for assessing the validity of knowledge in the Western world. From the early seventeenth century through the end of the twentieth century, science achieved greater cultural authority in the Western world than any other form of intellectual activity, and the authority and application of scientific knowledge became one of the defining characteristics of modern Western civilization.

Although new knowledge emerged in many areas during the sixteenth and seventeenth centuries, including medicine, chemistry, and natural history, the scientific achievements that most captured the learned imagination and persuaded people of the cultural power of natural knowledge were those that occurred in astronomy.

Nicolaus Copernicus Rejects an Earth-Centered Universe

Nicolaus Copernicus (1473–1543) was a Polish priest and an astronomer who enjoyed a high reputation during his life, but who was not known for strikingly original or unorthodox thought. He had been educated first at the University of Kraków in Poland and later in Italy. In 1543, the year of his death, Copernicus published *On the Revolutions of the Heavenly Spheres*, which has been described as "a revolution-making rather than a revolutionary text."[1] What Copernicus did was to provide an intellectual springboard for a complete criticism of the then-dominant view of the position of the earth in the universe. He had undertaken this task to help the papacy reform the calendar, so that it could correctly calculate the date for Easter based on a more accurate understanding of astronomy.

The Ptolemaic System In Copernicus's time, the standard explanation of the place of the earth in the heavens combined the mathematical astronomy of Ptolemy, contained in his work entitled the *Almagest* (150 C.E.), with the physical cosmology of Aristotle. Over the centuries, commentators on Ptolemy's work had developed several alternative **Ptolemaic systems**, on the basis of which they made mathematical calculations relating to astronomy. Most of these writers assumed the earth was the center of the universe, an outlook known as *geocentrism*. Drawing on Aristotle, these commentators assumed that above the earth lay a series of concentric spheres, probably fluid in character, one of which contained the moon, another the sun, and still others the planets and the stars. At the outer regions of these spheres lay the realm of God and the angels. The earth had to be the center because of its heaviness. The stars and the other heavenly bodies had to be enclosed in the spheres so they could move, since nothing could move unless something was actually moving it. The state of rest was presumed to be natural; motion required explanation. This was the astronomy found in such works as Dante's *Divine Comedy*.

The Ptolemaic model gave rise to many problems, which had long been recognized. The most important was the observed motions of the planets. At certain times the planets appeared to be going backwards. The Ptolemaic model accounted for these motions primarily through epicycles. The planet moved uniformly about a small circle (an *epicycle*), and the center of the epicycle moved uniformly about a larger circle (called a *deferent*), with the earth at or near its center. The combination of these two motions, as viewed from the earth, was meant to replicate the changing planetary positions among the fixed stars—and did so to a high degree of accuracy. The circles employed in Ptolemaic systems were not meant to represent the actual paths of anything; that is, they were not orbits. Rather, they were the components of purely mathematical models meant to predict planetary positions. Other intellectual, but nonobservational, difficulties related to the immense speed at which the spheres had to move around the earth. To say the least, the Ptolemaic systems were cluttered. They were effective, however, as long as one assumed Aristotelian physics to be correct.

[1]Thomas S. Kuhn, *The Copernican Revolution: Planetary Astronomy in the Development of Western Thought* (New York: Vintage, 1959), p. 135.

Copernicus's Universe Copernicus's *On the Revolutions of the Heavenly Spheres* challenged the Ptolemaic picture in the most conservative manner possible. He adopted many elements of the Ptolemaic model, but transferred them to a *heliocentric* (sun-centered) model, which assumed the earth moved about the sun in a circle. Copernicus's model, which retained epicycles, was actually no more accurate than Ptolemy's. However, Copernicus could claim certain advantages over the ancient model. In particular, the epicycles were smaller. The retrograde motion of the planets was now explained as a result of an optical illusion that arose because people were observing them from earth, which was itself moving. Furthermore, Copernicus argued that the farther planets were from the sun, the longer they took to revolve around it. The length of these individual revolutions made it easier to determine the order of the planets, how they ranked in terms of distance from the sun.

The repositioning of the earth had not been Copernicus's goal. Rather, he appears to have set out to achieve new intelligibility and mathematical elegance in astronomy by rejecting Aristotle's cosmology and by removing the earth from the center of the universe. His system was no more accurate than the existing ones for predicting the location of the planets. He had used no new evidence. The major impact of his work was to provide another way of confronting some of the difficulties inherent in Ptolemaic astronomy. The Copernican system did not immediately replace the old astronomy, but it allowed other people who were also discontented with the

This 1543 map of the heavens based on the writings of Nicholas Copernicus shows the earth and the other planets moving about the sun. Until well into the 1600s, however, astronomers continued to debate whether the sun revolved around the earth.
British Library, London, UK/Bridgeman Art Library

Ptolemaic view to think in new directions. Indeed, for at least a century, only a minority of natural philosophers and astronomers embraced the Copernican system.

Tycho Brahe and Johannes Kepler Make New Scientific Observations

The Danish astronomer Tycho Brahe (1546–1601) took the next major step toward the conception of a sun-centered system. He did not embrace Copernicus's view of the universe and actually spent most of his life advocating an earth-centered system. He suggested that Mercury and Venus revolved around the sun, but that the moon, the sun, and the other planets revolved around the earth. In pursuit of his own theory, Brahe constructed scientific instruments with which he made more extensive naked-eye observations of the planets than anyone else had ever done. His labors produced a vast body of astronomical data from which his successors could work.

When Brahe died, his assistant, Johannes Kepler (1571–1630), a German astronomer, took possession of these tables. Kepler was a convinced Copernican and a more consistently rigorous advocate of a heliocentric model than Copernicus himself had been. Like Copernicus, Kepler was deeply influenced by Renaissance Neoplatonism, which held the sun in special honor. In keeping with this outlook, Kepler was determined to find in Brahe's numbers mathematical harmonies that would support a sun-centered universe. After much work, Kepler discovered that to keep the sun at the center of things, he must abandon the circular components of Copernicus's model, particularly the epicycles. Based on the mathematical relationships that emerged from his study of Brahe's observations, Kepler set forth the first astronomical model that actually portrayed motion—that is, the path of the planets—and those orbits were elliptical, not circular. Kepler published his findings in his 1609 book entitled *The New Astronomy*. He had used Copernicus's sun-centered universe and Brahe's empirical data to solve the problem of planetary motion.

Kepler had also defined a new problem. None of the available theories could explain why the planetary orbits were elliptical or, for that matter, why planetary motion was orbital at all rather than simply moving off along a tangent. That solution awaited the work of Sir Isaac Newton.

Galileo Galilei Argues for a Universe of Mathematical Laws

From Copernicus to Brahe to Kepler, there had been little new information about the heavens that might not have been known to Ptolemy. In 1609, however, the same year that Kepler published *The New Astronomy*, an Italian mathematician and natural philosopher named Galileo

Galilei (1564–1642) first turned a telescope on the heavens. Using that recently invented Dutch instrument, he saw stars where none had been known to exist, mountains on the moon, spots moving across the sun, and moons orbiting Jupiter. The heavens were far more complex than anyone had suspected. These discoveries, with some work, could have been accommodated into the Ptolemaic model. Such accommodation would, however, have required a highly technical understanding of Ptolemaic astronomy. Galileo knew that few people who controlled patronage possessed such complex knowledge. Consequently, in the *Starry Messenger* (1610) and *Letters on Sunspots* (1613), he used his considerable rhetorical skills to argue that his newly observed physical evidence, particularly the phases of Venus, required a Copernican interpretation of the heavens.

Galileo's career illustrates that the forging of the new science involved more than just presenting arguments and evidence. In 1610, he had left the University

Galileo Galilei achieved a Europeanwide reputation as a mathematician, instrument maker, and astronomer. His use of the telescope revealed sights of objects in the heavens never previously viewed by human beings. His writings in defense of the Copernican system became increasingly controversial and eventually led to his condemnation by Roman Catholic authorities.   Justus Sustermans (1597–1681), "Portrait of Galileo Galilei." Galleria Palatina, Palazzo Pitti, Florence, Italy. Nimatallah/Art Resource, NY.

of Padua for Florence, where he became the philosopher and mathematician to the Grand Duke of Tuscany, who was a Medici. Galileo was now pursuing natural philosophy in a princely court and had become dependent on princely patronage. To win such support both for his continued work and for his theories, he named the moons of Jupiter after the Medicis. As a natural philosopher working with the new telescope, he had literally presented recently discovered heavenly bodies to his patron. By his political skills and his excellent prose, he had transformed himself into a high-profile advocate of Copernicanism. Galileo's problems with the Roman Catholic Church (see page 424), arose from both his ideas and his flair for self-advertisement.

Galileo not only popularized the Copernican system, but he also articulated the concept of a universe subject to mathematical laws. More than any other writer of the century, he argued that nature displayed mathematical regularity in its most minute details.

Philosophy is written in that great book which ever lies before our eyes—I mean the universe—but we cannot understand it if we do not first learn the language and grasp the symbols in which it is written. This book is written in the mathematical language, and the symbols are triangles, circles, and other geometrical figures, without whose help it is impossible to comprehend a single word of it; without which one wanders through a dark labyrinth.[2]

The universe was rational; however, its rationality was not that of medieval scholastic logic, but of mathematics. Copernicus had thought that the heavens conformed to mathematical regularity; Galileo saw this regularity throughout physical nature.

A world of quantities was replacing one of qualities. All aspects of the world—including color, beauty, and taste—would increasingly be described in terms of the mathematical relationships among quantities. Mathematical models would eventually be applied even to social relations. The new natural philosophy portrayed nature as cold, rational, mathematical, and mechanistic. What was real and lasting was what was mathematically measurable. For many people, the power of the mathematical arguments that appeared irrefutable proved more persuasive than the new information from physical observation that produced so much controversy. Few intellectual shifts have wrought such momentous changes for Western civilization.

Isaac Newton Discovers the Laws of Gravitation

The question that continued to perplex seventeenth-century scientists who accepted the theories of Copernicus, Kepler, and Galileo was how the planets and

other heavenly bodies moved in an orderly fashion. The Ptolemaic and Aristotelian answer had been the spheres and a universe arranged in the order of the heaviness of its parts. Many unsatisfactory theories had been set forth to deal with the question. It was this issue of planetary motion that the Englishman Isaac Newton (1642–1727) addressed and, in so doing, established a basis for physics that endured for more than two centuries.

In 1687, Newton published *The Mathematical Principles of Natural Philosophy*, better known by its Latin title of *Principia Mathematica*. Much of the research and thinking for this great work had taken place more than fifteen years earlier. Galileo's mathematical bias permeated Newton's thought, as did his view that inertia applied to bodies both at rest and in motion. Newton reasoned that the planets and all other physical objects in the universe moved through mutual attraction, or gravity. Every object in the universe affected every other object through gravity. The attraction of gravity explained why the planets moved in an orderly, rather than a chaotic, manner. Newton had found that "the force of gravity towards the whole planet did arise from and was compounded of the forces of

Sir Isaac Newton's experiments dealing with light passing through a prism became a model for writers praising the experimental method. CORBIS/Bettmann

---

[2]Quoted in E. A. Burtt, *The Metaphysical Foundations of Modern Physical Science* (Garden City, NY: Anchor-Doubleday, 1954), p. 75.

gravity towards all its parts, and towards every one part was in the inverse proportion of the squares of the distances from the part."[3] Newton demonstrated this relationship mathematically; he made no attempt to explain the nature of gravity itself.

Newton was a mathematical genius, but he also upheld the importance of empirical data and observation. Like Francis Bacon, he believed in empiricism—that one must observe phenomena before attempting to explain them. The final test of any theory or hypothesis for him was whether it described what was actually observed. Newton was a great opponent of the rationalism of the French philosopher René Descartes (see page 414), which he believed included insufficient guards against error. Consequently, as Newton's own theory of universal gravitation became increasingly accepted, so, too, was Baconian empiricism.

▼ Philosophy Responds to Changing Science

The revolution in scientific thought contributed directly to a major reexamination of Western philosophy. Several of the most important figures in the scientific revolution, such as Bacon and Descartes, were also philosophers discontented with the scholastic heritage. Bacon stressed the importance of empirical research. Descartes attempted to find certainty through the exploration of his own thinking processes. Newton's interests likewise extended to philosophy; he wrote broadly on many topics, including scientific method and theology.

Nature as Mechanism

If a single idea informed all of these philosophers, though in different ways, it was the idea of *mechanism*. The proponents of the new science sought to explain the world in terms of mechanical metaphors, or the language of machinery. The image to which many of them turned was that of the clock. Johannes Kepler once wrote, "I am much occupied with the investigation of the physical causes. My aim in this is to show that the machine of the universe is not similar to a divine animated being, but similar to a clock."[4] Nature conceived as machinery removed much of the mystery of the world and the previous assumption of the presence of divine purpose in nature. The qualities that seemed to in-

here in matter came to be understood as the result of mechanical arrangement. Some writers came to understand God as a kind of divine watchmaker or mechanic who had arranged the world as a machine that would thereafter function automatically. The drive to a mechanical understanding of nature also meant that the language of science and of natural philosophy would become largely that of mathematics. The emphasis that Galileo had placed on mathematics spread to other areas of thought.

This new mode of thinking transformed physical nature from a realm in which Europeans looked for symbolic or sacramental meaning related to the divine into a realm where they looked for utility or usefulness. Previously, philosophers had often believed a correct understanding of the natural order would reveal divine mysteries or knowledge relating to sacred history. Henceforth, they would tend to see knowledge of nature as revealing nothing beyond itself—nothing about divine purposes for the life of humankind on earth. Natural knowledge became the path toward the physical improvement of human beings through their ability to command and manipulate the processes of nature. Many people associated with the new science also believed such knowledge would strengthen the power of their monarchs.

Francis Bacon: The Empirical Method

Bacon (1561–1626) was an Englishman of almost universal accomplishment. He was a lawyer, a high royal official, and the author of histories, moral essays, and philosophical discourses. Traditionally, he has been regarded as the father of **empiricism** and of experimentation in science. Much of this reputation was actually unearned. Bacon was not a natural philosopher, except in the most amateur fashion. His real accomplishment was setting an intellectual tone and helping create a climate conducive to scientific work.

In books such as *The Advancement of Learning* (1605), the *Novum Organum* (1620), and *The New Atlantis* (1627), Bacon attacked the scholastic belief that most truth had already been discovered and only required explanation, as well as the scholastic reverence for authority in intellectual life. He believed scholastic thinkers paid too much attention to tradition and to the knowledge of the ancients. He urged contemporaries to strike out on their own in search of a new understanding of nature. He wanted seventeenth-century Europeans to have confidence in themselves and their own abilities rather than in the people and methods of the past. Bacon was one of the first major European writers to champion innovation and change.

Bacon believed that human knowledge should produce useful results—deeds rather than words. In particular, knowledge of nature should be enlisted to improve

[3]Quoted in A. Rupert Hall, *From Galileo to Newton, 1630–1720* (London: Fontana, 1970), p. 300.
[4]Quoted in Steven Shapin, *The Scientific Revolution* (Chicago: University of Chicago Press, 1996), p. 33.

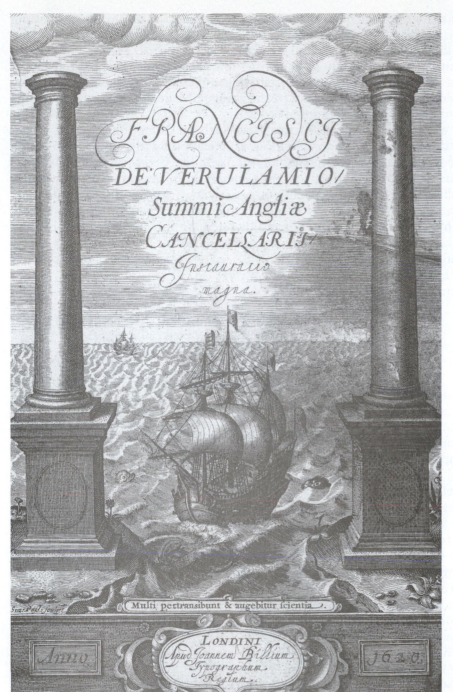

Published in 1620, *Novum Organum* ("new organ or instrument") by Francis Bacon is one of the most important works of the scientific revolution. In this and other works Bacon attacked the long-held belief that most truth had already been discovered. This allegorical image, from the frontispiece of *Novum Organum*, shows a ship striking out for unknown territories, seeking, as did Bacon, for a new understanding of the natural world. The ship is flanked by the mythical pillars of Hercules that stand at the point where the Mediterranean meets the Atlantic—the realm of the unknown and unexplored.   Courtesy of the Library of Congress

than to help the search after truth."[5] Scholastic philosophers could not escape from their syllogisms to examine the foundations of their thought and intellectual presuppositions. Bacon urged that philosophers and investigators of nature examine the evidence of their senses before constructing logical speculations. In a famous passage, he divided all philosophers into "men of experiment and men of dogmas" and then observed,

The men of experiment are like the ant, they only collect and use; the reasoners resemble spiders, who make cobwebs out of their own substance. But the bee takes a middle course: it gathers its material from the flowers of the garden and of the field, but transforms and digests it by a power of its own. Not unlike this is the true business of philosophy.[6]

By directing natural philosophy toward an examination of empirical evidence, Bacon hoped it would achieve new knowledge and thus new capabilities for humankind.

Bacon boldly compared himself with Columbus, plotting a new route to intellectual discovery. The comparison is significant, because it displays the consciousness of a changing world that appears so often in writers of the late sixteenth and early seventeenth centuries. They were rejecting the past not from simple contempt or arrogance, but rather from a firm understanding that the world was much more complicated than their medieval forebearers had thought. Neither Europe nor European thought could remain self-contained. Like the new worlds on the globe, new worlds of the mind were also emerging.

Most of the people in Bacon's day, including the intellectuals influenced by humanism, thought that the best era of human history lay in antiquity. Bacon dissented vigorously from that view. He looked to a future of material improvement achieved through the empirical examination of nature. His own theory of induction from empirical evidence was unsystematic, but his insistence on appealing to experience influenced others whose methods were more productive. He and others of his outlook received almost daily support from the reports not only of European explorers, but also of ordinary seamen who now sailed all over the world and could describe wondrous

the human condition. These goals required modifying or abandoning scholastic modes of learning and thinking. Bacon contended, "The [scholastic] logic now in use serves more to fix and give stability to the errors which have their foundation in commonly received notions

[5]Quoted in Franklin Baumer, *Main Currents of Western Thought*, 4th ed. (New Haven, CT: Yale University Press, 1978), p. 281.
[6]Quoted in Baumer, *Main Currents of Western Thought*, p. 288.

cultures, as well as plants and animals, unknown to the European ancients.

Bacon believed that expanding natural knowledge had a practical purpose and its goal was human improvement. Some scientific investigation does have this character. Much pure research does not. Bacon, however, linked science and material progress in the public mind. This was a powerful idea that still influences Western civilization. It has made science and those who can appeal to the authority of science major forces for change and innovation. Thus, although not making any major scientific contribution himself, Bacon directed investigators of nature to a new method and a new purpose. As a person actively associated with politics, Bacon also believed the pursuit of new knowledge would increase the power of governments and monarchies. Again, his thought in this area opened the way for the eventual strong links between governments and the scientific enterprise.

René Descartes: The Method of Rational Deduction

Descartes (1596–1650) was a gifted mathematician who invented analytic geometry. His most important contribution, however, was to develop a scientific method that relied more on deduction—reasoning from general principle to arrive at specific facts—than empirical observation and induction.

In 1637, he published his *Discourse on Method*, in which he rejected scholastic philosophy and education and advocated thought founded on a mathematical model. (See "Compare & Connect: Descartes and Swift Debate the Scientific Enterprise," pages 422–423.) The work appeared in French rather than in Latin because Descartes wanted it to have wide circulation and application. In the *Discourse*, he began by saying he would doubt everything except those propositions about which he could have clear and distinct ideas. This approach rejected all forms of intellectual authority, except the conviction of his own reason. Descartes concluded that he could not doubt his own act of thinking and his own existence. From this base, he proceeded to deduce the existence of God. The presence of God was important to Descartes because God guaranteed the correctness of clear and distinct ideas. Since God was not a deceiver, the ideas of God-given reason could not be false.

On the basis of such an analysis, Descartes concluded that human reason could fully comprehend the world. He divided existing things into two basic categories: thinking things and things occupying space—mind and body, respectively. Thinking was the defining quality of the mind, and extension (the property by which things occupy space) was the defining quality of material bodies. Human reason could grasp and understand the world

of extension, which became the realm of the natural philosopher. That world had no place for spirits, divinity, or anything nonmaterial. Descartes separated mind from body to banish nonmaterial matters from the realm of scientific speculation and analysis. Reason was to be applied only to the mechanical realm of matter or to the exploration of itself.

Descartes's emphasis on deduction, rational speculation, and internal reflection by the mind, all of which he explored more fully in his *Meditations* of 1641, have influenced philosophers from his time to the present. His deductive methodology, however, eventually lost favor to **scientific induction**, whereby scientists draw generalizations derived from and test hypotheses against empirical observations.

Queen Christina of Sweden (r. 1632–1654), shown here with the French philosopher and scientist René Descartes, was one of many women from the elite classes interested in the new science. In 1649 she invited Descartes to live at her court in Stockholm, but he died a few months after moving to Sweden.   Pierre-Louis the Younger Dumesnil (1698–1781), *Christina of Sweden (1626–89) and her Court: detail of the Queen and René Descartes (1596–1650) at the Table.* Oil on canvas. Chateau de Versailles, France/Bridgeman Art Library

Thomas Hobbes: Apologist for Absolute Government

Nowhere did the impact of the methods of the new science so deeply affect political thought as in the thought of Thomas Hobbes (1588–1679), the most original political philosopher of the seventeenth century.

An urbane and much-traveled man, Hobbes enthusiastically supported the new scientific movement. During the 1630s, he visited Paris, where he came to know Descartes, and Italy, where he spent time with Galileo. He took special interest in the works of William Harvey (1578–1657), who was famous for his discovery of the circulation of blood through the body. Hobbes was also a superb classicist. His earliest published work was the first English translation of Thucydides' *History of the Peloponnesian War* and is still being reprinted today. Part of Hobbes's dark view of human nature would appear to derive from Thucydides' historical analysis.

Hobbes had written works of political philosophy before the English Civil War, but the turmoil of that struggle led him in 1651 to publish his influential work *Leviathan.* His aim was to provide a rigorous philosophical justification for a strong central political authority. Hobbes portrayed human beings and society in a thoroughly materialistic and mechanical way. He traced all psychological processes to bare sensation and regarded all human motivations as egoistical, intended to increase pleasure and minimize pain. According to his analysis, human reasoning penetrated to no deeper reality or wisdom than those physical sensations. Consequently, for Hobbes, unlike both previous Christian and ancient philosophers, human beings exist only to meet the needs of daily life, not for higher spiritual ends or for any larger moral purpose. Only a sovereign commonwealth established by a contract between the ruler and the ruled could enable human beings to meet those needs by limiting the free exercise of the natural human pursuit of self-interest with all its potential for conflict.

According to Hobbes human beings in their natural state are inclined to a "perpetual and restless desire" for power. Because all people want and, in their natural state, possess a natural right to everything, their equality breeds enmity, competition, diffidence, and perpetual quarreling—"a war of every man against every man," as Hobbes put it in a famous summary.

In such condition there is no place for industry, because the fruit thereof is uncertain; and consequently no culture of the Earth; no navigation nor use of the commodities that may be imported by sea; no commodious building; no instruments of moving and removing such things as require much force; no knowledge of the face of the Earth; no account of time; no arts; no letters; no society; and, which is worst of all, continual fear and danger of violent death; and the life of man solitary, poor, nasty, brutish, and short.[7]

[7]Thomas Hobbes, *Leviathan*, Parts I and II, ed. by H. W. Schneider (Indianapolis: Bobbs-Merrill, 1958), pp. 86, 106–107.

The famous title page illustration for Hobbes's *Leviathan.* The ruler is pictured as absolute lord of his lands, but note that the ruler incorporates the mass of individuals whose self-interests are best served by their willing consent to accept him and cooperate with him.   Courtesy of the Library of Congress

As seen in this passage, Hobbes, contrary to Aristotle and Christian thinkers like Thomas Aquinas (1225–1274), rejected the view that human beings are naturally sociable. Rather, they are self-centered creatures who lack a master. Thus, whereas earlier and later philosophers saw the original human state as a paradise from which humankind had fallen, Hobbes saw it as a state of natural, inevitable conflict in which neither safety, security, nor any final authority existed. Human beings in this state of nature were constantly haunted by fear of destruction and death.

Human beings escaped this terrible state of nature, according to Hobbes, only by entering into a particular kind of political contract according to which they agreed to live in a commonwealth tightly ruled by a recognized sovereign. This contract obliged every person, for the sake of peace and self-defense, to agree to set aside personal rights to all things and to be content with as much liberty against others as he or she would allow others against himself or herself. All agreed to live according to a secularized version of the golden rule, "Do not that to another which you would not have done to yourself."[8]

Because, however, words and promises are insufficient to guarantee this agreement, the contract also established the coercive use of force by the sovereign to compel compliance. Believing the dangers of anarchy to be always greater than those of tyranny, Hobbes thought that rulers should be absolute and unlimited in their power, once established as authority. Hobbes's political philosophy has no room for protest in the name of individual conscience or for individual appeal to some other legitimate authority beyond the sovereign. In a reply to critics of his position on sovereign authority, Hobbes pointed out the alternative:

The greatest [unhappiness] that in any form of government can possibly happen to the people in general is scarce sensible in respect of the miseries and horrible calamities that accompany a civil war or that dissolute condition of masterless men, without subjection to laws and a coercive power to tie their hands from rapine and revenge.[9]

The specific structure of this absolute government was not of enormous concern to Hobbes. He believed absolute authority might be lodged in either a monarch or a legislative body, but once that person or body had been granted authority, there existed no argument for appeal. For all practical purposes, obedience to the Hobbesian sovereign was absolute.

Hobbes's argument for an absolute political authority that could assure order aroused sharp opposition. Monarchists objected to his willingness to assign sovereign authority to a legislature. Republicans rejected his willingness to accept a monarchical authority. Many Christian writers, including those who supported the divine right of kings, furiously criticized his materialist arguments for an absolute political authority. Other Christian writers attacked his refusal to recognize the authority of either God or the church as standing beside or above his secular sovereign. The religious critique of Hobbes meant that his thought had little immediate practical impact, but his ideas influenced philosophical literature from the late seventeenth century onward.

John Locke: Defender of Moderate Liberty and Toleration

Locke (1632–1704) proved to be the most influential philosophical and political thinker of the seventeenth century. Although he was less original than Hobbes, his political

[8]Hobbes, *Leviathan*, Parts I and II, p. 130.
[9]Hobbes, *Leviathan*, Parts I and II, p. 152.

writings became a major source of criticism of absolutism and provided a foundation for later liberal political philosophy in both Europe and America. His philosophical works dealing with human knowledge became the most important work of psychology for the eighteenth century.

Locke's family had Puritan sympathies, and during the English Civil War his father had fought for the parliamentary forces against the Stuart monarchy. Although a highly intellectual person who was well read in all the major seventeenth-century natural philosophers, Locke became deeply involved with the tumultuous politics of the English Restoration period. He was a close associate of Anthony Ashley Cooper, the earl of Shaftesbury (1621–1683), considered by his contemporaries to be a radical in both religion and politics. Shaftesbury organized an unsuccessful rebellion against Charles II in 1682, after which both he and Locke, who lived with him, were forced to flee to Holland.

During his years of association with Shaftesbury and the opposition to Charles II, Locke wrote two treatises on government that were eventually published in 1690. In the first of these, he rejected arguments for absolute gov-

John Locke (1632–1704), defender of the rights of the people against rulers who think their power absolute. *John Locke (1632–1704)*. By courtesy of the National Portrait Gallery, London ernment that based political authority on the patriarchal model of fathers ruling over a family. After the publication of this treatise, no major political philosopher again appealed to the patriarchal model. In that regard, though not widely read today, Locke's *First Treatise of Government* proved enormously important by clearing the philosophical decks, so to speak, of a long-standing traditional argument that could not stand up to rigorous analysis.

In his *Second Treatise of Government*, Locke presented an extended argument for a government that must necessarily be both responsible for and responsive to the concerns of the governed. Locke portrayed the natural human state as one of perfect freedom and equality in which everyone enjoyed, in an unregulated fashion, the natural rights of life, liberty, and property. Locke, contrary to Hobbes, regarded human beings in their natural state as creatures of reason and basic goodwill rather than of uncontrolled passion and selfishness. For Locke, human beings possess a strong capacity for dwelling more or less peacefully in society before they enter a political contract. What they experience in the state of nature is not a state of war, but a condition of competition and modest conflict that requires a political authority to sort out problems rather than to impose sovereign authority. They enter into the contract to form political society to secure and preserve the rights, liberty, and property that they already possess prior to the existence of political authority. In this respect, government exists to protect the best achievements and liberty of the state of nature, not to overcome them. Thus, by its very foundation, Locke's government is one of limited authority. (See "John Locke Denounces the Idea of Absolute Monarchy" in the previous chapter, page 387).

The conflict that Hobbes believed characterized the state of nature emerged for Locke only when rulers failed to preserve people's natural freedom and attempted to enslave them by absolute rule. The relationship between rulers and the governed is that of trust, and if the rulers betray that trust, the governed have the right to replace them. In this regard, Locke's position resembled that of Thomas Aquinas, who also permitted rebellion when government violated laws of nature.

In his *Letter Concerning Toleration* (1689), Locke used the premises of the as yet unpublished *Second Treatise* to defend extensive religious toleration among Christians, which he saw as an answer to the destructive religious conflict of the past two centuries. To make his case for toleration, Locke claimed that each individual was required to work out his or her own religious salvation and these efforts might lead various people to join different religious groups. For its part, government existed by its very nature to preserve property, not to make religious decisions for its citizens. Governments that attempted to impose religious uniformity thus misunderstood their real purpose. Moreover, government-imposed religious uniformity could not achieve real religious ends, because assent to religious truth must be freely given by the individual's conscience rather than by force. Consequently, Locke urged a wide degree of religious toleration among differing voluntary Christian groups. He did not, however, extend toleration to Roman Catholics, whom he believed to have given allegiance to a foreign prince (i.e., the pope), to non-Christians, or to atheists, whom he believed could not be trusted to keep their word. Despite these limitations, Locke's *Letter Concerning Toleration* established a powerful foundation for the future extension of toleration, religious liberty, and the separation of church and state. His vision of such expansive toleration was partially realized in England after 1688 and most fully in the United States after the American Revolution.

Finally, just as Newton had set forth laws of astronomy and gravitation, Locke hoped to elucidate the basic structures of human thought. He did so in the most immediately influential of his books, his *Essay Concerning Human Understanding* (1690), which became the major work of European psychology during the eighteenth century. There, Locke portrayed a person's mind at birth as a blank tablet whose content would be determined by sense experience. His vision of the mind has been aptly compared to an early version of behaviorism. It was a reformer's psychology, which contended that the human condition could be improved by changing the environment.

Locke's view of psychology rejected the Christian understanding of original sin, yet he believed his psychology had preserved religious knowledge. He thought such knowledge came through divine revelation in Scripture and also from the conclusions that human reason could draw from observing nature. He hoped this

---

MAJOR WORKS OF THE SCIENTIFIC REVOLUTION

1543	*On the Revolutions of the Heavenly Spheres* (Copernicus)
1605	*The Advancement of Learning* (Bacon)
1609	*The New Astronomy* (Kepler)
1610	*The Starry Messenger* (Galileo)
1620	*Novum Organum* (Bacon)
1632	*Dialogue on the Two Chief World Systems* (Galileo)
1637	*Discourse on Method* (Descartes)
1651	*Leviathan* (Hobbes)
1687	*Principia Mathematica* (Newton)
1689	*Letter Concerning Toleration* (Locke)
1690	*An Essay Concerning Human Understanding* (Locke)
1690	*Treatises of Government* (Locke)

interpretation of religious knowledge would prevent human beings from falling into what he regarded as fanaticism arising from the claims of alleged private revelations and irrationality arising from superstition. For Locke, reason and revelation were compatible and together could sustain a moderate religious faith that would avoid religious conflict.

▼ The New Institutions of Expanding Natural Knowledge

One of the most fundamental features of the expansion of science was the emerging idea that *genuinely new knowledge* about nature and humankind could be discovered. In the late Middle Ages, the recovery of Aristotle and the rise of humanistic learning looked back to the ancients to rediscover the kind of knowledge that later Europeans needed. Luther and other Reformers had seen themselves as recovering a better understanding of the original Christian message. By contrast, the proponents of the new natural knowledge and the new philosophy sought to pursue what Bacon called the advancement of learning. New knowledge would be continuously created. This outlook required new institutions.

The expansion of natural knowledge had powerful social implications. Both the new science and the philosophical outlook associated with it opposed Scholasticism and Aristotelianism. These were not simply disembodied philosophical outlooks, but ways of approaching the world of knowledge most scholars in the universities of

the day still believed in. Such scholars had a clear, vested interest in preserving those traditional outlooks. As they saw it, they were defending the ancients against the moderns. Not surprisingly, the advanced thinkers of the seventeenth century often criticized the universities. For example, in his *Discourse on Method*, Descartes was highly critical of the education he had received. Hobbes filled the *Leviathan* with caustic remarks about the kind of learning then dominating schools and universities, and Locke advocated educational reform.

Some of the criticism of universities was exaggerated. Medical faculties, on the whole, welcomed the advancement of learning in their fields of study. Most of the natural philosophers had themselves received their education at universities. Moreover, however slowly new ideas might penetrate universities, the expanding world of natural knowledge would be taught to future generations. With that diffusion of science into the universities came new supporters of scientific knowledge beyond the small group of natural philosophers themselves. Universities also provided much of the physical and financial support for teaching and investigating natural philosophy and employed many scientists, the most important of whom was Newton himself. University support of science did, however, vary according to country, with the Italian universities being far more supportive than the French.

Yet because of the reluctance of universities to rapidly assimilate the new science, its pioneers quickly understood that they required a framework for cooperating and sharing of information that went beyond existing intellectual institutions. Consequently, they and their supporters established what have been termed "institutions of sharing" that allowed information and ideas associated with the new science to be gathered, exchanged, and debated.[10] The most famous of these institutions was the Royal Society of London, founded in 1660, whose members consciously saw themselves as following the path Bacon had laid out almost a half century earlier. The Royal Society had been preceded by the Academy of Experiments in Florence in 1657 and was followed by the French Academy of Science in 1666. Germany only slowly overcame the destruction of the Thirty Years' War, and the Berlin Academy of Science was not founded until 1700. In addition to these major institutions, the new science was discussed and experiments were carried out in many local societies and academies.

These societies met regularly to hear papers and observe experiments. One of the reasons many early experiments achieved

Colbert was Louis XIV's most influential minister. He sought to expand the economic life of France and to associate the monarchy with the emerging new science from which he hoped might flow new inventions and productive technology. Here he is portrayed presenting members of the French Academy of Science to the monarch. On the founding of the French Academy. Henri Testelin (1616–1695). (after Le Brun). Minister of Finance Colbert presenting the members of the Royal Academy of Science (founded in 1667) to Louis XIV. Study for a tapestry. Photo: Gerard Blot. Chateaux de Versailles et de Trianon, Versailles, France. Reunion des Musées Nationaux/Art Resource, NY

[10]Lewis Pyenson and Susan Sheets-Pyenson, *Servants of Nature: A History of Scientific Institutions, Enterprises, and Sensibilities* (New York: W. W. Norton, 1999), p. 75.

credibility was that they had been observed by persons of social respectability who belonged to one or more of the societies and who, because of their social standing, were presumed to be truthful witnesses of what they had observed. These groups also published information relating to natural philosophy and often organized libraries for their members. Perhaps most important, they attempted to separate the discussion and exploration of natural philosophy from the religious and political conflicts of the day. They intended science to exemplify an arena for the polite exchange of ideas and for civil disagreement and debate. This particular function of science as fostering civility became one of its major attractions.

The activities of the societies also constituted a kind of crossroads between their own members always drawn from the literate classes, and people outside the elite classes, whose skills and practical knowledge might be important for advancing the new science. The latter included craftspeople who could manufacture scientific instruments, sailors whose travels had taken them to foreign parts and who might report on the plants and animals they had seen there, and workers who had practical knowledge of problems in the countryside. In this respect, the expansion of the European economy and the drive toward empires contributed to the growth of the scientific endeavor by bringing back to Europe specimens and experiences that required classification, analysis, and observation.

In good Baconian fashion, the members of the societies presented science as an enterprise that could aid the goals of government and the growth of the economy. For example, mathematicians portrayed themselves as being useful for solving surveying and other engineering problems and for improving armaments. Furthermore, people who had ideas for improving production, navigation, or military artillery might seek the support of the associated societies. In the English context, these people became known as *projectors* and were often regarded as people simply eager to sell their often improbable ideas to the highest bidder. Nonetheless, their activities brought the new science and technology before a wider public. (See "Compare & Connect: Descartes and Swift Debate the Scientific Enterprise" pages 422–423.)

The work, publications, and interaction of the scientific societies with both the government and private business established a distinct role and presence for scientific knowledge in European social life. By 1700, that presence was relatively modest, but it would grow steadily during the coming decades. The groups associated with the new science saw themselves as championing modern practical achievements of applied knowledge and urging religious toleration, mutual forbearance, and political liberty. Such people would form the social base for the eighteenth-century movement known as the **Enlightenment**.

▼ Women in the World of the Scientific Revolution

The absence of women in the emergence of the new science of the seventeenth century has been a matter of much historical speculation. What characteristics of early modern European intellectual and cultural life worked against extensive contributions by women? Why have we heard so little of the activity by women that did actually occur in regard to the new science?

The same factors that had long excluded women from participating in most intellectual life continued to exclude them from working in the emerging natural philosophy. Traditionally, the institutions of European intellectual life had all but excluded women. Both monasteries and universities had been institutions associated with celibate male clerical culture. Except for a few exceptions in Italy, women had not been admitted to either medieval or early modern European universities; they would continue to be excluded from them until the end of the nineteenth century. Women could and did exercise influence over princely courts where natural philosophers, such as Galileo, sought patronage, but they usually did not determine those patronage decisions or benefit from them. Queen Christina of Sweden (r. 1632–1654), who brought René Descartes to Stockholm to provide the regulations for a new science

Margaret Cavendish, who wrote widely on scientific subjects, was the most accomplished woman associated with the new science in seventeenth-century England. ImageWorks/Mary Evans Picture Library Ltd.

academy, was an exception. When various scientific societies were founded, women were not admitted to membership. In that regard, there were virtually no social spaces that might have permitted women to pursue science easily.

Yet a few isolated women from two different social settings did manage to engage in the new scientific activity—noblewomen and women from the artisan class. In both cases, they could do so only through their husbands or male relatives.

The social standing of certain noblewomen allowed them to command the attention of ambitious natural philosophers who were part of their husband's social circle. Margaret Cavendish (1623–1673) actually made significant contributions to the scientific literature of the day. As a girl she had been privately tutored and become widely read. Her marriage to the duke of Newcastle introduced her into a circle of natural philosophers. She understood the new science, quarreled with the ideas of Descartes and Hobbes, and criticized the Royal Society for being more interested in novel scientific instruments than in solving practical problems. Her most important works were *Observations Upon Experimental Philosophy* (1666) and *Grounds of Natural Philosophy* (1668). She was the only woman in the seventeenth century to be allowed to visit a meeting of the Royal Society of London. (See "Margaret Cavendish Questions the Fascination with Scientific Instruments.")

MARGARET CAVENDISH QUESTIONS THE FASCINATION WITH SCIENTIFIC INSTRUMENTS

Margaret Cavendish, duchess of Newcastle, was the most scientifically informed woman of seventeenth-century England. She read widely in natural philosophy and had many acquaintances who were involved in the new science. Although she was enthusiastic about the promise of science, she also frequently criticized some of its leading proponents, including Descartes and Hobbes. She was skeptical of the activities of the newly established Royal Society of London, which she was once permitted to visit. She believed some of its members had become overly enthusiastic about experimentation and new scientific instruments for their own sakes and had begun to ignore the practical questions that she thought science should address. In this respect, her criticism of the Royal Society and its experiments is a Baconian one. She thought the society had replaced scholastic speculation with experimental speculation and that both kinds of speculation ignored important problems of immediate utility.

Why might Margaret Cavendish think that the experiments which were reported about new optical instruments dealt with superficial wonders? Why does she contrast experimental philosophy with the beneficial arts? Do you find a feminist perspective in her comparison of the men of the Royal Society with boys playing with bubbles?

Art has intoxicated so many men's brains, and wholly imployed their thoughts and bodily actions about phaenomena, or the exterior figure of objects, as all better Arts and Studies are laid aside. ... But though there be numerous Books written of the wonder of these [experimental optical] Glasses, yet I cannot perceive any such; at best, they are but superficial wonders, as I may call them. But could Experimental Philosophers find out more beneficial Arts then our Fore-fathers have done, either for the better increase of Vegetables and brute Animals to nourish our bodies, or better and commodious contrivances in the Art of Architecture to build us houses, or for the advancing of trade and traffick . . . it would not only be worth their labour, but of as much praise as could be given to them: But, as Boys that play with watry Bubbles . . . are worthy of reproof rather than praise, for wasting their time with useless sports; so those that addict themselves to unprofitable Arts, spend more time than they reap benefit thereby.

From Margaret Cavendish, *Observations Upon Experimental Philosophy*, to which is added, *The Description of a New Blazing World* (London, 1666), pp. 10–11, as quoted in Anna Battigelli, *Margaret Cavendish and the Exiles of the Mind* (Lexington: University of Kentucky Press, 1998), p. 94.

Women associated with artisan crafts actually achieved greater freedom to pursue the new sciences than did noblewomen. Traditionally, women had worked in artisan workshops, often with their husbands, and might take over the business when their spouse died. In Germany, much study of astronomy occurred in these settings, with women assisting their fathers or husbands. One German female astronomer, Maria Cunitz, published a book on astronomy that many people thought her husband had written until he added a preface supporting her sole authorship. Elisabetha and Johannes Hevelius constituted a wife-and-husband astronomical team, as did Maria Winkelmann and her husband Gottfried Kirch. In each case, the wife served as the assistant to an artisan astronomer. Although Winkelmann discovered a comet in 1702, it was not until 1930 that the discovery was ascribed to her rather than to her husband. Nonetheless, contemporary philosophers did recognize her abilities and understanding of astronomy. Winkelmann had worked jointly with her husband who was the official astronomer of the Berlin Academy of Sciences and was responsible for an official calendar the academy published. When her husband died in 1710, Winkelmann applied for permission to continue the work, basing her application for the post on the guild's tradition of allowing women to continue their husbands' work, in this case the completion of observations required to create an accurate calendar. After much debate, the academy formally rejected her application on the grounds of her gender, although its members knew of her ability and previous accomplishments. Years later, she returned to the Berlin Academy as an assistant to her son, who had been appointed astronomer. Again, the academy insisted that she leave, forcing her to abandon astronomy. She died in 1720.

Such policies of exclusion, however, did not altogether prevent women from acquiring knowledge about scientific endeavors. Margaret Cavendish had composed a *Description of a New World, Called the Blazing World* (1666) to introduce women to the new science. Other examples of scientific writings for a female audience were Bernard de Fontenelle's *Conversations on the Plurality of Worlds* and Francesco Algarotti's *Newtonianism for Ladies* (1737). During the 1730s, Emilie du Châtelet (1706–1749) aided Voltaire in his composition of an important French popularization of Newton's science. Her knowledge of mathematics was more extensive than his and crucial to his completing his book. She also translated Newton's *Principia* into French, an accomplishment made possible only by her exceptional understanding of advanced mathematics.

Still, with few exceptions, women were barred from science and medicine until the late nineteenth century, and not until the twentieth century did they enter these fields in significant numbers. Not only did the institutions of science exclude them, but also, the ideas associated with medical practice, philosophy, and biology suggested that women and their minds were essentially different from, and inferior to, men. By the early eighteenth century, despite isolated precedents of women pursuing natural knowledge, reading scientific literature, and engaging socially with natural philosophers, it had become a fundamental assumption of European intellectual life that the pursuit of knowledge about nature was a male vocation.

▼ The New Science and Religious Faith

For many contemporaries, the new science posed a potential challenge to religion. Three major issues were at stake. First, certain theories and discoveries did not agree with biblical statements about the heavens. Second, who would decide conflicts between religion and science—church authorities or the natural philosophers? Finally, for many religious thinkers, the new science seemed to replace a universe of spiritual meaning and significance with a purely materialistic one. Yet most of the natural philosophers genuinely saw their work as supporting religious belief by contributing to a deeper knowledge of the divine. Their efforts and those of their supporters to reconcile faith and the new science constituted a fundamental factor in the spread of science and its widespread acceptance in educated European circles. The process was not an easy one.

The Case of Galileo

The condemnation of Galileo by Roman Catholic authorities in 1633 is the single most famous incident of conflict between modern science and religious institutions. For centuries it was interpreted as exemplifying the forces of religion smothering scientific knowledge. More recent research has modified that picture.

The condemnation of Copernicanism and of Galileo occurred at a particularly difficult moment in the history of the Roman Catholic Church. In response to Protestant emphasis on private interpretation of Scripture, the Council of Trent (1545–1563) had stated that only the church itself possessed the authority to interpret the Bible. Furthermore, after the Council, the Roman Catholic Church had adopted a more literalist mode of reading the Bible in response to the Protestant emphasis on the authority of Scripture. Galileo's championing of Copernicanism took place in this particular climate of opinion and practice when the Roman Catholic Church, on the one hand, could not surrender the interpretation of the Bible to a layman and, on the other, had difficulty moving beyond a literal reading of the Bible, lest the Protestants accuse it of abandoning Scripture.

In a *Letter to the Grand Duchess Christina* (1615), Galileo, as a layman, had published his own views about how scripture should be interpreted to accommodate the new science. (See "Galileo Discusses the Relationship of Science to the Bible," page 424.) To certain

Descartes and Swift Debate the Scientific Enterprise

THROUGHOUT THE SEVENTEENTH and eighteenth centuries various writers asserted that the growth of natural knowledge held the promise of improving the human situation. Others, who did not dispute the truth or correctness of the new natural knowledge, nonetheless questioned whether it could actually improve the human situation. In these two documents the French philosopher René Descartes upholds the former position while many decades later the English satirist Jonathan Swift questions the usefulness of the new natural knowledge pursued by the Royal Society of London and by implication by other European scientific academies.

QUESTIONS

1. How does Descartes compare the usefulness of science with previous speculative philosophy?

2. What, if any, limits does he place on the extension of scientific knowledge?

3. Why might Swift have so emphasized what he saw as the impracticality of science?

4. How might Swift's presentation be seen as manifesting jealousy of a literary figure toward the growing influence of science?

5. How does Swift's passage serve as an effort to refute the promise of science championed by Bacon and Descartes?

I. Descartes Explores the Promise of Expanding Natural Knowledge

In 1637, Descartes published his Discourse on Method. *He wrote against what he believed to be the useless speculations of scholastic philosophy. He championed the careful investigation of physical nature on the grounds that it would expand the scope of human knowledge beyond anything previously achieved and, in doing so, make human beings the masters of nature. This passage contains much of the broad intellectual and cultural argument that led to the ever-growing influence and authority of science from the seventeenth century onward.*

My speculations were indeed truly pleasing to me; but I recognize that other men have theirs, which perhaps please them even more. As soon, however, as I had acquired some general notions regarding physics, and on beginning to make trial of them in various special difficulties had observed how far they can carry us and how much they differ from the principles hitherto employed, I believed that I could not keep them hidden without grievously sinning against the law which lays us under obligation to promote, as far as in us lies, the general good of all mankind. For they led me to see that it is possible to obtain knowledge highly useful in life, and that in place of the speculative philosophy taught in the Schools we can have a practical philosophy, by means of which, knowing the force and the actions of fire, water, air, and of the stars, of the heavens, and of all the bodies that surround us—knowing them as distinctly as we know the various crafts of the artisans—we may in the same fashion employ them in all the uses for which they are suited, thus rendering ourselves the masters and possessors of nature. This is to be desired, not only with a view to the invention of an infinity of arts by which we would be enabled to enjoy without heavy labor the fruits of the earth and all its conveniences, but above all for the preservation of health, which is, without doubt, of all blessings in this life, the first of all goods and the foundation on which the others rest. For the mind is so dependent on the temper and disposition of the bodily organisms that if any means can ever be found to render men wiser and more capable than they have hitherto been, I believe that it is in the science of medicine that the means must be sought. . . . With no wish to depreciate it, I am yet sure there is no one, even of those engaged in the profession, who does not admit that all we know is almost nothing in comparison with what remains to be discovered; and that we could be freed from innumerable maladies, both of body and of mind, and even perhaps from the infirmities of age, if we had sufficient knowledge of their causes and of the remedies provided by nature.

Source: From René Descartes, *Discourse on Method*, in Norman Kemp Smith, ed., *Descartes's Philosophical Writings* (New York: The Modern Library, 1958), pp. 130–131. Reprinted by permission of Macmillan Press Ltd.

An illustration from *Discourse on Method* by René Descartes (1637). Courtesy of the Library of Congress

II. Jonathan Swift Satirizes Scientific Societies

Swift, the greatest author of English satire in the eighteenth century, was a deeply pessimistic person who thought much of the promise held forth for scientific enterprise would never be realized. In the Third Voyage of Gulliver's Travels, *published in 1726, Swift portrays Gulliver as visiting the land of Lagardo where he encounters a learned academy filled with scholars pursuing outlandish projects. Swift lists the efforts of a whole series of Projectors each of which is more impractical than the next. This passage in which Swift pillories the various people who hoped to received patronage for project from persons associated with the Royal Society of London remains one of the most famous satires of science in the English language. That Swift wrote it is a testimony to the cultural authority that science had achieved by the early eighteenth century.*

Gulliver reports a conversation he encountered while visiting Lagardo:

"The Sum of his Discourse was to this Effect. That about Forty Years ago, certain Persons went up to *Laputa,* either upon Business or Diversion; and after five Months Continuance, came back with a very little Smattering in Mathematics, but full of Volatile Spirits acquired in that Airy Region. That these Persons upon their Return, began to dislike the Management of every Thing below; and fell into Schemes of putting all Arts, Sciences, Languages, and Mechanics upon a new Foot. To this End they procured a Royal Patent for erecting an Academy of *Projectors* in *Lagado*; And the Humour prevailed so strongly among the People, that there is not a Town of any Consequence in the Kingdom without such an Academy. In these Colleges, the Professors contrive new Rules and Methods of Agriculture and Building, and new Instruments and Tools for all Trades and Manufactures, whereby, as they undertake, one Man shall do the Work of Ten; a Palace may be built in a Week, of Materials so durable as to last for ever without repairing. All the Fruits of the Earth shall come to Maturity at whatever Season we think fit to chuse; and increase an Hundred Fold more than they do at present; with innumerable other happy Proposals. The only Inconvenience is, that none of these Projects are yet brought to Perfection; and in the mean time, the whole Country lies miserably waste, the Houses in Ruins, and the People without Food or Cloaths. By all which, instead of being discouraged they are Fifty Times more violently bent upon prosecuting their Schemes, driven equally on by Hope and Depair. . . ."

Gulliver then reports what he found occurring in the rooms of an academy in Lagardo:

"The first Man I saw . . . had been Eight Years upon a Project for extracting Sun-Beams out of Cucumbers, which were to be put into Vials hermetically sealed, and let out to warm the Air in raw inclement Summers. . . .

"I saw another at work to calcine ice into Gunpowder . . .

"There was another most ingenius Architect who had contrived a new Method for building Houses, by beginning at the Roof, and working downwards to the Foundation. . . .

In another Apartment I was highly pleased with a Projector, who had found a Device of plowing the Ground with Hogs, to save the Charges of Plows, Cattle, and Labour. The Method is this: In an Acre of Ground you bury at six Inches Distance, and eight deep, a quantity of Acorns, Dates, Chesnuts, and other Masts or Vegetables whereof these Animals are fondest; then you drive six Hundred or more of them into the Field, where in a few Days they will root up the whole Ground in search of their Food, and make it fit for sowing, at the same time manuring it with their Dung. It is true, upon Experiment they found the Charge and Trouble very great, and they had little or no Crop. However, it is not doubted that this Invention may be capable of great Improvement."

Source: Jonathan Swift, *Gulliver's Travels*, Part III, chaps. iv and v (New York: The Heritage Press, 1960), pp. 193–194, 197–199.

GALILEO DISCUSSES THE RELATIONSHIP OF SCIENCE TO THE BIBLE

The religious authorities were often critical of the discoveries and theories of six-teenth- and seventeenth-century science. For years before his condemnation by the Roman Catholic Church in 1633, Galileo had contended that scientific theory and re-ligious piety were compatible. In his Letter to the Grand Duchess Christina *(of Tus-cany), written in 1615, he argued that God had revealed truth in both the Bible and physical nature and that the truth of physical nature did not contradict the Bible if the latter were properly understood. Galileo encountered difficulties regarding this letter because it represented a layman telling church authorities how to read the Bible.*

Is Galileo's argument based on science or theology? Did the church believe that nature was as much a revelation of God as the Bible was? As Galileo describes them, which is the surer revelation of God, nature or the Bible? Why might the pope reject Galileo's argument?

The reason produced for condemning the opin-ion that the Earth moves and the sun stands still is that in many places in the Bible one may read that the sun moves and the Earth stands still. . . .

With regard to this argument, I think in the first place that it is very pious to say and prudent to af-firm that the holy Bible can never speak untruth—whenever its true meaning is understood. But I believe nobody will deny that it is often very ab-struse, and may say things which are quite differ-ent from what its bare words signify. . . .

This being granted, I think that in discussions of physical problems we ought to begin not from the authority of scriptural passages, but from sense experiences and necessary demonstrations; for the holy Bible and the phenomena of nature proceed alike from the divine Word, the former as the dictate of the Holy Ghost and the latter as the observant executrix of God's commands. It is nec-essary for the Bible, in order to be accommodated to the understanding of every man, to speak many things which appear to differ from the absolute truth so far as the bare meaning of the words is concerned. But Nature, on the other hand, is inex-orable and immutable; she never transgresses the laws imposed upon her, or cares a whit whether her abstruse reasons and methods of operation are understandable to men. For that reason it appears that nothing physical which sense-experience

sets before our eyes, or which necessary demon-strations prove to us, ought to be called in ques-tion (much less condemned) upon the testimony of biblical passages which may have some differ-ent meaning beneath their words. For the Bible is not chained in every expression to conditions as strict as those which govern all physical effects; nor is God any less excellently revealed in Na-ture's actions than in the sacred statements of the Bible. . . .

From this I do not mean to infer that we need not have an extraordinary esteem for the passages of holy Scripture. On the contrary, having arrived at any certainties in physics, we ought to utilize these as the most appropriate aids in the true expo-sition of the Bible and in the investigation of those meanings which are necessarily contained therein for these must be concordant with demonstrated truths. I should judge the authority of the Bible was designed to persuade men of those articles and propositions which, surpassing all human reason-ing, could not be made credible by science, or by any other means than through the very mouth of the Holy Spirit. . . .

But I do not feel obliged to believe that the same God who has endowed us with senses, reason, and intellect has intended to forgo their use and by some other means to give us knowledge which we can attain by them.

Roman Catholic authorities, his actions resembled those of a Protestant who looked to himself rather than the church to understand the Bible. In 1615 and 1616, he visited Rome and discussed his views openly and aggressively. In early 1616, however, the Roman Catholic Inquisition formally censured Copernicus's views, placing *On the Revolutions of the Heavenly Spheres* in the Index of Prohibited Books. The ground for the condemnation was Copernicus's disagreement with the literal word of the Bible and the biblical interpretations of the Church Fathers. It should be recalled that at the time fully satisfactory empirical evidence to support Copernicus did not yet exist, even in Galileo's mind.

Galileo, who was not on trial in 1616, was formally informed of the condemnation of Copernicanism. Exactly what agreement he and the Roman Catholic authorities reached as to what he would be permitted to write about Copernicanism remains unclear. It appears that he agreed not to advocate that Copernican astronomy was actually physically true, but only to suggest that it could be true in theory.

In 1623, however, a Florentine acquaintance of Galileo's was elected as Pope Urban VIII. He gave Galileo permission to resume discussing the Copernican system, which he did in *Dialogue on the Two Chief World Systems* (1632). The book clearly was designed to defend the physical truthfulness of Copernicanism. Moreover, the voices in the dialogue favoring the older system appeared slow-witted—and those voices presented the views of Pope Urban. Feeling humiliated and betrayed, the pope ordered an investigation of Galileo's book. The actual issue in Galileo's trial of 1633 was whether he had disobeyed the mandate of 1616, and he was held to have done so even though the exact nature of that mandate was less than certain. Galileo was condemned, required to renounce his views, and placed under the equivalent of house arrest in his home near Florence for the last nine years of his life.

Although much more complicated than a simple case of a conflict between science and religion, the condemnation of Galileo cast a long and troubled shadow over the relationship of the emerging new science and the authority of the Roman Catholic Church. The controversy continued into the late twentieth century, when Pope John Paul II formally ordered the reassessment of the Galileo case. In 1992, the Roman Catholic Church admitted that errors had occurred, particularly in the biblical interpretation of Pope Urban VIII's advisers.

Blaise Pascal: Reason and Faith

Blaise Pascal (1623–1662), a French mathematician and a physical scientist who surrendered his wealth to pursue an austere, self-disciplined life, made one of the most influential efforts to reconcile faith and the new science. He aspired to write a work that would refute both dogmatism (which he saw epitomized by the Jesuits) and

skepticism. Pascal considered the Jesuits' casuistry (i.e., arguments designed to minimize and excuse sinful acts) a distortion of Christian teaching. He rejected the skeptics of his age because they either denied religion altogether (atheists) or accepted it only as it conformed to reason (deists). He never produced a definitive refutation of the two sides. Rather, he formulated his views on these matters in piecemeal fashion in a provocative collection of reflections on humankind and religion published posthumously under the title *Pensées (Thoughts)*.

Pascal allied himself with the Jansenists, seventeenth-century Catholic opponents of the Jesuits. (See Chapter 13.) His sister was a member of the Jansenist convent of Port-Royal, near Paris. The Jansenists shared with the Calvinists Saint Augustine's belief in human beings' total sinfulness, their eternal predestination to heaven or hell by God, and their complete dependence on faith and grace for knowledge of God and salvation.

Pascal believed that in religious matters, only the reasons of the heart and a "leap of faith" could prevail. For him, religion was not the domain of reason and science. He saw two essential truths in the Christian religion: A loving God exists, and human beings, because they are corrupt by nature, are utterly unworthy of God. He believed the atheists and the deists of his age had overestimated reason. To Pascal, reason itself was too weak to resolve the problems of human nature and destiny. Ultimately, reason should drive those who truly heeded it to faith in God and reliance on divine grace.

Pascal made a famous wager with the skeptics. It is a better bet, he argued, to believe God exists and to stake everything on his promised mercy than not to do so. This is because, if God does exist, the believer will gain everything, whereas, should God prove not to exist, comparatively little will have been lost by having believed in him.

Convinced that belief in God improved life psychologically and disciplined it morally (regardless of whether God proved in the end to exist), Pascal worked to strengthen traditional religious belief. He urged his contemporaries to seek self-understanding by "learned ignorance" and to discover humankind's greatness by recognizing its misery. He hoped thereby to counter what he believed to be the false optimism of the new rationalism and science.

The English Approach to Science and Religion

Francis Bacon established a key framework for reconciling science and religion that long influenced the English-speaking world. He argued there were two books of divine revelation: the Bible and nature. In studying nature, the natural philosopher could achieve a deeper knowledge of things divine, just as could the theologian studying the Bible. Because both books of revelation shared the same author, they must be compatible. Whatever discord might first appear between science and

A Closer ▶ LOOK

THE SCIENCES AND THE ARTS

PAINTERS DURING THE seventeenth century were keenly aware that they lived in an age of expanding knowledge of nature and of the world. Adriaen Stalbent (1589–1662) portrayed this close interrelationship of *The Sciences and the Arts*. Across Europe various societies were founded to study the expanding realm of natural knowledge. As in this painting, women only were rarely admitted to the meetings of these societies or to the rooms where the new natural knowledge was pursued or discussed.

The paintings on the wall illustrate the great masters of the day, some of whom drew on ancient mythological themes, others biblical scenes, and still others contemporary landscapes. Sophisticated viewers would have been able to identify each painting and its artist. The themes from the Bible and ancient mythology here are intended to contrast with the symbols of modern knowledge displayed elsewhere in the room.

On the red, covered table stands an astronomical instrument that natural philosophers used to illustrate the theories of Copernicus, Kepler, and Galileo.

On the table on the right stands a globe and volumes of maps that allow observers to trace the explorations of the Americas and other parts of the non-European world.

Adriaen Stalbent (1589–1662), *The Sciences and the Arts*. Wood, 93 × 114 cm. Inv. 1405. Museo del Prado, Madrid, Spain. Photograph © Erich Lessing, Art Resource, NY

To examine this image in an interactive fashion, please go to www.myhistorylab.com

myhistorylab

religion must eventually be reconciled. Natural theology based on a scientific understanding of the natural order would thus support theology derived from Scripture.

Later in the seventeenth century, with the work of Newton, the natural universe became a realm of law and regularity. Most natural philosophers were devout people who saw in the new picture of physical nature a new picture of God. The Creator of this rational, lawful nature must also be rational. To study nature was to come to a better understanding of that Creator. Science and religious faith were not only compatible, but also mutually supportive. As Newton wrote, "The main Business of Natural Philosophy is to argue from Phaenomena without feigning Hypothesis, and to deduce Causes from Effects, till we come to the very first Cause, which certainly is not mechanical."[11]

The religious thought associated with such deducing of religious conclusions from nature became known as *physico-theology*. This reconciliation of faith and science allowed the new physics and astronomy to spread rapidly. At the very time when Europeans were finally tiring of the wars of religion, the new science provided the basis for a view of God that might lead away from irrational disputes and wars over religious doctrine. Faith in a rational God encouraged faith in the rationality of human beings and in their capacity to improve their lot once liberated from the traditions of the past. The scientific revolution provided the great model for the desirability of change and of criticism of inherited views.

Finally, the new science and the technological and economic innovations associated with its culture came again, especially among English thinkers, to be interpreted as part of a divine plan. By the late seventeenth century, natural philosophy and its practical achievements had become associated in the public mind with consumption and the market economy. Writers such as the Englishman John Ray in *The Wisdom of God Manifested in His Works of Creation* (1690) argued it was evident that God had placed human beings in the world to understand it and then, having understood it, to turn it to productive practical use through rationality. Scientific advance and economic enterprise came to be interpreted in the public mind as the fulfillment of God's plan: Human beings were meant to improve the world. This outlook provided a religious justification for the processes of economic improvement that would characterize much of eighteenth-century Western Europe.

▼ Continuing Superstition

Despite the great optimism among certain European thinkers associated with the new ideas in science and philosophy, traditional beliefs and fears long retained their hold on Western culture. During the sixteenth and

seventeenth centuries, many Europeans remained preoccupied with sin, death, and the devil. Religious people, including many among the learned and many who were sympathetic to the emerging scientific ideas, continued to believe in the power of magic and the occult. Until the end of the seventeenth century, almost all Europeans in one way or another believed in the power of demons.

Witch Hunts and Panic

Nowhere is the dark side of early modern thought and culture more strikingly visible than in the witch hunts and panics that erupted in almost every Western land. Between 1400 and 1700, courts sentenced an estimated 70,000 to 100,000 people to death for harmful magic (*maleficium*) and diabolical witchcraft. In addition to inflicting harm on their neighbors, witches were said to attend mass meetings known as *sabbats*, to which they were believed to fly. They were also accused of indulging in sexual orgies with the devil, who appeared in animal form, most often as a he-goat. Still other charges against them were cannibalism—particularly the devouring of small Christian children—and a variety of ritual acts and practices, often sexual in nature, that denied or perverted Christian beliefs.

Why did witch panics occur in the sixteenth and early seventeenth centuries? The disruptions created by religious division and warfare were major factors. (The peak years of the religious wars were also those of the witch hunts.) Some argue that the Reformation spurred the panics by taking away the traditional defenses against the devil and demons, thus compelling societies to protect themselves preemptively by searching out and executing witches. Political consolidation by secular governments and the papacy played an even greater role, as both aggressively conformed their respective realms in an attempt to eliminate competition for the loyalty of their subjects.

Village Origins

The roots of belief in witches are found in both popular and elite culture. In village societies, feared and respected "cunning folk" helped people cope with natural disasters and disabilities by magical means. For local people, these were important services that kept village life moving forward in times of calamity. The possession of magical powers, for good or ill, made one an important person within village society. Those who were most in need of security and influence, particularly old, impoverished single or widowed women, often made claims to such authority. In village society witch beliefs may also have been a way to defy urban Christian society's attempts to impose its orthodox beliefs, laws, and institutions on the countryside. Under church persecution local fertility cults, whose semipagan

[11]Quoted in Baumer, *Main Currents of Western Thought*, p. 323.

practices were intended to ensure good harvests, acquired the features of diabolical witchcraft.

Influence of the Clergy

Popular belief in magical power was the essential foundation of the witch hunts. Had ordinary people not believed that "gifted persons" could help or harm by magical means, and had they not been willing to accuse them, the hunts would never have occurred; however, the contribution of Christian theologians was equally great. When the church expanded into areas where its power and influence were small, it encountered semipagan cultures rich in folkloric beliefs and practices that predated Christianity. There, it clashed with the cunning men and women, who were respected spiritual authorities in their local communities, the folk equivalents of Christian priests. The Christian clergy also practiced high magic. They could transform bread and wine into the body and blood of Christ (the sacrament of the Eucharist) and eternal penalties for sin into temporal ones (the sacrament of Penance or Confession). They also claimed the power to cast out demons who possessed the faithful.

In the late thirteenth century, the church declared its magic to be the only true magic. Since such powers were not innate to humans, the theologians reasoned, they must come either from God or from the devil. Those from God were properly exercised within and by the church. Any who practiced magic outside and against the church did so on behalf of the devil. From such reasoning grew allegations of "pacts" between nonpriestly magicians and Satan. Attacking accused witches became a way for the church to extend its spiritual hegemony.

In working its will, the church had an important ally in the princes of the age, who were also attempting to extend and consolidate their authority over villages and towns within their lands. As the church sought to supplant folk magic with church magic, the princes sought to supplant customary laws with Roman law. Here the stage was set for a one-sided conflict. Witch trials became one of the ways church and state realized their overlapping goals. To identify, try, and execute witches was a demonstration of absolute spiritual and political authority over a village or a town.

Who Were the Witches?

Roughly 80 percent of the victims of witch hunts were women, most single and aged over forty. This has suggested to some that misogyny fueled the witch hunts. Inspired by male hatred and sexual fear of strong women, and occurring at a time when women were breaking out from under male control, witch hunts were a conspiracy of males against females.

A perhaps better argument holds that women were targeted in higher numbers for more commonsensical reasons. (See "Why More Women Than Men Are Witches.") Three groups of women appear especially to have drawn the witch-hunters' attention. The first was widows, who, living alone in the world after the deaths of their husbands, were often dependent on help from others, unhappy, and known to strike out. A second group was midwives, whose work made them unpopular when mothers and newborns died during childbirth. (See "Encountering the Past: Midwives," page 430.) Surviving family members remembered those deaths. Finally, there were women healers and herbalists, who were targeted because their work gave them a moral and spiritual authority over people whom the church wished to reserve for its priests. These women found themselves on the front lines in disproportionate numbers when the church declared war on those who practiced magic without its special blessing. Social position, vocation, and influence, not gender per se, put old, single women in harm's way. Nowhere do we find women being randomly rounded up for burning. The witch hunts targeted specific women.

End of the Witch Hunts

Several factors helped end the witch hunts. One was the emergence of a more scientific point of view. In the seventeenth century, mind and matter came to be viewed as two independent realities, making it harder to believe that thoughts in the mind or words on the lips could alter physical things. A witch's curse was mere words. With advances in medicine, the rise of insurance companies, and the availability of lawyers, people gained greater physical security against the physical afflictions and natural calamities that drove the witch panics. Finally, the witch hunts began to get out of hand. Tortured witches, when asked whom they saw at witches' sabbats, sometimes alleged having seen leading townspeople there, and even the judges themselves! At this point the trials ceased to serve the interests of those conducting them, becoming dysfunctional and threatening anarchy as well.

▼ Baroque Art

Art historians use the term *baroque* to denote the style associated with seventeenth-century painting, sculpture, and architecture. As with other terms used in art history, the word *baroque* covers a variety of related styles that developed during the century and moved in different directions in different countries. Baroque painters depicted their subjects in a thoroughly naturalistic, rather than an idealized, manner. This faithfulness to nature paralleled the interest in natural knowledge associated with the rise of the new science and the deeper understanding of human anatomy that was achieved during this period. These painters, the most famous of whom was Michelangelo Caravaggio (1573–1610), also were devoted to picturing

WHY MORE WOMEN THAN MEN ARE WITCHES

A classic of misogyny, The Hammer of Witches *(1486), written by two Dominican monks, Heinrich Krämer and Jacob Sprenger, was sanctioned by Pope Innocent VIII as an official guide to the church's detection and punishment of witches. Here, Krämer and Sprenger explain why they believe most witches are women rather than men.*

Why would two Dominican monks say such things about women? What are the biblical passages that they believe justify them? Do their descriptions have any basis in the actual behavior of women in that age? What is the rivalry between married and unmarried people that they refer to?

Why are there more superstitious women than men? The first [reason] is that they are more credulous; and since the chief aim of the devil is to corrupt faith, therefore he rather attacks them. . . . The second reason is that women are naturally more impressionable and ready to receive the influence of a disembodied spirit. . . . The third reason is that they have slippery tongues and are unable to conceal from their fellow-women those things which by evil arts they know; and since they are weak, they find an easy and secret manner of vindicating themselves by witchcraft. . . . [Therefore] since women are feebler both in mind and body, it is not surprising that they should come more under the spell of witchcraft. For as regards intellect, or the understanding of spiritual things, they seem to be of a different nature from men, a fact which is vouched for by the logic of the authorities, backed by various examples from the Scriptures. . . . .

But the natural reason [for woman's proclivity to witchcraft] is that she is more carnal than a man, as is clear from her many carnal abominations. And it should be noted that there was a defect in the formation of the first woman, since she was formed from a bent rib, that is, a rib of the breast, which is bent as it were in a contrary direction to a man.

And since through this defect she is an imperfect animal, she always deceives. . . . .

As to her other mental quality, her natural will, when she hates someone whom she formerly loved, then she seethes with anger and impatience in her whole soul, just as the tides of the sea are always heaving and boiling. . . . .

Truly the most powerful cause which contributes to the increase of witches is the woeful rivalry between married folk and unmarried women and men. This [jealousy or rivalry exists] even among holy women, so what must it be among the others . . . ?

Just as through the first defect in their intelligence women are more prone [than men] to abjure the faith, so through their second defect of inordinate affections and passions they search for, brood over, and inflict various vengeances, either by witchcraft or by some other means. Wherefore it is no wonder that so great a number of witches exist in this sex. . . . [Indeed, witchcraft] is better called the heresy of witches than of wizards, since the name is taken from the more powerful party [that is, the greater number, who are women]. Blessed be the Highest who has so far preserved the male sex from so great a crime.

From *Malleus Maleficarum*, trans. by Montague Summers (Bungay, Suffolk, UK: John Rodker, 1928), pp. 41–47. Reprinted by permission.

sharp contrasts between light and darkness, which created dramatic scenes in their painting. Consequently both baroque painting and sculpture have been seen as theatrical and intending to draw the observer into an emotional involvement with the subject that is being portrayed.

The work of Baroque artists served both religious and secular ends. Baroque painters, especially in Roman Catholic countries, often portrayed scenes from the Bible and from the lives of saints intended to instruct the observer in religious truths. Artists used the same style of painting, however, to present objects and scenes of everyday life in new realistic detail. Such was the case with Dutch painters of still lifes who portrayed all manner of elaborate foodstuffs as well as with artists

MIDWIVES

ALTHOUGH WOMEN IN early modern Europe generally found themselves excluded from the world of the new science, midwives across Europe oversaw the delivery of children until well into the eighteenth century. Often known as *wise women* because of their knowledge and medical skills, midwives were among the few women who carried out independent economic and public roles.

Midwifery was a trade, often pursued by elderly or widowed women of the lower social classes, for which women apprenticed for several years. In the 1630s, the Hôtel Dieu, a public hospital near Paris, set up a basic course for training midwives. Unlike other skilled workers and tradesmen, however, midwives were not allowed to organize guilds or associations to protect their trade, pass on their skills, and stabilize their incomes. Instead, civil or church authorities, who were invariably men, licensed midwives and often appointed upper-class women, known as honorable women, to supervise them.

Personal respectability and respect for the privacy of the women they attended were essential qualities for successful midwives. They were present at some of the most private moments in the lives of women and their families and were expected not to gossip about family secrets. Furthermore, women from all social classes feared that if their attending midwives were not of good character their own babies might be stillborn or imperfectly formed. Careless or incompetent midwives who injured mother or child could lose their license.

Midwives also performed important religious and civic functions at births. In emergencies they could baptize a frail newborn. They also often registered births and were officially required both to discourage abortion and infanticide and to report those activities when they occurred to the authorities. The respectability of midwives also gave them legal standing to testify to a child's legitimacy or illegitimacy.

Midwifery was one of numerous skills and occupations associated with women in early modern Europe that men took over during the eighteenth century. (See Chapter 16.) Male medical practitioners claimed to possess better training, which was available to them in medical schools, and more professional knowledge about delivering children. Over time, civil and medical authorities began to demand that people who delivered children be trained as doctors in medical schools, which women were not allowed to attend until well into the nineteenth century. In particular, the use of forceps by male surgeons to deliver a child involved a level of training unavailable to women. Yet even as medical professionalization became entrenched, midwives continued to provide their services to the poor and rural populations of Europe.

Linda Schiebinger, *The Mind Has No Sex? Women in the Origins of Modern Science* (Cambridge, MA: Harvard University Press, 1989); Hilary Marland, ed., *The Art of Midwifery: Early Modern Midwives in Europe* (London: Routledge, 1993).

What types of women became midwives in early modern Europe? How did the authorities regulate the practice of midwifery?

Why did male professionals gradually replace midwives in delivering babies?

Until well into the eighteenth century, midwives oversaw the delivery of most children in Europe. CORBIS

Bernini designed the elaborate Baldacchino that stands under the dome of St. Peter's Basilica. It is one of the major examples of baroque interior decoration.   Scala/Art Resource, NY

such Louis LeNain (1593–1648) who painted scenes of French peasant life (see Chapter 15, page 440).

Baroque art became associated, rightly or wrongly, with both Roman Catholicism and absolutist politics. Baroque art first emerged in papal Rome. Gian Lorenzo Bernini's work (1598–1680) in St. Peter's Basilica there was the most famous example of baroque decoration. At the direction of Pope Urban VIII (r. 1623–1644), during whose reign Galileo was condemned, Bernini designed and oversaw the construction of the great tabernacle that stands beneath the church's towering dome and directly over the space where St. Peter is said to be buried. Behind the tabernacle, Bernini also designed a monument to papal authority with the chair of St. Peter resting on the shoulders of four of the church fathers. In front of the cathedral, he designed the two vast colonnades that he said symbolized the arms of the church reaching out to the world. In the church of Santa Maria de la Vittoria in Rome, Bernini created the dramatic sculpture of the Spanish mystic St. Teresa of Avila (1515–1582), depicting her in religious ecstasy.

The association of baroque art with Roman Catholicism had its counterpart in the secular world. Charles I (r. 1625–1649) of England during the 1630s when he ruled as an all-but absolute monarch without calling Parliament employed the Roman Catholic Flemish artist Peter Paul Rubens (1577–1640) to decorate the ceiling of the Banquet-ing Hall at his palace in London with paintings commemorating his father James I (r. 1603–1625). Rubens was the leading religious painter of the Catholic Reformation. Charles's employment of him fed Puritan suspicions that the king harbored Roman Catholic sympathies. Consequently, it was not by coincidence that Charles I was led to his execution in 1649 through the Rubens-decorated Banqueting Hall to his death on the scaffold erected outside.

The most elaborate baroque monument to political absolutism was Louis XIV's palace at Versailles. (See Chapter 13.) The exterior of the palace was classical in its restrained design. Room after room on the interior, however, was decorated with vast, dramatic paintings and murals presenting Louis as the Sun King. The Hall of Mirrors, which runs across the entire rear of the palace, allowed for a glittering and elaborate play of light whose purpose was to reflect the power of the monarch. In the gardens of Versailles fountains depicted mythical gods as if they had come to pay court or to amuse the Sun King. Monarchs across Europe, Protestant as well as Catholic, who hoped to imitate Louis's absolutism in their own domains, erected similar, if smaller, palaces filled with elaborate decoration. Baroque architecture dominated the capitals of the rulers of the smaller German states as well as the imperial court of the Habsburgs in Vienna.

In Perspective

The scientific revolution and the thought of writers whose work was contemporaneous with it mark a major turning point in the history of Western culture and eventually had a worldwide impact. The scientific and political ideas of the late sixteenth and seventeenth centuries gradually overturned many of the most fundamental premises of the medieval worldview. The sun replaced the earth as the center of the solar system. The solar system itself came to be viewed as one of many possible systems in the universe. The new knowledge of the physical universe gave rise to challenges to the authority of the church and Scripture. Mathematics began to replace theology and metaphysics as the tool for understanding nature.

Parallel to these developments and sometimes related to them, political thought became much less concerned with religious issues. Hobbes's theory of political obligation made virtually no reference to God. Locke's theories about politics recognized God, but paid little attention to Scripture. He also championed greater freedom of religious and political expression. Locke's ideas about psychology emphasized the influence of environment on human character and action. All of these new ideas gradually displaced or reshaped theological and religious modes of thought and placed humankind and life on earth at the center of Western thinking. Intellectuals in the West consequently developed greater self-confidence in their own capacity to shape the world and their own lives.

None of this change came easily, however. The new science and enlightenment were accompanied by new anxieties that were reflected in a growing preoccupation with sin, death, and the devil. The worst expression of this preoccupation was a succession of witch hunts and trials that took the lives of as many as 100,000 people between 1400 and 1700.

REVIEW QUESTIONS

1. What did Copernicus, Brahe, Kepler, Galileo, and Newton each contribute to the scientific revolution? Which do you think made the most important contributions and why? What did Francis Bacon contribute to the foundation of scientific thought?

2. How would you define the term *scientific revolution*? In what ways was it truly revolutionary? Which is more enduring, a political revolution or an intellectual one?

3. What were the differences between the political philosophies of Thomas Hobbes and John Locke? How did each view human nature? Would you rather live under a government designed by Hobbes or by Locke? Why?

4. Why were women unable to participate fully in the new science? How did family relationships help some women become involved in the advance of natural philosophy?

5. Why did the Catholic Church condemn Galileo? How did Pascal seek to reconcile faith and reason? How did English natural theology support economic expansion?

6. How do you explain the phenomena of witchcraft and witch hunts in an age of scientific enlightenment? Why did the witch panics occur in the late sixteenth and early seventeenth centuries? How might the Reformation have contributed to them?

SUGGESTED READINGS

R. Ashcraft, *Revolutionary Politics and Locke's Two Treatises of Government* (1986). A major study emphasizing the radical side of Locke's thought.

J. Barry, M. Hester, and G. Roberts, eds., *Witchcraft in Early Modern Europe: Studies in Culture and Belief* (1998). A collection of recent essays.

M. Biagioli, *Galileo Courtier: The Practice of Science in the Culture of Absolutism* (1993). A major revisionist work.

J. A. Conner, *Kepler's Witch: An Astronomer's Discovery of Cosmic Order Amid Religious War, Political Intrigue, and the Heresy Trial of His Mother* (2005). Fascinating account of Kepler's effort to vindicate his mother against charges of witchcraft.

P. Dear, *Revolutionizing the Sciences: European Knowledge and Its Ambitions, 1500–1700* (2001). A broad-ranging study of both the ideas and institutions of the new science.

M. Feingold, *The Newtonian Moment: Isaac Newton and the Making of Modern Culture* (2004). A superb, well-illustrated volume.

S. Gaukroger, *The Emergence of a Scientific Culture: Science and the Shaping of Modernity* (2007). A challenging book exploring the differing understanding of natural knowledge in early modern European culture.

S. Gaukroger, *Francis Bacon and the Transformation of Early-Modern Philosophy* (2001). An excellent, accessible introduction.

J. Gleik, *Isaac Newton* (2003). Highly accessible to the general reader.

I. Harris, *The Mind of John Locke: A Study of Political Theory in Its Intellectual Setting* (1994). The most comprehensive recent treatment.

J. L. Heilbron, *The Sun in the Church: Cathedrals as Solar Observatories* (2000). Explores uses made of Roman Catholic cathedrals to make astronomical observations.

K. J. Howell, *God's Two Books: Copernican Cosmology and Biblical Interpretation in Early Modern Science* (2002). The clearest discussion of this important subject.

L. Jardine, *Ingenious Pursuits: Building the Scientific Revolution* (1999). A lively exploration of the interface of personalities, new knowledge, and English society.

A. C. Kors and E. Peters, eds., *European Witchcraft, 1100–1700* (1972). Classics of witch belief.

T. S. Kuhn, *The Copernican Revolution: Planetary Astronomy in the Development of Western Thought* (1957). Remains the classic work.

B. Levack, *The Witch Hunt in Early Modern Europe* (1986). Lucid survey.

P. Machamer, ed., *The Cambridge Companion to Galileo* (1998). Essays that aid the understanding of the entire spectrum of the new science.

J. Marshall, *John Locke, Toleration and Early Enlightenment Culture* (2006). A magisterial and challenging survey of the background of seventeenth-century arguments for and against toleration.

J. R. Martin, *Baroque* (1977). A classic introduction to Baroque art.

M. Osler, *Rethinking the Scientific Revolution* (2000). A collection of revisionist essays particularly exploring issues of the interrelationship of the new science and religion.

R. Popkin, *The History of Scepticism: From Savonarola to Bayle* (2003). A classic study of the fear of loss of intellectual certainty.

L. Pyenson and S. Sheets-Pyenson, *Servants of Nature: A History of Scientific Institutions, Enterprises, and Sensibilities* (1999). A history of the settings in which the creation and diffusion of scientific knowledge have occurred.

J. Repcheck, *Copernicus' Secret: How the Scientific Revolution Began* (2007). A highly accessible biography of Copernicus.

L. Schiebinger, *The Mind Has No Sex? Women in the Origins of Modern Science* (1989). A major study of the subject.

S. Shapin, *The Scientific Revolution* (1996). A readable brief introduction.

W. R. Shea and M. Artigas, *Galileo in Rome: The Rise and Fall of a Troublesome Genius* (2003). Argues that Galileo in part brought about his own condemnation.

T. Sorell, *The Cambridge Companion to Hobbes* (1994). Excellent essays on the major themes of Hobbes's thought.

R. S. Westfall, *The Construction of Modern Science: Mechanisms and Mechanics* (1971). A classic work.

For additional learning resources related to this chapter, please go to www.myhistorylab.com

GLOSSARY

absolutism   Term applied to strong centralized continental monarchies that attempted to make royal power dominant over aristocracies and other regional authorities.

Acropolis (ACK-row-po-lis)   The religious and civic center of Athens. It is the site of the Parthenon.

Act of Supremacy   The declaration by Parliament in 1534 that Henry VIII, not the pope, was the head of the church in England.

agape (AG-a-pay)   Meaning "love feast." A common meal that was part of the central ritual of early Christian worship.

agora (AG-o-rah)   The Greek marketplace and civic center. It was the heart of the social life of the *polis*.

Agricultural Revolution   The innovations in farm production that began in the eighteenth century and led to a scientific and mechanized agriculture.

Albigensians (Al-bi-GEN-see-uns)   Thirteenth-century advocates of a dualist religion. They took their name from the city of Albi in southern France. Also called *Cathars.*

Anabaptists   Protestants who insisted that only adult baptism conformed to Scripture.

anarchism   The theory that government and social institutions are oppressive and unnecessary and society should be based on voluntary cooperation among individuals.

Anschluss (AHN-shluz)   Meaning "union." The annexation of Austria by Germany in March 1938.

anti-Semitism   Prejudice, hostility, or legal discrimination against Jews.

apartheid (a-PAR-tid)   An official policy of segregation, assignment of peoples to distinct regions, and other forms of social, political, and economic discrimination based on race associated primarily with South Africa.

apostolic primacy   The doctrine that the popes are the direct successors to the Apostle Peter and as such heads of the church.

Apostolic Succession   The Christian doctrine that the powers given by Jesus to his original disciples have been handed down from bishop to bishop through ordination.

appeasement   The Anglo-French policy of making concessions to Germany in the 1930s to avoid a crisis that would lead to war. It assumed that Germany had real grievances and Hitler's aims were limited and ultimately acceptable.

Areopagus   The governing council of Athens, originally open only to the nobility. It was named after the hill on which it met.

arete (AH-ray-tay)   Manliness, courage, and the excellence appropriate to a hero. It was considered the highest virtue of Homeric society.

Arianism (AIR-ee-an-ism)   The belief formulated by Arius of Alexandria (ca. 280–336 C.E.) that Jesus was a created being, neither fully man nor fully God, but something in between. It did away with the doctrine of the Trinity.

aristocratic resurgence   Term applied to the eighteenth-century aristocratic efforts to resist the expanding power of European monarchies.

Asia Minor   Modern Turkey. Also called *Anatolia.*

assignats (as-seen-YAHNTS)   Government bonds based on the value of confiscated church lands issued during the early French Revolution.

Atomists   School of ancient Greek philosophy founded in the fifth century B.C.E. by Leucippus of Miletus and Democritus of Abdera. It held that the world consists of innumerable, tiny, solid, indivisible, and unchangeable particles called *atoms.*

Attica (AT-tick-a)   The region of Greece where Athens is located.

Augsburg (AWGS-berg) **Confession**   The definitive statement of Lutheran belief made in 1530.

Augustus (AW-gust-us)   The title given to Octavian in 27 B.C.E. and borne thereafter by all Roman emperors. It was a semireligious title that implied veneration, majesty, and holiness.

Ausgleich (AWS-glike)   Meaning "compromise." The agreement between the Habsburg emperor and the Hungarians to give Hungary considerable administrative autonomy in 1867. It created the Dual Monarchy, or Austria-Hungary.

autocracy (AW-to-kra-see)   Government in which the ruler has absolute power.

Axis   The alliance between Nazi Germany and fascist Italy. Also called the *Pact of Steel.*

banalities   Exactions that the lord of a manor could make on his tenants.

baroque (bah-ROWK)   A style of art marked by heavy and dramatic ornamentation and curved rather than straight lines that flourished between 1550 and 1750. It was especially associated with the Catholic Counter-Reformation.

Beguines (bi-GEENS)   Lay sisterhoods not bound by the rules of a religious order.

benefice   Church offices granted by the ruler of a state or the pope to an individual. It also meant *fief* in the Middle Ages.

bishop   Originally a person elected by early Christian congregations to lead them in worship and supervise their funds. In time, bishops became the religious and even political authorities for Christian communities within large geographical areas.

Black Death   The bubonic plague that killed millions of Europeans in the fourteenth century.

blitzkrieg (BLITZ-kreeg)   Meaning "lightning war." The German tactic early in World War II of employing fast-moving, massed armored columns supported by airpower to overwhelm the enemy.

Bolsheviks   Meaning the "majority." Term Lenin applied to his faction of the Russian Social Democratic Party. It became the Communist Party of the Soviet Union after the Russian Revolution.

bourgeois A French word used as an adjective describing something associated with the middle class or as a noun to describe a middle-class person.

boyars The Russian nobility.

Bronze Age The name given to the earliest civilized era, c. 4000 to 1000 B.C.E. The term reflects the importance of the metal bronze, a mixture of tin and copper, for the peoples of this age for use as weapons and tools.

Bundesrat (BUHN-dees-raht) The upper house of the German federal parliament whose members are appointed by the various state governments.

Caesaropapism (SEE-zer-o-PAY-pi-zim) The direct involvement of the ruler in religious doctrine and practice as if he were the head of the church as well as the state.

cahiers de doléances (KAH-hee-ay de dough-LAY-ahnce) Meaning "lists of grievances." Petitions for reforms submitted to the French crown when the Estates General met in 1789.

caliphate (KAH-li-fate) The true line of succession to Muhammad.

capital goods Machines and tools used to produce other goods.

Carbonari (car-buh-NAH-ree) Meaning "charcoal burners." The most famous of the secret republican societies seeking to unify Italy in the 1820s.

categorical imperative According to Emmanuel Kant (1724–1804), the internal sense of moral duty or awareness possessed by all human beings.

catholic Meaning "universal." The body of belief held by most Christians enshrined within the church.

Catholic Emancipation The grant of full political rights to Roman Catholics in Britain in 1829.

censor Official of the Roman republic charged with conducting the census and compiling the lists of citizens and members of the Senate. They could expel senators for financial or moral reasons. Two censors were elected every five years.

Chartism The first large-scale European working-class political movement. It sought political reforms that would favor the interests of skilled British workers in the 1830s and 1840s.

chiaroscuro (kyar-eh-SKEW-row) The use of shading to enhance naturalness in painting and drawing.

civic humanism Education designed to promote humanist leadership of political and cultural life.

civilization A form of human culture marked by urbanism, metallurgy, and writing.

civilizing mission The concept that Western nations could bring advanced science and economic development to non-Western parts of the world that justified imperial administration.

clientage (KLI-ent-age) The custom in ancient Rome whereby men became supporters of more powerful men in return for legal and physical protection and economic benefits.

Cold War The ideological and geographical struggle between the United States and its allies and the USSR and its allies that began after World War II and lasted until the dissolution of the USSR in 1989.

collectivization The bedrock of Stalinist agriculture, which forced Russian peasants to give up their private farms and work as members of collectives, large agricultural units controlled by the state.

coloni (CO-loan-ee) Farmers or sharecroppers on the estates of wealthy Romans.

Commonwealthmen British political writers whose radical republican ideas influenced the American revolutionaries.

concentration camps Camps first established by Great Britain in South Africa during the Boer War to incarcerate noncombatant civilians; later, camps established for political prisoners and other persons deemed dangerous to the state in the Soviet Union and Nazi Germany. The term is now primarily associated with the camps established by the Nazis during the Holocaust.

Concert of Europe Term applied to the European great powers acting together (in "concert") to resolve international disputes between 1815 and the 1850s.

conciliar theory The argument that General Councils were superior in authority to the pope and represented the whole body of the faithful.

condottieri (con-da-TEE-AIR-ee) Military brokers who furnished mercenary forces to the Italian states during the Renaissance.

congregationalist A congregationalist puts a group or assembly above any one individual and prefers an ecclesiastical polity that allows each congregation to be autonomous, or self-governing.

Congress System A series of international meetings among the European great powers to promote mutual cooperation between 1818 and 1822.

conquistadores (kahn-KWIS-teh-door-hez) Meaning "conquerors." The Spanish conquerors of the New World.

conservatism Support for the established order in church and state. In the nineteenth century, it implied support for legitimate monarchies, landed aristocracies, and established churches. Conservatives favored only gradual, or "organic," change.

Consulate French government dominated by Napoleon from 1799 to 1804.

consuls (CON-suls) The two chief magistrates of the Roman state.

Consumer Revolution The vast increase in both the desire and the possibility of consuming goods and services that began in the early eighteenth century and created the demand for sustaining the Industrial Revolution.

containment The U.S. policy during the Cold War of resisting Soviet expansion and influence in the expectation that the USSR would eventually collapse.

Convention French radical legislative body from 1792 to 1794.

Corn Laws British tariffs on imported grain that protected the price of grain grown within the British Isles.

corvée (cor-VAY) A French labor tax requiring peasants to work on roads, bridges, and canals.

Council of Nicaea (NIGH-see-a) The council of Christian bishops at Nicaea in 325 C.E. that formulated the Nicene Creed, a statement of Christian belief that rejected Arianism in favor of the doctrine that Christ is both fully human and fully divine.

Counter-Reformation The sixteenth-century reform movement in the Roman Catholic Church in reaction to the Protestant Reformation.

coup d'état (COO DAY-ta) The sudden violent overthrow of a government by its own army.

creed A brief statement of faith to which true Christians should adhere.

Creoles (KRAY-ol-ez) Persons of Spanish descent born in the Spanish colonies.

Crusades Religious wars directed by the church against infidels and heretics.

culture The ways of living built up by a group and passed on from one generation to another.

cuneiform (Q-nee-i-form) A writing system invented by the Sumerians that used a wedge-shaped stylus, or pointed tool, to write on wet clay tablets that were then baked or dried (*cuneus* means "wedge" in Latin). The writing was also cut into stone.

Curia (CURE-ee-a) The papal government.

Cynic (SIN-ick) **School** A fourth-century philosophical movement that ridiculed all religious observances and turned away from involvement in the affairs of the *polis*. Its most famous exemplar was Diogenes of Sinope (ca. 400–325 B.C.E.).

deacon Meaning "those who serve." In early Christian congregations, deacons assisted the presbyters, or elders.

decolonization The process of European retreat of colonial empires following World War II.

deism A belief in a rational God who had created the universe but then allowed it to function without his interference according to the mechanisms of nature and a belief in rewards and punishments after death for human action.

Delian (DEE-li-an) **League** An alliance of Greek states under the leadership of Athens that was formed in 478–477 B.C.E. to resist the Persians. In time the league was transformed into the Athenian Empire.

deme (DEEM) A small town in Attica or a ward in Athens that became the basic unit of Athenian civic life under the democratic reforms of Clisthenes in 508 B.C.E.

demesne (di-MAIN) The part of a manor that was cultivated directly for the lord of the manor.

divine right of kings The theory that monarchs are appointed by and answerable only to God.

Domesday (DOOMS-day) *Book* A detailed survey of the wealth of England undertaken by William the Conqueror between 1080 and 1086.

domestic system of textile production Method of producing textiles in which agents furnished raw materials to households whose members spun them into thread and then wove cloth, which the agents then sold as finished products.

Donatism The heresy that taught the efficacy of the sacraments depended on the moral character of the clergy who administered them.

Duce (DO-chay) Meaning "leader." Mussolini's title as head of the Fascist Party.

Duma (DOO-ma) The Russian parliament, after the revolution of 1905.

electors Nine German princes who had the right to elect the Holy Roman Emperor.

émigrés (em-ee-GRAYS) French aristocrats who fled France during the Revolution.

empiricism (em-PEER-ih-cism) The use of experiment and observation derived from sensory evidence to construct scientific theory or philosophy of knowledge.

enclosure The consolidation or fencing in of common lands by British landlords to increase production and achieve greater commercial profits. It also involved the reclamation of waste land and the consolidation of strips into block fields.

encomienda (en-co-mee-EN-da) The grant by the Spanish crown to a colonist of the labor of a specific number of Indians for a set period of time.

ENIAC The Electronic Numerical Integrator and Computer. The first genuine modern digital computer, developed in the 1940s.

Enlightenment The eighteenth-century movement led by the *philosophes* that held that change and reform were both desirable through the application of reason and science.

Epicureans (EP-i-cure-ee-ans) School of philosophy founded by Epicurus of Athens (342–271 B.C.E.). It sought to liberate people from fear of death and the supernatural by teaching that the gods took no interest in human affairs and that true happiness consisted in pleasure, which was defined as the absence of pain. This could be achieved by attaining *ataraxia*, freedom from trouble, pain, and responsibility by withdrawing from business and public life.

equestrians (EE-quest-ree-ans) Literally "cavalrymen" or "knights." In the earliest years of the Roman Republic those who could afford to serve as mounted warriors. The equestrians evolved into a social rank of well-to-do businessmen and middle-ranking officials. Many of them supported the Gracchi.

Estates General The medieval French parliament. It consisted of three separate groups, or "estates": clergy, nobility, and commoners. It last met in 1789 at the outbreak of the French Revolution.

Etruscans (EE-trus-cans) A people of central Italy who exerted the most powerful external influence on the early Romans. Etruscan kings ruled Rome until 509 B.C.E.

Eucharist (YOU-ka-rist) Meaning "thanksgiving." The celebration of the Lord's Supper. Considered the central ritual of worship by most Christians. Also called *Holy Communion*.

Euro The common currency created by the EEC in the late 1990s.

European Economic Community (EEC) The economic association formed by France, Germany, Italy, Belgium, the Netherlands, and Luxembourg in 1957. Also known as the *Common Market.*

European Union The new name given to the EEC in 1993. It included most of the states of Western Europe.

excommunication Denial by the church of the right to receive the sacraments.

existentialism The post–World War II Western philosophy that holds human beings are totally responsible for their acts and that this responsibility causes them dread and anguish.

Fabians British socialists in the late nineteenth and early twentieth centuries who sought to achieve socialism through gradual, peaceful, and democratic means.

family economy The basic structure of production and consumption in preindustrial Europe.

fascism Political movements that tend to be antidemocratic, anti-Marxist, antiparliamentary, and often anti-Semitic. Fascists were invariably nationalists and exalted the nation over the individual. They supported the interests of the middle class and rejected the ideas of the French Revolution and nineteenth-century liberalism. The first fascist regime was founded by Benito Mussolini (1883–1945) in Italy in the 1920s.

fealty An oath of loyalty by a vassal to a lord, promising to perform specified services.

feudal (FEW-dull) **society** The social, political, military, and economic system that prevailed in the Middle Ages and beyond in some parts of Europe.

fief Land granted to a vassal in exchange for services, usually military.

foederati (FAY-der-ah-tee) Barbarian tribes enlisted as special allies of the Roman Empire.

Fourteen Points President Woodrow Wilson's (1856–1924) idealistic war aims.

Fronde (FROHND) A series of rebellions against royal authority in France between 1649 and 1652.

Führer (FYOOR-er) Meaning "leader." The title taken by Hitler when he became dictator of Germany.

gabelle (gah-BELL) The royal tax on salt in France.

Gaul (GAWL) Modern France.

German Confederation Association of German states established at the Congress of Vienna that replaced the Holy Roman Empire from 1815 to 1866.

ghetto Separate communities in which Jews were required by law to live.

glasnost (GLAZ-nohst) Meaning "openness." The policy initiated by Mikhail Gorbachev (MEEK-hail GORE-buh-choff) in the 1980s of permitting open criticism of the policies of the Soviet Communist Party.

Glorious Revolution The largely peaceful replacement of James II by William and Mary as English monarchs in 1688. It marked the beginning of constitutional monarchy in Britain.

gold standard A monetary system in which the value of a unit of a nation's currency is related to a fixed amount of gold.

Golden Bull The agreement in 1356 to establish a seven-member electoral college of German princes to choose the Holy Roman Emperor.

Great Depression A prolonged worldwide economic downturn that began in 1929 with the collapse of the New York Stock Exchange.

Great Purges The imprisonment and execution of millions of Soviet citizens by Stalin between 1934 and 1939.

Great Reform Bill (1832) A limited reform of the British House of Commons and an expansion of the electorate to include a wider variety of the propertied classes. It laid the groundwork for further orderly reforms within the British constitutional system.

Great Schism The appearance of two and at times three rival popes between 1378 and 1415.

Great Trek The migration by Boer (Dutch) farmers during the 1830s and 1840s from regions around Cape Town into the eastern and northeastern regions of South Africa that ultimately resulted in the founding of the Orange Free State and Transvaal.

Green movement A political environmentalist movement that began in West Germany in the 1970s and spread to a number of other Western nations.

grossdeutsch (gross-DOYCH) Meaning "great German." The argument that the German-speaking portions of the Habsburg Empire should be included in a united Germany.

guild An association of merchants or craftsmen that offered protection to its members and set rules for their work and products.

hacienda (ha-SEE-hen-da) A large landed estate in Spanish America.

Hegira (HEJ-ear-a) The flight of Muhammad and his followers from Mecca to Medina in 622 C.E. It marks the beginning of the Islamic calendar.

heliocentric (HE-li-o-cen-trick) **theory** The theory, now universally accepted, that the earth and the other planets revolve around the sun. First proposed by Aristarchos of Samos (310–230 B.C.E.). Its opposite, the geocentric theory, which was dominant until the sixteenth century C.E., held that the sun and the planets revolved around the earth.

Helots (HELL-ots) Hereditary Spartan serfs.

heretic (HAIR-i-tick) A person whose beliefs were contrary to those of the Catholic Church.

hieroglyphics (HI-er-o-gli-phicks) The complicated writing script of ancient Egypt. It combined picture writing with pictographs and sound signs. Hieroglyph means "sacred carvings" in Greek.

Holocaust The Nazi extermination of millions of European Jews between 1940 and 1945. Also called the "final solution to the Jewish problem."

Holy Roman Empire The revival of the old Roman Empire, based mainly in Germany and northern Italy, that endured from 870 to 1806.

home rule The advocacy of a large measure of administrative autonomy for Ireland within the British Empire between the 1880s and 1914.

Homo sapiens (HO-mo say-pee-ans)   The scientific name for human beings, from the Latin words meaning "Wise man." *Homo sapiens* emerged some 200,000 years ago.

honestiores (HON-est-ee-or-ez)   The Roman term formalized from the beginning of the third century C.E. to denote the privileged classes: senators, equestrians, the municipal aristocracy, and soldiers.

hoplite phalanx (FAY-lanks)   The basic unit of Greek warfare in which infantrymen fought in close order, shield to shield, usually eight ranks deep. The phalanx perfectly suited the farmer-soldier-citizen who was the backbone of the *polis*.

hubris (WHO-bris)   Arrogance brought on by excessive wealth or good fortune. The Greeks believed it led to moral blindness and divine vengeance.

Huguenots (HYOU-gu-nots)   French Calvinists.

humanism   The study of the Latin and Greek classics and of the Church Fathers both for their own sake and to promote a rebirth of ancient norms and values.

humanitas (HEW-man-i-tas)   The Roman name for a liberal arts education.

humiliores (HEW-mi-lee-orez)   The Roman term formalized at the beginning of the third century C.E. for the lower classes.

Hussites (HUS-Its)   Followers of John Huss (d. 1415) who questioned Catholic teachings about the Eucharist.

Iconoclasm (i-KON-o-kla-zoom)   A heresy in Eastern Christianity that sought to ban the veneration of sacred images, or icons.

id, ego, superego   The three entities in Sigmund Freud's model of the internal organization of the human mind. The id consists of the amoral, irrational instincts for self-gratification. The superego embodies the external morality imposed on the personality by society. The ego mediates between the two and allows the personality to cope with the internal and external demands of its existence.

Iliad (ILL-ee-ad) **and the *Odyssey*** (O-dis-see), **The**   Epic poems by Homer about the "Dark Age" heroes of Greece who fought at Troy. The poems were written down in the eighth century B.C.E. after centuries of being sung by bards.

imperator (IM-per-a-tor)   Under the Roman Republic, it was the title given to a victorious general. Under Augustus and his successors, it became the title of the ruler of Rome meaning "emperor."

imperialism   The extension of a nation's authority over other nations or areas through conquest or political or economic hegemony.

Imperialism of Free Trade   The advance of European economic and political interests in the nineteenth century by demanding that non-European nations allow European nations, most particularly Great Britain, to introduce their manufactured goods freely into all nations or to introduce other goods, such as opium into China, that allowed those nations to establish economic influence and to determine the terms of trade.

imperium (IM-pear-ee-um)   In ancient Rome, the right to issue commands and to enforce them by fines, arrests, and even corporal and capital punishment.

indulgence   Remission of the temporal penalty of punishment in purgatory that remained after sins had been forgiven.

Industrial Revolution   Mechanization of the European economy that began in Britain in the second half of the eighteenth century.

Inquisition   A tribunal created by the Catholic Church in the mid-twelfth century to detect and punish heresy.

insulae (IN-sul-lay)   Meaning "islands." The multistoried apartment buildings of Rome in which most of the inhabitants of the city lived.

Intolerable Acts   Measures passed by the British Parliament in 1774 to punish the colony of Massachusetts and strengthen Britain's authority in the colonies. The laws provoked colonial opposition, which led immediately to the American Revolution.

investiture controversy   The medieval conflict between the church and lay rulers over who would control bishops and abbots, symbolized by the ceremony of "investing" them with the symbols of their authority.

Ionia (I-o-knee-a)   The part of western Asia Minor heavily colonized by the Greeks.

Islam (IZ-lahm)   Meaning "submission." The religion founded by the prophet Muhammad.

Italia irredenta (ee-TAHL-ee-a ir-REH-dent-a)   Meaning "unredeemed Italy." Italian-speaking areas that had been left under Austrian rule at the time of the unification of Italy.

Jacobins (JACK-uh-bins)   The radical republican party during the French Revolution that displaced the Girondins.

Jacquerie (jah-KREE)   Revolt of the French peasantry.

Jansenism   A seventeenth-century movement within the Catholic Church that taught that human beings were so corrupted by original sin that they could do nothing good nor secure their own salvation without divine grace. (It was opposed to the Jesuits.)

Judah (JEW-da)   The southern Israelite kingdom established after the death of Solomon in the tenth century B.C.E.

Julian Calendar   The reform of the calendar by Julius Caesar in 46 B.C.E. It remained in use throughout Europe until the sixteenth century and in Russia until the Russian Revolution in 1917.

July Monarchy   The French regime set up after the overthrow of the Bourbons in July 1830.

Junkers (YOONG-kerz)   The noble landlords of Prussia.

jus gentium (YUZ GEN-tee-um)   Meaning "law of peoples." The body of Roman law that dealt with foreigners.

jus naturale (YUZ NAH-tu-rah-lay)   Meaning "natural law." The Stoic concept of a world ruled by divine reason.

Ka'ba (KAH-bah)   A black meteorite in the city of Mecca that became Islam's holiest shrine.

Keynesian economics   The theory of John Maynard Keynes (CANES) (1883–1946) that governments could spend their economies out of a depression by running deficits to encourage employment and stimulate the production and consumption of goods.

kleindeutsch (kline-DOYCH) Meaning "small German." The argument that the German-speaking portions of the Habsburg Empire should be excluded from a united Germany.

Kristallnacht (KRIS-tahl-NAHKT) Meaning "crystal night" because of the broken glass that littered German streets after the looting and destruction of Jewish homes, businesses, and synagogues across Germany on the orders of the Nazi Party in November 1938.

kulaks (koo-LAKS) Prosperous Russian peasant farmers.

Kulturkampf (cool-TOOR-cahmff) Meaning the "battle for culture." The conflict between the Roman Catholic Church and the government of the German Empire in the 1870s.

laissez-faire (lay-ZAY-faire) French phrase meaning "allow to do." In economics the doctrine of minimal government interference in the working of the economy.

Late Antiquity The multicultural period between the end of the ancient world and the birth of the Middle Ages, 250–800 C.E.

latifundia (LAT-ee-fun-dee-a) Large plantations for growing cash crops owned by wealthy Romans.

Latium (LAT-ee-um) The region of Italy in which Rome is located. Its inhabitants were called *Latins*.

League of Nations The association of sovereign states set up after World War I to pursue common policies and avert international aggression.

Lebensraum (LAY-benz-rauhm) Meaning "living space." The Nazi plan to colonize and exploit the Slavic areas of Eastern Europe for the benefit of Germany.

levée en masse (le-VAY en MASS) The French revolutionary conscription (1792) of all males into the army and the harnessing of the economy for war production.

liberal arts The medieval university program that consisted of the *trivium* (TRI-vee-um): grammar, rhetoric, and logic, and the *quadrivium* (qua-DRI-vee-um): arithmetic, geometry, astronomy, and music.

liberalism In the nineteenth century, support for representative government dominated by the propertied classes and minimal government interference in the economy.

Logos (LOW-goz) Divine reason, or fire, which according to the Stoics was the guiding principle in nature. Every human had a spark of this divinity, which returned to the eternal divine spirit after death.

Lollards (LALL-erds) Followers of John Wycliffe (d. 1384) who questioned the supremacy and privileges of the pope and the church hierarchy.

Lower Egypt The Nile delta.

Luftwaffe (LUFT-vaff-uh) The German air force in World War II.

Magna Carta (MAG-nuh CAR-tuh) The "Great Charter" limiting royal power that the English nobility forced King John to sign in 1215.

Magna Graecia (MAG-nah GRAY-see-a) Meaning "Great Greece" in Latin, it was the name given by the Romans to southern Italy and Sicily because there were so many Greek colonies in the region.

Magyars (MAH-jars) The majority ethnic group in Hungary.

Mandates The assigning of the former German colonies and Turkish territories in the Middle East to Britain, France, Japan, Belgium, Australia, and South Africa as de facto colonies under the vague supervision of the League of Nations with the hope that the territories would someday advance to independence.

mannerism A style of art in the mid- to late-sixteenth century that permitted artists to express their own "manner" or feelings in contrast to the symmetry and simplicity of the art of the High Renaissance.

manor Village farms owned by a lord.

Marshall Plan The U.S. program named after Secretary of State George C. Marshall of providing economic aid to Europe after World War II.

Marxism The theory of Karl Marx (1818–1883) and Friedrich Engels (FREE-drick ENG-ulz) (1820–1895) that history is the result of class conflict, which will end in the inevitable triumph of the industrial proletariat over the bourgeoisie and the abolition of private property and social class.

Mein Kampf (MINE KAHMFF) Meaning *My Struggle*. Hitler's statement of his political program, published in 1924.

Mensheviks Meaning the "minority." Term Lenin applied to the majority moderate faction of the Russian Social Democratic Party opposed to him and the Bolsheviks.

mercantilism Term used to describe close government control of the economy that sought to maximize exports and accumulate as much precious metals as possible to enable the state to defend its economic and political interests.

Mesopotamia (MEZ-o-po-tay-me-a) Modern Iraq. The land between the Tigris and Euphrates Rivers where the first civilization appeared around 3000 B.C.E.

Messiah (MESS-eye-a) The redeemer whose coming Jews believed would establish the kingdom of God on earth. Christians considered Jesus to be the Messiah (*Christ* means Messiah in Greek).

Methodism An English religious movement begun by John Wesley (1703–1791) that stressed inward, heartfelt religion and the possibility of attaining Christian perfection in this life.

millets Administrative units of the Ottoman Empire that were not geographic but consisted of ethnic or religious minorities to whom particular laws and regulations applied.

Minoans (MIN-o-ans) The Bronze Age civilization that arose in Crete in the third and second millennia B.C.E.

missi dominici (MISS-ee dough-MIN-ee-chee) Meaning "the envoys of the ruler." Royal overseers of the king's law in the Carolingian Empire.

mobilization The placing of a country's military forces on a war footing.

modernism The movement in the arts and literature in the late nineteenth and early twentieth centuries to create new aesthetic forms and to elevate the aesthetic experience of a work of art above the attempt to portray reality as accurately as possible.

moldboard plow A heavy plow introduced in the Middle Ages that cut deep into the soil.

monasticism A movement in the Christian church that arose first in the East in the third and fourth centuries C.E. in which first individual hermits and later organized communities of men and women (monks and nuns) separated themselves from the world to lead lives in imitation of Christ. In the West the Rule of St. Benedict (c. 480–547) became the dominant form of monasticism.

Monophysite (ma-NO-fiz-it) Adherent of the theory that Jesus had only one nature.

monotheism The worship of one universal God.

Mycenaean (MY-cen-a-an) The Bronze Age civilization of mainland Greece that was centered at Mycenae.

"mystery" religions The cults of Isis, Mithra, and Osiris, which promised salvation to those initiated into the secret or "mystery" of their rites. These cults competed with Christianity in the Roman Empire.

nationalism The belief that one is part of a nation, defined as a community with its own language, traditions, customs, and history that distinguish it from other nations and make it the primary focus of a person's loyalty and sense of identity.

natural selection The theory originating with Darwin that organisms evolve through a struggle for existence in which those that have a marginal advantage live long enough to propagate their kind.

naturalism The attempt to portray nature and human life without sentimentality.

Nazis The German Nationalist Socialist Party.

Neolithic (NEE-o-lith-ick) **Revolution** The shift beginning 10,000 years ago from hunter-gatherer societies to settled communities of farmers and artisans. Also called the Age of Agriculture, it witnessed the invention of farming, the domestication of plants and animals, and the development of technologies such as pottery and weaving. The earliest Neolithic societies appeared in the Near East about 8000 B.C.E. "Neolithic" comes from the Greek words for "new stone."

Neoplatonism (KNEE-o-play-ton-ism) A religious philosophy that tried to combine mysticism with classical and rationalist speculation. Its chief formulator was Plotinus (205–270 C.E.).

New Economic Policy (NEP) A limited revival of capitalism, especially in light industry and agriculture, introduced by Lenin in 1921 to repair the damage inflicted on the Russian economy by the Civil War and war communism.

New Imperialism The extension in the late nineteenth and early twentieth centuries of Western political and economic dominance to Asia, the Middle East, and Africa.

nomes Regions or provinces of ancient Egypt governed by officials called *nomarchs*.

oikos (OI-cos) The Greek household, always headed by a male.

Old Believers Those members of the Russian Orthodox Church who refused to accept the reforms of the seventeenth century regarding church texts and ritual.

Old Regime Term applied to the pattern of social, political, and economic relationships and institutions that existed in Europe before the French Revolution.

optimates (OP-tee-ma-tes) Meaning "the best men." Roman politicians who supported the traditional role of the Senate.

orthodox Meaning "holding the right opinions." Applied to the doctrines of the Catholic Church.

Ottoman Empire The imperial Turkish state centered in Constantinople that ruled large parts of the Balkans, North Africa, and the Middle East until 1918.

Paleolithic (PAY-lee-o-lith-ick) **Age, The** The earliest period when stone tools were used, from about 1,000,000 to 10,000 B.C.E. From the Greek meaning "old stone."

Panhellenic (PAN-hell-en-ick) ("all-Greek") The sense of cultural identity that all Greeks felt in common with each other.

Pan-Slavism The movement to create a nation or federation that would embrace all the Slavic peoples of Eastern Europe.

papal infallibility The doctrine that the pope is infallible when pronouncing officially in his capacity as head of the church on matters of faith and morals, enumerated by the First Vatican Council in 1870.

Papal States Territory in central Italy ruled by the pope until 1870.

parlements (par-luh-MAHNS) French regional courts dominated by hereditary nobility. The most important was the *Parlement* of Paris, which claimed the right to register royal decrees before they could become law.

parliamentary monarchy The form of limited or constitutional monarchy set up in Britain after the Glorious Revolution of 1689 in which the monarch was subject to the law and ruled by the consent of parliament.

patricians (PA-tri-she-ans) The hereditary upper class of early Republican Rome.

Peloponnesian (PELL-o-po-knees-ee-an) **Wars** The protracted struggle between Athens and Sparta to dominate Greece between 465 and Athens's final defeat in 404 B.C.E.

Peloponnesus (PELL-o-po-knee-sus) The southern peninsula of Greece where Sparta was located.

peninsulares (pen-in-SUE-la-rez) Persons born in Spain who settled in the Spanish colonies.

perestroika (pare-ess-TROY-ka) Meaning "restructuring." The attempt in the 1980s to reform the Soviet government and economy.

petite bourgeoisie (peh-TEET BOOSH-schwa-zee) The lower middle class.

pharaoh (FAY-row) The god-kings of ancient Egypt. The term originally meant "great house" or palace.

Pharisees (FAIR-i-sees) The group that was most strict in its adherence to Jewish law.

philosophes (fee-lou-SOPHS) The eighteenth-century writers and critics who forged the new attitudes favorable to change. They sought to apply reason and common sense to the institutions and societies of their day.

Phoenicians (FA-nee-shi-ans) The ancient inhabitants of modern Lebanon. A trading people, they established colonies throughout the Mediterranean.

physiocrats Eighteenth-century French thinkers who attacked the mercantilist regulation of the economy, advocated a limited economic role for government, and believed that all economic production depended on sound agriculture.

plantation economy The economic system stretching between Chesapeake Bay and Brazil that produced crops, especially sugar, cotton, and tobacco, using slave labor on large estates.

Platonism Philosophy of Plato that posits preexistent Ideal Forms of which all earthly things are imperfect models.

plebeians (PLEB-bee-ans) The hereditary lower class of early Republican Rome.

plenitude of power The teaching that the popes have power over all other bishops of the church.

pogroms (PO-grohms) Organized riots against Jews in the Russian Empire.

polis (PO-lis) (plural, *poleis*) The basic Greek political unit. Usually, but incompletely, translated as "city-state," the Greeks thought of the *polis* as a community of citizens theoretically descended from a common ancestor.

politique Ruler or person in a position of power who puts the success and well-being of his or her state above all else.

polygyny (po-LIJ-eh-nee) The practice of having two or more wives or concubines at the same time.

polytheism (PAH-lee-thee-ism) The worship of many gods.

pontifex maximus (PON-ti-feks MAK-suh-muss) Meaning "supreme priest." The chief priest of ancient Rome. The title was later assumed by the popes.

Popular Front A government of all left-wing parties that took power in France in 1936 to enact social and economic reforms.

populares (PO-pew-lar-es) Roman politicians who sought to pursue a political career based on the support of the people rather than just the aristocracy.

positivism The philosophy of Auguste Comte that science is the final, or positive, stage of human intellectual development because it involves exact descriptions of phenomena, without recourse to unobservable operative principles, such as gods or spirits.

postimpressionism A term used to describe European painting that followed impressionism; the term actually applies to several styles of art all of which to some extent derived from impression or stood in reaction to impressionism.

Pragmatic Sanction The legal basis negotiated by the Emperor Charles VI (r. 1711–1740) for the Habsburg succession through his daughter Maria Theresa (r. 1740–1780).

predestination The doctrine that God had foreordained all souls to salvation (the "elect") or damnation. It was especially associated with Calvinism.

presbyter (PRESS-bi-ter) Meaning "elder." A person who directed the affairs of early Christian congregations.

Presbyterians Scottish Calvinists and English Protestants who advocated a national church composed of semiautonomous congregations governed by "presbyteries."

proconsulship (PRO-con-sul-ship) In Republican Rome, the extension of a consul's imperium beyond the end of his term of office to allow him to continue to command an army in the field.

protectorate (pro-TEC-tor-ate) A non-Western territory administered by a Western nation without formal conquest or annexation, usually a de facto colony.

Protestant Ethic The theory propounded by Max Weber in 1904 that the religious confidence and self-disciplined activism that were supposedly associated with Protestantism produced an ethic that stimulated the spirit of emergent capitalism.

Ptolemaic (tow-LEM-a-ick) **System** The pre-Copernican explanation of the universe, with the earth at the center of the universe, originated in the ancient world.

Punic (PEW-nick) **Wars** Three wars between Rome and Carthage for dominance of the western Mediterranean that were fought from 264 B.C.E. to 146 B.C.E.

Puritans English Protestants who sought to "purify" the Church of England of any vestiges of Catholicism.

Qur'an (kuh-RAN) Meaning "a reciting." The Islamic bible, which Muslims believe God revealed to the prophet Muhammad.

racism The pseudoscientific theory that biological features of race determine human character and worth.

realism The style of art and literature that seeks to depict the physical world and human life with scientific objectivity and detached observation.

Reformation The sixteenth-century religious movement that sought to reform the Roman Catholic Church and led to the establishment of Protestantism.

regular clergy Monks and nuns who belong to religious orders.

Reichstag (RIKES-stahg) The German parliament, which existed in various forms, until 1945.

Reign of Terror The period between the summer of 1793 and the end of July 1794 when the French revolutionary state used extensive executions and violence to defend the Revolution and suppress its alleged internal enemies.

relativity The scientific theory associated with Einstein that time and space exist not separately but as a combined continuum whose measurement depends as much on the observer as on the entities that are being measured.

Renaissance The revival of ancient learning and the supplanting of traditional religious beliefs by new secular and scientific values that began in Italy in the fourteenth and fifteenth centuries.

reparations The requirement incorporated into the Versailles Treaty that Germany should pay for the cost of World War I.

revisionism The advocacy among nineteenth-century German socialists of achieving a humane socialist society through the evolution of democratic institutions, not revolution.

robot (ROW-boht) The amount of labor landowners demanded from peasants in the Habsburg Monarchy before 1848.

Romanitas (row-MAN-ee-tas) Meaning "Roman-ness." The spread of the Roman way of life and the sense of identifying with Rome across the Roman Empire.

romanticism A reaction in early-nineteenth-century literature, philosophy, and religion against what many considered the excessive rationality and scientific narrowness of the Enlightenment.

SA The Nazi parliamentary forces, or storm troopers.

sans-culottes (SAHN coo-LOTS) Meaning "without knee-breeches." The lower-middle classes and artisans of Paris during the French Revolution.

Schlieffen (SHLEE-fun) **Plan** Germany's plan for achieving a quick victory in the West at the outbreak of World War I by invading France through Belgium and Luxembourg.

Scholasticism Method of study based on logic and dialectic that dominated the medieval schools. It assumed that truth already existed; students had only to organize, elucidate, and defend knowledge learned from authoritative texts, especially those of Aristotle and the Church Fathers.

scientific induction Scientific method in which generalizations are derived from data gained from empirical observations.

scientific revolution The sweeping change in the scientific view of the universe that occurred in the sixteenth and seventeenth centuries. The new scientific concepts and the method of their construction became the standard for assessing the validity of knowledge in the West.

scutage Monetary payments by a vassal to a lord in place of the required military service.

second industrial revolution The emergence of new industries and the spread of industrialization from Britain to other countries, especially Germany and the United States, in the second half of the nineteenth century.

secular clergy Parish clergy who did not belong to a religious order.

seigneur (sane-YOUR) A noble French landlord.

Sejm (SHEM) The legislative assembly of the Polish nobility.

serfs Peasants tied to the land they tilled.

Shi'a (SHE-ah) The minority of Muslims who trace their beliefs from the caliph Ali who was assassinated in 661 C.E.

Sinn Fein (SHIN FAHN) Meaning "ourselves alone." An Irish political movement founded in 1905 that advocated complete political separation from Britain.

Social Darwinism The application of Darwin's concept of "the survival of the fittest" to explain evolution in nature to human social relationships.

Sophists (SO-fists) Professional teachers who emerged in Greece in the mid–fifth century B.C.E. who were paid to teach techniques of rhetoric, dialectic, and argumentation.

soviets Workers and soldiers councils formed in Russia during the Revolution.

spheres of influence A region, city, or territory where a non-Western nation exercised informal administrative influence through economic, diplomatic, or military advisors.

spinning jenny A machine invented in England by James Hargreaves around 1765 to mass-produce thread.

SS The chief security units of the Nazi state.

Stoics (STOW-icks) A philosophical school founded by Zeno of Citium (335–263 B.C.E.) that taught that humans could only be happy with natural law. Human misery was caused by passion, which was a disease of the soul. The wise sought *apatheia*, freedom from passion.

studia humanitatis (STEW-dee-a hew-MAHN-ee tah-tis) During the Renaissance, a liberal arts program of study that embraced grammar, rhetoric, poetry, history, philosophy, and politics.

Sturm und Drang (SHTURM und DRAHNG) Meaning "storm and stress." A movement in German romantic literature and philosophy that emphasized feeling and emotion.

suffragettes British women who lobbied and agitated for the right to vote in the early twentieth century.

Sunna (SOON-ah) Meaning "tradition." The dominant Islamic group.

Sunnis Those who follow the "tradition" (sunna) of the Prophet Muhammad. They are the dominant movement within Islam to which the vast majority of Muslims adhere.

symposium (SIM-po-see-um) The carefully organized drinking party that was the center of Greek aristocratic social life. It featured games, songs, poetry, and even philosophical disputation.

syncretism (SIN-cret-ism) The intermingling of different religions to form an amalgam that contained elements from each.

syndicalism French labor movement that sought to improve workers' conditions through direct action, especially general strikes.

Table of Ranks An official hierarchy established by Peter the Great in imperial Russia that equated a person's social position and privileges with his rank in the state bureaucracy or army.

tabula rasa (tah-BOO-lah RAH-sah) Meaning a "blank page." The philosophical belief associated with John Locke that human beings enter the world with totally unformed characters that are completely shaped by experience.

taille (TIE) The direct tax on the French peasantry.

ten lost tribes The Israelites who were scattered and lost to history when the northern kingdom of Israel fell to the Assyrians in 722 B.C.E.

tertiaries (TER-she-air-ees) Laypeople affiliated with the monastic life who took vows of poverty, chastity, and obedience but remained in the world.

tetrarchy (TET-rar-key) Diocletian's (r. 306–337 C.E.) system for ruling the Roman Empire by four men with power divided territorially.

Thermidorian Reaction The reaction against the radicalism of the French Revolution that began in July 1794. Associated with the end of terror and establishment of the Directory.

thesis, antithesis, and synthesis G. W. F. Hegel's (HAY-gle) (1770–1831) concept of how ideas develop. The *thesis* is a dominant set of ideas. It is challenged by a set of conflicting ideas, the *antithesis*. From the clash of these ideas, a new pattern of thought, the *synthesis*, emerges and eventually becomes the new thesis.

Third Estate The branch of the French Estates General representing all of the kingdom outside the nobility and the clergy.

Third Reich (RIKE) Hitler's regime in Germany, which lasted from 1933 to 1945.

Thirty-Nine Articles (1563) The official statement of the beliefs of the Church of England. They established a moderate form of Protestantism.

three-field system A medieval innovation that increased the amount of land under cultivation by leaving only one third fallow in a given year.

transportation The British policy from the late eighteenth to the mid–nineteenth centuries of shipping persons convicted of the most serious offenses to Australia as an alternative to capital punishment.

transubstantiation The doctrine that the entire substances of the bread and wine are changed in the Eucharist into the body and blood of Christ.

tribunes (TRIB-unes) Roman officials who had to be plebeians and were elected by the plebeian assembly to protect plebeians from the arbitrary power of the magistrates.

ulema (oo-LEE-mah) Meaning "persons with correct knowledge." The Islamic scholarly elite who served a social function similar to the Christian clergy.

Upper Egypt The part of Egypt that runs from the delta to the Sudanese border.

utilitarianism The theory associated with Jeremy Bentham (1748–1832) that the principle of utility, defined as the greatest good for the greatest number of people, should be applied to government, the economy, and the judicial system.

utopian socialism Early-nineteenth-century theories that sought to replace the existing capitalist structure and values with visionary solutions or ideal communities.

vassal A person granted an estate or cash payments in return for accepting the obligation to render services to a lord.

vernacular The everyday language spoken by the people as opposed to Latin.

vingtième (VEN-tee-em) Meaning "one twentieth." A tax on income in France before the Revolution.

Vulgate The Latin translation of the Bible by Jerome (348–420 C.E.) that became the standard bible used by the Catholic Church.

Waldensians (wahl-DEN-see-ens) Medieval heretics who advocated biblical simplicity in reaction to the worldliness of the church.

war communism The economic policy adopted by the Bolsheviks during the Russian Civil War to seize the banks, heavy industry, railroads, and grain.

war guilt clause Clause 231 of the Versailles Treaty, which assigned responsibility for World War I solely to Germany.

water frame A water-powered device invented by Richard Arkwright to produce a more durable cotton fabric. It led to the shift in the production of cotton textiles from households to factories.

Weimar (Why-mar) **Republic** The German democratic regime that existed between the end of World War I and Hitler's coming to power in 1933.

White Russians Those Russians who opposed the Bolsheviks (the "Reds") in the Russian Civil War of 1918–1921.

zemstvos (ZEMPST-vohs) Local governments set up in the Russian Empire in 1864.

Zionism The movement to create a Jewish state in Palestine (the Biblical Zion).

Zollverein (TZOL-fuh-rine) A free-trade union established among the major German states in 1834.

INDEX